THE LETTERS OF ROBERT LOUIS STEVENSON

Stevenson in 1872, aged 21. (Photo
J. Moffatt, Edinburgh)

THE LETTERS
OF
ROBERT LOUIS
STEVENSON

edited by

BRADFORD A. BOOTH AND ERNEST MEHEW

VOLUME ONE

1854–April 1874

YALE UNIVERSITY PRESS
NEW HAVEN AND LONDON
1994

Set in Bembo by Best-set Typesetter Ltd, Hong Kong
Printed and bound in Great Britain by the Bath Press, Avon

Library of Congress Cataloging-in-Publication Data

Stevenson, Robert Louis, 1850–1894.
    The letters of Robert Louis Stevenson/edited by Bradford A.
Booth & Ernest Mehew.
        p. cm.
    Includes bibliographical references and index.
    Contents: v. 1. 1854–April 1874—v. 2. April 1874–July 1879.
    v.1 ISBN 0–300–05183–2. v.2 ISBN 0–300–06021–1.
        1. Stevenson, Robert Louis, 1850–1894—Correspondence.
    2. Authors, Scottish—19th century—Correspondence. I. Booth,
Bradford Allen, 1909– . II. Mehew, Ernest. III. Title.
PR5493.A3 1994
828'.809—dc20
    [B]   93–45419
                                                                                                  CIP

A catalogue record for this book is available from the British Library.

CONTENTS

THE LETTERS

NOTE

This new edition of Stevenson's letters has been many years in the making. Professor Bradford A. Booth began work on the project in the 1950s and had largely completed his version by 1966. Following a report I made on two samples of his version, I was asked by Yale University Press to revise Professor Booth's work in co-operation with him and given the status of assistant editor. Professor Booth died in 1968. The following year his material was handed over to me and an agreement was reached between Yale, Professor Booth's widow and myself that I should revise and complete the edition.

Professor Booth carried out with energy and enthusiasm the arduous task of locating Stevenson's letters and collecting photocopies of them from libraries and private collectors throughout the world. To these I have added many new letters or copies of letters which have since come to light through the sale-room or as a result of my own enquiries.

The work of editing the letters has been carried out afresh according to different editorial principles from those originally adopted by Professor Booth. The dating and annotation, including the identification of people mentioned, is based largely on my own researches, although I have benefited from the enquiries Professor Booth had made. I have checked and made many corrections to his transcriptions of the letters he had collected. Although I am completely responsible for this final version and for all the introductory material, Professor Booth's name has been retained on the title page along with mine in recognition of the fact that he initiated the project and in accordance with the agreement made.

ERNEST MEHEW

ACKNOWLEDGEMENTS

I should like to thank all the institutions and private owners listed on pp. 73–6, who made their Stevenson letters available to Professor Booth or to me.

A small group of friends deserve a special acknowledgement. It was thanks to Sir Rupert Hart-Davis that I first became involved in this project, and over the years I have benefited enormously from his friendly help and wise counsel. My editorial procedures have been closely modelled on those in his edition of *The Letters of Oscar Wilde*. I owe an immense debt of gratitude to the American scholar Roger Swearingen and his wife Sarah, who have taken a close and enthusiastic interest at every stage of my work, and generously provided hospitality to my wife and myself during our stay in California. Roger has shared with me his encyclopaedic knowledge of Stevenson's life and work, and made available the detailed notes of his meticulous research. His major bibliography, *The Prose Writings of Robert Louis Stevenson* (1980) and his other specialised studies have been invaluable. Kenneth Mackenzie, a Canadian historian, made available his original research on Stevenson's involvement in Samoan politics, and drew my attention to letters I would otherwise have missed. His thesis, 'Robert Louis Stevenson and Samoa' (1974) has been a valuable guide. Horst Schroeder, a German scholar, has been a mine of information and erudition. He carried out detailed research on RLS's visit to Frankfurt in 1872, identified out-of-the-way quotations from Heine and others, and laboured long on my behalf in seeking information about the Russians RLS met at Mentone in 1874.

It is a pleasure to record the assistance I have had from Stevenson's relatives. Jean Leslie, granddaughter of Stevenson's cousin Charles Stevenson, and Michael Balfour, son of Stevenson's cousin and first biographer Sir Graham Balfour, have shown me many kindnesses. They provided copies of letters and much information about the Stevenson and Balfour families, including family trees.

Many librarians and curators, whose names are listed below, have helped me. Two of them have become close friends. I have been extremely fortunate to have had the whole-hearted co-operation of Marjorie G. Wynne, the former Research Librarian of the Beinecke Rare Book and Manuscript Library, Yale University. I cannot sufficiently thank her for all the kindness she has shown and the trouble she has taken in facilitating my research and in providing hospitality to my wife and myself during our visits to New Haven. Another good friend has been Ellen Shaffer, the former Curator of the Silverado Museum, St Helena, California, whose efforts and enthusiasm have made that Museum a centre for Stevenson studies. She, too, has been immensely helpful, and she made my wife and myself very welcome during our stay at St Helena. The late Norman Strouse, founder of the Silverado Museum, went to endless trouble on my behalf and was generous in providing hospitality.

Professor Booth would have wanted to thank all the librarians and the many other people, including his colleagues in the University of California, Los Angeles, who helped him in his research. My own gratitude for the provision of letters, and help and kindnesses, both large and small is due to the following:

David Angus; the late Jean Baird-Smith; Alan Bell, when at the National Library of Scotland and later; Mary A. Benjamin; John W. Bicknell; Iain Brown, National Library of Scotland; Patrick Cadell, National Library of Scotland; Herbert Cahoon, Pierpont Morgan Library, New York; Robert Campbell, The University of Wyoming; Morton N. Cohen; Janet Corran; Hunter Davies; Rodney G. Dennis, Houghton Library, Harvard University; Marsha Donaldson, Alexander Turnbull Library, Wellington, N.Z.; Donald D. Eddy, Cornell University; Penelope Feltham, Alexander Turnbull Library; Elizabeth E. Fuller, the Rosenbach Museum and Library, Philadelphia; J. C. Furnas; Vincent Giroud, Yale University Library; the late Roger Lancelyn Green; Ronald Haralson; the late James D. Hart, the Bancroft Library, University of California, Berkeley; Cathy Henderson, Harry Ransom Humanities Research Center, the University of Texas at Austin; Robin Hill, when at Lady Stair's House Museum Edinburgh, and later; Sara Hodson, the Huntington Library; the late Roy Holland; Brian Hughes, Director of Education, Bolton; Elisabeth Inglis, University of Sussex; Richard Jackson; Lord and Lady Jenkin of Roding; Dorothy Jenkinson; David Jenson; Kathleen Johnston (Lady Dunpark); Mary Lanch; H. Jack Lang; Alexandra Lapierre; Cecil Y. Lang; Henry Maas; the late William H. McCulloch; James M. MacGlone; the late Elinor McIntire; the late Paul Maixner; David Masson, The Brotherton Library, University of Leeds; K. M. Elisabeth Murray; Scott Allen Nollen; W. Park, National Library of Scotland; Roger Peers, Dorset County Museum, Dorchester; Carolyn Powell, the Huntington Library; Nicholas Rankin; the late Gordon N. Ray; Michelle Redwood, National Archives of New Zealand, Wellington; Richard Reilly, the James S. Copley Library, La Jolla, California; James Ritchie, National Library of Scotland; Augustus Saint-Gaudens; Margaret M. Sherry, Princeton University Library; Janet Adam Smith; Marion Kingston Stocking; Louis Stott; Michael Turner, Bodleian Library; Alexander D. Wainright, Princeton University Library; and Elizabeth Stuart Warfel.

I apologise to any of my helpers whose names have been inadvertently omitted from the above list. I should like to thank them collectively. Much of the research work for this edition was carried out in the London Library, and the British Library (including the Newspaper Library at Colindale); I should like to thank the staff at these and other libraries where I have worked. I should also like to thank the staff at the Public Record Office, Kew. Crown copyright material in the Public Record Office is reproduced by permission of the Controller of Her Majesty's Stationery Office.

I owe a special word of thanks to Ann Grindrod for typing my Notes and a number of the letters, to Robyn Marsack, the copy-editor at Yale University Press, and to Douglas Matthews for taking on the formidable task of preparing the Index. I am grateful to Michael Balfour, Richard Garnett, Sir Rupert Hart-Davis, Robyn Marsack and Roger Swearingen for the care and expertise they have brought to the reading of the proofs.

Without the devoted support and encouragement of my wife Joyce I would have found it impossible to bring this edition to completion. She has helped me to check and date the letters, carried out much individual research, and criticised and improved my editorial work at every stage. No words can adequately express my gratitude to such an ideal collaborator.

December 1993.   ERNEST MEHEW

Stevenson's parents, Thomas and
Margaret Stevenson. ('Robert Louis
Stevenson Collection', Edinburgh
City Museums)

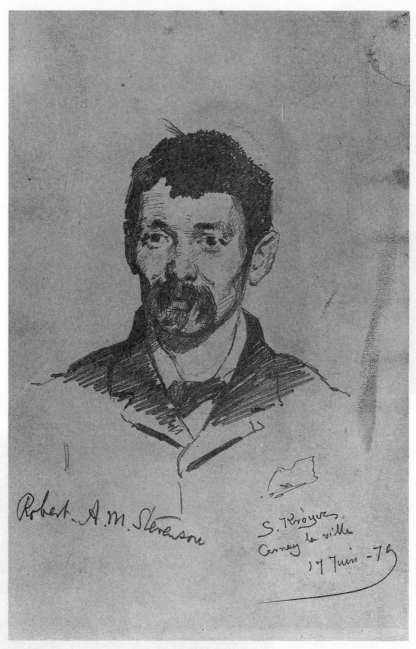

Bob Stevenson. Drawing by Peter Severin Krøyer, 1879. (Hirschprung Museum, Copenhagen. Photo: Hans Petersen)

Charles Baxter. (From *W.E. Henley* by John Connell, 1949)

W.E. Henley. (Hulton–Deutsch)

Sidney Colvin. Drawing by Alphonse
Legros, 1893. (British Museum)

Frances Sitwell (later Lady Colvin). (From
The Colvins and Their Friends by E.V. Lucas,
1928)

Fanny Van de Grift Osbourne (later Stevenson) in the early 1870s. (Beinecke Rare Book and Manuscript Library, Yale University)

INTRODUCTION

In the years since the War we have seen many editions of the collected letters of the great literary figures of the Victorian period and others are still in progress. Such editions are indispensable as the basis of accurate biographies and they make an interesting contribution to the social and publishing history of the time, but as yet another heavy and expensive volume appears we have to admit that although their authors are major writers, not all of them are inspired letter-writers. There can be no such reservations in the case of Robert Louis Stevenson. As Henry James said in his review of Sidney Colvin's edition of *Letters to His Family and Friends* in 1899: 'The shelf of our library that contains our best letter-writers is considerably furnished, but not overcrowded; and its glory is not too great to keep Stevenson from finding there a place with the very first.'[1]

Previous editions of Stevenson's collected letters have been linked with the name of his close friend and literary mentor, Sidney Colvin, who was Stevenson's own choice as editor of his correspondence. In Tahiti in November 1888, 'rather out of health and a little downcast', Stevenson had left a sealed 'letter of direction' to his stepson Lloyd Osbourne advising him of possible ways of raising money in the event of his death. The suggestions included a popular volume of 'my *reliquiae*, little verses; certain of my letters etc.' to be edited by Colvin and prefaced by a sketch of his life for which 'Colvin is again the boy'. The idea was repeated and extended in January 1893 when, following 'a turn of influenza', RLS was again anxious about future provision for his family. In a letter to his old friend and business agent, Charles Baxter, he suggested that after his death there should be an edition of his letters edited by Colvin, of which 'the *pièce de résistance* would probably be my long monthly budgets to Colvin, though I have no doubt a good many amusing or characteristic extracts could be made from earlier periods.' Baxter promptly squashed a proposal by Fanny Stevenson, put forward in the same letter, that Stevenson himself might call in his letters in his lifetime and excerpt and arrange them for publication. Stevenson had already recognised that the long diary-letters to Colvin from Samoa 'would make good pickings after I am dead' and he begged Colvin (in a letter of June 1892) 'for God's sake' not to lose them.

After Stevenson's death in December 1894, Colvin was duly appointed by Fanny Stevenson as the official biographer and editor of the letters. In less

---

[1] Review in the *North American Review*, January 1900, reprinted in *Notes on Novelists* (1914) and in *Henry James and Robert Louis Stevenson*, ed. Janet Adam Smith (1948).

than a year he had fulfilled Stevenson's wishes by publishing in November 1895 *Vailima Letters*, comprising in expurgated form forty-five journal letters to himself covering the period from November 1890 to October 1894. In spite of his poor health and his scanty leisure from his duties as Keeper of Prints and Drawings at the British Museum, Colvin accomplished a great deal in a few years. He edited and saw through the press by May 1898 the twenty-eight volumes of the Edinburgh Edition of Stevenson's works (including much unpublished material); he edited and published the two unfinished novels, *St Ives* and *Weir of Hermiston*, and made good progress with the collection and editing of the letters, which proved greater in volume than had been expected. He did virtually no work on the biography, now more and more spoken of as a full-scale work rather than the introductory sketch to the letters envisaged by Stevenson himself. Fanny and Lloyd were angry at what they saw as Colvin's delay, and after an acrimonious dispute the writing of the Life was finally entrusted to Stevenson's cousin, Graham Balfour.[2] It was left for Colvin to produce two volumes of letters.

These appeared in November 1899 as *The Letters of Robert Louis Stevenson to His Family and Friends*. In May 1911 Colvin combined the 1899 *Letters* and the *Vailima Letters* into one series, added 150 new letters and published them in four volumes as *The Letters of Robert Louis Stevenson*. This remained the basic edition to which new letters were added in successive collected editions of Stevenson's work. In the Swanston Edition of 1912 Sir Sidney Colvin (as he had now become) added seven new letters, including a fine letter to himself of August 1892 omitted from the original *Vailima Letters*. The 1911 *Letters* were reprinted again in the Vailima Edition produced in America by Scribner's in 1923 under the nominal editorship of Lloyd Osbourne. To this, independently of Colvin, were added among others forty-eight new letters to Stevenson's parents and nine to Fanny Stevenson, which had come into the hands of private collectors following the dispersal of Stevenson's papers by auction in New York after Fanny's death in 1914. Meanwhile Colvin himself published forty new letters to Mrs Sitwell (now Lady Colvin) in the *Empire Review* of June–August 1923 (reprinted in *Scribner's*). The five volumes of *Letters* published as part of the Tusitala Edition in 1924 incorporated all this new material plus a few other letters from printed sources. It was the final version produced by Colvin and has remained the standard text. The volumes were reprinted in America as part of the South Seas Edition published by Scribner's in 1925.

The only new volume of Stevenson's letters published since that time has

---

[2] See Michael Balfour, 'How the Biography of Robert Louis Stevenson Came to be Written', *TLS* 15 and 22 January 1960, and 'The First Biography' in *Stevenson and Victorian Scotland*, ed. Jenni Calder (1981).

been the scholarly edition of the full text of his letters to Charles Baxter, edited by DeLancey Ferguson and Marshall Waingrow in 1956.

Colvin's editions of the letters have given great pleasure to several generations of Stevenson's admirers. His introduction and biographical summaries are still of value, reflecting as they do the impressions of a close friend (himself a distinguished critic) of Stevenson's character and personality; but the imperfections in his editing of the letters themselves and the extent of his expurgations have become more and more apparent as the manuscripts have passed from private hands into public collections. Even when the 1899 *Letters* were published, Henry James, another close friend, wondered whether Colvin in his discretion had not 'erred a little on the side of oversuppression' and perceptively commented: 'One has the vague sense of omissions and truncations – one *smells* the things unprinted.'[3]

On several occasions, ironically enough, Colvin made it clear that he was not in favour of what he called 'sugaring' the facts in regard to key episodes in Stevenson's life. To Stevenson's mother, pained by a reference in the Editorial Note to *Weir of Hermiston* to her son's strained relations with his father, he bravely wrote: 'I would not willingly hurt you for the world . . . but if I am to handle Louis's memory at all, I cannot tell a glozing tale: I must indicate – I hope in due proportion and with the due tenderness – the things which I know to be vitally true as to certain difficult and troubled periods of his life.' He wrote in a similar vein to Lloyd Osbourne in July 1899: 'I am afraid it is not possible, with any regard to essential truth, to avoid upsetting the idyllic fictions about Louis's Edinburgh days . . . derived from Aunt Maggie [Stevenson's mother] whose peculiar gift of disguising all facts at all unpleasant, whether from others or from herself, you must have known by your own experience.'

Lloyd Osbourne, on behalf of his mother, interfered in detail when the 1899 edition of the letters was in proof and Colvin was forced to amend his account of the love affair with Fanny and the events leading to her divorce. Colvin wrote to Lloyd: 'the changes in this bit of the introduction are altogether somewhat against my judgment. I think they "sugar" the facts more than is wise or quite honest, and may invite contradiction from the unfriendly.'[4]

Against these firmly expressed opinions about biographical integrity must be set Colvin's strong, somewhat arrogant views about the suppression, indeed the destruction, of letters *he* considered unworthy of publication or

---

[3] James to Colvin [?1 November 1899] (MS Yale). Published in *The Letters of Henry James*, ed. P. Lubbock (1920), I, 339.
[4] Colvin to Mrs M.I. Stevenson 5 May 1896; to Osbourne 13 July 1899 and 5 September 1899 (MSS Yale).

of preservation. When Mrs W.E. Henley wrote to him in 1911 about the arrangements for the presentation to the Advocates' Library in Edinburgh of Stevenson's letters to her husband, he replied that he personally would go a great deal farther than her adviser, Stevenson's old friend Lord Guthrie, in 'readiness to destroy':

> Had I my will, I should . . . destroy a good many R.L.S. letters that have been through my hands, – either as too trivial, or too intimate and unveiled for the eyes of strangers either now or hereafter, or as reflecting on persons in a way which the writer never dreamed of allowing to be known by any one but his correspondent. And I expect that were I dealing with those written to your husband, I should feel the same desire. Above all I should dislike the idea of future commentators coming and rooting out things for publication which the writer's own representatives had not chosen to publish. Any advice I could give would be coloured by this general preference for destroying everything that is not manifestly worthy and suitable for preservation.[5]

These views obviously influenced Colvin's selection of letters for publication and the extent to which he felt it necessary to expurgate the letters he did publish. As he explained in his Introduction, he was strongly influenced by Stevenson's own attitude: 'Public prying into private lives, the propagation of gossip by the press, and the printing of private letters during the writer's lifetime were things he hated.' Colvin agonised at some length as to the extent to which he was justified in making public 'that which had been held sacred and hitherto private among his friends.' In view of the fact that the letters were being published so soon after Stevenson's death, when Fanny Stevenson and most of the people mentioned were still alive, a good deal of discretion was obviously necessary and many personal and family details had perforce to be omitted. There is, inevitably, no reference to the bitter quarrel with Henley, no indication of the seriousness and the nature of Fanny's illness at Vailima or of the problems with Joe Strong, the ne'er-do-well husband of Fanny's daughter, Belle. Many of the details of the dispute with his father over religion are omitted and the long emotional outpourings to Mrs Sitwell are heavily cut. Bearing in mind, no doubt, Stevenson's admonition in the 1885 Codicil to his will (Letter 1465), 'It is never worth while to inflict pain even upon a snail for any literary purpose', Colvin omitted forthright comments on fellow-authors like Hardy, criticism of missionaries and officials in Samoa and disputes with publishers.

But when every allowance has been made for the various special factors and for the restrictions imposed by Victorian standards of propriety,

---

[5] Colvin to Mrs Henley 29 September 1911 (MS Morgan).

Colvin's cavalier treatment of the text and the extent of his bowdlerisation are at times baffling to the modern reader. He cut out words, sentences and whole passages from letters without any indication of omission ('I have used the editorial privilege of omission without scruple where I thought it desirable'). He omitted or softened Stevenson's mild profanity and vulgarity: 'bloody', for example, usually becomes 'beastly'; 'behind' or 'bottom' becomes 'back' or 'posteriors'; 'constipation' is amended to 'indigestion', and even 'God grant' has to be altered to 'I only hope'. It is difficult to understand why Colvin delicately thought it necessary in Letter 1481 to Henry James to delete all but the first five words of the following: 'Likewise there is a cat, now, all unconscious of its doom, awaiting the knife of the Gelder. You shall see it when the sting has been extracted: not before.' In the same letter he altered a reference to RLS as a 'bawdy writer' to read 'immoral writer'. What possible harm to Stevenson's reputation would have resulted from the retention in a letter to his artist friend Will H. Low (Letter 1172) about Art and honesty of the following exuberant comment: 'It is idle to pretend; I love fun, wine, debauchery, and slumming from my soul's centre; but if Villon (for example) had continued to be an honest man, we should not now look, almost with pity, on that pitiful apology for a life's work.'

The letters to Mrs Sitwell suffered severely from Colvin's editorial attentions. Originally he published short extracts from them; in 1923 he added further extracts but muddled the texts in a maddening way: a passage from a letter of January 1874 is printed twice within eight pages; in other cases he added part of one letter on to part of another without explanation, or treated a further extract from a partly published letter as a new letter. Survival of the typescript of the letters to Mrs Sitwell published in the *Empire Review* in 1923 shows how the worst example of confusion occurred:[6] the pages were sent to the printer in the wrong order with the result that a letter of March 1875 has tacked onto it the conclusion of a letter of April 1879 (which Colvin misdates 1878) and the error was not picked up when the letter was published in the Tusitala Edition. It is only fair to say that the worst mistakes were made in Colvin's old age, when his memory must have been failing, and the publishers of the Tusitala Edition made no attempt to provide competent editorial assistance.

To minimise the apparent extent of Stevenson's emotional dependence on Mrs Sitwell, Colvin cut out the references to her as 'madonna', but the word slipped through in some letters added in later editions. If he had not omitted a few earlier references to her as 'Claire', we should have been spared much foolish speculation by G.S. Hellman and others in the 1920s.

[6] The typescript is at Yale.

In his essay on Samuel Pepys, Stevenson castigated the editor of a new edition of the famous diary for his expurgations, pointing out that it was 'no part of the duties of the editor of an established classic to decide what may or may not be "tedious to the reader" ', or to seek to justify omissions by the use of the 'time-honoured phrase "unfit for publication" '; he considered that readers who had bought the expensive volumes were 'entitled to be treated more like scholars and rather less like children.'

A hundred years after Stevenson's death, the problems that beset Colvin as editor have long disappeared; Stevenson himself is an 'established classic' and widely recognised, even by those who know his letters only through Colvin's truncated versions, as one of the finest letter-writers of the nineteenth century. The time has come to publish his letters in full.

In his last edition Colvin printed about 800 letters. Another 220 were added in the separate volume of letters to Charles Baxter and a number have appeared in memoirs and biographies. The total of published letters probably does not exceed 1100, many of them in sadly mutilated form. By contrast, the present edition will contain nearly 2800, of which about 2300 are taken from the original manuscripts and the rest from a variety of printed sources and copies. This number must represent only a small proportion of those he actually wrote. In an untraced letter quoted in Balfour's *Life*, RLS says that in three of his last days at Saranac in April 1888 he 'sent away upwards of seventy letters' but so far as I can tell only fifteen of these are included in this edition. Some correspondents destroyed their letters. There are over a hundred letters from Andrew Lang to Stevenson but only half a dozen from Stevenson to Lang; all but two of the letters to Professor Fleeming Jenkin have been destroyed (fortunately there is a fine series to his wife) and very few of the many that must have been written to such close friends as Sir Walter Simpson and Walter Ferrier have survived.

Over half of the manuscripts of the letters that have been traced are in the great treasure-house of Stevenson material bequeathed to Yale University Library by Edwin J. Beinecke. Next in importance, appropriately enough, comes the National Library of Scotland (successor to the Advocates' Library). There is a wide range of material in many other libraries, including the Harry Elkins Widener Collection at Harvard University, Princeton University Library (incorporating the collections of Henry E. Gerstley and Morris L. Parrish), the Huntington Library, the Pierpont Morgan Library, the Berg Collection in the New York Public Library, the Mitchell Library, Sydney, and the British Library (incorporating the Ashley Library formed by Thomas J. Wise). American collectors have performed a notable role in collecting and preserving Stevenson material and special mention must be made of the great Stevenson collector, Norman Strouse, who sadly died as this edition was nearing publication; his valuable collection is in the Silverado Museum, St Helena. One major collection of letters is still in the hands of a descendant of the original correspondent and some other descendants have a few letters. Letters in the possession of private collectors are the most difficult to trace: Stevenson has long been a sentimental favourite and many autograph-collectors have wanted an example of a letter by the man who wrote *Treasure Island*; there must still remain a number of untraced letters in private hands.

There are two important sources for the texts of letters of which the manuscripts have not been traced (and in some cases may not survive). In 1898, when preparing his edition of the 1899 *Letters*, Colvin had the texts of letters to each correspondent set up in type in galley sheets, arranged for the most part alphabetically by recipient. The text seems to have been set up by the printers – T. and A. Constable, Edinburgh – directly from the original letters, and the galleys served the same purpose as a typed copy would today. A complete set of 192 galleys formerly belonging to Lloyd Osbourne and also used by Graham Balfour for the biography came to light in California in 1979 and was acquired by the Silverado Museum.[7] In many cases they provide a fuller text than that finally printed by Colvin and the punctuation is probably closer to Stevenson's original. I have used these galleys to provide better texts for those letters partially published by Colvin for which the manuscripts have not been traced. They also provide the only available texts for a number of previously unknown letters (including some to Henley) which Colvin omitted from his edition. Among the materials collected by Balfour when writing the biography (presented to the National Library of Scotland by his son, Michael) are a great many typed transcripts of excerpts of letters to Stevenson's parents and others, and the biography itself has provided some extracts from letters not available elsewhere.

Approximately one-third of the letters are addressed to four close friends: Sidney Colvin, Frances Sitwell, W.E. Henley and Charles Baxter. When we add the letters to his father and mother (by far the largest single group) we account for almost half the known letters. The bulk of Stevenson's correspondence to the four friends has happily remained largely intact.

Colvin disposed of his letters in two main blocks. The majority of those written to him from 1873 to 1888 were sold to a bookseller in 1919 and after going through various hands were bought by Mr Beinecke for Yale in 1949. A second group, comprising the letters from the South Seas from 1888 to 1894, were sold to the Widener family for presentation to Harvard in 1913; a further eight letters or portions of letters complementing those at Harvard were sold after Colvin's death and are now at Yale. Some thirty other known letters, sold or given away by Colvin, are dispersed in various

---

[7] A section of Colvin's own copy of the galleys (containing letters to himself and a few others) was given by him to the Stevenson Club, Edinburgh and disposed of by them when the Birthplace Museum was sold in 1963. It has ended up in the library of the Trinity Academy, an Edinburgh school.

libraries including Yale.[8] A volume of typed transcripts made for Colvin
(also at Yale) has supplied the text of three untraced letters, and for some
dozen others I have had to rely on Colvin's published texts supplemented
where possible from his galleys.

Colvin bequeathed most of the letters to his wife, the former Mrs Sitwell,
to the National Library of Scotland, and they are still preserved there in the
large envelopes inside the mahogany box in which he kept them. The
National Library has acquired a number of others and has a total of 106. Ten
of the fifteen others which have been traced are at Yale, and for another
thirteen I have relied mainly on Colvin's published texts and his galleys.

Mrs Henley presented a large number of the letters to her husband to the
Advocates' Library in 1912, and a few have been acquired since; these
together with a group given by Mrs Henley to Lord Guthrie (who helped
her with the arrangements) now in Lady Stair's House Museum, Edinburgh, make up the bulk of the letters to Henley. Yale has another sixteen,
and there are a few in other libraries. The texts of seventeen untraced letters
have been taken from the published texts and the galleys.

The letters to Charles Baxter constitute the largest group to a friend.
Although he was not a wealthy man, Baxter refused to make any money
from his Stevenson letters and gave them (together with a mass of related
letters) to the Savile Club London, in 1906. The Club sold them to Mr
Beinecke in the 1930s and they are now at Yale. They were published in
full together with three letters at Princeton and four from printed sources in
1956. For this edition it has been possible to print one of these from the
manuscript in the British Library (overlooked by the editors of the 1956
volume) and to add seven new letters which have since come to light or
were overlooked in 1956.

The *Baxter Letters* also published for the first time in full the letters to and
from Baxter, Henley and others relating to the quarrel with Henley in 1888
from the originals presented by Baxter to the Advocates' Library. To these
I have been able to add a small group of previously unknown letters and
drafts acquired by Yale in 1980.

Sadly, the letters to his parents which Stevenson's mother treasured so
proudly have been widely scattered. After being used by Balfour, they were
returned to Fanny Stevenson and on her death in 1914 were put up for
sale by auction by Fanny's daughter, Belle, in the three sales of Stevenson's
books and manuscripts at the Anderson Galleries, New York, 1914–16.
Although a great number have ended up in Yale and other American

---

[8] The Yale collection (Beinecke 7971) includes one crude forgery purporting to be a letter to
Colvin from 608 Bush Street, San Francisco. The main body of the letter consists of an extract (set
out as prose) from RLS's poem 'If This Were Faith', written in 1893 (*Songs of Travel* XXVI) and
it is signed 'Yours very truly', never used in genuine letters to Colvin. It was obviously put
together from various published facsimiles.

libraries, many have not been seen by scholars since their appearance in the sale catalogue. I have put together the fullest text possible for these untraced letters from Colvin's text and galleys, Balfour's excerpts and the brief entries in sale catalogues.

Colvin was allowed to publish only nine of Stevenson's letters to his cousin Bob Stevenson, the closest friend of his youth: Bob's family were in financial difficulties after his death, and the guardians of his young son felt they could raise more money by the sale of the letters if they remained unpublished. The letters were sold off – many through Maggs, the London bookseller – and are widely dispersed. Fortunately Charles C. Osbourne, one of the guardians, had a set of typed transcripts made which he presented to the British Museum in 1922: this has provided the text for six untraced letters. Yale has the largest number of originals (twenty-two); the rest are to be found (often as one example) in eleven other libraries. Included in those at Yale are thirteen early letters which were completely unknown until they were discovered, along with the early play *Monmouth*, in 1922.

Stevenson wrote a large number of letters to Edmund Gosse, nearly half of which remained unpublished. Gosse gave many of them to T.J. Wise and as a result the British Library has the largest single collection. A few letters remain among Gosse's family papers in the Brotherton Library, Leeds, but the rest were widely dispersed after Gosse's death, often pasted into his books. Fortunately Gosse had a very accurate typed transcript made of all his letters from Stevenson and this volume (at Yale) has provided the text of thirteen untraced letters. All but one of Stevenson's letters to his American artist friend Will H. Low are in the Huntington Library; while all but one of those to the closest new friend of his later years, Henry James, are in the family papers at Harvard.

Anne Jenkin, widow of Stevenson's friend Fleeming Jenkin, gave a few of her letters for auction in aid of the Red Cross in 1918; for these untraced letters I have relied on Colvin's galleys. A large number of warmly affectionate letters remain in the possession of her great-grandson and these are mostly published for the first time. A series of letters to a Bournemouth friend, Adelaide Boodle, a number of which were unpublished, were sold at auction in 1976; most of these are at Silverado and Yale. Five early letters dating from 1872–4 to a previously unknown correspondent, Elizabeth Crosby, came to light in 1969 and are now at Yale. They throw interesting light on Stevenson as a young man and on the religious difficulties with his parents.

Most of the letters to Messrs Cassell were lost in the London Blitz, but a small group preserved by Sir Newman Flower are at Silverado. The letters to Messrs Chatto and Windus are widely dispersed but fortunately a manuscript copy made in the Chatto office of a number of the letters is at Yale. The long series of letters to Messrs Scribner and Sons (including the letters to Edward L. Burlingame, editor of *Scribner's Magazine*) were bought from the firm by Mr Beinecke and are at Yale; a few strays remain in the Scribner archives at Princeton.

Given the strong views about the destruction of letters expressed in his letter to Mrs Henley in 1911, it seems likely that Colvin destroyed a few of Stevenson's letters to himself and Mrs Sitwell. In the manuscripts of the letters to Mrs Sitwell he obliterated what were obviously expressions of affection; in one case (Letter 333) the deleted word 'Madamina' (evidently a forerunner of 'madonna'), unreadable in the manuscript, still survives in an earlier typed copy (at Yale). In the letters to himself Colvin made deletions in ink ranging from a single word (often an individual name) to a complete phrase or sentence. In those destined for Harvard he went to great lengths to conceal, as he explained in a covering letter, matters 'with which outsiders have in my judgment no concern, either now or hereafter.' In some cases he achieved his object by obliterating a word or phrase in ink or by cutting away part of the page and pasting down the manuscript. In what he obviously considered the more serious cases Colvin pasted two strips of paper – the first black, the second white – over the offending passage. In 1962, at the request of Professor Booth, the authorities at Harvard allowed manuscript experts to remove the paper strips and this was accomplished without damage to the letters. The most important passage revealed is a long account in a letter of April 1893 of Fanny Stevenson's mental illness; other passages refer to this and other domestic problems, to the dispute with the missionary A.E. Claxton, or give unflattering descriptions of acquaintances; Colvin even masked out of the last letter a passage critical of his editorial procedures in preparing the Edinburgh Edition.[9]

Fanny Stevenson, when sending Anna Henley a batch of Henley's letters to RLS, told her that she had burned two or three that she knew 'William Ernest would have liked me to destroy, being too personal and intimate' and she asked Mrs Henley 'to do the same with any you have of Lou's that you think should be destroyed.'[10] Lord Guthrie told Colvin that he had destroyed a few of Stevenson's letters to Henley before they were presented to the Advocates' Library[11] and it must have been Guthrie who went through the letters resolutely rubbing out swear-words and other improprieties. It is a pity Mrs Henley did not choose a more tolerant advisor; ribaldries which amused RLS and Henley must have shocked Guthrie, who was a strict Free Churchman and Sunday School Superintendent.

Stevenson's mother destroyed the letters her son wrote home from America at a time of family distress and dissension. She censored a few other

---

[9] See Bradford A. Booth, 'The Vailima Letters of Robert Louis Stevenson', *Harvard Library Bulletin*, April 1967.
[10] Undated letter at Yale.
[11] Lord Guthrie to Colvin 14 September 1919 (MS NLS).

letters before parting with them either by cutting away part of the manuscript or by writing over a sentence or paragraph in ink. One such passage that has been deciphered is an innocuous reference to an Edinburgh family, presumably deleted to protect their privacy (Letter 480); others may well fall into the same category.

In a number of cases the manuscript of one letter has become muddled with that of another to the same correspondent and sometimes half of a letter has ended up in one library and half in another. Sometimes, too, letters have been attributed to the wrong recipient: the last four pages of a letter to his parents has been catalogued at Yale as part of a letter to Colvin and in the same library a letter to Colvin of December 1874 is listed as being to Bob Stevenson in January 1869.

These are the least of the problems that face the editor of Stevenson's letters. A major problem is his handwriting. This is never easy to read and gets worse in the Samoan period when he suffered from writer's cramp. At times one despairs of ever being able to decipher what he actually wrote: his u's, v's and n's are often interchangeable as are his o's and a's; one cannot readily distinguish between his p's and f's, his b's and h's and his capital K's and R's. Often it is only the context or familiarity with RLS's turn of phrase that enables one to guess at the right word. Colvin, for all his familiarity with Stevenson's hand, made many mistakes and others have done no better: a few examples will illustrate the problem. One of the most amusing of Colvin's misreadings occurs in a letter to him of 20 June 1891, when in a list of chapter headings for *In the South Seas* Stevenson is made to refer to 'The Palace of Mary Warren' instead of 'The Palace of Many Women'; this mistake went through all editions from 1895 onwards and was not corrected until 1923. There is a more serious error in a letter to Lady Taylor in December 1886 (Letter 1732). RLS, commenting on Dowden's recently published life of Shelley, is made to say that he 'was weary at my resemblances to Shelley' instead of 'uneasy'. In the same letter Stevenson refers to the mixture of stories published in *The Merry Men*: 'The tales are of all dates and places; they are like the fox, the goose, and the cabbage of the ferryman; and must go floating down time together as best they can.' He is obviously referring to the old puzzle of how a ferryman could get a fox, goose and cabbage across the river without the fox eating the goose and the goose eating the cabbage. Colvin makes nonsense of this by printing 'the box, the goose and the cottage'.[12]

The editors of the Vailima Edition made some ludicrous errors in the letters they published. Even though the manuscript of Letter 65 of September 1868 has not been traced, one can guess that they were misled

---

[12] John Sparrow (who had not seen the MS) pointed out the error in a letter to the *TLS*, 11 September 1959.

by the long S, which Stevenson often used at this time, into printing 'Harbour Compinpéon' instead of 'Harbour Commission' and 'Adam Rupel' instead of 'Adam Russel'. In October 1882 (Letter 995) RLS is, amusingly, made to tell his wife, 'The Doctoribus just left me' (which is just what it looks like), instead of 'The Doctor has just left me.' Although the editors of the *Baxter Letters* generally provided a more accurate text than Colvin, there is a sprinkling of small errors, like 'Fichra' for the Scottish island of Fidra and 'nine' for the Pacific island of Niue, and confusingly in Letter 115 of December 1872 Stevenson is made to describe himself 'in a hell of a state – venus, mind and body', instead of the more prosaic 'nerves, mind and body'. Sometimes recognition of an obscure phrase can help solve an otherwise illegible word. In a passage in a letter to Baxter of February 1890 (omitted by Colvin) the editors of the *Baxter Letters* make Stevenson call Joe Strong and his wife Belle 'the worst in the lot today' – a meaningless phrase; what Stevenson actually wrote was 'the crook in the lot today', a Scottish phrase meaning a trial or an affliction.

In the face of all the errors made by my predecessors it is too much to hope that there are no misreadings of Stevenson's handwriting but I have done my best not to make him write nonsense. To add to the problem Fanny Stevenson's hand is often difficult to read, as is that of such friends as Henley.

The other major problem is dating. Until he reached Samoa, when mail was collected only on set sailing dates each month, Stevenson rarely dated his letters even though his correspondents begged him to do so; 'a date' he told Will H. Low 'is a thing to which I rise easily superior.' At best he gives the day of the week, and even that is sometimes wrong. This habit ('the despair of editors' in Colvin's phrase) did not stop him from advising others to date their letters. At times an exasperated editor feels like calling down upon him the fate he refers to in a piece of doggerel to Baxter, making fun of the latter's meticulous business habits:

> All who go in for dates and dockets
> Glory in well-filled guts and pockets;
> But they who do not date their letters
> Perish at last in straw and fetters!

Very few postmarked envelopes survive and one cannot always be sure that they relate to the correct letters. Fortunately some recipients recorded dates. Stevenson's mother went through the letters to herself and her husband, noting places and dates (presumably from envelopes later destroyed) or guessing at approximate dates. Charles Baxter also noted postmarks or recorded dates of receipt. Colvin is often wildly wrong, even in the dating of letters to himself and Mrs Sitwell, and when the date is approximately right he often gets the actual sequence of letters badly muddled; this is particularly true of the letters from Hyères and Bournemouth.

In dating the letters I have had to rely on a wide variety of factors ranging from the handwriting and paper to internal evidence, for example, of work in progress or events mentioned in other letters written at the same time as well as references to external events recorded in the wonderfully detailed newspapers of the time. It has been possible to date the early letters from Wick by references in the local press to the events – a storm, a shipwreck and a riot of discontented fishermen – described in them. A number of letters to Mrs Sitwell have been dated by the details in the Edinburgh papers of the concerts Stevenson attended and a few letters to his mother from Paris by information about the plays he saw at the Comédie Française. Australian, New Zealand and San Francisco papers have been invaluable for details of the sailing dates of steamers to Hawaii and Samoa.

But the greatest source of information, both for dating the letters and for setting them in their context by annotation, has been the wealth of contemporary documentation (much of which is at Yale) by Stevenson's relatives and friends. It includes a vast collection of letters *to* Stevenson, letters between his friends about him, the many letters that Fanny Stevenson wrote to her mother-in-law, Colvin and other friends (although like her husband she rarely dated them), and the series of pocket diaries kept by his mother in which she faithfully recorded her son's movements. Further details of this and other material used are provided in the section on Editorial Procedures.

Many of the letters to his parents after Stevenson's marriage were joint letters with his wife and she sometimes added postscripts in letters written to his friends. I have printed all or part of Fanny's contribution when it helps to explain references in Stevenson's own letter, gives background information, or is amusing or interesting in its own right. I have also published a few of Fanny's letters to her mother-in-law, Colvin, Henley, Baxter and others when she tells them what was happening during Stevenson's severe illnesses or when, as was sometimes the case during the Pacific voyages, friends depended on her letters for news of their travels. I have given the key letters written by Stevenson's father and others at the time of his first visit to America and subsequent marriage and a few exchanged between his friends later which throw light on their views of that marriage. I have also included the letters by Henley, Baxter, Fanny and Katharine de Mattos during the quarrel with Henley.

I have taken the opportunity to publish as enclosures in the letters to Baxter six previously unpublished 'Brashiana' sonnets in addition to the five already included in *Collected Poems* (1950) and in an Appendix the six uncollected Prose Poems of 1875 (three of which were previously unpublished).

In his published prose we find Stevenson, the literary stylist and craftsman
dedicated to his art, who has redrafted and polished his work in order to
convey his ideas in the most effective way. In a number of early letters –
some of those to his cousin Bob, the travel accounts to his mother on the
journey in the lighthouse steamer in 1869, and in the set pieces of descriptive writing in the letters to Mrs Sitwell – we can watch the prentice writer
still learning his trade, but in most of them (in Colvin's words) 'Stevenson
the deliberate artist is scarcely forthcoming at all.' In the Introduction to his
edition, Colvin gives a summary of their qualities which applies even more
strongly to the uncut letters than it does to his own selection:

> He does not care a fig for order or logical sequence or congruity, or for
> striking a key of expression and keeping it, but becomes simply the most
> spontaneous and unstudied of human beings. He has at his command the
> whole vocabularies of the English and Scottish languages, classical and
> slang, – the slang both of general use and of a kind of private code current
> among his intimates, – with good stores of the French, and tosses and
> tumbles them about irresponsibly to convey the impression or affection,
> the mood or freak of the moment; pouring himself out in all manner of
> rhapsodical confessions and speculations, grave or gay, notes of observa-
> tion and criticism, snatches of remembrance and autobiography,
> moralisings on matters uppermost for the hour in his mind, comments on
> his own work or other people's, or mere idle fun and foolery.

Elsewhere, quoting a letter to Henley (Letter 1145) which he omitted from
his own edition, Colvin tells us that Stevenson's letters 'are the only things
left of him that convey any impression of his talk':

> When I open a letter at random and find it beginning, 'My bosom's lord'
> (bosom's lord, you remember, is from the great speech of Romeo on the
> fatal morning) – when I read, 'My bosom's lord is literally swipey with
> elevation', I catch a far off but a genuine note of that flood of mingled
> poetry and slang which used to pour from him in speech.[13]

The Stevenson who emerges from this full edition of his letters is
essentially the same Stevenson we already knew from Colvin's edition and
from his own writings. But we see him in sharper focus as a far more human
figure, highly emotional and given to quick outbursts of anger, more
irreverent and ribald in language and more critical and forthright in his
comments on people and events. We watch him responding to the concerns
of everyday life (including many family problems) as well as to the special
difficulties and anxieties that face an author. What comes across strongly is

[13] Colvin's lecture to the Royal Institution, 10 February 1911, published in its *Notices of the
Proceedings* . . . (1914), XX, 48–9.

his sense of fun and the shared jokes with his family and friends, his great zest for life under conditions that would daunt most people, and his many enthusiasms. In almost every letter in the last fourteen years of his life there is some reference to his own health: there is little or no bitterness in these comments and no self-pity, but certainly nothing of the cheerful optimist of legend. Underlying it all is a more serious, even solemn, attitude which leads him to drop without warning into passages of moralising or wry reflection on the ironies and absurdities of life. Over-riding everything else is Stevenson's dedication from his early days to what he called 'my trade of words'. He sums it up in a letter to Meredith in September 1893:

> For fourteen years I have not had a day's real health; I have wakened sick and gone to bed weary; and I have done my work unflinchingly. I have written in bed, and written out of it, written in hemorrhages, written in sickness, written torn by coughing, written when my head swam for weakness; and for so long, it seems to me I have won my wager and recovered my glove.

When he was twenty-two Stevenson told Elizabeth Crosby (Letter 117) 'My letters have a trick of lapsing away from me in tranquil egotism, with never a currant of information in the whole unleavened pudding.' Thirteen years later he wrote to his parents (Letter 1509), 'I deny that letters should contain news (I mean mine – those of other people should). But mine should contain appropriate sentiments and humorous nonsense or nonsense without the humour. When the house is empty, the mind is seized with a desire – no that is too strong – a willingness to pour forth unmitigated rot, which constitutes (in me) the true spirit of correspondence.' These are important elements in the charm of Stevenson's letters, but there is much more.

In a letter to Mrs Sitwell in 1883 (Letter 1168) he mentions facetiously another element: 'There is nothing like a good correspondent; absence is destroyed: why it's like living in the same house! All the details of your friend's life unroll before you like a panorama; you know his thoughts, his feelings, his minutest habits and surroundings.' Up to his thirtieth year, in spite of some fascinating glimpses, Stevenson's letters cannot be said to provide such a picture of his life: but from the time of his marriage until his death they give us the fullest possible record of his thoughts and feelings, so far of course as he was prepared to divulge them to his correspondents. Because of his opposition to what he called 'sordid facts', we often have to rely on his wife or mother for some of the actual events and essential dates, but once he begins his long journal-letters to Colvin from Samoa even this biographical element is supplied. We can watch his slow progress to maturity, his struggles to achieve success as an author through to the world-wide fame he had reached at the time of his sudden death. Recent biographers have used some of these letters to good effect, but no-one can tell the story as well as Stevenson himself.

Many foolish books have been written about Stevenson. In the years immediately following his death he was sentimentalised by extreme admirers as 'Velvet Jacket', the long-haired, loveable eccentric and Bohemian; as the near-saintly optimist – the 'Seraph in Chocolate' of Henley's gibe, and as 'Tusitala', the white chief of Vailima beloved by missionaries and worshipped by the Samoans. In reaction, the debunkers of the 1920s and later created another unreal figure – the sensualist and poseur dominated by his wife. Soon after the centenary of his birth the publication of J.C. Furnas's major biography, *Voyage to Windward*, provided us with a balanced picture of the man freed from these legends and most later biographers have continued to redress the balance. In spite of this some of the old legends still linger and as we reach the centenary of his death I hope that the publication of the complete letters will sweep them away for ever.

Henry James deplored the fact that interest in Stevenson as a personality and picturesque character had effectively killed serious consideration of him as a literary artist.[14] The publication of his letters will inevitably feed interest in Stevenson as a character as attractive as any that he created in his fiction; but I hope the many comments he makes in them on his own work and the way he discusses the technical problems facing the author will lead some people at least to read or re-read that work with a greater regard for Stevenson as a serious writer. But there is surely no reason why in reading his letters we should not combine both interests: his superb skill as a letter-writer is now an important part of his literary fame. We can continue to indulge our fascination in Stevenson as a person (already roused by his autobiographical essays) by reading about him directly in his own words in his letters.

Long ago George Saintsbury (a friend and correspondent) expressed the view that Stevenson's letters were 'almost as good as his fiction' and that he would hold his own as a letter-writer 'as long as English literature lasts'.[15] It is surely ironic that through his letters, hurriedly and casually written without thought of publication, Stevenson should have attained a place in English literature as secure as that already achieved through his carefully composed masterpieces of formal prose.

ERNEST MEHEW

---

[14] James to Gosse 20 November 1901. *Letters*, ed. Lubbock, I, 395.
[15] George Saintsbury, *A Letter Book* (1922), 81, 303.

EDITORIAL PROCEDURES AND SOURCES OF INFORMATION

As stated in the Introduction, Stevenson's letters were often hurriedly and carelessly written and include notes scribbled in pencil from his sick-bed on scraps of paper. Any attempt to reproduce in type on a different page-size the layout and vagaries of the manuscript would result in an unreadable text without conveying the flavour of the original. The following editorial procedures have been adopted.

The letters have been numbered consecutively with occasional letters by others included in the numeration. A few letters overlooked or which came to light at a late stage have been given a number followed by an A. Below the heading the location of the manuscript or other source of the text has been given in abbreviated form, followed by information about previous publication. References to Colvin's edition are to the five-volume edition of *Letters* included in the Tusitala Edition of Stevenson's works, 1924. Previous partial publication in newspapers, sale catalogues or published library catalogues has been ignored.

The address and date are given in italics at the head of the letter, regardless of where they appear in the manuscript. The address, printed on the right, is given in full the first time it occurs and thereafter abbreviated to the essential minimum. No attempt is made to distinguish between printed or written addresses. The date is given in standardised form on the left. Dates or locations supplied editorially are enclosed in square brackets and queried when doubtful; when such information is recorded by the recipient this is indicated by an asterisk to the left of the square bracket. Dates or addresses provided in the course of journal-letters are standardised in the same way.

To save space, the beginning and ending of each letter have been run into the body of the letter, and punctuation and capitalisation provided where necessary. Superior letters have been lowered and contractions and abbreviations (including abbreviations for books and articles) have been expanded save in such standard cases as 'Mr', 'Dr' and so on; ampersands have been expanded except where they are used in names of firms. I have retained a few favourite contractions such as 'vol' for volume and 'Mag' for 'magazine'. Contractions and abbreviations used for comic effect have also been retained. Figures of small numbers are usually written out in words.

Where ellipses occur in the body of the letter they are Stevenson's own, except when a fragment of a letter is being printed or the text is incomplete because of deletions made by later hands. False starts or inserted words are not indicated as such. Words or passages deleted by Stevenson are (where legible) given in a footnote if they seem of interest or significance, or where they help to explain an allusion in the letter; otherwise they are ignored. Words or passages cancelled by others, notably Colvin, Lord Guthrie and Mrs M.I. Stevenson (see p. 10 above) are incorporated into the main text so far as they can now be read, with an explanatory footnote. Slips of the pen are usually silently corrected; words inadvertently omitted are supplied in square brackets, as are words lost through damage to the manuscript. In a few places a guess is made at an illegible word or indication given that the word is illegible.

Postscripts are printed at the end of the letter wherever they occur in the original, save in a few cases where a note at the head of the letter makes better sense. It is not possible to reproduce all the manual flourishes, doodles, variations in the size of writing and comic signatures of which Stevenson was so fond. A number of his comic drawings are reproduced in facsimile where they add to the interest or gaiety of the letter. Childish drawings enclosed in early letters are not reproduced.

Words underlined by Stevenson have usually been printed in italics regardless of the number of times they have been underlined, save where the use of capitals seems appropriate. The printing of titles has been standardised: those of poems, stories and articles are in quotation marks; those of books, plays and periodicals in italics. Foreign words are printed in italics except where the whole letter is in French.

Stevenson set great store by his own idiosyncratic punctuation and was annoyed when printers changed it. He wrote angrily to Henley in 1881 (Letter 882): 'Your printer is a bloody insolent dog, whom I could smite on the mouth. Who is he to alter all my punctuation . . . I made two table-spoonfuls of bad blood over the bitch.' When he returned proof to the publisher's reader for *Scribner's Magazine* in the winter of 1887 he wrote: 'I must suppose my system of punctuation to be very bad; but it is mine; and it shall be adhered to with punctual adherence by every created printer who shall print for me.' In the face of these admonitions I have tried to be as faithful as possible to Stevenson's punctuation, but since we are dealing with hurriedly written letters, not material prepared for the press, I have not scrupled to add or delete an occasional punctuation mark without comment, for ease of reading, and to supply opening or closing brackets and full-stops omitted through carelessness. Letters dictated to others, especially those to his stepdaughter Belle Strong at Vailima, have been re-punctuated where necessary. I have regularised Stevenson's use of initial capital letters where his practice seems to have no significance and provided some initial capitals where these seemed necessary. I have re-paragraphed some long letters.

Colvin commented: 'As all his friends are aware, to spell in a quite accurate and grown-up manner was a thing which this master of English letters was never able to learn.' In the mid-1870s RLS was still having problems with words like easily, hastily, readily and steadily, which he spelled with two l's, and he tended to write 'litterature' and 'litterary'. He cured himself of these mistakes but all his life he was uncertain of the spelling of 'ei' words like neighbour, leisure, seize and weigh; he often wrote 'excercise', 'carreer', 'adition' and 'quarreled'. Another idiosyncrasy was to hyphenate a great many words beginning with 'dis', as dis-cover, dis-gusting, dis-cussions and dis-cretion; and also a few beginning with 'mis', like mis-giving. To perpetuate such misspellings would merely distract the reader's attention and I have silently corrected them. Misspellings deliberately used for comic effect have been retained, as have a few deliberate archaic spellings and words adapted from the French that he liked to use when corresponding with Henley or Bob Stevenson. I have provided some missing accents for French words but have not corrected mistakes in his use of French or Latin. Mistakes in the spelling of people's names have been silently corrected except where Stevenson could not have known the true spelling. The original misspellings have been retained in the letters written in childhood in Part I.

Letters written wholly or mainly in French have been translated as have phrases or passages in Latin or German. Words or phrases in Scots, the meaning of which cannot easily be guessed by English readers from the context have been glossed.

The question of the amount of annotation necessary in an edition of this kind is always a matter of dispute; what one reader will find helpful another will find merely irritating; I hope I have struck a reasonable balance. It has been strongly represented to me that present-day readers will not always understand literary and historical references or allusions to the nineteenth-century background that would not have needed annotation a generation ago, and I have also borne in mind that the letters will be read on both sides of the Atlantic. My aim has been to explain RLS's references to his family, his work, books read and contemporary events and to identify people mentioned (except where they are major literary or historical figures). I have set the letters in a biographical framework and in doing so established what I believe is the fullest and most accurate chronology of his life. Quotations have been identified so far as possible, except where they seem too obvious. From his upbringing Stevenson's mind was full of Biblical phrases and his letters are larded with them, sometimes for comic effect. I have thought it useful to identify such references.

The notes have been kept as factual as possible but it is not practicable for reasons of space to give the source of all the information provided.

A wealth of documentation has been drawn upon for the dating and annotation of the letters. The main sources used are as follows.

1. *Stevenson's own writings*   Stevenson's manuscripts, notebooks and books from his library were dispersed in three sales at the Anderson Galleries New York, 1914–16, following Fanny Stevenson's death. A great deal of this material is now at Yale, and other libraries have useful collections. As well as using Stevenson's published works, I have made use of this unpublished material, including fragments of autobiography (MSS Rosenbach and Yale), early recollections of childhood, a diary for 1883 (Yale) and many of his notebooks (mainly Yale).

Unless otherwise indicated it can be assumed that all published work referred to in the Notes can be found in the Tusitala Edition of 1923–4. For the published poems I have used the *Collected Poems*, ed. Janet Adam Smith (1971), supplemented by vol. XXIII of the Tusitala Edition.

2. *Graham Balfour's papers*   The material collected by Balfour when writing the official biography is in the National Library of Scotland. It includes his Biography Notebook, establishing the main events in Stevenson's life; recollections by his friends; correspondence and comments by Fanny Stevenson, Lloyd Osbourne and others; and Balfour's own recollections (originally written for Colvin). The biography itself has been a valuable source.

3. *His mother's diaries and letters*   The pocket diaries kept by Mrs M.I. Stevenson from 1853 to her death in 1897 are at Yale. They carefully record her son's movements and give a mass of information on relatives and friends. She summarised the information about RLS from these diaries up to the year 1888 in her *Diary Notes* (Yale) compiled for Colvin's use in 1896; the summary was published (with many misreadings) in vol. 26 of the Vailima Edition (1923). The diaries are usefully supplemented by the journal-letters she wrote to her sister, Jane Balfour (originals untraced), published as *From Saranac to the Marquesas and Beyond* (1903) and *Letters from Samoa* (1906), and by her letters to Baxter (Yale).

4. *His wife's diaries and letters*   The diary kept intermittently by Fanny Stevenson at Vailima from September 1890 to July 1893 (MS Stevenson House, Monterey) was published as part of *Our Samoan Adventure*, ed. Charles Neider (1956); a few pages of an unpublished fragmentary continuation are at Silverado. Silverado also has the original diary which Fanny published in part as *The Cruise of the 'Janet Nichol'* (1915). Copies of Fanny's letters to Timothy Rearden are at Yale and Silverado. Her letters to Dora Norton Williams, Charles Baxter and W.E. Henley are at Yale, as are most of those to Colvin and Mrs Sitwell. Especially useful are her many letters to RLS's mother (with a few to his father) divided between Yale and Silverado. Fanny's introductions to the Biographical Edition of her husband's work (1905) were reprinted in the Tusitala Edition and the

biography by her sister Nellie Van de Grift Sanchez (1920) has some material not available elsewhere.

5. *Diaries and letters by his stepchildren*   Isobel Strong's journal, *Grouse in the Gun-room*, covering the period from October 1892 to January 1895, is at Yale; a few extracts were published in *Memories of Vailima* (1902). Her letters to Charles Warren Stoddard are at Silverado and Yale. In old age she published her reminiscences, *This Life I've Loved* (1937). Lloyd Osbourne's diary for 1889 is at Yale. His letters to his mother (with some later ones to her and RLS) are at Silverado and Yale, as are a few letters to Stevenson's mother; his letters to Baxter are at Yale. Lloyd's recollections, which cannot be relied on for detail, were contributed as introductions to various volumes of the Tusitala Edition; they were collected as *An Intimate Portrait of R.L.S.* (1924).

6. *Letters to and about Stevenson*   There exists a rich collection of letters to Stevenson and his wife, most of which is at Yale. It includes a great many letters from Henley, Baxter, Bob Stevenson, Will H. Low and Andrew Lang; regrettably only a few from Colvin have survived. The letters from Stevenson's parents are at Yale and the Bancroft Library, and those from his wife are at Yale and Silverado. The office copies of letters from the Scribner archives (including letters from E.L. Burlingame and Charles Scribner) are at Yale. For letters from famous literary figures I have used the collected editions of their correspondence (but I have also seen the originals of those at Yale): volumes II and III of *The Letters of George Meredith*, ed. C.L. Cline (1970); volumes II and III of *The Letters of John Addington Symonds*, ed. H.M. Schueller and R.L. Peters (1968 and 1969), plus two uncollected letters at Princeton and Silverado; volume III of *Henry James Letters*, ed. Leon Edel (1981), supplemented by a great many others at Yale. For letters from Edmund Gosse (originals untraced) I have used Evan Charteris, *The Life and Letters of Sir Edmund Gosse* (1931), supplemented by transcripts by Balfour in the National Library. After my own work had been completed, Andrew Lang's letters to RLS were published as *Dear Stevenson: Letters from Andrew Lang to Robert Louis Stevenson with Five Letters from Stevenson to Lang*, ed. Marysa Demoor (Louvain, Belgium, 1990).

There are many references to Stevenson in the letters exchanged between his friends. Yale has typed transcripts of the letters from Colvin to Baxter and a long series of original letters from Henley to Baxter. Extracts from correspondence exchanged between Colvin and Henley are published in E.V. Lucas, *The Colvins and Their Friends* (1928) and there are some originals at Yale, which also has some letters from Henry James to Colvin, and Lucas prints some others. The Brotherton Library, Leeds, has a long series of letters to Gosse from both Henry James and Colvin. Those by James have been partly published in *Selected Letters of Henry James to Edmund Gosse 1882–1915*, ed. Rayburn S. Moore (1988). Lady Stair's House,

Edinburgh has some letters from Charles Baxter to Lord Guthrie which throw some interesting light on the quarrel with Henley.

7. *Reviews*   Another example of his mother's devotion is to be found in the six scrapbooks in which she collected reviews of Stevenson's books and newspaper references to him: volumes I and III belong to the Stevenson Society, Saranac Lake and volumes II, IV–VI, plus a separate volume of family obituary notices, are at Stevenson House, Monterey (xerox copy at Yale). *Robert Louis Stevenson: The Critical Heritage*, ed. Paul Maixner (1981) reprints some major reviews.

8. *Bibliographies*   I am deeply indebted to Roger Swearingen's *The Prose Writings of Robert Louis Stevenson: A Guide* (1980). He and I used much of the same material and it has been an inestimable advantage to be able to check my own research against his; where we occasionally differ over details, I have had access to information not available to him. The material in the Beinecke Collection at Yale is mostly listed in *A Stevenson Library: Catalogue of a Collection . . . Formed by Edwin J. Beinecke*, compiled by George L. McKay, 6 vols (1951–64). Volumes I and II, listing printed material, largely supersede the standard bibliography by W.F. Prideaux (rev. 1917).

9. *Other Works*   The published reminiscences by Stevenson's friends include: Colvin, *Memories and Notes* (1921); Gosse, *Critical Kit-Kats* (1896); Henley, 'R.L.S.' in the *Pall Mall Magazine*, December 1901; and Will H. Low, *A Chronicle of Friendships* (1908). Amidst much dross, *I Can Remember Robert Louis Stevenson*, ed. Rosaline Masson (1925) contains some items of value, as does *Stevensoniana*, ed. J.A. Hammerton (1907). Other works dealing with specific periods of Stevenson's life are mentioned in the Parts concerned but special acknowledgment must be made of my debt to Kenneth S. Mackenzie's Ph.D. thesis, 'Robert Louis Stevenson and Samoa' (Dalhousie University, 1974). *The Edinburgh Academy Register* (1914) has been invaluable in the identification of Edinburgh friends.

Unless otherwise indicated, letters quoted in the notes are at Yale.

THE STEVENSON FAMILY

When working on his family history (posthumously published as *Records of a Family of Engineers*) in the last years of his life, Stevenson traced his paternal ancestors back to James Stevenson, a tenant farmer living at Nether Carsewell, in the Parish of Neilston, south-west of Glasgow, in the seventeenth century. Some of his descendants became maltmen in Glasgow, among them his grandson, Robert Stevenson (1720–64), who had ten children by his second wife, Margaret Fulton. Two of the children, Hugh (born 1749) and Alan (born 1752), were West India merchants and ship-owners in Glasgow who both died tragically of a fever in the West Indies in 1774 while pursuing two merchants who had swindled them. Alan had married in 1771 Jean, daughter of David Lillie, a Glasgow builder who was several times 'Deacon of the Wrights', and their son, Robert Stevenson (RLS's grandfather), was born in 1772. The death of her husband, followed in the same year by that of her father, left Jean in straitened circumstances and she married James Hogg, a Glasgow manufacturer (a marriage unknown to RLS). By 1778 she had moved to Edinburgh with her six-year-old son, and appears to have divorced Hogg later.

In Edinburgh she became on friendly terms with Thomas Smith and his wife, Elizabeth, who like her were devout church-goers. Thomas Smith (1753–1815) was a remarkable man who established a successful business in Edinburgh as tinsman and maker of oil-lamps. In 1786, having designed a system of reflector oil-lights to replace the primitive coal fires, he was made Engineer to the recently formed Board of Northern Lights. As his business expanded he took as his apprentice the young Robert Stevenson. In 1792 (not 1787 as RLS has it), following the death of his second wife, Thomas Smith married the forty-one-year-old Jean Stevenson, and Robert thus became his stepson as well as his apprentice. The two families became even closer when Robert married in 1799 his stepsister Jean (Jane), Thomas Smith's eldest daughter from his first marriage. As RLS put it, 'the marriage of a man of twenty-seven and a girl of twenty who have lived for twelve years [in fact seven] as brother and sister is difficult to conceive.'

Robert Stevenson became Thomas Smith's partner and took over more and more responsibility for the lighthouse work. He succeeded his step-father as Engineer to the Northern Lighthouse Board and held the position for nearly half a century until 1843, during which time he may be said to have been mainly responsible for the inauguration of the Scottish lighthouse system. The greatest achievement of his long career was the building under hazardous conditions of the Bell Rock lighthouse, 1807–11. He built some

twenty lighthouses in all and made major improvements in lighting, including the invention of intermittent and flashing lights. From 1811 onwards he
took on a wide range of other civil engineering work, including the design
of bridges and roads – he was responsible for the eastern approaches to
Edinburgh – and the improvement of harbours, rivers and canals.

Only five of Robert and Jean Stevenson's thirteen children survived
infancy. Three of the sons – Alan, David and Thomas (RLS's father) –
joined their father in the family firm as civil engineers, becoming in their
turn Engineers to the Northern Lighthouse Board. The family tree shows
Thomas Stevenson's sister and brothers and those members of their families
mentioned in Stevenson's letters. Details about them are provided in the
annotation to the letters.

[The history of the Stevenson family is given in Craig Mair's *A Star for
Seamen* (1978) and in RLS's *Records of a Family of Engineers*. There is an
article on Robert Stevenson by D.A. Stevenson in the *DNB*.]

THE STEVENSON FAMILY

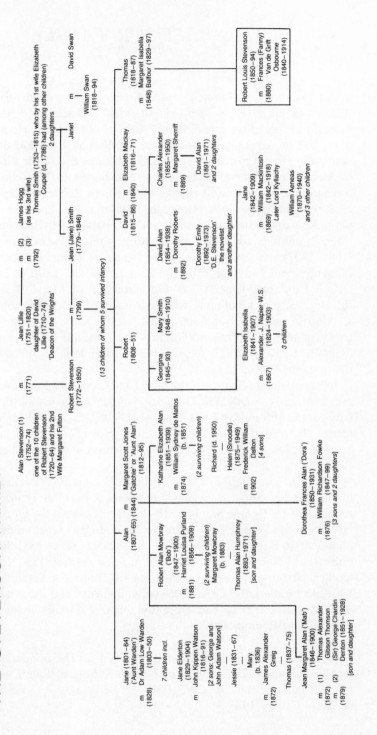

THE BALFOUR FAMILY

In his 'Memoirs of Himself' RLS described his mother's family, the Balfours of Pilrig, as 'good provincial stock' and said he believed them 'related to many of the so-called good families of Scotland'. He said he had never had the curiosity to look at the family tree. If he had done so he would have found that this branch of the Balfours trace their ancestry back to Alexander Balfour of Inchrye, near Newburgh in Fife, who is almost certainly the man placed in charge of the King's Cellar by King James IV in 1499 and later years. Although RLS did not know it when he wrote *Kidnapped*, Alexander's son was David Balfour. His descendants were mainly ministers, advocates or merchants. One of them, James Balfour (1681–1737), bought the house and estate of Pilrig, halfway between Edinburgh and Leith, in 1718 and became the first Laird of Pilrig. The second Laird was James (1705–95), Professor of Moral Philosophy at the University of Edinburgh, who is visited by his fictional cousin David at Pilrig in chapter 3 of *Catriona*. His wife, Cecilia Elphinstone, was a granddaughter of Sir Gilbert Elliot of Minto, enabling RLS to say (in 'The Manse'), 'I have shaken a spear in the Debateable Land and shouted the slogan of the Elliots'.

John Balfour (1740–1814), the third Laird, a commission agent and corn merchant, had five children. The eldest, James, became the fourth Laird and father of the fifth and last Laird, James (1811–93), who added Melville to his name. The second son of the third Laird, John (1776–1859), also a corn merchant, was the grandfather of RLS's cousin and biographer Graham Balfour.

The third son, the Revd Lewis Balfour, became RLS's grandfather. At his first parish, Sorn in Ayrshire, he married in 1818 Henrietta Scott, daughter of Dr George Smith (1748–1823) of Galston, the Dr Smith who (as RLS liked to remember) 'opens out his cauld harangues on practice and on morals' in Burns's 'The Holy Fair'. In 1823 he moved to Colinton, four miles from Edinburgh, where he lived until his death in 1860. Stevenson's mother, Margaret Isabella, was their twelfth child. The family tree shows her eight brothers and sisters who survived infancy and those members of their families mentioned in Stevenson's letters. Details about them are provided in the annotation to the letters.

[The history of the Balfour family is given in *The Balfours of Pilrig* by Barbara Balfour-Melville (1907), supplemented from Balfour, I, 10–13, and Michael Balfour, 'The First Biography' in *Stevenson and Victorian Scotland*, ed. Jenni Calder (1981).]

THE BALFOUR FAMILY

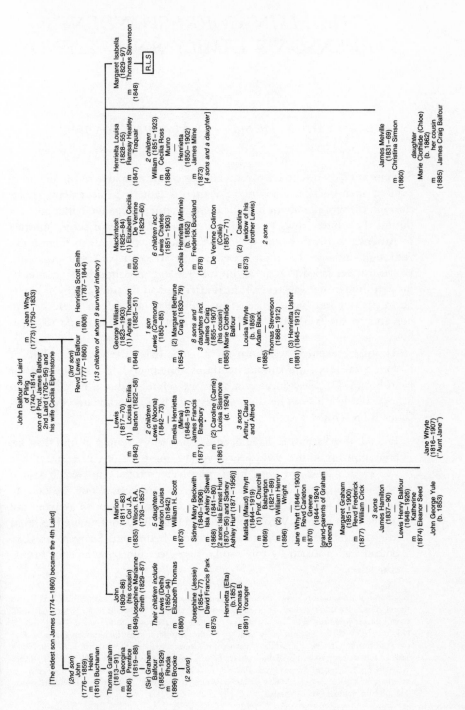

John Balfour 3rd Laird
of Pilrig
(1740–1814)
son of Prof. James Balfour
2nd Laird (1705–95) and
his wife Cecilia Elphinstone
m Jean Whyte
(1773) (1750–1833)

[The eldest son James (1774–1860) became the 4th Laird]

(2nd son)
John
(1776–1859)
m Helen
(1810) Buchanan

(3rd son)
Revd Lewis Balfour m Henrietta Scott Smith
(1777–1860)   (1808)   (1787–1844)
[13 children of whom 9 survived infancy]

Margaret Isabella
(1829–97)
m Thomas Stevenson
(1848) R.L.S

Thomas Graham
(1813–91)
m Georgina
(1856) Prentice
(1819–88)

(Sir) Graham
Balfour
(1858–1929)
m Rhoda
(1896) Brooke
(2 sons)

John
(1809–86)
(his cousin)
m Josephine Marianne
(1849) Smith (1829–87)

Their children include
Lewis (Delhi)
(1850–94)
m Elizabeth Thomas
(1880)

Josephine (Jessie)
(1854–77)
m David Francis Park
(1875)

Henrietta (Etta)
(b.1857)
m Thomas B.
(1891) Younger

Marion
(1811–83)
m Col J.A.
(1835) Wilson, R.A.
(1793–1857)

5 daughters
Marion Louisa
(b1842)
m William H. Scott
(1873)

Sidney Mary Beckwith
(1840–1908)
m Isla Ashley Sitwell
(1868) Isla Ernest Hurt
(1870–95) and Sidney
Ashley Hurt (1871–1956)]

Matilda (Maud) Whyt
(1844–1919)
m (1) Prof. Churchill
(1869) Babington
(1821–89)
m (2) William Henry
(1896) Wright

Lewis
(1817–70)
m (1) Louisa Emilia
(1842) Barton (1822–58)

2 children
Lewis (Noona)
(1842–73)
—
Emelia Henrietta
(Mina)
(1848–1917)
m James Francis
(1871) Bradbury

m (2) Caroline (Carrie)
(1861) Louisa Sissmore
(d. 1924)

3 sons
Arthur, Claud
and Alfred

George William
(1823–1903)
m (1) Agnes Thomson
(1848) (1825–51)

1 son
Lewis (Cramond)
m (2) Margaret Bethune
(1854) Craig (1830–79)

*8 sons and
3 daughters incl.*
James Craig
(1855–1907)
(his cousin)
m Marie Clothilde
(1885) Balfour

Louisa Whyte
(b. 1859)
m Adam Black
(1885)

Thomas Stevenson
(1868–1912)
m (3) Henrietta Usher
(1881) (1845–1912)

Mackintosh
(1825–84)
m (1) Elizabeth Cecilia
(1850) De Verinne
(1829–60)

6 children incl.
Lewis Charles
(1851–1903)
—
Cecilia Henrietta (Minnie)
(b. 1862)
m Frederick Buckland
(1878)

De Verinne Colinton
(Collie)
(1857–71)

m (2) Caroline
(1873) (widow of his
brother Lewis)

2 sons

Henrietta Louisa
(1828–55)
m Ramsay Heatley
(1847) Traquair

William (1851–1923)
m Cecilia Ross
(1884) Munro
2 children

Henrietta
(1850–1902)
m James Milne
(1873)
[4 sons and a daughter]

Jane Whyte
(1816–1907)
("Aunt Jane")

Margaret Graham
(1851–1900)
m Revd Frederick
(1877) William Crick

Jane Whyt (1846–1903)
m Revd Carleton
(1870) Greene
(1844–1924)
[grand-parents of Graham
Greene]

James Hamilton
(1837–90)
—
Lewis Henry Balfour
(1848–1926)
m Katherine
(1874) Eleanor Seed
3 sons

John George Yule
(b. 1853)

James Melville
(1831–69)
m Christina Simson
(1860)

daughter
Marie Clothilde (Chloe)
(b. 1862)
her cousin
m (1885) James Craig Balfour

THE MAIN CORRESPONDENTS:
STEVENSON'S FAMILY AND FRIENDS

Stevenson's Parents: Thomas and Margaret Stevenson[1]

Stevenson's closeness to his parents and his continuing love for them is very evident in his letters, and his pride in his father's achievements shines through his writings about him. The estrangement between father and son during their bitter rows over religion and at the time of RLS's journey to America to marry Fanny Osbourne caused deep distress to them both. Although usually the most careless and irregular of correspondents, he hardly ever failed to write to his mother and, as Balfour says, 'master of his pen though he was, several times after he had become a man of letters he bursts out into impatience at the difficulty he finds in expressing to her and to his father the depth of his affection and gratitude to them both'.

Thomas Stevenson was born on 22 July 1818, the youngest child of Robert Stevenson, the famous lighthouse engineer, and his wife Jean (or Jane) Smith. He was educated at a private school and at Edinburgh High School, but like his son he was indifferent to it all. In some notes about his father RLS wrote:

> Indeed, there seems to have been nothing more rooted in him than his contempt for all the ends, processes, and ministers of education. Tutor was ever a by-word with him; 'positively tutorial', he would say of people or manners he despised; and with rare consistency, he bravely encouraged me to neglect my lessons, and never so much as asked me my place in school. What a boy should learn in school he used to say is 'to sit upon his bum'. It could scarce be better put. So were his days bound each to each by this natural suspicion and contempt for formal education.

[1] Biographical information about Thomas Stevenson comes from the article in the *DNB* by his friend Alexander Buchan, and the obituary notice by his cousin William Swan (which has a full record of his professional achievements) in *Proceedings of the Royal Society of Edinburgh*, vol. 20 (1895), 61–78. RLS's account of his father's childhood (intended for inclusion in a later chapter of the unfinished *Records of a Family of Engineers*) is extensively quoted in Balfour, I, 16–20. I have added a few words, omitted by Balfour, from the original MS in a notebook in Huntington. RLS's essay on his father is in *Memories and Portraits*. Colvin's comments are in *Letters* I, 1–2. Further information is given in Craig Mair's *A Star for Seamen* (1978); Mair considers that David Stevenson was a better engineer than Thomas.

It is not surprising that his cousin, William Swan, should record that 'his position was at best that of respectable mediocrity'; and that in later life Thomas 'might be heard to say that none of the troubles and trials of his manhood were so hard to bear as the sufferings he had endured at school.'

RLS considered that the 'truly formative parts' of his father's education 'lay entirely in his hours of play' and conceives him as 'a very sturdy and madly high-spirited boy'. He goes on to describe Robert Stevenson's house, No. 1 Baxter's Place in Leith Walk, as 'a paradise for boys' where Thomas and his cousins enjoyed many games together:

> It was of great size, with an infinity of cellars below, and of garrets, apple-lofts, etc., above; and it had a long garden, which ran down to the foot of the Calton Hill, with an orchard that yearly filled the apple-loft, and a building at the foot frequently besieged and defended by the boys, where a poor golden eagle, trophy of some of my grandfather's Hebridean voyages, pined and screamed itself to death.

The pranks that Thomas and his friends played were very similar to those RLS and his cousin Bob were to play later: among them was the diversion of making up little parcels of ashes, labelling them 'Gold Dust', leaving them in the street and then watching the reactions of those who found them. As Balfour pointed out, 'The characteristics of the father in his boyhood might be ascribed with little alteration to his son. The circumstances differed, but the spirit, the freaks, and the idleness were the same.'

For a short period Thomas worked in a printing office in Edinburgh, but before he had completed his eighteenth year he entered his father's office and began his life's work as an engineer. He served his apprenticeship 1836–9 and during the same period studied at Edinburgh University. By the end of his stringent apprenticeship he had become a valued member of the family firm, alongside his two older brothers Alan and David, and following his father's retirement in 1846 he was made a junior partner. From 1853, after Alan's ill-health caused his retirement, David and Thomas ran the family firm of D. and T. Stevenson with David as the senior partner until 1872 when (in RLS's words) his father '*by a great fight* carried his point of an equal division'. There seems to have been some bitterness on Thomas's part about the delay in obtaining the same share in the profits as his brother. In 1881 David himself fell ill and was unable to take any part in the firm's activities, but continued as partner to draw half of the profits until he retired in 1883. At that time RLS wrote to his mother, 'my heart is angry with Uncle David; it is cruel he should thus hang on, and spoil the end, as he spoiled the beginning of my father's life.' After David had retired Thomas became the senior partner, taking the bulk of the profits, with David's son, David Alan, as junior partner. When Thomas in his turn became ill in the last years of his life there was a further dispute over remuneration, this time between Thomas and his nephew David Alan; the dispute continued after Thomas's death and is referred to in some of RLS's letters to Charles Baxter.

Robert Stevenson's position as Engineer to the Northern Lighthouse Board was taken in their turn by his sons Alan and David; in 1855 Thomas joined David as joint engineer and they also held the joint position of Engineer to the Fishery Board of Scotland. In addition to their major work as lighthouse engineers, the Stevensons were engaged in the construction of harbours and docks and the improvement of rivers and estuaries. Thomas served under his brother Alan in the building of Skerryvore (called by RLS 'the noblest of all extant deep-sea lights'), and he and David were responsible for the construction of two more deep-sea lights under difficult conditions – Dhu Heartach and the Chicken's Rock. They erected no fewer than twenty-seven shore lights and about twenty-five beacons.

Thomas Stevenson's great achievement as an inventor was in the field of optics as applied to lighthouse illumination, which earned him from his son (in the dedication to him of *Familiar Studies of Men and Books*) the tribute '. . . by whose devices the great sea lights in every corner of the world now shine more brightly.' RLS called his 'holophotal revolving light' his 'most elegant contrivance' but his crowning invention, perfected after some thirty years of work, was 'the azimuthal condensing system'. These inventions were all the more remarkable in that Thomas was no mathematician and had to rely on his friends, Professor Swan and Professor P.G. Tait, to calculate the mathematical formulae for the instruments he had conceived. His main scientific interest outside engineering was meteorology and he was a founder-member of the Scottish Meteorological Society and its honorary secretary from 1871. His best known contribution in this field was the louvre-boarded Stevenson Screen for the protection of thermometers, which is still in use. He was a prolific contributor to scientific journals on a great number of subjects including lighthouse and harbour engineering, lighthouse optics, experiments in the force of waves (he invented an instrument, the Marine Dynamometer, for this purpose) and meteorology. He published two major books: *The Design and Construction of Harbours* (1864, 1874, and 1886) and *Lighthouse Construction and Illumination* (1881). As an engineering expert he was greatly in demand to give evidence to Parliamentary Committees.

Thomas met his future wife by chance on a railway journey to Glasgow in September 1847, when the eighteen-year-old girl was in the charge of an aunt and uncle, and after a few more meetings he proposed to her on a country walk with the Balfour family in the Pentlands.[2] They were married on 28 August 1848.

---

[2] This information comes from J. Pope Hennessy, *Robert Louis Stevenson* (1974), 26–7, from an account by MIS's sister, Jane Balfour.

Margaret Isabella Balfour was born on 11 February 1829, the twelfth child (out of thirteen) and fourth daughter of the Revd Lewis Balfour who had been the minister at Colinton, four miles from Edinburgh, since 1823, and his wife, Henrietta Scott Smith. She was known as 'Maggie' by her family; later RLS's stepchildren and the family generally at Vailima affectionately called her 'Aunt Maggie'. It has been said that not a line was written about her by her son. In fact in about 1884 he did jot down a hurried note about her in completing a printed questionnaire on the subject of family characteristics:[3] this accounts for the staccato nature of his comments. He described her as 'tall, slim, aquiline, handsome' and said that in temperament she was 'sanguine, cheerful, very fond of amusement, [and] very easily amused'; her energy was 'much above the average' and she had a 'remarkable, though not universal, fairness of mind'. He said that her favourite pursuit was 'organisation' for which she had a 'marked talent'. He considered that she had 'no musical ear; no dexterities whatever' and was 'fond of literature of a smiling order'. Colvin complements this description by calling her 'capable, cultivated, companionable, charming . . . a determined looker at the bright side of things, and hence better skilled, perhaps, to shut her eyes to troubles or differences among those she loved than to understand, compose, or heal them.' Balfour says that 'her face and fair complexion retained their beauty, as her figure and walk preserved their elasticity, to the last' and that 'her vivacity and brightness were most attractive'.

RLS has left us far more information about his father. He was, he says, five feet ten inches tall, stout, broad-shouldered and florid in appearance.[3] He gives us a vivid pen-picture in the essay he wrote immediately after Thomas Stevenson's death:

> He was a man of a somewhat antique strain: with a blended sternness and softness that was wholly Scottish and at first somewhat bewildering; with a profound essential melancholy of disposition and (what often accompanies it) the most humorous geniality in company; shrewd and childish; passionately attached, passionately prejudiced; a man of many extremes, many faults of temper, and no very stable foothold for himself among life's troubles. Yet he was a wise adviser; many men, and these not inconsiderable, took counsel with him habitually . . . He had excellent taste, though whimsical and partial; . . . took a lasting pleasure in prints and pictures . . . and though he read little, was constant to his favourite books. He had never any Greek; Latin he happily re-taught himself after

---

[3] *Record of Family Faculties* by Francis Galton (1884). This contained a number of tables for the reader to record the physical attributes and mental faculties of his ancestors in order to forecast those of his children. In his copy of the book at Yale, RLS completed only the forms relating to his parents; the entries are wrongly catalogued as being in the hand of Fanny Stevenson.

he left school, where he was a mere consistent idler . . . He was a strong
Conservative, or, as he preferred to call himself, a Tory; except in so far
as his views were modified by a hot-headed chivalrous sentiment for
women. He was actually in favour of a marriage law under which any
woman might have a divorce for the asking, and no man on any ground
whatever; and the same sentiment found another expression in a
Magdalen Mission in Edinburgh, founded and largely supported by
himself.

Later in the essay RLS describes his father's daily walks, 'which now
would carry him far into the country with some congenial friend, and now
keep him dangling about the town from one old book-shop to another, and
scraping romantic acquaintance with every dog that passed.' He describes
his talk, 'compounded of so much sterling sense and so much freakish
humour, and clothed in language so apt, droll and emphatic'. Thomas
Stevenson was clearly a man of strong and unusual personality. Colvin sums
him up as 'despotic, even in little things, but withal essentially chivalrous
and soft-hearted; apt to pass with the swiftest transition from moods of
gloom or sternness to those of tender or freakish gaiety, and commanding
a gift of humorous and figurative speech second only to that of his famous
son.'

Thomas Stevenson was a deeply religious man, although RLS later made
the distinction that he was not a pious one. His adherence to the harsh and
gloomy dogmas of Scottish Calvinistic Christianity, as set out in the Shorter
Catechism, dominated his whole attitude to life. RLS says that his father's
'morbid sense of his own unworthiness' prevented him from holding any
office in the Church of Scotland, but he served on many committees and his
advice was often sought. He studied the work of obscure theologians in the
original Latin and was extremely proud of his own writings in defence of
Christianity, many of them published under the pseudonym 'A Layman'. In
them, as one obituarist pointed out, 'the much-vexed question of the
compatibility of Predestination and Free-Will . . . [was] almost always impending, if not actually present'. His book *Christianity Confirmed by Jewish
and Heathen Testimony and the Deductions from Physical Science* (2nd edition,
1879) was part of the meagre luggage carried by RLS on his defiant journey
to America and he gave it to the clergyman who married him.

Colouring Thomas Stevenson's approach both to religion and life was
the 'profound underlying pessimism' which RLS thought was a characteristic of the Stevenson family: 'the future is *always* black to us' he wrote to
his cousin Bob in 1894. He described his father's 'sense of the fleetingness
of life and his concern for death' as 'morbid': 'He had never accepted the
conditions of man's life or his own character; and his inmost thoughts were
ever tinged with the Celtic melancholy.' Coupled with this was his marked

hypochondria, which made his last years (when he was genuinely ill) very difficult for his wife and family. To this period belongs the story of how he woke his wife in the night and announced, 'My dear, the end is now come; I have lost the power of speech.'

Fanny Stevenson, in a letter to her friend Dora Williams from Strathpeffer in September 1880, gives us a lively picture of her parents-in-law soon after her first meeting with them:

> The father is a most lovely old person . . . and is hustled about, according to the humour of his wife and son, in the most amusing way; occasionally he comes in with twinkling eyes and reports a comic verse of his own making with infinite gusto. Mrs Stevenson is a much more complex creature, much more like Louis. She is adored by her husband who spoils her like a baby; both, I can see, have spoiled Louis.

Many years later in a preface to *Treasure Island* she wrote:

> I shall always believe that something unusual and great was lost to the world in Thomas Stevenson. One could almost see the struggle between the creature of cramped hereditary conventions and environment, and the man nature had intended him to be. Fortunately for my husband he inherited from his tragic father his genius and wide humanity alone. The natural gaiety of Margaret Stevenson, who lived as a bird sings, for very joy of it, she passed down to her son.

The relationship between RLS and his parents had been a very close and happy one during his childhood and the strains only began to appear as he entered into manhood. Margaret Stevenson recorded in her diary that her husband was 'wonderfully resigned' following RLS's decision not to become an engineer; although there was no quarrel he was bitterly disappointed, feeling, as she later told Colvin, 'that it was a cutting short of his own life, as he had looked forward to its being continued in his son's career'.[4] It was the quarrel over religion – fully recorded in RLS's letters to Baxter and Mrs Sitwell – that caused so much pain to both men and brought RLS (in the period before he went to Mentone) near to nervous collapse. Given the nature of Thomas Stevenson's religious beliefs, there could be no compromise on his part. A flavour of the argument is given in a letter from RLS to Mrs Sitwell in September 1873 (Letter 143):

> He said tonight, 'He wished he had never married', and I could only echo what he said. 'A poor end,' he said, 'for all my tenderness.' And what was there to answer? 'I have made all my life to suit you – I have worked for you and gone out of my way for you – and the end of it is

[4] MIS to Colvin 3 May [1896].

that I find you in opposition to the Lord Jesus Christ – I find everything gone – I would ten times sooner have seen you lying in your grave than that you should be shaking the faith of other young men and bringing such ruin on other houses, as you have brought already upon this.'

Margaret Stevenson was present at many of these arguments but later claimed to Colvin that she never knew until she was living with him at Vailima how painful the discussions had been to her son.

Thomas Stevenson reacted with equal vehemence to RLS's journey to America, calling it in a letter to Colvin 'this sinful mad business' and linking it with the earlier religious problems: 'I lay all this at the door of Herbert Spencer. Unsettling a man's faith is indeed a *very* serious matter.' Several months of family dissension were ended by the news of RLS's serious illness and of his impending marriage. Putting the best face on it they could, Stevenson's parents sent their cable, 'Count on 250 pounds annually'. It is greatly to Thomas Stevenson's credit that from this point there seems to have been not a word of recrimination. The prodigal son, accompanied by his wife and stepson, was welcomed home with warmth and affection. Fanny made a conquest of her father-in-law and was thereafter treated indulgently like a favourite daughter (see p. 67). Within a few months Fanny was writing to her daughter Belle of her husband's parents in moving terms: 'They are the best and noblest people in the world, both of them, and I can hardly write about them now without tears in my eyes. Every day, almost, I come upon fresh proofs of their thought for our comfort or pleasure.'

This close and happy relationship continued for the rest of Thomas Stevenson's life, marred only by the worries caused by RLS's serious illnesses and by the problems of Thomas's own breakdown in health in the last two years of his life, which was finally mental as well as physical. In spite of his increasing success as an author, RLS was still to some extent financially dependent upon his father and never looked to him in vain. Thomas loved to give his son advice about his work (he was enthusiastically involved with *Treasure Island*), to send him books, to pour out his thoughts on religion and his depression over his illness and to indulge in family jokes. The relationship between father and son became an increasingly tender and gentle one and all trace of the disagreements that had affected their earlier close companionship had long disappeared. Thomas Stevenson died in Edinburgh on 8 May 1887.

After her husband's death, Maggie Stevenson gamely accompanied RLS and Fanny to America and the South Seas and finally settled with them as one of the family at Vailima. She took all the adventures and hardships in her stride, meeting with near-naked former cannibals, and rough traders as if they were a normal part of her world. To a certain extent she brought her existing social conventions with her and wherever she went she was able to find a church, native or otherwise, where she could worship. As a minister's daughter she had always been a devout Christian but in a gentler way than her husband. She had been a member of Women's Committees organising Church Bazaars and supporting foreign Missions; it was a wonderful realisation of the missionary hymns she had sung all her life to meet and see missionaries 'in action' in these far-away places. Her letters and diaries show how closely she became involved in all the day-to-day happenings at Vailima and the interest she took in Samoan affairs.

Her lifelong devotion was to her husband and her son. She treasured RLS's letters, stuck reviews of his books into a succession of scrapbooks and meticulously recorded details of his life in her diaries. RLS's own love for his mother continued unabated to the end and she was with him when he died. She returned to Edinburgh after his death to live with her sister; his name was on her lips when she died of pneumonia on 14 May 1897.

Robert Alan Mowbray (Bob) Stevenson[1]

In a fragment of autobiography Stevenson described his cousin, Bob Stevenson, as 'the man likest and most unlike me that I have ever met. Our likeness was one of tastes and passions, and for many years at least, it amounted in these particulars to an identity.' Introducing him to Sidney Colvin in 1874 he wrote: 'You know *me* now. Well, Bob is just such another mutton, only somewhat farther wandered and with perhaps a little more mire on his wool.'

Bob was born in Edinburgh on 25 March 1847, the only son of Alan Stevenson and his wife Margaret Scott Jones (known as 'Aunt Alan' and 'Gatchie'). RLS and Bob became close companions in the winter of 1856–7 when Bob stayed at Inverleith Terrace and attended Edinburgh Academy. RLS later described this 'great holiday' in his life:

---

[1] The fullest biography of Bob is in the essay by Denys Sutton prefixed to the revised edition of his *Velasquez* (1962); this repeats the error made by Colvin in the *DNB* that Bob accompanied RLS on the 'Inland Voyage' canoe journey. There is a fine article (reprinting a talk on the radio) by J. Isaacs in *The Listener*, 27 November 1947. The quotations from RLS come from his fragment of autobiography, 'Memoirs of Himself', written in 1880, Book I (MS Harvard, published in *Vailima* and other collected editions) and Book III (MS Rosenbach, quoted in Balfour, I, 86–8); and from published essays and his letters. The other material comes from Will H. Low, *A Chronicle of Friendships* (1908); H.G. Wells, *Experiment in Autobiography* (1934); Elizabeth Pennell, *Nights* (1916); Henley, *Views and Reviews* (1902); *The Letters of Sir Walter Raleigh* (1926); Fanny Stevenson's introduction to *New Arabian Nights*; Gosse, *Biographical Notes* (1908); W. B. Yeats, *Autobiographies* (1926).

[Bob] was three years older than I, an imaginative child who had lived in a dream with his sisters, his parents, and the *Arabian Nights*, and more unfitted for the world, as was shown in the event, than an angel fresh from heaven. . . . We lived together in a purely visionary state. We had countries; his was Nosingtonia, mine Encyclopaedia; where we ruled and made wars and inventions, and of which we were perpetually drawing maps. . . . We were never weary of dressing up. We drew, we coloured our pictures; we painted and cut out the figures for a pasteboard theatre.

Bob was the cousin in RLS's essay 'Child's Play' who ate his porridge with sugar, explaining it 'to be a country continually buried under snow', while Louis took his with milk explaining it 'to be a country suffering gradual inundation.'

Bob was educated at Windermere College and went up to Sidney Sussex College, Cambridge in 1866, taking his B.A. degree in 1871; at Cambridge he excelled as a gymnast and light-weight athlete and his favourite exercise was canoeing. Bob returned to Edinburgh in 1871 to live with his widowed mother (his father had died in 1865) and sisters, and spent the next two years studying painting at the School of Art. RLS later described the return of Bob as having changed the course of his life by providing him with a friend and confidant. It was the period of 'Jink' and of the mysterious secret society called the L.J.R. (see Part III) but (in Stevenson's words) 'under all this mirth-making, there kept growing up and strengthening a serious, angry, and at length a downright hostile criticism of the life around us.' Bob played a major part in helping RLS break out from the restrictions and conventions of his Edinburgh background and, as the letters show, Thomas Stevenson blamed Bob for his influence especially in religious matters.

There are in fact indications that by this time RLS was the dominant partner. When Bob went to Antwerp in November 1873 to study at the École des Beaux Arts, he wrote disconsolately that he could not get on without RLS who had been the whole world for him. The following year he enrolled in the studio of the portrait painter Carolus-Duran in Paris and was soon in his element in the Bohemian life of his fellow-students. Under Bob's tutelage RLS became part of that world; in April 1875 he paid his first visit to the artist haunts of the forest of Fontainebleau and for the next few years, whenever he could escape from Edinburgh, he spent his time with Bob and his friends in Paris and in the art-colonies at Barbizon and later at Grez. Their life is reflected in *The Wrecker*, where they figure as Stennis *aîné* and Stennis *frère*, 'a pair of hare-brained Scots', who showed their independence of haversacks by travelling with 'nothing but greatcoats and tooth-brushes' and every time they had to change their linen bought a new shirt and threw the old one away. At Grez in the summer of 1876 Bob met

RLS's future wife, Fanny Osbourne, before his cousin arrived on the scene, and her letters show that she was strongly attracted to him; Bob in his turn was half in love with Fanny's daughter, Belle. Bob was the only one of RLS's friends who showed sympathy and understanding of his journey to America to marry Fanny.

Bob himself married on 27 August 1881 Harriet Louisa Purland, a dentist's daughter.[2] They kept the marriage secret at first and lived apart. When RLS told his mother about it the following year he described her as a 'far stronger person than Bob' and hoped it would 'kick him into getting on.' To the despair of his friends Bob seemed to lack ambition and drive; he later told his American artist friend Will H. Low that he 'limited his effort to the amount of work necessary to the needs of his little family.' Although he exhibited at the Royal Academy from 1879 to 1885, he had no success as a painter and the desperate need for money forced him into writing for a living. RLS told Low in March 1885: 'We do not think he will ever make anything of painting; and we are all in a plot, sugaring him off on literature . . . Of course he is yet awkward at the trade . . . hates the slavery of writing; hates to give up the time when he should paint; but the one brings in something, the other nix . . . A little while ago, Henley and I remarked about Bob, "how strange it was that the cleverest man we knew, should be starving."' Henley (who was editor) persuaded him to write for the *Magazine of Art* in 1885 and he went on to contribute articles on both art and music (he was a keen amateur musician) to the *Saturday Review*. His articles won him a considerable reputation as an art critic and in 1888 he was elected to the Roscoe Chair of Fine Art at the University College, Liverpool. The atmosphere of genteel conformity eventually proved too much for him and he resigned in 1892. He explained his reasons to Low: 'What I found was that, in addition to my definite work in the college, I was expected to wear a high hat and a carnation in my buttonhole, and talk mild gossip about Botticelli, Burne-Jones and Frith – actually Frith – at garden-parties and afternoon teas. . . . I held out as long as I could and then I simply cut it, for no human being could have stood it any longer.' From 1893 until 1899 Bob was the art critic for the *Pall Mall Gazette* and he also contributed to *The Studio*, the *Art Journal* and Henley's *National Observer*. He crowned his reputation as a critic with his study of *Velasquez* (1895), which D.S. MacColl proclaimed as 'the most substantial contribution to the theory and defence of modern painting since Ruskin's *Modern Painters*.' Its continuing

[2] In Colvin's article in the *DNB* the name was misprinted 'Pyrland' and the error has often been repeated. In his autobiography, *Bone of Contention* (1969), written when he was ninety, the musician Cyril Scott remembered his meetings with the widowed Louisa Stevenson in about 1903. He described her as an entertaining conversationalist, with advanced views on sexual freedom in marriage, who fulminated against the 'frightful humbug and hypocrisy' of the age. She died in 1909.

relevance is shown by the fact that it was reprinted in a fine new edition as recently as 1962. At that time the reviewer in the *Times Literary Supplement* called him 'Apart from Ruskin . . . quite certainly the best professional British critic [of art] of the nineteenth century.' *Velasquez* was followed by a study of *Rubens* (1898) and there was a posthumously published book on *Raeburn* (1900).

In the fragment of autobiography already quoted, RLS described his cousin as having 'the most indefatigable, feverish mind I have ever known; he had acquired a smattering of almost every knowledge and art; he would surprise you by his playing, his painting, his criticism, his knowledge of philosophy, and above all, by a sort of vague, disconnected and totally inexplicable erudition.' Sir Walter Raleigh (who was Professor of English Literature at Liverpool in Bob's day) told Gosse that he had learned more from Bob '(pastors and masters included) than from any single person I ever met' and he dedicated his *Milton* (1900) 'To R.A.M. Stevenson, whose radiant and soaring intelligence enlightened and guided me during the years of our lost companionship.' Henley, who extravagantly claimed that 'we shall get ten Lewises, or a hundred even, or ever we get a Bob', said, 'Nothing like him has ever passed through my hands.' All Bob's friends agreed with Henley that 'his true gift was that of Talk.' RLS put him into his essay 'Talk and Talkers' as 'Spring-Heel'd Jack':

> I know not which is more remarkable; the insane lucidity of his conclu-
> sions, the humorous eloquence of his language, or his power of method,
> bringing the whole of life into the focus of the subject treated, mixing
> the conversational salad like a drunken god. He doubles like the serpent,
> changes and flashes like the shaken kaleidoscope, transmigrates bodily
> into the views of others, and so, in the twinkling of an eye and with a
> heady rapture, turns questions inside out and flings them empty before
> you on the ground, like a triumphant conjuror.

Elizabeth Pennell, who delighted in Bob's company when he was an art critic, attempted to describe his talk:

> The talk came in a steady stream, laughter occasionally in the voice, but
> no break, no movement, no dramatic action – the sanest doctrine set
> forth with almost insane ingenuity . . . extraordinary things treated quite
> as a matter of course; brilliant flashes of imbecility passed for cool well-
> balanced argument. . . . And he would tell the most extravagant tales, he
> would confide the most paradoxical philosophy, the most topsy-turvy
> ethics, with a fantastic seriousness . . .

H.G. Wells, who remembered especially 'a dissertation upon how he would behave if he was left nearly two millions' tried to give 'a faint impression of his style of imaginative talking in Ewart's talk about the City of Women' in his novel *Tono-Bungay*; but he explained in his autobiography, 'Ewart is not even a caricature of Bob; only Bob's style of talk was grafted on to him.' W. B. Yeats, who also recalled Bob's fantasy about what he would do with two million pounds, said that it was generally felt among his friends that Bob was a better talker than Wilde: '[Wilde's] charm was acquired and systematised, a mask which he wore only when it pleased him, while the charm of Stevenson belonged to him like the colour of his hair.'

New Arabian Nights was very appropriately dedicated to Bob, 'in grateful remembrance of their youth and their already old affection', and the stories had their origin, as RLS later reminded his cousin, in their talks together. Bob was the original of The Young Man with the Cream Tarts in the first story; Gosse confirmed it was 'a life-like portrait of one of the rarest of human kind.' Fanny Stevenson later noted: 'Whenever my husband wished to depict a romantic, erratic, engaging character, he delved into the rich mine of his cousin's personality. Robert Alan served, not only for the young man with the cream tarts, but as Paul Somerset in *The Dynamiter* and appeared in certain phases of *Prince Otto*.'

Bob's many letters to Louis are rambling and incoherent and convey no idea of his brilliance as a talker or his imaginative flow of ideas; but RLS's letters to his cousin, with their exuberant use of slang and private jokes give some impression of what their discussions must have been like. The old close relationship continued well into the Bournemouth days but by the summer of 1886 RLS evidently hinted to Will H. Low that he had noticed a change in Bob's attitude. When Low, who was planning to visit London, questioned Stevenson further on this, he replied in vague terms that Bob was 'gentle, intelligent as ever, and (as never before) industrious' even if 'somewhat withdrawn from the touch of friendship'. It may be that Bob was weighed down by the responsibility of having to earn his living and care for his family – a much-loved daughter had been born in 1883; but the main change in the warmth of the relationship must surely have been due to the fact (as RLS later told Baxter) that Bob's wife disliked Stevenson.

Bob and Henley (who lived near each other) had become very close friends, and RLS's bitter quarrel with Henley in 1888, involving as it did a story written by Bob's sister, Katharine de Mattos, was a further factor in the clouding of the friendship; it is clear that Bob was helping Henley and Katharine draft their replies to RLS's angry letters of reproach. There must also have been some embarrassment: from the time he left England in 1887 until his death Stevenson was paying Bob an allowance of £10 a quarter. In 1890 RLS wrote to Baxter about the loss of friends: 'Even Bob writes to me with an embarrassment which communicates itself to my answers. Our relation is too old and close to be destroyed; I have forgiven him too much – and he me – to leave a rupture possible; but there it is – the shadow.' In 1893 he complained to Baxter again that Bob never answered his letters.

Friendlier (if still slightly constrained) relations were resumed in 1894, following the birth of Bob's son the previous year. RLS wrote a long friendly letter in June 1894 recalling their past, seeking news of Bob's work and activities and retailing his own: 'Still I would like to hear what my *alter ego* thought of it; and I would sometimes like to have my old *maître es arts* express an opinion on what I do.' Bob sent a friendly reply (which has not survived) and RLS wrote his final letter to Bob – a long, serious, philosophical one about their differing attitudes to life – two months before his death.

When the news of his cousin's death reached him, Bob sent a sad letter of sympathy to Aunt Maggie, saying how the world seemed 'changed and deadened' at the loss 'of him who was my first and best friend': 'There was no one else like him to me and . . . I can think of nothing else but the long off past of friendship and the bitter present for all of you in Samoa.'

Bob died in London on 18 April 1900 following a stroke.

Charles Baxter

In his fragment of autobiography written in 1880 Stevenson gave the following pen picture of Charles Baxter:

> I cannot attempt to characterise a personality so unusual in the little space that I can here afford. I have never known so odd a creature; one of so mingled a strain; one so sure and yet so unsure in friendship; so clear-headed and yet so stark mad; so sentimental and yet at the same time so basely material. As a companion, when in spirits, he stands without an equal in my experience; he is the only man I ever heard of who could give and take in conversation with the wit and polish of style that we find in Congreve's comedies; and he has probably both said and done the most brilliantly laughable things in my generation. He is likewise the only person I ever knew who could *advise*; or to explain more perfectly my meaning, who could both make helpful suggestions, and at the same time hold his tongue when he had none to offer.[1]

In a letter written two years later he compared him to Pepys: 'Pepys was a decent fellow; singularly like Charles Baxter, by the way, in every character of mind and taste, and not unlike him in face.'

---

[1] 'Memoirs of Himself', Book III (MS Rosenbach, quoted in Balfour, I, 87–8).

Baxter was born in Edinburgh on 27 December 1848, the son of Edmund Baxter (1813–94) and his wife Mary Turnbull (died 1879). Edmund Baxter's original surname was Cockshot; he came to Edinburgh as a boy from Liverpool and assumed the name Baxter when he was adopted by his uncle, Charles Baxter, a lawyer. Edmund Baxter was a well-known and respected Edinburgh lawyer who became a Writer to the Signet (W.S.) – the elite of Scottish solicitors[2] – in 1837 and was auditor of the Court of Session from 1866 until his death.

Charles Baxter was educated at the Edinburgh Academy 1860–66 and then went on to Edinburgh University. He followed his father in becoming a Writer to the Signet in 1871 and after his apprenticeship joined his father's law firm of Mitchell and Baxter. Edmund Baxter was an elder of St Stephen's Church where the Stevensons worshipped from 1869, so the two families would have known each other. RLS and Baxter were both members of the University debating club, the Speculative Society – RLS from 1869 and Baxter from 1870 – but they do not seem to have become close friends until 1871, and the earliest of the surviving letters dates from that year. In 1883, writing to Henley about his friends, Stevenson recalled: 'Well do I remember telling Walter [Ferrier] I had unearthed a W.S. that I thought would do.' Baxter himself (in a letter over forty years later to a fellow-member of the Speculative Society, Lord Guthrie) dated the beginning of the friendship to a visit to the Stevensons' summer home, Swanston Cottage:

> I was often at Swanston, and it seems but yesterday that at the west end of Princes St, Louis stood by me tracing with his stick on the pavement the plan of the roads by which I was to come on my first visit. I had known him long before, but then began our friendship. It was that night, late, in his bedroom, after reading to me (I think) 'The Devil on Cramond Sands', he flung himself back on his bed in a kind of agony exclaiming, 'Good God, will any one ever publish me!' To soothe him, I (quite insincerely) assured him that of course someone would, for I had seen worse stuff in print myself.[3]

This may well have been the visit recorded in Margaret Stevenson's diary for 15 July 1871: 'Charles Baxter comes to dinner and stays the night.'

From this point Baxter was one of the little group of close friends comprising Bob Stevenson, Walter Ferrier and Walter Simpson who shared

---

[2] A Writer to the Signet (W.S.) is a member of an ancient society of solicitors in Edinburgh. Originally they were clerks in the Secretary of State's office who prepared writs to pass the Royal Signet; later they were given powers to conduct cases before the Court of Session and to prepare crown writs and charters.

[3] Baxter to Lord Guthrie 25 March 1914 (MS Edinburgh); Baxter told a similar story in a letter to Guthrie of 16 October 1907.

with RLS the experience of growing up in Edinburgh. Baxter was not only
the careful and methodical Secretary of the 'Spec' but the boon companion
in the pubs of the Lothian Road. From the South Seas in 1890 RLS
addressed to Baxter his poem 'To My Old Familiars', beginning:

> Do you remember – can we e'er forget? –
> How, in the coiled perplexities of youth,
> In our wild climate, in our scowling town,
> We gloomed and shivered, sorrowed, sobbed and feared?
> . . . Do you remember? – Ah, could one forget!

Stevenson never did forget the 'bygone adventures' of their youth and
referred to them nostalgically in letters to Baxter for the rest of his life.
These were the days of public houses with names like the 'Gay Japanee' and
'The Green Elephant', of Brash the bad-tempered publican, to whom
Stevenson later wrote a series of mock sonnets, and of the mysterious and
short-lived secret society the L.J.R., which met at a pub in Advocates'
Close (see Letter 98). RLS remembered those days in a letter of July
1877: 'the past where we have been drunk and sober, and sat outside of
grocers' shops on fine dark nights, and wrangled in the Speculative, and
heard mysterious whistling in Waterloo Place, and met missionaries from
Aberdeen.'

The friendship that began against a background of youthful foolishness
and dissipation when (in Stevenson's later phrase) they were 'a couple of
heartless drunken young dogs' developed into a close and lasting relationship. Baxter's sympathy and understanding never failed RLS or Fanny
Stevenson. This was particularly so at the time of the quarrel with Henley,
when Baxter's affection and his wise and friendly counsel steered Stevenson
safely through the emotional crisis caused by this break with his old friend.
Baxter was himself an old crony of Henley's, but while remaining loyal to
RLS he did not lose Henley's friendship.

With the growth of Stevenson's success as a writer, Baxter became not
only a friend but his legal, business and financial adviser. To him were sent
the cheques from publishers and magazine editors; he kept the accounts,
handled the investments and made payments to a bewildering number of
people – doctors, school-masters, relatives and friends. With Stevenson's
isolation in the South Seas these responsibilities increased – requests for
books, research on the family history, and all the business complications of
Vailima from the running of the estate to the ordering of wine. Baxter had
always filed Stevenson's publishing contracts, but from 1892 RLS made
him responsible for handling all negotiations with publishers and editors.
Baxter drove hard bargains with publishers, and at a time when RLS was
pressed for money he conceived the idea of the Edinburgh Edition. He
must at times have been sorely tried by the unbusinesslike ways of the

Stevenson household where papers were mislaid, receipts lost and queries went unanswered. As the letters show, Baxter coped with it all patiently and efficiently, earning himself the title of 'The Flower of Doers'.

One feels that Stevenson was more at ease with Baxter than with any of his other correspondents; with him he could always let off steam and write anything he pleased, polite or otherwise. In their letters they created the characters of Thomson and Johnstone, a pair of dissolute and disreputable Church elders who wrote to each other in broad Scots. RLS managed to smuggle a reference to Mr Thomson into *Kidnapped* and introduced Baxter into the preface of *The Master of Ballantrae* as his friend Mr Johnstone Thompson W.S. Baxter more than held his own in the foolery of these comic letters. Baxter's part in the series of hoax letters which RLS perpetrated at Bournemouth in 1886 illustrate his skill as a letter-writer. Stevenson paid tribute to that skill in a letter of 1892: 'I have appeared rather freely lately as an insulting letter writer, but I do not consider I am fit to black your shoes.' Underneath the façade of the serious and successful Edinburgh lawyer we glimpse through the letters the very different person described in Stevenson's pen picture. This side of his character is brought out in Michael Finsbury (for which he was the original) in *The Wrong Box*, the comic masterpiece Stevenson wrote in collaboration with his stepson, Lloyd Osbourne. Michael is a witty young lawyer (frequently drunk) who handles with imperturbable presence of mind and an air of solemn absurdity the problem of disposing of an unwanted corpse.

The measure of Stevenson's regard for Baxter is shown by his dedication to him of two of his finest novels, *Kidnapped* and *Catriona*; in both of them he recalled with affection their youth in Edinburgh. One of Stevenson's strongest expressions of that friendship was in a letter of February 1890:

> I take this blank corner to add a warmer expression of my thanks for your friendship; so much has fallen away, death and the worse horror of estrangement have so cut me down and rammed me in, that you and Colvin remain now all in all to me . . . I beg of you, dear old friend, to take care of your health physical and moral; you do not know what you become to me, how big you bulk; . . . you remain alone of my early past, truer now than ever, and I cling to the thought of you.

Fanny Stevenson later called Baxter her husband's 'friend of the heart'[4] and Stevenson inscribed his special set of the Edinburgh Edition, '*Amicus amico*' (A friend to a friend).

---

[4] Fanny wrote to Graham Balfour when he was preparing the biography, 'Colvin was a friend of the intellect, but Charles of the heart. Louis's affection for Charles never wavered' (Balfour's papers, NLS).

On 24 July 1877 Baxter married Grace Roberta Louisa Stewart, with RLS as best man. They had two sons, and a daughter (who died in infancy). He was one of the group of well-to-do Edinburgh citizens who helped to found and finance the *Scots Observer*, of which Henley was editor. He was a stalwart member of the Church of Scotland and served on Committees connected with it and (as befitted a former member of the L.J.R) he became an enthusiastic Freemason and achieved high office. In the 1890s various personal troubles beset him. His wife died in 1893 and he lost money through Bank failures; a year later his father died and Baxter suffered an emotional collapse. He gave way to heavy drinking and his continual drunkenness caused great anxiety. He decided to visit Stevenson in Samoa, carrying with him the first two volumes of the Edinburgh Edition; tragically enough he had only got as far as Aden when the news of Stevenson's death reached him in December 1894.

Baxter's heavy drinking continued to cause serious problems during the period following Stevenson's death, when he acted as executor of the estate. He retired from his legal business in Edinburgh and lived for a time in London. In October 1895 he married Marie Louise Gaukroger of Longniddry; they had one daughter. They lived first in Paris and then moved to Siena in Italy (presumably because it was possible to live more cheaply abroad). He returned to England during the First World War and died in London on 29 April 1919.

Sidney Colvin and Frances Sitwell[1]

In a fragment of autobiography dictated to his stepdaughter at Vailima (probably in 1892), Stevenson said of Sidney Colvin:

It is very hard for me, even if I were merely addressing the unborn, to say what I owe to and what I think of this most trusty and noble-minded man. If I am what I am and where I am, if I have done anything at all or done anything well, his is the credit. It was he who paved my way in letters; it was he who set before me, and still, as I write, keeps before me, a difficult standard of achievement; and it was to him and to Fleeming Jenkin that I owed my safety at the most difficult periods of my life.

[1] *The Colvins and Their Friends* by E.V. Lucas (1928) has been supplemented by obituaries in *The Times* of 4 August 1924 and 12 May 1927 and by the entry on Colvin in the *DNB* by Campbell Dodgson, his successor as Keeper of Prints at the British Museum. The quotations from RLS come from the fragment of autobiography dictated to Belle at Vailima, added to 'Memoirs of Himself' in *Vailima* and later collected editions, and from his letters. Colvin's surviving letters to RLS are at Yale.

In a poem a dozen years earlier he had called Colvin 'the perfect friend', and time and again in the last years of his life he referred to him in moving terms as the 'most beloved' of all his friends. In August 1890 he wrote: 'understand once and for all, that since my dear wild noble father died, no head on earth, and not my wife's, is more precious to my thought than yours.' A little earlier, in December 1889, he made it clear that when he thought of 'home' it was Colvin and his house in the British Museum he had in mind.

Sidney Colvin was born on 18 June 1845. He was the youngest son of Bazett David Colvin, a partner in a leading London firm of East India merchants, and his wife, Mary Steuart Bayley. Both sides of the family had been connected with India, either as merchants or as administrators in the old East India Company: among them were Colvin's uncle, John Russell Colvin, who was Lieutenant-Governor of the North-West Provinces, and his mother's father, William Butterworth Bayley, who was for a few months in 1828 acting Governor-General of India and for many years Chairman of the Board of Directors of the East India Company. Colvin spent his childhood at the family home, The Grove, Little Bealings near Woodbridge in East Suffolk, a country house set in five hundred acres. He went up to Trinity College, Cambridge in 1863 and was third in the first class of the Classical Tripos of 1867; he was made a Fellow of Trinity in 1868.

On leaving Cambridge, Colvin settled in London and soon established a reputation as a critic of the fine arts. He wrote regularly for the *Pall Mall Gazette*, the *Fortnightly Review*, the *Portfolio* and other magazines. As a boy he had worshipped Ruskin, who was a family friend. His next great admiration was for the work of Burne-Jones, who became a close friend; Burne-Jones introduced him to Rossetti, and Colvin saw much of him during his early years in London in 1868–72. In 1869 he joined the recently-founded New Club, which became the Savile Club two years later; he became Honorary Secretary in 1871 and remained a member all his life. In January 1873 Colvin was elected Slade Professor of Fine Art at Cambridge; he was re-elected four times and from 1876 to 1884 he was also Director of the Fitzwilliam Museum. The obituarist in *The Times* says that although Colvin was neither brilliant nor eloquent as a speaker, 'his enthusiasm and the thoroughness which characterized everything that he did made him an inspiring teacher.' A special interest was the sculpture and archaeology of ancient Greece; in March 1875 he visited Greece and saw the excavations in progress at Olympia.

Some time in the late 1860s Colvin met and fell in love with Frances Sitwell, the wife of a clergyman at Stepney in the East End of London, but he was unable to marry her until over thirty years later. Frances Jane Fetherstonhaugh, born on 25 January 1839, was a daughter of Cuthbert Fetherstonhaugh, a member of a long-established Anglo-Irish family who had fallen on hard times. In 1843 he sold the family home in County Westmeath, Ireland and took his large family of three sons and five daughters to Frankfurt in Germany but the revolution of 1848 drove them back to Ireland. In 1852 he went off to Australia with two sons to try his luck in the goldfields; he failed to find gold but succeeded in being made a police magistrate at the Buckland River and spent the rest of his life there, achieving great popularity as an 'Irish gentleman' and sportsman. His wife and daughters joined him in 1856. Frances soon returned home in order to marry in 1859 the Revd Albert Hurt Sitwell (1834–94), to whom she had been betrothed before leaving Ireland. Sitwell was the third son of Captain William Hurt Sitwell of Barmoor Castle, Northumberland, who was the nephew of Sir Sitwell Sitwell, 1st Baronet of Renishaw (ancestor of Osbert and Edith). He was educated at Dublin University and took his B.A. there in 1858. The young couple went out to Calcutta, where the husband had a chaplaincy, but an outbreak of cholera soon forced them to return to England. Sitwell served as a curate in Stepney as well as acting as private secretary to the Bishop of London, before becoming in 1863 the Vicar of St Stephen's Stepney. Two sons were born – Frederick in 1861, and Francis Albert (Bertie) in 1862 – but the marriage ran into difficulties. *The Times* obituarist says that Mrs Sitwell was 'not well matched with a husband whose manner of life . . . made it difficult to remain with him' and E.V. Lucas says that Sitwell was 'a man of unfortunate temperament and uncongenial habits'. Whatever the problem (it may have been drink), the marriage fell into greater strain when in 1869 Sitwell was given the living of Minster, a village in the Isle of Thanet near Ramsgate; Frances seems to have decided to break away from her husband following the death of their elder son in April 1873.

It was at this sad and difficult time in her own life that Mrs Sitwell came to Cockfield Rectory in Suffolk to stay with her close friend, Maud Babington, who was one of RLS's Balfour cousins. They had become friends because Maud's sister, Sidney Wilson – they were both daughters of Margaret Stevenson's sister, Marion Wilson – had married Isla Sitwell, one of Albert Sitwell's brothers. By fortunate chance Stevenson also came to stay at Cockfield Rectory at the end of July 1873. At a critical point in his own life, when he was deeply hurt by the bitter religious disagreements with his father and uncertain about his future career, RLS found two devoted friends to steady and guide him. The introduction to Part IV tells the story of the fateful first meetings with Frances Sitwell and Sidney Colvin at the Rectory in Suffolk.

Colvin was evidently bowled over by the young Scot and recognised his potential as a writer. With characteristic generosity and kindness he helped and encouraged him in his literary aspirations by introducing him to publishers and editors and tirelessly promoting his interests. For the rest of his life RLS looked to Colvin as his mentor as well as his closest friend. Colvin was unwavering in his loyalty, even though it soon became apparent that RLS had fallen in love with the woman he himself loved and hoped to marry.

The picture of Frances Sitwell presented by her friends is of someone who was a paragon of all the virtues; even when allowance has been made for the affectionate exaggerations in the tributes paid at the time of her death, it is clear that she was a truly remarkable woman. She is described as having 'a sibylline beauty over which time had no power' – Sir John Squire, reviewing Furnas's biography in 1952, said that she 'was like an enchanting girl, even when she was eighty' – with a 'fine aquiline profile', a 'wonderful smile', and an 'irradiating charm'. The impression is of a person not only of wit and intelligence but also of great tenderness, warmth and vitality, with a sympathetic understanding of other people's problems. Hugh Walpole, who became a friend of the Colvins in their old age, wrote:

[Lady Colvin] had a deep understanding of all the complexities of modern life; you could not tell Colvin everything, because to shock him was to hurt him too deeply; but there was nothing that you could not tell to her. . . . She had to the last that certain stamp of a great character, an eager acceptance of the whole of life. Every little pleasure was exciting to her; she was like a child going to the world for the first time over a new play, a new book, a new picture.[2]

Stopford Brooke, the popular Victorian preacher and man of letters, who had known Frances Sitwell as a young woman in Ireland, said that she had more men in love with her than any other woman he knew. Colvin in a pen-portrait has a relevant passage about her sexual attractiveness:

In the fearlessness of her purity she can afford the frankness of her affections, and shows how every fascination of her sex may in the most open freedom be the most honourably secure. Yet in a world of men and women, such an one cannot walk without kindling once and again a dangerous flame before she is aware. As in her nature there is no room for vanity, she never foresees these masculine combustions, but has a wonderful tact and gentleness in allaying them, and is accustomed to convert the claims and cravings of passion into the lifelong loyalty of grateful and contented friendship.[3]

---

[2] The descriptions of Mrs Sitwell (including Hugh Walpole's tribute) are in Lucas, Sir Osbert Sitwell's *Great Morning* (1948) and Sir John Squire's review of Furnas in *The Illustrated London News*, 11 October 1952.

[3] Stopford Brooke's description comes from Furnas, citing *The Bookman* (London), April 1928. Colvin's pen-picture is in Lucas.

All we know about the relationship between RLS and Mrs Sitwell is derived from the rather cryptic references in his letters to her; her letters to him have not survived because he destroyed them as she requested him to do. Furnas and later biographers have speculated from this evidence that there was an emotional crisis, of the kind euphemistically described in Colvin's note, when he came to London in June 1874, and that he was warned not to overstep the boundary between passionate friendship and a physical love affair, and perhaps reminded too that her loyalties were to Colvin; certainly RLS seems to have gone off on his yachting cruise with Simpson in July in a mood of black depression. In the 1930s, before the full text of Stevenson's letters had become available, G.S. Hellman suggested that there had been such an affair. Furnas dismissed the suggestion as 'most unlikely', but still earned himself a rebuke from Sir John Squire (in the review already quoted): 'if Mr Furnas had known her he wouldn't even have allowed himself to discuss the question, although deciding in her favour, as to whether she had had "carnal" relations with RLS: gentle as she was, I can see her lips curl and her eyes flash at the mere suggestion.'

The long diary-letters that RLS wrote to Mrs Sitwell from the time of their first meeting for the next two years constitute a remarkable and touching record of the young man's slow growth to maturity. They are written in the language of love and adoration, with Mrs Sitwell progressing from 'Claire' (the name also written on a poem from Mentone which led Hellman astray) to 'Consuelo' (the heroine of a George Sand novel) and eventually, in a bid to change the nature of the relationship, to 'madonna' and 'mother', with RLS as a loving son rather than a lover. Although there can be no doubt of his love and emotional dependence on Mrs Sitwell, the way in which he addresses her sometimes seems unreal; he treats her with the reverence and adoration accorded a goddess rather than in the way a lover writes to a flesh-and-blood woman. To her he poured out all his feelings of unhappiness and near-despair over the religious conflict with his father and what he saw as his parents' lack of understanding; he confided his ambitions and disappointments in his literary work, and received encouragement in return; he wrote of the details of his daily life including his own ill-health; he sympathised over her bad health and her marriage problems. In these letters, particularly those from Mentone about the guests at the hotel and in his observations about the people he meets in Edinburgh, we find RLS beginning to show his skill at bringing people to life that was to become an important element in his travel writings. The letters also contain remarkable passages of 'fine prose' in descriptions of scenery and analyses of his feelings which show the apprentice stylist developing his powers as a writer.

Colvin is constantly mentioned in the letters to Mrs Sitwell and RLS was writing to him regularly. Their growing friendship was strengthened by their meetings in London and the time they spent together at Mentone in the winter of 1873–4. After the intensity of the friendship with Mrs Sitwell had ended Colvin became the main friend and correspondent, but RLS always saw the two of them together in his mind, and the letters to Colvin from the South Seas were also intended for Mrs Sitwell. In the early days RLS was, as he later admitted, somewhat in awe of Colvin, and he described him as having 'the air of a man accustomed to obedience'. RLS wrote to Bob Stevenson in April 1879: 'I get fonder of Colvin steady, and wish he was one to whom one could talk more equally. He is a person in whom you must *believe* like a person of the Trinity, but with whom little relation in the human sense is possible. A difficult, shut up, noble fellow.' In August 1886, introducing Colvin to Will H. Low, his American artist friend, he wrote: 'He (Sidney Colvin) is to call on you when he goes through Paris. You must not be affected by his manner; his is a heart of gold.' He found it necessary also to warn another friend in the South Seas who was due to meet Colvin: 'if you find him at the first sight anyway dry it is a question of manner and you will soon see how very noble and kind a nature lies behind. I have seen many men; never a finer; nor is there any more dear to me.' In the fragment of autobiography already quoted, RLS wrote of Colvin: 'A great shrewdness, a great simplicity of character, were conjoined in him . . . there is no man whose trenchant insight I more fear, none at whose childishness I have more often smiled.' Clearly Colvin was a man very different in character and manner from RLS and it says a great deal for both men that they became such close friends in spite of the difference in their temperaments. In appearance Colvin was tall and thin with a pointed beard and he was, according to a colleague, 'in manner animated and nervous, sometimes irritable, but charming in demeanour to those whom he liked.' Another friend, Sir Edward Marsh, commented: 'His dry but vibrant voice, and the chiselled face on which the dry skin was tightly stretched over the thin cover of flesh that revealed the neatness of his small domed skull, seemed emblems of the tense control which his inward fires were never very long in evading.'[4]

In July 1883 Colvin was appointed Keeper of the Department of Prints and Drawings at the British Museum but he did not take up the position until 1884 when he left the Fitzwilliam Museum; he held the Slade Professorship until 1885. The Keepership carried with it a residence in the Museum precincts. It was in this house – jokingly called 'The Monument' by him – that RLS stayed during his visits to London from Bournemouth. In his poem 'To S.C.', written from the South Seas in October 1889, RLS remembered with affection and nostalgia awakening there in the mornings:

---

[4] The colleague was Dodgson in the *DNB*. Sir Edward Marsh's description is in his *A Number of People* (1939).

> Most of all,
> For your light foot I wearied and your knock
> That was the glad réveillé of my day.

Mrs Sitwell had made the final break with her unsatisfactory husband in 1874, taking her surviving son, Francis Albert (Bertie), with her; he was to die tragically at Davos of tuberculosis in April 1881, at the age of eighteen, while the Stevensons were staying there. Mrs Sitwell became Secretary of the College for Working Women (later the New College for Men and Women) in Queen's Square, Bloomsbury and also worked as a translator and reviewer. She lived apart from Colvin in London but acted as his visiting hostess, and thanks to her influence his house became a literary and artistic centre, 'her social tact and ready sympathy' supplying, as Colvin's oldest friend, Basil Champneys, put it, 'whatever might have seemed lacking in him of the lighter graces which conduce to enjoyable social intercourse.' Their liaison was accepted without scandal and approved by their friends. The Revd Albert Sitwell died in January 1894 but, strange as it may seem to modern minds, Colvin and Mrs Sitwell did not marry until July 1903, when he was fifty-eight and she was sixty-four.

The reason for the delay given by their biographer E.V. Lucas was Colvin's 'straitened circumstances due to certain family claims'; apparently Colvin did not feel able to support a wife as well as his mother and therefore did not marry until his mother died. The clue to Colvin's financial problem is to be found in Stevenson's letters. In May 1878, when at the Fitzwilliam Museum, Colvin lost a portfolio of engravings borrowed on approval from a London print-dealer. He put them into a cab and the driver went off with them. Although the thief was caught and sentenced, the prints were never recovered and Colvin had to bear the loss of £1500, an enormous sum for those days. RLS lent him £400 and he repaid it by instalments.[5] The second financial misfortune was in February 1888. Colvin's brother, Bazett, had over the years got deeper and deeper into debt, speculated on the Stock Exchange and dissipated all the money in various family trusts. As a result Colvin's mother was left penniless and dependent on him for support. Colvin was particularly worried about being able to maintain the life insurance premiums to secure a sum for his mother in the event of his death. RLS told Baxter that he was 'to strain my credit to bursting, and mortgage all I possess' if Colvin needed help. Baxter made annual payments, on RLS's behalf, of £137 to cover Colvin's insurance premium and these continued until Stevenson's death.

Colvin had been strongly opposed to RLS's journey to America in 1879 and to his marriage, but behind the scenes he worked hard to reconcile

[5] Details of the theft of the prints are given in the annotation to Letter 529.

Thomas Stevenson to what was happening. Although, like Henley, he privately criticised Fanny Stevenson in the early days, he at length recognised her good qualities and paid generous tribute to her in his memoirs (see p. 66). Colvin had been the only one of Stevenson's friends to welcome RLS and Fanny when they arrived in Liverpool in August 1880 on their return from America. RLS had been well aware of the feelings with which Colvin had regarded the appearance of a wife by his side. In January 1889, writing to Colvin from the South Seas about their planned return to England the following year (which never materialised), he commented: 'I would like fine to see you on the tug: ten years older both of us than the last time you came to welcome Fanny and me to England, but I, if all goes well, in better health, and you glad to see Fanny this time, and she I can promise you burning to see you.'

Colvin appears to have had a serious breakdown in health in 1888–9 during the first part of Stevenson's Pacific voyages. The young Rudyard Kipling (in a letter of November 1889) gives an unattractive picture of him: 'The same [Colvin] is an allfired prig of immense water and suffers from all the nervo-hysterical diseases of the 19th Century. . . . He recounted all his symptoms and made me sick. A queer beast with match-stick fingers and a dry unwholesome skin.'[6]

Strangely Colvin does not seem to have fully recognised the seriousness of Stevenson's own ill-health and when RLS, realising that a return to Europe could mean his death, wrote announcing his plan to settle in Samoa, Colvin wrote a bitter letter of recrimination (which has not survived), apparently blaming Fanny for the decision. Colvin explained in his memoirs that he had felt that RLS's work would suffer because of his absence from 'cultivated society' and he had suggested that RLS no longer valued his own suggestions and criticism of his work. RLS and Fanny wrote a long affectionate letter to Colvin, assuring him of their love and seeking to justify their decision. Part of what Stevenson wrote has already been quoted. He concluded his letter by saying that if Colvin were ever dangerously ill, he must be summoned: 'I can see no harm in my dying like a burst pig upon some outlandish island, but if you died, without due notice and a chance for me to come and see you, I should count it a disloyalty; no less.' Reading this letter thirty years later Colvin found 'the terms infinitely touching and too sacred almost to quote' and it was excluded from his edition. It was in order to maintain the intimacy of their friendship that RLS began, when he settled in Samoa, the long monthly journal-letters which were published in expurgated form as *Vailima Letters* in 1895.

---

[6] Kipling to Edmonia Hill 9 November 1889. *The Letters of Rudyard Kipling*, ed. Thomas Pinney, vol. I (1990).

Colvin was out of sympathy with much of Stevenson's work in Samoa and says so in his essay on RLS in *Memories and Notes*:

> On the side of his friends at home, speaking at least for myself, I fear that our joy in the news of his returning strength and activity had been tempered by something of latent jealousy that so much good could befall him without help of ours and at a distance of half the world away from us. I know that I was inclined to be hypercritical about the quality and value of some of the work sent home from the Pacific.

Many critics have agreed with Colvin that the series of papers constituting *The South Seas* were 'overloaded with information and the results of study' and not the lively accounts of his personal experiences that readers had expected. He deplored Stevenson's continued involvement in the political affairs of Samoa, his letters to *The Times*, and the time spent in writing the specialised account of recent Samoan history, *A Footnote to History*. In spite of this, he worked hard through contacts with senior Foreign Office officials to promote Stevenson's interests and to keep him informed of their views. Anxious for news of RLS's work in progress and of the books he had read, he wrote in March 1894 in a burst of irritation that Stevenson's last three letters had been concerned with nothing else but 'your beloved blacks – or chocolates – confound them.' This evoked a rebuke from RLS that Colvin was being 'a little too Cockney with him' and asking him to remember that his life was passed among his 'blacks or chocolates' and that not to write about them would cut off Colvin entirely from his life. Colvin apologised at once for having been a 'beast' and asked him to put his remark down to 'the mere clumsiness of an over-anxious affection'.

Colvin's narrow views and his slightly fussy pedantry did not make him a good judge of some of RLS's later work, especially that set in the South Seas. Colvin's condemnation of *The Ebb-Tide* led RLS to write to Baxter: 'Colvin (between ourselves) is a bit of an old wife, and has so often predicted that a book would be my ruin in January, and by July defied me to do anything as good, that I have ceased to pay very much regard.' Colvin quoted both of Stevenson's comments and good humouredly admitted his faults in his introduction to *Vailima Letters*: '*Tibi Palinure* [Palinurus was Aeneas's pilot] – so, in the last weeks of his life, he proposed to inscribe to me a set of his collected works. Not Palinurus so much as Polonius may perhaps – or so I sometimes suspect – have been really the character.'

Much has been made of the fact that Baxter was addressed as 'Dear Charles' and Henley as 'Dear Lad' but that Colvin remained more formally 'My dear Colvin' (although he himself wrote to 'My dear Louis'). Fanny lent support to this view by telling Graham Balfour that 'Colvin was a friend of the intellect, but Charles of the heart'. Too much should not be read into this. Colvin was never a crony in the sense that Baxter and Henley were because he was not the sort of man one could get drunk with, but there is no doubt from his letters of the love and admiration felt by RLS for the rather austere man who had become his close friend. The closeness of that friendship is shown by the fact that it was to Colvin and no other friend that he confided the details of Fanny's serious illness in 1893 and other personal and family problems. Colvin's own unselfish devotion both to Stevenson himself and later to his memory never faltered.

In his memoirs Colvin relates how on 'one gloomy, gusty, sodden December day in 1894', after lunching with a friend, he came out of a Government Office in Westminster 'and saw newspaper posters flapping dankly in the street corners, with the words "Death of R.L. Stevenson" printed large upon them.' As he later told Stevenson's mother in his letter of condolence, 'I knew from the first moment that it was not like former tales, I saw that it was true, and that half the light of my world had gone out.' The next few years (as related in the Introduction, p. 2) were fully taken up by the completion of the Edinburgh Edition, seeing through the press previously unpublished works by RLS and editing his letters; all done in addition to his official duties and in spite of poor health. The task of undertaking the biography – described by him as 'the great hope and interest of my life' – was finally relinquished after acrimonious rows with Fanny and Lloyd over the delay. There was also a dispute with Lloyd over payment to Colvin for his work on the *Letters*, Lloyd insisting on taking into account the payments RLS had made for Colvin's insurance policies, although RLS had never regarded them as a loan. Michael Balfour has shrewdly suggested that it was not just 'want of health and leisure' that induced Colvin to agree to give up the biography but 'the prospect of a long series of battles with Fanny and Lloyd as to what went in and what did not.'[7] After publication of the *Letters* in November 1899 Colvin wrote to Baxter: 'D—d idiots Lloyd and his mother. Had they only waited they would have had within a couple of years or so (quite soon enough) another book from me which would have made quite as great a mark; would have lived with the language; and would have brought them (which is all *he* cares about) pots of money.'[8]

Colvin was disappointed that he had not reached the highest position in his chosen career. In 1894 he failed to become Director of the National Gallery and in 1909 he was an unsuccessful candidate for the directorship of the British Museum. He was knighted in 1911 and retired from the British Museum in 1912. His retirement enabled him to resume his interest in

[7] Michael Balfour, 'The First Biography' in *Stevenson and Victorian Scotland*, ed. Jenni Calder (1981).
[8] Colvin to Baxter 15 November 1899 (copy sent by Baxter to Lord Guthrie, MS Edinburgh: published in *TLS* 12 February 1960).

literature, which had been his first love. He had published short biographies of Landor (1881) and Keats (1887) and the major work of his retirement was his lengthy *John Keats. His Life and Poetry, His Friends, Critics and After-Fame* (1917). This was the standard biography in its day but has long been superseded. It was followed in 1921 by *Memories and Notes*, a volume of reminiscences which contains a chapter on Stevenson.

Colvin's most attractive quality, according to the *Times* obituarist, 'was his loyal constancy to his friends, whom he was never tired of helping and encouraging.' He and Lady Colvin became famous for their championing of young and unappreciated talent. The closest friend of their later years was Joseph Conrad, who became in a sense Stevenson's successor in Colvin's loving admiration. The Colvins were a very devoted couple and Lady Colvin's death on 1 August 1924 was a great blow to Sir Sidney. His own last years were marred by deafness and growing loss of memory. He died on 11 May 1927.

William Ernest Henley[1]

On 12 February 1875 Leslie Stephen, then editor of the *Cornhill Magazine*, took Stevenson to visit another young man who was a patient in the Royal Infirmary in Edinburgh. It was the beginning of a famous friendship that was to alter both their lives. RLS described the meeting the next day to Mrs Sitwell:

> Yesterday, Leslie Stephen, who was down here to lecture, called on me and took me up to see a poor fellow, a bit of a poet who writes for him, and who has been eighteen months in our Infirmary and may be, for all I know, eighteen months more. It was very sad to see him there, in a little room with two beds, and a couple of sick children in the other bed; . . . the gas flared and crackled, the fire burned in a dull economical way; Stephen and I sat on a couple of chairs and the poor fellow sat up in his bed, with his hair and beard all tangled, and talked as cheerfully as if he had been in a King's Palace, or the great King's Palace of the blue air. He has taught himself two languages since he has been lying there. I shall try to be of use to him.

[1] The standard biography by John Connell (1949) is inaccurate in a number of details, especially those relating to RLS; he also has the wrong date for Henley's marriage. It has been supplemented by earlier biographies by Kennedy Williamson (1930) and L. Cope Cornford (1913) and the article in the *DNB* by T.F. Henderson. There is a valuable study by J.H. Buckley (1945).

William Ernest Henley was born on 23 August 1849 in Gloucester, the eldest of the five sons of William Henley, a feckless and unsuccessful stationer and bookseller and his wife, Emma Morgan (died 1888). He was educated at the Crypt Grammar School, Gloucester where the Manx poet T.E. Brown ('A garden is a lovesome thing, God wot!') was headmaster. From the age of twelve he was never wholly free from pain and illness caused by a tuberculous disease. He left school in 1867 and for the next few years, in conditions of extreme poverty and ill-health, earned a precarious living by hack-journalism in London. In 1868 his left leg was amputated three or four inches below the knee and thereafter he had a wooden leg and walked painfully with the aid of crutches. A few years later the disease threatened his right foot and he was told by the doctors in Margate (whence he had gone in search of health) that amputation was the only remedy for necrosis of the bone. Henley refused to accept this and in August 1873 he bravely went up to Edinburgh to seek treatment at the Royal Infirmary from Professor Joseph Lister (later Lord Lister), the great pioneer of anti-septic surgery. Lister managed to save his foot, but Henley had to spend nearly two years in bed receiving treatment and convalescing.

As his biographer pointed out, Edinburgh was to change Henley's whole life. His schooling had been brief and scrappy; the enforced leisure of his sick-bed enabled him to study and served as his university. The sufferings and experiences in the Old Infirmary gave rise to the remarkable sequence of 'In Hospital' poems which established his worth as a poet. To the same period (1875) belong the verses entitled 'Invictus', by which Henley is now best remembered and for which he is derided. The references to his 'unconquerable soul' his head being 'bloody, but unbowed' and the conclusion that he is 'the master of my fate . . . the Captain of my soul' are now hackneyed through repetition; but they have a different feel when it is remembered that they were written by a poor, lonely man bravely fighting a painful disease.

The meeting with Stevenson brought immense benefits to Henley. He was drawn into the close circle of RLS's friends; his links with two of them – Bob Stevenson and Charles Baxter – resulted in lifelong friendships; and Colvin helped through his contacts with London publishers and editors. With the encouragement of Stevenson and his friends Henley was launched on his literary career of poet, journalist, critic and, in due course, editor. The friendship between RLS and Henley was a very special one for both young men and in its emotional warmth and spontaneity evidently supplied for RLS some element missing from his other relationships; in their letters they became 'Dear Lad' and 'Dear Boy' and this romantic, rather adolescent character of their friendship contained the seeds of their later discord. Henley's biographer, John Connell, shrewdly observed: 'Close and high-wrought as their friendship was, practical and fruitful of good literary work

as it undoubtedly was, through it there ran all the time a streak of highly
revealing boyishness, whose most frequent expression was a shrill jocosity –
occasional fifth-form smut, obscure puns, funny little rhymes, and mock-
pompous signatures such as "H. Lufton Duckworth."' Henley never
reconciled himself to the later, more mature person that Stevenson was to
become; the Stevenson he loved and remembered (as he wrote in his
notorious *Pall Mall Magazine* article of 1901) was 'the unmarried and
irresponsible Lewis: the friend, the comrade, the *charmeur*' and the 'riotous,
intrepid, scornful Stevenson'. This was the youthful Stevenson whom
Henley portrayed in his poem 'Apparition' (written within a year of their
meeting); although it has been reprinted by all the biographers it still
deserves its place here:

> Thin-legged, thin-chested, slight unspeakably,
> Neat-footed and weak-fingered: in his face –
> Lean, large-boned, curved of beak, and touched with race,
> Bold-lipped, rich-tinted, mutable as the sea,
> The brown eyes radiant with vivacity –
> There shines a brilliant and romantic grace,
> A spirit intense and rare, with trace on trace
> Of passion and impudence and energy.
> Valiant in velvet, light in ragged luck,
> Most vain, most generous, sternly critical,
> Buffoon and poet, lover and sensualist:
> A deal of Ariel, just a streak of Puck,
> Much Antony, of Hamlet most of all,
> And something of the Shorter-Catechist.

RLS's own impression of Henley as a talker was written after they had
known each other for seven years. He put him into his essay 'Talk and
Talkers' as 'Burly', classifying him along with Bob Stevenson as a 'loud,
copious, intolerant' talker:

Burly is a man of great presence; he commands a larger atmosphere, gives
the impression of a grosser mass of character than most men. It has been
said of him that his presence could be felt in a room you entered
blindfold; and the same, I think, has been said of other powerful con-
stitutions condemned to much physical inaction. There is something
boisterous and piratic in Burly's manner of talk which suits well enough
with this impression. He will roar you down, he will bury his face in his
hands, he will undergo passions of revolt and agony; and meanwhile his
attitude of mind is really both conciliatory and receptive; . . . and you
end arm-in-arm, and in a glow of mutual admiration.

This accords with Wilde's later comment: 'His personality is insistent. To converse with him is a physical no less than an intellectual recreation.'[2]

Stevenson's most famous partial portrait of Henley is in *Treasure Island*. In a letter of May 1883 he confessed: 'It was the sight of your maimed strength and masterfulness that begot John Silver in *Treasure Island*. Of course, he is not in any other quality or feature the least like you; but the idea of the maimed man, ruling and dreaded by the sound, was entirely taken from you.' Sir Herbert Stephen (a journalistic colleague) has a good description:

> The skin of his face was decidedly more red than yellow. His eyes were blue, and very clear and vivacious. His hair was of such colours as are indicated by the words light-yellow, golden, or red, and his full beard and moustache were rather less yellow and more red than his hair. Nothing in his appearance was more characteristic than his hair. It grew plentifully, with manifest strength and insistence. . . . As he talked it usually became extensively ruffled, and stood up all over his head in generous profusion. . . . He was lively, impulsive, enthusiastic, vigorous, full of vehement tastes and distastes, affectionate, and largely dominated by sentiment.[3]

To complete the picture it must also be said that he was extremely touchy and quick to take offence and quarrelled at one time or another with most of his friends. George Saintsbury commented: 'It was very possible to quarrel with him – or rather for him to quarrel with you – but it was strangely impossible to dislike him'[4]; his worst failing in Stevenson's eyes was his habit of indiscreet gossip and backbiting.

The progress of the friendship and of Henley's literary career are chronicled in the letters; they need only be briefly summarised here. Henley had been discharged from hospital in April 1875 and after a short period of hack-work for the *Encyclopaedia Britannica* in Edinburgh he returned to London. For the rest of his life he earned a fairly precarious living as a journalist and editor. He was a prolific contributor to the *Athenaeum*, the *Saturday Review* and other journals and did dramatic criticism for the *Pall Mall Gazette*. His first spell as editor was on the short-lived and little-known magazine *London* (1877–9); Henley contributed many poems and articles but it is now remembered only because it published Stevenson's *New Arabian Nights* and some early essays. Henley came into his own as editor of the *Magazine of Art* (1881–6) where he assembled a fine team of writers and championed Rodin and Whistler.

---

[2] Wilde to Will Rothenstein 14 August 1897. *The Letters of Oscar Wilde*, ed. Rupert Hart-Davis (1962).

[3] Sir Herbert Stephen, 'William Ernest Henley' (*The London Mercury*, February 1926).

[4] George Saintsbury, 'R.L.S., Henley and Sir Walter Raleigh' (*University of Edinburgh Journal*, 1927; reprinted in *George Saintsbury: The Memorial Volume*, ed. A. Muir *et al*, 1945).

The most important consequence of Henley's stay in Edinburgh was his meeting with his future wife, Anna Boyle, when she was visiting her brother, a captain in the merchant navy, who was a fellow patient with Henley in the Old Infirmary. They were married on 22 January 1878 in the Roman Catholic Pro-Cathedral in Edinburgh, with Charles Baxter and Anne Jenkin as witnesses. They set up home in Shepherd's Bush, the first of many rented houses they were to occupy in this dismal area of London. RLS stayed with them before and after his 'Travels with a Donkey' journey in France in that year and paid tribute in a letter to his mother to the kindness and graciousness of Anna Henley. One of Henley's brothers described the marriage as a 'bold action for a lame man with a family on his back'. Henley's widowed mother and his four brothers had joined him in London and looked to him for financial help: two of the brothers figure in Stevenson's letters – Anthony, an artist who was at Grez with RLS, and Edward (Teddy), a ne'er-do-well actor whose misconduct was a great trial to both RLS and Henley. The only sorrow for many years in Henley's very happy marriage was the absence of children; his wife suffered a succession of miscarriages. On 4 September 1888 their daughter Margaret Emma – 'The Golden Child' – was born and became the focus of all Henley's hopes; she died on 11 February 1894 and the light went out of his life.

Like RLS's other friends, Henley was strongly opposed to his journey to California in 1879 and his marriage to Fanny Osbourne. After Stevenson's return as a married man, the correspondence between the two men was in the warmest terms and relations between Henley and Fanny seem (on the surface at least) to have been friendly, even though in the early days he was describing her to Baxter as feckless and irresponsible and later, like Colvin, thought her an 'alarmist' in her attitude to her husband's illnesses. It was to Henley that Fanny turned for help in 1884 when RLS was seriously ill at Hyères and she looked to him for advice on later occasions.

At this time, when Stevenson was mostly living abroad, Henley performed a valuable service by acting as his unpaid literary agent (he refused the offer of a commission) and he was indefatigable in negotiations with publishers. It was thanks to him that Chatto and Windus became Stevenson's publishers and he secured the contract with Cassell for *Treasure Island* and with Longmans for *A Child's Garden of Verses*. As editor of the *Magazine of Art* Henley provided an outlet for a number of articles, although in some instances (as had happened with the magazine *London*) it could be argued that RLS was providing much-needed 'copy' to help Henley.

The friendship entered a new phase with Stevenson's return to England in July 1884 and the move to Bournemouth. It coincided with the London production (for one performance) of the play *Deacon Brodie* that RLS and Henley had written in collaboration in 1879. From almost the beginning of the friendship Henley had seen the theatre as the way to financial success and the letters are full of ideas for possible future plays. Most of August and September 1884 were spent by RLS and Henley, in a mood of great enthusiasm (in which Fanny shared), writing *Beau Austin* and *Admiral Guinea*; early in 1885, at the suggestion of Beerbohm Tree, they wrote *Macaire*. RLS later told Baxter that he had gone on writing the plays 'without hope because I thought they kept him [Henley] up' and that he 'thought these days and months a sacrifice'. This seems to have been an exaggeration, written in bitterness after the event, but it is true that RLS soon lost his initial enthusiasm, and realising the plays had little merit was embarrassed by Henley's continued attempts to interest theatrical managers in them. At the beginning of the Bournemouth period the friendship between Stevenson and Henley was at its closest; letters seem to have been exchanged almost every day and there were frequent visits by Henley to Bournemouth and even Fanny twice stayed with the Henleys in London. By the end of it the friendship was under severe strain. In later letters to Baxter, RLS makes it clear that in the winter of 1886–7 there was a serious estrangement followed by reconciliation and it seems there were earlier lesser quarrels.

The final quarrel, which effectively ended the friendship, came in March 1888 when RLS was at Saranac Lake in the United States. All the available documents relating to it (including a few not previously published) are given in Part XXII. It concerned an accusation by Henley, made almost casually in the course of a long letter, that Fanny was guilty of plagiarism in publishing under her own name a short story, 'The Nixie', based on an earlier story by RLS's cousin, Katharine de Mattos; RLS and Fanny claimed that Katharine had in effect given up the story and consented to Fanny's use of it (although RLS admitted to Baxter that Katharine's consent had been an unwilling one and he had asked Fanny not to write the story); Henley was convinced that Fanny was guilty and that the story should have had Katharine's name as well as Fanny's on it. The rights and wrongs cannot now be determined. The issue for Stevenson was that Henley had been disloyal as a friend in making such an accusation against Fanny, and he saw it as the latest example of what he regarded as Henley's penchant for stirring up trouble behind his back and speaking ill of him to his friends; he wrote bitterly to Baxter about Henley and the clique of his family and friends in Shepherd's Bush: 'There is not one of that crew that I have not helped in every kind of strait – with money, with service . . . and every year there is a fresh outburst against me and mine.' RLS agonised at great length over the affair in his letters to Baxter and made himself ill with distress and bitterness. To make matters worse, Katharine de Mattos (who was Henley's protégée) refused to confirm Stevenson's version of events; meanwhile Fanny in San Francisco was writing hysterical letters to Baxter.

Colvin saw the chief reason for the quarrel as Henley's resentment of the way Fanny, in the interests of her husband's health, had treated him at Bournemouth:

Henley's crippled boisterousness consoled itself at all times by a large indulgence in whisky and tobacco and uproarious talk. When he used to stay for long whiles with the Stevensons at Bournemouth . . . it was always a matter of just and anxious doubt to Mrs RLS whether the rackety and inconsiderate company of this friend might not at any moment bring on one of those hemorrhages of the lungs which from time to time threatened her husband's life. She was obliged for his health's sake in some degree to discourage and put restrictions on their intercourse.[5]

Another factor (mentioned by both Colvin and Baxter) was Henley's jealousy of RLS's growing fame and success, coupled with bitterness over the failure of the plays. Linked with this must have been resentment and embarrassment over the fact that RLS was providing him with financial help. Baxter commented: 'Poverty *is* a hard thing, but I think I have noticed that it is a dangerous thing for a rich man as you now are, or seem to him, to give money, and I'm afraid that the recent gifts which it gave you so much pleasure to suggest, and me to carry out, may have carried a certain gall with them.'

The old cordial relations were never restored, but matters were patched up to the extent of the exchange of a few letters in the early days in the South Seas. The last straw came in December 1890 when RLS learned that Henley, by this time living in Edinburgh, had failed to call on his mother when she returned to Scotland from Honolulu. There was another outburst of anger in a letter to Baxter and what RLS regarded as the final breach took place. In spite of this he continued to make references to Henley in letters to Baxter. In March 1891, for instance, he wrote: 'As for Henley, what a miss I have of him. The charm, the wit, the vigour of the man haunt my memory; my past is all full of his big presence and his welcome, wooden footstep. Let it be past henceforward: a beloved past, without continuation.' There were a few more brief letters to Henley himself (including a letter of congratulation in August 1892 about his poems) and a final letter in 1894.

Henley's career had meanwhile taken a more successful turn. His *A Book of Verses* published in 1888 had been well received and was followed by further collections. He produced three volumes of art criticism (collected in *Views and Reviews* II, 1892). In November 1889 he began to edit *The Scots Observer*, which later changed its name to *The National Observer*; when he lost the editorship in 1894 he took over *The New Review*, which lasted until

[5] Colvin to Clayton Hamilton 15 February 1923 (Colvin's file copy, Yale).

1898. In these nine years he showed himself to be an editor of genius: in the lively pages of the *Observer* and the *New Review* readers were introduced to the work of many new young writers – H.G. Wells, Kipling, Yeats, Conrad, among others. In this period of editorship Henley was surrounded by a group of young men – called the Henley Regatta by Max Beerbohm – who flattered him and hero-worshipped him and treated him as a great man.

To complete the picture it should be recorded that Henley did some editorial work of distinction. In collaboration with T.F. Henderson he edited a major edition of Burns (1896–7); with J.S. Farmer he edited *Slang and its Analogues* (1894–1904); he began an important series of Tudor Translations with an edition of Florio's *Montaigne*, dedicated to RLS (1892); among a number of anthologies he produced the once-famous *Lyra Heroica*.

Following the loss of Henley's daughter in February 1894, RLS sent a letter of sympathy which has not survived. Henley responded with a long letter of gossip about literary projects and news which may well have been a 'feeler' towards better relations. RLS sent a friendly but fairly impersonal reply in July 1894, addressed to 'My dear lad'. He told Baxter at the same time that he thought Henley's letter 'in very good taste and rather touching' but that Fanny 'thought it was a letter preparatory to the asking of money'. Realising that it could bear that construction, 'with a great deal of distaste' RLS authorised Baxter 'to pay (when necessary) five pounds a month to Henley. He can't starve at that; . . . and if I gave him more, it would only lead to his starting a gig and a Pomeranian dog.'

The phrase, in slightly garbled form with the deletion of the name, was quoted by Graham Balfour in his official biography as an example of Stevenson's generosity. J.C. Furnas shrewdly guessed that it was the recognition of the phrase as applying to himself that led to the fury and special vindictiveness of Henley's onslaught on the memory of his old friend in his review in the *Pall Mall Magazine*. Baxter in letters to Lord Guthrie in 1914[6] had in fact already recognised this and considered it an intentional slight on the part of Fanny Stevenson – 'It could not have passed to the printers' hands without her knowledge.' Henley's biographer in his turn saw the article as having been written 'to savage Fanny'. Henley's friends and apologists for him in more recent times have tried to justify the article on the grounds that he was attacking the attempt to canonise Stevenson on the part of his more fanatical and sentimental admirers; Henley's gibe about 'this Seraph in Chocolate, this barley-sugar effigy of a real man' was not really true of the figure presented in Balfour's biography, despite the obvious reticences inevitable at the time it was written. Henley went on to write patronisingly and contemptuously about Stevenson's personal qualities and

[6] Baxter's letters to Lord Guthrie 25 March and 4 April 1914 (MSS Edinburgh).

to belittle his work. A truer comment was surely that made by Henley in a letter to Charles Whibley in December 1894 when he first heard of Stevenson's death: 'It has upset us not a little; for though there had been differences, he was, save for my wife, the oldest friend, as he had been the dearest, I had on earth.'

Henley died in Woking, after several years of increasing ill-health and pain, on 11 July 1903. His ashes were interred in his daughter's grave in the churchyard of Cockayne Hatley in Bedfordshire; Anna Henley's joined them in 1925.

Fanny Stevenson and her Children[1]

Fanny Stevenson has been savagely treated by some of her husband's biographers. They have represented her as a selfish, jealous woman who dominated and controlled Stevenson's life, alienated him from his friends and censored and sometimes suppressed his work in the interests of respectability and commercial success. It is difficult to reconcile this dreadful creature with the real woman whom (despite her faults) Stevenson loved. This love is consistently shown throughout his letters. In January 1880 he wrote to Gosse: 'I do not think many wives are better loved than mine will be.' In April 1884 he wrote to his mother from Hyères:

> The great Cassandra is in pretty good feather; I love her better than ever and admire her more; and I cannot think what I have done to deserve so good a gift. This sudden remark came out of my pen; it is not like me; but in case you did not know, I may as well tell you, that my marriage has been the most successful in the world. I say so, and being the child of my parents, I can speak with knowledge. She is everything to me: wife, brother, sister, daughter and dear companion; and I would not change to get a goddess or a saint. So far, after, I think four years of matrimony.

[1] *The Life of Mrs Robert Louis Stevenson* by Nellie Van de Grift Sanchez (1920) gives the whitewashed family version of Fanny's biography but is the only source for some details of her early life. It reprints extracts from Fanny's autobiographical fragment, 'A Backwoods Childhood'. In *The Violent Friend* (New York, 1968; abridged edition London, 1969) Margaret Mackay collects together a rag-bag of material mainly about Fanny's life with RLS, but she is unselective, uncritical and unscholarly in her use of it. Alexandra Lapierre's *Fanny Stevenson. Entre Passion et Liberté* (Paris, 1993), although partly fictional in form, is based on meticulous research and has been invaluable for information on Fanny's life before the meeting with RLS. J.C. Furnas, *Voyage to Windward* (1952) gives an excellent summary, incorporating some original research.

He was still of the same opinion eight years later, in December 1892, when he wrote to Mrs Jenkin, troubled about the marriage of one of her sons:

> I should like to remind you of another thing; my marriage was hugely in the teeth of what my parents wanted; they were deeply hurt – I think they were near despairing over it. And now, as I look back, I think it was the best move I ever made in my life. Not only would I do it again; I cannot conceive the idea of not doing it.

Fanny had already lived for half of her life and had many and varied experiences and adventures before her first meeting with RLS in 1876; in old age she said that her life had been too much 'like a dazed rush on a railroad express' for her to be able to write her memoirs. Frances Matilda Vandegrift was born in Indianapolis, the capital of Indiana, on 10 March 1840 to Jacob Vandegrift (1816–76) and his wife Esther Thomas Keen (1811–94) and was the eldest of six surviving children (five daughters and one son). She always called herself 'Fanny' and later adopted the earlier and more aristocratic-looking spelling of her surname 'Van de Grift'. Both families came from Philadelphia and traced their descent from early Dutch and Swedish settlers. Jacob Vandegrift was a lumber merchant and dealer in real-estate who also acted as purchasing agent for the railroad company; he owned a farm in Hendricks County.

When Fanny was born Indianapolis was only twenty years old but it was growing rapidly and by the time she was seven it boasted 3000 inhabitants. J.C. Furnas says that Fanny's autobiographical fragment, 'A Backwoods Childhood', curiously misrepresents the 'pioneering background' of her early days and that although 'raw', life in Indianapolis was in no sense 'pioneering'; even so it must have been a fairly primitive, rough life that helped to develop qualities of independence and self-reliance. Her sister Nellie (who wrote her biography) says that Fanny was 'a high-spirited, daring creature, a little flashing firefly of a child, eagerly seeking for adventure' who became something of a tomboy. She was 'a brilliant but not an industrious pupil' at school but with her father's encouragement she was an avid reader. Under her mother's tuition she developed into an excellent needlewoman and a good cook and either now or later she became a keen gardener, skills that were to stand her in good stead. By the conventions of her time she was not beautiful, being dark-complexioned and dark-haired; as a child she had wanted to be a lily but had to content herself with being a tiger-lily.

On 24 December 1857, at the age of seventeen, Fanny married in Indianapolis Samuel Osbourne, a tall, handsome twenty-year-old from Kentucky who was private secretary to the Governor of Indiana and was later deputy clerk to the State Supreme Court. They lived in Indianapolis for the early years of their marriage and their daughter Isobel (Belle), a lively, dark-complexioned little girl like her mother, was born on 18 September 1858.

In November 1861, following the outbreak of the Civil War, Sam joined a local regiment, the 46th Indiana, to fight on the side of the North and was commissioned as a captain, but he saw no action and resigned after six months; a year later he enrolled in the Indiana Legion, a locally raised 'home guard'. In the winter of 1863 he left his wife and family to accompany his friend George Marshall (recently married to Fanny's sister, Josephine), who was seriously ill with tuberculosis, to California. George died in Panama in January 1864 but Sam continued alone to San Francisco, and then, attracted by the lure of silver-mining, moved on to the mining-camp of Austin in Nevada. Fanny with her young daughter made the difficult journey there by steamer from New York, by rail across the isthmus of Panama and then by steamer again to San Francisco; from San Francisco she went by stage-coach via Carson City and finally joined her husband in June 1864. Fanny was later to describe the Reese river district where Austin was situated as 'an arid stretch of alkali desert, where no green thing was to be seen on the face of the earth'.[2] Here, in the most primitive conditions in a little cabin on the mountainside, Fanny performed wonders of housekeeping, learning, it was said, to cook beef (along with bread virtually the only food available) in fifteen different ways. Here too, she learned to roll and smoke cigarettes – thereafter a lifelong habit – and to fire a revolver. Sam lost most of his money in the failure of his mining ventures in Austin and in 1865 they moved on to Virginia City – the rough, lawless silver-mining boom town, with its gambling saloons and brothels, established a few years earlier on the site of the fabulous Comstock lode, where fortunes were made and lost. Sam bought a silver mine but failed to make his fortune and took a job as Deputy City Clerk. Fanny, as before, created a comfortable home in a mining shack.

It was in Virginia City that Fanny first discovered that her husband had been unfaithful. The depressing pattern of infidelities, recriminations and reconciliations that was to characterise the next ten years of their marriage had begun. Perhaps as a result of that first row, in March 1866 Sam left on a prospecting trip to the Coeur d'Alene mountains in Montana where he joined up with Samuel Orr, a fellow prospector who was later to marry Fanny's sister, Cora. Fanny stayed on in Virginia City without news of her husband but by the end of the year she moved to San Francisco. Here a false report reached her that Sam had been killed by Indians; she went into mourning, took a room in a cheap boarding-house and representing herself as French earned a precarious living by dressmaking. Some time in 1867 Sam turned up again – 'a tall handsome man in high boots and a wide

---

[2] 'Life Abroad – The Far West' by Fanny in *The Queen*, 31 March 1894.

hat' – and caught up Belle in his arms with the cry, 'Is this my little girl?'
A reconciliation followed and on 7 April 1868 their son Samuel Lloyd
Osbourne (later known as Lloyd) was born; he was given the name Lloyd
after John Lloyd, a young Welshman (at this time a lawyer's clerk) who
had become friendly with the Osbournes in Austin and Virginia City and
befriended Fanny (with whom he was 'somewhat resentfully' in love) when
she was alone in San Francisco.

Soon after her son's birth Fanny caught Sam out in fresh philanderings
and she returned with her children to her father's farm in Clayton,
Hendricks County, Indiana. After a year away she rejoined her husband in
San Francisco in June 1869. Sam Osbourne, remembered with affection by
his children as a man of great kindness and charm, was obviously unsatisfactory as a husband and it seems that the marriage never recovered from the
strains put upon it by his unfaithfulness. He had by this time secured a
position as an official shorthand reporter in the District Court and was a
popular member of the Bohemian Club. In their cottage in East Oakland –
later remembered by RLS in the dedication to *Prince Otto* as the 'old
wooden house embowered in creepers . . . [that] had come round the Horn
piecemeal in the belly of a ship' – Fanny was able to develop a wide range
of interests and activities. Her greatest joy was in her garden, but according
to her sister Nellie she also dabbled in photography, set up and practised at
a rifle-range, made clothes on her sewing-machine, and when the servant
was away did the cooking. She became friendly with a group of people
(who were also Sam's friends) prominent in the cultural life of San Francisco; they included the artist Virgil Williams, Director of the School of
Design, and his artist wife Dora Norton (with whom she corresponded for
the rest of her life), and Timothy Rearden, a lawyer who was librarian of
the Mercantile Library and teased her and flirted with her. With Rearden's
encouragement she tried (not very successfully) to write stories. A more
important step was to join her daughter Belle in studying art at Virgil
Williams's School. Belle was to show the greater talent but Fanny did
sufficiently well to gain a silver medal for drawing.

A second son, Hervey, had been born in June 1871 but the marriage
continued to deteriorate and in 1875 Fanny made the decision not only to
leave her husband again but to travel with her children to Europe, where
she and Belle could continue their art studies. No doubt the advantage for
Belle of art instruction in Europe played some part in what seems a puzzling
decision. After a brief visit to Indianapolis to see her parents, Fanny travelled
from New York to Antwerp, arriving there in August 1875. After three
months in Antwerp she moved on to Paris, where she and Belle enrolled as
art students in the Atelier Julian. Sam seems to have paid her an allowance
throughout her stay in France but they were often desperately poor. In
April 1876 the beautiful but delicate Hervey died after a long and painful

illness; Sam joined his wife in Paris and was with her when their son died but he returned to America almost immediately. In order to recuperate after the grief of Hervey's death Fanny went to Grez in July 1876. A few weeks later came the first meeting with Stevenson. The story of their love affair, so far as it can now be pieced together, is told in Part VIII, and Part X tells of RLS's journey to America as an 'Amateur Emigrant' to make her his wife.

Fanny's appearance and personality made a strong impression on all who met her. In a private letter to Henley written aften he had met RLS and Fanny off the ship at Liverpool in August 1880, Colvin referred to her 'little determined brown face and white teeth and grizzling hair', but in his *Memories and Notes* (1921), long after her death, he gave a more considered portrait:

> Deep and rich capacities were in her, alike for tragedy and humour; all her moods, thoughts and instincts were vividly genuine and her own, and her daily talk, like her letters, was admirable both for play of character and feeling and for choice and colour of words. On those who knew the pair first after their marriage her personality impressed itself almost as vividly as his; and in my own mind his image lives scarce more indelibly than that of the small, dark-complexioned, eager, devoted woman his mate. In spite of her squareish build she was supple and elastic in all her movements; her hands and feet were small and beautifully modelled, though not meant for, or used to, idleness; the head, under its crop of close-waving thick black hair, was of a build and character that somehow suggested Napoleon, by the firm setting of the jaw and the beautifully precise and delicate modelling of the nose and lips: the eyes were full of sex and mystery as they changed from fire or fun to gloom or tenderness; and it was from between a fine pearly set of small teeth that there came the clear metallic accents of her intensely human and often quaintly individual speech.

Edward Marsh recorded what Edmund Gosse had told him about Fanny: 'He said she was one of the strangest people who had lived in our time, a sort of savage nature in some ways, but very lovable – extraordinarily passionate and unlike everyone else in her violent feelings and unrestrained way of expressing them – full of gaiety, and with a genius for expressing things picturesquely, but not literary.'[3]

Henry James described Fanny to Owen Wister in December 1887 as 'a strange California wife fifteen years older than Louis himself, but almost as interesting' and added: 'If you like the gulch and the canyon you will like

[3] Edward Marsh to Neville Lytton, 1 June 1898, quoted in Christopher Hassall, *Edward Marsh* (1959).

her.' Most biographers, especially those hostile to Fanny, quote James's later casual remark about her as 'Poor lady, poor barbarous and merely instinctive lady' but they do not give the context. James was commenting in 1907 on Fanny's eccentric behaviour while visiting Europe in withholding her address and trying to avoid meeting her friends; he went on to regret that he would fail to see her — 'and yet, with a sneaking kindness for her that I have, shall be sorry wholly to lose her.'

The best word-picture of Fanny is, not surprisingly, that given by Stevenson himself in a letter to J.M. Barrie in April 1893 as part of his humorous catalogue of the Vailima family:

> If you don't get on with her, it's a pity about your visit. She runs the show. Infinitely little, extraordinary wig of gray curls, handsome waxen face like Napoleon's, insane black eyes, boy's hands, tiny bare feet, a cigarette . . . Hellish energy; relieved by fortnights of entire hibernation. Can make anything from a house to a row, all fine and large of their kind. My uncle, after seeing her for the first time: 'Yes Louis, you have done well. I married a besom[4] myself and have never regretted it.' . . . Doctors everybody, will doctor you, cannot be doctored herself. The Living Partizan: A violent friend, a brimstone enemy. . . . Is always either loathed or slavishly adored; indifference impossible. The natives think her uncanny and that devils serve her. Dreams dreams, and sees visions.

In spite of the background of family distress against which the marriage had taken place, Stevenson's parents welcomed Fanny warmly and treated her with great kindness and indulgence. Fanny's letters show how genuine was her own affection for them. She was quickly drawn into the intimacy of family jokes and nicknames. Thomas Stevenson, who shared her own gloomy and pessimistic view of life, called her 'Cassandra' and 'The Vandergrifter' while she called him 'Mr Tommy'.

Fanny did not make as good an impression on Stevenson's friends as she had made on his parents. At their first meeting in October 1880 in their London hotel *en route* for Davos, her main concern was to try to prevent them overtiring her husband. She was, as she wrote to her mother-in-law, 'all the time furtively watching the clock, and thirsting for their life's blood because they stay so late'. This set the pattern for Fanny's married life. It was well summarised by Lloyd Osbourne, in a letter to G.S. Hellman in the 1920s: 'As to my mother . . . whatever you may find to criticise in her remember always that it was she who kept Stevenson alive; and in keeping him alive — guarding him, watching over him, subordinating her whole life to him, she necessarily offended many people. Her life in many ways was a

---

[4] A broom, but when applied to a woman it means she is a little tart in temper, 'a handful'.

very sad one – a life of unending apprehension; death was always snatching at Stevenson, and there she was always interposing herself.' In the early days his friends did not always recognise the seriousness of his illness and regarded Fanny's attitude as 'alarmist'; undoubtedly she over-reacted at times and was given to exaggeration and over-dramatisation, but Stevenson's illness was real enough and at moments of crisis Fanny's care and determination helped him to survive. The physical demands made on her when nursing RLS were considerable and the nervous strains in coping with an often bad-tempered and difficult patient cannot be over-emphasised. Well ahead of the scientists Fanny realised that colds were infectious and went to great lengths to prevent anyone with a cold from seeing RLS; although this was treated humorously, as one of her eccentricities, it must have offended many people.

In his reminiscences Colvin wrote that although Fanny could be 'a dragon indeed' to those of her husband's friends who ignored the precautions necessary for his health, 'the more considerate among them she made warmly her own and was ever ready to welcome'. Colvin himself fell into the latter category and, whatever his reservations, he and Fanny were on close and friendly terms. The affectionate references to Colvin (and the awe at his scholarship) in her letters to Dora Norton Williams seem perfectly genuine, as do the letters she wrote in rather emotional terms to both Baxter and Colvin in 1890 when the Stevensons made their decision to settle in Samoa. Even with Henley Fanny seems to have been on terms of affectionate banter at first, and she was deeply grateful for his help when RLS was seriously ill at Hyères in 1884; the strains came at Bournemouth following the collaboration over the plays and his resentment at the curbs she found it necessary to place on the relationship in the interests of her husband's health.

There were elements in Fanny's character with which RLS's friends found it difficult to come to terms. She was outspoken and dogmatic in her views and defended her opinions vigorously and passionately. She was quick to take offence, leading RLS to remark at the height of the quarrel with Henley, 'I envy you flimsy people who rage up so easily with hate'. In his essay 'Talk and Talkers II' (1882) RLS wrote:

Marriage is one long conversation, chequered by disputes. The disputes are valueless; they but ingrain the difference; the heroic heart of woman prompting her at once to nail her colours to the mast. But in the intervals, almost unconsciously and with no desire to shine, the whole material of life is turned over and over, ideas are struck out and shared, the two persons more and more adapt their notions one to suit the other, and in process of time, without sound of trumpet, they conduct each other into new worlds of thought.

RLS and Fanny argued fiercely throughout their marriage, about his conduct, about his work and everything else under the sun. Graham Balfour,
who was a member of the family at Vailima, wrote to Colvin in 1915:
'Louis and Fanny were high-tempered, outspoken people but their affection
nobody but a fool could doubt.'

Fanny liked to think that she could have earned her living as a writer, but
apart from one children's story published before her marriage, the few
stories she had published were no doubt accepted on the strength of her
husband's name. Her letters and her published diaries are lively and amusing
and her contribution to *The Dynamiter* shows she had a vivid imagination
for fantastic stories. She also had great pretensions as a literary critic,
especially as a judge of her husband's work; RLS seems to have valued her
opinion even though he did not necessarily accept it. In January 1885 she
wrote to her mother-in-law about their collaboration on *The Dynamiter*:

> I always have to fight hard for my changes, but in most Henley has borne
> me out. If I die before Louis my last earnest request will be, if I can make
> one . . . that Louis shall publish nothing without his father's approbation.
> I know that means little short of destruction to both of them, but there
> will be no one else. The field is always covered with my own dead and
> wounded, and often I am forced to a compromise. Still I make a very
> good fight.

The most famous example of Fanny's influence on her husband's work is
her criticism of the first draft of *Dr Jekyll and Mr Hyde* and his rewriting of
it to bring out the allegory. There is absolutely no evidence to support
Malcolm Elwin's speculation that the first draft contained specific details of
Jekyll's sexual excesses and that Fanny censored these in the interests of
respectability and the possible effect on Stevenson's reputation as an author
of children's books.[5]

No love letters between RLS and Fanny have survived and RLS even
told Colvin '. . . to F. I never write letters. . . . All that people want by
letters has been done between us. We are acquainted; why go on with more
introductions? I cannot change so much, but she would still have the clue
and recognise every thought.' RLS's letters to Fanny after their marriage (so
far as they have survived) are usually brief notes about day-to-day events,
written in unsentimental terms but with an undercurrent of affection often
expressed in a humorous way; they show how close and interlinked their
lives were and how much they relied on each other. They also show that
in spite of the stresses caused by RLS's constant ill-health there was a good
deal of shared family fun expressed in the form of nicknames – like Folly
Vandegrift – and jokes, often at Fanny's expense. She seems to have taken

[5] Malcolm Elwin, *The Strange Case of Robert Louis Stevenson* (1950).

these in good part. Fanny had an enormous admiration for her husband's work and pride in his achievements. He in his turn was fiercely protective of her, as shown in his angry reaction to Henley's accusation of plagiarism. His love and devotion is shown in the many references in his letters and in the poems he wrote to her, culminating in his dedication to her of what he considered would be his masterpiece – *Weir of Hermiston*.

This love was strongly shown in his reaction to her serious mental breakdown in 1893. Throughout her marriage Fanny was plagued by bad health and biographers have speculated about the nature of it. There was (understandably) a breakdown at the time of Hervey's death in 1876, when she suffered from giddy spells and blackouts of memory. She seems to have had another breakdown of some kind in 1879, after her return to California, and in letters expressed her troubles with Sam in emotional and hysterical terms. In a letter to Colvin from New York in August 1879, on his way to her, RLS says she had inflammation of the brain 'from anxiety and wretchedness' and in a later letter to Henley in January 1880 he wrote: 'Fanny is so much better, so almost quite well – in spite of another fit; I count these damned fits like coffin nails – that my heart is very light.' No more is heard of the fits but Fanny had a background of emotional instability characterised by black moods and gloomy forebodings, and was given to over-dramatising of events and exaggeration of some of her illnesses. Like her father-in-law, Thomas Stevenson, she was something of a hypochondriac and enjoyed exchanging information with him about symptoms and remedies. But there were obviously a number of illnesses with a physical basis. At both Davos and Saranac she had heart trouble from the high altitudes; she had recurrent problems with her gall-bladder, liver and other internal troubles which were obviously not helped by some of the barbarous medicines prescribed by the doctors, and she suffered severely from rheumatism. One can only speculate about the reasons for the serious mental illness at Vailima in April 1893, which was the culmination of some eighteen months of trouble. The only information about it is given in a letter to Colvin (published in full in this edition for the first time) and in a more guarded letter to his mother. There may have been some element of jealousy, but underlying it must surely have been the stress of caring for RLS over all the years of their married life; although he was much better in the South Seas, life was punctuated by colds, influenza and threatenings of hemorrhage with Fanny continually on her guard to protect him. In addition there were the real hardships of life at sea and in the early months at Vailima. Although she revelled in the 'pioneering' aspects of it, Fanny worked hard organising and working in the garden, and there seems no doubt that much of the planning of the plantation and the running of Vailima fell upon her. She seems to have pulled herself out of the mental trouble very quickly and there is no further mention of it in Stevenson's letters. A doctor in Honolulu in

October 1893 diagnosed Fanny as suffering from Bright's disease, but no more is heard of this either.

Fanny, Belle and Lloyd stayed on at Vailima for a few months after Stevenson's death. They went to San Francisco in April 1895 and then to Honolulu, where in April 1896 Lloyd married Katharine Durham. They returned to Vailima a month later and Lloyd served briefly as American Vice Consul. His first son, Alan, was born in March 1897. Vailima was finally given up in September 1897 and in 1898 all the family went to England. Here Fanny had a serious operation for the removal of gall-stones, performed free of charge by Sir Frederick Treves; she gave him a set of the Edinburgh Edition. There was a prolonged dispute with Colvin over his delay in producing the official biography and the task was handed over to Graham Balfour. On her return to San Francisco Fanny had a house built 'like a fort on a cliff' at the corner of Hyde and Lombard Streets; she also acquired a ranch in the Santa Cruz mountains which she called Vanumanutagi (vale of the singing birds), after the property adjoining Vailima which RLS had bought in 1893 and left to Belle in his will.

As the widow of RLS Fanny was a formidable figure (Henry James called her 'an old grizzled lioness') but she still had the power to attract men. Her first protégé was Gelett Burgess (1866–1951), the journalist and humorist once famous as the author of the quatrain about the 'Purple Cow', who designed the two bronze panels for Stevenson's tomb. The second protégé was Edward (Ned) Salisbury Field (1880–1936), the son of an old school friend from Indianapolis, who caused some gossip by becoming her companion and secretary from 1903 until her death; he was later to become the successful author of lightweight plays such as *Twin Beds* and *Wedding Bells* and worked on film scripts in Hollywood. With Field and Lloyd Fanny paid her last visit to Europe in 1907. The next year she moved to a house called Stonehedge, near Santa Barbara, California. She wrote a series of prefaces for the Biographical Edition of RLS's works published by Scribner's in 1905, and prepared for publication her journal of the cruise of the *Janet Nicoll*. Fanny died at Stonehedge on 18 February 1914. Six months later, on 29 August 1914, the fifty-six-year-old Belle married the thirty-four-year-old Ned Field; the following year they took Fanny's ashes to Samoa for interment in her husband's grave.

In the 1920s oil was found on land owned by Ned Field and Belle became a rich woman. Field died in 1936. The following year Belle published her gossipy and attractive memoirs, *This Life I've Loved*. She lived to a great age, long enough to see the celebration of the centenary of her stepfather's birth and to correspond with Graham Greene. She died on 26 June 1953.

Lloyd's second son, Louis, was born in 1900, but the marriage ended in bitterness and eventually there was a divorce. Katharine Osbourne hated her

mother-in-law and all the Osbourne family, but claimed to know more
about Stevenson (whom of course she never met) than any of them. Her
malicious stories about Fanny were published by G.S. Hellman and still turn
up in some biographies of RLS. Lloyd went on to write over a dozen novels
and collections of short stories. They include some good short stories of the
South Seas such as *Wild Justice* (1906), and light novels reflecting his
enthusiasms as a pioneer motorist, such as *Baby Bullet: the Motor of Destiny*
(1905) and *Three Speeds Forward: An Automobile Love Story with one Reverse*
(1907); his last novel, *Peril*, was published in 1929. They do not seem to
have been very successful and are forgotten today. Lloyd later married Ethel
Head, a young protégée of Fanny, but this marriage also ended in divorce.
He was a well-known member of the Lambs Club in New York, and spent
much time in Europe, particularly in the South of France, where in old age
he had a third son, Samuel, by a French girl. He is remembered as having
a sharp eye for royalties from the immensely valuable Stevenson estate
which passed to him after Fanny's death, and was said never to have let a
quotation from RLS pass without extracting a fee. He was the rather
careless editor of the Vailima Edition (1922–3), and his warmly affectionate
memories of his stepfather were published as *An Intimate Portrait of R.L.S.*
(1924). He died in California 22 May 1947.

The youngest member of the Vailima family, Belle's son Austin Strong,
was trained in New Zealand as a landscape architect but became a successful
playwright with plays such as *Three Wise Fools* (1918) and *Seventh Heaven*
(1927). He died 18 September 1952.

SOURCES OF LETTERS AND
OTHER MATERIAL

Institutions

Academy	The Edinburgh Academy
Auckland	Auckland Public Library, New Zealand
Bancroft	The Bancroft Library, University of California, Berkeley
Berg	Henry W. and Albert A. Berg Collection, New York Public Library
BL	British Library, London
Bodley	Bodleian Library, Oxford
Bolton	Archive Service, Bolton Metropolitan Borough
Boston Athenaeum	The Library of the Boston Athenaeum
Brinton	Bradford Brinton Memorial Ranch, Wyoming
Bristol	University of Bristol
Brotherton	The Brotherton Library, University of Leeds
Brown	Brown University, Providence, Rhode Island
Buffalo	State University of New York, Buffalo
Buffalo and Erie	Buffalo and Erie County Public Library, Buffalo, N.Y.
Chicago	The University of Chicago Library
Clark	William Andrews Clark Memorial Library, University of California, Los Angeles
Cleveland	Case Western Reserve University Libraries, Cleveland, Ohio
Clifton	Clifton College, Bristol
Colby	Colby College, Waterville, Maine
Columbia	Columbia University, New York
Congress	Library of Congress, Washington, D.C.
Copley	The James S. Copley Library, La Jolla, California
Cornell	Cornell University Library, Ithaca, N.Y.
Dartmouth	Dartmouth College, Hanover, New Hampshire
Davis	University of California, Davis
Dickinson	Dickinson College, Carlisle, Pennsylvania
Dixson	Dixson Library, Public Library New South Wales, Sydney

Dorset	Dorset County Museum, Dorchester
Dublin	Trinity College, Dublin
Edinburgh	Lady Stair's House Museum, Edinburgh
Edinburgh CL	Edinburgh City Libraries
Fales	The Fales Collection, New York University
Fitzwilliam	Fitzwilliam Museum, Cambridge
Folger	Folger Shakespeare Library, Washington, D.C.
Harvard	Harvard University Library
Hawaiian Mission	Hawaiian Mission Children's Society Library, Honolulu
Hopkins	The John Hopkins University, Baltimore
Huntington	The Huntington Library, San Marino, California
Illinois	University of Illinois
Knox	Knox College, Galesburg, Illinois
Longmans	Messrs Longmans, Green & Co Ltd.
Massachusetts	Massachusetts Historical Society, Boston
McGill	McGill University, Montreal
Mills College	Mills College, Oakland, California
Mitchell	The Mitchell Library, Sydney
Monterey	Stevenson House, Monterey
Morgan	The Pierpont Morgan Library, New York
NLS	National Library of Scotland, Edinburgh
NYPL	New York Public Library
NZ Archives (BCS)	National Archives of New Zealand, Wellington (Records of British Consulate Samoa)
Northwestern	Northwestern University, Evanston, Illinois
Pennsylvania	The Historical Society of Pennsylvania, Philadelphia
Princeton	Princeton University Library
PRO (CO) and (FO)	Public Record Office, London. Colonial Office and Foreign Office files
Rosenbach	Rosenbach Foundation, Philadelphia
Rowfant	The Rowfant Club, Cleveland, Ohio
St Andrews	University of St Andrews
San Joaquin	San Joaquin Pioneer Museum, Stockton, California
Saranac	Saranac Memorial Cottage, Saranac Lake, N.Y.
Silverado	The Silverado Museum, St Helena, California
Speculative	The Speculative Society, Edinburgh
Sussex	University of Sussex, Brighton
Temple	Temple University, Philadelphia
Texas	Harry Ransom Humanities Research Center, The University of Texas at Austin

Texas CU	Texas Christian University, Fort Worth, Texas
Trinity Academy	Trinity Academy, Edinburgh
Trinity	Trinity College, Cambridge
Turnbull	The Alexander Turnbull Library, Wellington, New Zealand
[UCLA]	Formerly owned by University of California, Los Angeles (dispersed)
USC	University of Southern California, Los Angeles
Virginia	University of Virginia, Charlottesville
Washington	Washington University Libraries, Saint Louis, Missouri
Wellesley	Wellesley College Library, Wellesley, Mass.
Williams College	Williams College Library, Williamstown, Mass.
Yale	Yale University Library (Beinecke Library)

Private Owners

M. Balfour	Mr Michael Balfour
Baker	Mrs Nettie Doud Baker
Bangs	Miss Mary Bangs
[Block]	Formerly owned by the late Mr Gordon A. Block, Jr. (dispersed)
Cameron	Mr Waverley B. Cameron
Charnwood	The late Lady Charnwood's Autograph Collection (on loan to BL)
Dalton	Mr Chris Dalton
Furnas	Mr J.C. Furnas
Graham	Mrs Muriel Graham
[Greene]	The late Mr Graham Greene
[Haggard]	The late Sir Godfrey Haggard
Haralson	Mr Ronald Haralson
Jenkin	Lord Jenkin of Roding
Leslie	Mrs Jean Leslie
Mehew	Mr Ernest Mehew
Milne	Mr Ramsay Milne
Murray	Miss K.M. Elisabeth Murray
Nollen	Mr Scott Allen Nollen
[Osbourne]	The late Mr Alan Osbourne
Pennycuik	Brigadier J.A.C. Pennycuik

Saint-Gaudens	Mr Augustus Saint-Gaudens
Sinclair	Mr Gregg M. Sinclair
Vail	Mr R.W.G. Vail
Williams	Mrs Martha R.C. Williams

Note: Some of the private owners listed above made their letters available to Professor Booth many years ago, and the letters may have changed hands by sale or death since then.

SHORT TITLES

AAA Catalogue	American Art Association, New York, Sale Catalogue.
Accounts Current	Mitchell and Baxter's record of Stevenson's Account, December 1877–December 1884; September 1887–December 1888; June 1891–July 1894 (MS Yale).
Anderson I–III	Sale catalogues, The Anderson Galleries, New York: Stevenson's letters, MSS, books etc., sold by Isobel Strong. I, November 1914; II, January 1915; III, February 1916 (the lot no. is given in brackets).
Balfour I–II	Graham Balfour, *The Life of Robert Louis Stevenson*, 2 vols (London, 1901).
Baxter Letters	*R.L.S. Stevenson's Letters to Charles Baxter*, ed. DeLancey Ferguson and Marshall Waingrow (New Haven and London, 1956).
BBS	Boston Bibliophile Society.
BBS I–III	*Poems by Robert Louis Stevenson Hitherto Unpublished* privately printed, The Bibliophile Society, Boston, 2 vols (1916), 1 vol. (1921).
Beinecke I–VI	*A Stevenson Library. Catalogue of a Collection of Writings By and About Robert Louis Stevenson Formed by Edwin J. Beinecke*, compiled by George L. McKay, 6 vols (New Haven, Yale University Library, 1951–64).
Collected Poems	Robert Louis Stevenson, *Collected Poems*, ed. Janet Adam Smith (London, 1950; second edition, 1971).
Diary	Mrs M.I. Stevenson's pocket diary for the year concerned (Yale).
Diary Notes	The summary of her son's life up to 1888, compiled by Mrs M.I. Stevenson from her diaries in 1896 (MS Yale). Published (inaccurately) in vol. 26 of the Vailima Edition (1923).
Edinburgh	The Edinburgh Edition of Stevenson's Works, 28 vols (1894–8).
From Saranac	*From Saranac to the Marquesas and Beyond*, Mrs M.I. Stevenson's letters to her sister, Jane Balfour, 1887–8 (London, 1903).

Furnas	J.C. Furnas, *Voyage to Windward. The Life of Robert Louis Stevenson* (London, 1952).
ICR	*I Can Remember Robert Louis Stevenson*, ed. Rosaline Masson (Edinburgh, enlarged edition, 1925).
Letters I–V	*The Letters of Robert Louis Stevenson*, ed. Sir Sidney Colvin, 5 vols; vols XXXI–XXXV of the Tusitala Edition (1924).
Lucas	E.V. Lucas, *The Colvins and Their Friends* (London, 1928).
Mackenzie	Kenneth S. Mackenzie, 'Robert Louis Stevenson and Samoa'. Ph.D. thesis (Dalhousie University, 1974).
Maixner	*Robert Louis Stevenson: The Critical Heritage*, ed. Paul Maixner (London, 1981). Reviews are identified by number.
Masson	Rosaline Masson, *The Life of Robert Louis Stevenson* (Edinburgh and London, 1923).
Prideaux	W.F. Prideaux, *A Bibliography of the Works of Robert Louis Stevenson* (London, 1903, revised edition 1917).
Sanchez	Nellie Van de Grift Sanchez, *The Life of Mrs Robert Louis Stevenson* (New York and London, 1920).
Scrapbook I–VI	Mrs M.I. Stevenson's collection of press-cuttings of reviews and other references (Saranac and Monterey).
Stevensoniana	*Stevensoniana*, ed. J.A. Hammerton (Edinburgh, revised edition 1907).
Swearingen	Roger G. Swearingen, *The Prose Writings of Robert Louis Stevenson: A Guide* (Hamden, Conn. and London, 1980).
This Life	Isobel Field, *This Life I've Loved* (New York, 1937).
Tusitala	The Tusitala Edition of Stevenson's Works, 35 vols (London, 1923–4).
Tusitala Poems II	Vol. XXIII of the Tusitala Edition. Contains posthumously published poems not included in *Collected Poems*.
Vailima	The Vailima Edition of Stevenson's Works, 26 vols (New York and London, 1923).
Widener Catalogue	*A Catalogue of the Books and Manuscripts of Robert Louis Stevenson in the Library of the Late Harry Elkins Widener* (Philadelphia, 1913). Now in the Widener Collection, Harvard.

Abbreviations of Names

Belle	Isobel (Belle) Osbourne, later Strong, RLS's step-daughter.
Bob	Robert Alan Mowbray Stevenson, RLS's cousin.
Fanny	Fanny Van de Grift Osbourne, later RLS's wife.
Lloyd	Samuel Lloyd Osbourne, RLS's stepson.
MIS	Margaret Isabella Stevenson, RLS's mother.
TS	Thomas Stevenson, RLS's father.

THE LETTERS

I. EARLY YEARS 1854–1867

Thomas Stevenson and Margaret Isabella Balfour were married on 28 August 1848. Their only child, Robert Louis Stevenson (Robert Lewis Balfour to give him all the Christian names bestowed at his baptism)[1] was born on 13 November 1850 at 8 Howard Place, Edinburgh. In January 1853 the family moved to 1 Inverleith Terrace, but following the doctor's advice that the house (at the end of the Terrace) was too cold for the delicate child, they moved in May 1857 to the familiar address, 17 Heriot Row.

The childish letters printed in this first section show a lively, imaginative, much-loved child on close and happy terms with his parents. Many of them were written to his father, who was frequently away from home on business connected with the family engineering firm. The clumsy handwriting and bad spelling reflect the lack of formal education because of his ill-health. There is little in them to indicate the future author and literary stylist, and they give a very imperfect record of his childhood.

For the full picture we must turn to Stevenson's autobiographical writings[2] and to the details faithfully recorded in his mother's diaries. RLS later recalled three main impressions of these years – his ill-health, the nightmares and other nocturnal terrors inspired by morbid religious fears, and the delights of convalescence at his grandfather's manse at Colinton:

> All this time, be it borne in mind, my health was of the most precarious description. Many winters I never crossed the threshold; but used to lie on my face on the nursery floor, chalking or painting in water-colours the pictures in the illustrated newspapers; or sit up in bed, with a little shawl pinned about my shoulders, to play with bricks, or dolls, or what not. . . . My ill-health principally chronicles itself by the terrible long nights that I lay awake, troubled continually with a hacking, exhausting

---

[1] Balfour says (I, 29–30) that the change of name from Lewis to Louis was made when RLS was about eighteen: 'The alteration was due, it is said, to a strange distaste, shared by his father for a fellow-citizen, who bore the name in the form in which Lewis had received it.' Lord Guthrie says that the 'fellow-citizen' was 'a certain Bailie David Lewis', a Radical and Dissenter regarded by Thomas Stevenson 'as the incarnation of everything dangerous in Church and State' (*Robert Louis Stevenson*, 1920, 24). For the final dropping of the third name see Letter 127.

[2] The quotations come largely from RLS's 'Notes of Childhood' [Balfour's title] dated 18 May 1873 (MS Yale) from which extensive extracts were published in Balfour, I, 32–4, 40, supplemented from Book I of 'Memoirs of Himself', 1880 (MS Harvard) published in *Vailima* and later collected editions.

cough, and praying for sleep or morning from the bottom of my shaken little body. . . . [I] cannot mention [these nights] without a grateful testimony to the unwearied sympathy and long-suffering displayed to me on a hundred such occasions by my good nurse . . . How well I remember her lifting me out of bed, carrying me to the window and showing me one or two lit windows, up in Queen Street across the dark belt of gardens; where also, we told each other, there might be sick little boys and their nurses, waiting, like us, for the morning. Other night-scenes connected with my ill-health, were the little sallies of delirium that used to waken me out of a feverish sleep, in such agony of terror as, thank God, I have never suffered since. . . . My father had generally to come up, and sit by my bedside and feign conversations with guards or coachmen or innkeepers, until I was gradually quieted and brought back to myself; but it was long, after one of these paroxysms, before I could bear to be left alone.

The 'good nurse' to whom tribute is paid in these reminiscences was Alison Cunningham (1822–1913), daughter of a weaver of Torryburn, Fife, who joined the Stevenson household when RLS was eighteen months old. Her devoted care is celebrated in the Dedication to *A Child's Garden of Verses*, where she is described as

> My second Mother, my first Wife,
> The angel of my infant life –

and in the many loving letters RLS wrote to her. There was, unfortunately, a darker side to Cummy's influence. A devout member of the Free Church, she was much stricter and narrower in her religious views than Stevenson's parents, and it was to her influence that he owed 'the high-strung religious ecstasies and terrors' that disfigured his early years. He had 'an extreme terror of Hell . . . which used to haunt me most terribly on stormy nights, when the wind had broken loose and was going about the town like a bedlamite':

I would not only lie awake to weep for Jesus, which I have done many a time, but I would fear to trust myself to slumber lest I was not accepted and should slip, ere I awoke, into eternal ruin. I remember repeatedly . . . waking from a dream of Hell, clinging to the horizontal bar of the bed, with my knees and chin together, my soul shaken, my body convulsed with agony. It is not a pleasant subject. I piped and snivelled over the Bible, with an earnestness that had been talked into me . . . I shook my numskull over the spiritual welfare of my parents, because they gave dinner parties and played cards, things contemned in the religious biographies on which my mind was fed.

The deeply religious atmosphere in which RLS was brought up was not one of unrelieved piety. Thomas Stevenson (in spite of his moods of religious melancholy) had a great sense of fun and romance, and Cummy, for all her strictness, was (in Balfour's words) 'full of life and merriment. She danced and sang to her boy and read to him most dramatically.' She read to him from the Bible, the Shorter Catechism, *Pilgrim's Progress* and from her favourite religious books, but such books were not his sole diet. At an early age he was introduced to the pleasures of *Robinson Crusoe*, the adventure stories of R.M. Ballantyne and Captain Mayne Reid, and the bound volumes of *Punch* in his father's library. All his life he remembered the serial stories Cummy read to him in *Cassell's Illustrated Family Paper*, and it was because he was so anxious to find out what the pictures were about in two bound volumes of the paper that he finally learned to read when he was eight, while recovering from an attack of gastric fever.

Stevenson's later writings (particularly *A Child's Garden of Verses* and his essay on 'Child's Play') show that he had a highly imaginative love of games. Many of these games (as the verses on 'The Child Alone' show) were solitary pleasures, but when he was well enough there was no shortage of playmates from among a small army of young cousins. RLS usually insisted on taking the lead in their games and was 'invariably exhausted to death by the evening'.

Both parents came from large families, and his mother's diaries show a constant flow of visits between relatives both in Edinburgh and at holiday resorts. On the Stevenson side there were the children of his father's brother David and his sister Jane Warden. A very special cousin was Bob Stevenson, the only son of Alan Stevenson. Bob spent the winter of 1856–7 at Inverleith Terrace; together they shared the delights of the toy theatre given to RLS by Aunt Warden on his sixth birthday and later described as 'one of the dearest pleasures of my childhood'.

There were even more cousins on the Balfour side. Chief among them were Willie and Henrietta (later to be commemorated in one of the envoys to *A Child's Garden*), the children of Margaret Stevenson's sister Henrietta who had married Ramsay Traquair, a farmer at Colinton, and died when the children were very young. Together with other cousins, the children of Mrs Stevenson's brothers who worked in India, they were often to be found at Colinton Manse, the home of their grandfather, the Revd Lewis Balfour. Here they were looked after by his unmarried daughter, Jane Balfour: 'The children of the family came home to her to be nursed, to be educated, to be mothered, from the infanticidal climate of India. There must sometimes have been half a score of us children about the Manse; and all were born a second time from Aunt Jane's tenderness.' In *Memories and Portraits* RLS devoted an essay to 'The Manse' but his more personal reminiscences were written when he was twenty-three:

One consequence of my ill-health was my frequent residence at Colinton Manse. Out of my reminiscences of life in that dear place, all the morbid and painful elements have disappeared. I remember no more nights of storm; no more terror or sickness. Beyond a thunderstorm when I was frightened, after a half make-believe fashion, and huddled with Willie and Henrietta underneath the dining-room table; and a great flood of the river, to see which my father carried me wrapped in a blanket through the rain; I can recall nothing but sunshiny weather. That was my golden age; *et ego in Arcadia vixi*.[3] There is something so fresh and wholesome about all that went on at Colinton, compared with what I recollect of the town that I can hardly, even in my own mind, knit the two chains of reminiscences together.

Throughout Stevenson's childhood his mother suffered from a 'weak chest' and it was on her account as much as his that the family spent a good deal of time away from Edinburgh. In the summer months they would usually take a furnished house at one of a number of Scottish health or holiday resorts; two favourite places were Bridge of Allan and North Berwick, and in 1864 and 1865 they were at Peebles. It was his father's ill-health that led to RLS's first experience of foreign travel. In July 1862 Thomas Stevenson was ordered by his doctor to take the waters at Homburg, where RLS (as he was to recall thirty years later) was fascinated to watch the gambling. In January 1863, because of his mother's illness, there was a visit to Nice and Mentone which lasted three months. It was followed by a tour of Italy, taking in Genoa, Naples, Rome, Florence and Venice; they crossed the Alps by the Brenner Pass and came home via Munich and Nuremberg and down the Rhine. Mrs Stevenson had to go back to Mentone in November 1863, and RLS joined her there from school at the end of the year; they remained in the South of France until the beginning of May 1864. In the spring of 1865 and 1866 (as the letters show) they stayed, again because of Mrs Stevenson's health, on the south coast of England at Torquay.

His mother records that he went to school for the first time on 30 September 1857, to Mr Henderson's preparatory school in India Street. He did not stay for more than a few weeks and was not well enough to return until October 1859. During his many absences he was taught by private

---

[3] In an earlier unpublished MS (Yale) written in 1870, RLS had applied the phrase to the whole of his childhood: 'For one thing else I thank Hazlitt: for these words "*Et ego in Arcadia vixi*". Surely all my childhood was a golden age to me; and, except a storm or two whose grandeur, I suppose, impressed them upon my imagination, the whole time seems steeped in sunshine, and I have to come far forward in my memories to find the chronicle of a single shower of rain. If I desire a long life, it is that I may have the longer retrospect. Ninety years of life might be a burden; but ninety years of recollection must be heaven.'

tutors. On 1 October 1861 he went to Edinburgh Academy and stayed there (with interruptions) for about fifteen months. In the autumn of 1863 (as we see from the letters) he spent one term at an English boarding school at Isleworth. By this time his health had shown considerable improvement, and in October 1864 he resumed his regular education in Edinburgh at Robert Thomson's private school in Frederick Street; he continued there until he went to University in 1867.

Even before he could write, as well as dictating letters, RLS was dictating stories and accounts of his thoughts and doings to two willing amanuenses, his mother and his nurse. He won a prize, given by David Stevenson, for his 'History of Moses' dictated to his mother when he was six: 'from that time forward it was' (in her words) 'the desire of his heart to be an author.' A number of manuscript magazines illustrated in colour, and other childish efforts still survive; when he was in his teens he moved on to more ambitious works. As a child, he had been introduced by Cummy to the writings about the Covenanters by Patrick Walker, Robert Wodrow and others.[4] Their influence remained with him all his life; it was thanks to her, as he later wrote, that he had a 'Covenanting childhood'. A long novel about the Pentland rising was converted into an historical essay and published anonymously in 1866 at his father's expense, in pamphlet form, as *The Pentland Rising: a Page of History, 1666.*

---

[4] The Covenanters were the adherents of the two Covenants setting out and defending the Protestant faith and the Presbyterian organisation of the Scottish Church, which formed the background to the complex religious disputes in seventeenth-century Scotland. The National Covenant (1638) was a national protest specifically against a new prayer-book but more generally against the attempts of Charles I to make the government and rituals of the Scottish Church conform with those of the Church of England. The Solemn League and Covenant (1643) was the treaty made between the Scots (who had won their own conflict over religion with the King) and the English Parliamentarians under which the strict Presbyterianism practised in Scotland was to be imposed in England and Ireland in return for Scottish military aid in the Civil War. The Covenanters in whom RLS was interested (and to whom the name is now usually applied) were the extremists, mainly in the south-west of Scotland, who resisted the religious settlement made by Charles II at the Restoration (1660). Charles had reintroduced episcopacy, but had not interfered with the form of worship. Nearly 300 ministers who refused to accept the authority of the bishops or to renounce the Covenants were ejected from their parishes. Secret meetings (known as conventicles), often attended by hundreds of people, were held out of doors by these 'outed' ministers, and the authorities took harsh measures to suppress them and to punish the participants. The growing discontent led to the ill-fated Pentland Rising (1666) chronicled by the youthful RLS, and there was a later uprising crushed at Bothwell Bridge (1679) which was the subject of Scott's *Old Mortality* (1816). The Covenanters endured many years of brutal persecution culminating in the notorious 'Killing Time' (1685) when they were hunted down by troops. There were hideous tortures and executions (following the callous customs of the period) and the surviving memorials bear witness to the many 'martyrs' to the cause. Great cruelty and intolerance was shown by both sides, and fanatical Covenanters were themselves responsible for such atrocities as the assassination of Archbishop Sharp (cf. Letter 39, n. 8). The Covenanting writers recounted the dreadful stories of what happened to their heroes in a vivid self-righteous phraseology reminiscent of that of the Old Testament prophets.

So far as is practicable, the childish spelling and punctuation has been retained in the early letters.

1   To his Father[1]

MS USC.

[*Dictated to his mother*]
28 March 1854   [*1 Inverleith Terrace, Edinburgh*]

Dear Papa, Do come home to see me. My dear Papa will you bring a book to Mama too. I do want you to come home very soon *very*. If you could bring a humming top to me I would like to have it. I have drawed a picture to you and it's called a cross.[2] I'm your dear son and affectionate son

Robert Lewis Balfour Stevenson

Every word dictated by Mr Peter Sprook.[3]

2   To his Father

MS Bancroft.

[*Dictated to his mother*]
29 March 1854   [*1 Inverleith Terrace*]

Do come home dear Papa very soon. I want a kind of Swiss cottage that won't break to be sent along with the humming top. I was feinds with a shopman today and he gave me a great many pictures and he wanted me to be a little cashier. I think I will go but if I don't run fast I don't think they'll keep me. Dear Papa I want you to come home soon and see all those pictures. Dear Papa I shall be delighted to see you. Poor Bo[1] is ill and he is not better yet. I am your affectionate son   Robert Lewis Stevenson[2]

[1] TS was visiting Dumfries 28–31 March 1854.

[2] A few scribbles on the back of the letter.

[3] TS was fond of inventing nicknames for his son. MIS noted 'Boulibasker-Smoutie-Baron Broadnose-Signor Spruckie otherwise Maister Sprook . . . but Smoutie stuck to him till he was about 15' (MIS, *Baby's Record*, reproduced in *Stevenson's Baby Book*, San Francisco, 1922).

[1] Robert James Stevenson (born 1850) a young son of TS's brother David, died on 12 April 1854.

[2] MIS adds: 'I send you a pattern of Smout's new frock, do you like it.'

3   *To his Father*

MS Bancroft.

[*Dictated to his mother*]
30 March 1854   [*1 Inverleith Terrace*]

Dear Papa, Do come home very soon. If I could remember about the cross that I drawed. Papa will you do a thing that I want you to do. It's to come home and see the pictures that I got from the shopman. I would like you dear Papa to come along and get this letter.

I am your son that's going to try to be good   Baron Broadnose

4   *To Jane Whyte Balfour*[1]

MS Silverado.

[*Dictated to his mother*]
[*? October 1855*][2]   [*1 Inverleith Terrace*]

My dear Auntie, It's wonderful to know how you took that thought of rising and going into town for it makes me quite thunderstruck at the thought of it.

Do you know I've been writing a letter to Henrietta[3] and Papa forgot to put it in the post and one Sunday Mama scolded him about it. When we were at Portobello before we went away to Craggan some of the Rhinds told me we would not get the train and I said we would and I was right and they were wrong. Just this moment I was thinking to tell you of one disaster that I forgot in my letter to Henrietta it was to ask Billy how he likes his cards. Auntie I was intending to build a large tower today but now it is far too late. I've been all the day playing with paints and the like of these trash. How are Johnnie and Noona keeping?[4] I hope they've got no fleas about

[1] Jane Whyte Balfour (1816–1907), celebrated in *A Child's Garden of Verses* as 'Chief of our Aunts'. MIS's spinster sister kept house for her father at Colinton Manse and mothered her many nephews and nieces.
[2] Although dated September 1854 in an unknown hand, it cannot be earlier than October 1855. The Stevensons stayed at Portobello – the 'seaside' of Edinburgh – in the summer of 1855 and were at Craggan (near Grantown on Spey in the Highlands) 20–28 September 1855.
[3] Henrietta Traquair (1850–1902) and her brother William (1851–1923) were the children of MIS's sister Henrietta (1828–55), married to Ramsay Traquair, a farmer at Colinton.
[4] John Boyle (1839–60). The Revd Lewis Balfour (RLS's grandfather) was his guardian. 'Noona' was the nickname for Lewis Balfour (1842–73), eldest son of MIS's brother Lewis. Both boys attended the Edinburgh Academy 1852–6.

them for we were most awfully harbashered with them when we were at Colinton. Your affectionate nephew RLBS-Stevenson[5]

5 To Jane Whyte Balfour

MS Yale.

[*Dictated to his mother*]
[c. *6 February 1856*][1]   [*1 Inverleith Terrace*]

A present to Auntie on her birthday and it is a thing that Auntie may pull open any side and she puts her pen in it, then she shuts it down and draws the pen out and that makes it clean. There are a great many holes for the pen to go in at and a picture with a ship and rocks in the sea. Its mast is tumbling down with the wind because it is very stormy. It is raining too. I am your affectionate nephew   R.L.B.S.

The above has been dictated *word by word*.

6 To his Father

MS Yale.

[*Dictated to his mother*]
7 *August 1856*   *21 Pitt Street* [*Portobello*]

My dear Papa, I hope you are quite well and how do you like your voyage.[1] I hope it isn't windy or anything of that kind. When do you think you will arrive at Oban? Whether do you like steamers or ships better Papa? How are you keeping? Whether do you like railway ship or coach or steamer? If you were here just now you would have seen a boat and it had its sails up at first and a red flag and then it took down its sails and left the red flag up. Do you know that there is very few ladies' machines either on the sands or either in the sea. Do you know what I am going to get, Papa, if I am good all the time till you come back. I am going to get a game and there are pictures about Robinson Crusoe in it.   Your affectionate son   R.L.B.S.

---

[5] The crude signature is in RLS's hand. He first wrote and smudged 'R.L.S.B.' From this point all dictated letters bear crude initials or signatures by RLS. The letter was accompanied by a childish drawing of a ship and a rowing-boat, with another drawing of a sailing-ship on the back.

[1] Aunt Jane's birthday was on 6 February. The MS carries a typed note that it was dictated by RLS at the age of five.

[1] From 5 to 16 August 1856 TS was on a journey 'round the north' in the *Pharos*, the steam-yacht of the Commissioners of Northern Lights.

7   To his Father[1]

Text: extract in Catalogue of Brick Row Bookshop, New York, 1921 (1).

[*Dictated to Alison Cunningham*]
[*? August 1856*]   [*? Portobello*]

I am wearying for an answer to my last letter . . . I am making myself very happy tonight. I am wondering how Englishmen can attend to their work and beat on drums because there is a picture in *Punch* and it is a man beating a great many drums on an engine . . .   Robert-Lewis B. Stevenson

8   To his Father

MS Bancroft.

[*Dictated to his mother*]
[*27 September 1856*]   [*Innerleithen*][1]

My dearest Papa, If you look at these pictures which I have been drawing[2] you will see the inscriptions upon them. Papa do you know that I went with them a very nice picnic. We went to Ashiestiel and Yair Bridge. It was very pretty and we saw some salmon catchers. They were wading in the water up to the top of their legs. I have been trying to fish and I caught one trout[3] and Cousin Jessie gave me one that she got. Mama did not get any at all and neither did Mr Swan.[4]

This is a very bad day and we can't get out to fish. Your affectionate son
R.L.B.S.

[1] According to the catalogue and Anderson I (16), this letter was dictated to his nurse, Cummy, and dated in pencil in another hand.

[1] A health resort in Peeblesshire where the Stevensons were staying. TS was on a visit to Londonderry.

[2] The first drawing, captioned 'Our picnic', shows a horse and carriage. The second is entitled 'A Steamer bound for Londonderry'. Someone (apparently not MIS) has added a note: 'This steamer may be bound for Londonderry but I fear she will never reach it.'

[3] On 27 September MIS records in her diary: 'A pouring wet day. Last night Smout tried to fish in the Tweed with a string and a crooked pin. Tom Warden made him believe he had caught a fish and he was much charmed.' Thomas Warden (1838–75), who became a surgeon in the Royal Navy, and Jessie Warden (1831–67) were two of the five children of Dr Adam Warden and TS's sister Jane (1800–64).

[4] William Swan (1818–94), Professor of Natural Philosophy at St Andrews University, 1859–80. His mother and TS's mother were daughters of the Thomas Smith who became Robert Stevenson's stepfather (see p. 23). Swan's father died when he was three and he spent much time as a boy with Robert Stevenson and his family. He and TS were close and lifelong friends.

9   To Jane Whyte Balfour

MS Yale.

[*Dictated to Alison Cunningham*]
Friday night [*1856 or 1857*][1]   *1 Inverleith Terrace*

My dearest Auntie, Mama and us all are very much disappointed because we
can't get to Colinton tomorrow. So dear Auntie if you would like to send
the phaeton down on Monday morning we will be very glad to come and
stay a while, but you know we will have to come home again in the
afternoon. Papa and Mama are out dining tonight at General Graham's, and
that is why Mama has not written you herself. Noona seems to have a very
interesting story in his bound up *Cassell's Paper*, and I think we have one of
them in our own.[2] Cummy gives me my lessons, and I've good behaviour
ones and bad behaviour ones. Dear Auntie I'm coming on Monday to
spend the forenoon with you. Are you better of that same horrible thing
because I would like if you were. Please tell the boys to say to Jackie that
I'm coming on Monday, and will have some fun with him. Your very
affectionate nephew   R.L.B. STEVENSON

10   To Lewis Balfour[1]

MS Yale.

[*Dictated to Alison Cunningham*]
[*1856 or 1857*]   [*1 Inverleith Terrace*]

My dearest Granpa, I hope you are quite well and preaching every Sunday.
Did you preach about David last Sunday? I'm wondering if you did. My
tongue is tired and can't dictate any more. Your affectionate Granson. I'm
not a Grandson but only a Granson   R.L.B. STEVENSON

[1] This letter and the two following cannot be dated precisely, but they must have been written
before the Stevensons left Inverleith Terrace in May 1857.
[2] *Cassell's Illustrated Family Paper* began publication in December 1853. Cummy read the stories
aloud to him.
[1] Lewis Balfour (1777–1860), RLS's maternal grandfather, minister at Colinton for thirty-seven
years. This letter is written on the last page of the folded sheet containing the previous
letter.

11   To his Father

MS Bancroft.

[*Dictated to Alison Cunningham*]
Monday noon [*1856 or 1857*]   *1 Inverleith Terrace*

My dearest Papa, I've been thinking all this day if the fuses took fire in your bag it would make your sherry rather hot for drinking. This morning Mama and me took some of your books up to the library that you had brought down. And I saw a *Punch* which I thought I would like so much. So dear Mama gave it to me to amuse myself with while she was away and there was one queer picture in *Mr Punch* which I must tell you about. Well dear Papa it was a great many rabbits running about their houses, and there was one, such a bit oddity, peeping out of his window – and you could only see his head. Dear Papa I've been very happy all this day – and Aunty sent for me – but it was too cold and too bad a day for me to go so dear Mama just went without me. Dear Cummy and me are going to play at looking at Punch. Last Sunday I found an old pocket book and I dusted it. I got it from Mr Constable[1] long ago. And I hope you are not tired with your long jaunt. And I hope the axle of the engine has not gone to smash this time as it did when you went to Dumfries.[2] And I am dearest Papa, ever your affectionate son   R.L.B. STEVENSON

12   To Jane Whyte Balfour[1]

Facsimile. Pentland Edition of Stevenson's Works (1907), XX.

6 February 1860   [*17 Heriot Row, Edinburgh*]

my dear auntie
    i hope you are quite well. i wish you many happy returns of the day i hope grand papa is well mister coolin is well[2]
    i am your affecte nephew
               ROBERT LEWIS B. STEVENSON C.E. F.R.S.E.
               BARON OF BROADNOSE CASTLE

---

[1] Probably David Constable (1795–1867), eldest son of Archibald Constable the publisher. He lived at Portobello and Cummy often took RLS to visit him.

[2] The front axle of the railway engine broke during a journey TS made to London on 8 May 1855. He wrote a letter to his son about it.

[1] The first surviving letter completely written in RLS's own handwriting. He has copied the family arms with the motto *Coelum non Solum.*

[2] MIS records in her *Baby's Record*: 'Coolin a Skye terrier was given him just before he was seven years old and was his constant companion ever after.' When the dog was killed in 1869, RLS provided a tombstone complete with Latin epitaph.

Facsimile of Letter 12

13   To his Parents

MS Princeton. Quoted in Balfour, I, 55.

Wedensday [? September 1863]   *[Spring Grove, Isleworth]*[1]

My dearest Papa and Mama, I am getting on very well. I hope Papa's cold is better and that Mama is keeping well. Yesterday I was playing at football. I have never played at Cricket so Papa may comfort himself with that. I like football very much[2] and it seems nicer than

[1] The Stevensons had spent two months at Mentone in 1863 because of MIS's ill-health. She was advised to spend the winter of 1863–4 there and it was decided to send RLS to school in England. On 28 August 1863 TS took him to the Burlington Lodge Academy, Spring Grove, Isleworth, near London, where Mr Thomas Wyatt was headmaster. MIS's brother, Mackintosh Balfour (1825–84), temporarily home from India (where he was a bank manager) lived nearby, and three of his sons, looked after by 'Aunt Jane', attended the school as day pupils. Another brother, Lewis (see Letter 20), also lived in Spring Grove.

[2] Against this has to be set the confession in 'Child's Play': 'I knew at least one little boy who was mightily exercised about the presence of the ball, and had to spirit himself up, whenever he came to play, with an elaborate story of enchantment, and take the missile as a sort of talisman bandied about in conflict between two Arabian nations.' There is a drawing of a game of football on the last page of the letter.

Just now a boy came up here and as he was looking for something, he held up his prayer book and said

Dialogue

He. Isn't this a nice P.B.

Me. I have a nicer.

He. Is it here.

Me. I never use it at home.

He. Oh yes I forgot you had a different church there. I think you only use the bible.

Me. Yes.

He. Well there can be no harm in that.

I will write again on Saturday. Love to all. I remain your loving son

R. Stevenson

(excuse grammar and writing)

14   *To his Parents*

MS Yale.

Wedensday [? September 1863]   [*Spring Grove*]

My dear Parients, I have received your three kind letters – four I mean for I was forgetting a note from Coolin. I have got the book from Mrs Bell[1] it is *Martin Rattler*.[2] I have been afraid to write to her till I got your advice about it as I do not know whether to tell her I had it or not, please tell me. I am getting on very well, but my cheif amusement is when I am in bed then I think of home and the holidays. On Saturday I was invited to go to the house of one of the boys but it was wet so I could not go.

BURLINTON LODGE ACADEMY

– Headmaster –

Mr Wyat

– Classical –   – French –

Mrss Beton and Hunter   M. Trautvetter

– Parlour Boarders –

Mackenzie. Yarker

– Big Boys –

[1] Mrs Helen Cecilia Bell (died 1878), a great friend and fellow church worker of MIS, often mentioned in her diary.

[2] *Martin Rattler or a Boy's Adventures in the Forests of Brazil* by R.M. Ballantyne, 1858.

Hepburn. Hume. M. Field.
—Midling Size—
Bec. Swinton. Newberry. Stevenson.
Balfour. F. Field.
—Smal fry lots—

Love to all. I remain your afft. son   R. Stevenson[3]

15   To his Parents

MS Washington.

Thursday [*September or October 1863*]   [*Spring Grove*]

My dear Parients, I am getting on very well here. You I think asked me
what kind of a game dibbs was, there are five stones or bones and you take
them in your hand, fling them up and catch as many as you can on the back
of your hand, you put all those aside that you have caught eccept one which
you fling up and while it is in the air pick up the others and then catch the
flung up one. There are other things to be done but all somewhat of the
same kind. I was so delighted to get your present of the ring. We had a
grand match yesterday of which I send you a picture.[1]

Dialogue
Mr Hunter (en riant). Collie[2] be quiet or I'll lick you.
Collie. I'll lick *you*.
Mr Beton. Collie be quiet.
Collie. Yes.

Mr Beton can make Collie do anything. Mr Hunter nothing. Love to all.
Yours   R. Stevenson

16   To his Mother

MS Yale.

Saturday [*September or October 1863*]   [*Spring Grove*]

My dear Mama, I could not write to you on Wednesday this week as I had
a headache and had to go to bed. Both Mr and Mrs Wyat were very kind
to me and Mrs Wyat came in after tea with some tea for me. I got some

---

[3] On the last page there is a drawing of a 'Game of Dibbs'.
[1] There is a drawing of a cricket match on the last page.
[2] De Verinne Colinton Balfour (1857–71), Mackintosh Balfour's third son.

rhubarb and soda. At breakfast next morning I had an egg and as everyone
had finished I could help myself to bread butter sugar tea etcetera. I am
getting on very well with Ovid and also with greek they are at the verbs, I
am at the adjectives. I *have* written to Mrs Bell how is Papa, has he come
back and how is Cummy. I hope Coolin is all well and that he will send me
another letter. I was very much obliged to you for your letters.

I am obliged to send this letter to the post so good-bye. I remain

R. Stevenson[1]

17   *To his Father*

Text: extract in Anderson I (20).

15 October 1863   [*Spring Grove*]
[*Tells of a school row which caused two of the boys to leave*]

Will you bring down my coins and *The Young Voyageurs*[1] and any other
book you think would suit . . .

18   *To his Father*

MS Yale.

Friday [? *October 1863*]   [*Spring Grove*]

Pater meus, I received your kind letter to-day with the amusing account of
Coolin's encounter with the dog. I wish you would keep a diary of Coolins
for me. You can direct his paw and make him write every day a short
account of his adventures if it is not too much trouble will you do this. I
send you some specimens of Latin Excercise of course they are my own
unassisted uncorrected ones.

Good Ones
Qui non colit suum agrem, frustra sperat fruges.
Est turpe fidem fallere Portalemus nostro omnia nobiscum. Audient
pauca dicent multa.
Turpe est bonos et sapientes expellere ex civitate.
Tu, quae tua est humanitas, pollicitus es conficere negotium.

---

[1] There is a drawing of a game of football on the last page.
[1] *The Young Voyageurs, or the Boy Hunters in the North* (1853), by Captain Mayne Reid. Reid was a
childhood favourite, and RLS records that one of the stories he dictated as a child, 'The
Adventures of Basil', was a 'bungling adaptation' from him ('Reminiscences of Colinton Manse'
quoted in Balfour, I, 45).

Bad Ones

Audio te fidem praes tandem ense.

boo! boo!

(What this means deponent knoweth not).

If you please will you bring me my coins and the books I mentioned in my last letter. I have done something! I have made a grand step! I have appeared before the eyes of the publick not only as an author but[1]

Monday

I have received Mama's letter yesterday. In addition to my coins I have got another. Love to Mama, Cummy, and Coolin, if you see Willie Traquair ask him how the boats are getting on. Good-bye. I remain, your afft. son   R. Stevenson[2]

19   To his Parents

MS Yale. Published in *Letters*, I, 3–4.

12 November 1863   [*Spring Grove*]

Ma chere Maman, J'ai recu votre lettre Aujourdhui et comme le jour prochaine est mon jour de naisance je vous ecrit ce lettre. Ma grande gatteaux est arivé il leve 12 livres et demi le prix etait 17 shillings. Sur la soirée de Monseigneur Faux il y etait quelques belles feux d'artifice. Mais les polissons entrent dans notre champ et nos feux d'artifice et handkercheifs disappeared quickly but we charged them out of the feild. Je suis presque driven mad par un bruit terrible tous les garcons kik up comme grand un bruit qu'il est possible.

I hope you will find your house at Mentone nice.[1] I have been obliged to stop from writing by the want of a pen but now I have one so I will continue.

My dear Papa you told me to tell you whenever I was miserable. I do not feel well and I wish to get home. Do take me with you.   R. Stevenson

---

[1] This unfinished sentence has been crossed out and blotted, probably by RLS himself. It presumably refers to a contribution to *The School Boys' Magazine*, which he wrote at Spring Grove. The only number of this to survive is at the Pierpont Morgan Library, New York.

[2] There is a drawing of 'The Walk' on the last page.

[1] The Stevensons came south at the end of October. On 31 October they visited Spring Grove and found their son, as MIS records, 'looking well but his shoulders very round'. MIS left England on her way to Mentone on 6 November. She was accompanied by Jessie Warden and Cummy.

20   To his Mother

MS Silverado.

Sunday [? 29 November 1863]   *Rostrevor House, Spring Grove*[1]

My dear Mama, I hope you are enjoying yourself at Mentoni? I hear you have got the sitting room now. *Do* tell me in your next letter about some excursion. Is Massaniello still to the fore, if so is he catching much? I long so to see dear old Mentoni again with the olives and the oranges. Is the prince's palace not bought yet? Do the frogs make as much noise as last year? We are to begin examination on Monday: have you been out [on] any donkey excursions? I like coming to Aunt Carries on Sundays very much. I have been having such fun watching Arty. Last night Aunt Carry had such a jolly party last night with a lot of schoolboys there. In the dressing up Moyle came in with a crinoline and gown on and in the middle the crinoline dropped off. Leslie Gordon had on one of the manservant's coats when suddenly he thrust his hand right through the sleeve. Love to all. I remain your afft. son   R. Stevenson

21   To his Mother

Text: *Letters*, I, 4.

[? 6 December 1863]   *Rostrevor House, Spring Grove*

My dear Mam, I hope that the sitting room has got a good view of 'La Mediteranee'. I was at the Hilburys[1] to tea yesterday. We had parlour croquet and Mrs Hilbury called me the turk, because I used to croquet everyone. After that we had some Old Maid and then such an amusing game called 'Fright'. Janey Wilson[2] is staying at Uncle Mack's and her brother sent a telegram about some trains at which he was to meet her. It arrived at Aunt Carry's after they were all in bed and all the servants and Aunt Carry were in such a fright till they found out what it was. My dear Mama I am to send 7 loves from 7 different people. I remain, your afft. son   R. Stevenson

---

[1] The home of MIS's brother, Lewis Balfour (1817–70), a merchant of Calcutta. He had married as his second wife Caroline Louisa Sissmore (died 1924). 'Arty' was their young son, Arthur. Carrie later married her brother-in-law, Mackintosh Balfour (see Letter 149, n. 3).

[1] James William Ilbery was one of the masters at the school. RLS wrote to Mrs Ilbery from Vailima in March 1894.

[2] Jane Wilson (1846–1903), one of the daughters of MIS's sister Marion. She became the grandmother of Graham Greene (see Letter 86). She had three brothers and it is not possible to identify the one referred to here.

22   To his Mother

Text: extract in Catalogue of Brick Row Bookshop, New York, 1921 (4).

Sunday [? 13 December 1863]   [Spring Grove]

I hope that Papa is well for he has not written to me for nearly three weeks. I will have finished work on Friday the 18th and the boys are to go away on Saturday. I hope Papa will come for me soon as I wish to spend Christmas at Mentoni . . . I am wearying very much you may be sure for the time when I am to come to Mentoni . . .   R. Stevenson

23   To his Mother

MS Yale.

Sunday [20 December 1863]   Craven Hotel, [London][1]

Mamma, I have left Springrove at last. I was the last boy to leave school and papa came so late that I had given up all hope of his coming that night.[2] Poor papa had toothache today so he went to the dentists who took out the tooth. Papa gave me a George II halfpenny today. I have much pleasure in stating that Mr Coolin is much better having now recovered so much as to be able to go up stairs as well as down. We are both very glad to hear that your hot spots are getting better. Lewis Charles[3] has been very much troubled with the same thing. Papa's toothache is quite away since the tooth was taken out. I remain, your afft. son   R. Stevenson

24   To his Father

MS Yale.

[17 February 1864][1]   [Mentone]

My dear Papa, I hope that your chest will be better before this letter arrives. Mamma does not like your 'caffe au Stevenson' ni moi, ni Jessie non plus. I am very much obliged to you for your nice letter you sent me. I got a Valentine from Arty. I send you a picture. Yesterday when we, that is

[1] The Stevensons often stayed at the Craven Hotel on their visits to London. Silas Q. Scuddamore stays there in 'New Arabian Nights'.
[2] TS was taking his son to Mentone for the Christmas holidays. The boy did not return to Spring Grove. TS has written to his wife on the same sheet of paper.
[3] Lewis Charles Balfour (1851–1903), eldest son of Mackintosh Balfour. He later became a bank manager in Calcutta.
[1] Dated from references in MIS's diary. TS had returned home at the beginning of February.

ourselves and the Shortings[2], were up the valleys one of the donkeys ran off and played about till a man enticed it with a loaf and received the wretched pittance of 4 pence for it. No one was on it at the time.

Dialogue

Mama. Sit down and rest and be thankful.

Jessie. Would you like to be there.[3]

Mamma. Yes if I had Tom with me!

Lewis. Oh Mama that's tiresome.

Jessie. Oh man can ye no gie us something new.

I have made an enigma. My first is the work of the Burntisland steamers.[4] My second is a part of the human countenance, and my whole is an English seaport town. Grillier[5] is back and I read and translate till my cough is troublesome and then there is a kind of play hour till the end. One day he taught me a little dancing! If Jessie wasn't more dead than alive, have no doubt she would join me in well wishes to Edinburgh. There are some new people here who give Jessie riddles every day which, have no doubt are the causes of Jessie's present dwām.[6] The cursed souries are as troublesome as ever and ten times more cunning. I am making a cardboard windmill and a lot of cardboard soldiers which C.J. bought for me. I remain, dear sir, ever your afft. son   R.L. Stevenson

P.S. I am ever so angry at you for not bringing my things from Wyatts – recollect my coins.[7]

25   To his Father

Text: Sotheby Catalogue, 29 May 1956 (1721).

[21 or 28 February 1864][1]   *Mentone*

My dear Papa, This is most awful weather it is raining however, which will do good. We had church in the house today. Mr Shorting officiated and the congregation were as follows

---

[2] The Revd Charles Shorting (1810–64), Rector of Stonham Aspel, Suffolk 1836–64, an Evangelical clergyman of 'unusual earnestness' (*Gentleman's Magazine*, June 1864). He married (1837) Elizabeth Harriet Cobbald (1817–1910).

[3] I.e. at Rest-and-be-Thankful, a point on Corstorphine Hill commanding a fine view of Edinburgh. David and Alan part there at the end of *Kidnapped*.

[4] Burntisland, on the northern shore of the Firth of Forth opposite Edinburgh, was the terminus of the railway steam-ferry before the Forth Bridge was built.

[5] M. Grillière was giving RLS French lessons. RLS gave the name to a character in his story 'The Banker's Ward' in *The Sunbeam Magazine*, 1866.

[6] A swoon or fainting fit (Scots).

[7] At the end of the letter there is a comic sketch of a head, labelled 'Design for Lady's Brooch'. In the body of the letter there is a crude sketch of men fighting, captioned 'Danish War'.

[1] MIS records the Revd Charles Shorting as reading a sermon in the house on both these Sundays.

Our noble selves,
Lady Emily Brown[2]
Mrs and Miss Shorting

Cummy, the Howth and Shorting Lady's maids. Jessie tumbled down two
terraces about a foot high each roaring with laughter all the time. I have
a headache so good bye. Love to all [*word illegible*] I remain, ever your
afft. son   R. Stevenson

26   *To his Father*

MS Yale.

[*2 March 1864*][1]   [*Mentone*]

Scene from 'The Unsociable Grosbeak of Menton'
A room in Morgan Villa

Mrs Morgan[2] a sour favoured woman discovered toiling at a pillow cover.
Sound of wheels without.
Mrs M. (starting up) Another visitor (going to window) Oh those tiresome
Stevensons. Would they were at the bottom of the sea. (rushes to bell pulls
violently)
Enter servant.
Mrs M. Therese I'm out if ever them people come again rec'lect I'm not at
home.[3]

My dear papa, We have got a general 'de la suite de l'empereur de Russie'
by name Czywpsknipolski or Czypski or something of that sort. He is
covered from head to foot with contusions at least he has one on both of
these two usefull members.

   Mamma got your Sunday letter today and read it over three times. You
have not given me your opinion about the Danish war or of my picture
of it.[4]

---

[2] Lady Emily Charlotte Brown (1829–1916) was a daughter of the second Marquess of Sligo. Her
mother's sister was the Countess of Howth, and Lady Emily probably had one of her Howth
cousins with her.

[1] Dated from references in MIS's diary. 2 March: 'Damp with a little rain in the morning. At home
all day.' 3 March: 'Go to see a Prestidigitateur at the Cercle.'

[2] The Revd D.F. Morgan, who settled with his family at Mentone in 1857, was one of the founders
of Mentone as an English colony. He was the chaplain of the first English church opened in the
eastern bay in 1863. MIS records a visit to Mrs Morgan on 29 February.

[3] There follows a crude sketch of a woman sewing with the caption, 'The "unsociable grosbeak"
working an antimacassar for the english Bazaar.'

[4] See Letter 24, n. 7. The short-lived war between Denmark and Prussia and Austria in the early
months of 1864 over Schleswig-Holstein.

It is raining today which is a sell as we were going on a donkey excursion. I am making experiments on the temperature. I have made two new scents called Quintessence of Assafoedita and Collett bouquet both stooks especially Collett Bouquet. Fancy. I am going to the Prestidigitateur. Grilliers showed me some tricks and he is teaching me Piquet and he has introduced me to the capitaine of the garrison of Mentone. Love to all at home. I remain, Your affectionate son   R. Stevenson[5]

27 To Henrietta Traquair

MS Milne.

[*? June 1864*][1]   *Colinton*
I don't know the date.

My dear Cat, I am at present watching other people taking tea and hearing Willie saying, in a dolefull tone, 'I don't know what to say.' But as I am in the same state I can not afford to laugh at him. Mamma says you wish to know what is going on so here goes – Mr Traquair[2] is reading the newspaper, Jessie is clearing away the tea things, Uncle Ramsay is looking at the cattle, and the rest are all writing to a certain person called puss. Pray tell me whether *Rosa Lind* is sister of Jenny Lind. We are going to look at Whiteside Cottage tomorrow as perhaps we shall take it; it is said to have the finest garden in [Perthshire *crossed out*] Mama says it's in Stirlingshire however (slightly altering the old proverb) Geography is all a matter of opinion some likes Pershire and some likes Stirlingshire.

'Oh my vessel's on the say says the shan van voght
And I do not know what to say says the shan van voght'[3]

Nothing to say this letter ought to be in French but you can translate it for yourself which is all the same. All's well with everybody. Good bye.
                                                              R.S.

---

[5] On the last page there are two drawings: 'Jessie falling down terraces, a real incident' and 'Mamma and Jessie throwing themselves into violet beds'.
[1] MIS recorded in her diary on 31 May 1864: 'Lou and I go to Colinton today. Henrietta is at Islay.' I assume that this and the next letter were written during this stay at Colinton Farm. MIS and RLS returned briefly to Edinburgh 6–10 June but seem to have been back at Colinton for the rest of June.
[2] Ramsay Traquair's unmarried brother William Traquair, W.S. [i.e. Writer to the Signet – see p. 41, n. 2] (1810–95).
[3] 'Shan Van Voght', the famous Irish revolutionary song (1798).

28   *To Henrietta Traquair*

MS Milne.

[*? June 1864*]   [*Colinton*]

My dear puss as we were driving in the dog cart across Redford Bridge
Willie saw a Pigeon on the parapet he pointed it out to me. I had a stone
in my catty so I let fly and down went the Pigeon 'Stop I've killed it' yelled
I. 'Shut up' screamed Willie 'it is not ours.' And so we drove away and left
the Fish pie dieing. Contrary to my expectations the ghost has not as yet
appeared if it does I have a ready answer; all that I'll say will be '*temporary
insanity* my good pigeon.' Bryce's breakfast consisted of an artichoke and
oyster (hearty choke and hoister). Will has discovered that dogs can eat
Henbane with impunity. Solve that?

[*portion missing*]

   all the rest of it   R. Stevenson

to Mistress Puss v.b.g.

29   *To H.B. Baildon*[1]

MS Yale. Short quotation published in H.B. Baildon, *Robert Louis Stevenson* (1901), 23.

[*22 March 1865*]   [*Glen Villa, Torquay*][2]

> From Baildon I
> Received a high-
> Ly finished rhyming letter
> Than which I'm sure
> And can assure
> I never read a better
> Recounting how
> With mournfull row
> I left my native city
> And saying how

---

[1] Henry Bellyse Baildon (1849–1907), the son of an Edinburgh chemist, became Lecturer in
English at Vienna University and at University College, Dundee. He and RLS were fellow-pupils
in 1864–5 at a day school for backward or delicate boys in Frederick Street, Edinburgh, run by
Mr Robert Thomson. They collaborated in a school magazine, first called *The Trial* and later *Jack
o' Lantern*.

[2] This year, instead of going abroad, MIS had been advised to go to the south of England for her
health. The Stevensons arrived in Torquay on 16 March and took lodgings at Glen Villa,
Meadfoot Road. The address and date have been added by MIS.

My leaving now
Was a most monstrous pity
He also put
That my sad foot
Went towards the *Sunny* south
But now my dear
Will wish that ne'er
These words had left his mouth
For, ah! dear me!
How little we
Have seen of Sols bright face
Though for that thing
As you did sing
We came to this poor place
But at this time
As though my rhyme
Made angry this Torquay
The sun shines out
And with a shout
Is hailed by joyfull we. (poetic licence)

E'er since I left
Of freinds bereft
I've pined in melancholly
And all Torquay
It's rocks and sea
Have witnesséd my folly
I do not say
That all the day
I weep and pine in grief
But now and then
I say again
The greek for 'Stop the thief.'
And then I sigh
And wipe my eye
And drown the thoughts in cider
And if *that* fails
When grief assails
I just have to abide 'er

The sea the sea
Is near Torquay
In fact 'tis in a bay sirs
And vessels ply

Before my eye
Throughout the livelong day sirs
The hills behind
With houses lined
Hold up their pines on high sirs
But even here
As you might fear
For Frederick Street I sigh sirs
The cliffs that bound
The ocean's sound–
Ing mass are very red sirs
Much I've not seen
For ill I've been
And kept within my bed sirs
So now adieu
To all of you

And thanks for what you've said sirs

R. Stevenson

30   To Mrs Robert Cunningham[1]

Text: W.H. Arnold, *Ventures in Book Collecting* (1923), 260–61 (apparently from the untraced original), checked against MS copy by MIS, Yale.

March [1865]   [*Glen Villa, Torquay*]

This rhyming letter's writ to the[e]
From Glen Villa at Torquay.
It is raining plashing pouring
And without the wind is roaring
Among the cliffs that bound the sea
And through the boughs of every tree
With an untuneful melody
Not peculiar to Torquay
Oft I've heard it midst the shades

[1] Arnold records that his MS bore the superscription, 'Mrs Cunningham, Torryburn, from Lewis'. MIS noted on her copy, 'Written at Torquay in March 1865 and sent to several people. I have lost the first edition which was the best. This one was sent to Cummy's mother.' Alison Hastie (died 1870) was the wife of Robert Cunningham, a weaver of Torryburn on the northern shore of the Firth of Forth. RLS gave her name to the girl who rowed David and Alan across the Forth in *Kidnapped*.

Of Dreghorn's[2] lovely wooded glades
And now again we've got it here
Quite as bad as there I fear.
Imagine to yourself a hill
And then another and one more still
Then mix together houses white
And cliffs of a stupendous height
And just as red as red can be
And then a landlocked bit of sea.
Mix these together with each hill
And place three capes beyond that still
And then you'll have the fair Torquay
That is as near as near can be
But I've forgot the Port to add
Which really is a deal too bad.
Our ill luck never seems to leave us
The weather here is just as grievous
As it was in Edinburry
Which we left in such a hurry
For to try if we could find
A place more suited to Ma's mind.
But now the lunch has been brought in
With bread and cheese and Burtons beer
So I must leave this pretty[3] letter
And occupation for a better.

I being feasted take again
The Ink the paper and the pen
So now you see I've writ to thee
A letter very long Ma'am
And as this rhyme took up much time
It needed patience strong Ma'am
As[4] I am ill I stay my fill
In Glen Villa Meadfoot Road
Which as you see will need to be
Till I get round again Ma'am.

Robert Louis Balfour Stevenson

---

[2] Dreghorn Castle near Colinton.
[3] Arnold: 'preely'.
[4] Arnold: 'its'.

31　To his Father

MS Yale.

[*25 March 1865*]　　　　　　　　　　　　　　　　[*Glen Villa, Torquay*]

Dear Papa, I am in daily hourly expectation of Jessy,[1] so is Mama; who was so overcome last night as to admit that she wished the letter had been sent sooner! What a triumph! We spent a rather miserable day Mama on the sofa myself on a chair both reading. The stillness only broken by the noise of turning the pages, or a sigh from Mama. And every now and then 'I wish Jessie was here' from me. Dinner left us a little merrier and we had a lot of écarté in the evening. The sky is a fine, dull, gloomy, leaden, gray without the faintest trace of a beginning of a commencement of a dawn of blue anywhere. Bon jour. Love to the purfessor.[2] Your afft. son

　　　　　　　　　　　　　　　　　　　　　　　　　　R. Stevenson

32　To his Father

MS Yale.

Sunday [*2 April 1865*][1]　　　　　　　　　　*Glen Villa,* [*Torquay*]

Mein guter Väter, I take the opportunity of writing to you and reporting to you my progress. First and foremost comes Mister Mistowski, who teaches me German and French and gives me a large quantity, say two pounds a week, of butter on my 'bonne volonté'. What I have to do for him, however is I can assure you no child's play and takes me about two hours and a half.

　　I'm getting on famously with my German and Mistertowski says I'll be able to speak it in 3 months, that remains to be proved however. The next one Dart[2] is a very different specimen of humanity and when I tell you that his name should be Machriebeg I think I am giving the best possible description. He wears a hideously ill-made wig of brown hair from which circumstance I have named him Browniwig under which cognomen he is alone spoken of. He teaches arithmetic and mathematics, and is an exceedingly rummy looking antiquated chap. The other for drawing I have not yet

[1] TS returned to Edinburgh on 24 March and Jessie Warden, who was staying at Exmouth with her family, came to Torquay to be with RLS and his mother the next day.

[2] Possibly Professor Swan.

[1] Dated from references in MIS's diary. Jessie Warden left on 8 April.

[2] Mr Mistowsky was charging 5/-a lesson and Mr Dent ('commonly called Dart') 2/6 per lesson (MIS's diary).

seen. I can assure you that my hands are just as full as they can be. Preparing till twelve, out till one, lunch time, driving till three, French till four, preparing till five, Machriebeg from 6½ to 7½ and then I'm jolly tired however one day I'll only have Mistertowski and then I'll be able to write letters. I sketch allways when we're out, so there's no danger of my being dull. The weather is beautiful now driving in an open carriage just like Mentone.

I'm very tired so addio. I remain, your afft. son   R. Stevenson

P.S. Jessie has gone to church in Mama's clothes. Is'n't good?

33   To his Father

MS Yale.

[? 1865]

Allways an eye to business

My dear papa, I am a great deal better but I have begun to despair of 5/-, which is a disappointment, however I can claim -/1 for being called Smout.[1] I am going to send doctor Paul's story of Dr Muir to the magazine (of course suppressing names).[2] Remember the old houses please. I have no more news so good bye.   R.L.B. Stevenson

34   To his Father

MS Yale. Published in *Letters*, I, 5.

Thursday [*March or April 1866*]   *2 Sulyarde T[errace, Torquay]*[1]

Respected paternal relative, I write to make a request of the most moderate nature.

[1] RLS disliked his childish nickname and now exacted a penalty from his parents when they used it.

[2] If the conjectural date of 1865 is correct, this must refer to the school magazine he produced in collaboration with H.B. Baildon. It is tempting to suppose that the story is 'Anecdote of a Sermon' in a surviving number of the magazine at Yale dated 5 June 1865. This relates how a succession of visiting clergymen to a particular parish preached the same sermon from a copy left behind by the previous minister. John Paul, D.D. (1795–1873), was minister of St Cuthbert's, Edinburgh, 1828–73. His wife, Margaret Balfour, was MIS's cousin and their son was Sir James Balfour Paul. William Muir, D.D. (1787–1869), was minister of St Stephen's, Edinburgh, 1829–69.

[1] The Stevensons went to Torquay again in 1866, arriving on 7 March and taking lodgings at 2 Sulyarde Terrace. TS returned to Edinburgh on 26 March but RLS and his mother stayed until the end of April. The house is now part of the Torbay Hotel.

Every year I have cost you an enormous – nay, elephantine – sum of money for drugs and physician's fees: and the most expensive time of the twelve months was March.

But this year the biting oriental blasts, the howling tempests, and the general ailments of the human race have been successfully braved by yours truly.

Does not this deserve remuneration?

I appeal to your charity, I appeal to your generosity, I appeal to your Justice, I appeal to your accounts, I appeal, in fine, to your purse.

My sense of generosity forbids the receipt of more – my sense of Justice forbids the receipt of less – than half-a-crown.

Greeting, from, sir, your most afft. and needy son

R. Stevenson

Thomas Stevenson Esq.
17 Heriot Row
Edinburgh.

35   To Bob Stevenson[1]

MS Yale.

[? 1866]   [Edinburgh]

My dear Bob, All's right! When I came home I told it to Mamma: she was very sorry for you. Ditto Papa. You see these Lieth Boats used allways to sail at four, and have done so regularly for a long time. So *Fortuna favet fortibus*, behold you all serene. With the David S.'s[2] I told the 'wan smile' .story. Janey, whose opinion I heard alone, seemed inclined to laugh at you and call you 'foolish boy'. Uncle David alone remains, but his opinion will be something like Papa's.

After I had told Mamma, she called Papa into her room. When I came down I heard Papa say, in a rageful voice: 'If that's the way he conducts business.' Of course I thought this was you, and trembled, but I was wrong. I don't know who it was. I remain, your afft. cousin

R. Stevenson

Written at my solitary breakfast. All round me slumber. I have thought much on the complications but can get no idea.

---

[1] Robert Alan Mowbray Stevenson (1847–1900), the son of TS's brother Alan and RLS's closest friend in his youth. See p. 35.

[2] David Stevenson (1815–86), TS's brother and the senior partner in the family firm. His daughter Jane (1842–1909) married William Mackintosh. See Letter 355, n. 2.

36   *To Bob Stevenson*[1]

MS Yale.

Monday 26 November [*1866*]   *17 Heriot Row*

My dear Bob, Being in the house with cold, I take the opportunity for discharging my debt to you – a duty hitherto prevented by excess of work and paucity of time. When you answer me, please give me the following items of information

I   What sort of place is Cambridge?
II Describe your domicile?
III — your work?
IV — your amusements?
V   — your companions?
VI Do Cambridge students indulge in a private magazine: if so, full
    particulars?

Have you ever read *Alroy* by Disraeli? It is a novel and in prose(?) Take the following extract: it is unaltered, except that I have divided it into lines; –

Part the Fifth
Chapter I
'Now our dreary way is over,
Now the desert's toil is past.
Soon the river broadly flowing,
Through its green and palmy banks,
To our wearied limbs shall offer
Baths which Caliphs cannot buy
Allah-illah, Allah-hu. Allah-illah, Allah-hu'

*   *   *   *

Again

Part the Eighth
Chapter I
'The waving of Banners, the flourish of trumpets,
  The neighing of steeds, and the glitter of spears.
On the distant horizon they gleam like the morning,
  When the gloom of the night shivers bright into day.'

*   *   *   *

[1] Bob had gone to Sidney Sussex College, Cambridge, in October 1866. He took his B.A. in 1871.

Again

Part the Tenth
Chapter I
'She comes not yet! her cheerful form,
Not yet it sparkles in our mournful sky.
She comes not yet! the shadowy stars seem sad
And lustreless without their queen.
   She comes not yet!'
'We are the watchers of the moon,
And live in loneliness to herald light.'

*   *   *   *

'She comes, she comes! her beauteous form
Sails with soft splendour in the glittering air.
She comes, she comes! The beacons fire,
And tell the nations that the month begins!
   She comes, she comes!'

*   *   *   *

There are three very beautiful specimens of three different kinds of blank verse, but what they have to do in one of the dullest historical romances that ever was penned, deponent knoweth not!

I have read *Bragelonne*.[2] The conversations are certainly wonderful, but the strength of the plot is frittered away, and the whole story is lengthened out to a most unconscionable and dreary extent. The strength of Porthos, and the furiously acute intellects of Aramis and D'Artagnan are singularly overdone. There are too many conversations in which the latter braves the King, and, when he has thoroughly failed in his object, succeeds all at once by shamming that he is going to stick himself, or throwing up his situation. Had I been Louis, I should have had his brains blown out for one half of the cheek which he gives. Fouquet, who is a wicked man (as manners stand at present, and should stand always), becomes at the end superhuman. In spite of all these defects, I grant, the book displays a wonderful amount of genius, and imagination. Did you ever observe the different ranges of intellect displayed by Aramis and D'Artagnan.

[2] Alexandre Dumas's *Le Vicomte de Bragelonne* (1848–50) was later to become one of RLS's favourite novels. In 'A Gossip on a Novel of Dumas's' RLS says that on his first perusal he understood 'but little of the merits of the book.' After he had read it five or six times he could write: 'No part of the world has ever seemed to me so charming as these pages, and not even my friends are quite so real, perhaps quite so dear, as d'Artagnan.'

Aramis is creative; his huge plot, his manifold dodges, and sub-plots, and the way in which he finds an excuse for everything all prove it. D'Artagnan, on the other hand, – like Poe's Dupin – is profoundly analytical; the way in which he finds out about the duel between Guiche and Wardes, and especially the way in which he defeats the greater mind of Aramis in all their conversations, in which he finds out the real fortifier of Belle Isle, and fathoms so much of the plot – all demonstrate it.

The author is much to be praised for the way in which he has preserved the distinction. The only thing in which he seems to transgress is, in truth, no transgression at all. This is D'Artagnan's plot for setting that ruffian Charles II on the throne. But a moment's consideration will show to you that the plan was very simple, and that it was merely the daring with which it was carried out which is to be admired – indeed the plot was bad, for it was not likely that Monk would keep any promise made under compulsion.

At present I am going in for Macaulay's *History*[3], and no novels at all. Do likewise! Stick in! Go it, my tulip! With which classical and encouraging remarks begins and ends the moral part of this here epistle.

Picture to yourself Davie and Charlie[4] entering church in immense chimney pots every Sunday. Here is the proportion; –

I go from nine to ten to Lang's mathematics in George Street. Then I go out to the Sciennes (an aristocratic part of the Royal burgh of Edinburgh lying at the South East corner of the meadows) where I learn practical mechanics. Picture 'yoors trooly' in apron and shirt sleeves planing, sawing and hammering at a deal box! From one to half past three I go to Roland, who by

---

[3] RLS had been given Macaulay's *History of England* (1848–61) by his parents on his sixteenth birthday.

[4] David Alan Stevenson (1854–1938) and Charles Alexander Stevenson (1855–1950) were sons of David Stevenson. They both became lighthouse engineers.

the by retains a recollection of you: from 3.30 to five, to classics. In the evening German and General preparation.[5]

We had a Reform Demonstration here[6] – Horror of Horrors! Here is the chorus of their song, in its original and as altered by 'yoors trooly.'

> While angel voices shout aloud,
>   Amid the gath'ring storm,
> 'Upraise once more, ye British Men,
>   The Banner of Reform.'

*   *   *   *

> While husky voices hiccup out,
>   Amid the alehouse storm,
> 'Upraise once more ye tippling brutes
>   The Banner of Reform!'

Write to John Hughes. Upon my word it is disgraceful never to have written to him. Just a line would still his wrath. I remain, Your affectionate cousin   R. Stevenson

37   To his Father

MS Yale.

Wednesday [*10 April 1867*]   *Darnley House, Bridge of Allan*[1]

My dear Papa, I wish you to go to Roland's; get my foil and mask and glove; and buy me another foil mask and glove from the Captain. Then please bring them out with you when you come, for Davie is able to fence, and I am fearfully in want of some such employment. I have told Mary[2] to 'nag' you till you go and do it. Vide last page where you will find an important legal document empowering you to expend the sum necessary for these purchases and signed by the heed o' th' Hoose.

---

[5] 'In October he goes to Mr Thomson for Latin and Greek, to old Mr Lang for mathematics, to young Mr Lang for practical mechanics and to Mr Roland for gymnastics. The outcome of the practical mechanics was that he made a box which is now at Vailima – he was always making mistakes which caused the size of the box to be reduced, so at last some extraneous aid had to be called in lest it should disappear altogether!' (MIS, *Diary Notes*). The box is now in the Silverado Museum. George Roland (1819–82), and his brother Henry (1827–81), taught fencing and gymnastics at the Edinburgh Academy and other Edinburgh schools.

[6] The years 1866 and 1867 saw great demonstrations in favour of parliamentary reform before the passage of the Reform Bill. There was a demonstration in Edinburgh on 17 November.

[1] The Stevensons stayed at the Bridge of Allan from 16 March to 27 April 1867. The Bridge of Allan, three miles north of Stirling – at this period a fashionable spa – was one of their favourite holiday places.

[2] Mary Smith Stevenson (1848–1910), another daughter of David Stevenson, and her sister Janey had been staying at the Bridge of Allan with RLS and his mother. They left on 10 April.

Le temp est ici tragique. Je veux exclamer avec le poete: 'Ah! ce climat atroce!' Nous sommes tous seules: nous sommes reduits a nos dernieres resource. Je mane, votre fils   R. Stevenson

Buy a foil, mask, and glove from Captain George Roland for R.L. Stevenson.[3]   M.I. Stevenson
                    Mother of the above mentioned R.L. Stevenson.
To T. Stevenson
Father of the above mentioned
R.L. Stevenson.

38   To his Mother

MS Yale. Published in *Letters*, I, 12–13.

Sunday evening [? Autumn 1867]   *Anchor House, [North Berwick]*[1]

My dear Mamma. Got here all right. Was it not funny that I saw the Murrays at Leadburn?[2] After they left I got awful dull and, Blow! (I mean blow my nose)* I was constrained to jump about, walk up and down and box the air. Suddenly in the middle of these evolutions, the train stopped, and I thought it as well to guard against interruptions by casting myself down in a position at once dignified and graceful. As well I did it! An old man came in, tall, thin, cadaverous, in clothes made for St Edmund the pride of our city, the choice of our electors. I addressed to him some remarks on the subject of the weather; but he appeared completely shut up by the novelty of my views on the subject, as he said no more till the end of our journey. By dwelling upon this subject, it seems that his mind, too weak to grapple with such subjects, became entirely deranged; for he suddenly began to talk aloud to himself and to snap his fingers, and to nod his head in an encouraging manner. At first I expected to be Mullered;[3] but the journey ended too soon and I was rescued.

---

[3] The rest of this 'certificate' is in the hand of MIS, who has written a letter to her husband on the inside pages.
[1] A holiday resort (then little more than a fishing village) at the entrance to the Firth of Forth, noted for its golf links. The Stevensons often stayed there and RLS recorded his boyhood memories in 'The Lantern Bearers'. Anchor House was the house at North Berwick rented by the David Stevensons. RLS certainly stayed there in July 1866 after his parents returned home and he went there again in September 1870. I cannot date this particular visit with certainty: the detailed record in the 1868 diary rules out that year; the diary for 1867 breaks off in July.
[2] A village and railway junction south of Edinburgh but not on the direct route to N. Berwick. RLS knew several Murrays: MIS records his friendship with Janey and Bob Murray at Peebles in 1865; he visited them from North Berwick in September 1869.
[3] Franz Muller murdered Thomas Briggs in a London railway carriage in July 1864. He attempted to escape to America but was arrested on arrival in New York. The case excited great public interest.

I had an ice at Blairs[4] as I said I would.

Tell Degenerate Douglas[5] that here no Romola drinks behind doors and here no Tito raves and tells lies – that, in a word, this is the land of freedom.

Tell Romola that Beales was playing golf here yesterday with Prince Alfred.[6] B. had been drinking and knocked the Prince down for a blow'd aristocrat – so she needn't laugh at me any more for my word: it is a word hallowed by the usage of a patriot and a reformer.

Mary is seedy; and Dr Hislop[7] has been here. It is a headacher – her ailment (second thought): silence reighens (reigns).[†] Your affectionate son

R.L. Stevenson

Luck to Papa!

N.B. I am not going to ask for messages as I am tired of writing. Used all my paper: can't write again.

By the by I'm becoming radical too. Nothing about anything but *subjects* in the first sheet.

* Penny enclosed.[8]
† Please Excuse after dinner.

---

[4] A restaurant in George Street, Edinburgh.
[5] Apparently another nickname for Lewis (Noona) Balfour; it must derive from Wordsworth's sonnet on Neidpath Castle, Peebles (where RLS played as a boy). Tito is a character in George Eliot's *Romola* (1863).
[6] Edmond Beales (1803–81), barrister and political campaigner, who achieved notoriety as President of the Reform League during the agitation of 1866–7. Alfred (1844–1900), second son of Queen Victoria, was created Duke of Edinburgh during a visit to the city in May 1866. There was an attempt on his life in Australia in March 1867 and he returned to England briefly that summer. Electioneering was in progress for several months in 1867, culminating in the General Election of November 1867.
[7] John Crallan Hislop (1811–69) was a doctor at North Berwick mentioned in MIS's diary as attending the Stevenson family during their visits. 'Mary' was presumably David Stevenson's daughter.
[8] A penny fine for using the word 'blow'. A penny stamp is stuck to the last page of the letter.

II. THE EDUCATION OF AN ENGINEER
December 1867–April 1871

Stevenson was enrolled as a student at Edinburgh University in November 1867. In 'The Foreigner at Home' he was to contrast the experience of an 'English lad' at Oxford or Cambridge 'in an ideal world of gardens . . . costumed, disciplined and drilled by proctors' with that of his Scottish equivalent:

> At an earlier age the Scottish lad begins his greatly different experience of crowded class-rooms, of a gaunt quadrangle, of a bell hourly booming over the traffic of the city to recall him from the public-house where he has been lunching, or the streets where he has been wandering fancy-free. His college life has little of restraint, and nothing of necessary gentility . . . All classes rub shoulders on the greasy benches. The raffish young gentleman in gloves must measure his scholarship with the plain, clownish laddie from the parish school.

For the next three-and-a-half years, Stevenson (in Colvin's words), 'tried dutifully if half-heartedly, to prepare himself for the family profession.' The letters in this section mainly relate to his experiences in the summer months when an attempt was made to teach him something of the practical side of the engineering business: visits to the harbour works at Anstruther and Wick in 1868; his journey with his father on board the lighthouse steamer to the Orkney and Shetland islands in 1869; and his visit to the Isle of Earraid in 1870. These experiences were vividly remembered in 'The Education of an Engineer', written twenty years later. In that essay, RLS summarised the pleasures of the engineer's way of life:

> It takes a man into the open air; it keeps him hanging about harbour-sides, which is the richest form of idling; it carries him to wild islands; it gives him a taste of the genial dangers of the sea; it supplies him with dexterities to exercise; it makes demands upon his ingenuity; it will go far to cure him of any taste (if ever he had one) for the miserable life of cities. And when it has done so it carries him back and shuts him in an office! From the roaring skerry and the wet thwart of the tossing boat, he passes to the stool and desk; and with a memory full of ships, and seas, and perilous headlands, and the shining pharos, he must apply his long-sighted eyes to the petty niceties of drawing, or measure his inaccurate mind with several pages of consecutive figures. He is a wise youth, to be sure, who can balance one part of genuine life against two parts of

drudgery between four walls, and for the sake of the one, manfully accept the other.

Stevenson regarded his formal education as 'a mangle through which I was being slowly and unwillingly dragged' (cf. Letter 817) and he acted (as he was later to write in 'Some College Memories') 'upon an extensive and highly rational system of truantry, which cost me a good deal of trouble to put in exercise . . . and sent me forth into the world and the profession of letters with the merest shadow of an education'. But while he was neglecting with such ingenuity his formal education he was (as he relates in a famous passage in 'A College Magazine') seriously and conscientously setting about the task of learning to write:

> I kept always two books in my pocket, one to read, one to write in. As I walked, my mind was busy fitting what I saw with appropriate words; when I sat by the roadside, I would either read, or a pencil and a penny version-book would be in my hand, to note down the features of thescene or commemorate some halting stanzas. Thus I lived with words. . . . Description was the principal field of my exercise; for to any one with senses there is always something worth describing, and town and country are but one continuous subject. . . . Whenever I read a book or a passage that particularly pleased me, in which a thing was said or an effect rendered with propriety, in which there was either some conspicuous force or some happy distinction in the style, I must sit down at once and set myself to ape that quality. I was unsuccessful, and I knew it; and tried again, and was again unsuccessful and always unsuccessful . . . I have thus played the sedulous ape to Hazlitt, to Lamb, to Wordsworth, to Sir Thomas Browne, to Defoe, to Hawthorne, to Montaigne, to Baudelaire and to Obermann.

Only one of these prentice efforts seems to have survived: the play *Monmouth* in which, so he tells us, he 'reclined on the bosom of Mr Swinburne.' The genesis of this is described in Letters 40 and 41. Other letters (e.g. 72, 76, 77) give us examples of his attempts at descriptive writing.

39   *To Bob Stevenson*

MS Yale (first 4 pp.); Morgan (last 4 pp.).

Saturday Evening [21 December 1867][1]   *17 Heriot Row*

My dear Bob, Thaw: a thick yellow mist between us and Queen Street: continual sharp drizzle: streets one sheet of two inch liquid ooze. The

[1] There was snow in Edinburgh on Friday 20 December 1867, and another slight fall on the Saturday afternoon: it quickly changed to sleet and then to rain (Edinburgh newspapers).

Porters walk up and down before their corners, stamping their chilled feet and blowing their rain-wet noses. The message girls have hoisted umbrellas and scud about something like this: –

Yesterday was Sellar's Exam.[2] I send you the paper, as it may amuse. I have noted what I did, from which you can see that I am sure of the medal.

On Thursday night, I was at the Terrace.[3] Aunt E. played the River piece. Janie and Mary have a slap up duet – J. on the piano, M. on the harp – from *I Puritani*.[4] Isn't the Harmonious Blacksmith[5] first class: you hear the clink of hammer and anvil; and I, for one, felt my face burned by the roaring furnace. How very seldom it is that either composers or writers convey the meaning they intended to other people's minds. There is a nice little bit of poetry about that in an old number of *Good Words*. A fellow plays; and we are told what he and his two hearers heard in the notes and cadences of his music. Ensample: poor old Jack Sheppard. I doubt not Ainsworth meant to be moral: Heu! Heu!

Have you seen anything of the *Broadway*: I rather like it. You should at any rate get No. 3 (November) and read Buchanan's review of Walt Whitman.[6]

Sunday [29 December 1867]

This yepistle has been lying by all Christmas week from a number of reasons. First, Mamma has been anything but well. A *very* bad sore throat. We were quite in a fright about her; but I am glad to say that she is a good deal better now. The second reason is – business, perhaps I ought rather to say busy-ness – a very different thing. I am writing the life of a fellow – outlaw, soldier,[7] martyr. Getting authorities is incredible trouble. I spent

[2] William Young Sellar (1825–90) was Professor of Humanity (i.e. Latin) at Edinburgh University 1863–90.
[3] David Stevenson and his wife Elizabeth (1816–71) lived at 25 Royal Terrace, Edinburgh. For their daughters Jane and Mary, see Letters 35, n. 2 and 37, n. 2.
[4] Bellini's opera (1835), based ultimately on Scott's *Old Mortality*.
[5] The popular name for Handel's Suite for Harpsichord in E.
[6] This monthly magazine first appeared in September 1867. The November issue contained a review by Robert Buchanan of Whitman's *Leaves of Grass*, which he reprinted in *David Gray and other Essays* (1868). Buchanan (1841–1901), poet, novelist and playwright, later achieved notoriety with his attack on the Pre-Raphaelites in 'The Fleshly School of Poetry' (1871).
[7] The Yale MS ends at this point.

most of yesterday in the Advocates' Library and got about half way through the catalogue. This is the easiest bit: when it comes to reading the MSS it's frightful.[8]

A letter of mine to you has somehow or other gone astray. I gave it to a girl to post: it was acknowledging Hughes's letter. It was carefully worded fortunately.

Looking over some MSS of mine lately I came upon four beginnings of letters to you. Most of them didn't turn the page.

N.B. 'scud' on p.1 is an unhappy word: limp would better express the motion.

Do you know Henry Kingsley. Read *Mademoiselle Mathilde* by him, now coming out in the *Gentlemen's Magazine*,[9] which, I doubt not, some library whereto thou hast access, will afford to thee. It is first class. M. D'Isigny is a portrait and a perfect portrait.

Pity me: I have a broken pen. I remain, your affectionate cousin, and friend   R.L. Stevenson

What day will your friend in the canoe pass the Port of Leith: I think he is bound for D. Jones Esquire.

40   *To Bob Stevenson*

MS of letter, Harvard. Printed (with facsimile of first page) in Widener Catalogue (1913), 234–8. MS of poem, Princeton. Privately printed (with facsimile) in *An Ode of Horace* (Clement Shorter, 1916).

[*? March 1868*]   [*Edinburgh*]

My dear Bob. It is your turn to write; but I am in the house with cold; which makes a difference.

I suppose you are all right now; and the *corpus sanum* has returned.

I got *Atalanta in Calydon*[1] yesterday. What a wonderful master of language and measure Swinburne is; and what a pity he is such a sensual brute.

---

[8] At this period RLS was fascinated by the Covenanters (see p. 87 n. 3). *The Pentland Rising* had been published in 1866 and he wrote 'the bulk of a Covenanting novel' in 1868. A special hero was David Hackston of Rathillet, executed in 1680 for his part in the murder of Archbishop Sharp. In 'The Coast of Fife' RLS writes: 'With incomplete romances about Hackston, the drawers of my youth were lumbered. I even dug among the Wodrow manuscripts . . . keenly conscious of my youth in the midst of other and (as I fondly thought) more gifted students.' The voluminous papers of the historian Robert Wodrow (1679–1734) were preserved in the Advocates' Library and it seems likely that RLS is referring to his research in these MSS for his projected life of Hackston.
[9] It appeared from April 1867 to May 1868. Henry Kingsley (1830–76), younger brother of the famous author, was himself a prolific novelist. *Mademoiselle Mathilde* is a historical novel about the French Revolution.
[1] Published in 1865. *Poems and Ballads* appeared in 1866.

All the choruses are splendid: what a power, what cadence, what melody! Meleager's account of Jason's voyage is very fine. Here are some lines that strike me.

1.

'for thy sacrifice
With sanguine-shining steam divides the dawn.'

2.

'The mother of months in meadow and plain
Fills the shadows and windy places
With *lisp of leaves and ripple of rain*'

3.

'And dust divided by hard light and spears
That shine and shift as the edge of wild beast's eyes
Smite upon mine.'

4.

'And the first furrow in virginal green sea
Followed the plunging ploughshare of hewn pine
And closed . . . . Doubtful Gods
Risen out of sunless and sonorous gulfs
Through waning water into shallow light
That watched us . . . .'

And dozens of others.

There is not much of the metaphysician in him; but oh, what a versifier he is! I suppose *Poems and Ballads* will stand in the way of a Laureateship.

By the way what awful trash Tennyson's serial poetry is just now. To think of the man who wrote the 'Lotos Eaters' 'St Simeon Stylites' *et caetera*, 'blowing and roaring' such cursed nonsense as the last thing in *Good Words*.[2] Oh! Alfred Tennyson! Alfred Tennyson, oh![3]

I send you three translations of a bit of Horace, in order to hear what you think of the last measure. Of course it is unfit for longer pieces.

Don't you think you and I might collaborate a bit this summer. Something dramatic, blank verse and Swinburne choruses. I think we might do worse. We must take care in the first place to have a plot full of violent passion and situation, and occupying the shortest possible time.

[2] The last two lines of Tennyson's '1865–1866' published in *Good Words*, March 1868, are: 'Old year roaring and blowing, / And New Year blowing and roaring.'
[3] Cf. 'Oh! Sophonisba! Sophonisba, Oh!', the much parodied line from James Thomson's play *Sophonisba* (1730).

Suggestions.

I.

Scene a dreary sea beach, with a grey sea in front and low grey hills behind. A wrecked galley sitting, all draped with sea-weed, just above the surf. A.'s father was found in the cabin of this vessel murdered, when it came ashore. A. finds out that B. has done it, and has come down to beard him. C. – a girl, with whom A. is in love – comes down and tells him that she loves B. and B. loves her and asks his assistance with crusty father. Conflicting passions. She leaves him, surprised and puzzled by his behaviour. B. comes. Accusations, fight, *et caetera*. That one won't do I see. I think the next one better it is founded on poor Monmouth.

II.

Scene, a palace chamber. Without famine and revolt and an enemy investing the plains. A. found making love to B. Enter Prince who overhears. P. and A. quarrel, P. being also in love with B. Swords are drawn but D., who resembles A. very closely separates them. Exit P., cursing and muttering: exit A. to his lady love. D. sits down in a curtained nook, re-enter P. with the King his father. P. makes K. believe that A. is a conspirator and in league with the ruffians who are stirring sedition in the city. Exit P. and K. Re-enter A.   D. warns him. Whilst they speak, P. is seen looking through a door. Arrest of A. He is simply kept in a strong-room with a grated window opening into the great hall. D. proposes to go instead of him. Especially as men are executed masked in that land; and, by working on him by his love to B., gets A. to consent. Some trickery with the guards and the thing is managed. A. goes to B. Grand scene. D. was her brother! Awful conversation, amidst the crash of arms and shouts. The mob are attacking the palace. They burst into the hall. Seeing him in D.'s uniform, they slay him; for D. was odious to them; and he falls across B.'s feet.

Write me your opinion of the thing and I will write the first scene which nothing can alter. I'll then send it to you for alteration, amendment and addition, and we can parcel out the rest of the thing or alter it. There will be the chorus of citizens without; the chorus of priests during the execution; the chorus of the rebels during the attack; and the chorus of priests again to wind up with.

Do write soon; and give me your opinion of the plot and suggestions: in no time, I will send the first scene; and we shall see what can be done. I think we should parcel the different scenes out: by lot, if we can't agree. When the first fellow has written the second gets it to correct, alter, and re-write; but if a dispute arises, he who was first at that scene will have the casting vote.

Please also tell me how your holidays go: Mamma is still too weak for us to ask you here;[4] but still we might contrive a meeting; and I wish of course to speak of this *magnum opus*.

I am your affectionate Cousin and, I hope, your successful collaborator
                                                                R.L. Stevenson

P.S. Get *Atalanta* and you will see the genius of the thing I want; but of course ours will be more exciting, more *plotty* and I hope better!

[*Enclosure*]

BOOK II. ODE III.[5]

I
(Ordinary ten syllable blank verse)

Where the high pine and the white poplar mix,
With twining bows, their hospitable shade,
And bright streams flee between the crooked banks,
Bid them bring wines and unguents rich, and flowers;
While age and wealth and the black, fateful threads
Of the three sisters join to suffer you.
For soon you leave your purchased groves, and home,
Your villa, which the yellow Tiber laves;
And heirs will seize upon the hoarded gold.

II
(Iambic feet: eight syllable rhymed verse)

Where mix the pine and poplar white,
    With boughs, their hospitable shade,
And where the gleaming water flees
    In crooked banks adown the glade.
Ah! *there* command thy slaves to bring
    The jars of wine that pass the hours
And unguents rich to smear the hair
    And scented roses' short-lived flowers.

Too poor to go on with. I was so hampered with the rhyme.

III

$$-\breve{}\,|-\smile\smile|-\smile\smile|-\breve{}$$

Where the pine and the shivering poplar
Love to join with their branches their shadow;

---

[4] MIS records in her *Diary Notes* that she had an attack of diphtheria in December 1867 'which leaves me very weak for a long time'.
[5] The third version of the ode was first published in *Collected Poems*, 1950.

Where through glimmering valleys, the water,
Glass-clear, hurries, in murmur, toward Ocean –
Thither command them carry the wine jars –
Wine jars full of the juice of *Falernum*(?) –
Unguents, roses to bind in our chaplets,
Bid your slaves carry down to the margin.
Now, we glory in youth and in riches:
Now, the sisters are merciful toward us.
Soon, our Fortune shall turn from us coldly:
Soon, we leave our groves and our houses,
Soon, our gardens by yellow old Tiber;
While our gold that we hoarded so closely
Gladly seizes the joyful successor.

41   *To Bob Stevenson*

MS Yale. The enclosure privately printed in *Monmouth* (1928), 76–9.

Friday 17 April 1868   [*Edinburgh*]

My dear Bob, I entirely agree with your strictures on the form of play. So
I send you the programme, the division, and the *first sketch* for scene I of
Monmouth: A Tragedy.[1] The plot was arranged and the programme written
yesterday: the scene was scribbled off in about an hour and a half this
afternoon; so you must excuse it. Don't you think Henrietta will make a
nice character?[2] If you wish to change plot or anything vital, write at once:
if you wish to shirk anything, I'll take either VII or VIII. I wish to have
every word of it in blank verse, and indeed do not understand that part of
your letter. Too much dramatic action for blank verse? Did you ever read
the 'works of a nameless fellow called Shakespeare' – to quote Nahum Tate,
in the preface to his *King Lear?*[3] I find myself utterly unable to write really
dramatically. I go off into long soliloquies, descriptions of scenery, emotion
et caetera. Is not the motto cute? Mind you know it is only the first sketch

[1] The MS of this play (now at Yale) came to light, with a number of previously unknown letters
to Bob Stevenson, in 1922. The announcement of its impending sale at Christie's brought forth
letters in *The Times* from Gosse and Colvin protesting at the possible publication of what they
considered, though they had not read it, a worthless piece of juvenilia. It was eventually printed
by W.E. Rudge in 1928. The theme of RLS's play (which was still in his mind ten years later –
see Letter 568) is completely unhistorical. James, Duke of Monmouth (1649–85), illegitimate son
of Charles II, led an unsuccessful rebellion in the west of England against his uncle James II and
was beheaded.
[2] Monmouth's mistress, Henrietta Wentworth.
[3] Nahum Tate (1652–1715), playwright and poet laureate, adapted several of Shakespeare's plays.
His version of *King Lear*, which held the stage for many years, ends happily. It does not contain
the comment RLS quotes.

of I; and when you have altered send back as soon as possible and let me rewrite and alter, too. You see I made a sort of beginning for II, which is simply sickening: only keep in the joke about the 'little black box'[4] – of course you twig the allusion. Do mind and make Lambourne and everybody moral – no Swinburnism. Ever yours, Collaboratorially

R.L. Stevenson

P.S. If you can manage to make any character say aught witty, humorous or bright, for Heaven's sake do so: I can't. I'm going on with III.

I have agreed to withhold I till I have rewritten and polished it, as I am not pleased and as II does not really require a sight of it. You go on with II; and I will rewrite I.   R.L.S.

Make one of the conspirators tell how the crowd at Ringwood greeted him: 'one fellow cried "He'll get the little black box now!"' twig the goak?[5]

I hope you understand that I'm frightfully busy and can only give an hour a day to this sort of amusement.

[*Enclosure*][6]

MONMOUTH:
A Tragedy.
'Whoso will save his life shall lose it'[7]

I.

Old house in London, deserted. Henrietta and her attendants. The news of his capture arrives. *Mine.*

II.

The loft of a house on Tower Hill. The conspirators plotting a way of escape. Michael Lambourne stands forth and offers if all other plans fail to die for him: general astonishment: conspirators go away: Michael and Sir William Gervase left alone. Gervase wondering at his courage – his, a man of letters', a pamphleteer's. Michael tells that he is the illegitimate brother of Henrietta. *et caetera. Yours.*

III.

Whitehall: the scene between Monmouth and James: that between Grey and James. James sums up betwixt the two. *Mine.*

---

[4] There were rumours at the time of a black box containing the certificate of Charles II's marriage to Monmouth's mother, Lucy Walter.

[5] 'Goak' – a characteristic mis-spelling by the American humorist Artemus Ward. See Letter 63, n. 6.

[6] The synopsis is now linked with the MS of the play but it was evidently an enclosure to this letter. The final version differs a good deal from the synopsis. Lambourne is no longer Henrietta's brother but is in love with her.

[7] Matthew 16:25.

IV.

Cell: the prisoner and the divines: more of Monmouth's character. *Yours.*

V.

Old house again: Henrietta is told of his baseness: excuses it: the conspirators say that there is no means of saving him: Michael comes in and tells that there is one way: gets a letter from her. *Mine.*

VI.

Cell: the temptation. *Mine.*

VII.

Loft on Tower Hill: Monmouth sees the execution: irresolution. *Yours.*

VIII.

Old house: Henrietta hears: enter Monmouth: she tells him that, not content with robbing her honour, he has slain her brother – that God is punishing them. Soldiers enter to arrest *Lambourne.* Monmouth despairing flings himself on their swords and dies fighting.

The Duke of Monmouth.
James II.
Michael Lambourne, a Whig pamphleteer, attached to Monmouth, illegitimate brother of Henrietta, resembling Monmouth.
Sir William Gervase, a Whig conspirator, friend to Lambourne.
Lord Grey of Wark.
Conspirators.
Bishops Ken and Turner.
Officers and soldiers.
Henrietta, Lady Wentworth.

All the reading up is Macaulay, p. 530 to 535 and then p. 616 to 630. Of course Lady Wentworth was not in London; but that doesn't matter. During the whole time I must have Monmouth and Henrietta doubting when there was none to hear of the propriety of their relation. Make Lambourne keenly alive to it in Scene II. Make him mock you know at their test by praying, and doubt if he will not give his body to buy his sister's and his friend's perdition. And at the end make her say that God *et caetera.* If you positively object to the arrangement of scenes, write what you'd like better. Scene VII is fine – work it up. At the beginning of Scene II, I'd make a little work of this kind you know.

'Put your cloak before the window.'

twig? As well to have it graphic – it may be acted you know. Last words, let the verse be smooth as glass, and O! write distinctly, I can't decipher your letters often. So write plainer than that. I'll try and copperplate my scenes.

BYELAWS.

I. He who wrote the scene has the casting vote on any difficulty.

II. It is requested that this casting vote be used as little as possible.

III. Corrections not merely verbal and additions exceeding a line in length to be put on a paper apart and pinned on.

42   *To his Mother*

MS Yale.

[*1 July 1868*]   *Kenzie House, Anstruther*[1]

My dear 'Madame', I got here all right: met the Stirlings and the Crawfords on the way – in which last detachment Miss Lizzie invited me to come to 12 Alexander Place, if I ever came to St Andrews, where they are going to summer. There was not much to be done at the works today; and I was tired so little has been done on that head.

Anster[2] seems the very stronghold of the Pledge. Mackintosh, Mitchell, and Bailie Brown my Landlord (whom I *will* persist in calling Wood, because he's a carpenter and *ought to have been called* some name which I don't know, and *is called* some name which I can't recollect) are all T-T's.

I dined at the inn and have tea'd here in honour of my distinguished host's predilection; but I've ordered up half a dozen of 'Pell-ell',[3] and, as it has not yet compeared, don't know how he'll receive it.

Anstruther may produce a gentleman, even, perhaps, a lady, but of neither genus have I as yet encountered a specimen.

Bye-the Bye – this here is wrote to Mr S. – they fired a shot to slap the wall for a drain this afternoon; and a curious old man came forward and asked questions about it. Thinks I: 'when have I seen that cove before?' Says I to Mitchell: 'Who is that?' 'O!' replied Mitchell, 'That's a man they call "the professor" here: he's something to do with Edinburgh College.'

---

[1] RLS went to Anstruther on the northern shore of the Firth of Forth on 1 July to gain engineering experience from the building of a breakwater by the family firm. In 'The Education of an Engineer' (1888) he looks back at his youthful self: 'I lodged with a certain Bailie Brown, a carpenter by trade; and there, as soon as dinner was despatched, in a chamber scented with dry rose-leaves, drew in my chair to the table and proceeded to pour forth literature, at such a speed, and with such intimations of early death and immortality, as I now look back upon with wonder. . . . Late I sat into the night, toiling (as I thought) under the very dart of death, toiling to leave a memory behind me.'

[2] The local pronunciation of Anstruther.

[3] I.e. pale ale.

It was Lindsay,[4] rusticating, and wearing out a suit of antiquated swallow-tails amid the savoury wynds of Cellardyke.

Tonight I saw Kirk-Yetton[5] quite distinctly and thought I caught the shadow of the belt of wood that lies athwart the hollow; so after all I'm near you all you see – within sight. Love to all. Believe me Your affectionate son

R.L. Stevenson

On reading over my epistle,[6] it seemed curt, and I feared it might engender wrathful and improper thoughts in your heart too desirous of letters. I think there's a text which tells you not to lay temptation in your brother's way;[7] so I'll make it apply to your mother and spin a platitude or two to salve the sore.

Miss Robertson knew me.

Mrs Wood – (Just look at that!) – Mrs Brown I mean, said: 'Is it your father – no, it'll be your grandfather – that has charge of the Northern Lights?'

I put her right.

'Aye,' quoth she, 'I kent the name – Stevison' (The mischief she did! It's more than I do!) 'It's jist a household word, so to speak.'

So much for belonging to the Aristocracy of Merit.

Has not this mansion a daft like name? I asked the servant. 'Kenzie House,' she said. 'That'll be somewhere about Mac-kenzie, with the "Mac" off?' I asked. But the handmaiden dissolved into idiotic giggling.   R.L.S.

43   *To his Father*

MS Yale. Published in *Letters*, I, 10–11.

First Sheet: *Thursday* [*2 July 1868*]   *'Kenzie House, or whatever*
Second Sheet: *Friday*   *it is called, Anstruther*

My dear Father, My lodgings are very nice and I don't think there are any children. There is a box of mignonette in the window and a factor of dried rose-leaves which make the atmosphere a trifle heavy but very pleasant.

---

[4] James Lindsay (1799–1877), a native of Anstruther, worked at Edinburgh University from 1814 until 1872 and for most of this time was mechanical assistant to successive Professors of Natural Philosophy. During the summer he supplemented his scanty income by working at Anstruther as a fisherman and when too old to go to sea he acted as an agent for the fish-curers. (Obituary by P.G. Tait in *The Scotsman*, 5 January 1877.) RLS writes of him with affection in 'Some College Memories'.

[5] 'Kirk Yetton (Caer Ketton, wise men say)' – RLS in 'Pastoral' – one of the Pentland Hills with the village of Swanston at its foot. TS took a lease of Swanston Cottage in 1867 and it was a much-loved country home until 1880.

[6] The postscript exists as a separate MS but it seems to belong to this letter.

[7] Cf. Romans 14:13 – '. . . that no man put a stumblingblock, or an occasion to fall, in his brother's way'.

When you come, bring also my paint box – I forgot it.

I am going to try the travellers and Jennies, and have made a sketch of them and begun the drawing. After that I'll do the staging.[1] This morning I walked over with Mitchellins and young Morrison to the Quarry where Mit and I bathed: Mor unbuttoned his waistcoat and then funked.

Mrs Brown 'has suffered herself from her stommik, and that makes her kind of think for other people.' She is a motherly lot. Her motherliness and thought for others displays itself in advice against hard-boiled eggs, well-done meat and late dinners, these being my only requests. Fancy – I am the only person who dines in the afternoon in Anstruther.

[*Second sheet begins*]

If you could bring me some wine when you come 'twould be a good move: I fear *vin d'Anstruther*; and having procured myself a severe attack of gripes by two days total abstinence on chilly table beer, I have been forced to purchase Green Ginger ('Somebody or other's "celebrated"'), for the benefit of my stomach, like St Paul.[2]

There is little or nothing doing here to be seen. By heightening the corner in a hurry to support the staging they have let the masons get ahead of the divers and wait till they can overtake them. I wish you would write and put me up to the sort of things to ask, and find out. I received your registered letter with the £5: it will last forever. Tomorrow I will watch the masons at the pier-foot and see how long they take to work that Fifeness stone you ask about: they get sixpence an hour; so that is the only datum required.

It is awful how slowly I draw and how ill: I am not nearly done with the travellers and have not thought of the Jennies yet. When I'm drawing I find out something I have not measured, or, having measured, have not noted, or, having noted, cannot find; and so I have to trudge to the pier again, ere I can go further with my noble design.

I had a ride today on Morrison's pony. He gave me rather a dismal account of its temper, mouth *et caetera*. Mitchellins told me, I must not believe it all for Mor: was 'not a very daring horseman', he thought. His own groom was more explicit.

'Has Mr Morrison a good seat,' I asked.

'Him? Heck no! By G—, he's a puir show i' the saidle, him!'

After the way Morrison had hinted at his horsemanship, this was too much; and I could scarcely mount for laughter.

Mitchellins says the divers can't work when the tide's out because of the

---

[1] Engineering terms. A traveller is a piece of mechanism designed to 'travel' or slide along a support; a jenny is a crane which moves backwards and forwards and moves heavy weights. The staging is the scaffolding.

[2] 'Drink no longer water, but use a little wine for thy stomach's sake and thine own infirmities' – I Timothy 5:23.

weight. It has occurred to me that a great part of the weight at least might be taken off: it seems such a pity to lose all the time.

I haven't *seen* fruit since I left. Love to all, Your affectionate son

R.L. Stevenson

44   *To his Mother*

MS Yale.

Tuesday [7 July 1868]   *'Kenzie House*

My dear Mama, I got here in safety, box, pockmantie and all.[1] Your letter came here on Saturday. Mrs B. sent it all round; for I had forgotten to leave mine address. Mitchell addressed it to 'Clarendon Crescent'! I suppose it will be in the dead letter office, get it out and forward it again. One wants all the letters in 'furrin parts'. There [is] tonight a heavy westerly gale, with a storm of small close rain which is lashed against my window at every gust with a noise like a theatre-hailstorm.

> My heart is sair: I daurna tell;
> I fear the ugly westerly swell,
> May make Davie and Charlie not quite well.[2]

Tell Papa that a westerly wind brings the swell down here in no time, owing to which some work was done today at the pier by the masons – the first time since I came.

Wednesday

All afternoon in the office trying to strike the average time of building the edge work. I see that it is impossible. The average that we got was: 12 masons in 1 month would build 100 cubic yards. 15 cubic inches; but it is utterly untrustworthy, looks far wrong and could not be compared with any other decision as to the time of the flat work.

Old Lindsay, with whom I have had plenty of talk,[3] remembers the coal fire on the May: he said Grandpapa, the most benevolent man he ever saw, met him one day in the road, he driving, L. walking, and said: 'If we had

---

[1] RLS had been at home from Saturday till Monday.

[2] The first line is from Burns's 'For the Sake o' Somebody'.

[3] 'His reminiscences were all of journeys on foot or highways busy with post-chaises – a Scotland before steam; he had seen the coal fire on the Isle of May, and he regaled me with tales of my own grandfather. Thus he was for me a mirror of things perished' (RLS in 'Some College Memories'). The first Scottish lighthouse, a coal-burning beacon, was set up on the Isle of May at the entrance to the Forth in 1636. The coal fire was replaced by oil-lamps in 1816.

been goin' the same, you would have got a lift.' Papa, he says, 'was a studious boy; and so was David' – He's very irreverend and a trifle blasphemous – 'But I didn't know David so well. Some of them, ye see, comes up to the stove and cracks a bit, some isn't so intimit, ye see.'

'Did Tait do so?'

'Tait? Ah he was a rum student! He came fresh from the High School and went to Forbès.[4] "I want to join," he says. "That'll be the third division" says Forbès. "The first," says he. "O my dear boy" says Forbès, "that's out of the question: you haven't had the *training*, you see. The second is the highest you could possibly try." "Never mind" says Tait, "we'll try the first." "Well, you won't do any good," says Forbès; but he took the second prize.' Tait, it seems, is a great golfer and a good musician, has a huge head and a great fondness for jokes. Lindsay has been 54 years in the College.

The low water is late just now. So I shall be out till eleven at least to-night.

I have taken your room. I remain, Your affectionate son

R.L. Stevenson

I enclose a flower and want to know its name.

45   *To his Mother*

MS Yale. Partly published in *Letters*, I, 14 and I, 11–12 (with Letter 50).

Tuesday [*14 July 1868*]   [*Anstruther*]

My dear Mother, Tell Papa that his boat-builders are the most illiterate brutes with whom I ever had any dealing. From beginning to end of their precious specification, there was no stop whether comma, semi-colon, colon, or point; and to tell whether the adjectives belonged to the previous or the subsequent noun, was work for five experienced boat-builders. However, I made daylight of it, copied it and sent it to Porringer: it took me and Mitchell two hours to understand the part called 'the specification' and there were several parts in the 'offer' or 'tender' which had to be copied as well. So confused, indeed, and so insufficient was the whole thing that the saving clause, smuggled in in the tender, 'and things not fully specified needful for efficient service,' forms its whole value. Have you sent the Essays off? Do see to it?

---

[4] Peter Guthrie Tait (1831–1901), mathematician and physicist, was Professor of Natural History at Edinburgh University 1860–1901. He was a friend of TS. James David Forbes (1809–68) was his predecessor in the chair 1833–60.

Can you find and send to me the last lines of Longfellow's *Golden Legend*, beginning 'It is Lucifer, son of the air,' and so on. 'Since God put him there, he is God's minister for some good end.'[1]

Wednesday [*15 July*]

Tonight I went with the youngest Morrison to see a strolling band of players in the town-hall. A large table placed below the gallery with a print curtain on either side of the most limited dimensions was at once the scenery and the proscenium. The manager told us that his scenes were sixteen by sixty-four, and so could not be got in. Though I knew or at least felt sure that there were no such scenes in the poor man's possession, I could not laugh, as did the major part of the audience, at this shift to escape criticism. We saw a wretched farce; and some comic songs were sung. The manager sang one but it came grimly from his throat. The whole receipt of the evening was 5 and 3d., out of which had to come room, gas and town drummer.

We left soon; and I must say came out as sad as I have been for ever so long: I think that manager had a soul above comic songs. I said this to young Morrison, who is a 'Phillistine' (Matthew Arnold's Philistine you understand)[2] and he replied, 'how much happier would he be as a common working man'. I told him, I thought he would be less happy earning a comfortable living as a shoe-maker, than he was starving as an actor, with such artistic work as he had to do. But the Phillistine wouldn't see it. You observe that I spell Philistine turn about with one and two l's.

As we went home, we heard singing, and went into the porch of the school-house to listen. A fisherman entered and told us to go in. It was a psalmody class. One of the girls had a glorious voice. We stayed for half an hour.

I have got Porringer's answer but will not send it till I get back the specification I gave him. It is £100 and he says he will give every advantage and make it very superior. The other was £115. I remain, Your affectionate son   R.L. Stevenson

---

[1]
                It is Lucifer,
                The son of mystery;
                And since God suffers him to be,
                He too, is God's minister,
                And labours for some good
                By us not understood!

[2] 'Philistine' in the sense of a person deficient in liberal culture was used by Matthew Arnold in *Essays in Criticism*, 1865.

46   To his Father

MS Yale.

Friday 17 July [1868]   *Office Anster*

My dear Father, We had an accident here today: a truck went over and
knocked in the divers' assistants. Two men seem pretty severely hurt; and
one or two others are slightly bruised. I have written an account to Uncle
David. I am, Your affectionate son   R.L. Stevenson

The whole town is in an uproar; and, as I passed one little girl said to
another: 'There's the man that has the charge o't'!!

47   To his Mother

MS Yale.

Sunday Evening [19 July 1868]   *Leven*[1]

My dear Mamma, If I am to write the essay, I require Carlyle's *Heroes and
Hero Worship* and that shortly. Can you send it to me? The divers' assistants
all escaped unhurt: only one of the men is still unwell, but I hope he too will
recover.

Old woman (to Aunt Josey): 'Eh mem! your dochter is indeed a bright
spark! an' the doctor was so prood of her too!'

What a lucky person you are always getting one compliment or another!

Last night, Aunt Josey took me up along the river, a most delightful walk
under great, green *willies*, and up to a place a little like Homburg
embosomed in trees. A tree is a perfect wonder to me now; and I return to
Anster still more dissatisfied by the contrast.

Pittenweem[2] Church is even more curious than Anster: it is, I should
think, unique. Such a strange, quaint mixture of ecclesiastical architecture
with the architecture of the later Scoto-French baronial buildings should
surely be in what I used to call 'the Baronials'.[3]

When I went to Robertsons to get the brush, which you – careless
creature! – left behind, I heard a piece of news. Fancy! Old Robertson is

---

[1] A town thirteen miles west of Anstruther, the home of MIS's brother John Balfour (1809–86) and
his wife (and cousin) Josephine Marianne Smith (1829–87). John Balfour had a distinguished
career in the East India Company and the British army and was in Delhi at the time of the Mutiny
(referred to by RLS in 'The Coast of Fife'). He retired to Leven in 1866 and practised there as a
doctor until his death. RLS's parents visited him at Anstruther on 10 July and they all spent the
weekend at Leven. The letter is written on notepaper bearing the Balfour family crest *Adsit Deus*.
[2] A village one mile west of Anstruther.
[3] RLS uses the phrase 'Scottish Baronial style' in an account dictated to his mother in 1861 of 'The
Antiquities of Midlothian' (Yale).

going to make the Bow window in the Coffee Room, and wondered if Papa would make the drawings for him.

I enclose a ticket thing. Aunt Josey expects Papa to make a large subscription.

Did my report give satisfaction at headquarters?

Have the *Essays* been sent away?

Tell Cummy, that she is not the only person who forgets to fill the ewers: I've almost always to ring when I'm going to wash my face: also impress upon her that I go to the theatre every night except when I play cards!

Talking of that, I forgot to tell you that I tea'd, croquet'd, supper'd and whist'ed at the Morrisons the other night: it was near twelve, when I got home; and the family, in virtuous indignation, had drawn their skirts away from the malefactor and put out their gas! There is a Miss Maggie in the question, not altogether bad looking.

A poor woman was there on Friday with a baby and a very neat and clean little girl asking after her husband who had bolted. We all agreed he should be flogged. James Nichol was his name. I'm glad to see Lord Stanley is so well received.[4] Have the boat-offers and estimates come to hand all right? I remain, Your affectionate son   R.L. Stevenson

I hope you are all right again.

48   *To his Mother*

MS Yale. Published in *Letters*, I, 14–15.

Thursday [*23 July 1868*]   *Kenzie House, Anster*

My dear Mère,[1] I don't remember whose turn it is. It is as well 'twas you that reproached me about the legibility of my hand and not the other parient: his last letter, though of commendable brevity, took me two hours to decipher finally: verily he must have been hurried that day: such a scrawl it has been seldom my fate to decipher.

I shall want some more money soon. My next Saturday's excursion will make me unable to meet Mrs Brown on Monday.

I got a very kind note from Mrs Fortune, addressed 'Lewis Balfour'! – asking me next Saturday but Aunt Josey had made an engagement for me to go with her somewhere *some* 'Hall' or another; so I was obliged to refuse.

All is going on well.

[4] Edward Henry Stanley (1826–93) who succeeded his father as fifteenth Earl of Derby 1869, was at this time Foreign Secretary in Disraeli's Tory ministry.
[1] 'Père et' deleted.

I got Carlyle and am duly obliged.

I wish this to go tonight. So excuse brevity: I only follow the example of both parents. Give my love to Auntie. Ask Papa why the stones of the last kant[2] are placed flat. Your affectionate son   R.L. Stevenson

49   *To his Mother*

MS Yale.

Sunday [*26 July 1868*]   *Leven*

My dear Mother, I do envy you all the fun you must be having. Is it Dick *ex officino* or John Dick[1] who is staying?

Tell Papa that an accident delayed my getting to Fifeness till Friday; but that I shall have the information ere I leave.

Uncle John will come by the 10:45. Adam to be at Lynedoch Place by three. I am not perfectly sure whether I shall be able to leave on the same day: it is possible I may want to stay longer.

Send me more money.

The Diving Bell is coming down on Monday and will be at work on Wednesday at latest.

We had a no end day of it yesterday. Newton Hall[2] is a very pretty place, on the side of a hill, with a fine view in front, a garden and a plantation on either hand, and wide, rich meadows, divided by belts of woodland, up behind it. We had some good games of croquet. Minnie Kerr is a very nice girl and very pretty: fair hair, freckles, and one of those infinitesimal squints Papa and I admire.

Tell Uncle John[3] that I hope he likes Swanston: a halfpenny worth of our hill air is worth 'a cycle in Cathay',[4] Glasgow or 'any other place'; and it will set him on his legs again.

The sea, being 'fanged with hideous stones'[5] – like Cologne – and otherwise marred, does *not* make up for Swanston. My letter today was a swindle and certainly not for Sunday reading.

[2] An oblique arm of a pier.
[1] James Dick was TS's chief clerk. Another family called Dick sometimes stayed at Swanston. The reference may be to John Dick whose wife Elspeth (died 1873) was for many years the servant of the Revd Lewis Balfour.
[2] A mansion in the village of Kennoway, near Leven.
[3] MIS's maternal uncle John Smith (1800–80), a Glasgow merchant, and his wife Jessie had stayed with the Stevensons 23–29 July.
[4] 'Better fifty years of Europe than a cycle of Cathay' – Tennyson, 'Locksley Hall'.
[5] 'In Köhln, a town of monks and bones, / And pavements fang'd with murderous stones' – Coleridge, 'Cologne'.

I have heard Fergusson, the Free cove,[6] and do not like him near so well as the 'stablished. He is sensational, in bad taste and, to my mind, undoctrinal or rather not the whole doctrine.

Aunt Josey wants Papa's picter. Your affectionate son   R.L. Stevenson

50   To his Mother

MS Yale. Published in *Letters*, I, 12 (with part of Letter 45).

Toosda [28 July 1868]   *Kenzie House, Anstruther*

I am utterly sick of this grey, grim, sea-beaten hole. I have a little cold in my head which makes my eyes sore; and you can't tell how utterly sick I am and how anxious to get back among trees and flowers and something less meaningless than this bleak fertility.

Papa need not imagine that I have a bad cold or am stone blind from this description; which is the whole truth.

Last night, Mr and Mrs Fortune called in a dog cart, Fortune's beard and Mrs F.'s brow glittering with mist-drops, to ask me to come next Saturday. Conditionally, I accepted. Do you think I can cut it? I am only anxious to go slick home on the Saturday. Write by return of post and tell me what to do. If possible, I should like to cut the business and come right slick out to Swanston.[1]

Mr Fisher got his levels all right and dined with me. Roast lamb: peas: cauliflower: bread: pudding: brandy and soda: beer: port. What a bill of fare!

I got the £3: much beholden.

I went to see the grotto room, which is a hum.

My second bottle of port is nigh an end; but the third and the brandy will be a horrid trouble coming home. Were I to live long by myself as I live just now, I fear I should grow awfully stingy about eating and drinking. I get worse and worse that way, and feel inclined almost to stint myself if a dish is nearly done.

Gogus is away today. He was a man called Melville whom we met, a very pleasant fellow, and a mystery. His name came out by chance, and what he is a complete and utter puzzle. I remain, Your affectionate son
                                                            R.L. Stevenson

I wrote to Janey today.

---

[6] Donald Ferguson (1811–97), Free Church minister at Leven from 1865.
[1] RLS returned home to Swanston on Friday 31 July.

51   To his Mother

MS Yale.

Friday [28 August 1868]   *New Harbour Hotel,*
No. I   *Pulteney, Wick*[1]

My dear Mamma, Today Papa left in the morning before I was up to go south.[2] It has been a frightful day of rain and wind: rain at intervals, wind continuously. I breakfasted, lunched and dined at the Hotel, all which with beer and wine cost me 4 shillings 4 pence – immense total! It can't pay 'em, that's one thing. Perhaps they overcharged Papa so fearfully in the morning that they desired to make '*l'amende honorable*' in under-charging me.

If D. Douglas Balfour Esq[3] is still with you, you can tell him, for his delectation, that I possess from my windows a monopoly of the ancient and fish-like smells[4] of this charming locality, as the house looks out on all the herring cureries (if such a word is allowed) and every gust is laden with the same delicate perfume with a luxuriance that reminds one of the scented south!!

It seems about an hour since the last sentence was begun; and I dare not read it over to see how it follows, as I forbode some doleful trap, pitfall or hollow midway.

My room is eight paces by five and nearly twelve feet high. It is adorned with pictures representing young ladies who have draped themselves with little care and whose habillements are deserting them in a very elegant fashion. One of them looks like a shop girl presenting and holding up some red stuff for the admiration of her customers. Another clad in wreaths of a very äerial blue veil or very material blue cloud, is taking a header across a globe, which she embraces in a tender and *dégagé* fashion. A third, lying on her face upon a 'purple couch' and surrounded by Cimmerian darkness, is holding a torch above her head: to add to her troubles, in addition to the

---

[1] Herring fishing port and county town of Caithness in the extreme north of Scotland. Pultneytown, the commercial and fisheries area, was built by the British Fisheries Society. The Society had ambitious plans for building a breakwater as part of a new harbour and employed the Stevenson firm as engineers. Construction began in 1863 but in December 1868 a considerable portion was swept away in a great storm; further gales in 1871 and 1872 continued the damage and the work was abandoned in 1874. RLS wrote in his essay on his father: 'The harbour of Wick, the chief disaster of my father's life, was a failure; the sea proved too strong for man's arts; and after expedients hitherto unthought of, and on a scale hyper-cyclopean, the work must be deserted and now stands a ruin in that bleak, God forsaken bay.'

[2] TS accompanied by RLS left Edinburgh on Tuesday 25 August and arrived in Wick on Thursday for what the local paper called 'his yearly inspection of the Harbour Works'. He left on Friday. Many of the dates supplied by MIS must have been added years later and are not always reliable. She misdates this letter 3 September.

[3] See Letter 38, n. 5.

[4] Cf. *The Tempest*, II.ii.27.

common grievance of her clothes coming off, this lady is tortured by the coming down of her back hair. The jewels of these nymphs – distributed with a liberality that would lead you to suppose the artist was either Croesus or Baron Rothschild – are represented by spangles of gilt paper; and, on a nearer inspection, I discover that the cloud-veil or veil-cloud of the second damsel – at once the most beautiful and the least clad – is adorned at regular intervals with similar *plaques* of Dutch leaf, giving it an appearance half way between a cloud with small-pox and a bottle of that liquor that papa tasted at Meurices.[5] There is a portrait of the Queen, one of Prince Albert, three or four of members of the family: two German prints of children, a German print of Balmoral, and the two German prints – well kent in lodging houses purporting to show forth and depict morning and evening in some apocryphal district of Scotland. These last, like the nymphs, are coloured. Follows a picture of Queen Mary, two photographs of Wick Harbour, pictures of Thurso and another German print of another angelic child. There are glass walking sticks, stuffed birds, shell boxes, jars, flower glasses, paper flowers, real flowers in pots and a profusion of similar ornaments fit to make you giddy. There are four tables, three of which and a sideboard groan and totter beneath the lumber above enumerated. There are twelve chairs and a sofa: four rugs, three of them fur: an acre and a half of whitish crumb cloth, three quarters of an acre of wax-cloth (different patterns) and a few patches of geometrical carpet seen hovering in the distance on the shores of the broad sea of crumb cloth and half-hid by the various islands of wax-cloth. Ask Papa about the token of love.

Young MacDonald[6] came here tonight and smoked: I thought he was never going away and I should never get the letter done; but at last he went, saying, as he left, with a glance of fiendish malignity at my note-paper, 'You're too late for the post!' Love to all, I remain, Your affectionate son
R.L. Stevenson

P.S. MacDonald guv me four pund for to go on with.

52   To his Father

MS Yale. Partly published in *Letters*, I, 15 and 17–18 as two separate letters.

No. II
[*1 September 1868*]   *New Harbour Hotel, Pulteney*

My dear Father, I hope your asthma is all right now. I think what you say about the diving is nonsense: I should only try in shallow water and if any

---

[5] A hotel in Paris. The Stevensons stayed there on their journey to the continent in 1863.
[6] David MacDonald, the son of the engineer in charge of the harbour works. The father (also David) is referred to in the postscript.

effect were produced could go out immediately: if all were right, should go in deeper gradually.[1] Besides if I don't get a shot at it, I lose great part of my idea of the work.

Wednesday [2 September]

I went and saw Rutherford yesterday.[2] He was very kind and friendly. I was introduced to Madame and Mademoiselle, and took lunch: he guv me advice. So you see, so far at least, that has been a better speculation than was expected.

What is the weight of a square foot of *salt* water? and how many lbs are there to a ton?

I think you had better not send that certificate of extra work till the cross wall is finished. Take care how you word it: my soul is not mine own down here; and 'him and I' will do his best to him–and-I it.[3]

Is it on the line BD, bisecting ABD, or on the line AE, bisecting WAB that the second station is to be put? Fig 2, I suppose.

Would it not interest you and be of use in some future report to have the measurements and calculated weight of any stones which have been evidently moved by the sea.

There is a Free Church minister here just now. Ah fie! what a creed! He

[1] In 'The Education of an Engineer', RLS gives a vivid description of his experiences when he achieved his ambition of going down in a diving dress – 'It was one of the best things I got from my education as an engineer.'

[2] Gilbert Brydone Rutherford (1816–95) retired from the Royal Navy in 1866 with the rank of Captain (but was subsequently promoted to Admiral). He was appointed by the British Fisheries Society as their agent and Superintendent Harbour Master at Pultneytown.

[3] David MacDonald, the engineer (see Letter 51, n. 6).

told me point blank that all Roman Catholics would be damned. I'd rather have MacDonald's amiable infidelity, than this harsh, judging, self-righteous form of faith. (I don't mean him-and-I, you know, but George MacDonald, the writer.)[4] I remain, Your affectionate son   R.L. Stevenson

P.S. Remove your veto from the diving, by doing it in that cautious way, no harm could ensue. Ask G.B.[5]

53   To his Mother

Text: brief extract in Balfour's Biography Notebook, NLS.

[*Early September 1868*][1]   [*Wick*]

Address me 'Robert Lewis' not 'R.L.B.' The other is so much nicer.

54   To his Father

Text: Balfour, I, 71.

[c. *4 September 1868*]   [*Wick*]
[*Postscript to a short business letter*]

P.S. I was forgetting my only news. A man fell off the staging this forenoon. I heard crying, and ran out to the end. By that time a rope had been lowered and the man was holding himself up by it, and of course wearing himself out. Some were away for a boat. 'Hold on, Angus,' they cried. 'I can NOT do it,' he said, with wonderful composure. I told them to lower a plank; everybody was too busy giving advice to listen to me; meantime the man was drowning. I was desperate, and could have knocked another dozen off. One fellow, Bain, a diver,[1] listened to me. We got the plank out and a rope round it; but they would not help us to lower it down, when some one cried, 'Hold your hand, lads! Here comes the boat.' And Angus was borne safely in. But my hand shook so, that I could not draw for some time after with the excitement.   R.S.

---

[4] George MacDonald (1824–1905), poet and novelist, now best remembered for his stories for children. He began his career as a Congregationalist minister but was rejected by his congregation and resigned. According to the *DNB* his novels of humble Scottish life were notable for his 'stern opposition to the rigid theology of Scottish orthodoxy'.
[5] MIS's brother, Dr George William Balfour (1823–1903) – 'that wise youth my uncle' – an authority on diseases of the heart; physician to Royal Infirmary Edinburgh 1867–82.
[1] Dated 7 September by Balfour, presumably on the authority of MIS. In view of Letter 57 this date seems to be incorrect.
[1] Bob Bain was the 'handsome scamp of a diver' who took RLS down with him as a diver.

55   *To his Mother*

MS Yale. Published in *Letters*, I, 18–20.

Saturday [5 September 1868][1]   [*Wick*]

My dear Mother, To go on with my description: – Wick lies at the end or
elbow of an open triangular bay, hemmed on either side by shores, either
cliff or steep earth-bank, of no great height. The grey houses of Pulteney
extend along the southerly shore almost to the cape; and it is about half-way
down this shore – no six-sevenths way down that the new breakwater
extends athwart the bay. A in the plan[2] represents my present domicile.

Certainly Wick, in itself, possesses no beauty: bare, grey shores, grim
grey houses, grim grey sea: not even the gleam of red tile: not even
the greenness of a tree.[3] The southerly heights when I came here, were
black with people, fishers waiting on wind and night. Now all the SYs[4]
(Stornaway boats) have beaten out of the bay and the Wick men stay
indoors or wrangle on the quays with dissatisfied fish-curers, knee-high in
brine, mud and herring refuse. The day when the boats put out to go home
to the Hebrides, the girl here told me there was 'a black wind'; and on going
out, I found the epithet as justifiable as it was picturesque. A cold, *black*
southerly wind, with occasional rising showers of rain: it was a fine sight to
see the boats beat out a-teeth of it.

In Wick I have never heard anyone greet his neighbour with the usual
'fine day' or 'Good morning'. Both come shaking their heads and both say:
'Breezy, breezy!'[5] And such is the atrocious quality of the climate, that the
remark is almost invariably justified by the fact.

The streets are full of the Highland fishers, lubberly, stupid, inconceiv-
ably lazy and heavy to move. You bruise against them, tumble over them,
elbow them against the wall – all to no purpose: they will not budge; and
you are forced to leave the pavement every step.

To the south however is as fine a piece of coast scenery as I ever saw.
Great black chasms, huge black cliffs, rugged and over-hung gullies, natural
arches and deep green pools below them, almost too deep to let you see the
gleam of sand among the darker weed: there are deep caves too. In one of
these lives a tribe of gypsies. The men are *always* drunk, simply and

---

[1] Misdated 11 September by MIS, who altered 'Saturday' to 'Friday' apparently from a misreading
of Letter 64. The arrival of the gunboat and the expected riot provide the correct date.

[2] A crude sketch by RLS.

[3] In 'The Education of an Engineer' RLS calls Wick 'one of the meanest of man's towns, and situate
certainly on the baldest of God's bays.'

[4] SY is the identification code for ships from Stornaway.

[5] This anecdote is repeated in 'On the Enjoyment of Unpleasant Places', where RLS (without
naming it) gives a description of the bleak scenery and unpleasant climate of Wick.

truthfully always. From morning to evening, the great villainous looking fellows are either sleeping off the last debauch, or hulking about the cove 'in the horrors'. The cave is deep, high and airy and might be made comfortable enough. But they just live among heaped boulders, damp with continual droppings from above, with no more furniture than two or three tin pans, a truss of rotten straw and a few ragged cloaks. In winter, the surf bursts into the mouth and often forces them to abandon it.

An *émeute* of disappointed fishers was feared; and two ships of war are in the bay to render assistance to the municipal authorities.[6] This is the ides; and to all intents and purposes, said ides have passed. Still there is a good deal of disturbance, many drunk men and a double supply of police. I saw them sent for by some people and enter an inn in a pretty good hurry: what it was for I do not know.

You would see by Papa's letter about the carpenter who fell off the staging: I don't think I was ever so much excited in my life. The man was back at his work and I asked him how he was; but he was a Highlander, and – need I add it? – dickens a word could I understand of his answer. What is still worse I find the people here about – that is to say the Highlanders, not the northmen – don't understand *me*.

Have you seen or heard any more of the American?

I have lost a shilling's worth of postage stamps, which has damped my ardour for buying big lots of 'em: I'll buy them one at a time as I want 'em for the future.

The Free Church minister and I got quite thick. He left last night about two in the morning. When I went to turn in, he gave me the enclosed. I remain, Your affectionate son   R.L. Stevenson

56   To Bob Stevenson

MS Yale.

Private
Sunday [*6 September 1868*]   *New Harbour Hotel, Pulteney Town, Wick*
                                                                          Caithnesshire
                                        (don't know mine own address by Jove!)[1]

My dear Bob, I received your kind letter some time ago; but ever since have been too busy to reply. Hegel must either be frightfully clever, or a most egregious ass: I incline to the latter opinion. The great old question

[6] Because of the failure of the fishing season many of the Highland fishermen could not be paid. There were fears of a riot and the gunboat the *Lizard* joined the gunboat *Netley* off Wick on Saturday 5 September. It left on the Monday.
[1] RLS originally wrote part of the word 'Sutherland' (the next county to Caithness), crossed it out and substituted 'Caithnesshire'.

of the Almighty, which has found an echo in every age and in every heart, ever since it rang to Job upon his dungheap, would seem to apply full well: 'Who is this that darkeneth counsel with words without knowledge?'[2] Do you observe? 'Who is/ this that/ darkeneth/ counsel with/ words without/ knowledge.' It is one of those natural hexameters which throng the splendid prose of our English version of the greatest poem in the world.

Monmouth is finished. A spasmodic effort, not a sustained and completed work. There are pieces in it which I think decent enough, some little touches of nature and an end sufficiently sensational to satisfy all lovers of poetic justice, of which I am one. But the play has somehow *crined in* – to use our Scotch expression. The characters do not come forth on the stage: they are only seen peeping out of a window. They are not developed, they are merely roughly and hastily sketched. With the versification, except in some parts, I am tolerably pleased; and the little touches of description also give me satisfaction. You see I am frank and praise myself: did I ever grow great, this letter would figure in my life.

Strange how my mind runs on this idea. Becoming great, becoming great, becoming great. A heart burned out with the lust of this world's approbation: a hideous disease to have, even though shielded, as it is in my case, with a certain imperturbable something – self-consciousness or common sense, I cannot tell which, – that would prevent me poisoning myself like Chatterton or drinking like Burns on the failure of my ambitious hopes. My nature is at once sanguine and ambitious; but I do not think I am so great a fool as to become my own dupe. Even in my vilest and most shameful thoughts – and who suffers more from such? – there is a something nobler intermixed; it may be but the next Spirit's last endeavours to raise me: it may be something intrinsically good. At least, it is the only thing in my nature that gives me hope, the only thing that I see and cannot trace back to absolute self-love and bald, unholy self-seeking. And yet what is it, merely the returning pang of conscience that bids me communicate my own fears to those who ought to share them. Would God it were more! [*Rest of MS missing*]

57   *To his Mother*

MS Yale. Partly published in *Letters*, I, 20–21.

Monday [7 September 1868]   [*Wick*]

My dear Mamma, I wish you would put the dates in days of the week as well as in days of the month.

[2] Job 38:2.

Your rebuke about writing oftener seems uncalled for. Papa has only been nine days away; and I have written three letters of two sheets to you, and two or three letters to him: if that is not enough, I don't know what you want. I begin to fear lest some of mine should have gone astray: tell me what you have received, not by the dates which I don't remember but by some slight synopsis of what was in 'em.

This morning, I got a delightful haul: your letter of the fourth (surely mis-dated): Papa's of same day: Virgil's *Bucolics* very thankfully received; and Aikman's *Annals*,[1] a precious and most acceptable donation, for which I tender my most ebullient thanksgivings. I almost forgot to drink my tea and eat mine egg. It contains more detailed accounts than anything I ever saw, except Wodrow,[2] without being so portentously tiresome and so desperately overborne with foot-notes, proclamations, Acts of Parliament and citations as that last history.

I have been reading a good deal of Herbert. He's a clever and a devout cove; but in places awfully twaddley (if I may use the word). Oughtn't this to rejoice Papa's heart.

> 'Carve or discourse; do not a famine fear.
> Who carves is kind to two, who talks to all.'[3]

You understand? the 'fearing a famine' is applied to people gulping down solid vivers without a word, as if the ten lean kine began tomorrow. Do you remember condemning something of mine for being too obtrusively didactic. Listen to Herbert.

> Is it not verse $\begin{Bmatrix}\text{unless}\\ \textit{except}\end{Bmatrix}$ enchanted groves
> And sudden arbours shadow coarse-spun lines?
> Must purling streams refresh a lover's loves?
> *Must all be veiled, while he that reads divines*
> *Catching the sense at two removes?*[4]

You see 'except' was used for 'unless' before 1630.

Tuesday [8 September]

The riots were a hum. No more has been heard; and one of the war-steamers has deserted in disgust. *The Moonstone* is frightfully interesting: isn't

---

[1] James Aikman, *Annals of the Persecution in Scotland from the Restoration to the Revolution* (1842).

[2] Robert Wodrow, *The History of the Sufferings of the Church of Scotland from the Restoration to the Revolution* (1721–22).

[3] George Herbert, *The Temple*: 'The Church Porch', xxii. RLS's copy of *The Poetical Works of George Herbert; and the Synagogue, by C. Harvey* (1863), a gift from Cummy 1 January 1866, was in Anderson II (249).

[4] *The Temple*: 'Jordan (I)'.

the detective prime?[5] Don't say anything about the plot; for I have only read on to the end of Betteredge's narrative; so don't know anything about it yet.

I thought to have gone on to Thurso tonight; but the coach was full; so I go tomorrow instead.

Today I had a grouse: great glorification.

There is a drunken brute in the house, who disturbed my rest last night. He's a very respectable man in general; but when on the 'spree' a most consummate fool. When he came in he stood on the top of the stairs and preached in the dark with great solemnity and no audience from 12 P.M. to half past one. At last I opened my door. 'Are we to have no sleep at all for that *drunken brute*?' I said. As I hoped, it had the desired effect. 'Drunken brute!' he howled, in much indignation: then after a pause, in a voice of some contrition, 'Well, if I am a drunken brute, it's only once in the twelvemonth!' And that was the end of him: the insult rankled in his mind; and he retired to rest. He is a fish-curer, a man over fifty and pretty rich, too. He's as bad again today; but I'll be shot if he keeps me awake, I'll douse him with water if he makes a row.[6] Ever your affectionate son

R.L. Stevenson

58   *To his Father*

MS Buffalo.

Wednesday [9 September 1868]   *Wick*
No. IV

My dear Father, What is the use of these fly-ropes with bladders at 'em. In [vain] have I, in vain has MacDonald striven to make head or tail of them. Tell that and send certificate of extra-work for making them and the experiments, and we shall get to work. MacDonald seems to think it will need four of the guys, but I consider that a piece of nonsense. Are these bladder-ropes merely for tightening the others? If so, why the middle one?

Weather favourable; the cross wall gets on well.

Have you asked Uncle George about the diving? If I go in cautiously it can't do any harm.

I'm off to Thurso tonight. Till tomorrow night at least. I remain, Your affectionate son   R.L. Stevenson

[5] Wilkie Collins's novel had been serialised in *All the Year Round* from January to August 1868; it appeared in book form in December.

[6] TS replied on 11 September: 'Do not interfere with that drunk man. You may get into trouble. I never should have acted as you have done. You may get your head broken before you know where you are.'

59   To his Father

MS Washington.

[*10 September 1868*]   *Royal Hotel, Thurso*

My dear Father, I came on here yesterday (Wednesday) night. This morning I went on to Scrabster, and, taking tutorial advice, 'had a note-book and
a well-nibbed pencil – a black lead pencil with me, Willee.' The ministrations of Doctor Leith[1] were pretty satisfactory but I am to hear from him
[on] the subject and will [r]eport[2] when I have got the rest of the information. Mean to stay till tomorrow. I remain, Your affectionate son

R.L. Stevenson

60   To his Mother

MS Yale. Partly published in *Scribner's Magazine*, XXV (January 1899), 34–7.

[*13 September 1868*]   *New Harbour Hotel, Pulteney*

My dear Mother, My trip to Thurso took up so much of my time, that I
have been rather remiss in my correspondence. I had good fun there. There
was a Colonel M—, an awful swearer, who was very good fun; and five
bagmen, with whom I dined the second day. The bagmen told some good
stories; and two or three of them nearly took apoplexy over Story of
Roseneath[1] and his *Cattenary* parishioner and two or three more of Mr
Swan's duly detailed to them. As this is Sunday I shall say no more on that
head. Colinton for length of service is a joke to Wick. Two hours morning
and evening. This afternoon we had two hours all but three minutes. I did
not look [at] my watch at the sermon till I was pretty tired, certainly not less
than twenty minutes; and the discourse lasted three quarters of an hour and
two or three minutes after that! O Lillo! Lillo![2]

The girl here tells me that she was a fortnight in bed of the Wick
Revival. She had been in the country and went to a week-day evening
service. A fearful sermon was given; and a woman near the pulpit began
screaming in a dreadful manner. It worked so strongly on her that she took
a trembling fit and had to be helped home.

---

[1] Possibly William Leith, Harbour Master at Scrabster. See also Letter 61.
[2] The corner of the letter is torn away and this word is not completely clear.
[1] Robert Henry Story (1835–1907) succeeded his father as minister of Rosneath 1860–86. He was
subsequently Professor of Church History and then Principal of Glasgow University. Rosneath is
a village on the Gare Loch opposite Helensburgh, where Professor Swan lived.
[2] Possibly a reference to William Lillie (1801–75), the minister at Wick. RLS remembered the
length of the sermon in 'The Education of an Engineer': 'The old minister of Keiss would not
preach, in these degenerate times, for an hour and a half upon the clock.'

I asked if she knew any of the people who had made a vow during the period and if there were any change in 'em. She knew scores of them, she said, young men and young women and, if anything, they were worse – a statement I can quite believe from all I have heard and seen.

After all this is a mere stirring of emotional fibre: like one crying over a novel.

> 'Tyrants no more their savage nature kept
> And, foes to virtue, wondered why they wept.'[3]

Aye, aye, but wait till tomorrow morning and see how his savage nature is then! For some good things on this, see one of Bulwer Lytton's essays: 'On the *sympathetic* (?) Temperament.'[4] See what a very Sunday letter 'tis!

It has been bitterly cold today.

Monday [14 September]

— And is bitterly ditto today. I have drawn the table up to the fire, and my hands are sore and stiff: we had a fire in the office.

Account of one of my days? very well. Breakfast: moveable feast 9 to 9.30. Tea, herring, finnan haddock, eggs, rolls, salt butter to which I am now entirely acclimatised. After breakfast: breakwater, drawing, general loafing and inspection. One P.M. lunch. Sherry, Latheron cheese, rolls, salt butter. After lunch: breakwatering again. Five: dinner heaps o' things (N.B. curds called 'yearned milk' hereaway). After dinner, letters, algebra, reading smoking, waiting for bed-time. Now and then a walk. 9.30 or 10, tea, rolls, butter, cheese. Nightcap in requisition about 11 or 11.30 or 10.30.

Was there anything worth in this month's *Good Words*. When should I call on the Rutherfords again?

Tell Myrrha[5] that when she came to envying G. Henry his hand, I wept – positively wept – so just, so well-founded did that envy appear – so truly did I respond the wish at that moment, then labouring in the depths. I lost I fear some of the choicest witticisms of the epistle. Indeed my state of mind put me deeply in mind of the Sweet Singer's description of a storm at sea. – vide Psalmn (any more dumb consonants required? It would look better thus Psalolmn) 107. Don't you think, by the bye, that David must have been sick: it *is* so life-like. 'They go down into the depths.' O yes, but what about their stommiks? 'They reel to and fro like a drunken man.' I declare I can almost hear a faint voice cry 'steward!' at that part. You see that

---

[3] Pope, 'Prologue to Addison's *Cato*'.

[4] 'The Sympathetic Temperament', *Caxtoniana* (1863, reprinted from *Blackwood's Magazine*), *Miscellaneous Prose Works* (1868). This essay gives the quotation from Pope.

[5] Identified by MIS as Mary Warden, another daughter of Adam and Jane Warden, TS's sister (see Letter 117).

Myrrha's letter has produced a healthy effect upon my spirits; but I'm not going to mention her again: it costs such labour to spell it. Fancy, I had to ring the bell and ask the girl how she spelt 'myrrh': I question much if she told me right. But what between it and the *Psalmmns*, my mind about spelling is lost.

D. Douglas Balfour disappears mysteriously from your correspondence: what has become of him? Did his corporeal and bodily presence take leave of Swanston in a similarly unaccountable manner.

Isn't it *prime* about Lockyer.[6] I hooted, raved, roared with laughter over it. The infernal scoundrel! Most say he'll get off under insanity. I remain, Your affectionate son   R.L. Stevenson

P.S. I can't help making this over weight. I forgot to tell such a first class joke.
Young MacDonald: 'Where is Dhuheartach?'[7]
Yours truly: 'O Ultima Thule.'
Y. M: 'Whereabouts *is* that? It's a bit of a wild place, isn't it? Bryson was up there the last time he was away. They're making a railway there, and MacDonald's got the contract.'

Isn't it *trooly* good!
Old MacDonald him-and-I's it a little. I was very strong for doing away with the stones at bottom of the gauge-pole and putting an iron collar of some sort instead, to give it weight. He pooh-pooh'd it. Today, he proposed a waggon wheel and went on enumerating reasons.

'It's quite useless to say any more,' I said. 'I quite agree with you. I proposed the same thing myself at first, you remember!'

But he took no notice, and bored on with his reasons, and has now got his patent for it, as an original invention. Your affectionate son   R.L.S.

61   *To his Father*

MS Yale. Excerpt published in Balfour, I, 71.

Thursday [*17 September 1868*]   [*Wick*]

My dear Father, I have had a long hard day's work in cold, wind and almost incessant rain.

---

[6] Edmund Beatty Lockyer, one of the candidates for Wick in the Parliamentary Elections then in progress, had been arrested for intercepting and opening letters addressed to a Miss Sinclair whom he had shortly before prosecuted for breach of promise of marriage. He was sentenced to a year's imprisonment the following year.
[7] The rocky islet in the Atlantic fifteen miles south-west of Iona, where David and Thomas Stevenson were building a lighthouse. It was completed in October 1872.

Two poles were placed on the staging to give us the right angle; and then I hit on this plan for the 45° one: the cosin and sin 45° being the same, then if we get AB, A being the point where we are going to measure, we have only to measure off an equal length BC, put up a pole at C and drop second gauge pole in the line AC. When these points and stations were erected it was about four. We got a lighter and a boat and were out till half past seven, doing labourers' work, pulling, hauling and tugging. We have got one up so far.

It was past eight before I got dinner, as I was soaking and bathed with mud to the ears; but, beyond being tired with the unusual exertion, I am all right now.

If the swell which is rising doesn't knock our labour down we shall get our observations started by tomorrow afternoon.

Leith has never sent me the rest of his information. It does first class for a year there is no mistake. The barnacles do not get through the coating at all; but MacDonald says that is always the way.

Too late for post tonight. I remain, Your affectionate son

R.L. Stevenson

62   *To his Mother*

MS Yale. Partly published in *Letters*, I, 22–3.

Saturday [actually Friday 18 September 1868][1]   [*Wick*]
10 A.M.

My dear Mother, The last two days have been dreadfully hard; and I was so tired in the evenings that I could not write. In fact *last* night, I went to sleep immediately after, or very nearly so. My hours have been 10–2 and 3–7 out

[1] The date is corrected in Letter 64.

in the lighter or the small boat, in a long, heavy roll from the nor'-east. When the dog was taken out, he got awfully ill, and cowed to particulars promiscuously, involving many kicks and much swabbing: one of the men, Geordie Grant by name and surname, followed *shoot* with considerable *éclat*; but, wonderful to relate! I kept well. My hands are all skinned, blistered, discoloured and engrained with tar, some of which latter has established itself under my nails in a position of such natural strength that it defies all my efforts to dislodge it. The worst work I had was when David (MacDonald's eldest) and I took the charge ourselves. He remained in the lighter to tighten or slacken the guys as we raised the pole towards the perpendicular, with two men. I was with four men in the boat. We dropped an anchor out a good bit, then tied a cord to the pole, took a turn round the sternmost thwart with it and pulled on the anchor line. As the great, big, wet hawser came in it soaked you to the skin: I was the sternest (used, by way of variety, for sternmost) of the lot and had to coil it – a work which involved, from *its* being so stiff and *your* being busy pulling with all your might no little trouble and an extra ducking. We got it up; and, just as we were going to sing 'Victory!', one of the guys slipped in, the pole tottered – went over on its side again like a shot, and behold the end of our labour.

You see I have been roughing it; and, though some parts of the letter may be neither very comprehensible nor very interesting to *you*, I think that perhaps it might amuse Willie Traquair, who delights in all such dirty jobs.

The first day, I forgot to mention was like mid-winter for cold, and rained incessantly so hard that the livid white of our cold-pinched faces wore a sort of enflamed rash on the windward side.

I am not a bit the worst of it, except fore-mentioned state of hands, a slight crick in my neck from the rain running down and general stiffness from pulling hauling and tugging for dear life.

We have got double weights at the guys and hope to get it up like a shot.

We had twelve men on at last.

I'm going to call on the Rutherfords today.

What fun you three[2] must be having. I think I see — cheating at cards! I hope the cold don't disagree with you. I remain, my dear Mother your affectionate son   R.L. Stevenson

A letter came to me today addressed thus:

Mr J. Henderson.
Mechanic

And another:

Mr R.L. Stevenson.

Didn't I foam!

---

[2] TS was on a business visit to the west coast. MIS and Mary Warden (who was with the Stevensons throughout September) went with him and were busy sightseeing.

Was ultima thule grand? The *Courant*[3] must have been exciting lately. I said to send whenever there was a review, a piece of literary intelligence or anything interesting. It has never come: consequently there has never been a review or anything interesting in the *Courant* since I left. Good luck to it! I wish the paper all success; but this doesn't promise well for an extended circulation.   R.L.S.[4]

63   To Bob Stevenson

MS Yale. The dedication verses privately printed in *Monmouth* (1928), xv.

Friday [?18][1] *September 1868*   [*Wick*]

My dear Bob, When I wrote you my last letter I was under the influence of a morbid frame of mind which attacks me often. Try to forget it. The morbid frame comes from solitude in great part: for the rest, takes its rise in an insane lust after human approbation, as I said before. When it is on me, I write, write, write – no matter what, under a vain delusion that my name will live in proportion to the number of foolscap pages covered with sprawling and half-illegible handwriting.

I must say you are a noble correspondent. One would have imagined now that such a letter as mine, if it did not deserve a strait-waistcoat, at least merited a pretty speedy answer. Well – let us take a man as we find him – I find you a bad correspondent: you find me morbidly insane on one point.

A propos, I have dedicated the rotten play of *Monmouth* to a friend of mine – the deedest correspondent I ever met with: it is enclosed for your approbation, condemnation or correction.

> 'Tis thus and thus that I shall sing:
> It don't require much predication
> To tell I'll have a dedication;
> For – p'raps it comes from eddication –
> I like the sort of thing.

Last letter I was melancholy mad: 'tonight my heart is merry', and I shall speak in a composed manner a few notions that have come into my head: they are what I would call 'Holmeisms' after Oliver Wendel H. – author of the thing I sent you about John's John, William's John and the real John.[2]

There are two English epics: *Paradise Lost* and *Jack the Giant Killer*.

Do you know I am entirely incapable of lyric verse – cannot even command lyric measures – cannot even appreciate it. Horace of course I

---

[3] An Edinburgh newspaper.
[4] The letter contains three 'Illustrative Diagrams' explaining how the pole was erected.
[1] A conjectural date. It may have been written on the following Friday.
[2] Oliver Wendell Holmes, *The Autocrat of the Breakfast-Table* (1858), ch. 3.

like; because he is *so supremely a gentleman*: that I think is Horace's charm; but of both Horace and Pope, something may be said, and I daresay has been said. It is not so much the thing they say, as the way they say it. Thus it is that they are so necessary to read, so intensely useful for quotation. The dicta are often trivial and commonplace, or so undeniably true as become part of orthodox-boredom; but when you find an idea put in either of them, *it is put in its optimum form*. Strive for years and you will not put it so well: Labour for centuries and you will not put it better. And this in different ways: both for brevity and concentration: Horace for felicity of epithet: Pope for close epigrammatic, antithetical writing. But Horace is an easy polished gentleman: Pope something of a mouthing, pompous school-master.

'Christy Minstrels', 'Star Slave Troups', 'Nigger-Break-down men' and the like existed in Shakespeare's age. To the proof, *Winter's Tale*, Act I, scene 1. 'But were they *false as o'er-dyed blacks*, as winds, as waters'.[3]

Do you think Job's birthday was the 29th of February 'As for that night let darkness seize upon it: let it not be joined to the days of the year, let it not come into the number of the months.'[4]

What a noble book that old tragedy is! I have a pocket edition: it is everything: at once the truest poetry, the most animated and natural controversy, the subtlest philosophy, and the voice of God. Observe to write a commentary – an appreciative commentary – you would require the poet, the philosopher, the theologist, the devotee. I find my answer to many a vext question in the pages of the grand old play. How true is everything said on either side! So with men's views in all things. Again, when I hear a man prating about his reason in connexion with the almighty polity, clipping this doctrine and rejecting that, I say to him in spirit the noble, glorious speech of God with which the whole concludes. 'Where wast thou when I laid the foundations of the earth? . . . Whereupon are the founda-tions thereof fastened? or who laid the corner stone thereof; when the morning stars sang together and all the sons of God shouted for joy?' And so on to the end: 'Shall he that contendeth with the Almighty answer him? He that reproveth God, let him answer it.'[5]

The prose of this Job is something beyond praise. How superior really

---

[3] The Christy Minstrels were one of the most famous of the troupes of 'Negro Minstrels', originating in the USA but equally popular in Britain, who were in their heyday at this time; in Britain the name was often used to describe any such show. White men with blackened faces performed a highly ritualized entertainment of what purported to be Negro songs and dances (including a riotous dance called a 'breakdown'), accompanied by banjos and other primitive musical instruments and interspersed with simple jokes and wisecracks. The Shakespearian refer-ence is *The Winter's Tale*, I.ii.131–2.

[4] Job 3:6.

[5] Job 38:4 and 40:2.

noble prose is to the noblest verse: verse after all is but a gelding (comic epigram: I charge exstry for this).

Imagine monsters who don't think Artemus Ward funny![6] I must tell you a good story in dialogue *formâ*. Characters represented myself, a young fellow. Y.F. 'Where is Dhuheartach?' M. 'O! Ultima Thule!' Y.F. 'Where is that place? It's a wildish bit, I guess; but they're going to make a railway to it and MacDonald's got the contract!' All this in good faith and earnest: I grew pale. Ever your affectionate friend and cousin   R.L. Stevenson

R.A.M. Stevenson Esq.

To R.A.M.S.
I dedicate this play

Worthier had been this offering of thee,
   Clad in the fancied colours that it wore,
Whilst it was still a glorious dream to be
   Hereafter carried forth − a hope before
And not the fragments, thin and ill-combined,
Of an unremedied defeat behind.

Worthier had been this offering of thee −
   A fairer garland for a nobler brow −
Hadst thou agreed to share the work with me
   And been co-author and not critic now:
Therefore, if aught is bad, the fault is thine:
Remember that and spare me, critic mine.

Such as it is, to thee I offer it,
   The worthiest offering that I could make,
A pledge of friendship of itself unfit:
   Not for its own, but for its author's sake,
Accept this now; and let me hope again
To dedicate to thee some nobler strain.

Since I have come here, I have written next to nothing: I am engaged on other work. I tried two metrical narratives, with what success I cannot judge. The subject of the one is 'Jeroboam and Ahijah' 1st Kings XIV, 1 to 18 − a splendid story: the other is Chaucer's tale of the three young men who rode out to find death.[7] The one in heroic quatrains, a little irregular in parts: the other in heroic couplets − a measure I do not like. I can write nothing but heroics.   R.L.S.

[6] Pen name of Charles Farrar Browne (1834−67), American humorist and lecturer who used comic mis-spellings. RLS was evidently reading *Artemus Ward: His Book* (1862). A number of RLS's intentional comic mis-spellings in letters of this period and for the rest of his life come from Ward.
[7] 'The Pardoner's Tale' in *The Canterbury Tales*.

64   *To his Mother*[1]

MS Yale. Partly published in *Letters*, I, 24–6 as part of Letter 67.

Read letter first

A Monody
On the Death of Mr Pogue O'Nelle[2]
In the Augustan Taste

Good

Ye nymphs that haunt this barren coast around
Wake briny bays to elegiac sound,
While, in unwilling and funereal verse
The virtues I, of Pogue O'Nelle rehearse.
Ah too-soon-snatched-away! the cruel fate
When with sharp scissor, on a mournful date,
She clipped the cord that held your joyous life
With poison first had smeared the fatal knife.
Say, was it not enough that you should die?
Must spite insult thy spirit ere it fly?
Must gloomy death with gloomier shame be padded,
And insult to the injury be added?
To men of honour – (all who hear this verse) –
The way we die makes death the best or worse.
Then what a trick of cruel-hearted fate,
To hurl inglorious death on glorious pate!
And make an honest dog – ('tis past belief!) –
Expire by hanging like a common thief!
Each mournful brow with fancied cypress drape,
And wreathe my pen with folds of sombre crape,
With grief imaginary cloud each face
And time thy walk to sad funereal pace.

Good

Do all thou canst and, all thou canst not, try
To make the manner of his ending die.
But still henceforward, legends must relate
And cold historians tell with pompous state
And fervid poets murmur on the gale:
Pogue was found hanging on an area rail.

---

[1] The first part of this letter (mis-dated 12 September by MIS) is written on a large sheet of paper with the poem on the reverse. The continuation of it, written on Sunday and Monday on small sheets of paper, has become mixed up with the MS of another Sunday letter (Letter 67) about another storm.

[2] Identified by MIS as the Wardens' dog.

Pieces marked are considered really Pope'ian.

The verses must be read with solemnity, emphasis and deliberation.

Robert's voice must be impressive.[3]

Saturday [19 September 1868]   [*Wick*]

My last letter should have been dated Friday.

My dear Mother, On the reverse you will find an exact imitation of Pope: in spite of the intrinsic difficulty of the subject I have succeeded in preserving the pompous, empty and magniloquent rhythm and language. It is the real outcome of my feelings: as I said before, I cannot sufficiently regret the unfortunate manner of his death.

I found only Miss Rutherford in, when I called – the Capting and his Missis being away from home. After a *tête-a-tête* of a certain stookiness, I left. The visit has borne fruits. Miss Russel – *Sheriffi fillia*[4] – was in the house, took home the news to her mother. In the afternoon the card of 'A. Sedgwick Russel, Esq., 9 Breadalbane Terrace' was on my table. That evening I went up to Macdonalds. During my absence the Russels sent down to ask me to come up for an hour as the Sinclairs of Dunbeath[5] were there. When I came up, I said with Polyphemus in *Acis and Galatea*:

> 'Torture! Fury! Rage! Despair!
> I cannot, cannot, cannot bear!'

(Kookler[6] was very fine in that song: he appeared to draw torture, fury, rage and despair from some dyspeptic sufferance at an unfathomable depth in his stomach). Of course after they had sent twice, I called this morning. Saw old R., his Missis, Miss R., A. Sedgwick – all very nice people indeed, I think. They asked me to come to tea tonight; so I've been overhauling my costume. No more yenow, but remains. After tea will tell ye.[7]

Sunday [20 September]

Storm without: wind and rain: a confused mass of wind-driven rain-squalls, wind-ragged mist, foam, spray and great, grey waves. Of this hereafter: in the meantime let us follow the due course of historic narrative.

---

[3] In 'Rosa Quo Locorum', RLS recalls an occasion at school when his reading aloud was commended by the master: ' "Robert's voice," said the master on this memorable occasion, "is not strong, but impressive": an opinion which I was fool enough to carry home to my father; who roasted me for years in consequence.' MIS records in her diary, 7 March 1861: 'Mr Henderson says "Robert's reading is not loud but it's *impressive*." '

[4] Hamilton Russel W.S. (1801–81) was Sheriff-Substitute of Caithness 1849–80. He married (1839) Mary Poole Blackburne (died 1883). Their only daughter, Sara Elizabeth Walrond, died in 1872, aged twenty.

[5] Presumably Sir John Sinclair, 6th Bt., of Dunbeath (1794–1873).

[6] Probably Heinrich Kuchler (1815–73), a popular music teacher, conductor and baritone singer who lived in Edinburgh. The reference is to Handel's oratorio.

[7] The letter continues on smaller paper, headed 'Sheet 2'.

Seven P.M. found me at 9 Breadalbane Terrace, clad in spotless blacks, white tie, shirt, *et caetera*, and finished off below with a pair of navvies' boots. How true that the devil is betrayed by his feet! A message to Cummy at last: Why O traitorous woman! were my dress boots withheld? Dramatis personae: père Russel, amusing, long-winded, in many points like papa: mère Russel, nice, delicate, Aunt Margaret, likes hymns, knew Aunt Margaret[8] (t'ould man knew Uncle Alan): fille Russel: nomine Sara (no h), rather nice, lights up well, good voice, *interested* face: Miss Latta, poor dependent, kind of slavey to Miss Sara, nice also, washed out a little and, I think, a trifle sentimental: fils Russel, Adam Sedgwick, in a Leith office, smart, full of happy epithet, amusing, pompous, tuft-hunter. The last applies to Madame and Mademoiselle who, in showing photograph book, said with a certain air: 'Lord Clarence Paget, my mother's uncle.'[9] It is Sir John and Sir George and Sir Gregory till I feel inclined to put in a crasher: I could spoke the wheel with considerable ease too: 'tis an awful temptation. Nevertheless, they are very nice and very kind, asked me to come back – 'any night you feel dull; and any night doesn't mean no night: we'll be so glad to see you' – *C'est la mère qui parle.* Mademoiselle, Miss Latta, and Miss Rutherford, to whom they put the question today, without any connivance all guessed my name to be William; but the two former, at least, were kind enough to express themselves vastly pleased with Lewis.

From the remark about Miss Rutherford, you will see I was back there again tonight. It wasn't my fault: Adam would have me in; and Sunday evenings are so dull. There was hymn singing, and general religious contro-versy till eight: after which talk was secular. Besides the elegant compliment about my name, and the unconscious confession of the rarity and interest of a stranger conveyed in carrying the question to Miss R., I have got a second go for my feet. Mrs Sutherland[10] was deeply distressed about the boot business. She consoled me by saying I should not fall in love with Sara, because she thought I was gey particular – not logic though – and by saying that many would be glad to have such feet, whatever shoes they had on. Unfortunately fishers and seafaring men are too facile to be compared with! This looks like enjoyment: better speck than Anster.

I have done with frivolity. This morning I was awakened by Mrs S. at the door. 'There's a ship ashore at Shaltigoe!'[11] As my senses slowly flooded, I

---

[8] Margaret Scott Stevenson (1812–95), daughter of Humphrey Jones of Llynon, Anglesey (Comp-troller of Customs, Holyhead), widow of Alan Stevenson and mother of Bob. Usually known as 'Aunt Alan' and later as 'Gatchie'.

[9] Lord Clarence Edward Paget (1811–95), son of the Marquess of Anglesey; Commander-in-Chief in the Mediterranean 1866–9, Admiral 1870. I can find no family link between the Pagets and the Russels.

[10] George Sutherland was the proprietor of the New Harbour Hotel.

[11] The loss of the *Sophia* from Drammen, Norway, with a cargo of battens, at the height of the storm on Sunday morning 20 September, is reported in the local press.

heard the whistling and the roaring of wind, and the lashing at the wind of gust-blown and uncertain flaws of rain. I got up, dressed and went out. The mizzled sky and rain blinded you.

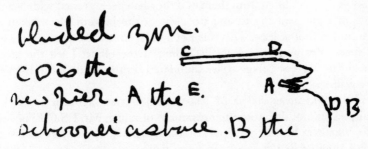

C D is the new pier. A the schooner ashore. B the salmon house.

She was a Norwegian: coming in she saw our first gauge pole, standing at point E. Norge skipper thought it was a sunk smack, and dropped his anchor in full drift of sea: chain broke: schooner came ashore. Insured: laden with wood: skipper owner of vessel and cargo: bottom out.

I was in a great fright at first lest we should be liable; but it seems that's all right.

Some of the waves were twenty feet high. The spray rose eighty feet at the new pier. Some wood has come ashore, and the roadway seems carried away. There is something fishy at the far end where the cross wall is building; but till we are able to get along, all speculation is vain.

I am so sleepy I am writing nonsense.

I stood a long while on the cope watching the sea below me – I hear its dull, monotonous roar at this moment below the shrieking of the wind – ; and there came ever recurring to my mind, the verse I am so fond of:

> But yet the Lord that is on high
> Is more of might by far,
> Than noise of many waters is
> Or great sea-billows are.[12]

The thunder at the wall when it first struck – the rush along ever growing higher – the great jet of snow-white spray some forty feet above you – and the 'noise of many waters', the roar, the hiss, the 'shrieking' among the shingle as it fell head over heels at your feet. I watched if it threw the big stones at the wall; but it never moved them.

Monday [21 September]

The end of the work displays gaps, cairns of ten ton blocks, stones torn from their places and turned right round. The damage above water is

---

[12] Scottish metrical version of Psalm 93:4.

comparatively little: what there may be below, *on ne sait pas encore*. The roadway is torn away, cross-heads broken, planks tossed here and there, planks gnawn and mumbled as if a starved bear had been trying to eat them, planks with spales lifted from them as if they had been dressed with a ragged plane, one pile swaying to and fro clear of the bottom, the rails in one place sunk a foot at least. This was not a great storm, the waves were light and short. Yet when we were[13] standing at the office, I felt the ground beneath me *quail* as a huge roller thundered on the work at the last year's cross-wall.

How could *noster amicus M. maximus* appreciate a storm at Wick. It requires a little of the artistic temperament of which Mr T.S.C.E. possesses some, whatever he may say. I can't look at it practically however: that will come I suppose like gray hair or coffin nails.

That man Holmes is really splendid. 'To be married into some families is next door to being canonized.'[14] Couldn't I name the family! Our pole is snapped: a fortnight's work and the loss of the Norge schooner all for nothing! – except experience and dirty clothes. Your affectionate son

R.L. Stevenson

P.S. *Monday Evening.* Asked to go to Ackrigale (Sir G. Dunbar's)[15] tomorrow or next day. *Le ciel s'ouvre!*

65   *To his Parents*

Text: *Letters*, I, 15–17.[1]

Wednesday [*23 September 1868*]   *Wick*

My dear Father, I am awfully sorry about Anstruther. It was that confounded Billow Ness-hearting[2] – so much sand, French chalk coagulated with water! It is the very last stuff to put for hearting at any rate; for it will crush to bits. I suppose it washed out from the open end; and the sea *exploded* the Inner-wall. I fancy Adamson's face! Poor, poor bankrupt Harbour Commission! I am glad the sea-wall stood; but I quake for it tonight: the wind is up again, and the sea; the men could do nothing today. *J'espère qu'il tiendra!*

---

[13] MS: are.

[14] Oliver Wendell Holmes, *The Guardian Angel* (1867), ch. 35.

[15] Sir George Dunbar, 4th Bt., of Hempriggs (1799–1875) lived at Ackergill Tower two miles north of Wick. This postscript is written at the top of the first page.

[1] I have corrected three misreadings in the text first published in the Vailima Edition: 'Ivory-wall' for 'Inner-wall'; 'Harbour Compinpéon' for 'Harbour Commission' and 'Adam Rupel' for 'Adam Russel'.

[2] Billow Ness is the western headland of Anstruther bay; 'hearting' is the filling.

There is an awful mess below water here; but him–and–I is in great glee about it. 'When he seen the account, he took the arm of (someone not known action illustrated on me) and he pointed to the breakwater': 'Sixty pounds'll do us' was his remarkable speech. It was awfully decent of him to write that about me;[3] and I am glad it went through the hands of somebodee!

My dear Mother, The rest of the letter will be more acceptable to you. Did you not get my letter about the lighter work the one I told you to show to Willie? If you did not, it has gone astray and should be seen to.

Mrs Wemyss (Sir George Dunbar's niece and house keeperess) asked me on Monday to go to Ackergill Tower either on Tuesday or Wednesday. On Wednesday[4] I and Adam Russel got a boat and took Sara R. and the latter person (in future I shall call them the former and the latta) out for a row. I reckoned that decidedly 'cuter; and elected Wednesday for Ackergill. To-day it blew, it rained. What could I do? Rain excused today; but what about yesterday? So I e'en trudged it. Mrs Wemyss is so nice and so kind that I was not sorry I had persevered. She has a son there, the handsomest lad I ever saw, a midshipman in the *Warrior*.[5] Poor fellow! he burst a blood vessel some time ago. He does not know it is in his lungs. It is very sad to see him. His breathing becomes sometimes very short and bad, and he has a hard, painful cough. Poor Mrs W. looks so very much put about when he coughs. She has the prettiest little children I ever saw. I was there till about four, lunched in a panelled 'baronial' hall quite scenic in its appearance. It is a delightful old house with a green room and a red room, the spectre of a black cook who fell into the well-hole and the ghost of an interesting young lady who flung herself off the top of the tower, because she had been *abduced* or abducted, or whatever it is, and kept in durance vile by its amiable possessor. She asked me to come back again before I left, lent me books and said that 'Will' (name of the sick fellow) should call on me the first time he was out. I got a lift in, in a 'gig' – merciful powers, a gig! and from a tower! extremes meet – such is life! (which I take it is not the *first* time that the last ingenious remark has been made).

The row was no end: seven feet of a swell: imagine Mademoiselle teasing me by saying: 'Tell us something to make us laugh, Mr Stevenson.' Adam the first said it was as bad as being introduced to a girl as 'a very funny

---

[3] In a letter to TS of 12 September reporting the previous week's activities, David MacDonald wrote: 'Master Stevenson is taking much interest in the matter and also in all that is going on he is most attentive.'

[4] A mistake for Tuesday.

[5] *HMS Warrior*, the first all-iron warship, launched in 1860. She has recently been fully restored and is on show at Portsmouth.

person.' What wit is it that says it should be said to you ere you sit to be photographed, in order to induce a fitting solemnity of visage.

I am glad Papa is better: the sea-side does not agree so well as the hills with him. Your affectionate son   R.L. Stevenson

66 To his Mother

MS Yale.

Saturday ＊[26 September 1868]   *New Harbour Hotel [Wick]*

My dear Mother, *Inspice inclusam (epistolam* understood): *responsionem demisi: nullum dicandum habeo: hic incipit fabula mea: nullum dicandum habeo: hic explicit fabula mea (traductio in linguam vulgi:-*

> 'Nothing have I for to say:
> In this my story doth begin:
> Nothing have I for to say:
> This my story endeth in')

Hope to get pole up today – the broken half of it, I mean to splice another end on. But 'tis the workmen's pleasure, ma'am, that we have to attend on (twig: pothry). Nomore yenow, bot melancoli thochtes in the mattere of myn unhappie bootes, ones more to be displaide. Your affection-ate son   R.L. Stevenson

67 To his Mother

MS Yale. Partly published in *Letters*, I, 23–4, with part of Letter 64.

Sunday [27 September 1868]   *Pulteney*

My dear Mother, Another storm: wind higher, rain thicker: the wind still rising as the night closes in and the sea slowly rising along with it: it looks like a three days' gale. Where and how, O Anstruther?

Last week has been a blank one: always too much sea.

I enjoyed myself very much last night at Rutherfords. There was a little dancing, much singing and supper. Present four Rutherfords two Cox's (Inspector of Customs daughters),[1] former and latter, Russel and I. Three gentlemen to seven ladies! The species is extinct in Wick; and even ladies are I believe bounded by the seven who were present. I had a headache, and *positively could* not have eaten one morsel. The situation was awkward. Had

[1] Caleb Cox, Collector of Customs and Landing Surveyor.

they been your pressing people where should I have been? Neither of them pressed me, proving that he was a gentleman and she was a lady. I explained to the capting after his missus had left and so got out of an awkward fix. Such prime cigars Rutherford gave us! two of 'em, nine inches long if they were one! Manillas.

Tuesday [29 September]

MacIntosh came yesterday: I dined with him at the New Hotel.

Are you not well that you do not write? I haven't heard from you for near a fortnight.

The wind fell yesterday and rose again today; it is a dreadful evening; but the wind is keeping the sea down as yet. Of course nothing more has been done to the poles; and I can't tell when I shall be able to leave, not for a fortnight yet I fear, at the earliest, for the winds are persistent. Where's Murra?[2] Is Cummie struck dumb about the boots? I wish you would get somebody to write an interesting letter and say how you are, for you're on the broad of your back I see.

There hath arrived an inroad of farmers tonight; and I go to avoid them to MacIntosh if he's disengaged, to the Russels if not.[3]

68   *To his Father*

MS Buffalo.

Thursday night [1 October 1868]   [*Wick*]

My dear Father, This has been a great day in Wick. The foreman joiner went to the review and by so doing prevented me. It was a perfectly calm day; and both poles might have been up by this time. I was awfully angry. I stayed at the works and got everything ready for him in case he should deign to appear on the afternoon shift; but my gentleman had washed his hands. It is a shamefully mismanaged work – nobody in charge, you know. If *I* ask a workman to do anything (aye – or even MacDonald) O! it can't be done – 'Mr Robertson said something about it: we'd better wait till he comes' or 'I must get on with the crane.'

We have had continual heavy sea here, and only one day for the divers, since the Sunday before last. The work has stood splendidly. The whole seaward or north-easterly corner is torn up to the bottom course; but the

---

[2] Another nickname for Mary Warden.

[3] The end of this sentence is written across the top of the first page, suggesting that there was no more to this letter, even though it is unsigned. The MS has become muddled with that of Letter 64.

cross wall is intact. MacDonald was measuring today; and he found that the building had *spread* two or three inches.

I hear the steamer saves a great deal of money: if these dilatory vagabonds would only gird up their loins I might leave on Tuesday which would be very nice as Miss Russel and some others are going at the same time: if not, I think I should get away by the Thursday boat.

Is Mamma well; and why do I never get a letter. I haven't had one since Monday.

Lord Caithness[1] called in yesterday at the Harbour Office about something; and he did me the honour of asking for me: I was out: his Lordship having spent the whole afternoon previous within sight of me on the staging. Lady Caithness had made him promise not to go down this last, so he halted near shore. Your affectionate son   R.L. Stevenson

69   *To his Mother*

MS Silverado. Published (with a few omissions) in *Letters*, I, 26–9.

Friday 2 October 1868   *Pulteney Hotel*
11.30 P.M.

My dear Mother, 'Ha my prophetic soul!'[1] how true thou prophesied! or prophesiedest; but the latter is bad orthography and spoils the Alexandrine (*Nota Bene*: Papa will again object to poetry). I knew you were on the broad of your back. Second withering blast of prophecy: – *you have been at church!*!! I am glad you are better.

To desert these windy and perilous heights of prophecy and grandeur, let me court the hum-drum muse of epistolary diction: you see I am still a little Poped: indeed he fairly *pooped* me! (Beg pardon.)

Miss J.J.? Where are thy thoughts? – Miss Janie Jamieson, to be sure!

On Wednesday, the Russels sent for me to come at eight. Wondering, I went. (Stay – a little gossip first. . . .[2] Enough – more than enough of gossip! To go on.) Forma and Latta (forma translates nicely: supposing an elision thus – '(*pulcherrima*) *forma*',[3] which Papa will translate) Miss Cox, Adamus et ego were to go a walk *per amica silentia lunae*, 'under the friendly

[1] The Earl of Caithness reviewed the Caithness Volunteers at Wick on 1 October – a great social occasion. James Sinclair (1821–81), 14th Earl of Caithness, was Lord Lieutenant of the county and Governor of the British Fisheries Society. He was the inventor of a steam carriage, a gravitating compass and a tape-loom.

[1] *Hamlet*, I.v.40.

[2] Two lines (eight or nine words) deleted by MIS.

[3] Most lovely.

silence of the moon' – ahem! Virgil![4] to quote Pangloss[5] – to the Old Man of Wick, a ruinous Tower on a neck of beetling cliff, with two roaring chasms of foam and a wild coast of crag and cave and boulder trending away on either hand (Papa here once more condemns Tatleranean tendency and deplores same). I entertained Sara and the latter woman: Adamus, Miss Cox. Or course on occasions, it faded into an insipided party of five; but that was the usual arrangement. We sat down outside the tower and watched 'The moon-chased shadows fly across the white fields of foam'. The latter, who is very romantic and likes Byron, Scott, dim moonlight and faded lovers, found her heart too full for words and retired to a far pinnacle, like Elijah the Tishbite, alone.

I was so much amused at Mrs Russel (who is a very nice body, albeit a Paget of the Pagets and the real Pagets, whence comes the tuftism): she was so frightened: we were to keep away from the rocks: we were to do this: I was to put on her shawl (which however I secreted in the lobby): we were to do that; but, above all, was she distressed over a portion of Sara's attire, a garment called, I am told, a p-t-c-t. This part of her apparel had been scrupulously cleansed for Germanee, and they feared that, passing through the mire, it might become soiled. In my eagerness to oblige not only did I become bound to wear the shawl and become answerable for the necks and future health of the whole party; but I actually offered a guarantee for the safe return of the said portion of attire or wearing apparel or the aforesaid garment, namely the p-t-c-t: whereat, *on rit*. We had a very pleasant walk.

So you left Swanston yesterday. *Heu scelerata jacet sedes in Heriot Row*! (How classical I have become – haven't I) As this substitution makes the line a foot too short, you will be pleased to proceed on the 'Murray of Murray's Ha-ha' principle, and say 'Row-ow,' which makes it correct. The line is the beginning of Ovid's description of Tartarus;[6] so it's rather hard on 'sweet seventeen' after all. And left it yesterday, while I was moiling for Mr Robieson, absent foreman-joiner. Well! well! troubles never come singly!

Today the two poles were put up: the levels taken: the gauges up-fixed; and, with these hands, I cut the paper strips! Tomorrow and Monday we take the observations.

David MacD. and I pulled out in the boat to the bay's mouth when the men were done. The moon rose, red and 'rideeclous magnified' from the

---

[4] *Aeneid*, II.255.

[5] Dr Pangloss, the pompous tutor in George Colman's play *The Heir-at-Law* (1797), was fond of using quotations and then identifying the author.

[6] '*At scelerata jacet sedes in nocte profunda*' (But the accursed place lies in deep gloom) is in fact from Tibullus, I.iii.67. Ovid's phrase from *Metamorphoses* iv.257 is '*sedes scelerata vocatur*' (the place is called accursed).

breast of the sea. It was a lovely night. A lugger out for the night's fishing passed close by: it looked tall, filmy and unnatural in the dim light: we could only see the outline. At last, it drove 'betwixt the moon and us' – ahem! Coleridge![7] (Pangloss again) –: you would have been delighted. We pulled back, moored the boat at the outmost ladder and walked in along the staging. Suddenly D.M. stopped; I thought he looked livid about the gills. 'The dog!' he gasped.

'What about the dog? The dog knows *you*?' said I, a little chilled.

'I don't know that though,' he said; 'and even when he wasn't so fierce, I seen★ him set on a young man that came down with me.'

Didn't I feel happy: we armed ourselves with stones; and very cautiously crept down the staging, trying to whistle and look calm.

After all we did not see him.

Mrs Wemyss and her son called here today. I must go out either on Saturday or Monday whichever day I can get the time. For I am to leave on Toosda and chaperone Forma and Latta down: that's rather a spec., isn't it?

This here letter has been intended to be very witty, very amusing, very romantic, very entertaining in general. The only thing that broke down was the gossip; I had an awful vision of parental brows in awful anger bent; and parental lips saying: 'Put nothing in black and white.' Besides what it seems but little malicious to say, seems perfectly diabolical on paper – the mean, low hits that flourish in the bitter satire of the satanic Byron. But isn't it true about Southey for all that. 'Immortal Hero' – this is Thalaba '. . . for ever reign. . . . Since startled metre fled before thy face!'[8]

I could not write to Myrrha; her name is so hard to spell. I remain, Ever your affectionate son   R.L. Stevenson

'*Parcite, ab urbe venit, jam parcite* epistolae, Robert.'[9] Another Hexameter neatly altered. If Papa could only scan, he would admire it.

When your letter came I said, '*Demum!*'[10] followin' my present classical bent.

★ As the old cock, etc. '*Le coq chanter*'.[11]

---

[7] 'Betwixt us and the sun' – Coleridge, 'The Ancient Mariner', Part III.

[8] Byron, 'English Bards and Scotch Reviewers', ll. 215–18.

[9] '*Parcite, ab urbe venit, jam parcite carmina, Daphnis*' (Cease, cease your songs; Daphnis is coming from the town) – Virgil, *Eclogues*, viii.109.

[10] At last.

[11] Cf. the proverb 'As the old cock crows the young cock learns', quoted by Scott in *The Pirate*, ch. 18. RLS presumably means that young MacDonald was speaking like his father.

70   To His Mother

MS Silverado.

Toosda *[6 October 1868]   *Pulteney*

My dear Mother, Come by land – leave tonight – shall be home about Saturday I think – all well – hope you're ditto. Ever your affectionate son
R.L. Stevenson

P.S. Accounts is confusion.

71   To Bob Stevenson

MS Yale. Published (with omission of the postscript) in G.S. Hellman, *The True Stevenson* (1925), 119–22.

Thursday 2 [?22] October 1868[1]   *17 Heriot Row*

My dear Bob, Your very friendly and interesting letter has at once pleased and disappointed me more than I can tell.[2] For a long time back my mind has been in an unhealthy state of agitation and filled with a silent shifting of squadrons, if so I may speak, that seems to shadow forth some great advance or some great retreat. Let me hope the former. Among the subjects which particularly disturbed me and gave me pain was the fact that my life, though by me most keenly enjoyed was of use to no one else. A dead pandering to the senses: simply such life as we see shadowed forth in the works of Keats, who, by the way, I almost think more destructive than Swinburne. In the latter, although we have all the fiery maddening pleasure of sin burning on the paper, there is still a tang of bitter remorse, a loathsome something that draws the veil aside and lets us see the white ashes gushing from the Sodom's apple, and the clanking bones of the skeleton below the fair, white, smooth skin and flesh on which the sensual poet gloats. To read Swinburne long would either make you mad or moral. The meretricious hand burns the sense as it fondles it, like the hand of the spectre knight in Scott's grand ballad.[3] Swinburne's sensualism is too deep: it works its own cure. Far

---

[1] RLS did not arrive home from Wick until 10 October. This letter is in reply to one from Bob dated 18 October. Thursday 22 October seems the most likely date.

[2] An eighteen-page letter of incoherent outpourings on philosphy and religion in response to RLS's Letters 56 and 63. In the course of it, Bob wrote: 'Oh if I had talent and if I could overcome my fearful foe indolence I would write and write preach and speak to the world. . . . I have given up all ideas of talented execution of anything only I hope with God's Grace and as far as my indolence permits me to live and *think* up to as high a standard as I can and to read aright those helps which God has given even to those least talented to live independent of the narrow views of worldly interest and worldly philosophy and in a measure to cast off weight of low thoughts.'

[3] 'The Eve of Saint John'.

otherwise is it with Keats. He is the sensuous poet, Swinburne the sensual. He is soft, dreamy, delicious. Summer breezes fan you to an idle languour, as they lisp and murmur through the music of his lines. There is, to use his own overstrained expression, 'a leafy pleasure'[4] in his works. You sleep in long forest alleys: you hear the murmur of rivers and the slumbrous drone of bees: you are introduced into not higher company than the worthless old classic gods. In a word he lulls where he should arouse and relaxes where he should brace. His highest ideal is beauty.

> 'A thing of beauty is a joy forever.'

And again,

> 'Beauty is truth, truth beauty – that is all
> Ye know on earth and all ye need to know.'

What a grovelling ideal! What an enervating atmosphere!

In such a mock paradise, shut out from what was harsh and dissonant, I have hitherto been living. But I am shaking up a little. I have wakened and am in a transition. Your letter has helped to brace and strengthen me: I thank you for it most sincerely. It is all very well to write and write: that is what I like. To do good by writing besides one must write little. I am entering on a profession which must engross the strength of my powers and to which I shall try to devote my energies. What I should prefer would be to search dying people in lowly places of the town and help them; but *I cannot trust myself* in such places. I told you my weak point before and you will understand me. This is a great clog to me. How can a man take any step, when he has not full faith that he can maintain an openly reputable 'walk and conversation'? This I have not, very much the reverse. Now the utmost I contemplate at present is a very low step – teaching in a Sunday school. I think it is always doing something – nay always doing a very great deal. But – have I a right to talk theology *ex cathedra* to poor boys when my own account is not made up, when my own life is a mere tissue of appearances and flimsy barriers that the first breath of temptation may blow to the winds? Again, have I a right for that to hold back my labour from the vineyard, and condemn others whom my services might help, because my own soul is not well. Again, is it not always something? 'That which a man doeth affects himself, but that which a man sayeth shall shake the very world.' If it was a reproach when hurled from head-wagging priests and Pharisees to our Saviour on the cross, might it not be even a boast to such as I: 'Himself he could not save; and yet he saved others.'[5]

I think I shall take it up; and so, may God assist me.

[4] RLS is probably thinking of 'A leafy luxury' in Keats's 'Dedication to Leigh Hunt'.
[5] Matthew 27:42.

For yourself, I have something to say. Our worthy old minister is accustomed to pray for 'those who are kept from church by indolence mistaken for indisposition.' May I apply it? You have no talents, you say, and you have given up all attempts to be distinguished. Is this right? You *have* intellect, a more powerful mind that I by a very long way, though I know well what your defects are: it was given you to use. Remember the servant who had one talent may have plied her broom very well, yet the unused talent condemned her, and the one who had only gained two was less praised than he who gained five. 'To whom much has been given'[6] – *et caetera*. Your indolence was given you to conquer not to bewail: your talents were given you to use. With best wishes, ever believe me, your affectionate friend and cousin   R.L. Stevenson

P.S. As to what you said, in re relationship: relationship is but the body, friendship the soul; without the latter, the former is a corpse too heavy for the pair to drag between them and often corrupting in their very hands.

I shall copy out the bit about Keats and Swinburne. I may write an article in which it would suit.

Your letter shall be preserved among my treasures. Believe me your friendship and the kind interest you display in me will not be forgotten.

Monmouth already stinks a little in my nostrils. Your letter has helped it. It was meant to shadow forth good lessons and true; but they are feeble and too feebly put. They disappear someyon.[7] I shall see however to sending it.

                                                                              R.L.S.

This is quite in your style, Bob. This letter written weeks ago got astray and I haven't sent it off till today.[8]

72   To Bob Stevenson[1]

MS Yale.

17 November 1868   *Edinburgh*

My dear Bob, I have been for a fortnight past confined to bed and the house, a fact which must explain the lateness of my last letter. As a sort of indication of my frame of mind I send you a piece of trash I wrote and wish your solemn criticism with regard to the question touched on in the last

---

[6] 'For unto everyone that hath shall be given, and he shall have abundance . . .' – Matthew 25:29.

[7] I can make no sense of this word which may be a misreading.

[8] A note in pencil at the bottom of the page.

[1] At the top of the letter there is a note by MIS: 'Read the last page first.'

lines. It was first suggested to me by the fact, mentioned in the piece, that I wrote about the sea whilst at Swanston, and about hills, wood etc. while at Anstruther and Wick. I suppose the real truth is that the objects themselves are far too complex for our comprehension, how much more for our description: five square feet of Scotch hillside would take a man a lifetime to describe, and even then how lame, how empty: after he had chronicled heather, whin, bracken, juniper, grass, these little yellow flowers and the rest, it would only be to find that each of these objects taken separately are indescribable, and that their combination is as much above human powers as flying. It is the very weakness of our memories, which by forgetfulness simplifies the scene, that enables us to grasp or to paint the very feeblest piece of nature.

Lying here in my bed, I have been brooding over past walks. Especially our walk *up* the Allan – you remember it? And how after having passed all the wooded banks, we came out past a cavern on a bit of river-meadow 'edged with Poplar pale',[2] surrounded on three sides by the retiring and then re-advancing wooded banks, and on the fourth by the brawling river and the high ground on the farther side. We passed through the meadow and came to a road betwixt two walls and two woods that sloped up the hillside precisely after the fashion of the 'strait and narrow way' between the Interpreter's house and Beëlzebub's garden, in our delightful edition of the delightful book.[3] Only one fault have I to find with the artist's conception: it is too much of a 'deadman's lane', fitter for a bloody robbery than the trashy surfeit of apples, British cholera and pill-boxes with which it is connected in the text. But where I chiefly long to be is at the immediate exit from the wood, where the river splashes through some rapids dewing with spray the over-hanging trees, and you see it bearing away its *taches* of foam, in a slow brown stream between 'the nodding horror of *two* shady brows'.[4]

I am mad for nature just now, have been this summer. I am never satisfied, you understand. I only long and long and long to do something with the beauty that I see, and don't know what to do. I grow delirious over a woodland aisle and foam at the mouth over a hillside, not with the hearty admiration of a genuine man, but a utilitarian, Benthamitical desire to take it and hug it and use and make it a part of myself; and as I cannot do this, lo! my lord waxeth wroth and the fire burns!

[2] Milton, 'Hymn on the Morning of Christ's Nativity', l. 185. For a description of this favourite walk see Letter 97.

[3] The copiously illustrated edition of *Pilgrim's Progress* first published by Samuel Bagster in 1845 had been given to RLS by his parents on 1 January 1858 (listed in Parke-Bernet Catalogue, 19 March 1952, 367, Edith Tranter Sale). RLS later wrote about the illustrations in this edition in *The Magazine of Art*, February 1882.

[4] Milton, *Comus*, l. 38. His mother had given RLS a three-volume edition of Milton's works for his eighteenth birthday (Anderson I, 418).

What an egotistical brute I am! self! self! self! That is the tune, the burthen, the fable, the moral. Self! self! Well you must take me as you find me. I have no confidant, and solemnly, with the exception of my father to whom such matters would be subject for scolding, no *friend* to whom I can speak; so I pour out all the watery and flaccid sentiment that I cook up within, upon you and in pen and ink. My daily life is one repression from beginning to end, and my letters to you are the safety valve. You do not know how few of them you get. I find them lying finished and half finished and scarce-begun among the mouldering remnants of gigantic novels and titanic Romances. Can you be troubled to read all this? The safety valves of a repressed soul, however necessary for its own happiness, do not usually emit a very attractive savour for those whose minds are in a healthy state. You have a rather sore task before you today, *mon ami*: there are plenty coals to be discharged; and discharge them I must and will.

I thank God I was never tempted to disbelieve. My difficulties are very different: I do not feel. Mine is 'a folding of the hands to sleep'.[5] Literature, Nature, Imagination, pretty gewgaws to spend a life upon, with an eternal hell below; yet so I do. God grant I may awake!

Your last letter is one I cherish much. Do you agree to something? If you keep my letters and I keep yours, what a curious retrospect it will be for us? My letters to you would form a history of myself, which, as I am too indolent to write a diary, I should like to have for future instruction and amusement. Perhaps you who know my weakness, too pitiable only to be ludicrous, may guess perhaps at another reason, too contemptible, too *small* for me, candid as I believe myself to be, to put in black and white.

Let me begin with a journey some memorial of which I desire to preserve (for it is a dream, a passionate longing realized) and some sketch of which I wish to send you – my Mail journey from Wick to Golspie.[6]

Night outside the Wick Mail.

The Wick Mail then, my dear fellow, is the last Mail Coach within Great Britain, whence there comes a romantic interest that few could understand. To me, on whose imagination positively nothing took so strong a hold as the Dick Turpins and Claude Duvals of last century, a Mail was an object of religious awe. I pictured the long, dark highways, the guard's blunder-buss, the passengers with three-cornered hats above a mummery of great-coat and cravat; and the sudden 'Stand and deliver!' – the stop, the glimmer of the coach lamp upon the horseman – Ah! we shall never get back to Wick.

[5] Proverbs 24:33.

[6] A fishing village fifty miles south of Wick. All the places mentioned are on the road from Wick to Golspie. The railway did not reach Wick until 1874.

All round that northern capital of stink and storm there stretches a succession of flat and dreary moors absolutely treeless, with the exception of above a hundred bour-trees[7] beside Wick, and a stunted plantation at Stirkoke, for the distance of nearly twenty miles south. When we left to cross this tract, it was cloudy and dark. A very cold and pertinacious wind blew with unchecked violence, across these moorlands. I was sick sleepy, and drawing my cloak over my face set myself to doze. Mine was the box-seat, desirable for the apron and the company of the coachman, a person, in this instance enveloped in that holy and tender interest that hangs about the *Last of the Mohicans* or the *Derniers Bretons*.[8] And as this example of the loquacious genus coachman was more than ordinarily loquacious I put down my hood again and talked with him. He had a philosophy of his own, I found, and a philosophy eminently suited to the needs of his position. The most fundamental and original doctrine of this, was as to what constitutes a gentleman. It was in speaking of Lockyer of Wenbury that I found it out. This man is an audacious quack and charlatan, destined for aught, I know, to be the Cagliostro[9] of the British Revolution; and, as such, Mr Lockyer is no favourite of mine: I hate quacks, not personally (for are they not men of imagination like ourselves?) but because of their influence; so I was rather struck on hearing the following. 'Well sir,' said the coachman, 'Mr Lockyer has always shown himself a perfect gentleman to me, sir – *his hand as open as you'll see, sir*!' In other words, half-a-crown to the coachman! As the pleasures of such philosophical talk rather diminished and the slumber increased, I buried my face again. The coach swayed to and fro. The wind battled and roared about us. I observed the difference in sounds – the rhythmic and regular beat of the hoofs as the horses cantered up some incline, and the ringing, merry, irregular clatter as they slung forward, at a merry trot, along the level.

First stage: Lybster. A Roman Catholic priest travelling within, knowing that I was delicate, made me take his seat inside for the next stage. I dozed. When I woke, the moon was shining brightly. We were off the moors and up among the high grounds near the Ord of Caithness. I remember seeing a curious thing: the moon shone on the ocean, and on a river swollen to a great pool and between stretched a great black mass of rock: I wondered

---

[7] Elder trees.

[8] Fenimore Cooper's novel (1826) and probably a memory of Balzac's *Le Dernier Chouan* (1829), the original title of the novel subsequently called *Les Chouans*.

[9] Giuseppe Balsamo (1743–95) who called himself Count Cagliostro. Italian charlatan who travelled widely in Europe posing as a physician, alchemist and wonder-worker and duped many people with his elixir of long life. He enjoyed enormous success in Parisian high society and was implicated in the plot known as the Affair of the Diamond Necklace, which (although she was innocent) helped to discredit the reputation of Marie Antoinette in the period just before the French Revolution. RLS had probably read the novels about him by Dumas, *Mémoires d'un Médecin: Joseph Balsamo* (1846–8) and *Le Collier de la Reine* (1849–50).

dimly how the river got out and then to doze again. When next I wake, we have passed the low Church of Berriedale, standing sentinel on the heathery plateau northward of the valley, and are descending the steep road past the Manse: I think it was about one: the moon was frosty but gloriously clear. In another minute –

Second stage: Berriedale.[10] And of all lovely places, one of the loveliest. Two rivers run from the inner hills, at the bottom of two deep, Killiekrankie-like gorges, to meet in a narrow bare valley close to the grey North Ocean. The high Peninsula between and the banks, on either hand until they meet, are thickly wooded – birch and fir. On one side is the bleak plateau with the lonesome little church, on the other the bleaker, wilder mountain of the Ord. When I and the priest had lit our pipes, we crossed the streams, now speckled with the moonlight that filtered through the trees, and walked to the top of the Ord. There the coach overtook us and away we went for a stage, over great, bleak mountains, with here and there a hanging wood of silver birches and here and there a long look of the moonlit sea, the white ribbon of the road marked far in front by the newly erected telegraph posts. We were all broad awake with our walk, and made very merry outside, proffering 'fills' of tobacco and pinches of snuff and dipping surreptitiously into aristocratic flasks and plebeian pint bottles.

Third stage: Helmsdale. Round a great promontory with the gleaming sea far away in front, and rattling through some sleeping streets that shone strangely white in the moonlight, and then we pull up beside the Helmsdale posting-house, with a great mountain valley behind. Here I went in to get a glass of whisky and water. A very broad, dark commercial said: 'Ha! do you remember me? Anstruther?'

I had met him five years before in the Anstruther commercial room, when my father was conversing with an infidel and put me out of the room to be away from contamination; whereupon I listened outside and heard the man say he had not sinned for seven years, and declare that he was better than his maker. I did not remember him; nor did he my face, only my voice. He insisted on 'standing me the whisky "for auld lang syne"'; and he being a bagman, it was useless to refuse. Then away again. The coachman very communicative this stage, telling us about the winter before, when the mails had to be carried through on horseback and how they left one of their number sticking in the snow, bag and all I suppose. The country here was softer; low, wooded hills running along beside the shore and all inexpressibly delightful to me after my six months of Wick barrenness and storm.

Fourth stage: name unknown. O sweet little spot, how often I have longed to be back to you! A lone farm-house on the sea-shore, shut in on three sides by the same, low, wooded hills. Men were waiting for us by the

---

[10] A small sketch map of Berriedale is inserted at this point.

roadside, with the horses – sleepy, yawning men. What a peaceful place it was! Everything *steeped* in the moonlight, and the gentle plash of the waves coming to us from the beach. On again. Through Brora, where we stopped at the Post-Office and exchanged letter-bags through a practicable window-pane, as they say in stage directions. Then on again. Near Golspie now, and breakfast, and the roaring railway. Passed Dunrobin, the dew-steeped, tree-dotted park, the princely cluster of its towers, rising from bosky plantations and standing out against the moon-shimmering sea – all this sylvan and idyllic beauty so sweet and new to me! Then the Golspie Inn, and breakfast and another pipe, as the morning dawned, standing in the verandah. And then round to the station to fall asleep in the train.

Such, my dear Bob, was my night journey on the last mail-coach in England. I do not know if I have made it interesting to you; but it has been a kind of era in my life, after a fashion. Believe me, Ever your affectionate friend and cousin   R.L. Stevenson

Read this first [11]

10 December

This unhappy letter has been delayed almost a month, till my mother should be well enough.

Can you make out the visit proposed and so unhappily interfered with last Xmas? We shall have plenty to say, I opine.

Please answer soon and tell us when your vacation begins that we may expect you? Your affectionate friend and cousin   R.L. Stevenson[12]

73   *To Henrietta Traquair*

MS Yale.

Saturday 5 December 1868   *17 Heriot Row*

My dear Henrietta, We're going to have some people at dinner on Saturday next, six o'clock,[1] and are very anxious for you to come in, help to entertain

---

[11] At the top of this last page there is the beginning of a poem in RLS's hand:

Autumn
In country sides, the long, wet, sunken lanes
Are heavy with November mud: the fields

[12] MIS has added a note inviting Bob to visit them.

[1] On 12 December MIS records: 'Lou's first dinner party of sixteen comes off today and is very successful.'

'em and stay till Monday. Ask Bessie Steen[2] also, please, and save Mamma writing. I remain, Your affectionate cousin   R.L. Stevenson

74   To Bob Stevenson

MS Yale.

13 January 1869   *17 Heriot Row*

My dear Bob, At last, a letter, and at last, the place? *Demum, Demum.* Up here we have all been wondering as to whether you were dead or alive.[1] Your room has been ready for a week: a denner was prepared for your delectation: a letter from your mother has rotted long on our mantelpiece. In despair it has been forwarded to Cambridge whence you had better get it.

I don't want to speak morality, but I don't think this was quite the ticket. Neither Papa nor U. David do, and they are prepared to walk into you on the subject.

It was arranged that you were to come to us first; and I suppose this arrangement still holds; so, unless you hear to the contrary from U.D., 17 Heriot Row is the goal.

I hope your mother has known of your address: if not let me advise you to correct that before you come here.

What a lark your voyage must have been. I was out with the hounds last Saturday which is the most of my news.[2] Talk about excitement. Ever your affectionate friend and cousin   R.L. Stevenson

R.A.M. Stevenson Esq.

75   To his Mother

MS Buffalo.

17 June 1869   *New Hotel, Wick*[1]

My dear Mamma, This is to be short as we are just about to leave for Scrabster. Mrs Russel tells me 'with her kind compliments' to advise you to

---

[2] Bessie Stein is mentioned several times in MIS's diary, usually in connection with the Traquairs.

[1] MIS records on 9 January: 'Lou has a young party . . . We expected Bob but he does not turn up.' Bob eventually came to stay on 25 January.

[2] 'Louis pretty well this winter, he rides pretty regularly and even occasionally follows the hounds, just to give him an object – not that he cares for the sport' (MIS, *Diary Notes*).

[1] RLS accompanied his father on a tour of inspection to the Orkney and Shetland islands on board the *Pharos*, the official steamer of the Commissioners of Northern Lights. They left home on 14 June and returned on 29 June.

read *Six Years in Russia* by a Lady – full of recipes and descriptions of Russian dinners.[2] She is so kind – asked me to stay with them if I came back for a short time, and was cut up at my looking ill – a thing I could not explain to her, as it was simple want of lunch. I remain, Your affectionate son   R.L. Stevenson

76   To his Mother

MS Yale. Partly published in *Scribner's Magazine*, XXV (January 1899), 41–4.

Friday 18 June 1869   *Lighthouse Steamer*
9 A.M.   *Between Cantick and Hoy*
                                                                  [Orkney islands]

Dear Mamma, I herewith begin my journal letter, which is intended to contain an account, full, true and particular, of all my 'sore journeying and perilous peregrination.'[1]

About ten, we came on board at Scrabster, after coming to Thurso by the Castleton Coach with a pretty little girl who knew every body on the road. 'That is the doctor.' 'That other is a farmer.' At Wick, at Keiss, at Castleton, at Thurso, she was equally well informed. It put me in mind of my similar journey last Autumn with fourteen Lews fishermen going back to the west, when we saw a still smoking whitely in the middle of a brown-looking moorland and met two Italian music boys within a mile or so of John o' Groat's House.[2] Our little fellow traveller ate many peppermint drops on the way, and offered some to my father; and, whenever anything was dropped or anyone wished out or in, she it was who picked it up or opened the door. Our last conversation was at Thurso, when she broke forth in hearty excitement and pointed out to us her sister who was there to meet her.

It was after sundown then, but still daylight; and we went to see Holburn Head. The man was in such a woundy fright, growing redder and redder

---

[2] *Six Years' Travels in Russia*, By An English Lady (1859). The 'English Lady' was Mary Ann Pellew Smith.

[1] Probably an imperfect recollection of the book by the Scottish traveller William Lithgow, *The Totall Discourse, of the Rare Adventures, and Painefull Peregrinations of long Nineteene Yeares Travayles* . . . (1632). RLS later owned his father's copy of the book (Anderson II, 288).

[2] RLS remembered these incidents twenty years later in 'The Education of an Engineer': 'A traveller today upon the Thurso coach would scarce observe a little cloud of smoke upon the moorlands, and be told, quite openly, it marked a private still: . . . [At Castleton] I saw, pursuing the coach . . . two little dark-eyed, white-toothed Italian vagabonds, of twelve to fourteen years of age, one with a hurdy-gurdy, the other with a cage of white mice.' Memory of the Italian boys was also in RLS's mind when he came to write 'The Pavilion on the Links'. See Letter 587, n. 3.

and breathing hard in mortal terror. Verily, *mon père* is a great man here: he putteth out his lip, and all men tremble.

We steamed across the Pentland Firth with Holburn Head behind us, Dunnet Head and Skerries on our right and Cantick Head in front. The vessel rolled a little; but the swell was nothing. There were squalls of rain all along the shore, and not a few of them where we were. Soon after there came a great white streak between two layers of cloud in the eastward, which widened and brightened into orange and red. This was the dawn. Just then, the bell rang for midnight. It was very picturesque: the decks all lucid and shining with the early shower, the dawn brightening feebly, and the ship rolling between the two low shorelines. Near one, we came round Cantick Head and dropped anchor in Kirk Hope with the light flashing on one side, and the dawn, orange and yellow and red, waxing brighter above a row of murkish clouds. Turned in, very sleepy.

This morning we landed and saw Cantick Head Light. The faces of the men was sufficient for inspection. You could see they were at their ease. The flag was hoist while we were in. We are now waiting for breakfast and running for Graemsay with the high land of Hoy on our right.

12 Noon

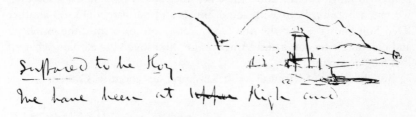

We have been at High and Low Hoy Sound Lights, Island of Graemsay. From the latter, which was in good order the view was very pretty. The water a sort of dark purple with here and there a streak of vivid emerald marking the position of some sandy shoal. The picture above is not the least like – not the slightest but I had no time. The hills behind are in Hoy and are the only Highlands of Orkney: the tower in front is the High Light mentioned above. Stromness is just opposite on the mainland a cluster of grey houses in the upper end of a bight – not very inviting.

At Cantick we were told that fush are plenty – an appetising remark which was not lost, I think; for when breakfast came, just as I finished my last entry, I ate three slices of toast and three helpings of salmon steak, and drank a cup and a half of tea – not bad that, I think: Mr Andrews and my father ate me down a long while though. I daresay this letter is not entertaining; but I am going to put down everything I can whether it be interesting or not.

4.30 P.M.

We are here in Scapa Flow, where we anchored about two, when the
Captain, Mr Andrews, Papa and I, together with Mr Henderson the
Steward in quest of cheese, landed on a shoaling beach and walked across an
isthmus to Kirkwall. The first sight one gets of Kirkwall is rather striking –
a cluster of grey roofs with the red Cathedral and a knot of umber ruin at
the top, and the sea at its foot, running into a long and shallow creek which
is severed from the open ocean by a ridge or bar of sand with some walls
atop.

The whole aspect of the town is distinctly English. The houses, white
with harl, present crowstepped gables and picturesque chimneys to the
street; while on one hand, through an arched gateway, one catches a cool
glimpse of a paven entrance court. Some of these arches are green with
burdock and grass, and even with fern; and, to render the likeness to a
village of the Riviera a thought more striking, on one occasion at least,
there was a secondary arch within the first uselessly spanning the stone
passage a nest for weed and a roosting place for fowls. The slates are greyish
white without the smallest tinge of colour; so it is a great relief to the general
whiteness of wall and roof, to see green trees of decent size spreading in the
court within. Above the doors there are inscriptions and emblems. On one,
we saw a burning heart with some initials and the date 1743; on another
'Deo Soli Gloria' – 'To the one God Glory'; and on a third the emphatic
and epigrammatic command 'Amet' – 'Let him love', the allusion whereof
it is hard to divine.

But the glory of Kirkwall, as of Salisbury, lies about its Cathedral.

The High Street – which, I omitted to observe, is narrow and paven with
the exception of a strip of causeway some two feet wide in the centre, so
that there are four lines of kerb-stone in the width – opens out on your left
into a sort of green. Just as you enter it, on the right, is the most noticeable
courtyard and gate (A) that we saw. Between two gables, rich in crowstep
and weighted with squat stone chimneys, the arch stretched across supporting a somewhat heavy balcony, in the centre of which was the inscription
'Except the Lord' etc., and the date 1574; while an iron lamp, of a battered
and rakish exterior was supported by an upright spike on the cornice. We

went down into the broad cool court, lined on three sides with white houses and on the fourth with a high brown wall, out of whose shadow you could see the sunshine on the streets through the old archway. But what struck us most was an inner bartizan or terrace behind the cornice of the gate, attained by a flight of foot-broad stone steps, which it seemed must have been meant for defence in the time when the burgher who held it had to make good his house against the drunken servants of the earl or the pirate crews of Captain John Goffe[3] and his like.

The Cathedral, then, drawing back its skirts from the street, stands apart on a raised green, with its face towards the picturesque gables of the High Street and bordered on another side by a broad road that runs betwixt the graveyard and the twin ruins of the Bishop's and the Earl's Palaces. At the corner of this green between the High Street and this roadway, stands an old white house (E) on a triple arcade closed with antique iron gratings and entered by an iron-studded door, which I believe I have identified with the Town House. The one remaining side of the High Street at this place is worthy of notice, because of two quaint old bow windows, projecting above the footway on massive corbelling; and between these houses and the church, within the two-foot wall that guards the precinct of the green, you see three broad stone steps, buried in dock and nettle, from the centre of which projects a forlorn spike of stone to show what was once the market cross (F). Going round the Town House again, turning up the road alongside of the burying ground, and passing an iron gate thereinto (D), somewhat in the fashion of the Town House rails and surmounted by a lamp similar to that above the old arch, you come to the twin palaces standing on either side of a pleasant looking lane. The Earl's Palace (C) stands among a thick grove of green plane trees, whence it shows its great corbelled bow windows, symptoms rather of manorial comfort than feudal warfare. The Bishop's (B) adjoins to an old inhabited house which gives an air of homeliness to its quaint outline; for what with the umber-brown walls contrasting with scarlet quoins, and little pieces of statuary let into the solid masonry of the round tower, and the confused whirl of corbel and corner and stair and ragged gable which forms the projecting summit, one rarely sees so bizarre and uncouth a ruin.

And now, having disposed of the minor curiosities that cluster like chickens round a hen, about its lordly shadow, I may go on to the grand old Cathedral, which towers, with narrow gables and slope slate roof and wonder of red stonework and white, above the little green and the little grey town on the seaboard. You enter through the usual triple door of Gothic churches at the foot of the tall, narrow gables with moulding of

---

[3] Captain John Gow, captured in the Orkney islands and executed for piracy in 1725. Scott, who also calls him Goffe, used the story as the basis of *The Pirate*.

alternate red and white and red columns crumbled down to the consistency of Madeira cake. Once in, you see the nave and the screen at the far end that shuts out the choir. It is as narrow and as tall as the outside has led you to expect. The roof, groined with red on dusky grey, is supported on tall black shafts, with no windows on the clerestory but a row of the dwarf Norman windows which prevail immediately above. In each aisle, there stands a row of dark monumental tablets. One in particular I noticed, showing the figure of a deformed woman with her back hair down weeping above a skull and cross bones, strangely mixed in with the following inscription: 'August 1756. Here was interred the corse of Margaret Young spouse of John Kiddoch, then one of the magistrates of Kirkwall and after Provost of the said Burgh. She lived regarded, and died regretted.' On a column not far distant was the tablet of another Kiddoch married to another Young: a system of intermarriage which seems in as great force now as ever, according to stories I was hearing today. For example, the two ministers of the Established Church have married sisters; and their brother-in-law has taken-to-wife a member of his mother's family which is in some way connected with one of them.

From the corner of the chancel just below the square tower you get the best look of the sombre church, with its black and scarlet stonework and its Catherine wheel at the chancel end; and hence you ascend to the belfry and the top of the church. And here I must fairly give up any hope, and my hope from the first has been feeble, to give you any idea of this delightful old church. From every corner of the tower, a corkscrew staircase ascends, giving admittance into passages along the blind clerestory of nave, choir and chancels: thence more stairs and narrower passages still – where one has to go on sidelong like a crab in a rock-cleft – leading along past the little windows of the nave, and between the double windows of the choir: thence more stairs to the dusty and lumbered lofts above the groined roof and to the belfry, criss-crossed by great unpainted wooden beams and hung with the big bells, on whose mellow sides the modern sacristan rings a stormy chime; and thence, by ladder to the outside of the tower. This is the climax: below you like a knife-edge the sharp ridge and swift slope of the two slate roofs each with its broad leaden gutters, the kirkyard with its stones, the little green, the ruins and the cluster of grey-slate roofs crouching at your feet. I wish I could let you feel, as I felt, these little stairs and passages – this network or web of dark and narrow alleys, with the very smallest windows sometimes, and sometimes with no windows at all. You expect to meet a 'priest in surplice white that defunctive music knows',[4] a sexton in hose and steeple hat, a tonsured monk, a mitred Bishop worn with conflict against Heathen Earls and savage boors, at every corner of the dusty maze;

[4] Shakespeare, 'The Phoenix and the Turtle', l. 14.

and when you come forth on the surface, the roof looks like that on which Dom Claude descends and breaks his fall, ere he plunges finally to the causeway below.[5] I know nothing so suggestive of legend, so full of superstition, so stimulating to a weird imagination, as the nooks and corners and bye-ways of such a church as St Magnus, in Kirkwall.

We then went down to the pier, where indeed we had a lamentable wakening and grievous revocation from Middle-Ages dreamland to everyday vulgarity and affectation. A London engineer has erected an iron jetty, like the ornamental bridge over the water in a cockney tea-garden – a gimcrack lane of carven lamp-posts – infinitely neat and infinitely shaky – a nursemaids' walk, that might have done at Greenwich, project-ing into the easterly surge from Pomona the mainland of Orkney. Alas! alas!

11.15 P.M.

We are running to Shetland. Fair Isle and Foula blots on the horizon before us and the tower of North Ronaldsay standing up clear behind with no land for it to stand upon. All round, a sphere of leaden sea. The flush behind the sunset and the flush before the dawn are both about equally clear and with only 62° between them. It is now the darkest of the night; and I have been reading small type on the bridge with the utmost ease. The *Pharos* rolls a little with the ocean swell, but, by good fortune, no more; though once I saw her put her nose in deep enough for a whiff of white spray to fly over the anchor davit. The moon is behind us, and comes out on the sea at intervals as she passes a rent in the clouds.

Saturday 19 June   *Blumel Sound*
10.10 A.M.

Last night, I must observe, the Captain told me, that, when steamers first came in, a half-wit in the west said he would shut himself into the hold and smoke for a week and then surely his boat would go too when he began to let it escape. He thought that it was the mere flight of the smoke that propelled the vessel.

We are now fairly in Shetland – a fair, cold day with a low, leaden sky such as I am told they have here all the summer through: a bountiful provision of nature, by the way, as a very little sunshine would scorch their crops to nothing. It is higher, bleaker, and darker than Orkney; but, for the rest, the same – an archipelago of bare islets, with ruinous-looking cottages and brown ends of cliff cropping up here and there along the beach – and

---

[5] Archdeacon Claude Frollo (pushed by the hunchback) falls from one of the towers of Notre-Dame in Hugo's novel.

divided too by the same winding sounds with blind angles and tide races every mile or half-mile.

We have just passed a ruined castle on a hillock, built of mixed red and black like St Magnus and the Bishop's Palace and clasping in its walls a modern mansion house, resplendent with whitewash and called Burg Hall. The cottages about it seem mostly deserted; and this I am told is very much the way; for life is nearly impossible in Shetland now-a-days. Before they lived on their knitting – took a pair of hose to the store and brought back meal in exchange, or gave three eggs and received a pirn of thread. In this way, however, they clad themselves and got everything but the potatoes which they planted and the fish they caught; and thus there was a man in Unst, whose yearly income was fifteen shillings and whose yearly rent was ten, leaving a margin of five solitary shillings – sixty copper pennies for himself and family. Nowadays, this is impracticable; and the reason I understand is want of wool to knit; but of this I am not sure.

This morning we landed on the Bound Skerry of Whalsey, a shelf of rock, the outmost of a group of islets to the east of Shetland. It is of quartzose rock, of a salmon colour at a fracture, but growing black with weather. Here the light was inspected, and the keepers took us down to show us the rock torn up by the sea.[6] One great big fellow ten feet long and between two and three feet deep had been shifted about tremendously, and had scored grooves, half an inch deep, wherever it went with its knife-like edges. (See dotted lines). This is some fifty feet above the sea.

10.50

We saw some black sea-birds called in local jargon Spotted Allans,[7] who never fish for themselves, but pursue the gulls who caught anything and make them give it up. On the South shore there was a smallish house in which Grahame[8] said Sir Jamset jee-jee-jee-jee-jee – *et caetera* – hee-boy[9] lived; but I doubt it is some small degree apocryphal. Coming out of Blumel Sound we met the tide, a long heavy roll, patches of water like oil and rips and creases of broken water all over the face of the sea.

45 minutes after midday

The coast beyond the embouchure of Blumel Sound, the western seaboard of Unst, is wild and rugged, dark cliffs riven with inky voes and

---

[6] RLS adds a rough sketch of the rock.

[7] Allan, Scouti-Allan, Dirty Allan (and many other variants) are local names for the Arctic or Richardson's Skua (known in North America as the Parasitic Jaeger).

[8] Captain of the *Pharos*.

[9] Sir Jamsetjee Jeejeebhoy (1783–1859), Bombay merchant and philanthropist, was the first Indian to be knighted and was later made a Baronet.

caverns, white with sea birds, marked here and there by natural arches, and crowned with round hills of sere sun-burnt grass. In about half an hour we sighted North Unst Lighthouse, the most northern dwelling house in Her Majesty's dominion. The mainland rises higher, with great seams and landslips; and from the norwestern corner runs out a string of shelving ledges, with a streak of green and purple seaweed and a boil of white foam about their feet. The Lighthouse stands on the highest – 190 feet above the sea; and there is only an uninhabited reef called the Out Stack between it and the Faroe Islands. The sketch is a little like their appearance as we steamed up to them from the south west, but wanting the jagged outline, and the rake to westward and the colouring.

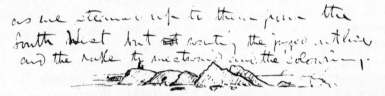

We steamed round between the lighthouse and the Out Stack (A in picture) with a great long swell from the northward splashing about her bows; and let the boat go from a point whence the reefs looked somewhat thus.[10]

We were pulled into the creek shown in the picture between the Lighthouse and the other rock, down the centre of which runs a line of reef marked B. This is very narrow, little broader than a knife edge; but its ridge has been cut into stone steps and laid with iron grating and railed with an iron railing. It was here that we landed, making a leap between the swells at a rusted iron ladder laid slant-wise against the raking side [of] the ridge. Before us a flight of stone steps led up the two hundred feet to the lighthouse in its high yard-walls across whose foot the sea had cast a boulder weighing twenty tons. On one side is a slippery face of clear sound rock; and on the other a chaos of pendulous boulder and rotten stone. On either side there was no vegetation save tufts of sea-pink in the crevices and a little white lichen on the lee faces. The lighthouse was in good order. We are now returning by Blumel Sound to Sunday at Lerwick.

[10] This sketch of North Unst Lighthouse was adopted by Mr E.J. Beinecke as his bookplate.

We saw one of the Spotted Allans chasing a gull. They are really entertaining birds, maritime cuckoos so far as want of principle goes – regular, habit and repute sorners.[11]

By the way, there is no part of Shetland three miles away from the sea: Mr Andrews and I tried it with the compass; so there is no mistake about it.

11.30 P.M.   *Off Lerwick*

Lerwick lies in the hollow angle of a winding sound between the mainland of Shetland and the Island of Bressay. As we came up we saw many people on a gravel spit at the corner, drying fish on the baked white stones. The houses present their one gable to the water which laves their foundations and their other to the main street which runs parallel to the line of the shore. When we landed – about eight – this narrow way was swarming with people. It is paved from wall to wall with broad flat paving stones; and the resemblance to a Riviera village is further heightened by the narrow side-lanes, which climb the hillside on long flights of ruinous steps between high houses on either hand. At the north of the town stands Fort Charlotte, founded, as I hear, by Cromwell. It overhangs the water with a circuit of heavy grass grown walls, backed by mounds supported by ruinous buttresses and pierced by some four arched gateways. The sea-pink blooms thickly among the lichened crevices of the old stonework. Inside there are two whitewashed buildings, a few sheds for the exercise of the naval reserve – four hundred of whom appear every winter on their return from the whale and seal fishing, and a great black looking tank, as old, I suppose, as the fort and lipping with repulsive looking water. The largest of these buildings is the jail and court-house – a long, low house with massive leaden gutters bearing the initials of George II[12] and the date seventeen hundred and eighty. The court is held in the upper part; and the lower windows each shaded by a wooden hutch have a melancholy interest in our eyes; for, not many days ago, a young man was sentenced to forty-five days imprisonment for shooting ducks at Unst, who hanged himself behind the midmost of these blank windows before the first night had come.

After seeing Fort Charlotte we took a walk with some gentlemen whom we had met and to whom Captain Grahame had introduced us. Among these was Captain McKinnon of the *Eaglet*, Revenue Cutter, who gave us some interesting particulars about the degenerate modern smuggling. On their first voyage to the Faroe fishing, they never smuggle; for should they be caught, they would be detained too long to get away again; but on their second, they bring home as much as they can get. They are not dishonest;

---

[11] Spongers or beggars (Scots).
[12] In fact George III: Fort Charlotte was named in honour of Queen Charlotte.

but they think smuggling their right, and give the Captain no little trouble. In these bright nights, of the north, he cannot get near them before they have thrown every thing overboard; but on some occasions he manages to catch them napping. One foggy night last summer, for example, he left the cutter behind an islet and took a circuit with his gig. They did not observe him till he was close at hand; but when they did, they lost no time. He saw them tumbling tobacco overboard out of a great big sack; and, when he boarded, the scuppers were a-wash with brandy and a man below was still staving in the casks. They got off easily on trial.

The Captain had had great trouble with one man called Preaching Peter, who whenever he got back with his spoils from Faroe sent round handbills to announce his coming, and went about the country preaching. After he had much prayed and much preached, he gave the benediction and then was the signal for all who knew him to crowd round 'How many gallons shall I give you?' 'How many do you want?' Such was the conversation; and so he sold his smuggled spirits, and improved the peoples' souls while he filled his own purse.

The four gentlemen whom we had met came out and took grog on board, when we had some interesting talk. George MacDonald, ill of inflamation of the knee-joint, passed here *en route* for Norway in a yacht a short time ago.[13] The doctor, who told us this, mentioned also that leprosy and lazar houses lingered into last century in this Ultima Thule of the ancients; and was succeeded by smallpox so violent that it swept away one third of the population. In Foula out of two hundred souls, there were left six men to bury friends, and relatives and neighbours. Shortly afterwards, inoculation was brought [in] in its more violent form when it killed one out of every four or five; and of course it became common in Shetland. Now, there was one, Patterson, I think, a jack of all trades – a tailor, a shoemaker, a fish curer, a doctor, who bethought him of weakening the matter introduced. He dried the pus on glass plates, mixed it with camphor, hung it for long in peat smoke and finally buried it for seven whole years. When this long ceremony was at an end, he used it and, out of three or four thousand, lost not one life; but his useful discovery was eclipsed by vaccination which followed so shortly after. Nowadays, the women suffer much from drinking too much tea. The Collector told us that the fishers of Dunrossness take cod-liver oil with them to drink, when they go out on a fishing cruise.

Four bells – midnight – has rung some time ago. Upstairs it is perfectly calm, the sky very dark with mottling of white and grey cirrus,[14] and the

---

[13] The yacht *Blue Bell* owned by John Stevenson, a Glasgow merchant, was at Lerwick on 13 June when a local doctor was called aboard to treat George MacDonald for a badly swollen knee.

[14] MS: surrus.

yellow moon half out, half in the clouds above the houses of the town – the whole thing mirrored to perfection in the water of the Sound. Some fishermen are singing on the shore, probably in imitation of Italy; for they please themselves by calling Lerwick the northern Venice. This appearance is heightened by the excessive lightness.

Tomorrow we shall send our letters off; so here I conclude and remain, Your affectionate son   R.L. Stevenson

77   *To his Mother*

MS Yale, plus 4pp. Edinburgh. Partly published in *Scribner's Magazine*, XXV (January 1899), 44–8.

Sunday 20 June 1869   *Off Lerwick*
11 P.M.

My dear Mamma, This night hath my first departed; and I shall begin my second by mentioning one or two facts about Lerwick which I omitted to chronicle therein. Between the house gables turned toward the Sound, there run down stairs and jetties every here and there, for more convenience of landing. One of these and that at which we have landed most frequently, was beside an old, square house with a belfry atop and a sort of terrace towards the street, with balustraded stair, used as the Town Hall. As with all the others, the green still water licks its very stones; but there is a projecting out house, butting forth among the wavelets, rendered noticeable by the wealth of some strange white blossom that hides its blue slate roof. The high street, too, as I forgot to notice, is not only irregular in direction, but also in width: sometimes a long house thrusts its gable far across and pens it in to a short ten feet; and sometimes the houses fall away in irregular open spaces, not unlike the little squares in the back slums of Venice.

On the Saturday evening, there were some hundred boats out before the town fishing herring with the bright hook – by which means, Mr Johnstone of the coast-guard told me he had caught three hundred the night before. Now the Shetland boats are crook-backed, with high stem and bow; and the appearance of this fleet upon the still, bright waters was as that of Indian canoes. It verily required the faint scent of peat smoke to remind you were still in Scotland.

Today, we landed and heard Mr Saunders[1] of the Established Church who gave us a most excellent sermon, swarming with epigrams. As instances, 'The Bible required the gloss of the great teacher: the book of Moses had to be set up in the Gospel type.' 'Yes, my friends, we find the

---

[1] Alexander Reid Saunders (1832–92), minister at Lerwick 1858–91.

devil in the narrow way as an angel of light – as a preacher extolling the righteousness of the everlasting God.' 'Men's consciences may be elastic; but Heaven's gate is not.' The seat in the gallery, kindly given us by Mr Hay was so low that my father wished to hold me when I stood up – true paternal solicitude. The women, who wear on the week-days white Shetland tippets, are very well dressed on Sunday and make a resplendent show.

In the afternoon, we heard Mr S. again after which Mr and Mrs Hay took us for a walk behind the town and showed us two little ponies. One a very pretty one might be up to my waist: the other, much smaller, with his tousy main, feathery head, bearded chin, and ragged tail, was a very walking jest; and a very scurvy jest too. We then said good-bye and walked out a bit to see a pict's house. The town of Lerwick stands on a low hill, circled in front by the sea, and behind by the loch of Klikomin[2] ('Klik'em in' is the way it's said), so that four roads alone join it to the island – one of them on an isthmus and the others on mere dykes. In this sheet of water, stands the Pict's House. On the next page is a rough – very rough, plan of its appearance.

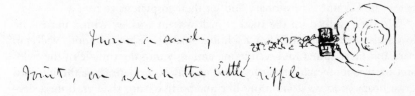

From a sandy point, on which the little ripple lays curves of strange looking emerald slime, there stretches out a causeway of rough stones, defended near the far end by two square piles of stones with a narrow pass between to act, I suppose, very much as the . . .[3] that covered the drawbridge of a feudal castle. The whole islet, thus joined to the mainland is buried in stones and stone ramparts, with many unroofed underground chambers; and the centre is occupied by a hollow round tower not unlike to a lime-kiln. In the thickness of its walls are passages along which I had to creep on all fours, stairs with steps three inches wide, round chambers buried in perfect darkness and small doorways, like coal hatches in a modern house, which seem to have led by covered ways to the outlying subterranean rooms. The people who built and occupied Maes-How[4] must have been two or three feet high at the outside; and there is I think something singularly disgusting in the whole idea. I fancied the place swarming with

---

[2] Clickhimin.

[3] RLS has left a blank in the letter at this point. Perhaps he was thinking of 'barbican'.

[4] Maes Howe, the great chambered tomb of the Neolithic period, had been uncovered in 1861.

little dirty devils talking outlandish jargon and brandishing their flint-head axes; and, with the natural human hatred for swarms of minute life, I confess that I brought myself to share in the horror of these old 'Peghts' which is felt in Orkney and Shetland to this day.

In a note to the *Pirate*[5] you will find a good story illustrative of this. There came a travelling missionary to the island of North Ronaldsha, and, being wearied with journeying, he went straightway to the house of the teacher and there lay down to sleep. But, as ill luck would have it, he had been observed by the people, who instantly concluded from his small frame and dark visage that he was one of the old Picts, whether in the body or out of the body they could not tell; so they gathered about the house with evil intentions. The schoolmaster feared for his guest's bodily safety, and, bethinking him of my grandfather, who was then in the island, he sent a messenger for him and asked him to pacify the angry Norsemen. Unwilling to wake the fatigued man, he tried to convince them of their mistake by showing them the clumsy boots which he had left outside the door; but they would not be persuaded; and at last he was obliged to go in. Fortunately he recognized the man as having been a shopkeeper in Edinburgh before he became a missionary and set their suspicions at rest.

We then walked up the road a small way in a valley with a burn. The lowlands were cultivated after a skimble-skamble fashion: ruinous walls ran here and there sometimes wandering aimlessly into the middle of the fields and there ending with as little show of reason, sometimes gathering into gross heaps of loose stone more like an abortive cairn than an honest dry-stone dyke; for crop, it seemed that docken and the yellow wild mustard, which made bright patches every here and there, were much more plentiful than turnip or corn. Mixed up with this unwholesome looking wilderness were thatched cottages bearing every sign of desertion and decay except the curl of smoke from the place where the chimney should be and was not; and in some cases presenting bare gables and roofless walls to the bitter ocean breeze. The uplands were a sere yellow brown, with rich full-coloured streaks of peat, and grey stretches of outcropping rock. The whole place looks dreary and wretched; for here, nature, as Hawthorne would have said, has not sufficient power to take back to herself what the idleness and absence of man has let go. There is no[6] ivy for the ruined cottage: no thorn or bramble for the waste way-side.

We returned again to the water-stair beside the town hall and waved a handkerchief for the gig,[7] a romantic action which made me remember

---

[5] Scott gathered his background information for *The Pirate* in 1814 when he accompanied RLS's grandfather, Robert Stevenson, and the Lighthouse Commissioners on their official voyage of inspection to lighthouses.
[6] The Edinburgh MS begins here – one folded sheet covering 4 pp. – and continues to [6] on p. 188.
[7] Cf. Letter 828.

many old daydreams when it was my only wish to be a pirate or a smuggler.

I forgot to say that in the afternoon the congregation was double the size; and that because the people, lured by the long clear night, sit up to all hours and do not rise till nine or ten.

Monday 21 June 1869   *Between Sumburgh and Fair Isle*
11.50 A.M.

This morning we have visited Sumburgh Head Lighthouse. This, the southermost point of Shetland as Unst is the most northerly, is joined to the mainland by a very narrow isthmus of low sandhills and thin bent grass. There is shoal water on either hand or the sea would soon carry it away. Inshore of this isthmus, the land is high and bare, with the huge crags of Fitful Head running out a few miles off. Among these sandhills, on a grassy mound, stand some low and ruinous house-walls, all that remains of Jarlshof, so often mentioned in the *Pirate*[8]; and a little way above it, an elegant new house built by Mr Bruce of Sumburgh.[9] During its erection, there was much disturbance among the masons; and the Aberdeen men, who were members of one Trade Union refused point blank to work with Shetland men who were not; so the curse of Bright and Broadhead[10] is felt even in Ultima Thule. The people call this house with a picturesque simplicity worthy of a primitive country and verily refreshing after miles of 'Laurel Groves' and 'Ivy Lodges', 'The new building' and 'the new building of Sumburgh'. By the way is there not something grand in that name of Sumburgh – a low hollow boom, as it were of bursting surf.

We pulled in to a small slip on the beach with some grey houses at its head, one of which purported to sell 'Tea and Tobacco' with blotches where 'Spirits and Ale' had been painted out – a silent commentary on the habits of the people. We had then two miles to walk along the narrow headland, which rises in precipitous cliffs to the east and on the west stretches down to the sea in a gentle sweep of spring turf. Here and there, however, the voes run in on either hand with a rush of water and a screaming of gulls, and leave but a neck of land three hundred feet above the surf. For all that, the spray flies over it in clouds. Down in these voes, we

---

[8] Better known since then as the site of important archaeological discoveries – a Bronze-Age village and a Viking settlement.

[9] John Bruce, J.P., D.L. (1798–1885), owner of Fair Isle.

[10] John Bright (1811–89), the great Liberal politician, had led the battle for parliamentary reform and was regarded as the champion of the working man. Trade Unions were much in the news at this time through the reports of the Royal Commission on Trade Unions 1867–9. A special enquiry in 1867 on outrages in Sheffield had shown that William Broadhead (1815–79), Secretary of the Saw Grinders' Union, had instigated attacks on employers and anti-Union workmen.

saw the white gulls sitting on their eggs and the young ones beginning to walk about. We then visited the light and went on board again, passing easily through a jabble of short cresting waves which, in spring tides and heavy gales, is the fatal Sumburgh Roost. The sketch represents the outmost spur of the head from the eastward. The light is three hundred feet high.

3.45 P.M.   *Between Fair Isle and Ronaldsha*

The coast of the Fair Isle is the wildest and most unpitying that we have yet seen.[11] Continuous cliffs from one to four hundred feet high, torn by huge voes and echoing caverns, line the bare downs with scarcely a cove of sand or a practicable cleft in the belt of iron precipice. At intervals it runs out into strange peninsulas, square bluff headlands, and plumb faces of stone, tinged with the[6] faint green of some sort of lichen.

Close by one of these was the long, bleak inlet into which the Duke of Medina Sidonia's vessel, the flagship of the great Armada, was driven in the storm. It was strange to think of the great old ship, with its gilded castle of a stern, its scroll-work and emblazoning and with a Duke of Spain on board, beating her brains out on the iron bound coast of the Fair Isle.

As we pulled into the cove, a tall thin gentleman and a small boy came down the beach as if to meet us. His clothes were of the oldest, and the date of his last shave would require a more daring conjecture than I am prepared to offer or at least to chronicle in black and white. He said he was only four days old in Fair Isle; and on our asking after his name and position, replied: 'I am a servant of the Lord Jesus Christ and have come here to preach his word.' He had been sent over in Mr Bruce of Sumburgh's sloop and occupied the room which that gentleman – to whom the island belongs – keeps for himself in the minister's house. To this, he showed us the way; and the minister himself, Mr Macfarlane,[12] led us to see whatever was interesting. The appearance from the landing place is very picturesque; for

---

[11] In 'The Coast of Fife' RLS writes: 'Half-way between Orkney and Shetland, there lies a certain isle; on the one hand the Atlantic, on the other the North Sea, bombard its pillared cliffs; sore-eyed, short-living, inbred fishers and their families herd in its few huts . . . there is nowhere a more inhospitable spot.'

[12] Andrew Macfarlane, minister of the Church of Scotland.

the land, sloping gradually upward, ends in the clear-cut, sharp and singularly wild and savage outline of the cliffs. It was towards this farther side that Mr Macfarlane escorted us. We first saw the schoolhouse, a dark, damp apartment, wet with rain droppings and half-roofed with wreck-timber thrown across the rafters: it required the 'tawse' and the ragged schoolbooks to remind you where you were. On our way thence to some strange holes in the land, we heard that our first friend was one Lord Teynham – the family name Curzon.[13] It was strange to find a nineteenth century nobleman, preaching the Gospel in the desolate Fair Isle. The people are very unwilling, Mr MacFarlane mentioned, to speak about the Armada sailors – indeed almost the only fact they will communicate is that, when hand in hand, the shipwrecked Spaniards reached right across the Island. Their reason for this is easily understood: they believe it throws discredit on their ancestors; for many of these unfortunate seamen were murdered in case of a famine, with so many extra mouths to fill. But there can be little question that the Duke himself must have consented to the deed; for how could the unarmed islanders – even now only 300 in number – have kept head against Medina Sidonia and his sailors and soldiers? and again, if such were the case, how did so many escape, by way of Kirkcaldy, to their own country? They seem to have left little traces, beyond a bayonet and the like, with the exception of the coloured woollen work which they are said to have taught to the islanders. It must have been a strange sight – all these southerners, fresh from the oranges of Seville, living in filthy cottages on the wildest island of our northern archipelago: very rusty, I doubt not, were their cuirasses and very ragged the lace, and ruffle and sash of the Spanish grandee officers ere they had done creeping about among the gios and caverns of the iron-bound coast-line.

Before all this was heard, we had reached what we had come to see. The land as I said, slopes almost continuously from the low shore on one side to the cliff top at the other; but in two places, the ground suddenly leaves your feet and you see a large rocky tank, some seventy feet deep, with a great arched doorway onto the ocean, right through the hill-side: the noise of a stone dropped in, reverberates with a hollow boom and splash up the rough sides on either hand. Close by there was a fine, graceful curve of beach, surrounded by red cliffs, and strangely marked by a great red stack or isolated pillar, standing among the heaped brown sea-weed on the sweep of the bay.

On our return we entered a house. They are here in three rooms. The first one is a byre; the second, the kitchen; the third, what they call 'the

---

[13] George Henry Roper-Curzon, 16th Baron Teynham (1798–1889). RLS describes him in 'The Coast of Fife' as 'an elderly gentleman, unshaved, poorly attired, his shoulders wrapped in a plaid'.

room'. This last was locked, so we did not see it; but the kitchen was open
to curious eyes, with no more inhabitants than a large yellow cat and a small
grey kitten.[14] You entered by the door from the byre – none of the doors
are above four feet high – and then saw opposite to you the door into 'the
room', with the fire immediately in front of it on some large flat stones
and with a stone standing upright behind it. The smoke escapes through
three holes in the thatch and hangs in blue clouds among the rafters. All
the furniture was on one side, and consisted principally of wooden arm-
chairs and Fair Isle arm-chairs – that is with a frame of wood and a back of
plaited straw. For such a cottage and croft, they only pay £4 or £3.10 a
year; and the rent of the whole island, exclusive of fishing, is no more than
£150.

As we went on, we found three women standing by a dyke side – two
of them young, one rather well-looking with a child, and the third old, pale
and haggard with a black shawl about her head and round her face. We
asked them if they had any coloured stockings.

Chorus from the two women knitting, in the negative.

The minister supposed that the merchants had got them away.

'Now that's just the very case, that is,' cried the old woman, unaccount-
ably exalted in manner and tone. 'The merchants has got 'em. That's the
very way as it lies, that is: that is the very way of it.'

The young knitter suggested that there were some at the store. Meantime, Mr Andrews had observed the child and said:

'This is an uncommonly sensible looking child. She's got the most
sensible eyes.'

The subject of discourse proceeded to illustrate its sensibility by attempting to swallow a penny which had been put into its hand by the panegyrist.

'Two and a half years, sir,' screamed the old woman.

'What do you mean,' cut in the mother in angry tones.

'It's two and a half years old she is,' reiterated the first.

'You shouldn't be saying the like o' that' and something very abusive
thereafter from the mother.

'The gentlemen were askin': you should listen to what the gentlemen
say.'

This was followed by a denial; and the dispute died out in grumbling.

The examination of the child was then continued; and Mr MacFarlane
told us that its father had died of consumption, adding that she was a young
woman and it was a pity she could get no work, during all which she sat
perfectly stolid and unmoved.

We then went on to the church, a cottage set with plain unvarnished
benches and a ditto pulpit – neat and tidy, however, and seated for two

[14] RLS adds a rough sketch of the floor plan.

hundred and fifty. Outside was a small graveyard, with headstones consisting of rough slates about a foot high thrust into the ground. On two alone are there any letters; and these two are made of wood and cut by a man in the island. They were two of the oldest men that had ever died in the place, and yet the ages were but 61 and 64 respectively. Intermarriage and bad houses makes them a weak lot; and almost none of the women, as I hear, have good eyes. One of these inscriptions I had the curiosity to copy, by reason of the error it contains. 'In Memor*ium* of T. Wilson. Born January 5th 1801. Died January 13th 1865. Aged 64 years and 8 days. Time flies.' My father took out his knife to alter the mistake; but Mr MacFarlane stopped him, as the people would have looked on it as insulting the dead. Apropos of tombstones, the same gentleman told us that there [were] some lettered stones on the hill top, but what the inscriptions meant he was unable to tell us.

From the church we proceeded to the store, where tea, teapots, linen and blankets are sold to the inhabitants; and where the inhabitants expose, on the other hand, their quaint-patterned parti-coloured knitted socks, cowls, gloves and mittens.

During our absence, his Lordship had been taking Mr Curry about among the sick folk; and he said that of all the miserable people he had ever seen, they were the worst. Two twin old women of six and eighty years, literal skeletons, lived in misery and sickness in a wretched den waited on by the daughter of one, now well up in years herself. One of these had burnt her foot the day before, and the cloth she had wrapped about it was no finer than ordinary sacking. Their only hope was in death.

Such more or less seems the condition of the people. Beyond reach of all communication, receiving such stray letters as may come not once in six long months, with diseased bodies, and wretched homes, they drag out their lives in the wildest and most barren island of the north. Their crops, raised after hard labour from a cold and stony soil, can only support them for three months out of the twelve. Indeed their only life is from the sea. It is the sea that brings the fish to their nets: it is the sea that strews their shore with the spoils of wrecked vessels (thus we saw in the minister's house, a huge German musical box saved from the wreck of the *Lessing*).[15]

Leaving a great parcel of papers, we went on board again.

Tuesday 22nd   *In Scrabster Roads*

This letter goes tonight: hoping all are well, Believe me, Ever your affectionate son   R.L. Stevenson

---

[15] The *Lessing* from Bremen was wrecked on Fair Isle on 23 May 1868.

78   To Bob Stevenson

MS Yale.

Friday 7 January 1870   *17 Heriot Row*

My dear Bob, I can't sufficiently apologize for my tardy answer; but somehow I am growing lazier and lazier as I go on.

Bradford works extraordinar'; and as I am smoking just now at the mean rate of twelve pipes a day, it came in very handy.

W. Murray,[1] whom I suppose you will see, will tell you of my news; and with that consideration I may salve my conscience and indulge my idleness.

Smoking – beer – occasional billiards – In fine ask W. Murray; and, with love to all your people, believe me, my dear Bob, Ever your affectionate friend and cousin   R.L. Stevenson

P.S. I am ashamed of this slender epistle, though indeed it is no worse than yours. The other day, methought it was the finest drunken man I met. He did nothing but quote Shakespeare, challenged people with 'Under which King Bezonian', reproved them with 'Thou friend of an ill-fashion',[2] and stood in the middle of the street spouting Hamlet's soliloquies. I made great friends with him and walked along Queen St in his most grandiloquent company. Ask Murray to describe the finale: it is side-splitting. I was up in Murray's room today, when in came a clerical employer of his and I had to take refuge in a coal place, where I kicked the coals about and yelled with laughter, and whence I kept injecting smoke into the main room to the no small amazement of the cleric. My reason for hiding Murray may perhaps also mention. By-the-by, of him it may be said,

> Of such gray seeming with so red a heart –
> It makes me wonder

                                                        R.L.S.

79   To Bob Stevenson

MS Yale.

Tuesday 29 March 1870   *17 Heriot Row*

My dear Bob, During almost the whole of this winter, I have been free from my usual attacks of morbid melancholy; to which circumstance you may

---

[1] Possibly William Hugh Murray (1850–1921), who became a Writer to the Signet. But the reference may be to W.B. Murray (see Letter 101, n. 7).
[2] *Henry IV*, V.iii.119 and *Two Gentlemen of Verona*, V.iv.60.

attribute the small number and the small size of my letters to you; but today
I was in the depths again. To what I should attribute this, I cannot think.
Yesterday, I was in high spirits writing 'Deacon Thin';[1] and today even, my
health is perfect. But from the morning I was gone, tried to find out where
I could get Haschish, half-determined to get drunk and ended (as usual) by
going to a graveyard. I stayed about two hours in Greyfriars Churchyard in
the depths of wretchedness.[2] If I had travelled a year, I could not have found
a better place. The castle, the old town, the spire of the Tolbooth Church,
loomed indistinctly through the cold grey mist. The grass was wet. A sexton
was at work upon a grave; and two wretched, filthy women, one of them
with a child were walking up and down there, with occasional harsh
strident laughters. As I walked towards the university, I looked down
College Wynd, with its clothes poles and harridan faces craning from
the windows and its steep narrow roadway clotted with fish barrows and
loafing prostitutes. Near the top, two small boys held a skipping rope. A
haggard sickly little girl was performing on it, with bouts of laughter
that reminded one fantastically of the old women in the graveyard, and
blaspheming with the most horrible and filthy oaths. Watching and listening
to this, was almost the only thing that interested me that morning. – At
the College I met a commonplace friend, who wished me to walk with
him. I told him I was not fit to walk with the devil; but he got me away.
He is a very nice fellow; but I must have rather astonished him. To begin
with, I scarcely spoke to him for about ten minutes. But the grand finale
was when I was getting better. I saw some children playing at marbles in a
stable lane; and I don't know why, the idea of playing pleased me. So I
insisted on going away and buying a half-penny worthy of marbles and
setting to work with my companion. By good luck, the shop I tried did not
possess the article; and my better angel (generally my worst) laziness,
prevented me from doing anything more. You should have seen my friend's
face!

I am better now; but it leaves me in a state of intellectual prostration, fit

---

[1] Posthumously published as 'The Builder's Doom' in the Edinburgh Edition (1898) and previously
thought to have been written as one of the Moral Tales during the Davos period 1881–2. The
version enclosed in this letter seems to be the MS of 'The Deacon's Crescent' described in Sotheby
Catalogue 27 July 1917 as longer than the published version and differing from it nearly all the way
through. The catalogue quotes the following note at the foot of the poem: 'No captious critics:
the irregularity of rhythm is intentional: Deacon Thin is an historical character . . . I suppose you
heard that I was had up for "snowballing, rioting, and resisting the police." It was rather an
excitement at the time . . . The paragraph in the story relating to the fall of number one, I may
remark, has been considered like Shelley, in its intensity and vividness; but Shelley wanted
realism . . .'. The snowballing incident took place on 26 February 1870. RLS and a number
of fellow students were charged on 1 March and RLS was bound over to keep the peace for a year.
[2] RLS often visited churchyards when he felt unhappy (see 'Old Mortality'). His description of
Greyfriars Churchyard is in *Picturesque Notes*, V. On 30 March MIS records: 'Lou still complaining
and in very low spirits.'

for nothing but smoking, and reading Charles Baudelaire. By the bye, I hope your sisters don't read him: he would have corrupted St Paul.

In literary work, I have two essays on 'The Right Conduct of the Imagination' simmering in my brain. One of them is in draught. When you come, you must bring me *Monmouth*. I have improved a little in dramatic diction – less of the buskin. So I must have a shot at that subject again. I see the possibilities of a first rate acting piece in it. Believe me, Ever your affectionate friend and cousin   R.L. Stevenson

Tell me what you think of 'Deacon Thin,' and write something interesting.

80   To Bob Stevenson

MS Yale.

Thursday 16 June 1870   *Swanston Cottage*

My dear Bob, I was very glad, excessively glad, to hear of your success; and I have only to apologize for being so long in writing to join my congratulations to those which you must already have received. I really never know what to say on such occasions. My art lies rather in things that sound artful than in things that sound really warm and heartfelt. And I can only tell you that the news has given me more pleasure than anything I have heard for years – it pleased me better than a large legacy would have done.

I have been shamefully lax in my correspondence for which I can offer no apology than the old original sin of idleness. To which I can only add that I have been very busy, and very much hit with a certain damsel who shall be nameless during the last month or so. This last obstacle is now removed, as the lady in question has been withdrawn to the paternal province; but the latter, od's fish! seems on the increase, as though to keep the balance square. I never was so nearly hooked, I may remark *en passant*, as I was by the damsel already noticed – indeed it was perhaps as well she left when she did, as I detected a nasty over-friendliness towards me on the part of her relations – one of the most sobering observations that the ardent youth can make. To be well received by the lady is pleasant; but it is appalling when the friends 'take up the wondrous tale'[1] and you find yourself gracefully sliding into the position of an acknowledged *shooter*.

You will observe, that finding the inclination of my hand becoming every day more and more alarming, I have given it a kant the other way – for a season.

[1] 'The moon takes up the wondrous tale' from Addison's hymn beginning 'The spacious firmament on high'.

When are we to see you up here, my dear Bob? Can you not spare us the light of your countenance a while, before you go to Avranches?[2] I have not seen you for so long that we shall be huge strangers when we meet; and I know nothing more disappointing than the first period after a long absence.

Will you tell your mother how much I was obliged to her for her kind letter, telling me the good news; and say also that I will write to her when next I can put on the spirt.

I am not in a mood to write somehow; but I wrote because I felt my congratulations could not decently wait longer. Therefore, good-bye, I am going to take my beer and sardines; after which to bed and a chapter or two of Fielding. Believe me, Ever your affectionate friend and cousin

R.L. Stevenson

81   To his Mother[1]

MS NLS.

Monday 27 June 1870   [*Swanston Cottage*][2]

My dear Mother, We are all doing extraordinary here, barring a most frantic ducking received *en route* for Roslin Chapel[3] yesterday. Sabbatic Peace was the order of the day: Cummy smiled and all faces relaxed in the genial sunshine of her favour. We envied not Lucullus his banquets, clearing out a gooseberry tart till it was 'pure in the last recesses of the dish,'[4] and disposing of divers other viands with like speed and in like proportion.

Robertson[5] bet sixpence all round he would go up to the top of Kirk Yetton and down again to our garden in half an hour. He lost his bet by one minute, no seconds which was good work. How are you getting on at Scarborough? Tell Puss that somebody was talking about her the other day in a most disrespectful manner.

I am getting on pretty well at Park's;[6] but these pines, Windau and Riga

---

[2] Bob was presumably going to France to further his studies in art. He had painted at Fontainebleau in the summer of 1869.

[1] MIS, who had not been well, went to Scarborough on 24 June 1870, accompanied by Henrietta Traquair (Puss). TS joined them and they all stayed till 4 July. RLS had various friends to stay with him at Swanston while his parents were away.

[2] Written on the official stationery of the family firm at 84 George Street, Edinburgh.

[3] Roslin Chapel in the village a few miles south of Swanston is famous for its rich and elaborate carving. Visitors to Swanston were often taken to see it.

[4] Cf. 'pure in the last recesses of the mind,' l. 133 of Dryden's translation of the Second Satire of Persius, quoted by Hazlitt in 'On the Pleasure of Painting I' (*Table Talk*).

[5] RLS was friendly with at least two Robertsons: Robert (see Letter 467, n. 3) and Charles (see Letter 551, n. 1).

[6] MIS records that RLS was attending a wood merchant's yard to learn to distinguish the different kinds of wood.

and American, white wood and red wood and yellow, are about the most utterly confusing things that one can see. However, as I found Park himself wrong on two occasions, I have plucked up courage a bit.

Talking about the rain yesterday and how we caught it, the following talk has just occurred.

Dick – It was a sort of judgment you know, for deserting the Established Church. What would your father think.

Yours Truly – O he would be pleased with the frugality. We saw the chapel for a mere song dropped in at the offertory.

Dick – Well, that's one way of looking at it; but (*chuckle*) that's not the view your father'll take.

I remain, Madam, Your respectful, respectable, dutiful and affectionate son   R.L. Stevenson

Mrs Stevenson

82   To Henrietta Traquair

MS Milne.

Friday 1 July 1870   *Swanston Cottage*
Eleven P.M.

My dear Pussy, I should perhaps have written to my father; but I know too well that I could write nothing that would please him and please the rest of you at the same time. I have nothing either new or important to say in the matter of business; so I shall content myself with bosh; which, for your sake and Madame's, I must try and make gossipy.

Aunt Kitty and Chloe[1] are out at Oxgangs; and on Monday evening a gang of them came up here. We walked down with them, had supper and offered the loan of the phaeton whenever they wanted it. The day they selected was yesterday. They went out, like the Higginses and Wigginses, sprightly and happy; but like the Higginses and Wigginses also, their return was in tears. It rained incessantly; and the very phaeton is still quite soaked; so what they must have been I leave you to imagine.

---

[1] Christina Simson (Kitty) married (1860) MIS's brother James Melville Balfour (1831–69), Marine Engineer to the Government of New Zealand. He was drowned in an accident in New Zealand in December. She had recently returned to Scotland with their only child, Marie Clothilde (born 1862), and had been staying with the Stevensons.

D.D.[2] is seated in the square chair reading a novel, I in the arm chair writing this epistle. On the table stand the chess-men, two empty tumblers and an empty canister of tobacco. A peculiar atmosphere pervades the room, which Cummy designates as a 'nasty, wauf smell'. – Huge ventilation schemes are going to be embarked in tomorrow, that the house may be garnished for the return of our absent lords and masters.

Brodie and Murray were out here on Wednesday. G. Scott, McAra, MacAra, or M'ara, and Watson dined with us on Thursday.[3] Tomorrow I must try and get Willie. This has been our list of guests – a distinguished list, you observe.

Tell my respected parents that, if they delay till next Monday, we shall still be able to cripple on – an affectionate message which, doubtless will afford them great satisfaction.

Down at Leith is pretty cold work in cold weather; and pretty hot work in hot weather. Apropos of which, I have never heard whether it was midsummer or midwinter at Scarborough.

The person who insulted you has been duly challenged; but (why should I deny it?) he took me on my weak side and silently extending his tobacco pouch, with a magnanimous gesture, overcame my scruples and left me helpless. If you should consider your interests culpably neglected in this matter, I see no better way of reparation, than my giving you a *fill* when you come back in return for the one that I purchased at the expense of your dignity.

Ask Mamma if the result of my writing *front*-hand is as festive as she seemed to hope. I know I can't read it myself; and I only hope she can.

You can also tell my respected mother than I have received a most satisfactory message from the north; whereupon my heart expandified.

And in the meantime,

    Believe me,

        dearest Madam,

           With feelings of the profoundest respect,

                Ever your most affectionate cousin   R.L. Stevenson

If that's not a good way of filling up paper, blame me! *My heart is in the Highlands. Impromptu goak.*

---

[2] Degenerate Douglas, i.e. Lewis (Noona) Balfour, who often stayed with the Stevensons at this period.

[3] MIS recorded these guests in her diary. John Wilson Brodie (1851–1937) became an Edinburgh stockbroker and company director; he was in RLS's class at the Academy (see Letter 1202). Also in this class was James Balfour Murray (1852–?). John Adam Watson was the son of TS's niece Jane (Warden) Watson. MIS also lists George Scott and Mr Macara.

83 To his Parents

MS Texas. Partly published in *Letters*, I, 30–35.

Thursday 5 [actually 4] August 1870   *Earraid*[1]

My dear Mother, I have so much to say, that needs must I take a large sheet; for the notepaper brings with it a chilling brevity of style. Indeed, I think, pleasant writing is proportional to the size of the material you write withal.

From Edinburgh to Greenock, I had the ex-secretary of the E.U. Conservative C[lub], Murdoch.[2] At Greenock I spent a dismal evening, though I found a pretty walk. The Tontine is a dirty uncomfortable house, and there was no one in the smoking room. Next day on board the *Iona*,[3] I had Maggie Thomson to Tarbert: Craig, a well-read, pleasant medical to Ardrishaig; and Prof., Mrs, and all the little Fleeming Jenkinseses.[4] Their oldest boy is a disgusting, priggish, envious, diabolically clever little specimen. For example, I asked what was the second one's *specialité*. 'Gardening,' quoth his father, 'I think his is the best garden.' 'My garden,' answers my young friend, 'is very good too.' 'Yes,' says the Professor; 'but Junior[5] is the best gardener.' 'Yes,' replies the young imp, with an inimitable sneer, 'I suppose Mr Brown *is* the best gardener.' 'At least, my son,' answered his father severely, 'whoever may be the best gardener, I

---

[1] The islet off the Isle of Mull near Iona was being used as a base for the construction of the Dhu Heartach lighthouse. RLS describes this visit in 'Memoirs of an Islet'. As Aros it became the setting for 'The Merry Men' and under its own name the scene of David Balfour's misadventures in ch. 14 of *Kidnapped*. MIS records that RLS left Swanston on Monday 1 August.

[2] Patrick Alexander Murdoch (1847–1912), practised as a surgeon in Fulham 1874–89, but later inherited the estate of Mount Annan, Dumfriesshire and changed his name to Pasley-Dirom. RLS was treasurer of the Edinburgh University Conservative Club in 1870, and made his first public speech there on 6 February 1871.

[3] Summer tours by steamer from Glasgow to Oban and the west coast and islands were very popular with Victorian tourists. The *Iona* was a luxuriously fitted paddle-steamer that took passengers from Glasgow and Greenock to Ardrishaig. Here they boarded a small steamer for the passage through the Crinan Canal and then went by another boat northwards to Oban. From Oban steamers made the round trip through the Sound of Mull and down the west coast of Mull to the island of Staffa (famous for Fingal's Cave) to the island of Iona and back to Oban. RLS disembarked at Iona and then went on to Earraid.

[4] Henry Charles Fleeming Jenkin (1833–85), a distinguished electrical engineer whose major work was in the manufacture, testing and laying of submarine telegraph cables. He became Professor of Engineering at Edinburgh University in 1868 where RLS was one of his students. He married (1859) Anne Austin (died 1921). She was a gifted amateur actress and the Jenkin theatrical productions were a feature of the Edinburgh social scene. The Jenkins warmly befriended RLS at a difficult period of his life. RLS wrote a 'Memoir' of Jenkin in 1887 and put him into his essay 'Talk and Talkers' as Cockshot. The Jenkins had three sons: Austin Fleeming (1861–1910) became a barrister; Charles Frewin (1865–1940) was the first Professor of Engineering Science at Oxford University 1908–29; Bernard Maxwell (1867–1951) was a Consulting Engineer. Colvin omitted the rest of this paragraph.

[5] I am not certain of this word.

don't like to see you the best runner-down of the family.' The little beggar knows geology; and apropos of Austin, Mrs F.J. told [me][6] a good story. 'I like your children very much,' said a friend to her: 'at least I like the two younger; and *respect* Osy.' Mrs Jenkin [is] very jolly. They went on to Corran Ferry, near which they have taken a farm, to which I stand invited.

At Oban, that night, it was delicious. Mr Stephenson's[7] yacht lay in the bay, and a splendid band on board played delightfully. The waters of the bay were as smooth as a millpond; and, in the dusk, the black shadows of the hills stretched across to our very feet and the lights were reflected in long lines. At intervals, blue lights were burned on the water; and rockets were sent up. Sometimes great stars of clear fire fell from them, until the bay received and quenched them. I hired a boat and sculled round the yacht in the dark. When I came in, a very pleasant Englishman on the steps fell into talk with me, till it was time to go to bed.

Next morning I slept on or I should have gone to Glencoe. As it was, it was blazing hot; so I hired a boat, pulled all forenoon along the coast and had a delicious bathe on a beautiful white beach. Coming home, I *cotoyai'd*[8] my Englishman, lunched alongside of him and his sister and took a walk with him in the afternoon, during which I find that he was travelling with a servant, kept horses *et caetera*. At dinner, he wished me to sit beside him and his sister; but there was no room. When we came out he told me why he was so *empressé* on this point. He had found out my name, and that I was connected with lighthouses, and his sister wished to know if I were any relative of the Stevenson in Ballantyne's *Lighthouse*.[9] All evening, he, his sister, I and Mr Hargrove, of Hargrove and Fowler, sate in front of the hotel. I asked Mr H. if he knew who my friend was. 'Yes,' he said, 'I never met him before; but my partner knows him. He is a man of old family; and the solicitor of highest standing about Sheffield.' At night, he said, 'Now if you're down in my neighbourhood, you must pay me a visit. I am very fond of young men about me; and I should like a visit from you very much. I can take you through any factory in Sheffield; and I'll drive you all about the *Dookeries*.' He then wrote me down his address; and we parted huge friends, he still keeping me up to visit him. Here is his address:

[6] The word is obscured by a large blot.

[7] George Robert Stephenson (1819–1905) of Glen Caladh Castle, Kyles of Bute, nephew of the famous railway engineer, was himself an engineer and proprietor of locomotive works at Newcastle upon Tyne.

[8] RLS must have been thinking of the French *côtoyer*. Colvin reads '*cotogai'd*'.

[9] R.M. Ballantyne's *The Lighthouse* (1865), an account of the building of the Bell Rock lighthouse by RLS's grandfather. In a fragment of autobiography dictated at Vailima (posthumously published as part of 'Memoirs of Himself'), RLS describes his tongue-tied meeting with Ballantyne while he was writing the book.

Henry Go Watson,[10] Shirecliffe Hall, Sheffield,
or, The Park Cottage, Worksop.

Saul also among the prophets, Mrs S.[11]

Hitherto, I had enjoyed myself amazingly; but today has been the crown. In the morning I met Bough[12] on board, with whom I am both surprised and delighted. He and I have read the same books, and discuss Chaucer, Shakespeare, Marlowe, Fletcher, Webster, and all the old authors. He can quote verses by the page, and has really a very pretty literary taste. Altogether, with all his coarseness and buffoonery a more pleasant, clever fellow you may seldom see. I was very much surprised with him; and he with me. 'Where the devil did you read all these books?' says he; and in my heart, I echo the question. One amusing thing I must say. We were talking about travelling; and I said I was so fond of travelling alone, from the people one met and grew friendly with. 'Ah,' says he, 'but you've such a pleasant manner you know – quite captivated my old woman, you did – she couldn't talk of anything else.'[13] Here was a compliment, even in Sam Bough's sneering tones, that rather tickled my vanity; and really my social successes of the last few days, the best of which is yet to come, are enough to turn anybody's head. To continue, after a little go in with Samuel, he going up on the bridge, I looked about me to see who there was; and mine eye lighted on two girls, one of whom was sweet and pretty, talking to an old gentleman. '*Eh bien,*' says I to myself, 'that seems the best investment on board.' So I sidled up to the old gentleman, got into conversation with him and so with the damsel; and thereupon, having used the patriarch as a ladder, I kicked him down behind me. Who should my damsel prove, but Amy Sinclair, daughter of Sir John George?[14] She certainly was the simplest, most naïve specimen of girlhood I ever saw. By getting brandy and biscuit and generally coaching up her cousin who was sick, I ingratiated myself; and

[10] Henry Edmund Watson (1815–1901), knighted 1886, Sheffield solicitor and company director. RLS seems to have written his second name as 'Go'.

[11] I Samuel 10:11.

[12] Sam Bough (1822–78), born in Carlisle, worked as a boy with his father as a cobbler and then briefly as a lawyer's clerk before abandoning it in favour of a Bohemian life wandering about the country, associating with gipsies while making water-colour sketches and working as a scene-painter in the theatre. Eventually he won recognition as a landscape painter of distinction and became a member of the Royal Scottish Academy, 1875. RLS wrote an affectionate obituary notice in the *Academy*, 30 November 1878, recording that Bough's rough and sarcastic manner 'was no more than a husk, an outer man, partly of habit, partly of affectation; and inside the burr there was a man of warm feelings, notable powers of mind, and much culture.'

[13] MIS records in her *Diary Notes*: 'In June while attending Prof. Jenkin's summer session and levelling on the Braid Hills, he ran a levelling rod into his leg and with some difficulty got as far as the house of Sam Bough, the artist. His wife is very kind and takes a great fancy to Lou.'

[14] Amy Camilla Sinclair (died 1925), elder daughter of Sir John George Tollemache Sinclair, Bt. (1824–1912). She married John Henry Fullarton Udny of Udny Castle, Aberdeen, in 1874. When Colvin published this letter (in part) in 1911 it was with her consent.

so kept by her the whole way to Iona, taking her into the cave at Staffa and generally making myself as gallant as possible. I never was so much pleased with anything in my life, as her amusing absence of *mauvaise honte*: she was so sorry I wasn't going on to Oban again: didn't know how she could have enjoyed herself if I hadn't been there: and was so sorry we hadn't met on the Crinan. When we came back from Staffa, she and her aunt went down to have lunch; and a minute after up comes Miss Amy to ask me if I wouldn't think better of it, and take some lunch with them. I could not resist that of course; so down I went; and there she displayed the full extent of her innocence. I must be sure to come to Thurso Castle the next time I was in Caithness, or The Mount, Upper Norwood (whence she would take me all over the Crystal Palace) when I was near London; and (most complete of all) she offered to call on us in Edinburgh! Imagine if Sir J.G. had been there and that beholding! Of course, I had to say we should be delighted and give our address, though I could scarce keep [from] laughing, and blushed, I must say, at her aunt's satyrical face and sharp ears on the other side. Wasn't it delicious? She is a girl of sixteen or seventeen, too, and the latter, I think.

In the meantime, Miss Amy has run away with my pen; and I must turn back to get into chronology. Coming off Staffa, Sam Bough (who had been in huge force the whole time, drawing in Miss Amy's sketchbook and making himself agreeable or otherwise to everybody) pointed me out to a parson and said, 'That's him!' This was Alick Ross and his wife. Ross seems very nice, but his wife is a horrid woman, so forward, pushing and brazen.

The last stage of the steamer now approached, Miss Amy and I lamenting pathetically that Iona was so near. 'People meet in this way,' quoth she, 'and then lose sight of one another so soon.' We all landed together, Bough and I and the Rosses with our baggage; and went together over the ruins. I was here left with the cousin and the aunt (a Mrs Malcolm) during which I learned that said cousin sees me *every* Sunday in St Stephens. Oho! thought I, at the 'every'. Mrs Malcolm was very anxious to know who that strange, wild man was? (didn't I wish Samuel in Tophet!) Of course in reply, I drew it strong about eccentric genius and my never having known him before, and a good deal that was perhaps 'strained to the extremest limit of the fact'. But Act Vth was yet to come, alas!

The steamer left, and Miss Amy and her cousin waved their handkerchiefs, until my arm in answering them was nearly broken. I believe women's arms must be better made for this exercise: mine ache still; and I regretted at the time that the handkerchief had seen service. Altogether, however, I was left in a pleasant frame of mind; but the disclosure of the Act Vth, above referred to, fell as a wet blanket on my hopes. Mrs Malcolm had thanked Bough for his attention; and what said the wild man of Jordan Lane to her, but this? 'I can only say in the words of Hamlet, "Fair maid, in thy orisons be all my sins remembered." '

Before I go to bed (for it is now near midnight) I shall epilogize on Miss Amy Sinclair. As a psychological study she was quite a discovery to me. I never yet saw a girl so perfectly innocent and fresh, so perfectly modest without the least trace of prudery. *Demain, Madame, j'espère de vous raconter ce qui reste (et ce n'est pas rien, ma foi) de nos aventures d'aujourdhui.*

Friday morning [*5 August*]

Being thus left alone, Bough, I, the Rosses, Professor Blackie,[15] and an English parson, called Malin. These people were going to remain the night, except the Professor who is resident there at present. They were going to dine *en compagnie* and wished us to join the party; but we had already committed ourselves by mistake to the wrong hotel and besides we wished to be off soon as wind and tide were against us to Earraid. We went up, Bough selected a place for sketching and blocked in the sketch for Mrs Ross; and we all talked together. Bough told us his family history and a lot of strange things about old Cumberland life; among others, how he had known 'John Peel', of pleasant memory in song and of how that worthy hunted. At five, down we go to the Argyll Hotel, and wait dinner. Broth, 'nice broth', fresh herrings, and fowl had been promised. At 5.50, I get the shovel and tongs and drum them at the stair-head till a response comes from below that the nice broth is at hand. I boast of my engineering and Bough compares me to the Abbot of Arbroath who originated the Inchcape Bell.[16] At last, in comes the tureen and the handmaid lifts the cover. 'Rice Soup!' I yell, 'O no! none o' that for me!' – 'Yes,' says Bough, savagely, 'But Miss Amy didn't take me downstairs to eat salmon.' Accordingly he is helped. How his face fell. 'I imagine myself in the accident ward of the infirmary,' quoth he. It was, purely and simply, rice and water. After this, we have another weary pause, and then herrings in a state of mash and potatoes like iron. 'Send the potatoes out to Prussia for grape-shot,' was the suggestion.[17] I dined off broken herrings and dry bread. At last 'the supreme moment comes', and the fowl in a lordly dish, is carried in. On the cover being raised, there is something so forlorn and miserable about the aspect of the animal that we both roar with laughter. Then Bough, taking up knife and fork, turns the 'swarry'[18] over and over, shaking doubtfully his head.

---

[15] John Stuart Blackie (1809–95), Professor of Greek at Edinburgh University 1852–82, was a much loved Edinburgh figure, famous for his eccentricities. RLS was a consistent truant from his classes.

[16] There is a tradition, commemorated by Southey in his ballad, that a bell was hung on the Inchcape or Bell Rock – the dangerous reef on which the lighthouse was built – by an Abbot of Arbroath, and that the pirate who removed it was himself wrecked on the rock.

[17] The Franco-Prussian war began in July 1870 and continued until January 1871.

[18] A humorous spelling of *soirée* in the sense of a social evening (cf. 'a friendly swarry', *Pickwick Papers*, ch. 37); here by extension the evening meal itself.

'There's an aspect of quiet resistance about the beggar,' says he, 'that looks bad.' However, to work he falls until the sweat stands on his brow and a dismembered leg falls, dull and leadenlike, onto my dish. To eat it was simply impossible. Toughness was here at its farthest. I did not know before that flesh could be so tough. 'The strongest jaws in England,' says Bough piteously harpooning his dry morsel, 'couldn't eat this leg in less than twelve hours.' Nothing for it now; but to order boat and bill. 'That fowl,' says Bough to the landlady, 'is of a breed I know. I know the cut of its jib whenever it was put down. That was the grandmother of the cock that firghtened Peter.' – 'I thought it was an historical animal,' says I, 'What a shame to kill it. It's as bad as eating Whittington's cat or the Dog of Montargis.'[19] – 'Na – na it's no old,' says the landlady, 'but it eats hard.' – 'Eats!' I cry, 'where do you find that? Very little of that verb with us.' So with more raillery, we pay six shillings for our festival and run over to Earraid, shaking the dust of the Argyll Hotel from off our feet.

I can write no more, just now and I hope you will be able to decipher so much; for it contains matter. Really the whole of yesterday's work would do in a novel without one little bit of embellishment; and, indeed, few novels are so amusing. Bough, Miss Amy, Mrs Ross, Blackie, Malin the parson, all these were such distinct characters, the incidents were so entertaining, and the scenery so fine, that the whole would have made a novelist's fortune. Believe me, Your very affectionate son

R.L. Stevenson

My dear Father, No landing today, as the sea runs high on the rock. They are at the second course of the first story on the rock. I have as yet had no time here; so this is α and ω of my business news. Your affectionate son

R.L. Stevenson

84   *To his Mother*

MS Yale.

[*August 1870*]   [*Earraid*]

My dear Mother, Young Brebner[1] is seated opposite to me, reading Shakespeare. A mug of porter stands conveniently at my right; and a stranger might detect the pleasant fragrance of S. Coltons' oriental mixture in active

---

[19] *The Forest of Bondy, or the Dog of the Montargis* was one of the juvenile dramas celebrated by RLS in 'A Penny Plain and Twopence Coloured'. Aubrey de Montidier was murdered in the Forest of Bondy near Montargis by Richard de Macaire. Aubrey's dog excited suspicion by always snarling at Macaire. The King ordered a judicial combat between dog and man; Macaire was overcome by the dog, confessed his guilt and died.

[1] Alan Brebner (born 1857), son of Alan Brebner, C.E. (1826–90), one of the engineers working on the Dhu Heartach lighthouse and later a partner in the family firm. He, too, became a distinguished lighthouse engineer.

deflagration. We are in the sitting room at Mrs Grant's, the leading master's wife: an apartment often honoured by the midnight, of Samuel[2] chanting 'John Peel' or 'If she be not fair to me, what care I how fair she be.'[3] The latter is now at Iona, where I spent Sunday with him, bringing a lay preacher over with me in the evening, of whom I shall say more when I have inclination to write you another 'long letter'. The manuscript you received must stand in stead for some time. What you say about Miss Sinclair, I cannot agree withal: teach her reticence and you spoil her. I am enjoying myself amazingly here, and could do so for some time. I really can't tell you much on this confounded note paper; but I can chronicle a remark of Sambo's which is too clever to be lost. 'Look at that miserable Yankee sinner, Benjamin Franklin,' he said, 'and the harm he has done. The devil never did a cleverer thing than the invention of the maxim, "Honesty is the best policy".'[4] Isn't that good and true? Mrs Brebner is awfully kind. I am getting red I understand from all parties.[5] On Sunday I was up at four in the morning and waited without any bother till nine for breakfast. Last year I should have been nearly dead ere that. Tomorrow we leave at seven for Skerryvohr.[6] At present I hear Mrs Grant locking the outer door. She is a very nice person, with an Aberdonian accent that always leaves me to guess wildly at her meaning. My dress would amuse you. I only put a collar on, on Sunday for service, and go about half the day in a Jersey with no coat, like a fisherman. Believe me, Your affectionate son

R.L. Stevenson[7]

85   To his Mother[1]

MS NLS.

Monday 3 October 1870   *Cockfield Rectory*

My dear Mother, There is no village of Cockfield (I go at once *in medias res*); but a number of delightful hamlets, each round its little patch of green: there

---

[2] Sam Bough.

[3] George Wither, 'The Shepherd's Resolution'.

[4] In his series *Poor Richard's Almanac* (1732–58), Benjamin Franklin wrote and collected many maxims and proverbs.

[5] In 'Memoirs of an Islet' RLS remembered his visit as mainly a holiday 'of sea-bathing and sun-burning'.

[6] Skerryvore lighthouse, 'the noblest of all extant deep-sea lights', was designed and built by Alan Stevenson 1838–43.

[7] RLS's parents visited Earraid on the *Pharos* on 19 August, and they all left the next day. They were back at Swanston on 25 August.

[1] On 30 September RLS went to Cockfield near Bury St Edmunds to visit his cousin Maud and to attend the wedding of her sister Jane Wilson. Matilda (Maud) Whytt Wilson (1844–1919) married (1869) Professor Churchill Babington (1821–89), Disney Professor of Archaeology at Cambridge 1865–80, and Rector of Cockfield 1866–89. She later married Colonel Henry Wright, and figures in Graham Greene's *A Sort of Life*.

is Great Green, Parsons Green, Windsor Green, Old Hall Green, Cross Green, and others.

Yesterday we had service in the barn, the church being under restoration; afterwards, Grahame Balfour[2] and I set forth and walked through the fields to Bradfield Combust, an old village, with a church, stone[3] antique cottages and a most beautiful avenue of elms.

Grahame (I know not if I spell his name aright) is very nice, I think: his wife, very much so. Babington is also a pleasant man but a pedant, objecting to Carlyle because he is not a scholar and for that reason, giving him no merit.

We breakfast at half-past eight. Then Grahame and I smoke a pipe in the garden; during which time he very pleasantly entertains me with tales reflecting his own renown in the most lively colours to my outland fancy. This not offensively, mark you; but as though finding a great and innocent satisfaction in his own success. At one, we lunch. At half-past six, dine: go into the drawing room for tea; and then return to the dining room for brandy and water, (or, in my case, beer) not unaccompanied with pipes. Babington and I smoke churchwardens, Grahame a red clay with a wooden stalk. These are not the least pleasant hours of the day. Today, we went in the morning, to the church. Professor Babington, being lame from a sprain, was not able to go. I shall tell you more of the church when I have large paper. I have before told you that I could not expatiate on note paper; but my next shall answer expectations. In the afternoon, we went to a croquet party; where I enjoyed myself much, the people were frank and pleasant. The place (Clopton Hall) pretty. So there was not much to cast reproach against.

Mr Babington is not so old as I expected; and is not at all disagreeable. Only one little disagreeable took place. I was carrying his footrest into the dining room; and, in turning round to remind Grahame that he should give him his arm, I struck a little stand laden with china. The professor's brow darkened. 'If you upset that and break my Wedgwood,' said he, 'I shall not thank you very much.' He and Maud get on well together.

I am very glad to hear of Bob's return.

Thanks for the stamps. Ever your affectionate son   R.L. Stevenson

No want of liquor; no objection to baccy, thanks.   R.L.S.

---

[2] Thomas Graham Balfour (1813–91), a nephew of RLS's grandfather Lewis Balfour, had a distinguished army career as surgeon and statistician. He was the first head of the new Statistical Branch of the Army Medical Service 1859–73; Surgeon-General 1873. He married (1856) Georgina Prentice (1819–88), and their only child, Graham, was to become RLS's biographer.

[3] RLS seems to have written 'of' after 'stone'. He may have written 'store of'.

86   *To his Mother*

MS NLS.

Thursday 6 October 1870   *Cockfield Rectory*

My dear Mother, The marriage went off exceedingly well, and the persons in question were sent off in triumph.[1] I like the service much. Maggie[2] is not bad looking: the belles of the marriage party were May and Nora Piers. James Wilson[3] was there, who is an ugly brute. After the marriage we all went off to Risbygate Street;[4] where we had refreshments and a photographer. First bride, bridegroom and horde of small bridesmaids were photographed: afterward, the residue of the company. All then came out to Cockfield where we had a luncheon and four croquet sets. The day including sixteen miles drive lasted from 7.30 to seven; and at the end of it, the greater part of us felt as though the labours of Hercules were at last eclipsed.

Yesterday, Grahame and I walked over to Lavenham, a most delightful old town; my spoil from which I enclose. I think it is the finest specimen of an old house I ever saw. Coming back we lost our way among the fields and had a sore trouble to extricate ourselves. One of the ditches took me over the head and I had to lie down on the far side and give Grahame my foot to struggle up by.

Grahame and Madame[5] are off this morning. I like both of them very much. She is great fun. Maud was sporting some views about community of church-sittings, when she turned to me and said, 'That's all very well; but the Baptists are the only people who could practise it – total immersion, you know.' These sort of sayings are never out of her mouth; and her Irish brogue and a strong emphasis give them a great deal more salt than they seem to have afterwards.

Dr Paul's remark was good: please include the two specimens sent me; or if you prefer it, we can find them Christian sepulture in Cockfield – consecrated ground being here as common as plough land.

Professor Babington is an innocent,[6] unworldly man (I withdraw the old,

---

[1] Jane Wilson (1846–1903) married on 4 October 1870 the Revd Carleton Greene (1844–1924), a solicitor's son from Bury. Graham Greene was their grandson.

[2] Margaret Graham Wilson (1851–1900). She married the Revd Frederick Crick in 1877.

[3] James Hamilton Wilson (1837–90).

[4] The mother of the bride, MIS's sister Marion Wilson (1811–83), was the widow of Col. J.A. Wilson, R.A. (1793–1857). She lived at 56 Risbygate Street, Bury St Edmunds, where she took as boarders children whose parents were in India. (Zoë Proctor, who was one of the children she cared for, gives an account of the household in *Life and Yesterday*, 1960, 26–31.)

[5] On a copy of this letter, Balfour noted that this was his mother's name among the Wilsons.

[6] 'old' deleted.

you see), who is really very kind, very merry and incredibly innocent: he knows about as much of the world as a child.

About my coming home, I don't know. I have an engagement for Wednesday forenoon, which I should like very much to keep. But as to that let me know. I could be in town I fancy by Thursday night. Believe me, Your affectionate son, In muckle haste   R.L. Stevenson

87   To Maud Babington

MS Yale.

26 November 1870   *17 Heriot Row*

My dear Maud, I know I am always in debt, always owing letters; still, I had so thoroughly convinced myself that your letter was duly answered and that you owed me another, that I was much astonied at my mother's message. However I am not obstinate in my beliefs. I accept what is inevitable; and, feeling very kind indeed, I agree to waive my doubts and write again.

News, I have not much – except, by the way, that we are now and for some time have been, in full seventh vial.[1] This is a consideration which I find very comfortable. Men have actually got through all the seals, all the trumpets, and 6.5 of the vials – and never found it out! I imagined us all fasting, and lying prostrate in sackcloth and ashes, and here we have been as well as usual, and as merry withal, through the whole performance. And to think now of how I have frightened myself with these same seals and vials, and read them with perspiration on my brow! I now begin to think that we may get through the last day, too, and never find it out.

If the Prussian war goes on, however, we shall probably have fully more vial than we want.

You observe that I have begun to write forwards; but I don't think the new incline so dignified, and I'm sure it's not so legible, as the old.

If your papers have been faithful, you will probably know how nicely woman's rights were received by some of my fellow students the other day. The female medicals were hooted, hissed and jostled till the police interfered and removed some of the aggressors to the place of condemnation. My views are very neutral. I quite believe that Miss Jex Blake,[2] and the rest

---

[1] Revelation, ch. 16.
[2] Sophia Louisa Jex-Blake (1840–1912) was one of the small group of women who studied medicine at Edinburgh under increasing difficulties, and who were refused permission to graduate in 1872. She founded the London School of Medicine for Women in 1874 and was the moving spirit behind the campaign which eventually led to all medical boards being empowered to admit women. Final victory came in 1894, when Edinburgh admitted women to graduation. She practised in Edinburgh 1879–99.

of our fellow-studentesses, are the first of a noble army – pioneers – Columbus's – and all that sort of thing. But, at the same time, Miss Jex Blake is playing for the esteem of posterity. *Soit.* I give her posterity; but I won't marry either her or her fellows. Let posterity marry them, if posterity likes – I won't. And if posterity gets hold of this letter, I shall probably be burnt in effigy by some Royal Female College of Surgeons of the future period; unless you save my credit and prevent them, by burning it at present.

I wish I could think of something to say. A person with earache, headache and his spinal marrow gradually liquifying before a fire heated seven times, can scarcely be expected to write either a very deep or a very festive epistle.

I am much concerned at the thought of not having sufficiently tipped Joyers;[3] so I wish you to expend what stamps you receive herewith, in the purchase of sweeties for his child – good, strong sickly lollipops, please – when I was a child I thought nothing of a sweet that could not make me ill – so keep that in view please in your choice for Miss Joyers – whatever you wouldn't eat yourself for a small fortune, that (be sure) she will roll under her tongue as a sweet morsel.

Remember me very kindly to Mr Babington and all folk about Bury, and, Believe me, Ever your most affectionate cousin   R.L. Stevenson

---

[3] 'Lou comes home from England this morning having travelled all night for want of *one shilling!*' (MIS, *Diary*, 15 October).

III. LEGAL STUDIES AND EDINBURGH FRIENDSHIPS April 1871–July 1873

On 27 March 1871, at a meeting of the Royal Scottish Society of Arts, Stevenson read his paper 'On a New Form of Intermittent Light for Lighthouses', for which he was later awarded a silver medal. A week later the University session ended with a supper (organised by RLS) for Professor Jenkin's engineering class and a class excursion to Glasgow to visit engineering works on 5/6 April: it was RLS's farewell to engineering.[1] On what he was later to describe as 'a dreadful evening walk' with his father, it came out that he was learning nothing: 'On being tightly cross-questioned . . . I owned I cared for nothing but literature. My father said that was no profession; but I might be called to the bar if I chose; so at the age of 21, I began to study law.'[2] In her diary for 8 April, his mother recorded: 'Hear today that Lou thinks of being an advocate and not a C.E. Tom wonderfully resigned'; on the 12th she noted, 'Lou's change of plan announced today.'

In November 1871, RLS began his Law classes at the University. A year later (on 9 November 1872) he passed the preliminary examination for the Scottish Bar.

In 1871 Bob Stevenson returned to Edinburgh after taking his degree at Cambridge. RLS (in the fragment of autobiography written in 1880)[3] described this as having changed the course of his life. Bob was an ideal confidant: 'The miserable isolation in which I had languished was no more in season; and I began to be happy . . . I was done with the sullens for good; there was an end of greensickness for my life as soon as I had got a friend to laugh with.' To this period belong the elaborate practical jokes called 'Jink' (cf. Letter 192). Soon RLS gathered round him (in addition to Bob) the group of special friends who were to play an important part in his life: Charles Baxter, who became a lawyer, RLS's financial agent, a close friend and lifelong correspondent (see p. 40); James Walter Ferrier (see Letter 111, n. 4) and Sir Walter Simpson (see Letter 101, n. 1). All three were fellow-members of the Speculative Society at the University.

---

[1] In an incomplete account of the supper and the excursion, RLS wrote of the drunken and rowdy behaviour of his fellow-students and commented: 'everything connected with this portion of my life is jaundiced in my eyes' (MS NLS).

[2] RLS to George Iles, 29 October 1887 (Letter 1928). E.B. Simpson (*The Stevenson Originals*, 1912, 59) says the walk was to Cramond.

[3] MS Rosenbach; extensively quoted in Balfour, I, 83–4, 86–94.

This famous literary and debating society was founded in 1764 and still flourishes. RLS became a member on 2 March 1869, and took an active part in its weekly meetings held every Tuesday from November to March. Proceedings included the reading of an essay by a member and a debate. Baxter records that RLS was never 'anything as a speaker. He was nervous and ineffective . . . but his papers were successful.'[4] RLS's continuing interest in the society is shown in his description in 'A College Magazine' and his references in the dedicatory letter to *Kidnapped* and in *Weir of Hermiston*. Another link between this group of friends was the mysterious society the L.J.R. (see Letter 98, n. 7).

In his later correspondence with Baxter RLS often remembered the fun they had together in the pubs in the Lothian Road when they were hard-put to find the few pennies needed to pay for their drinks. This 'low life', inevitably, finds no expression in these early letters. In his autobiography Stevenson tells us:

> I was always kept poor in my youth, to my great indignation at the time, but since then with my complete approval. Twelve pounds a year was my allowance up to twenty-three . . . and though I amplified it by a very consistent embezzlement from my mother, I never had enough to be lavish. . . . Hence my acquaintance was of what would be called a very low order; looking back upon it, I am surprised at the courage with which I first ventured alone into the societies in which I moved; I was the companion of seamen, chimney sweeps and thieves; my circle was being continually changed by the action of the police magistrate; I see now the little sanded kitchen, where 'velvet-coat', for such was the name I went by, has spent days together, generally in silence and making sonnets in a penny version book; and rough as the material may appear, I do not believe these days were among the least happy I have spent.[5]

Looking back from Vailima at this period of his life RLS told Balfour:

> You know I very easily might have gone to the devil: I don't understand why I didn't. Even when I was almost grown up I was kept so short of money that I had to make the most of every penny. The result was that I had my dissipation all the same but I had it in the worst possible surroundings. At the time I used to have my headquarters in an old public house frequented by the lowest order of prostitutes – threepenny whores – where there was a room in which I used to go and write. I saw

---

[4] *The Outlook*, 19 February 1898, 71.
[5] As in Note 3. I depend on Balfour for a number of words now lost when the corner of the MS was torn away. In a later note (dated 12 July 1925) in his papers, Balfour says that he deleted the word 'prostitute' between 'chimney sweeps' and 'thieves' and added: 'There is no question but that Louis had relations with girls of this class at this time of his life.' Strangely enough the word does not, in fact, occur at this point in the MS.

a good deal of the girls – they were really singularly decent creatures, not a bit worse than anybody else. But it wasn't a good beginning for a young man.[6]

Another aspect of RLS at this time must be mentioned – his shabby clothes. Colvin has a good summary:

There was something for strangers, and even for friends, to get over in the queer garments which in youth it was his whim to wear – the badge as they always seemed to me, partly of a genuine carelessness, certainly of a genuine lack of cash (the little that he had was always absolutely at the disposal of his friends), partly of a deliberate detachment from any particular social class or caste, partly of his love of pickles and adventures, which he thought befell a man thus attired more readily than another. But this slender, slovenly, nondescript apparition, long-visaged and long-haired, had only to speak in order to be recognised in the first minute for a witty and charming gentleman, and within the first five for a master spirit and a man of genius.

RLS scorned the polite Edinburgh society in which his parents moved and was contemptuous of its conventional entertainments (though he dined with the Jenkins and took part in their private theatricals). He preferred to go his own way, with his own small circle of friends, 'scraping acquaintance [as he later described himself in 'Lay Morals'] with all classes of man – and womankind.' In return, many of those in that society looked askance at the strange young man in his disreputable clothes and, failing to see the genius beneath the eccentricities, pitied the Stevensons for having such a wayward son.

In guarded phrases, Colvin sums up the inner conflicts at this period of RLS's life:

The ferment of youth was more acute and more prolonged in him than in most men even of genius. There met in him many various strains and elements, which were in these days pulling one against another in his half-formed being at a great expense of spirit and body. Add the storms, which from time to time attacked him, of shivering repulsion from the climate and conditions of life in the city which he yet deeply and imaginatively loved; the moods of spiritual revolt against the harsh doctrines of the creed in which he had been brought up, and to which his parents were deeply, his father even passionately, attached; the seasons of temptation, most strongly besetting the ardent and poetic temperament, to seek solace among the crude allurements of the city streets.[7]

---

[6] Recorded in Balfour's Reminiscences (NLS).
[7] Colvin's comments come from Letters, I, xxi, and 8.

In the first letter in this section we find RLS writing an earnest letter to a
Scottish religious paper. In one of the last (Letter 123) we see the beginnings
of the bitter conflict with his father over religion, which gave them both so
much distress.

88   *To the Editor of* The Church of Scotland Home and Foreign Missionary Record[1]

Text: above periodical, 1 May 1871, 349–50.

[*April 1871*]   [*Edinburgh*]

I have a proposal to make with regard to Parochial Organisation, which
is specially suitable in the present day, when the doctrine of humanity is
taking such large proportions, and when even our most forward unbelievers
make the backbone of their teaching a certain 'devout obligation and
service towards creatures that have only their own fellowship and mutual
ministry to lean upon.'[2]

We are kept in no doubt as to the touchstone on which the reality of our
faith – whether as individuals or body of individuals – whether as Church-
members or Church – is to be tried. Almost the last words of our Lord to
his disciples tell as exactly what charge we shall have to answer, what
outcome is required of our religion. 'Inasmuch as ye did it unto the least of
these,' is the trying clause.[3] Now, Sir, this test will be applied to us, as I have
said, not as individuals only, but as Churches. No body in this land is better
qualified, or stands in a more favourable position, for the care of the poor
and suffering, than our Established Church; and I would ask very seriously
whether it is doing all that it might do 'unto the least of these'. I think not.
Even supposing that our spiritual arrangements were not to be bettered, and
that our whole available strength was applied to the work of the religious
improvement of the people, there is still much to be done for their physical
needs. There is a large class of men who would be only too glad to visit
those that are sick or in prison, to clothe the naked, or feed the hungry; but
they are helpless – incapable of doing anything. An individual cannot well
enter into such tasks unaided. He cannot find an end of the skein to begin
upon. The doors of his suffering fellows are shut against him, or only

---

[1] Published anonymously under the heading 'Parochial Work and Organisation'. The editor noted:
'An earnest young "Student", not a "Divinity" student, he says, has sent us the following
interesting communication . . .'. MIS identifies it as by RLS in her *Diary Notes*.

[2] A footnote in the published text identifies this as 'Mr Morley in the *Fortnightly Review*'.

[3] Matthew 25:40. MIS noted that it must have been at this time that RLS was deeply influenced by
St Matthew's Gospel, as recorded in 'Books Which Have Influenced Me' (1887).

opened by greed and imposture. It is very easy for him to spend money, but very difficult for him to do good. It may be answered that such an one can always become a deacon or an elder, teach in the Sunday-school, or distribute tracts; but all these things are hampered with special qualifications. Many people find themselves unwilling or unfit for them. Perhaps from a morbid self-questioning, perhaps from too well-founded scruples, they hesitate to identify themselves so openly with the Church of Christ. Now it is not with regard to them, but with regard to those who might help, that I wish to move this question. It seems a pity to throw the willing helper into a false position. It seems a mere confusion of ideas to make a tract the only passport to a sick bed. You have nothing to do with the giver's frame of mind – what you have to consider is the possible benefit of the gift. You do not refuse every offering from the plate, until you know what feelings laid it there, until you are sure that mere cold habit, or the desire for a decent appearance, were not the actuating motives. It would be wrong to do so. In the same way, Sir, it seems to me, that the Church will be held answerable for all good work to which she has denied an outlet – for all help and comfort that her restrictions have withheld from '*the least of these*'. Now the proposal that I wish to make through your columns is one that would, I think, ameliorate the poor both physically and spiritually; for while it would bring in a large body of new assistants in the former branch, it would leave the minister and those who assist him even now, a full opportunity of devoting all their energies to the latter. It has the further merit of simplicity and absolute economy. Let the minister direct, assist, employ in every way, and assign fit districts to all who are willing to help in humane endeavours, without hampering their service by any burdensome titles, or committing them to any special profession. Let it be a work simply of humanity. Let the minister and the elders retain for themselves all the spiritual part of the parochial visitation. Let this be done, Sir, and I think we shall find much good result. First, the poor will be better cared for in every way. Second, there will grow up in each parish a body of men trained to such work, from whose number the eldership and the diaconate may in good time be reinforced. Third, and last, the Church itself will be strengthened. We must not forget that this is a time of much public feeling and public inquiry as to the fitness of our Established Churches, when the cry of inefficiency has been already raised against a sister body. It would be no small matter in the favour of our own Church if she could point to such a work as this.

Of course, this proposal demands no organisation or general understanding. Each good minister could find plenty of work in the dark places of his parish for any who were willing to join; and if two or three, or even one, would take the proposal up, and give it a fair trial, I am sure the example would spread.

89   To Maud Babington

Text: *Letters,* I, 35–7.

[*? Summer 1871*]   [*Swanston Cottage*]

My dear Maud, If you have forgotten the handwriting – as is like enough
– you will find the name of a former correspondent (don't know how to
spell that word) at the end. I have begun to write to you before now, but
always stuck somehow and left it to drown in a drawerful of like fiascos.
This time I am determined to carry through, though I have nothing
specially to say.

We look fairly like summer this morning; the trees are blackening out of
their spring greens; the warmer suns have melted the hoarfrost of daisies of
the paddock; and the blackbird, I fear, already beginning to 'stint his pipe
of mellower days'[1] – which is very apposite (I can't spell anything today –
one p or *two*?) and pretty. All the same, we have been having shocking
weather – cold winds and grey skies.

I have been reading heaps of nice books; but I can't go back so far. I am
reading Clarendon's *Hist. Rebell.*[2] at present, with which I am more pleased
than I expected, which is saying a good deal. It is a pet idea of mine that one
gets more real truth out of one avowed partisan than out of a dozen of your
sham impartialists – wolves in sheep's clothing – simpering honesty as they
suppress documents. After all, what one wants to know is not what people
did, but why they did it – or rather, why they *thought* they did it; and to
learn that, you should go to the men themselves. Their very falsehood is
often more than another man's truth.

I have possessed myself of Mrs Hutchinson,[3] which, of course, I admire,
etc. But is there not an irritating deliberation and correctness about her and
everybody connected with her? If she would only write bad grammar, or
forget to finish a sentence, or do something or other that looks fallible, it
would be a relief. I sometimes wish the old Colonel had got drunk and
beaten her, in the bitterness of my spirit. I know I felt a weight taken off my
heart when I heard he was extravagant. It is quite possible to be too good
for this evil world; and unquestionably, Mrs Hutchinson was. The way in
which she talks of herself makes one's blood run cold. There – I am glad to
have got that out – but don't say it to anybody – seal of secrecy.

---

[1] Cf. Shakespeare, Sonnet CII: 'As Philomel in summer's front doth sing / And stops her pipe in
growth of riper days.'
[2] The Earl of Clarendon's posthumously published *The True Historical Narrative of the Rebellion and
Civil Wars in England* (1702–4).
[3] Mrs Lucy Hutchinson's life of her husband Colonel John Hutchinson (1615–64), the Puritan
statesman and soldier (1806).

Please tell Mr Babington that I have never forgotten one of his drawings – a Rubens, I think – a woman holding up a model ship. That woman had more life in her than ninety per cent. of the lame humans that you see crippling about this earth.

By the way, that is a feature in art which seems to have come in with the Italians. Your old Greek statues have scarce enough vitality in them to keep their monstrous bodies fresh withal. A shrewd country attorney, in a turned white neckcloth and rusty blacks, would just take one of these Agamemnons and Ajaxes quietly by his beautiful, strong arm, trot the unresisting statue down a little gallery of legal shams, and turn the poor fellow out at the other end, 'naked, as from the earth he came'.[4] There is more latent life, more of the coiled spring in the sleeping dog, about a recumbent figure of Michael Angelo's than about the most excited of Greek statues. The very marble seems to wrinkle with a wild energy that we never feel except in dreams.

I think this letter has turned into a sermon, but I had nothing interesting to talk about.

I do wish you and Mr Babington would think better of it and come north this summer. We should be so glad to see you both. *Do* reconsider it. Believe me, my dear Maud, Ever your most affectionate cousin

Louis Stevenson

90   *To Mrs Alan Brebner*

MS NLS.

7 June 1871   *Swanston*

Dear Mrs Brebner, I hope you will please me by accepting the little brooch that my father will give you along with this, as a remembrance of my stay at Earraid. I shall always look back upon it, as one of the best times I ever had; and giving up the hope of such luck again, is one of the greatest griefs I have in my change of profession.

Will you tell Mr Brebner that my father has some tobacco in his portmanteau, which I hope he will accept and find good. I only wish I could be at the 'preeing'[1] somewhere in Earraid! Believe me, Yours sincerely

Robert Louis Stevenson

---

[4] 'Naked as from the earth we came,/And entered life at first' – Job, 1:21, in the Paraphrase sung in the Church of Scotland.
[1] Sampling or tasting.

91   To Charles Baxter

MS Yale. Published in *Baxter Letters*, 1.

31 October[1] *[1871]*   *17 Heriot Row*

My dear Baxter, Thursday the 16th is the important day.[2] 6.30 the eventful
hour. Be early, be early! Yours very sincerely   Louis Stevenson

92   To Henrietta Traquair

Facsimile, Yale.

[Postmark 8 November 1871]   *[Edinburgh]*

My dear Henrietta, I shall have much pleasure in dining with you on Friday
next. My classes do not finish till five; so that I have no choice as to how
I shall come. Besides, you seem to have only half a plan, when you propose
that I should drive out with your Uncle.[1] True enough, that would bring
me out to Colinton; but how should I get in again?

Consequently, I shall produce Mr 'Arrower[2] a carriage and two horses.
Believe me, Ever your affectionate cousin   Louis Stevenson

Talk about stupidity! I sat up till one last morning copying notes and I
was up at seven. I am somnambulous or somni-scribent or something.

R.L.S.

Give my respectful compliments to Mistress Thomson and kiss her hand
from me.   Charles Grandison[3]

93   To Henrietta Traquair

MS Yale.

[? December 1871]   *[Edinburgh]*

My dear Henrietta, I have got into the shadiest possible mess. Last night,
there came back upon me, like a hideous dream, the fact that nearly a week

---

[1] The date and address added by MIS.

[2] MIS records: 'Lou has his party to celebrate his birthday. We have 19 in all. It goes off well. A
good deal of singing.' The party also celebrated RLS's prize of £3 and silver medal from the Royal
Scottish Society of Arts for his paper 'On a New Form of Intermittent Light for Lighthouses'.

[1] See Letter 27, n. 2.

[2] MIS records on 12 November 1870: 'James Harrower comes as coachman.'

[3] The hero of Samuel Richardson's epistolary novel *Sir Charles Grandison* (1754).

ago, I got an invitation from the Ritchies,[1] which I forgot to answer and straightway thereafter, *lost*.

Do write and tell me what the day is, and suggest any falsehood or other crime by which you think I can get out of this.

I have not dared to tell my mother this – I do not pretend to be brave.

In looking back, I observe that every sentence ends with '*this*' – effects of mental agitation. Believe me, Your affectionate cousin

R.L. Stevenson

Are you going to Hallé's concerts?[2]

94   To Charles Baxter

MS Yale. Published in *Baxter Letters*, 1.

[*? 1871*]   [*Edinburgh*]

My dear Baxter, If you cannot bring down my copy tonight *in propria*, I shall call for it tomorrow a little after one. Yours sincerely   Louis Stevenson

95   To Charles Baxter

MS Yale. Published in *Baxter Letters*, 2–4.

Thursday 3 March (or April) 1872[1]   [*Edinburgh*]

My dear Baxter, Like one full of new wine[2] – and so indeed I was, for I had a cab at my disposal this lovely evening – I went and called on you. I learned you were out at dinner, and then indeed, O person well known unto R.L. Stevenson, then indeed did I remember the tale known unto men, how that on this night of all nights you should tread to the Thessalian measure, being girt with the skin of leopards and your temples girt with ivy leaves and

---

[1] A family mentioned a number of times by MIS but not otherwise identified. RLS did go to an evening party at the Ritchies' on 29 February 1872.

[2] Charles Hallé (1819–95), the German-born pianist and conductor who made his home in Manchester where he established the famous orchestra in 1857. Knighted 1888. He was closely associated on the concert stage for many years with Mme Norman-Neruda (1839–1911), the great violin virtuoso, who became his second wife in 1888. They gave regular recitals in Edinburgh during the winter months. MIS records on 16 December 1871: 'Lou at Hallé's concert. Charmed with Norman-Neruda.'

[1] 3 March was a Sunday, 3 April a Wednesday. RLS originally wrote 'Monday'! His mother was certainly ill in bed 'with a threatening of a cold' on Monday 4 March.

[2] Acts 2:13.

shining as to your face with ruddy Bacchus. Then indeed, then indeed did I recollect that you should deftly move forth your patent-leather footsteps, swaying as to your auburn head in the measure of them that touched the reed and your left arm curved about the slender waist of one fair among the virgins.

It is necessary to explain, O Argive youth, that I have been reading the translations of Bohn,[3] cunningly written with a reed upon the well-prepared tablets.

But wherefore, O son of Stephen, dost thou stay my footsteps, already bent, as it were unwillingly, unto the court of writers?[4]

He that is hasty with his questioning lips is not judged wise among the prudent.

Yea, but the man of many verbal words – he that explaineth nought with his much-sounding lips – what is he?

Thy words are sharp.

Thy words indeed, as it seemeth to me, are many; but the purport lingereth.

Hear then, O much writer, unto the plain sense that abideth ever behind my spoken words. Her that brought me forth, nowise unjustly judging herself indebted unto thee, bids me, touching the ground as to my forehead and as it were with the folded hands of him that hath an obligation, offer unto thee her gratitude, thus tardily, thus tardily coming toward thee, O thou crafty employer of scribes.

Now indeed, O son of Stephen, thou speakest well. But has the pious woman, her that intromits with furthest India, concealed with due regard my complicity in her diminutive game?

Truly thou art one of little reverence.

As why, O sick man?

Dost thou take us, perhaps, for those that have the colour in our eyes of dewy lawns, not trodden save by the flocks, whom the careful shepherds drive to and fro at morning and even?

Thou speakest doubtfully with thy lips.

Not so, O writer; but the doubtful hearer ever heareth things equivocal. Thy name, indeed, is hidden. And it seemeth, forsooth, a great thing, this name of thine; having once drawn forth the exchangeable money, what import, thinkest thou?, has the name of the son of him that checketh the doing of the writers.[5] Go to! thou art one of a swelling vanity, whom shall

---

[3] RLS was 'ignorant of Greek, and preferred the baldest of Bohn's translations to more literary versions that might come between him and his originals' (Balfour, II, 102).

[4] Baxter became a Writer to the Signet in July 1871.

[5] Baxter's father, Edmund Baxter W.S. (1813–94) was Auditor of the Court of Session 1866–94.

the gods chasten in due time. Neither is it for nothing that thou art held as a pointing of fingers, in that thou wearest the long robe called after him of Fame, the great chieftain, fiery as to his head, even him that, being great, is small. For thou also, though thou art great, art small, O employer of scribes.

R.L. Stevenson Bohn

Epilogue.

O thou, wearied with much Bohning, I am asked, I am asked that I should further open unto thee this riddle.

(*My mother has been ill*)

O thou etc . . . .

I could Bohn till doomsday.

(*and so could not write*)

O Bohn! Bohn! O Argive maidens!

(*herself*).

96   To Charles Baxter

MS Yale. Published in *Baxter Letters*, 7–10.

*[*28 March 1872*]   [*Edinburgh*]

My dear Baxter, Damn you for a cold-hearted knave. Quoy?[1] est ce qu'on escrit de telles espitres aux amys, qui sont malades et ont besoigne de consolations, de par dieu!, et non pas de telles inhumaines bouffees de vent mauldict de l'est. Ores, me vecy avant ung bien joli feu et qui fusmait a faire joye et lisait les *Contes Drolatique* de nostre feu Maistre de Balzac, qui etait ma foi homme de bien et scavoit a faire rire, si on le veult; et vecy qu'on m'apporte ung lettre de mon tres cher et tres respectez amy, le sieur de Baxter, que je jugeais de contentir moult jolis facons de parler et moult gentils proupos; et me vecy espouvantez d'y trouver rien que de choses sales et ordureuses et qui ne plaisent poinct aulx gens de bien et ceulx qui ont les haults gouts de la vie et sachent a vivre et a laisser vivre. Mais, suis gen de bien moi mesme, et sache pardonner, estant tres jolyment enseignez par la Soulffrance, en bon maistre d'escholle, qui est, pour vraye dire, restez chez moi et pas mesme mis pied hors la porte, pour ces darreniers cinq ou six jours. Et maintenant, faites ung peu le bonhomme et venez me visiter;

---

[1] An attempted imitation of Balzac's imitation of Rabelais in his *Contes Drolatiques* (1832–7). RLS lapses at times into shaky modern French.

et jectez par fenetres tout cettuy dignitez et froide pompe de secretaire[2] qui m'ha tant blesse, à ce que vous pouvez venir me veoir en bon amy et poinct aultre chose. Aulsi, vouldrai vous dire ung chose qui est bien proufictable a scavoir; que les dictes contes drolatiques sont on ne peult plus mieulx, et que debvrez les lire pour desvenir bon Pantagrueliste, ce que beucoulp de gens icy, qui sont aultrement assez drosles et bons viveurs, ne peuvent jamais, faulte de scavoir cette reine de langues, la langue galloise; qui faict grant pitiez ez coeurs de gens de biens. Vrayement, mon amy, suis jolyment villain moy, a escrire cettuy langue, mais fais toutsjours de mon mieulx et apprends tant bien de mal espeller; ce qui est ung mestier aulsi difficile a apprendre que son opposé, si vouldrez bien me croire. Aulsi vous dirai çy, ung petit moment, comment je me suis portez, pendant que je ne vous ai pas veu. Et premier, dans mon lict jusqu'au mardi soir: aspres suis ung peu mieulx a mon aise, mais toutsjours suis triste 'comme est la palumbe seule en son nid par mort du compaignon,' et bien resveurs, comme vous poulvez croire, ne pouvant moulvoir mon teste a cause de si grants douleurs et estant, pour en finir, plus mort que je ne fus vif.

A proupos, lisez 'La Connestable', belle conte, qui ne manque d'elements vrayements tragiques. Ça brusle a lire seulement. Si seulement nous n'estions pas icy tant preudes et de bonne mine, comme feu Messieurs Les Pharasiens, j'en resverais ung beau drame; mais ca n'ha poinct de fin, comme ça debvrez; aultrement c'est ung beau subject. Et maintenant, comment sont dejectez et aultrement detruicts touts nos beaux resves du Printemps! Sont depassez, ung apres l'aultre, et n'ont poinct laissez de successeurs! Et maintenant, beaux sire, qui est si grant homme et si redoubtable secretaire, debvrez vous humilier ung petit peu pour visiter les malades et les reconforter, eulx, et leurs donner touts ces jolys nolveutez qui sont en train dans la grante Ville. Moy, suys ung paulvre sourd a tous ces beaulx rumeurs, et ne voys poinct ces belles visions; estant icy comme en prison; et suys vrayement en prison sans detours comme je vous l'expliquerai.

Et esperai, beaulx sire, de vous reveoir bientost; aulsi que vous estes parvenuz a dechiffrer cettuy espitre, comme moultement me redoubte, et que sachez assez pour admirer tous mes laborieulx naivetez, qui me sont trez amables, a moy; et resterai toutsjours, si croyez, vostre escuyer ez arts et sciences.   Louis Stevenson

Translation

How is this? Does one write such epistles to friends who are sick and in need of consolation, by God, and not of such inhuman blasts from a cursed

---

[2] Baxter had just become Secretary of the Speculative Society.

east wind. Here I am before a pleasant fire, smoking to my heart's content and reading the *Droll Stories* of our late Master Balzac, who was indeed a good man and knew how to make one laugh, if one had the inclination; and here they bring me a letter from my very dear and respected friend, Mr Baxter, which I expected would contain many witty remarks and kind words; and here I am, horrified to find therein nothing but dirty, filthy things which would please no decent person nor those who have high standards and know how to live and let live. But, being a decent person myself, I know how to forgive, having been well taught by Suffering, a good schoolmaster, who in fact is staying with me and has not set foot outside the door for these past five or six days. And now, be a good fellow and come and visit me; throw out of the window all that dignity and cold pomp of the Secretary which has wounded me so much, so that you can come and see me as a good friend, and nothing else. Also, let me tell you something very profitable to know; that the said *Droll Stories* are as good as could possibly be and that you should read them to become a good Pantagruelist, which many people here, who are otherwise 'droll' enough and with a great relish for life, could never be, because they don't know this Queen of languages, the Gallic tongue; which arouses great pity in the hearts of good men. Truly, my friend, I write this language abominably, but I always do my best and am learning fairly well how to spell badly in it; which is as difficult a task as its opposite, believe me. Also I want to tell you, for a moment, how I've been since I last saw you. First of all, in bed until Tuesday night; after that, I was somewhat better but always sad, 'like the dove alone in its nest after the death of its companion', and very dreamy, as you can imagine, not being able to move my head because it hurt so much, and in short, feeling more dead than alive.

Apropos of which, read 'The High Constable's Wife', a fine tale, and not lacking in truly tragic aspects. Just to read it sets one aflame. If only we didn't have so many prudes and poker-faces, like the Pharisees of yore, I could dream up a fine play from it; but it doesn't have the ending it should; otherwise, it's an excellent subject. And now, how cast down and destroyed are our beautiful dreams of Springtime! They have passed by, one after another, without leaving any successors. And now, fine sir, you who are such a great man and redoubtable secretary, you must humble yourself a little to visit the sick and comfort them, and give them news of everything that's going on in the great city. I am a poor man, deaf to all those lovely rumours, and no longer see those beautiful sights; it is like a prison here, and I am really imprisoned without distractions, as I shall explain to you.

I hope, fine sir, to see you again soon; also that you have managed to decipher this epistle, which I very much doubt, and that you know enough to admire all my naive labours, which have been pleasant to me; and believe that I remain always your servitor in the arts and sciences.

97   To Charles Baxter

MS Yale. Partly published in *Letters*, I, 38–9; fully in *Baxter Letters*, 4–6.

Friday 5 March [actually April] 1872[1]   *Dunblane*

My dear Baxter, By the date you may perhaps understand the purport of my letter without any words wasted about the matter. I cannot walk with you tomorrow and you must not expect me. I came yesterday afternoon to Bridge of Allan, and have been very happy ever since, as every place is sanctified by the eighth sense, Memory.[2] I walked up here this morning (three miles, *tudieu*! a good stretch for me) and passed one of my favourite places in the world, and one that I very much affect in spirit, when the body is tied down and brought immovably to anchor in a sick-bed. It is a meadow and bank at a corner on the river, and is connected in my mind inseparably with Virgil's *Eclogues*. '*Hic corulis mistas inter consedimus ulmos*', or something like that the passage begins (only I know my short-winded Latinity must have come to grief over even thus much of quotation); and here, to a wish, is just such a cavern as Menalcas might shelter himself withal from the bright noon, and, with his lips curled backward, pipe himself blue in the face, while *Messieurs les Arcadiens* ('*Arcades ambo*') would roll out these cloying hexameters, that sing themselves in one's mouth to such a curious lilting chaunt.[3]

In such weather, one has the bird's need to whistle; and I, who am specially incompetent in this art, must content myself by chattering away to you on this bit of paper. All the way along I was thanking God that he had made me and the birds and everything just as they are and not otherwise; for although there was no sun, the air was so thrilled with robins and blackbirds that it made the heart tremble with joy, and the leaves are far enough forward on the underwood to give a fine promise for the future. Even myself, as I say, I would not have had changed in one *iota* this forenoon, in

---

[1] After his law classes finished in March, RLS was in poor health and Dr George Balfour advised him to 'have a change'. So he went to Dunblane and Bridge of Allan on 4 April, coming home every few days to take part in rehearsals for the amateur theatricals organised by Professor Jenkin. RLS had a minor part in *The Taming of the Shrew*. The year before he had acted as prompter.

[2] Cf. Letter 72.

[3] At the beginning of the Fifth Eclogue, Menalcas invites Mopsus to sit with him 'among these elms interspersed with hazels' (*Hic corylis mixtas inter consedimus ulmos*). Instead they chose to shelter in a small cave, where they sing and play on reed pipes. *Arcades ambo* (Both Arcadians) is in *Eclogues* VII.

spite of all my idleness and Guthrie's[4] lost paper, which is ever present with me – a horrible phantom; except perhaps in that one direction, in which I have so sorely over-ridden and disenchanted my poor mind and body.

No one can be alone at home or in a quite new place. Memory and you must go hand in hand with (at least) decent weather, if you wish to cook up a proper dish of Solitude. It is in these little flights of mine that I get more pleasure than in anything else; and yet I am not really happy. Happiness is a matter of bottled stout and roast beef – by the way, how memory loves to dwell over that rare joy, a really good roast of beef. Now, at present, I am supremely uneasy and restless – almost to the extent of pain; but O! how I enjoy it and how I *shall* enjoy it afterwards (please God) if I get years enough allotted to me for the thing to ripen in. When I am a very old and very respectable citizen, with white hair and bland manners and a gold watch and an unquestioned *entrée* to the Sacrament, I shall hear these crows cawing in my heart, as I heard them this morning. I vote for old age and eighty years of retrospect. Yet, after all, I daresay a short shrift and a nice, green grave are about as desirable.

Poor devil! how I am wearying you! Cheer up. Two pages more and my letter reaches its term, for I have no more paper. What delightful things inns and waiters and bagmen are! If we didn't travel now and then, we should forget what the feeling of life is. The very cushion of a railway carriage – 'The things restorative to the touch.'[5] I can't write, confound it.[6] That's because I'm so tired with my walk. I wish I could think of something else to say, for when this letter is done, I shall be handed over to my own restlessness for several hours, and then not all my weariness will be able to keep me still, and walking is the devil and all for my health. Such a nice little girl went past the window just now, in black and as *mignonne* as your warmest mood could fancy, that I felt inclined to run out and kiss her for her mother. I know exactly the sort of warm, brown, melting hand the little darling would and *must* have; but the gloomy waiter 'held me with his eye'.[7] He seemed to have all the beadle-staves and constable-batons of united respectability under his arm, instead of one poor napkin. Believe me, Ever your affectionate friend   R.L. Stevenson

---

[4] Charles John Guthrie (1849–1920), son of Thomas Guthrie, one of the leaders of the Free Church, was a fellow member of the Speculative Society. He had a distinguished legal career, becoming a Q.C. in 1899 and a Judge (as Lord Guthrie) in 1907. He lived at Swanston Cottage from 1908 and amassed a notable collection of Stevenson letters and relics (now in Lady Stair's House Museum, Edinburgh). His *Robert Louis Stevenson: Some Personal Recollections* appeared in 1920.

[5] 'The Thing's restorative, / I' the touch and sight' – Browning, *The Ring and the Book* (1868), I, 89.

[6] RLS crossed out and re-wrote two words in the preceding sentence.

[7] 'He holds him with his glittering eye . . .' – Coleridge, 'The Ancient Mariner', I, l.13. RLS has deleted 'glassy' before 'eye'.

98   To Charles Baxter

MS Yale. Partly published in *Letters*, I, 40; fully in *Baxter Letters*, 10–11.

Tuesday 9 April 1872   *Dunblane*

My dear Baxter, I don't know what you mean. I know nothing about the
Standing Committee of the *Spec.*,[1] did not know that such a body existed
and even if it doth exist, must sadly repudiate all association with such
'goodly fellowship'. I am a 'Rural Voluptooary', at present. *That* is what is
the matter with me. The Spec. may go whistle, may go be—. As for 'C.
Baxter Secy', who is he? I know one Charles Baxter (or Bagster), Jinkster,
Jokester, —ster, —ster; but I know nought of this '*Secy*'. 'One Baxter, or
Bagster, a secretary,' I say to mine acquaintance, 'is at present disquieting
my leisure with certain illegal, uncharitable, unchristian and unconstitu-
tional documents called *Business letters: the affair is in the hands of the
POLICE.*' Do you hear *that*, you evil-doer? Sending business letters is surely
a far more hateful and slimy degree of wickedness than sending threatening
letters: the man who throws grenades and torpedoes is less malicious: the
Devil in red-hot hell, rubs his hands with glee as he reckons up the number,
that go forth spreading pain and anxiety with each delivery of the Post.

I have been walking today by a colonnade of beeches, along the brawling
Allan.[2] My character for sanity is quite gone, seeing that I cheered my lonely
way, with the following, in a triumphant chaunt: 'Thank God for the grass,
and the fir-trees, and the crows, and the sheep, and the sunshine and the
shadows of the fir-trees.' I hold that he is a poor mean devil who can walk
alone, in such a place and in such weather, and doesn't set up his lungs and
cry back to the birds and the river. Follow, follow, follow me. Come hither,
come hither, come hither – here shall you see – No enemy – except a very
slight remnant of winter and its rough weather.[3] My bedroom, when
I awoke this morning, was full of bird-songs; which is the greatest
pleasure in life. Come hither, come hither, come hither, and when you
come bring the third Part of the *Earthly Paradise*:[4] you can get it for me in

[1] On 11 March 1872, RLS was elected one of the five Presidents of the Speculative Society for the
following session, and Baxter was elected Secretary. The five Presidents and the Secretary made
up the Standing Committee. The Minutes (in Baxter's hand) in the Society's records show that
RLS did in fact attend a meeting of the Standing Committee on 15 April.

[2] A notebook (Yale, RLS/P) carried by RLS on this visit contains law notes and rough drafts of a
number of poems. One begins:

> Calm runs my blood. By this high colonnade
> Of secular beeches that in order fair
> Follow the brawling river, I repair . . .

[3] Cf. *As You Like It*, II.v.5–8.

[4] Volume three of William Morris's poem had appeared in 1870. The notebook (RLS/P) contains
a page listing RLS's expenses connected with this visit. It includes 3/6d for *The Earthly Paradise*.

Elliots[5] for two and tenpence (2s/10d) (*business habits*). Also bring an ounce of Honey Dew from Wilsons.[6]

The whole of the latter part of this letter was written to a chaunt; and may be read in a similar style by the judicious reader, if he be as light-hearted.

Do come. I think you will find me nice, but know not, as I speak very little.

I send here competition sonnet to the *L.J.R.*[7]: you will soon get one from Bob, and will please consider yourself as Judge and lawgiver over us in this matter.

To the Members of the L.J.R.[8]

As Daniel, bird-alone in that far land,
Kneeling in fervid prayer, with heart-sick eyes,
Turned thro' the casement toward the westering skies;
Or as untamed Elijah, that red brand
Among the starry prophets; or that band
And company of faithful sanctities
Who, in all times, when persecutions rise
Cherish forgotten creeds with fostering hand;
Such do ye seem to me, light-hearted crew,[9]
O turned to friendly arts with all your skill,
That keep a little chapel sacred still,
One rood of Holy-ground in this bleak earth
Sequestered still (an homage surely due!)
To the twin Gods of mirthful wine and mirth.

R.L. Stevenson

---

[5] Andrew Elliot, bookseller, 17 Princes Street, had published *The Pentland Rising* by RLS in 1866.

[6] A tobacconist's shop in Leith Street, which RLS used as his 'headquarters'. He told Balfour at Vailima: 'The tobacconists' shops in Edinburgh used to be a curious institution. Young men who couldn't afford a club used to use them for the same sort of purposes. You used to have letters sent there, or meet friends whom you didn't want to bring to your father's house. You weren't expected to buy anything as long as the people knew you' (Balfour, Reminiscences, NLS).

[7] A mysterious society (commemorated in the dedication to *Kidnapped*), comprising RLS, Baxter, Bob, Ferrier and two others, which met at a pub in Advocates' Close. The initials signified Liberty, Justice and Reverence. Its tenets set out in the constitution (drafted by Baxter) included the abolition of the House of Lords and that its members were not to be bound by the doctrines of the Established Church. In correspondence in 1891, RLS and Baxter recalled the painful scene between father and son when TS discovered the document. RLS's thinly-fictionalised description is given in his *Edifying Letters of the Rutherford Family* (MS Yale, published 1982). Baxter gave an account in a letter to *T.P.'s Weekly*, 21 July 1911, and in a conversation with Balfour recorded in his Biography Notebook (NLS).

[8] A rough draft of this poem is in the notebook refered to in n. 2. Another MS (also at Yale) showing minor variations and dated 'Above Dunblane, by the riverside 1872' was printed in BBS II, 1916 (*Collected Poems*, 79). 'Bird-alone' or 'burd-alane' in l. 1 is a Scots phrase for the only child left in a family, hence 'all alone'.

[9] 'That follow joy with all your store of skill,' deleted.

99 *To Charles Baxter*

Text: *Letters*, I, 56–8, with additions from transcript by Balfour, NLS.

[c. *17 April 1872*][1]   *17 Heriot Row*

My dear Baxter, I am gum-boiled and face swollen to an unprecedented degree. One eye is levelled up all round so that it looks like a pool in a level plain. I look very stern, insomuch that it depresses me to see a mirror. I look sterner than anyone I ever saw. The result of staying in the house is gloom – indigestion – loss of appetite – *le vrai* (none others genuine) *diable*. It is very depressing and bad for you to suffer from gibber that cannot be brought to a head. I cannot speak it, because my face is so swollen and stiff, that enunciation must be deliberate a thing your true gibberer cannot hold up his head under; and writ gibber is somehow not gibber at all, it does not come forth – does not *flow*, with that fine irrational freedom that it loves in speech – it does not afford relief to the packed bosom.

Hence I am suffering from *suppressed gibber* – an uneasy complaint; and like all cases of suppressed humours (whether gouty, rheumatic or gibberous) this hath a nasty tendency to the brain. Therefore (the more confused I get, the more I lean on Thus's and Hences and Therefores) you must not be down upon me most noble Festus,[2] altho' this letter should smack of some infirmity of judgment. I speak the words of soberness and truth; and would you were not almost but altogether as I am except this swelling. Lord, Lord, if we could change personalities, how we should hate it! How I should rebel at the office, repugn under the Ulster coat, and repudiate your monkish humours thus unjustly and suddenly thrust upon poor, infidel me! And as for you – why, my dear Charles, 'a mouse that hath its lodging in a cat's ear'[3] would not be so uneasy as you in your new conditions. 'A man that lives in a windmill hath not a more whimsical abode'[4] than you would think yourself to be entered into as occupant. I do not see how your temperament would come thro' the feverish regret for things not done, the feverish longings to do things that cannot then (or perhaps ever) be accomplished, the feverish unrests and damnable indecisions, that it takes all my easy-going spirits to come comfortably through. A vane can live out anything in the shape of wind; and that is how I can be and am a more serious person than you. Just as the light French seemed very

---

[1] MIS records that on 13 April 1872 RLS had 'toothache and gumboil' and on 17 April 'he has a badly swelled face'. Colvin dates the letter 'October'.

[2] Acts 26:25 – 'But he said, I am not mad, most noble Festus; but speak forth the words of truth and soberness.'

[3] Webster, *The Duchess of Malfi*, IV. ii.134.

[4] 'A fellow that lives in a windmill, has not a more whimsical dwelling than the heart of a man that is lodged in a woman' – Congreve, *The Way of the World*, II. 2.

serious to Sterne,[5] light L. Stevenson can afford to bob about over the top
of any deep sea of prospect or retrospect, where ironclad C. Baxter would
incontinently go down with all hands. A fool is generally the wisest person
out. The wise man must shut his eyes to all the perils and horrors that lie
around him; but the cap and bells can go bobbing along the most slippery
ledges and the bauble will not stir up sleeping lions. Hurray! for motley, for
a good, sound *insouciance*, for a healthy philosophic carelessness!

My dear Baxter, a word in your ear – DON'T YOU WISH YOU WERE A FOOL?
God, how easy the world would go on with you – literally on castors. How
much less you would fear, and how much less you would require to drink.
The only reason a wise man can assign for getting drunk is that he wishes
to enjoy for a while the blessed immunities and sunshiny weather of the
land of fooldom. But a fool, who dwells ever there, has no excuse at all.
That is a happy land, if you like – and not so far away either.[6] Take a fool's
advice and let us strive without ceasing to get into it. Hark in your ear again.
'THEY ALLOW PEOPLE TO REASON IN THAT LAND.'

I wish I could take you by the hand, and lead you away into its pleasant
boundaries. There is no custom house on the frontier, and you may take in
what books you will. There are no manners and customs, but men and
women grow up, like trees in a still, well-walled garden, 'at their own sweet
will.'[7] There is no prescribed or customary folly – no motley, cap, or bauble:
out of the well of each one's own innate absurdity he is allowed and
encouraged freely to draw and to communicate; and it is a strange thing
how this natural fooling comes so nigh to one's better thoughts of wisdom;
and stranger still, that all this strange discord of people speaking in their own
natural moods and keys masses itself into a far more perfect harmony, than
all the dismal, official unison in which they sing in other countries. Part-
singing seems best all the world over.

I who live in England must wear the hackneyed symbols of the profession to show that I have (at least) consular immunities, coming as I do, out
of another land where they are not so wise as they are here, but fancy that
God likes what he makes and is not best pleased with us when we deface
and dissemble all that he has given us and put about us to one common
standard of – Heighty-Teighty, when was a jester obliged to finish his
sentence? I cut so strong a pirouette that all my bells jingle, and come down
in an attitude, with one hand upon my hip. The evening's entertainment is
over, 'and if our kyind friends –'[8]

[5] 'But the French, Mons. le Count, added I . . . have so many excellencies . . . they are a loyal, a
gallant, a generous, an ingenious, and good temper'd people as is under heaven – if they have a
fault – they are too serious' – Sterne, *A Sentimental Journey*, 'Character: Versailles'.
[6] Cf. 'There is a happy land,/ Far, far away', the well-known hymn (1838) by Andrew Young
(1807–89), Edinburgh schoolmaster and Sunday School Superintendant.
[7] Wordsworth, 'Composed Upon Westminster Bridge'.
[8] Thackeray, *Vanity Fair* ch. 8.

Hurrah! I feel relieved. I have put out my gibber, and if you have read thus far, you will have taken it in. I wonder if you will ever come this length. I shall try a trap for you, and insult you here, on this last page. 'O Baxter what a damned humbug you are!' There, – shall this insult bloom and die unseen, or will you come towards me, when next we meet, with a face deformed with anger and demand speedy and bloody satisfaction? *Nous verrons*, which is French.   R.L. Stevenson

100   *To Charles Baxter*

MS Yale. Published in *Baxter Letters*, 12–13.

28 April 1872   *17 Heriot Row*

My dear Baxter, Not being *in propria* able to appear before you and charm away your evil spirit, I must see what I can do by proxy; especially as I am myself somewhat gloomy owing to having had no sleep whatever last night with toothache. I had a pretty bad time of it. Could neither lie in bed nor stay out of it and passed a fairish slice of the night in dressing and undressing. About two I came downstairs and had a pipe and a couple of glasses of wine, which did me good for the time being; but I heard every hour until eight, which I missed dozing in the arm chair, waiting for breakfast. I kept pretty cheery until about five, when I began to throw pillows about and swear (in the words of Billy Taylor)[1] '*most horribel*'. I thought to myself that I should look pretty blue if this were some persistent malady and I were to be told next morning that I should spend all my remaining years without intermission of pain. However, I kept up my spirits by imagining worse cases: as, for example, the same degree of toothache in a draughty common stair – *Pouah! enfin, c'est assez, n'est-ce-pas?*

I don't know that I am very fit to write and I have a hideous tendency to relapse into bad French which I mean to resist and to keep on the Queen's Highway and Queen's English if I can.

In fact I can't write.   Yours very sincerely,
                                  Your most obedient servant,
                                        Yours faithfully,
                                              L.S.

(Second attempt)

I *will* write. Do you know what a hard thing it is to resist sleep and what a terrible thing it is to strive with wakefulness. I tried last night to play the

---

[1] Billy Taylor was a character in a number of comic plays of the period (including F.C. Burnand's *Military Billy Taylor*, 1869).

one off against the other and to pretend to my own heart that I wished to
keep awake in order to hear the next hour strike, in hopes that I should
cheat the devil and get to sleep; but it wouldn't do – he has not been going
to and fro upon the earth all these thousand years for nothing and he saw
thro' my honest deceit as tho' I had been glass. I could hear him sniggering
in the corner.

This morning, the *pain-wrinkle* that I have over one eye was deeper
than I have ever seen it. I shall pretty soon have a permanent brand
there. It is principally an autograph of Tick (tic, tik, tique, *comme vous
voulez*).

I can't help being egotistical, as you know already; but I feel that this
letter does require an apology. Pain concentrates one's feelings so inordin-
ately, that it takes one a while to get them spread again. One walk in the
sun, and a lungful or two of spring air, will send all the morbid de[vils . . .]
they [. . .].² I shall gradually recollect that there are other people in the
world besides myself and to like those other people (sometimes a great deal
too much) and to insist on speaking to them and hearing them speak. I have
written another page I see, but I am no nearer writing you a letter than I was
at the beginning, therefore,   *Ade,*

[*signature cut away*]

101   *To his Mother*

MS First 4 pp. Yale; last 2 pp. Silverado.

* [*Postmark 23 July 1872*]¹   *The Craven Hotel, Craven Street,*
                                                           Strand [*London*]

My dear Mother, I am very much ashamed that I have not sooner written;
but I have been in such a whirl with this town that I could not sit down
long enough to write.

All Sunday I spent alone and without speaking to a soul from ten in the
morning until I met a fellow at Simpson's Divan² in the evening. I walked

---

² The cutting away of the signature overleaf has affected two lines (about eight words).
¹ In May RLS's scheme of going to Germany for the summer had to be abandoned when MIS had
a fit of hysterics at the thought that she might never see him again. Eventually it was agreed that
he could go for a few weeks, and he left for London with Sir Walter Simpson on his way to
Germany on 20 July. Sir Walter Grindlay Simpson (1843–98) succeeded his father, Sir James
Young Simpson (the physician who pioneered the use of chloroform as an anaesthetic), as second
Baronet in 1870. He was one of RLS's special friends at this period and figures as Athelred in 'Talk
and Talkers'. He was a fellow-member of the Speculative Society and was also studying law,
becoming an advocate in 1873.
² The famous restaurant in the Strand.

all about Kensington and as several people had asked me the way to the Pro-Cathedral,[3] I thought I had better end by going thither myself. I did so; and the first thing I beheld was a Confessional with the 'Very Rev. Monsignor Capel'[4] over the door. But as I saw I was in for it, I just stayed. I went and sat down on a seat. A man comes up 'Sixpence for those seats, sir,' quoth he and I jumped up as if it had been red hot. He laughed and proceeded to inform me that some of the other seats were threepence and some of them nothing. I am very much pleased to say that I was strong enough to take the latter. The service was very well done, the music good; and altogether as I had not seen the R.C. service for a long time, I was pretty much interested, until I perceived a number of churchwardens stealing out of odd corners, – and, (every one with a plate in his hand) begin to pervade the whole place. The priests meantime lifted up their voices and prayed *at* us very hard. My first idea was flight, but I was too proud. My second was to throw in a shilling, as much as to say, 'You see it was no stinginess that kept me out of your confounded chairs.' But my mature determination was to face the matter boldly out and treat the churchwarden to a lofty, Protestant stare. This done, I thought I had sufficiently taken my position, and being somewhat aweary, I sneaked out.

Tell you all that I have done, say you? Impossible. I have been at the National Gallery, where I did *not* like the Turners and I refuse to conceal my feelings on that head. But Rembrandt, Velasquez, Hobbema, and Hogarth's 'Marriage à la Mode,' were an host in themselves of course. You must go to the Doré Gallery[5] when you come to[6] London. I think his 'Christ Leaving the Praetorium' will fetch you. I sat for nearly half an hour looking at it and I like it perhaps better than any other single picture in the world. As far as regards Christ, it is unsurpassable. The exhibition is very good too – really good. I recommend, Nos. 75, 183, 202, 223, 227, 266, 280, 416, 460, 492, 498, 580, 1043.

I had great work seeking W. Murray[7] and all without success; but I was very kindly received by one of the fellows in his club. I am too stupid to

---

[3] The Church of Our Lady of Victories in High Street Kensington was used as Pro-Cathedral until the consecration of Westminster Cathedral in 1903.

[4] Thomas John Capel (1836–1911), prominent Roman Catholic preacher, proselytizer and controversialist.

[5] The gallery at 35 Bond Street (now occupied by Sotheby's) which exhibited the large-scale religious paintings of Paul Gustave Doré (1833–83), the French illustrator and painter. On 9 September MIS recorded seeing 'Christ Leaving the Praetorium' – 'a splendid picture.'

[6] The rest of the letter is at Silverado.

[7] William Bazett Murray (1851/2–85), Scottish artist who contributed to the *Graphic* 1874–6 and *The Illustrated London News* 1873–85. He specialised in drawings of working-class and industrial scenes and was one of the magazine illustrators whose work was admired and collected by Van Gogh. (See R. Pickvance, *English Influences on Vincent Van Gogh*, Arts Council Catalogue, 1974.) He was a friend of Bob Stevenson.

write. I dine this afternoon with a Dr Black, a friend of Simpson's and tomorrow morning at three we leave London for Ostend.

With love to all, Believe me, Ever your affectionate son

R.L. Stevenson

102   *To his Mother*

MS Yale. Published (with deletions) in *Letters*, I, 41–2.

Thursday 25th [July] 1872   *Brussels*

My dear Madame, I am here at last, sitting in my room, without coat or waistcoat and with both window and door open and yet perspiring like a terra cotta jug or a gruyère cheese.

We had a very good passage, which we certainly deserved in compensation for having to sleep on the cabin floor and finding absolutely nothing fit for human food in the whole filthy embarcation. We made up for lost time by sleeping on deck a good part of the forenoon. When I woke, Simpson was still sleeping the sleep of the just, on a coil of ropes and (as appeared afterwards) his own hat; so I got a bottle of Bass and a pipe and laid hold of an old Frenchman of somewhat filthy aspect (*Fiat experimentum in corpore vili*)[1] to try my French upon. I made very heavy weather of it. The Frenchman had a very pretty young wife; but my French always deserted me entirely when I had to answer her, and so she soon drew away and left me to her Lord, who talked of French politics, Africa and domestic economy with great vivacity. From Ostend a smoking hot journey to Brussels. At Brussels we went off after dinner to the Parc. If any person wants to be happy, I should advise the Parc. You sit drinking iced drinks and smoking penny cigars, under great old trees. The band place, covered walks etc. are all lit up. And you can't fancy how beautiful was the contrast of the great masses of lamplit foliage and the dark sapphire night sky with just one blue star set overhead in the middle of the largest patch. In the dark walks, too, there are crowds of people whose faces you cannot see and here and there a colossal white statue at the corner of an alley that gives the place a nice, *artificial*, eighteenth-century sentiment. There was a good deal of summer lightning blinking overhead and the black avenues and white statues leapt out every minute into short-lived distinctness. This morning I was dressed by ten minutes past eight, went to the barber's and had my hair cut and my head shampoo'd, an awfully good move in hot weather, came back, had breakfast, smoked a pipe in the court with some friends of Simpson's whom he has met in the hotel, and then set off for the Bains St

[1] Let the experiment be tried on a worthless body.

Sauveur, Bassin de Natation. There we natated among many moustachio'd and facetious Belgians and now I am just delaying my siesta till I finish this sentence.

I get up to add one thing more. There is in the hotel a boy in whom I take the deepest interest. I cannot tell you his age, but the very first time I saw him (when I was at dinner yesterday) I was very much struck with his appearance. There is something very leonine in his face, with a dash of the negro especially, if I remember aright, in the mouth. He has a great quantity of dark hair, curling in great rolls not in little corkscrews, and a pair of large, dark, and very steady bold, bright eyes. His manners are those of a Prince. I felt like an overgrown ploughboy beside him. He speaks English perfectly but with I think sufficient foreign accent to stamp him as a Russian, especially when his manners are taken into account. I don't think I ever saw anyone who looked like a hero before. After breakfast this morning I was talking to him in the court; when he mentioned casually that he had caught a snake in the Riesengebirge.[2] 'I have it here,' he said. 'Would you like to see it.' I said yes; and putting his hand into his breast pocket he drew forth not a dried serpent skin, but the head and neck of the reptile writhing and shooting out its horrible tongue in my face. You may conceive what a fright I got. I send off this single sheet just now in order to let you know I am safe across; but you must not expect letters often.   R.L. Stevenson

P.S. The snake was about a yard long, but harmless and now, he says, quite tame.

103   To his Mother

MS Buffalo.

28 July 1872   *Hotel Landsberg, Frankfurt*

My dear Mamma, I enclose some cuttings from a newspaper, very smartly written they are, which will give you an idea of the heat if Monsieur can remember his formula for reducing Centigrade to Fahrenheit. I think the highest we have had is somewhere about 93 in the shade; but the calculation is Simpson's, not mine.

On Thursday afternoon, under a burning sun and refreshed by a wind that seemed to blow out of a furnace, we went all about the town on the outside of a tramway; and in the evening accompanied Simpson's friends to a concert in the zoological gardens. Next day, Simpson went to Antwerp and I spent the day in the swimming bath and at Café doors, drinking coffee and iced drinks under an awning. In the evening I went to a Garden

[2] A chain of mountains between Silesia and Bohemia.

Theatre and heard rather an amusing French farce; it was quite like an English one and tho' it turned on ticklish matters, was more moral than can be imagined.

That night, Friday, we left at half-past ten for Cologne. Up to the last moment we were undecided whether to go or stay and it was at last only my shame to own our indecision that decided us. I wonder how much of your boasted firmness comes from the same cause. In the carriage with us was a youth with a hundred horse power of somnolence, a handsome young Greek, his sister, his little boy and HIS WIFE. Simpson and I talked about her in whispers for near an hour, as she lay with her head on her husband's shoulder and her small white hand lying like a bird in the middle of his. She was one of the most perfectly pretty little women I ever saw; and with one accord we compared her to Dora in *David Copperfield* for both her prettiness and her stupidity. It was too much to suppose that she had any mind – one might as well expect cerebration in a violet. At Liège we got in a siphon of *eau de seltz*; and I gave some of this to our Greeks and got back some champagne in exchange. Madame looked at me with a sort of motherly interest all the time I was drinking it. '*Pas bon?*' she said when I had done; but I wish you could have heard the tone. It was the first time that I had profited by my youthful appearance. She was not a bit older than I, but she evidently looked upon me as *in loco filii*. All the next stage we dozed and looked at her; but at Verviers our twenty minutes' stoppage wakened us all up and we got fairly into conversation. I did the most of the talk on our side; for Simpson, with his charming characteristic prudence, had inwardly determined to have as little to do with her as possible, so as to guarantee peace of mind in the future. They had been the grand tour; and in talking over this place and that, we soon saw that we had underestimated her mind. At last, when I was making very very heavy weather of something, she said '*Parlez en anglais – je vous comprendrai.*' And then it turned out that she never travelled without some 'British Authors'[1] in her portmanteau, that she had read all Shakespeare twice and almost every novel we named, and (*enfin*) that her favourite novel was *David Copperfield* and one of her favourite characters was that very *Dora* to whom we had been profanely comparing her an hour or two before. She never read French novels unless she knew about them – '*il y a tant de mauvais auteurs en Français.*' Like you, Madame, she hated books that end badly. She has a sister who reads even more English than she – who *devours* 'British Authors'. I wish I could meet that sister. At last, the day breaking white and silent, here comes hateful Aachen. We shoot into the empty station. '*Et voilà l'oncle Fritz.*' L'oncle Fritz, in a big burly German voice, demands jocularly who is this that arrives '*à trois heures de matin*'. Much kissing on the platform. '*Bon voyage, messieurs*' from mad-

---

[1] Collections issued by continental publishers such as Tauchnitz.

ame. '*Serviteur, messieurs. Charmer d'avoir fait votre connaissance*' from monsieur. Tra-la-la on the ineffectual trumpet of the German railways; and

> 'Maid of Athens, ere we part
> Give, oh give me back my heart.'[2]

Simpson and I were left in a state of glorious excitement, I can tell you, and
kept debating what sort of an impression we had made, until we arrived at
a comfortable decision that she would tell her friends (*l'oncle Fritz*, I suppose
– happy uncle Fritz) that she had met '*deux bons écossais*' – compatriots of
Valter Scott. I am sure anyone who told us that she was laughing at us
would have had a warm reception.

And there is really all that I have to say about one of the most charming
people that I have ever seen. Three pages of small foreign letter paper and
even those written large, not to say written badly; and yet that night journey
will surely hold a place until the hour I die, among the most beautiful of my
remembrances. And so – these are the plain facts and an epilogue in my best
style.

For a long while we sat and talked of her, but at last we dropped over and
slept to Cologne, where we got up, dead with sleep and more filthy than
words can express. I shall never forget the sort of inane smile with which
Simpson staggered against the door post as we left the Station. Just outside
a commissionaire nailed us and took us to a pot house, close by the
Cathedral, where in a couple of rooms, which as Simpson said must have
been originally a balcony, we went incontinently into a pretty sleep. I was
dimly conscious through my slumber of a bell (as I then guessed it) about
the size of St George's Church being rung at my ear; but I clung hard to
Morpheus, got through its terrible brâm-brâm and did not waken till eleven
o'clock in the forenoon. We then had breakfast, saw the Cathedral, had a
swim in the Rhine and sat under a trellis in front of a hotel in Deutz,[3] for
about three hours, drinking a sharp, red German wine (not unpleasant) and
iced water. At last we found strength to move, and spent the afternoon
trying to find different objects of interest and finding none, except indeed
shady seats which, in this weather, are objects of more interest than anything
else. Simpson spent about fifteen minutes, on one of these seats, trying to
understand German money, a process by which he reduced himself to the
beasts of the field in intellect. He communicated to me the *fact* that while
one Groschen equalled twopence, *two* Groschen only equalled twopence
farthing. '*What*??' 'Yes' he replied, with the greatest *sérieux*. 'It's very
disheartening; but so it is.' I don't think I have laughed more for a month;
but as I did not want to bring him home in a strait waistcoat, I recom-

[2] Byron, 'Maid of Athens'.
[3] A suburb of Cologne on the right bank of the Rhine.

mended him to give over his financial studies; and he did. We dined at a
Restaurant and then went to the Tivoli Gardens where, in a Summer
Theatre we had the pleasure of hearing a Five Act play in German called
Mutter und Sohn.[4] In the first act, the son of a countess is discovered to have
stolen (so far as we could make out) a red, silk pocket handkerchief,
whereupon his mother and a fair percentage of the other relatives faint and
the curtain falls on a grand tableau. During the next four acts, this peculative
scion of the aristocracy makes himself a public nuisance by hanging about
his mother's house, in a white hat and a most wicked and harrowing necktie
and performing so far as I could see the most heroic and unnecessary acts of
self-sacrifice. Thro' these, or thro' the white hat, or thro' the restitution of
the pocket handkerchief or thro' something or other, he is at last reconciled
to his mother; whereat the audience testified lively pleasure. For my part,
I was only very tranquilly happy at this *dénouement*, as the hero by his
unjustifiable choice of clothing had long alienated all my sympathies.

That night, Saturday, I left Cologne at twelve, midnight, leaving
Simpson to follow in the steamer and join me, I don't quite know when,
at this hotel. I *did* the Rhine in grand style, seeing I never woke till I got
to Bingen, except when a brutal guard made me change carriages in a state
of somnambulism, I staggering in front with one eye open and the guard
walking behind to pick up my parcels as, one after another, I let them fall.
From Bingen to Mainz, I travelled with rather a nice Englishman, and from
Mainz to Frankfurt slept like a child. You can understand that in weather
like what we have been having, night travelling is almost the only possible
method of getting over the ground.

I enjoy the heat and agree with it very well. I have not heard from [you]
since London and I cannot get out my letters here till Simpson comes with
my letter of credit as a voucher.

Today it has thundered and rained much, and is a good deal cooler.
Sunday is observed in Frankfurt, just as it is in London – all the shops shut
except Cafés and Tobacconists. I saw a very exciting scene in the streets, a
man who had stabbed another being run down, captured, held until the
arrival of the police and then led away among a chorus of groans and hisses.
Believe me, Ever your affectionate son   R.L. Stevenson

[4] *Mutter und Sohn* (1843) by the prolific but now forgotten German actress and dramatist Charlotte
Birch-Pfeiffer (1800–68) was a free adaptation of *Grannarna* (*The Neighbours*) by the Swedish
author Fredrika Bremer (1801–65). In the play Bruno, the favourite son, takes some money from
his mother's money-box in order to prevent the disgrace of his half-brother, who has embezzled
money from his office. The half-brother, whose wedding-day it is, promises to replace the money
in a few days from his wife's dowry. Before he can do so, the 'theft' is discovered and Bruno
identified as the thief on the circumstantial evidence of a torn fragment of his handkerchief
jammed in the money-box; Bruno is disowned by the mother and disappears. Fifteen years later
he reappears as a mysterious stranger and is eventually reconciled with his mother after a deathbed confession by the half-brother.

104   To his Mother

MS Yale. Published in *Letters*, I, 42–4.

Monday 29 July 1872   *Hotel Landsberg, Frankfurt*

My dear Mamma, I think I shall get on pretty well with German. When I am not nervous, I can generally ask for anything I want, altho' it is indeed improbable that I shall be able to understand the answer. As for a conversation, as most gentlemen understand French tho' they do not speak it, I can get on wonderfully well, eking out with it whenever my German runs dry. The difficulty, here also, lies in what *they* say. In Frankfurt they pronounce very badly. This I was charmed to learn from a gentleman whom I met last night, and who besides this comfortable information gave me the greatest compliment that I think I ever received – he took me for a Frenchman. You will not be surprised to learn, after this, that he himself was not *de première force* in French, and indeed had to fall back upon Latin more than once in the course of our talk.

Last night, I met with rather an amusing adventurette. Seeing a church door open, I went in and was led by most importunate finger-bills up a long stair to the top of the tower. The father, smoking at the door, the mother and three daughters received me as if I was a friend of the family and had come in for an evening visit. The youngest daughter (about thirteen, I suppose, and a pretty little girl) had been learning English at the school and was anxious to play it off upon a real, veritable Englander; so we had a long talk and I was shown photographs etc, Marie and I talking and the others looking on with evident delight at having such a linguist in the family. As all my remarks were duly translated and communicated to the rest, it was quite a good German lesson. There was only one contretemps during the whole interview – the arrival of another visitor in the shape of (surely) the last of God's creatures, a wood-worm of the most unnatural and hideous appearance with one great striped horn sticking out of his nose like a boltsprit. If there are many wood-worms in Germany, I shall come home. The most courageous men in the world must be entomologists. I had rather be a lion-tamer.

I am waiting Simpson's arrival with impatience, as I have not heard from home for so long, and yet have not so much as an envelope to show in evidence at the Post Office.

Today, I got rather a curiosity – *Lieder und Balladen von Robert Burns*, translated by one Silbergleit, and not so ill done either.[1] Armed with which,

---

[1] *Robert Burns' Lieder und Balladen für deutsche Leser ausgewählt und frei bearbeitet von L.G. Silbergleit*, Leipzig [1869]. No. 184 in the popular cheap edition *Universal-Bibliothek* published by Philipp Reclam, jun.

I had a swim in the Main and then bread and cheese and Bavarian beer in a sort of Café, or at least the German substitute for a Café; but what a falling off after the heavenly forenoons in Brussels!

I have bought a Meerschaum out of local sentiment and am now very low and nervous about the bargain, having paid dearer than I should in England and got a worse article, if I can form a judgement.

Tuesday [30 July]

Only one letter: and that from my father and more technical than words can express. It contains however an account of the weather with you, that made both Simpson and me dance upon the streets. Compare this with what you have heard of from me and the newspaper slips.

My being taken for a Frenchman is no chance occurrence, and does not depend, alas! upon my admirable accent. Four or five people have already spotted me as sich and the most of these were people who could speak no French at all: very strange.

Do write some more, somebody. Tomorrow, I expect I shall go into lodgings as this hotel work makes the money disappear like butter in a furnace. Meanwhile believe me, Ever your affectionate son

R.L. Stevenson

105   To his Mother

MS Yale. Partly published in *Letters*, I, 44–7.

Thursday 1 August 1872   *Hotel Landsberg*

My dear Mother, You must indeed be having horrible weather. I am glad to hear you have got my letter from Brussels. I have only got three letters in all, one in London and two here; but I did not ask at Cologne because it was agreed that you were not to write to me there.

Yesterday I walked to Eckenheim, a village a little way out of Frankfurt and turned into the alehouse. In the room, which was just such as it would have been in Scotland, were the landlady, two neighbours, and an old peasant eating raw sausage at the far end. I soon got into conversation; and was astonished when the landlady, having asked whether I were an Englishman and received an answer in the affirmative, proceed to inquire farther whether I were not also a Scotchman. It turned out that a Scotch Doctor – a Professor – a poet – who wrote books, '*gross wie das*' had come nearly every day out of Frankfurt to the *Eckenheimer Wirthschaft* and had left behind him a most savoury memory in the hearts of all its customers. One man ran out to find his name for me, and returned with the news that it was

'*Cobie*' (Scobie, I suspect); and during his absence the rest were pouring into my ears the fame and acquirements of my countryman. He was, in some indecipherable manner, connected with the Queen of England and one of the Princesses. He had been in Turkey and had there married a wife of immense wealth. They could find apparently no measure adequate to express the size of his books. In one way or another, he had amassed a princely fortune and had apparently only one sorrow, his daughter to wit, who had absconded into a *Kloster* with a considerable slice of her mother's '*Geld*'. I told them we had no Klosters in Scotland, with a certain feeling of superiority. No more had they, I was told – '*Hier ist unser Kloster*,' and the speaker motioned with both arms round the taproom. Altho' the first torrent was exhausted, yet the Doctor came up again in all sorts of ways and with or without occasion throughout the whole interview; as for example when one man, taking his pipe out of his mouth and shaking his head, remarked *à propos* of nothing and with almost defiant conviction, '*Er war ein feiner mann, der Herr Doctor*' and was answered by another with '*Yaw, yaw, und trank immer rothen Wein.*'

Setting aside the Doctor, who had evidently turned the brains of the entire village, they were intelligent people. One thing in particular struck me, their honesty in admitting that here they spoke bad German and advising me to go to Coburg or Leipzig for German. '*Sie sprechen da rein, so rein*' (clean), said one; and they all nodded their heads together like so many mandarins, and repeated '*rein, so rein*' in chorus.

Of course we got upon Scotland. The Hostess said '*Die Schottländer trinken gern schnapps*', which may be freely translated 'Scotchman are horrid fond of whisky.' It was impossible of course to combat such a truism; and so I proceeded to explain the construction of toddy, interrupted by a cry of horror when I mentioned the *hot* water, and thence, as I find is always the case, to the most ghastly romancing about Scottish scenery and manners, the Highland dress and everything national or local that I could lay my hands upon. Now that I have got my German Burns, I lean a good deal upon him for opening a conversation and read a few translations to every yawning audience that I can gather. I am grown most insufferably national, you see. I fancy it is a punishment for my want of it at ordinary times. But really I don't see much to make a row about, except Burns, and perhaps John Knox. Now what do you think, there was a waiter in this very hotel, but alas! he is now gone, who sang (from morning to night, as my informant said with a shrug at the recollection) what but '*'S ist lange her*', the German version of Auld Lang Syne; so you see, Madame, the finest lyric ever written *will* make its way out of whatsoever corner of patois it found its birth in.

> '*Mein Herz ist im Hochland, mein Herz ist nicht hier.*
> *Mein Herz ist im Hochland im grünen Revier.*

Im grünen Reviere zu jagen das Reh;
Mein Herz ist im Hochland, wo immer ich geh.'[1]

I don't think I need translate that for you.

There is one thing that burthens me a good deal in my patriotic garrulage; and that is the black ignorance in which I grope about everything, as for example when I gave yesterday a full and I fancy a startlingly incorrect account of Scotch education to a very stolid German on a garden bench; he sat and perspired under it, however, with much composure. I am generally glad enough to fall back again after these political interludes, upon Burns, toddy and the Highlands. The conception of these last that I am spreading far and wide thro' astonished Teutonia, is a cross between the Alps and Central Africa, with a slight dash of Arcadia to stand for the sugar of its own tri-form beverage. No wonder, if it were only half as strange as my description, that '*Mein Herz ist im Hochland.*'

This is the first time since I left home that I have been in the mood to write and of course I have nothing particular to tell you about and am at the end of my paper!

I go every night to the Theatre, except when there is no opera. I cannot stand a play yet; but I am already very much improved and can understand a good deal of what goes on.

Friday 2 August[2]

Today, as I and Simpson were just sitting down to dinner in the café in the Schiller Platz, I looked across the room and there – yes – no – yes, behind a glass of ale and some bread and cheese, sat Duncan, the late Free-Church minister of Peebles's son.[3] He came over and sat beside us. He is master of a school at Offenbach near here and we are to go down there some day and see him. He pleased us both very much. I never saw a fellow more given to blurting things out and incontinently withdrawing them in confusion in my life. He seems the very soul of nervous simplicity.

In the evening, at the Theatre, I had a great laugh. Lord Allcash in *Fra Diavolo*,[4] with his white hat, red guide-books and bad German, was the *pièce-de-résistance* from a humorous point of view, and I had the satisfaction of knowing that in my own small way I could minister the same amusement whenever I chose to open my mouth.

I am just going off to do some German with Simpson. Your affectionate son   R.L. Stevenson

---

[1] Burns, 'My heart's in the Highlands' as translated by Silbergleit.
[2] The MS of this last section is torn and worn but the text is not in doubt.
[3] Either William Wallace or George Alexander Duncan, the sons of William Wallace Duncan (1808–64), Free Church minister of Peebles 1843–64. RLS spent the summers of 1864 and 1865 at Peebles.
[4] The Auber-Scribe comic opera about an Italian brigand and an English nobleman.

106   To his Father

MS Virginia. Partly published in *Letters*, I, 47–8.

4 August 1872   *Rosen Gasse 13, Frankfurt*[1]

My dear Father, I meant to write my dear Mother; so you can take it between you. And first, with regard to your letter of the 31st, I find myself always more gloomy after a letter from home. First, came gloomy analogies from the life of one Paul; and next (O shame!) reproaches about letters. 'I desire to cimply say' (after Artemus)[2] that I will not write any more, and unless a full retractation come speedily, I will e'en write less.

Second, you will perceive by the head of this page, that we have at last got into lodgings, and powerfully mean ones too. The Rosengasse (Rose street) is about twenty feet wide, I guess: at least if two drunk men were each to set a head against the houses their feet would overlap in the middle. Though we are in the second story and at the top of the house proper, yet the street has a fourth and yet a fifth row of windows in the slope of the steep roofs or in the slated gables. Story after story bulges out above the one below, till it looks as if the two sides would meet and shake hands above the roadway; and, as all the houses are built on a scale of their own, the slating joins the stonework at all sorts of elevations and the leaden rain gutters have to clamber up and down in the most fantastic fashion, till one wonders how gravity and the drip-water manage to come to an agreement at all. Yet withal the roadway is very clean; and what with town-gardens and bird cages at almost every window, the whole street looks rural and is full of twittering from morning to night.

We have here only one room between us, with two beds, two chairs, two receptacles (nameless I think) two basins and one ewer, two tumblers and one carafe, a stove, a spittoon, four sixpenny coloured prints representing the history of one Genevieve and her husband Siegfried,[3] one *ecce-homo* and one obtrusively amateur sketch of the Frauenberg at Fulda (whatever that may be).[4]

---

[1] This 'furnished room to be let to two gentlemen' was advertised in the local newspaper (*Intelligenz-Blatt der Stradt Frankfurt am Main*) on Friday 2 August. The Rosengasse was the centre of prostitution in Frankfurt from the Middle Ages to the 1930s. The alley was demolished in 1938.

[2] 'Artemus Ward in Richmond'.

[3] The medieval legend (widely popular in Germany) of St Genevieve (Genovefa) falsely accused of adultery and condemned to death by her husband Count Siegfried of Brabant. Spared by her executioners she is abandoned in the forest, where she gives birth to her son and is cared for by a doe. Six years later, while hunting the doe, her husband finds her in the forest and acknowledges her innocence: she dies soon afterwards. The cheap prints seen by RLS may have been the series of four coloured lithographs produced by Jean-Frederic Wentzel of Weissenburg, Alsace, *c.* 1845.

[4] A hill overlooking Fulda, a town seventy miles north-east of Frankfurt.

If I were to call the street anything but *shady*, I should be boasting; it is shady, powerful shady. The people sit at their doors in shirt sleeves smoking as they do in Seven Dials of a Sunday.

Bye the bye you had better still address Poste restante, as the intricacies of this are more than I can master.

Last night, we went to bed about ten, for the first time *householders* in Germany – real Teutons, with no deception, spring or false bottom. About half past one, there began such a trumpeting, shouting, pealing of bells and scurrying hither and thither of feet as woke every person in Frankfurt out of their first sleep with a vague sort of apprehension that the last day was at hand. The whole street was alive and we could hear people talking in their rooms or crying to passers-by from their windows all around us. At last I made out what a man was saying in the next room. It was a fire in Sachsenhausen, he said (Sachsenhausen is the suburb on the other side of the Main) and he wound up with one of the most tremendous falsehoods on record 'Hier alles ruht – here all is still.' If it can be said to be still in an engine factory, or in the stomach of a volcano when it is meditating an eruption, he might have been justified in what he said but not otherwise. The tumult continued unabated for near an hour; but as one grew used to it, it gradually resolved itself into three bells answering each other at short intervals across the town, a man shouting, at even shorter intervals, and with superhuman energy, 'Feuer – im Sachsenhausen' and the almost continuous winding of all manner of bugles and trumpets, sometimes in stirring flourishes and sometimes in mere tuneless wails. Occasionally, there was another rush of feet past the window and once there was a mighty drumming, down between us and the river, as tho' the soldiery were turning out to keep the peace. This was all we had of the fire, except a great cloud, all flushed red with the glare, above the roofs on the other side of the Gasse; but it was quite enough to put me entirely off my sleep and make me keenly alive to three or four gentlemen who were strolling leisurely about my person and everywhere and there, leaving me somewhat as a keepsake. What struck me most of all was their extremely *constitutional* rate of motion; and the time they took to get from one place to another made me expand in my own fancy till I felt as if the room could scarcely hold me. I have got quite used to being bitten, don't mind it, rather like the little titillation indeed; but these horrid journeys to and fro and especially the still more horrid little moments of debate they had with themselves as to their further route, worked very strongly in the state of nervous exaltation that always accompanies wakefulness. However everything has its compensation, and when day came at last, and the sparrows awoke with trills and *carol-ets*, the same nervous state made the dawn fall on me like a sleeping draught. I went to the window and saw the sparrows about the eaves and a great troop of doves go strolling up the paven Gasse, seeking what they might devour. And so to sleep, despite fleas and fire alarums and clocks chiming the hours of neighbouring houses at all sorts of odd times and with the most charming want of unanimity.

There is a complete account of our first night in our lodgings, written in sentences that it would exhaust the breath of a blacksmith's bellowses to read straight through. But there is no extra charge for this today as somehow I couldn't lay my hand upon anything shorter.

We have got settled down in Frankfurt and like the place very much. By the bye, we have been twice at the celebrated whisker shop; but they won't[5] [? shave] . . . there now at all – only [dr]ess and cut.

I am getting on slowly but I think decidedly with German. I can now make a flutter at almost anything I want to say, and already I begin to think a *little* (*very* little) about Grammar.

I send you herewith a card. Cards are so useful that I have had to indulge myself in half a hundred.

Simpson and I seem to get on very well together. We suit each other capitally; and it is an awful joke to be living (two would-be advocates and one a Baronet) in this supremely mean abode.

The abode is however a great improvement on the hotel and I think we shall grow quite fond of it. Ever your affectionate son   R.L. Stevenson

107   To his Mother

MS Texas. Published in *Letters*, I, 50–53.

Monday morning [*5 August 1872*]   *13 Rosen Gasse, Frankfurt*

My dear Mother, So, I have passed another night in our lodging and this time slept like a stone. I don't think I have much to say to you: in fact I question whether I have anything but it is a good habit to write a bit whenever you have nothing else to do. I am just going to do some Ollendorff[1] with Simpson; and so adieu.

Tuesday morning

Another letter. Good. I wish you would say in your letters, how many of mine you have received, not by date, which I do not remember, but by some recognisable headmark.

You ask if I am going to Leipzig, and I reply, yes. But you must tell me

---

[5] The corner of the page is torn affecting one or two words.
[1] Heinrich Gottfried Ollendorff (1803–65), a German language teacher in Paris who developed a simplified method of learning languages by examples and exercises rather than grammatical rules. His textbooks achieved immense popularity.

when Buchan[2] will pass thro' Frankfurt, and send me by him complete instructions and another £10 bill, if you please. It is very difficult to live cheaply here standing still; but when it comes to travelling all my economy goes to the winds, and whatsoever my heart desireth, that I purchase.

I don't think I have told you that our room is taken for a month; so I shall just stay here quietly, except the run to Leipsig and any excursion else that may turn up and look inviting, until a decent time to go quietly down to Baden for you.

Last night, I was at the theatre and heard *Die Jüdin* (*La Juive*)[3] and I was thereby most terribly excited. I was very near the tear point more than once, and at last in the middle of the Fifth Act, which is perfectly beastly, I had to slope. I could stand even seeing the cauldron with the sham fire beneath and the two hateful executioners in red, but when at last the girl's courage breaks down and, grasping her father's arm, she cries out, O, so shudder-fully! I thought it high time to be out of that *galère*; and so I do not know yet whether it ends well or ill, but if I ever afterwards find that they do carry things to the extremity, I shall think more meanly of my species. It was raining and cold outside, so I went into a *Bier Halle* and sat and brooded over a *Schnitt* (half-glass) for nearly half an hour. An opera is far more *real* than real life to me. It seems as if stage illusion and particularly this hardest to swallow and most conventional illusion of them all – an opera, would never stale upon me. I wish that life was an opera. I should like to *live* in one; but I don't know in what quarter of the globe I shall find a Society so constituted. Besides it would soon pall; imagine asking for three-kreuzer cigars in recitative, or giving the washerwoman the inventory of your dirty clothes in a sustained and *flourish-ous* aria.

I am in a right good mood this morning to sit here and write to you; but not to give you news. There is a great stir of life, in a quiet, almost country fashion, all about us here. Some one is hammering a beefsteak in the *rez-de-chaussée*: there is a great clink of pitchers and noise of the pump-handle at the public well in the little Square-kin round the corner. The children, all seemingly within a month and certainly none above five that always go halting and stumbling up and down the roadway, are ordinarily very quiet and sit sedately puddling in the gutter, trying, I suppose, poor little devils! to understand their cursed *mutter-sprache*; but they, too, make themselves heard from time to time in little incomprehensible antiphonies, about the drift that comes down to them by their rivers from the strange lands higher up the Gasse. Above all, there is here such a twittering of canaries (I can see

---

[2] There was a Meteorological Congress at Leipzig 14–16 August, which Buchan was expected to attend. Alexander Buchan (1829–1907), meteorologist, secretary of the Scottish Meteorological Society 1860 (of which TS was a member) librarian of the Royal Society of Edinburgh. Famous for his weather forecasting, particularly for his discovery of Buchan's 'cold spells'.

[3] The 'grand' opera by Jacques François Halévy (1835).

twelve out of our window) and such continual visitation of grey doves and big-nosed sparrows, as make our little bye-street into a perfect aviary. I would this were the only branch of natural history that could be advantageously prosecuted therein; but I have expatiated enough on that head, and perhaps too much, already. We are now finally settled down, we have given in our papers to the police and signed ourselves there as '*Rentiers*'; and, I suppose, if we only stay here long enough, we shall have something like the twentieth part of a vote at next election.

Alas, 'all my golden words are spent.'[4] I have no more to say. All I can do is to look across the Gasse at our opposite neighbour, as he dandles his baby about and occasionally takes a spoonful or two, of some pale slimy nastiness that looks like *dead Porridge*, if you can take the conception. These two are his only occupations. All day long you can hear him singing over the brat, when he is not eating; or see him eating when he is not keeping baby. Besides which, there comes into his house a continual round of visitors that puts me in mind of the luncheon hour at home. As he has thus no ostensible avocation, we have named him 'the W.S.', to give a flavour of respectability to the Street.

Enough of the Gasse. The weather is here much colder. It rained a good deal yesterday and though it is fair and sunshiny again, today, and we can still sit of course with our windows open, yet there is no more excuse for the Siesta; and the Bathe in the River, except for cleanliness, is no longer a necessity of life. The Main is very swift. In one part of the baths, it is next door to impossible to swim against it, and I suspect that, out in the open, it would be quite impossible. Adieu, my dear Mother, and believe me, Ever your affectionate son   Robert Louis Stevenson.

(*Rentier*)

Can you read my letters? I hope you can. Do tell me what you have received and let me have some remarks upon my doings.   R.L.S.

108   To his Mother

MS Buffalo.

Tuesday evening [*6 August 1872*]   *Rosen Gasse, Frankfurt*

My dear Mother, You can form no conception over there in dissipated England, of our early habits here. I have come back very leisurely from the Theatre (where, by the bye, I understood more than I have ever done before) and had some beer on the way; and, all done, it is not yet ten o'clock; yet would you believe it, the door was locked here, everyone was

[4] *Hamlet*, V. ii.136.

already safely housed in bed among their lively bedfellows, and I had to use my pass-key and slip in as shamefully as I might at home at half past one in the morning.

After having finished and posted my letter this morning, Simpson and I started and walked up the tow path on the Frankfurt side of the Main. We passed many barges, with their sail set to the favourable up-stream wind. The path winds up and down in a most unscientific fashion; so that sometimes the houses are on a level with the river, and sometimes twenty feet above it, the tow-rope rustling and whistling through the willow-tops along the bank. After about an hour's walk we got opposite Offenbach, where Duncan is a schoolmaster. On our side of the Main, an aisle of the most magnificent poplars, tall and straight as the columns of Cologne Cathedral, aye and yet taller and straighter, leads up to the Bridge of Boats. On the other side, lies the quiet, dead-alive town, where one wanders through three or four absolutely empty streets and then stumbles suddenly on a busy little market place, full of handsome Germans with every here and there one of those wonderfully malconstructed peasant women, whom to admit into our human family costs a sad struggle and, when done, represents a sad loss of self respect. We concluded it was too late to look up Duncan today; and dropped into the Golden Angel for some bread and cheese and beer. There we were very much pleased with two handsome *ouvriers* (a little run to fat, it is true) who came in to drink a glass and chaff the *Mädchen* at the bar. You cannot conceive anything freer or easier than their manner. Each of them looked as tho' he had conquered France with his own hand. I have been quite convinced, by the bye, by my stay here and far prefer the Germans to the French. I see in them almost everything that I liked with a considerable superstructure of honesty and with the enormous advantage of a fine physique.

Wednesday morning [7 *August*]

I have nothing to say. Simpson is stewing Ollendorff opposite to me. I have filled myself just as full of Ollendorff as I can hold. He is doubtless wholesome; but I think he is best in homoeopathic doses. I hate Ollendorff. Ollendorff was an ass. Ollendorff has written a dialogue between a father and mother, near the end of his Method which for downright laughableness has never been surpassed; but this is his best effort. His fun elsewhere seems forced, and his wit too often involves a want of courtesy. 'Is that your coat, or the Tailor's?' is certainly a hit – but how coarse, how vulgar!

Thursday 8 August

We have had a deal of trouble with the Police, in consequence of going into lodgings without a *passe-porte*. We have lived in an atmosphere of messages and official visits, till at last this morning we went up ourselves and, after an interview with a surly lieutenant, have got leave to stay. As usual our present amusement is the W.S. He is just now enticing pigeons to eat on his window sill for the entertainment of the eternal baby. He is certainly the most systematically idle man that I have ever seen. I suppose ravens come to him, morning and evening, with his daily bread. Perhaps, he is a conspirator − perhaps an exiled sovereign. There is nothing visible in his rooms to suggest industry of any description, except an ink bottle on the window sill. Even the baby cannot keep Mein Herr awake; for the other day when he had been left in charge he went peacefully asleep upon the sofa, and was awakened by his returning wife with a storm of contemptuous abuse and even an appeal to the next door neighbour; all which we heard thro' the open windows and my Lord accepted with an easy, sleepy smile and a yawn or two. He is becoming an object of morbid interest to me. I do so much long to know how he lives.

Outside, the W.S.: inside Ollendorff. Simpson is quite unsound in the mind about Ollendorff. He has already two colossal literary schemes, with regard to this great man. First an Ode, second an edition of the Method in verse.

Trouville-sur-Mer is the place you ought to go to. You can get there by rail from Boulogne.

Germany has some objections, two in particular, the language and the 'livin' wild beests of pray'.[1]

I am afraid my brief fit of letter-writing is now quite run dry. I can't find anything to say − no not a word.

So Adieu,
my dear mother,
and believe me,
Ever your affectionate son
R.L. Stevenson
Anything to fill up room.

109   To his Mother

MS Buffalo.

Saturday 9 August [*1872*]   *Rosen Gasse, Frankfurt*

My dear Mother, I have got fairly off writing principally perhaps because our way of life here has got into a set and has become already nearly as much

---

[1] A favourite phrase of Artemus Ward, who wrote in the character of an illiterate travelling showman with 'a wonderful colleckshun of livin wild Beests of Pray, snaix in grate profushun, a endless variety of life-size wax figgers, and the only traned Kangaroo in Ameriky' ('The Showman's Courtship').

of a mill round as the way of life at home. It is curious how soon you can raise habits; and how the mere fact of having done something yesterday, obliges you to repeat the same today. It requires as much energy for us now to alter our customary order, as it did to begin the whole journey. I feel just as if I had lived in Frankfurt all my life and just as if I should never leave it. Talking of which why is there no answer to my requests about Leipsig? But I suppose you have not yet got that letter.

The only thing worth telling is about an excursion, we made the other day, by way of change, down the Main. It was a very tiny affair, but I'm sure I regarded it quite as a journey. We walked about three miles down, crossing the river once in a Ferry; and found ourselves about five opposite a long village called Griesheim or Kriesheim,[1] I forget which. The evening was very still, and golden: the river just rippled with an upstream breeze; and the Taunus hills lying back in a perfect megilp of haze and sunshine. With one accord, we agreed that we could not go back to Frankfurt in such an idle evening; and so we got into the Ferry and were swung across to the village. The Ferry, you know, consists of one section of a Bridge of Boats, which is attached by a long string of skiffs, threaded on a strong rope, to a fixed point some hundred feet higher up the river; from this point by some wonderful mechanical contrivance, or perhaps by a law of nature, it pendulates backward and forward from one shore to the other. There was a *Gasthaus* close to the Ferry; but we must needs walk the whole village over in search of a better, and at last shamefully return to the point we started from. After some difficulty, we got dinner ordered and sat waiting for it, behind the inn looking out across the river, where the horizontal pendulum of the Ferry was slowly oscillating from shore to shore, picking up now a green-coated, fair-haired German and now a cart drawn by a couple of oxen and laden with great boughs of fire-wood. Right across by the roadside, a great white crucifix stood out from the shadow of the wood, the first I have seen. We had thought to dine out here, but the evening began to fall chilly and shortly after a smart plump of rain drove us inside. Two plates of sheep (I don't call it mutton, because I have associations with that name that are incongruous) in a not unsavoury sauce, half a loaf of black bread, a bottle of thin, sharp, white wine, a pudding dish full of small plums, whereof Simpson ate between twenty and thirty to his own check, and a glass of veritable Schnapps, was the *Menu*. Something English about the taste of the sheep, made my heart turn from cigars; and as I knew that sooner or later I must buy a German pipe I came to the conclusion that 'if it were to come, 'twere well that it came quickly'[2] and asked boldly where I could get hold of a '*Pfeife.*'

---

[1] Griesheim, a village south of Frankfurt.
[2] Cf. *Macbeth*, I. vii.1–2.

A small man who was drinking at a neighbouring table was on his legs in a moment to go with me; and no sooner had he got me outside than he stopped and asked me, with a mysterious twinkle in his eye, whether I were not an Englishman. On my pleading guilty, he immediately discharged the English numerals up to ten; and then, thinking apparently that I had not sufficiently appreciated the feat, he repeated the operation a second and third time with unabated vivacity. These English numerals were evidently a fixed idea with him, as he returned to his wallowing among them more than once afterwards and seemed vastly flattered when I told him that he knew more English than I knew German. I soon began to find however that it was not his own English only that he wished to show off; for as we went on, with ever a longer string of pretty children with fair hair, dark eyes and liver coloured faces admiringly following at our heels, I discovered that we were not going direct for the pipe but first of all to the house of a '*Musiker*' who spoke English. The house was in a court and there at the ground floor window (now I come to think of it there was only one story) sat *the* – well perhaps not that, but certainly *one* of the – very dirtiest man that I have ever put my eyes upon. This was the *Musiker*. Poor man! how his face fell when my conductor pointed out me, ever meekly following, and told him that this was an Englander who could speak no German (the sacrilegious dog!) and to whom he must therefore speak English. I saw the case in a moment. My poor, filthy fellow creature had evidently been gassing all round, about his powers and now when the time had come for him to justify his boasts, felt himself sadly wanting. It occurred to me that I might someday be in the same case myself on the head of German; and so I compassionately put my head well into the window and said to him as slowly and distinctly as I could 'You can speak English.' This was pretty elementary and the unclean *Musiker* leapt at it like a straw and answered with inconceivable difficulty. Our small friend wished him to come and join us and help to choose the pipe; but to this both I and the *Musiker*, for private reasons, had each the most emphatic objection; he, because he knew that his English would not last him thro' so long a proof; and I, from sanitary considerations. He said he was writing music – 'al-wes-Besy'; and I taking off my hat told him that I positively would not allow him to leave his work. Gratitude was stamped upon every line of his face, when I thus rescued him out of the very jaws of shame, and he laboured forth some statement that he would be glad to see me again. I do not know that I can put it quite so strong as that, but I have at least a curiosity to see that *Musiker* once more – I do so wonder whether he will be any dirtier. No sooner had we set out again, from this visit, than my conductor demanded eagerly whether his friend could not speak English very well. I gave the *Musiker* a character that would have rather surprised himself I fancy. I said he spoke it like a native. I did. It was wrong but I think it leaned to virtue's side; and I was amply repaid for my little peccadillo, by the relief that my guide displayed. He had evidently been hanging on the answer with almost apprehension, having probably been rendered suspicious by the *Musiker's* unconcealable want of volubility; but all was right now – Dagon was once more set up.[3] We had scarcely reached the shop, when everyone began asking my conductor about me; but alas! he had only a few words on that head and then shot off at a tangent to the *Musiker*, who, he said, had been interviewing me in '*recht gut English*', and then appealed to me for confirmation. So that I had several times to repeat my original somewhat highly-coloured testimonial.

> 'Ah what a tangled web we weave
> When first we venture to deceive.'[4]

At last, came the pipe choosing. Almost the first head that I saw was adorned with the picture of an old, white-haired man that fascinated me like a serpent. I couldn't get past it. I had eyes for none other; for I had never seen anything that went more directly against all the better feelings of my nature. Morally and aesthetically, that old man and his portrait are two of the hatefulest things on earth. The white-headed scoundrel I feel convinced, must have waded knee-deep, his whole life long, in innocent life-blood spilt by treachery; and his face is enough to embitter a whole Decameron of Dreams. Well, what did I do? The fascination was too strong, or my better Angel[5] was absent, or both perhaps, for *I bought him*, yes, and have him here in the room beside me, as I write. Frankenstein and his monster are not a circumstance to me and my old man. He has a dress-coat and a green cloak over it and – words fail me – you will see him soon enough and I only hope that he will not haunt your dreams, as already he begins gruesomely to people mine.

By the time I got back to the Inn, I was already doubting about the pipe; and before we got into Frankfurt, Despair was about my size.

I don't know what you mean by running amuck at our lodgings. It's a jolly little room with white curtains and as full of fleas —!

There's a long letter for you written straight off the nail and now going straight to post. Your affectionate son   R.L. Stevenson

Tell Cummy, I've been trying to find a message for her and will send a startler shortly.

---

[3] When the Philistines captured the Hebrew Ark they placed it in the temple of their own god Dagon. The next morning the statue of Dagon was found fallen on its face before the Ark and it was restored to its place. The following morning the statue was again found on the ground with its head and hands cut off (I Samuel 5:3–4).

[4] Scott, *Marmion* Canto VI. 17 slightly misquoted.

[5] Cf. Shakespeare, Sonnet CXLIV, l.3. The first line of the sonnet, 'Two loves I have, of comfort and despair,' is echoed in the later reference to Despair.

110   To his Father

MS Yale. Published in *Letters*, I, 49–50.

Sunday 11 August [1872]   *Rosen Gasse, Frankfurt*

My dear Father, I can scarcely tell you what a lucky thing your draft was; indeed the best way to explain it to you is to begin from the beginning and tell the affair consecutively through.

We were coming home from Bockenheim last night about ten, and in fine spirits, when my tobacco ran short and instead of going for our nightcap, we came up here. When I opened the door, there was a telegraph man standing inside in the lobby. Simpson's second brother was alarmingly ill.[1] We went straight to the Station but the last train was gone. This morning we were up by five (a needless nuisance, as we found afterwards that he would arrive equally soon by a later train and so he is still here – twelve o'clock); but then the following hitch was discovered. He had only four Napoleons in money; all the banks were shut of course, so that no draft could be cashed; and if I advanced him enough, I should be left here, with bills to pay and my Leipzig excursion before me, a great deal nearer penniless than would be pleasant. Ruminating over this, we turned in about nine to get some sleep, after a most wretched night and morning of uncertainty and botheration; but as luck would have it, out of mere restlessness, I determined to go first to the Post Office and so dressed myself again and arrived there, just in time – twenty minutes later would have done the trick – to get the £20 Draught which at once smoothed matters over.

We have both been much amused by your precautionary note.

Seeing matters are so, I shall probably get to Baden in seven or eight days; but this of course depends upon the length of the Congress and when you will be there,[2] as I should rather loiter on the way than arrive before you.

It is an awfully sad affair and has broken up our pleasant establishment in a sufficiently dismal manner. I hope he will pull through yet. Simpson, who believes in presentiments, seems to think he will.

If I get a letter with Buchan's address in it tomorrow, I shall go to Leipzig at eleven o'clock that night. If I don't, I shall probably wait another day. Poste Restante Leipzig is the next address of Your affectionate son

R.L. Stevenson

P.S. Write immediately you hear anything of poor Willy Simpson?

R.L.S.

[1] William Simpson (1850–1911), who became an artist.
[2] RLS joined his parents at Baden Baden on 23 August.

111   To Charles Baxter

MS BL. Privately printed by T.J. Wise as *Familiar Epistle in Verse and Prose* (1896); published less fully in *Letters*, I, 53–6, and in *Baxter Letters*, 13–16.[1]

Wednesday 3 or 4 September 1872 [actually 4]   *Boulogne sur Mer*[2]

> Blame me not that this epistle
>> Is the first you have from me.
>>> Idleness has held me fettered;
>>> But at last the times are bettered
> And once more I wet my whistle
>> Here, in France beside the sea.
>
> All the green and idle weather
>> I have had in sun and shower
>>> Such an easy, warm subsistence,
>>> Such an indolent existence
> I should find it hard to sever
>> Day from day and hour from hour.
>
> Many a tract-provided ranter
>> May upbraid me, dark and sour,
>>> Many a bland Utilitarian
>>> Or excited Millenarian,
> – '*Pereunt et imputantur*[3]
>> You must speak to every hour.'
>
> But (the very term's deceptive)
>> You at least, my friend, will see
>>> That in sunny grassy meadows
>>> Trailed across by moving shadows
> To be actively receptive
>> Is as much as man can be.
>
> He that all the winter grapples
>> Difficulties – thrust and ward –
>>> Needs to cheer him thro' his duty

---

[1] Baxter gave the MS to Clement K. Shorter, who sold it to Wise. Wise printed it without authority in a limited edition (allegedly of 27 copies) and Baxter and Colvin considered legal action. The editors of the *Baxter Letters* described the MS as untraced.

[2] After a week in Baden Baden the Stevensons returned home via Strasbourg, Paris and Boulogne. They reached Edinburgh on 11 September.

[3] '*Bonosque/Soles effugere atque abire sentit,/ Qui nobis pereunt et imputantur.*' (And he feels the good days are flitting and passing away, our days that perish and are scored to our account.) RLS was fond of this phrase from Martial (*Epigrams*, V. 20) and used it again in Letter 1517 as well as in 'A Christmas Sermon' (1888).

Memories of sun and beauty
Orchards with the russet apples
    Lying scattered on the sward.

Many such I keep in prison,
    Keep them here at heart unseen,
        Till my muse again rehearses
        Long years hence, and in my verses
You shall meet them rearisen
    Ever comely, ever green.

You know how they never perish,
    How, in time of later art,
        Memories consecrate and sweeten
        These defaced and tempest-beaten
Flowers of former years we cherish,
    Half a life, against our heart.

Most, those love-fruits withered greenly;
    Those frail, sickly amourettes,
        How they brighten with the distance
        Take new strength and new existence
Till we see them sitting queenly
    Crowned and courted by regrets!

All that loveliest and best is,
    Aureole-fashion round their head,
        They that looked in life but plainly,
        How they stir our spirits vainly
When they come to us Alcestis-
    Like returning from the dead!

Not the old love but another,
    Bright she comes at Memory's call,
        Our forgotten vows reviving
        To a newer, livelier living,
As the dead child to the mother
    Seems the fairest child of all.

Thus, our Goethe, sacred master,
    Travelling backward thro' his youth,
        Surely wandered wrong in trying
        To renew the old, undying
Loves that cling in memory faster
    Than they ever lived in truth.

So; *en voilà assez de mauvais vers*. Let us finish with a word or two in honest prose, tho' indeed I shall so soon be back again and, if you be in town as I hope, so soon get linked again down the Lothian road by a cigar or two and a liquor, that it is perhaps scarce worth the postage to send my letter on before me. I have just been long enough away to be satisfied and even anxious to get home again and talk the matter over with my friends. I shall have plenty to tell you; and principally plenty that I do not care to write; and I daresay you, too, will have a lot of gossip. What about Ferrier?[4] Is the L.J.R. think you to go naked and unashamed this winter? He with his charming idiosyncrasy was in my eyes the vine-leaf that preserved our self-respect. All the rest of us are such shadows, compared to his full-flavoured personality; but I must not spoil my own *début*. I am trenching upon one of the essayettes which I propose to introduce, as a novelty this year before that august assembly. For we must not let it die. It is a sickly baby, but what with nursing, and pap, and the like, I do not see why it should not have a stout manhood after all, and perhaps a green old age. Eh! when we are old (if we ever should be) that too will be one of those cherished memories I have been so rhapsodizing over. We must consecrate our room. We must make it a museum of bright recollections; so that we may go back there white-headed, and say '*Vixi*'. After all, new countries, sun, music, and all the rest can never take down our gusty, rainy, smoky, grim old city out of the first place that it has been making for itself in the bottom of my soul, by all pleasant and hard things that have befallen me for these past twenty years or so. My heart is buried there – say, in Advocate's Close!

I don't know why I write so sadly and sentimentally. Momus is absent on a journey and I may cut my flesh and wail to him as much as I like – he cannot hear me.[5] Talking about my flesh I am all out in [*one or two words obliterated*] the result of mosquito bites. I am a horrid spectacle and am haunted at bed and board by my resemblance to the 'Monarch'. Simpson and I got on very well together, and made a very suitable pair. I like him much better than I did when I started which was almost more than I hoped for.

If you should chance to see Bob, give him my news or if you have the letter about you, let him see it. Ever your affectionate friend

R.L. Stevenson

P.S. *He* can give you some of mine.

---

[4] James Walter Ferrier (1850–83), one of the small group of RLS's close Edinburgh friends, was a fellow-member of the Speculative Society and the L.J.R. His early death grieved RLS deeply and he paid tribute to his memory in 'Old Mortality'. See also Letter 689, n. 4.

[5] Momus was the Greek god of ridicule and fault-finding. RLS is also remembering the contest between Elijah and the priests of Baal (1 Kings 18:27–8). ›

112   To Bob Stevenson

MS Yale.

Tuesday October 1872[1]   [*Edinburgh*]

My dear Bob, A damned lot of waves and counter-waves have been beating upon me of late, and as this new creed of mine is not ballasted as yet with many Articles, it has tossed terribly about and made my heart sick within me. I am almost drifting back into my old introspective humour, perhaps opportunely, as I am now again thinking seriously of my duty; and here, as the symbol, comes another foolscap letter.

There are a sight of hitches not yet disentangled in this Christian skein. Somehow, after the last talk or two I have had, I have been half inclined to take that ready cheerful acceptance, that welcome as of an old friend, with which I had met my new views, not so much for a proof of their fitness, as for a suggestion of some possible dishonesty to myself in the means I took to find them. One does get so *mixed* – my ears begin to sing, when I think of all that can be said on either side; and I do feel just now that hopeless emptiness about the stomach and desire to sit down and cry, that always does and always will result from a succession of small and irritating obstacles. And yet, my God, here am I, well suppered, well clothed, with the white bed at my elbow, warm and soft, for me to lie down in when once I am so minded – educated – having little thought for the morrow – and a whole lot of poor devils outside, whoreson paupers, empty bellies, sleepers in common stairs, that are just turning in just now pleasantly dazed with whiskey or pleasantly lying down with contentment – and are ten times easier with ten times more to bother them.

It is all very well to talk about flesh and lusts and such like; but the real hot sweat must come out in this business, or we go alone to the end of life. *I* want an object, a mission, a belief, a hope to be my wife; and, please God, have it I shall. I will not be put aside and beaten down with such assaults as I have just now all about me. It would be much easier to give over the pursuit, to leave the windy hunting ground and go home to the warm ingle, to bid adieu to honesty and settle back to the old outward conformity; but I am damned if I don't carry it through, and to do this I want all the good steady talk you can give me, all the wind you can puff into the tattered sails of my enthusiasm. O I am so tired of this attempt to be honest and strike the bed rock, more weary than I could have fancied; and, kind and even sympathetic as my father has shown himself, the limits of his tolerance are so near to me, that I am always lingering about the

---

[1] The day seems to be in Stevenson's hand, but the month and year may have been added later.

landmark to pass which is to sour his half-hearted patience into petty persecution. We need to be helped in this matter. The work of judging truth needs such fair skies and favourable circumstances; and here at least it has to be conducted, somewhat as the boarding-school boy reads his novel, with the candle half up the chimney, the book in an illegible position and the 'dreadful looking for' of the pedagogue playing the very devil at his heart. Don't we need help and encouragement? I am very proud of my good spirits and ordinarily equable temper; but I begin to feel the truth of what you said the other day at the corner of Union Street – if we do go honestly and bravely through with this, we shall come out crushed and sad.

Here is another terrible complaint I bring against our country. I try to learn the truth, and their grim-faced dummies, their wooden effigies and creeds dead years ago at heart, come round me, like the wooden men in *Phantastes*[2], and I may cut at them and prove them faulty and mortal, but yet they can stamp the life out of me. What a failure must not this Christian country be, when I who found it easy to be a vicious good companion, find nothing but black faces and black prospects when once I try honestly to inquire into the words this very Christ of theirs spent all his life in speaking and repeating. When I think of this, look you, I grow as bitter against ministers and elders and the like as ever Falconer or you or Buckle. . . .[3] Why should I be sitting up here at midnight writing nearly such morbid rubbish as I wrote to you so many years ago; why, *messieurs les presbytères* – why, you black-coated, black-faced race?

Oh God, I am not the man for work like this. It needs a tougher fibre to handle such perilous stuff in such a shower of fire and brimstone; and I am so anxious to be happy and have blue skies about me and good wine and pretty *die-dies* of the grown-up sort, that I fear I shall not find enough nerve and patience and determination in my heart to carry it to an end.

Wednesday Morning

All my difficulties cleared away whenever I laid my head on the pillow. I saw at once that one must continue precisely what we have begun, silence and questions: we must always appear in character, as a point of interrogation. It never can be wrong to ask a question.

Excuse me for this gloomy epistle; but it was in me and had to come out of me. Ever your affectionate friend and cousin   R.L. Stevenson

---

[2] George MacDonald, *Phantastes: A Faerie Romance* (1858).
[3] On 9 December 1872 MIS records: 'Falconer, Bob and Noona at dinner.' This may be James Falconer who took his MA at Edinburgh University in 1875. RLS has blotted out two or three words at the end of the sentence.

Note

I am sorry Bob answered this in person, as I should like to have had his answer also as something to look on, if we ever come to a haven; but, merely with the note that he has had days of similar depression, I shall put this away in may desk as a *bonne-bouche* for better times.

113   To Charles Baxter

MS Yale. Published in *Baxter Letters*, 19–20.

Private
31 October 1872   *17 Heriot Row*

My dear Baxter, I have been quite depressed all day about this rotten, carious job of yours with that poor, honest, childish weakling, John Forman.[1] I can always say more in pen and ink that I can *viva voce*; and so I may say now (what I had on my tongue a dozen times this afternoon) that whereas this would have been a funny story to me in ordinary circumstances, it becomes a matter of great concern to me from the moment that my friend is involved in it. I do think, my dear Charles, that from beginning to end you have played neither a wise, nor a kindly part in the affair. (I know I am speaking like a parson; but I'm damned if I can help it.) You might, I think, have felt yourself above taking revenge on such a shorn lamb as J.F.; instead of answering his inefficacious pebbles with such a boulder as you sent upon his poor, frail head; and certainly, after you had done so – after you had played a part so far off magnanimity, you might have taken a lower key and done your best to heal your own bruises, by healing his.

I do wish you would think better of this matter and give Forman something in the way of reparation. Apology is from the strong to the weak. A big man is never so big as when he apologises to a little whelk of a creature such as our poor, *invalide* Forman. If you cannot see your way to writing something – for the love of God, old man, let me call and I'll eat all the necessary onion – yea, and relish it. I shall say that you were hasty and told a foolish story, without any wish to hurt his (J.F.'s) feelings, that you were riled at the way he took to shew his displeasure, that – *enfin*, old man, that you are plucky enough and *man* enough to apologise because you find yourself involved in a duel with a child. For God's sake, don't deny me this favour. I shall count it a real proof of friendship. I shall take it more gladly than I would a ten-pound note, and you know what that means for an

---

[1] Probably John Forman, W.S. (1838–82), who lived at 8 Heriot Row. His father John Nairne Forman, W.S. was (like Baxter's father) an elder of St Stephen's Church.

impecunious, extravagant, hand-to-mouth, poor devil, such as I. I know well enough that you are not so mean as to desire a fight with so feeble an adversary. I know that you must feel the *hate* of such a man, a slur upon your tact and magnanimity, and I want – I really do wish and hope, in spite of all this cursed pulpit phraseology, that you will either write or let me go on your part and do the immediate leek-eating.

Don't let me have a friend who isn't bold enough to say '*I was wrong*' to such a — as J.F.

For God's sake don't take this amiss. However much you dislike it or think it strained and foolish it is the best proof of friendship you have ever got, or are ever likely to get, from your affectionate friend

R.L. Stevenson

114   To James Walter Ferrier

MS Yale. Second half published in G.S. Hellman, *The True Stevenson* (1925), 122–3 (as a letter to Bob Stevenson).

Saturday 23 November 1872[1]   *17 Heriot Row*

My dear Ferrier, Our intentions must have been set close to each other in the infernal mosaic, for the removal of yours so loosened mine that it has only taken me a fortnight's labour to get the great big block dislodged and set before me. It looks very rough and shapeless; but I hope to carve it into a very comely epistle before I have made an end.

You did not come to Edinburgh? or, did you? It is conceivable to me that you may be lying *perdu* in some of these new and undiscoverable suburbs that are being wedged into all manner of odd corners about the town; on one of which, by the way, Bob and I stumbled the other afternoon. It lay between Leith Walk and the London Road; and, though split new in all its members, was already of a goodly size and possessed the necessary organs of life – a tobacconist's, the London Journal and a Public House.

And now, old man, how are you getting on? You are already so clouded over with myths and legends, that we rationalists of Edinburgh have begun to question your existence. By common repute, there is scarcely a crime that you have not committed. Simony, arson, fraud, adultery,

> 'Wi' mair o' horrible and awful',
> Which ev'n to name wad be unlawfu',[2]

---

[1] RLS must have begun the letter on 20 November (see n. 14).
[2] Burns, 'Tam o'Shanter', ll.141–2.

are already identified with your memory. If you go on at this rate, you will become a very famous man – a 'bug to frighten babes withal.'[3] If all this be true you seem to have run the race which is set before you,[4] with laudable industry and swiftness of foot.

Seriously, however, you have left a very motley reputation behind you; and godly people, when your name is mentioned, draw closer round the fire and look fearfully over their shoulders.

As for me, I suppose you knew that I *was* going away to Germany with Simpson; so I may now tell you that the plan was carried out; and a very good time we had of it – what with sunshine, idleness and amourettes. Sir W. however was telegraphed home, because the chinee-God was thought to be dying; so I left Frankfurt where we had been staying and proceeded onward to Leipzig and Dresden; then to B. Baden Esq., where I met my family; and thence home with them thro' France. This latter part was somewhat spoilt by the most inconceivable insubordination on the part of my liver – a lewd liver, indeed – who exhibited every form of misconduct that malice could suggest. I was not however quite clear in my own conscience; for I dined twice in the forenoon, a liberty always resented by the human organism.

I am now, *working hard* (*credite posteri!*)[5]. I am at Political Economy, which I love; and Scots Law, which is a burthen greater than I can bear. The large white head of the professor[6] relieved, in the pale gaslight, against the black board, is the one '*taedii dulce lenimen*'[7] that we poor students have. He is called 'The Bum-Faced', by those who know him.

I have served myself universal heir to you; but the assets consist of five Speculative keys, sent me in an envelope by your mother, and one eighteen-penny book on Spiritualism; while the liabilities, as far as yet disclosed, are a very fair, good, honest, downright pound or two and half a hundred weight of library books. I shall probably abscond.

And now for yourself.

Jowett is good and Malvern also is good.[8] Both of these are 'good holts' for you, my lad. But they are not what you want. What you want is to *publish that Heine manuscript of yours*.[9] There can be comparatively little difficulty about it for you, because you are your father's son, your grandfather's grandson, and the brother-in-law of him that married your

---

[3] 'As bugs to fearen babes withall' – Spenser, *Faerie Queene*, II.xii.25.
[4] Hebrews 12:1.
[5] Believe it, future generations – Horace, *Odes*, II.xix.2.
[6] Norman Macpherson (1825–1914), Professor of Scots Law 1865–88.
[7] Pleasant balm for tedium adapted from 'O *laborum dulci lenimen*' (O sweet balm of troubles), Horace, *Odes*, I.xxxii.15.
[8] Apparently essays by Ferrier.
[9] Ferrier read essays on Heine to the Speculative Society on 24 January 1871 and 16 January 1872.

sister.[10] Don't say who you are, but give a brief genealogy – give in an extract register of birth instead of a visiting card. Go to Grant's publisher, or your father's publisher – or, go to the devil if you like, but *publish that Heine*. Write a damned good witty critical thing for the beginning; but look sharp. I happen to[11] know that the Comptist club are at work on a complete edition of Heine; so you must get before them.

Now, old man, all this *is wrote* powerful serious. I know what you want, and I know what would do you more good than all the Malverns in the world in a brown paper parcel, or a luncheon box of concentrated essence of Jowett. You want to get your name up a bit – that's what's the matter with you, and that also is what is the matter with ever-yours-faithfully-R.L. Stevenson.

All which is good sense and very good sense, In Witness Whereof . . .

I am reading Herbert Spencer[12] just now very hard. I got over the fingers at the Spec., the other night. I proposed 'Have we any authority for the inspiration of the New Testament?' as a subject of debate; when I was not seconded and Colin Macrae[13] protested. The liberty of free speech is the greatest boon of this happy and glorious – happy and glorious – ever victorious – country of Pharisees and whiskey.

We have a sight of new men in that august Society; and black balled one named (with cheerful anachronism) Daniel Macbeth[14] no longer gone than last night; on which occasion it will interest you to hear that Omond[15] was inarticulate and foolish, and subsided gradually into an infantile slumber.

[10] Ferrier's father, James Frederick Ferrier (1808–64), Professor of Moral Philosophy and Political Economy at St Andrews, was a nephew of the novelist Susan Ferrier. He married (1837) his cousin Margaret Anne Wilson (1813–78), eldest daughter of John Wilson (1785–1854), the 'Christopher North' of *Blackwood's Magazine* and author of *Noctes Ambrosianae*. Their daughter Susan married Sir Alexander Grant (1826–84), classical scholar, Principal of Edinburgh University 1868–84.

[11] The rest of the MS was long separated from the first half and thought to be a letter to Bob Stevenson.

[12] 'Close upon my discovery of Whitman, I came under the influence of Herbert Spencer. No more persuasive rabbi exists, and few better. . . . His words, if dry, are always manly and honest . . . I should be much of a hound if I lost my gratitude to Herbert Spencer' – RLS, 'Books Which Have Influenced Me' (1887).

[13] Colin George Macrae (1844–1925), W.S. 1871; Chairman of Edinburgh School Board 1890–1900; knighted 1900. He was present at a Spec. meeting on 5 November. On 12 November RLS read an essay: 'Two Questions on the Relation between Christ's Teaching and Modern Christianity'.

[14] Daniel Macbeth (1851–1928) became an advocate. He was blackballed at the Spec. on 19 November.

[15] George William Thomson Omond (1846–1929), one of the founders, with RLS, Ferrier and Robert Glasgow Brown of the shortlived *Edinburgh University Magazine* (January–April 1871), to which RLS contributed some essays. He became an advocate and author. He was one of the few people RLS strongly disliked and was the original of Frank Innes in *Weir of Hermiston* (Balfour papers NLS; Baxter, *The Outlook*, 19 February 1898). Omond read an essay on 19 November on 'Church Tendencies in Scotland at the Present Time' and also put a question about library books.

Write again and (if you please) let me hear something definite about Heine. Ever yours truly   Louis Stevenson

P.S. As so long has elapsed, I think I shan't try the hotel but send this to Bonchurch.

115   To Charles Baxter

MS Yale. Published in *Baxter Letters*, 27–9 (misdated).

Private – a few![1]
Satingty [*7 or 14 December 1872*]   [*Edinburgh*]

My dear Charles, The doctor has just told me that I have succeeded in playing the devil with myself to a singular degree. That walk down from Queen Street has made a fine sore of my burning;[2] and here I am. There is not much gibber about me, alas! Like bad soda-water, the cork has come out and my spirit does not pour forth in foolery, as I had wished. It is difficult to gibber with a sore and after having written two and twenty pages for Hodgson.[3] Still I must do something light and festive.

Talking of soda-water, I have a vapid, dead taste in my mouth as if I had been drinking some and it was *very* bad. I see the colourless pools on the table with the bubbles in them, and the green bottle and the wire and the spitoons – *Fi! fermons les yeux!* We are in a public house, and somebody was drunk last night. This is a most intolerable vision, isn't it? I have had it about me all morning; and you never saw such a sour, saw-dusty, cold, matutinal public house in your life, as is this one that I inhabit in spirit. I cannot get rid of this.

The general chorus of all my thoughts just now is

'Over the hills and far away;'[4]

as it must be of any well-regulated person in this double-damned place at the beginning of winter. It is a terrible long dark vault, this winter, for a man to enter into; not so long, however, but what I can see – far away, at the other end – the sun shining in next spring. Aren't you made hungry, or thirsty, or something, by the mere word? Spring, that dear delusion, that

---

[1] I.e. a little. An Artemus Ward usage.
[2] On 4 December MIS records: 'Lou has burned his leg with iodine and can only go to Hodgson's class in a cab.' He was 'rather worse' on Saturday 7 December and on the following Saturday was 'ordered to lay himself up'.
[3] William Ballantyne Hodgson (1815–80), educational reformer, first Professor of Political Economy and Mercantile Law at Edinburgh 1871–80.
[4] Cf. RLS's use of the refrain from this popular song in 'A Song of the Road' (*Underwoods* II).

jolly old impostor, that I know will be cold and rainy and unutterably filthy after all!

I feel very sentimental. The sun is shining just now, by the bye, right into the room; and that has dispersed my visionary public and terrible depressing potash water – a new form of nightmare and very horrid.

I don't like the slowness with which this drivel comes away. Is the cask running dry? Is the issue of my foolishness ceased? God forbid.

You can't tell how much I want to stand on my head – just because I've got a sore; altho' you know I couldn't stand on my head even if I hadn't a sore.

Who the devil's that knocking in the lower flat? Knocking stopped. Do you remember the knocking in *Macbeth*? That is some pumpkins. There is not much knocking about the world that can come up to that. The porter is a man I have a great respect for. He had a great command of language. All that he says, curiously enough, my mother left out when she read *Macbeth* to me – I suppose it was too affecting. By jingo! I remember the day my mother read *Macbeth* to me.[5] A terrible, black, stormy day, when neither of us could go out of the house; and so we both sat over the fire and she read and I had snakes and newts and others to crawl up and down my spine.

There is blasted little to think about in this world. This letter is quite a chronicle of all my thoughts, except that whenever a cart passes I should like to go and look at it to see what is in it, and then don't go and then am sorry for not having done so.

I have left out some of my thoughts here. The spirit of the porter entered into me for a space. If I were a medium, I should call up the spirit of that porter and just sit and listen to him by the hour. I don't think anything could soothe me so.

Words can't express how empty my head is. I have entirely exhausted it over Political Economy. By the bye, wouldn't it be fun to borrow a motto for Hodgson from the porter's speech?

I feel as if I had taken hands with certain personified execrations and was dancing with them in a sort of Bacchanalian jinga-ring, all about the vacant but sensitive floor of my mind. *Damn* is a short, burly fellow; he is not much at dancing; he is sort of solid and serious and dances away with gravity.— is lean and feathers his toes like anything. But the life and soul of the party is my little immortal soul, who skips and leaps and cancanises and drags the whole ring hither and thither, and faster! faster! – step out, damn! – *Evoë*! round and round and round goes my immortal soul and all the personified oaths.

[5] 'I never supposed that a book was to command me until, one disastrous day of storm . . . my mother read aloud to me *Macbeth*. I cannot say I found the experience agreeable . . . it was something new and shocking to be thus ravished by a giant and I shrank under the brutal grasp' – RLS, 'Popular Authors' (1888).

The real truth is I was able to eat nothing at breakfast, and I am quite giddy and light-headed with work and tea and want of food. My head rolls about on my shoulders like a great, big, peony on the end of a blade of spear-grass. And O! I am in a hell of a state – nerves, mind and body. Distractedly yours   R.L. Stevenson

I shouldn't wonder if there are some oaths in this letter. I now believe that story about Swinburne and the bell-pull.[7]

I really am not drunk, altho' I feel quite drunk, for I have tasted *nothing* but tea today.

116   To Charles Baxter

MS Yale. Published in *Baxter Letters*, 20–21.

[? 18] *December 1872*   [*Edinburgh*]

Secretairy,
Quite contrairy,
How did the voting go?
Did the president's rule
Make you look like a fool?
Or were you at the head of the row?[1]

As for me, I am a harmless, necessary —ster. 'If you want to see – a—[2] come to me.' Seriously, old man, I'm limed, and my lookout for life is a pretty bad one. I gave myself a good cross-examination this morning, and ever since I have been – I don't say *indifferent*, for I should like to live – but *easy* as to the result. I don't take so unkindly to death, especially as I see a course about which anon and in your private ear. I don't think much of my own chance, for I think I have a regular skinful, and I fancy the doctor thinks so too. I feel somehow as if I were in the roads already, and casting anchor; but eh good God! they may be a long way off, and there may be a nasty surf on the bar when I come to cross. We shall hope, however, first for a good recovery, and second for an easy passage, if No. 1 be denied.

---

[7] In the last sentences of the fragment of autobiography dictated at Vailima (appended to 'Memoirs of Himself'), RLS regrets that he never met Swinburne: 'I could tell a lot of funny stories of the days when he was partial to the bottle, and I had rather not. Some other gentleman will probably preserve them'. This particular anecdote seems to be unknown.

[1] RLS was present at meetings of the Spec. on 3 and 10 December. He was not at the meeting on 17 December, when the Report of the Standing Committee (of which Baxter was Chairman) was approved.

[2] A series of squiggles which might be a drawn-out spelling of 'ruin'.

Enough of the mortuary. I have started an essay for Simpson's night, 'Law versus Legislation'.[3] It is *terribly* broad, and will bring anyone who may happen to listen on my head.

I wish to God I had five years more, for if I went on as I have been doing, I think I should not have been so useless – should not feel myself a cancelled cipher when I came to the end. Ever your sincere friend   R.L.S.

117   *To Elizabeth Crosby*[1]

MS Yale.

22 December 1872   *17 Heriot Row*

My dear Miss Crosby, We were very much pleased to hear from you; and I was not a little surprised to hear you were in Dresden, as I was there myself this summer. I cannot enter into your dislike of the place; for to me it was a place of refuge out of horrible Leipzig, and many concomitant disagreeables. I was only a few days in Dresden, as I was telegraphed for to meet my father and mother at Baden Baden; but (as far as I could see) it was a place where you could get eatables, where you might amuse yourself and where I was free from certain burthensome companionship; in all which it had the advantage of Leipzig.

I must tell you that I have twice before begun to write to you; but my letters have a habit of falling through at various different degrees of completion; and mighty few of them ever find their way into the letter box. So I hope you will credit me with good intentions, however little result they may have had.

I am writing (as I am begged to mention) for the family; and the selection of scribe has been very unfortunate for you, as my letters have a trick of lapsing away from me in tranquil egotism, with never a currant of information in the whole unleavened pudding. I am going to try my best, however, and will restrain my polysyllables as much as may be.

My father and mother, then, are very well; and my mother looks as young and pretty as ever, if my testimony is to be credited.

Mary I suppose you will hear from; she is looking wonderfully well, and is not at all changed by marriage. Indeed we refuse to call her anything but

[3] On 11 February 1873 RLS read an essay to the Spec. on 'Law and Free Will. Notes on the Duke of Argyll'. See Letter 143, n. 1.

[1] Elizabeth Russel Crosby (1845–1931), a London solicitor's daughter, was a friend of Mary Warden's; she stayed with the Stevensons 25 February–1 March 1871. She married (1878) Dr Hugo Müller, F.R.S. (1834–1915), a German-born chemist who was ultimately a partner in De la Rue & Co., and head of their stamp department. The letters to Miss Crosby were completely unknown until sold by Christie's in December 1969.

'Mary Warden' to this day, which is the source of much amusement of a *domestic* character.[2]

Bob is still at the School of Arts here, and is (I think and we all think) improving considerably, so I have some hope he may yet do something worthy of himself.

I am going on with my classes, and have besides been sometime in an office. I must say that the life of a copying clerk is the ideal of a placid, idle, equable existence. One's handwriting takes an unnatural interest to itself: you never think of the goodly matter that may be inditing;[3] and there is yet just a sufficient strain upon the attention to keep all other thoughts outside the gates. The mind is thus kept, swept and garnished[4] – nothing perturbs, nothing (except an occasional erasure) annoys. For a man who has no ambition, and loves peace, a copying clerk's is the most suitable condition out of question. Even for me, my copying days were a sojourn in the Vale of Avallon (or *Avalon*, or *a vallon*, or *whatever it is*).

It has rained pretty consistently here, ever since you left – Not but what it rained a bit, even when you were here. The only little blink of sunshine I have had, was during my two months on the continent this summer. I left Edinburgh, while it rained; and when I returned, it was raining.

Sir Walter Simpson and I left together and stayed a good while in Frankfurt; he was then telegraphed home to see his brother who was thought to be dying; and I went on to Leipzig and Dresden, then back to Baden and home with my father and mother thro' France.

And now, dear Miss Crosby, how have you been getting on yourself. You must have had a rare feast of art, all over Italy. You must have enjoyed living in a climate where you can sometimes see the sun, and where people are not all so very similar to English people, as English people are to one another. I daresay you have learned a great deal in many ways. Have you yet seen *Middlemarch*?[5] You would not be quite so unsophisticated a visitor to Rome as Miss Brooke?

I have been the eager missionary of 'Fröhlicher Landmann',[6] and have (in advertisement words) 'introduced it to many a family circle'; so that I have heard *that* often, since you left; but the *Gavotte en Ré*, only once. You see your pieces are still remembered.

I have been rather seedy and kept in the house for some time back but I hope to get away for a week to the country during these Christmas

---

[2] Mary Warden married James Alexander Greig of Terreglestown, Dumfries on 13 February 1872.
[3] Psalms 45:1. From 9 May to 5 July 1872, RLS was employed as a copyist by the Edinburgh law firm of Messrs Skene Edwards and Bilton, W.S.
[4] Matthew 12:44.
[5] George Eliot's novel was published in eight parts from December 1871 to December 1872.
[6] RLS wrote some verses headed 'Schumann's "Fröhlicher Landmann"'. They were posthumously published in part by BBS and reprinted in *Tusitala Poems II*, CLVIII – 'Come, here is adieu to the city'.

holidays; although as it never ceases raining here and generally blows very hard, it will not be an Arcadian affair, I fear. Believe me, my dear Miss Crosby, Ever yours very truly   R.L. Stevenson

118   *To his Mother*

MS Yale.

Xmas Day 1872   *B[ridge] of A[llan]*[1]

My dear Mother, I have had all things considered and thanks principally to *Philip*,[2] a very passable Christmas day. I find on enquiry that I must have missed last night's post – *a fortiori*, because I have missed tonight's. Town living breeds one into a very unlimited confidence in postal arrangements.

Bob left this morning and I sat in the porch for some time, then went upstairs and read *Phillip* till lunch time (you see I adhere to my own views as to how *Philip* should be spelt). At lunch, I went down to the coffee room, where there was a man in a highly seasonable condition, who *would* drink my sherry at any price, or no price, whether I would or not. He offered me with drunken conviviality and generosity a fresh pint for the two glasses or so that I had remaining. I said, I did not wish to explain matters again to him, but the sherry was mine. 'I say, Bob,' says he, turning to his companion, who had evidently done less reason to the holy festival, 'we must drink it – eh? – after interference, eh?' A course of reasoning that reminded me of Falstaff's 'reason under compulsion'.[3] His companion fortunately interfered at this stage and spared me the ridiculous issue that might have been.

The afternoon I spent over *Philip*. I had a first rate dinner and have just come up stairs after smoking and talking in the Billiard room. Many happy returns of the season to you all.

I saw that Mr E.B. Lockyer's charge had turned out blank cartridge.[4]

A cup of coffee is being brought me; which I mean to enjoy over the same Philipian pleasures.

Today, there has been much singing, whistling and snapping of castanets about the high street; and there is a ceaseless fresh sound of conversation in front of the hotel that keeps you in mind of your fellow creatures. The sounds are all individualised, not melted into a hum as they are in a town; and the tall trees above the low, opposite houses, are too tall for the window

---

[1] RLS went to Bridge of Allan with Bob on 24 December.

[2] Thackeray's novel *The Adventures of Philip* (1862).

[3] *I Henry IV*, II. ii.4.

[4] Edmund B. Lockyer (see Letter 60, n. 6) was sued for arrears of rent on a house at Thurso which he had taken for a Mrs Trotter. It was reported on 24 December that he had won his case by pleading that the house was uninhabitable. The Commissioner of Police gave evidence that 'the house was quite in a habitable condition for a tradesman, but not for a gentleman.'

and seem to go right up into the clouds; so I am at liberty to think myself
in California or any other *Pays de Cocagne* I like. It was very nice in the
forenoon to see people making their markets, old women and young,
smartly-dressed and meanly, and think of a whole lot of Christmas dinners
all about Bridge of Allan that these were catering for, getting in the last
raisins and suet for. I doubt tho' if any of them had so comfortable a dinner
as I.

It is amusing to see the unanimity with which everyone explains my stay
here as having reference to some unknown 'young lady' in 'one of the
villas'. Evidently Christmas courtship on the part of Glasgow clerks is here
largely practised. Ever your affectionate son   R.L. Stevenson

An atrocious pen.

119   To his Mother

MS Yale.

Friday 27 December 1872   *B. of Allan*

My dear Mother, Today, it has rained without intermission and shows no
symptom of stopping even now. The room is comfortable, however; and so
are we. Bob is painting a bit of wet road at the corner of the bridge, with
our window frame and the golden bird on the top of the hotel-door-lamp:
hitherto this performance has not offered much promise; but I suppose
something will soon issue from the wet mist: at present the canvas looks like
a mirror that somebody has been breathing on.

Right opposite to us, are the only other inhabitants of B. of A.
(nearly) – two girls in blue, who sit and sew all day long with a red table
cloth and a basket between them in the recess of a bow window. The
younger has her hair cut quite short, and looks like a very eccentric school
boy on the masquerade. They are in the house of 'P. Jaffray & Co,
Plumbers, Brass Founders, Gasfitters & Bell-hangers'; so they may be
P. Jaffray's daughters; or Co's, if you come to that. There is a cat also in
P. Jaffray's house, which I can see through the open door, exhibiting the
most extraordinary stealthiness about nothing, in the passage: I suppose it
is keeping its hand in; but it is just what I used to do at home, when I
was a child and went about the house more stealthily than words could
express.

In the evening, we have a charmingly light-hearted, if somewhat vulgar,
circle in the billiard room. I am getting delightfully into the spirit of it; and
jokes, which [were] somewhat slender at first, have now, at the seventh and
eighth repetition, gathered a good deal of humour about them. There is the

doctor. There is Mr Anderson,[1] with his slavish reproduction of all Mr John
Brand's witticisms. There is Mr John Brand, the funny man – licensed, none
others are genuine – himself, with his old billiard table jests – aye 'that's
rather *thin* this time, Jim,' when there's a total miss, or 'I've seen a better
stroke than that played with the handle of an old wife's um*ber*ella' – jests,
old, so very, very old, and here greeted with peals of laughter, and repeated
and going current as genuine original coin with John Brand's superscription
on them. O happy countrymen! *O fortunati nimium!*[2] Will nothing ever pall
upon them? Then there is Mr Brand's lantern and his Highland cloak; and
the tale of how he, John Brand, right royally attired in the garb of old Gaul,[3]
presented a nosegay of roses to the Queen of the Netherlands. And then
there are musty traditions of former memorable scores, and games, and
players; and sad, feeble gossip about the freemasons; and anything *fâde* and
stale that can be thought upon: all of which is received with a zest, 'never
ending, still beginning.'[4]

You see, we move in the best society o' nights. . . .[5] with Mr Pearson,
the real, genuine English traveller, fat, conservative, good-humoured, stupid, addicted to the nobility and to sports?—(A visitor in waterproof cloak
has just arrived for the Miss Jaffray's.) —

We were out for a drive this afternoon and were much edified.

Adieu, chère mère et croyez moi . . . [signature cut away]

120   To his Mother

MS Yale.

Monday [30 December 1872]   B. *of A.*

My dear Mother, On Saturday, Bob had to go into town for an hour
or two; but he had no time to go and give you our news; which indeed is
non-existent.

Sunday is not very different from other days in the B. of A. Except that
there was a little, but not very obtrusive jangling of bells, that the whole
Jaffray family came and talked in the window including a patriarchal Jaffray
with a white beard, and that John Brand was detected by Bob going
kirkward in a complete suit of glossy evening clo' surmounted by a tile hat

[1] Alexander Anderson was the proprietor of the hotel.
[2] '*O fortunatos nimium, sua si bona norint,/Agricolas*'. (Ah blest beyond all bliss the husbandmen did
they but know their happiness.) Virgil, *Georgics*, ii.458.
[3] I.e. in a kilt. 'The Garb of Old Gaul' is the name of a Scottish march with words by Sir Henry
Erskine. The Queen of the Netherlands paid a brief private visit to Keir House (the home of Sir
William Stirling Maxwell) near Bridge of Allan in November 1872.
[4] Dryden, 'Alexander's Feast', l.101.
[5] The signature has been cut away, affecting two lines (about ten words).

in company with offspring in miniature dress clo' with snout-caps – except for all this there was nothing remarkable but the weather. It certainly was a lovely day; and so we had a drive in an open carriage. Stirling was all in a lather of smoke and sunshine; and when we got away down by Logie and under that great wall of Ochils[1] – well, it was worth the carriage hire, that's all I can say. I certainly think Blair Logie, lying up in that rocky gorge, with an old orchard down in front of it, and two gigantic stone-pines standing up from among the apple trees, with bent red columns, is about as pretty a place as you will see. I haven't the heart to go back over that last sentence: I seemed just buried under adjectives when I was writing it.

Hodgson certainly seems to have disliked something powerfully. What could have disagreed so prodigiously with his critical stomach. As for a spirit of banter, I did not know I possessed the commodity. I know I hate being bantered myself, and generally fail when I try to make a return in kind; and now here is an apparently sane Economist talking as if I was one of the most bantery cusses in existence – a regular economical John Brand. He evidently doesn't like 'from grave to gay, from lively to severe'[2] work, at all. I do not think, however, that the kid gloves are the difficulty. I suspect my 'mouse-traps' were where he got his fingers into. But why such wrath? If he had been a mouse, he might have stood excused; but perhaps his father or grandfather, were in the mouse-trap-manufactory-line; and that, you see, would make the allusion almost as unpalatable. I am glad to see however that the small pieces of 'graver and more sedate' cheese, have been savoury enough to catch me nine marks: it is always better than eight.

Philip is a most delightful book. The story is not properly speaking told at all; you are only given occasional *aperçus*. Thackeray is a sort of photographer: he takes a brief daguerrotype from one point of view; and then, shouldering his camera, entertains you, as he marches to another, with the most charming and irrelevant of gossip. And yet somehow the characters seem to form themselves and become distinct in spite of the writer: Philip you get to know probably better than you know your dearest friend. And O! the gossip! it is better than twenty stories.

You may be interested to hear that the Miss Jaffrays are reading: having only eyes and not a 'pair of patent double magnifying microscopes'[3] (or

---

[1] A range of hills extending from the vicinity of the Bridge of Allan north-east in the direction of Perth.

[2] Pope, *Essay on Man*, Epistle IV.380.

[3] '"Yes, I have a pair of eyes," replied Sam, "and that's just it. If they wos a pair o' patent double million magnifyin' gas microscopes of hextra power, p'raps I might be able to see through a flight o' stairs and a deal door; but bein' only eyes, you see, my wision's limited."' *Pickwick Papers*, ch. 34.

whatever it was that dear Sam Weller said) I cannot tell you what they are reading. Perhaps *Queechy* or perhaps *The Mother's Something-or-other* by Grace Aguilar.[4]

Bob is out taking a walk; so I am on for prattling about anything or nothing just now.

I suppose there are not in Christendom two persons of a more nondescript appearance, than yours sincerely Robinson and his present Man Friday. I in a serge coat, jersey, straw-hat, and (if the pavement be quite dry) slippers, may be seen smoking unashamed in front of the hotel; but the desperate respectability of Bob's hat and coat – the one green with age, the other simply ragged – is, I flatter myself, much more mean and pitiable. I was so curious to know which looked worse, and whether it was possible to identify either as belonging to any definite class of society, that I hobbled down to the booth of one 'Andw Manson, photographer', to get this shady couple photographed. Andw Manson proved to be a very gloomy and depressed photographer indeed: he received us with a sort of heart-broken contempt, refused sadly to have anything to do with us, took no notice of our salutations when we left, and I suppose wrapped himself up again in his secret griefs, the moment he found himself alone. Andw Manson seems about as sorrowful a individual as can be found. I should not like to board and lodge with Andw.

How nice and fresh this frosty day is! The air here is quite still and clear and quite exhilarating to breathe. That's a very hard word to spell – a very hard word indeed: you can alter my spelling of it to suit your own taste. Adieu. Ever your affectionate son   R.L. Stevenson

P.S. Andw Manson is a very gloomy man.

I find I can't stop about Andw. I expect him to haunt my slumbers, coming forward and asking me, with outstretched, beseeching arms 'Am I not a man and a photographer?'[5]; which I suppose he is, and a *Manson* too, if you come to that. I thought at first that he must have a leash of bloody murders on his mind; but there were some enlarged, coloured portraits in his shanty that explain the matter in a more probable way. If these – these – *pictures*, were Andw Manson's own handiwork, then I wonder no longer at his hunted, timorous eye and gloomy manner. Poor Andw! surrounded by these memorials of shattered hopes and with the fear of a just vengeance

---

[4] *Queechy* (1852), one of the sentimental religious novels by the American author Susan Warner (1819–85), who wrote under the pseudonym Elizabeth Wetherell. *The Mother's Recompense* (1850) is a novel of the same type by the Anglo-Jewish writer Grace Aguilar (1816–47).

[5] A reminiscence of the legend 'Am I not a man and a brother' on a medallion issued by Josiah Wedgwood depicting a kneeling Negro slave in chains with both hands lifted up to heaven. This was adopted as a seal by the Anti-Slavery Society and widely used in propaganda for emancipation.

on the part of his victims, ever grislily haunting his imagination Poor Andw! He said he wouldn't photograph us because the day was too dark. I was just as glad to escape.   R.L.S.

How is Mary getting on? – you say nothing about her.[6]

121   To Charles Baxter

MS Yale. Published in *Baxter Letters*, 21–3.

16 January 1873   *Imperial Hotel, Great Malvern*[1]

My dear Baxter, Without, it rains – within, muddle o' the brains. The damp weather has played old billy with such gray matter or convolutions (or whatever it is) as I possess, and the result is incapacity to do more. I have been stewing up spiritualism and just began an article on it yesterday:[2] fresh, gay, breeze blowing, streamers flowing. And now O pitiable sight! – we have missed the tide and I and my new embarcation lie stranded together on the broad, wet flats of idiocy. No gibbering here – all things are too despondent and wet: it requires an effort but I shall throw off mine inactivity, drop down by the fore-chains and take a reach over the swampy sands – who knows but I may stumble on an oyster or two?

The fact is, I have a hidden grief and am letting concealment like a worm i' the bud, prey on my damask cheek.[3] But – chut! – not even in the privacy of this epistle can I be *base* enough to breathe – I really ought to be very glad and shall be by tomorrow or perhaps earlier; but in the meantime this blessing wears about as offensive a disguise as he could well have laid his hands upon – I should say, figuratively speaking, that he wore a white hat – and the double knocker of not being able to work coming on the back of it has played the devil with me altogether.

Charles Baxter, I am demoralised. There is no use attempting to deny it. I am unstrung, undone, mind and body. O Writer to the Signet, that thou wert here and this black hour consoling!

I shall go shortly and play billiards with the waiter, which is my one, forlorn, and dissipated amusement in this place. Said waiter is intelligent;

---

[6] Mary Greig was expecting her first baby.

[1] RLS returned from Bridge of Allan on 1 January 1873. He and his mother left Edinburgh on 9 January and arrived in Malvern the next day.

[2] RLS was Secretary for a short time of a small Spiritualist Society – the Psychological Society of Edinburgh – founded about 1872 (see J.W. Herries, *I Came, I Saw*, 1937, 286).

[3] Cf. *Twelfth Night*, II.iv.112–13.

but he has such good manners and talks so point-device, that I have to be on my ps and qs with him. He is too good society for me – is that waiter! It is such a strain to be always a gentleman and never to be allowed to say —.[4]

I had a card from Hodgson in which he said that he hungered and thirsted (Mrs H. *de même*) after my company on some specified evenings in the 'Halls of the Society of Art' – I *think* that was the expression, but as I had lost the ticket before I answered, I didn't of course enter these details. If you go you must tell me all about it.

I must say that I am damned tired of this place. My mother and I talk little except at meal times, and I write or read straight on, except when I betake me to my waiter.

But today, *O spes naufracta, O scribendum opus, O blokus pokendum!* (Please construe and parse.) *Nigri diaboli sunt in corde mea et illic saltant et ludunt veterem Henricum generaliter; quod est lugendum. 'Ne sit ancillae tibi amor pu–. Non plus, non plus – silentium est vestrum ludum, R.L. Stevenson, in meano tempore.*[5]

My brain is just like a wet sponge: soft, pulpy, and lying spread out, flat and flaccid, over my eyes.

If I could call up the devil just now, wouldn't I do it pretty quick, neither! The devil! why I'd be glad of John the Baptist. The fact is, that waiter is a strain on me. I am not framed for such damned good society. And it rains. And I can't walk – drink – work – play –; but I *can* smoke, and I'm going to.

I feel as if I could write poetry today: probably shall, before night.[6]

O Lord, old man, I'm getting tired of this whole life business. If I could find any other investment, I should take out my capital. When I think of how much country lies behind me since November, country that I had never thought to travel in at all, when I think of how deep a quagmire I have been puddling in this whole winter through – well you don't suppose the retrospect *égayant*, do you? O fie, fie upon the whole foolish, violent, and wearisome game, say I. Let me get into a corner with a brandy bottle; or down on the hearthrug, full of laudanum grog; or as easily as may be, into

---

[4] 'Lou plays billiards with the waiter who is most agreeable and gentlemanlike' (MIS, *Diary*, 11 January). RLS was later to write of him in his essay 'Gentlemen' (1888).

[5] 'O shipwrecked hope, O work to be written, O bloke to be prodded! Black devils are in my heart, and there dance and play Old Harry generally; which must be deplored. "You need not be ashamed [*pudori*] of your love for a servant lass" [Horace, *Odes*, II.iv.1.] No more, no more – silence is your game, R.L. Stevenson, in the meantime.'

[6] Cf. RLS's posthumously published verses, '*Ne Sit Ancillae Tibi Amor Pudori*', addressed to a 'graceful housemaid' at the hotel (*Collected Poems*, 332), and the verses to Charles Baxter, 'The wind is without there and howls in the trees' (*Tusitala Poems*, II, 121). A MS of the latter (Yale) is dated 'Malvern. January 1873' in pencil.

the nice, wormy grave. I give up my chair to whoever wants it – here gentlemen is the refuse of what was never a very good hand and the one or two counters still left to me – share them and Adieu! R.L.S.

Please see that I am not done brown at the Speculative. R.L.S.

122   To Bob Stevenson

MS Morgan.

January 1873 *Malvern*

My dear Bob, I send you the introductory part of Sperretooalism.[1] The second part, which will be the longest and hardest to write, will be on the explanation of all the game, by hysteria, legerdemain etc. It is wonderful how long and curious that might be made. Part III is 'the reconciliation', in Spencer's phrase, – a mean term between I and II, a minimistic retrospect on both.

I am afraid in health that I am rather bad. I have another sloughing sore, and a bad sore throat and something damnably like incipient roseola. In fact, I'm a budding Howden, I fancy. However, I expect the doctor in a minute or two; and he will likely say something definite, one way or other. Only how these medical men hedge – how they secrete themselves and bob behind their terms and phrases! You can't get at a man who fights behind a polysyllable, can you? The throat is very likely mercury poisoning; and so, like enough, with the roseola. It is wonderful how I keep my general health through it all and still continue to eat, drink, smoke and sleep like a gamecock.

You must send back Sperretualism again in a day or two, will you? I don't know if any of it is at all good. I think some of the introductory work is not so bad, however. I have had to write it all twice over already to get out the jesting with which the first copy was peppered all over, as thick as peas – or roseola, to take a simile more germane to my state. Poor, slaughtered witticisms, how I regret you!

That passage in the MSS about *cui bono*, I must take out. I don't know what made me write anything so shallow, after all the experience that man: . . . . [*MS incomplete*]

[1] Artemus Ward's spelling. The article does not survive.

123   To Charles Baxter[1]

MS Yale. Partly published in *Letters*, I, 58–9; fully in *Baxter Letters*, 23–5.

Sunday 2 February 1873   *17 Heriot Row*

My dear Baxter, The thunderbolt has fallen with a vengeance now. You know the aspect of a house in which somebody is still waiting burial – the quiet step – the hushed voices and rare conversation – the religious literature that holds a temporary monopoly – the grim, wretched faces; all is here reproduced in this family circle in honour of my (what is it?) atheism or blasphemy. On Friday night after leaving you, in the course of conversation, my father put me one or two questions as to beliefs, which I candidly answered. I really hate all lying so much now – a new-found honesty that has somehow come out of my late illness – that I could not so much as hesitate at the time; but if I had foreseen the real Hell of everything since, I think I should have lied as I have done so often before. I so far thought of my father, but I had forgotten my mother. And now! they are both ill, both silent, both as down in the mouth as if – I can find no simile. You may fancy how happy it is for me. If it were not too late, I think I could almost find it in my heart to retract; but it is too late; and again, am I to live my whole life as one falsehood? Of course, it is rougher than Hell upon my father; but can I help it? They don't see either that my game is not the lighthearted scoffer; that I am not (as they call me) a careless infidel: I believe as much as they do, only generally in the inverse ratio: I am, I think, as honest as they can be in what I hold. I have not come hastily to my views. I reserve (as I told them) many points until I acquire fuller information. I do not think I am thus justly to be called a 'horrible atheist'; and I confess I cannot exactly swallow my father's purpose of praying down continuous afflictions on my head.

Now, what is to take place? What a damned curse I am to my parents! As my father said, 'You have rendered my whole life a failure.' As my mother said, 'This is the heaviest affliction that has ever befallen me.' And, O Lord, what a pleasant thing it is to have just *damned* the happiness of (probably) the only two people who care a damn about you in the world. You see when I get incoherent, I always relapse a little into the Porter in *Macbeth*.

I should like to – blast!

---

[1] RLS and his mother returned home from Malvern on 29 January. Furnas links the letter with the discovery of the constitution of the L.J.R. (see Letter 98, n. 7). Perhaps, for the same reason, Balfour also says (I, 113) that TS discovered the constitution in February 1873. But the references in a letter to Baxter in 1891 (Letter 2364) do not fit well with this suggestion.

I think if Cambridge could be managed, it would be the best thing. A little absence is the only chance.

Imagine, Charles, my father sitting in the arm chair, gravely reading up Butler's *Analogy*[2] in order to bring the wanderer back. Don't suppose I mean this jocularly – damn you. I think it's about the most pathetic thing I ever heard of – except one; and *that* I could not tell, but I can write it. My mother (dear heart) immediately asked me to join Nicholson's[3] young men's class: O what a remedy for me! I don't know whether I feel more inclined to laugh or cry over these naivetés; but I know how sick at heart they make me.

What is my life to be, at this rate? What, you rascal? Answer – I have a pistol at your throat. If all that I hold true and most desire to spread, is to be such death and worse than death, in the eyes of my father and mother, what the *devil* am I to do? Here is a good heavy cross with a vengeance, and all rough with rusty nails that tear your fingers: only it is not I that have to carry it alone: I hold the light end, but the heavy burthen falls on these two.

Charles Baxter, if you think it likely that you will ever beget a child, follow Origen's specific;[4] it is painful, but there are worse pains in this world.

If PEOPLE ONLY WOULD admit in practice (what they are so ready to assert in theory) that a man has a right to judge for himself; and is culpable if he do not exercise that right – why, it would have been better for a number of people – better for Wycliffe and Servetus and even Whitefield,[5] nay and even me. Better on the other hand, for many a doubting Torquemada, and for my father and mother at the present date.

Don't – I don't know what I was going to say. I am an abject idiot; which all things considered is not remarkable. Ever your affectionate and horrible Atheist.   R.L. Stevenson, C.I., H.A., S.B., Etc.[6]

---

[2] Joseph Butler (1692–1752), Bishop of Durham; *The Analogy of Religion* (1736) is his famous defence of Christianity and divine revelation.

[3] Maxwell Nicholson (1818–74), minister of St Stephen's Church, Edinburgh 1867–74, where the Stevensons regularly worshipped from 1869.

[4] To avoid the temptations of the flesh Origen, the famous third century Church Father, endured castration, thus obeying the injunction in Matthew 19:12 to make oneself a eunuch 'for the kingdom of heaven's sake'. In a cynical footnote, Gibbon commented: 'As it was his general practice to allegorize Scripture, it seems unfortunate, that in this instance only, he should have adopted the literal sense.'

[5] All religious reformers.

[6] Careless Infidel, Horrible Atheist, Son of Belial(?).

124   To the Speculative Society[1]

MS Speculative.

4 February 1873   [*Edinburgh*]

I beg to request the honour of extraordinary privileges.

R.L. Stevenson

To The Office Bearers and Members
of the Speculative Society.

125   To Charles Baxter[1]

MS Speculative.

[?*25 March 1873*]   [*Edinburgh*]

Private
I think it wants being read with much deliberation.
Arrange about the chair; I am strictly on my back – have not turned on
either side, since yesterday morning. Very jolly, however.   R.L.S.

126   To Alexander Buchan[1]

Text: extract in Alwin J. Scheur Catalogue No. 2 (New York, 1926).

19 May [?1873][2]   *Swanston*

. . . I was no less surprised than pleased at your kind remembrance of me.
I hope I shall not altogether forget meteorology and your book will be only

---

[1] After three years' attendance an ordinary member may petition for the privileges of an extraordinary member. An extraordinary member retains all the rights of membership but is exempt from all the burdens including the annual subscription. RLS's petition was read for the first time on 4 February, and read again and granted on 11 February.

[1] This note is written on the back of the MS of RLS's Valedictory Address for the last meeting of the 1872–3 session of the Speculative Society on 25 March 1873. RLS, who was to have been President of the Day, was too ill to attend and Baxter read it for him. The Address was published (with introductory notes by Baxter) in *The Outlook* for 19 February 1898. Baxter found the MS at Vailima in 1895 and gave it to the Society. A copy made by MIS of an earlier draft was published with many misreadings by Katharine D. Osbourne as *The Best Thing in Edinburgh* (San Francisco, 1923).

[1] See Letter 107, n. 2.

[2] The year is an arbitrary one but it seems to fit the fact that on 19 May 1873 RLS read a paper before the Royal Society of Edinburgh 'On the Thermal Influence of Forests'. On 2 July he read a paper on 'Local Conditions Influencing Climate' at a meeting of the Scottish Meteorological

another incitement to keep me from altogether turning my back on science . . . The sight of your present is making me long still more for a little leisure . . .

127   To Charles Baxter

MS Yale. Published in *The Sphere* (22 April 1916), 96; *Baxter Letters*, 6–7.

[*June or July 1873*][1]   [*Edinburgh*]

Mon cher Baxter, After several years of feeble and ineffectual endeavour with regard to my third initial (a thing I loathe) I have been led to put myself out of the reach of such accidents in the future by taking my two first names in full. It is perhaps as well from another point of view, as I am going to land fame wholesale under the same designation; and as such will probably be the superscription on my tooomb in Westminster Abbey, as well as on the marble tablet, to be let into the front of the house of my birth – No. 8 Howard Place.[2]

I have seen nothing else to change except a numeral which you had omitted to change yourself, while working off the rest.

Your caution about being funny and clever on the proof, Dear C., was unnecessary. I call various celestial persons to witness that I would gladly be as funny as old Harry just now, if I could; and simply can't. If you want epitaphs, apply to sincerely-yours; but this is not the booth for humour. Life, my dear Charles, is real, life is earnest.[3] Death is a sort of roaring lion that produces itself between three and four in the morning and at divers other disrespectable hours. I may also observe, in the same connection, that the worm dieth-not quite free.[4] No-one is so good at not-dying as the

Society. The catalogue dates the letter 1867, but this is impossible since the Stevensons did not take up residence at Swanston Cottage until June of that year. It also identifies the book as Buchan's *Handy Book of Meteorology* (1867).

[1] I assume that the 'proof' RLS is commenting on is that of the Case Book giving the list of Office Bearers and Members of the Speculative Society, the Order of Business for the session beginning in November 1873, showing the authors of the weekly essays with the subjects for debate. This was prepared and discussed in draft in the closing weeks of the old session and printed and distributed to members by 31 July. In the Case Book for 1872–3 RLS is listed as 'R.L.B. Stevenson' but in that for 1873–4 he is shown as 'Robert Louis Stevenson'. RLS was certainly using the signature 'Robert Louis Stevenson' in 1872 and so signed the New Ledger of the Speculative Society on 18 June 1872. This led Baxter to date this letter '1872(?) (about that year, *certainly*)'. Balfour, who quotes the opening sentence (*Life*, I, 29), dates the change 'about 1873'.

[2] There is a tablet on 8 Howard Place, and until 1963 it was maintained as a museum.

[3] Longfellow, 'A Psalm of Life'.

[4] Mark 9:44.

worm. Even the devil requires a dyke-side[5] to do not–do it at for any considerable lapse of time. Yours gloomily and intellectually-feebly Flourish.[6]   R.L.S

128   To Elizabeth Crosby

MS Yale.

July 1873   *Speculative Society Hall. University Edinburgh*

My dear Miss Crosby, I was very glad to get your letter; and very sorry to read it. I cannot say I was surprised. When you were here, you were just escaping into a new world, and thought that all the dulness was owing to the restrictions you were going to throw aside; now, you have learned that the world at large is as wearisome as woman's world, and that the arts and manufactures are as unsatisfying as embroidery and making jam. So be it. I sympathise with you on the disillusion; but there is no cure for it. Any one has always the crew of the blue devils at his right hand, with MM. Werther, Obermann, René and company[1] ready to sicken him with insipid con-dolences. There is no door of escape from this ennui. I try to evade it by constant change; by science, law, literature, perfect sunshine idleness when the weather permits, science again, law again, literature again, and perhaps a little, at the end of the cycle, of what has been mendaciously called 'life'. But leap as I may from one to the other, disgust is always at my back.

It is a most hateful mood; and can only be cleaned out by a little wholesome laughter or still wholesomer sympathy. There is something too much in the notion of people in good health and not hungry, muling over life; life *is* a bad thing, and that's the end of it; but we are not the people who have to bear the worst. Things are so settled for us by an omniscient tradition, that the worst of life cannot be mentioned even in a letter; but you will believe me, at least, when I say that something I saw, a week ago, is enough to make any Werther ashamed of his sham sorrows.

I beg your pardon for preaching. I am not in the humour for much else, and your letter was sad enough to justify me perhaps. Of course, they are not satisfying; nothing is; those are the terms on which we have to make the best of a very bad bargain.

---

[5] 'Long e'er the Dee'l lie dead by the Dyke-side.' Scottish proverb.
[6] A scrawl round the initials.
[1] The melancholy and introspective heroes of Goethe's *Sorrows of Young Werther* (1774), Etienne Pivert de Senancour's *Obermann* (1804), and Chateaubriand's *René* (1802). The first page of an unpublished essay by RLS on Obermann written in 1870 is at Yale, and in 'Old Mortality' (1884) he speaks of having 'fed upon the cheerless fields of Obermann.' In his essay on Whitman RLS refers to 'this *Maladie de René* . . . the blue devils dance on all our literary wires.'

I shall be down in England, most likely, in July or August, and I should much like to see you.

The Physician has so utterly failed to cure himself that I have not the heart to go on. I must wait for a better humour before I finish, and not come to visit you metaphorically speaking, in a hearse. –

[2]Do you know I find it very difficult to write to you. It is so long since we have met, and now I am not the same person, and no more, I am sure, are you. I may be committing gaucheries at every word – you know what I mean? Correspondence is impossible by fits and starts; you cannot write to a person whom you have neither seen nor written to, for a year; and so I am afraid I simply cannot write to you.

I can only say that I am in good health, that I rise at half past six in the morning and walk into town alone before nine – the walk is very pleasant often – that I go to classes, or oftener stay away from them and sit smoking in the Public Princes Street Gardens, where one sees a great deal of easy life in shirt-sleeves, shop girls and shopmen during their interval, tract distributors, vague wandering old men with all the Ancient Mariner's desire to tell their story and no story after all to tell. I must begin a new sentence for breath's sake; though I don't think the last is finished. Then I am driven out to Swanston again, eat a very good dinner, smoke very placidly in the garden, read or write, and go early to bed. A life of beautiful regularity, is it not? and kept interesting by the daily contrast of town and country. It is especially pleasant to arrive in the outskirts of the town at that hour, before the day's dust has risen. I meet pleasant little circumstances, tramps, troops of German musicians and the like, going out for a day's round in the country; that sort of thing always makes you feel cool about the heart I think. I like especially to think over the German band, going out into the plain, every step new to them, playing in shadowy courts behind old country houses or creating a small stir in a village street. I remember having a fancy once for a sort of Hawthorne sketch; how some spoony, sentimental yokel in the country gets a small legacy from a distant relative and, his heart being very full and his head very empty, imagines the life of an organ grinder the most pleasant on earth – imagines him going about and visiting place after place like a sunbeam – a wandering providence to children. You can finish the story for yourself; after he has spent all his money and bought his organ, you can imagine how cruel a first day one might give him in the streets of a town.

I am very sorry, Miss Crosby, that I can do nothing but maunder today; and even that, so sicklily. I hope this letter will not find you in too rational a state, or in extra good spirits, as in either case, it will go hard with it.

Bob is well and doing – well, a little. I think he has been too long here,

---

[2] The beginning of a new page in different ink; the letter was apparently continued after an interval.

there is nothing here to spur him on the side of art; I am only a colossal distraction. He will go to Antwerp, I hope, this spring, and thence to London. It is very good of me to say *hope*, as with him I shall lose about a fifth of my waking life; and this town of ours will be duller than ever.

My mother bids me say that – I forget what – something about not being able to answer your letter. She has not been very well; but is getting all right again.

Do you know, by the way, that I have never been right round the Queen's Drive, since the day we played truant together.

I hope you will forgive this dreary letter and give me an answer in mercy, as family worship has it. Believe me, Yours very sincerely

Robert Louis Stevenson

What formidable paper to envelope!

129   To Alison Cunningham

MS Edinburgh. Published in *Letters*, I, 37–8.

[? 1873][1]   [*Edinburgh*]

My dear Cummy, I was greatly pleased by your letter in many ways. Of course, I was glad to hear from you; you know, you and I have so many old stories between us, that even if there was nothing else, even if there was not a very sincere respect and affection, we should always be glad to pass a nod. I say 'even if there was not.' But you know right well there is. Do not suppose that I shall ever forget those long, bitter nights, when I coughed and coughed and was so unhappy, and you were so patient and loving with a poor, sick child. Indeed, Cummy, I wish I might become a man worth talking of: if it were only that you should not have thrown away your pains.

Happily, it is not the result of our acts that makes them brave and noble; but the acts themselves and the unselfish love that moved us to do them. 'Inasmuch as you have done it unto one of the least of these.'[2] My dear old nurse, and you know there is nothing a man can say nearer his heart except his mother or his wife – my dear old nurse, God will make good to you all the good that you have done, and mercifully forgive you all the evil. And next time when the spring comes round, and everything is beginning once again – if you should happen to think that you might have had a child of your own, and that it was hard you should have spent so many years taking

[1] It is impossible to date this letter with certainty. Colvin guessed 1871, but on the evidence of the handwriting I put it two years later. MIS records that Cummy left the Stevensons on 14 November 1871 'to keep her brother's house at Swanston'.

[2] Matthew 25:40.

care of some one else's prodigal: just you think this: you have been for a great deal in my life; you have made much that there is in me, just as surely as if you had conceived me; and there are sons who are more ungrateful to their own mothers than I am to you. For I am not ungrateful, my dear Cummy, and it is with a very sincere emotion that I write myself Your little boy   Louis

IV. COCKFIELD RECTORY AND NEW FRIENDS *July–October 1873*

On 26 July 1873, Stevenson paid what he was later to call a 'very fortunate visit' to Cockfield Rectory in Suffolk, the home of his cousin Maud and her husband, Professor Churchill Babington (see Letter 85). It was a turning point in his life: at a critical time he gained the friendship of Mrs Sitwell and Sidney Colvin (see p. 44). Frances Jane Sitwell, a beautiful woman of thirty-four, estranged but not yet separated from her husband, the Revd Albert Sitwell, had come to the Rectory to stay with her close friend Maud Babington. She was recovering from the death of her elder son, Frederick, in April; with her was her surviving son 'Bertie', a boy of ten. Many years later, Lady Colvin (as she became) recalled:

> That afternoon I was lying on a sofa near an open window when I saw a slim youth in a black velvet jacket and straw hat, with a knapsack on his back walking up the avenue. 'Here is your cousin,' I said to Mrs Babington; and she went out through the open french window to meet him and bring him in. For a few minutes he talked rather shyly to us about his long walk out from Bury St Edmunds in the heat; and then my little boy . . . suddenly went up to him and said, 'If you will come with me, I'll show you the moat; we fish there sometimes.' Louis rather jumped at this, and . . . [they] went out together hand in hand, and came back in a little while evidently fast friends. From that moment Louis was at his ease . . .

RLS soon captivated the entire household, and between himself and Mrs Sitwell there sprang up what Colvin described as 'an instantaneous understanding'. Later biographers, on the evidence of the letters that follow, have said more simply that during the happy five weeks at Cockfield RLS fell in love.

Mrs Sitwell wrote to her friend Sidney Colvin begging him not to delay his promised visit to the Rectory if he wanted to meet a 'fine young spirit'. Colvin, a Fellow of Trinity College Cambridge, had been elected Slade Professor of Fine Art at Cambridge earlier in the year. Five years older than RLS, he had already established a reputation as a critic. In his own reminiscences, dictated nearly twenty years later, Stevenson remembered his admiration for the *Fortnightly Review* and for the critical notices in it by Colvin:

My visit to England was to a country rectory . . . I knew what I had to expect, croquet parties, the parsons' wives, the ecclesiastical celebrations; that I should there meet with the flesh-and-blood Colvin of the *Fortnightly Review*, was a thing beyond the bound of my extremest hopes.

Yet so it fell out. Not only that, but I was brought under his notice by a lady whose generous pleasure – perhaps I might almost say, whose weakness – it was to discover youthful genius. With a little goodwill and a little friendship, genius is mighty easily supplied. Mrs Sitwell found it or supplied it in my case, and announced the discovery or the attribution to Colvin. So it came about that when I went down to Cockfield Station, I was not only in a state of great agitation myself at the notion of meeting one of my great men, but the great man was prepared to notice me with favour. These preparations go a long way in life . . . Meeting as we did, I the ready worshipper, he the ready patron, we had not got up the hill to the rectory before we had begun to make friends.

Colvin remembered vividly how he 'landed from a Great Eastern train at a little country station in Suffolk, and was met on the platform by a slender youth in a velvet coat and straw hat, who walked up with me to the house . . .'. Colvin 'was not unused to the presence and ways of genius': he had received drawing lessons as a child from Ruskin, was 'a close intimate in the circles of Rossetti and Burne-Jones', and knew 'the great mathematician' W.K. Clifford.

But this new Scottish youth, his first shyness past, beat everything I had ever known. Genius shone from him, he held and drew you by the radiance of his eye and smile no less than by the enthralling quality of his conversation. The new company in which he found himself drew him out, and jest and earnest, wisdom and folly – folly of the illuminating kind which is sometimes wiser than wisdom itself – streamed and flashed from him . . . and all the while an atmosphere of goodwill, a glow of eager benignity and affectionate laughter, would diffuse itself from the speaker, till everyone about him seemed to catch something of his own gift and inspiration.

On further acquaintance it became clear to Colvin that under the gaiety and charm 'there lay a troubled spirit, in grave risk from the perils of youth, from a constitution naturally frail and already heavily overstrained, from self-distrust and uncertainty as to his own powers and purposes, and above all from the misery of bitter, heart- and soul-rending disagreements with a father to whom he was devotedly attached.'

His new friends saw their task as 'to strengthen, encourage and steady him.' Colvin's part was 'to make him known to editors and get him a start on the path of literature, to which his own instincts and private self-training were already diffidently pointing.'[1]

130   To his Mother

MS Yale. Published (with deletions) in *Letters*, I, 65.

Tuesday 28 [actually 29] July 1873   *Cockfield Rectory,*
                                                       Sudbury, Suffolk

My dear Mother, I am too happy to be much of a correspondent. Mrs Sitwell is most delightful; so is the small boy; so is the Professor; so is the weather; and the place.

On Sunday, we had two diets, two sermons from the Professor which would have been counted in Scotland as poor, but quite orthodox. Yesterday we were away to Melford and Lavenham; both exceptionally placid, beautiful old English towns; Melford scattered all round a big green, with an Elizabethan Hall and Park, great screens of trees that seem twice as high as trees should seem, and everything else like what ought to be in a novel, and what one never expects to see in reality, made me cry out how good we were to live in Scotland, for the manyhundredth time. I cannot get over my astonishment – indeed it increases every day, at the hopeless gulph that there is between England and Scotland, and English and Scotch. Nothing is the same; and I feel as strange and outlandish here, as I do in France or Germany. Everything by the wayside, in the houses, or about the people, strikes me with an unexpected unfamiliarity; I walk among surprises, for just where you think you have them, something wrong turns up.

I got a little Law read yesterday and some German this morning, but on the whole, there are too many amusements going for much work; as for correspondence I have neither heart nor time for it today. I enclose a *pièce justificative*, which was deposited in my room yesterday.   R.L.S.

---

[1] Lady Colvin's account comes from her contribution to *ICR*, 87–8. Colvin's account is taken largely from his lecture to the Royal Institution, 10 February 1911 (as published in its *Notices of the Proceedings . . .* (1914), xx, 33–4) supplemented from the condensed and revised version in his *Memories and Notes* (1921), 105, and his introduction in *Letters*, I, 63. RLS's reminiscences are from the fragment of autobiography dictated at Vailima *c.* 1892, added to the earlier 'Memoirs of Himself' in the *Vailima* and later collected editions (MS untraced).

131   *To his Mother*

MS Yale.

★[*31 July 1873*]   [*Cockfield Rectory*]

My dear Mother, I am ashamed of my bad correspondence but there is something to be said in excuse. We are really too busy doing nothing, to do anything. I hope you are quite well. I am quite well, thank you. How was you tomorrow. Five people are talking round me and pen and ink are both cruelly against me; I require to stick to my thema with my teeth in order to write at all.

An exodus of some of the more talkative has taken place through the drawingroom window: I shall get back to work again: –

I hope you are quite well. I am quite well, thank you. James Wilson is reading poetry outside in a very lamentable voice. Yours truly is utterly demoralised. Maud sends her love. It is only four in the afternoon – I say this in case you might think it was after dinner.

Without, the rain is falling fast and thick. It is as cold as December.

Babington is as jolly as anything.

[1]I try to keep Louis in good order and now I can sympathize with the task you have.   M.B.

He is a <u>nice</u> boy.

  J.H.W.   Francis A. Sitwell

I quite agree with my son but not with the dashes under the nice.

                                                                F.J. Sitwell

I am sorry for this. The *dashes* meant *very*.   J.H. Wilson

My letter is done.   R.L. Stevenson

132   *To his Mother*

MS Buffalo.

Tuesday 5 August [*1873*]   [*Cockfield Rectory*]

My dear Mamma, I own to the enormous advantages of Scotland, just as strongly as I hold to the opposite. The people in this parish are horridly

---

[1] From this point other hands take over – Maud Babington, Bertie (Francis Albert) Sitwell, James Hamilton Wilson (Maud's brother) and Mrs Sitwell.

debased, I must say; centuries of education would scarcely bring them up to our Scotch level.[1]

Mr Colvin comes here this afternoon;[2] and James Wilson goes. I don't know yet when I am to leave.

Tomorrow, there is to be a school treat, where all parish will assemble.

Friday [8 August]

A lot of things has prevented me from writing ever so long. My finger is all blistered with cutting up bread for 110 school children; and I am somewhat sore and weary after starting them at games (a hopeless task) and making them run races for penny toys.

You will be amused to hear that I breakfast almost entirely on Porridge or Porrage or however it should be spelt.

The Professor left this morning for Ireland on business. (I am so scrappy and uninteresting; but I can't help it.) Tell my father that I am being continually sat upon for my Scotch pronunciations. – father, book, full, Colvin – Colvin – that is, Sidney Colvin, Professor of Fine Arts in Cambridge, who is staying here.

I send herewith – no I shall send this to Londonderry[3] – No – I shan't. I shall send my corrected proof along with this. I wish my father to be kind and forget and forgive, and get the *Annales de Chemie et de P.*[4] reference at the foot of the second slip. He knows where he can find it, in Clerk Maxwell's *Heat.* When that is filled up I think the proof will be ready to forward. I suppose I shall get a revise. Ever your affectionate son

R.L. Stevenson

133   To Lewis Charles Balfour[1]

MS Yale.

Saturday *[9 August 1873]   Cockfield

My dear Lewis, Please excuse my writing, as I have blistered my finger in cutting bread for the school feast, to the tune of some 250 slices, so gravely

---

[1] RLS later worked some of his impressions of the contrasts between Scotland and England received during this visit into his essay 'The Foreigner at Home': 'The dull, neglected peasant, sunk in matter, insolent, gross and servile, makes a startling contrast with our own long-legged, long-headed, thoughtful, Bible-quoting ploughman. A week or two in such a place as Suffolk leaves the Scotsman gasping.'

[2] Maud Wright (formerly Babington), quoting dates from her diary, told Balfour that Colvin in fact arrived on Wednesday 6 August. (Letter dated 20 January 1900 in NLS.)

[3] The Stevensons were in Londonderry 4–5 August.

[4] RLS was correcting the proof of 'On the Thermal Influence of Forests' (see Letter 126) published in the *Proceedings of the Royal Society of Edinburgh. Annales de Chimie et de Physique* is one of the footnote references.

[1] RLS had a number of Balfour cousins named Lewis. The identification of Lewis Charles,

that I have to write with my pen between my middle and fourth fingers. We are having great fun here; and by 'we', I must explain I mean Maud, Mrs Sitwell, myself and Sidney Colvin Professor of Fine Arts at Cambridge; the Professor being gone on a little business journey to Ireland. A curate – one Mr Taylor – has just arrived to take his duties for tomorrow and is being regaled with tea in the drawing room.

The school feast was a great success; there were 110 children present. They ate bread and butter and cake and drank tea on the lawn; and I could not help feeling rather pathetically that this great treat of theirs (to which they look forward for 364 days out of the 365) was just like our ordinary, everyday teas at Wyatt's. After the eating was done, and some singing to let their digestions go *festina lente*, we all went into the meadow and gave a ten shilling box of penny toys among them, under the pretence of giving prizes for racing. I did the infant classes first, and stupider children it would be hard to imagine – I feel as if I could make brighter specimens myself with a little care. I had them separated into three divisions of ten each; but as often as I turned my back my tens got mixed up together and had to be rearranged from the beginning. It was only by turning round each individual infant that I could get my line of starters to face the same way; and even then, many of them could never be got to understand the signal but stood and stared stupidly while the others ran away from them.

Every attempt to interest the children in games utterly collapsed; but after the toys had been distributed, the harrowing noise of shouts laughters and above all of many lustily blown whistles and tin-trumpets showed that they could enjoy themselves after their own fashion. The Professor took to playing cricket and one swipe of his caught one of my little infants in the pit of the stomach; whereupon the sufferer lifted up his voice and wept.

We are just cleared out just now, because of many visitors who arrived in a waggonette. On all similar occasions, the company escapes, at the first sound of the wheels out of the drawing room windows.

I hope you will let my father and mother see this, as I am too – busy, I was going to say, but lazy would be the better word perhaps – to write another letter today and they have been scantily supplied this week.

Writing with these fingers grows curiously wearisome so I must shut up.

Good-bye, old man, I shall write again soon. Believe me, Ever your affectionate cousin   R.L. Stevenson

---

Mackintosh Balfour's eldest son, is confirmed by the fact that he was at Burlington Lodge Academy (Wyatt's). See Letter 23, n. 3.

134   To his Mother

Text: extract quoted in Letter 354.

Wednesday 13 August 1873   [*Cockfield Rectory*]

Today, is a grand warm sunshiny day, with great clouds, and a great, soft west wind. The rustle of all the trees in Suffolk seems to blow across to one's ears over the plains. I have had a long walk alone – while Professor Colvin was here I had grand walks with him. The way was very sweet and solitary; – the clover fields smelt down the wind for half a mile away; such curious carriers and men in gigs kept passing me too; and they, and the noise of the wind, kept my eyes open as I went.

135   To Frances Sitwell

MS Yale. Facsimile, Beinecke III, facing p. 1027. Published (with deletions) in *Letters*, I, 66–7.

Monday 1 September [1873][1]   *17 Heriot Row*

I have arrived, as you see, without accident; but I never had a more wretched journey in my life. We were packed very tightly all the way and I was haunted by a face that I saw looking out of a window in London and that made me very sad. I could not settle to read anything; I bought Darwin's last book[2] in despair, for I knew I could generally read Darwin, but it was a failure. However, the book served me in good stead, for when a couple of children got in at Newcastle, I struck up a great friendship with them, on the strength of the illustrations. These two children (a girl of nine and a boy of six) had never before travelled in a railway; so that everything was a glory to them and they were never tired of watching the telegraph posts and trees and hedges go racing past us to the tail of the train; and the girl I found quite entered into the most daring personifications that I could make. A little way on, about Alnmouth, they had their first sight of the sea; and it was wonderful how loath they were to believe that what they saw was water: indeed it was very still, and grey and solid-looking under a sky to match. It was worth the fare, yet a little farther on, to see the delight of the girl when she passed into 'another country', with the black Tweed under our feet crossed by the lamps of the passenger bridge; I remembered the first time I had gone into 'another country', over the same river from the other side.

[1] RLS spent a few days in London before returning home. He stayed with Colvin at his cottage in Norwood in South London, and apparently with the Sitwells.
[2] *The Expression of the Emotions in Man and Animals* (1872).

Bob was not at the station when I arrived; but a friend of his brought me a letter and he is to be in the first thing tomorrow. I am very tired, dear, and somewhat depressed after all that has happened. Do you know, I think yesterday and the day before were the two happiest days of my life. It seems strange that I should prefer them to what has gone before; and yet after all, perhaps not. O God, I feel very hollow and strange just now. I had to go out to get supper and the streets were wonderfully cool and dark, with all sorts of curious illuminations at odd corners from the lamps; and I could not help fancying as I went along all sorts of foolish things – *chansons* – about showing all these places to you, Claire,[3] some other night; which is not to be. Dear, I would not have missed last month for eternity.

I trust you were well all today and that le chapelain[4] did not trouble you. Give all sorts of good messages to the sole-lessee (B. Sitwell) and say what is necessary, if you like, or if you think anything necessary, to the Curate of Cumberworth and the Vicar of Roost.[5] Good-bye, my dear. Ever yours

R.L.S.

It is very hard to stop talking to you tonight; for I can't do anything else. Sleep well; and be strong. I *will* try to be worthy of you and of *him*.[6]

136   To Frances Sitwell

MS NLS. Partly published in *Letters*, I, 67–9.

Saturday 6 September 1873   *17 Heriot Row*

The day of the Panorama!

I have been today a very long walk with my father, through some of the most beautiful ways hereabouts; the day was cold with an iron, windy sky and only glorified now and then with autumn sunlight. For it is fully autumn with us, with a blight already over the greens and a keen wind in the morning that makes one rather timid of one's tub when it finds its way indoors. I think he has made up his mind to say nothing to me about the affair I mentioned.[1] My mother has already informed me officially that Bob

---

[3] In the 1920s G.S. Hellman and J.A. Steuart built up an elaborate story of a love affair of great importance between RLS and an Edinburgh prostitute (a blacksmith's daughter in some versions) called 'Claire'. This reference (omitted by Colvin) helped J.C. Furnas in *Voyage to Windward* to demolish the foolish story and to show that 'Claire' was in fact an 'emotion-charged pseudonym' for Mrs Sitwell.

[4] Her husband, the Revd Albert Hurt Sitwell, Vicar of Minster was also honorary chaplain to the Archbishop of Canterbury (see Letter 294, n. 4).

[5] The titles of two moral tales by the Revd Francis Edward Paget published anonymously in 1859. The first story concerns a self-opinionated clergyman and the second, a worldly vicar.

[6] I.e. Colvin.

[1] Lewis Balfour (Noona) had died in Edinburgh on 6 August 1873. On his deathbed, he had told TS of Bob's unorthodox views on religion and his influence on RLS.

and he are not to be allowed to meet. With the strangest readiness they have transferred all blame from me and have no censure for any one but him; as they have done all through, they are going to do to the end; and, after all, things perhaps lie out most easily on that slope. For me, they are very pleasant. It is a God's mercy I was not at home or things might have really come to a climax; so you see my six weeks in the sunshine have been a fortunate season for me in even more ways than I had fancied.

I was out this evening to call on a friend and, coming back through the wet, crowded, lamp lit streets, was singing after my own fashion '*Du hast diamenten und Perlen*';[2] when I heard a poor cripple man in the gutter wailing over a pitiful Scotch air, his club foot supported on the other knee and his whole woebegone body propped sideways against a crutch. The nearest lamp threw a strong light on his worn, sordid face and the three boxes of lucifer matches that he held for sale. My own false notes stuck in my chest.[3] How well off I am! is the burthen of my songs all day long – '*Drum ist['s] so wohl mir in der Welt!*';[4] and the ugly reality of the cripple man was an intrusion on the beautiful world in which I was walking. He could no more sing than I could; and his voice was cracked and rusty and altogether perished. To think that that wreck may have walked the streets some night years ago as glad at heart as I was and promising himself a future as golden and honourable!

I have to ask you pardon for my last letters. Believe me, I shall be more calm. And understand always, that a hint from you will stop this issue of gossip and reduce my letters to what is simply necessary.

'*Aus deinen schönen Augen*', I can draw no army of songs; but I hope to draw what is much better, a very great inspiration. I come always back to this; for it is the best I have to say. I try, even as hard as I can, to make things pleasant for those at home; but things have been hitherto against me; for neither my father nor I have been quite well and so we have been both a little snappish. Nothing however at all serious.

It makes me so glad to think of my letter travelling away to you and of the hope I have to hear again sometime from you.

Sunday. 11.20 A.M.

I wonder what you are doing now; in church likely – at the *Te Deum*. Everything here is utterly silent. I can hear men's footfalls streets away; the

---

[2] Heine, *Buch der Lieder*, '*Die Heimkehr*' [The Homecoming] LXII. In it the poet tells his love that she has diamonds and pearls and beautiful eyes on which he has written many poems (the phrase RLS quotes later); she has broken his heart and he asks her what more she wants. The poem has been set to music by many German composers.

[3] Two words heavily deleted.

[4] Goethe, '*Vanitas! vanitatum vanitas*' (1806), 1.2. RLS's 'How well off I am' is a rough translation of Goethe's 'Thus I am so happy in the world'. The reference is to emotional well-being rather than material wealth.

whole life of Edinburgh has been sucked into sundry pious edifices; the gardens below my windows are steeped in a diffused sunlight, and every tree seems standing on tip-toes, strained and silent, as though to get its head above its neighbours, and *listen*. You know what I mean, don't you? How trees do seem silently to assert themselves on an occasion; until literally you cannot 'see the wood for the trees'. I have been trying to write 'Roads'[5] until I feel as if I were standing on my head; but I mean 'Roads' and shall do something to them.

I wonder very much what advice this parson will give you. My dear, I can't bear to think of your life. You must not imperil your health and – yet I don't see what is to be done. I am becoming maudlin yet again; it seems to be my favourite mood.

I wish I could make you feel the hush that is over everything, only made the more perfect by rare interruptions; and the rich, placid light, and the still, autumnal foliage. Houses, you know, stand all about our gardens; solid, steady, blocks of houses; all look empty and asleep. I just feel as if I were alone with you. I know you would just see the same things and feel satisfied, as it were with drinking, by this great quiet, just as I do.

137   *To Frances Sitwell*

MS NLS. A few excerpts published in *Letters*, I, 69–70 as continuation of Letter 136.

Monday 8 September [*1873*]   *17 Heriot Row*

I must write you a little word again before I go to bed; although my last is not yet many miles on its southward journey. Blessings on the trains that go all night, through rain and moon-glimpse, over the sleeping country, to bring people so near together. The post office man is just now sorting the letters by the light of his lamp, as the whole thundering train goes swaying round the angles of the line; and some time soon, my letter will slip through his fingers and be thrown on the right heap to get safely to its happy destination: I wish I could go with it.

I want to say so many things to you, that I find it impossible to begin. I want to tell you how any little detail of your life makes absence a mere dream; but on that head, dear, you know already all that I feel. And I want to tell you what I hope to do and of what I fear to fail in the accomplishment. And again, I want to tell you all manner of small things out of my own life, all sorts of infinitesimal joys and sorrows and disappointments and happy surprises, that I desire to share with my dearest of all friends; and yet

---

[5] This essay, planned during walks at Cockfield, was ultimately published in the *Portfolio* and was RLS's first paid contribution to a periodical.

these and many other things (do you understand me?) it seems a sort of insincerity to write about between us two, as when people talk of the weather for a long while, warily avoiding something of superlative interest to both. Let us talk of the weather, however. And, at least, dear, I hope the weather is now warmer with you: it would be a real gladness to me to think of you in warm sunshine, and I should not feel so cold myself up here, if I could believe so. The drums and fifes up in the castle are sounding the guard-call through the dark, and there is a great rattle of carriages without. I have had (I must tell you) my bed taken out of this room, so that I am alone in it with my books and two tables, and two chairs, and a coal-*skuttle* (or *scuttle*) (?) and a *débris* of broken pipes in a corner, and my old school play-box, so full of papers and books that the lid will not shut down, standing reproachfully in the midst. There is something in it, that is still a little gaunt and vacant; it needs a little populous disorder over it, to give it the feel of homeliness and perhaps a bit more furniture, just to take the edge off the sense of illimitable space, eternity and a future state and the like, that is brought home to one, even in this small attic, by the wide, empty floor. I am not alone in it however; for I have three scraps of paper and two photographs, under my hands, as I write, in the table drawer, and a whole sunny world in my heart; not only fulfilment, but promise, believe that; not only the recollection, but the good, strong, faithful hope. You would require to know, what only I can ever know, many grim and many maudlin passages out of my past life to feel how great a change has been made for me by this past summer: I wish to God I could make you feel it. It is worth having lived for, to have thrown so much glory and gladness into another's thin existence, as you have thrown into mine. Mind what I say, and let no future doubt or regret obliterate it – it is worth having lived for, by God. Let me be ever so poor and threadpaper a soul, I am going to try for the best, and I hope more in the strong inspiration of your sympathy than ever Christian hoped out of his deity. I hope you do not think that I am phrasing; if I am phrasing, it is because (as Dr Watts says) 'it is my nature to'.[1] I don't write to you; I just think and conversationally blurt out my thoughts; and in consequence I have had to destroy, as you saw in my last letter, what I had written before. *Don't* think it phrasing! I wish I could write as you do, in that strong simplicity that goes to one's heart with a thrill of conviction; but I can't, my dear, and so you must be saved by faith. Whenever I weary you by writing, please tell me; remember it is not so cruel to say so – not by an infinity of difference – as to let a poor wretch go on warming his

---

[1]
        Let dogs delight to bark and bite,
        For God hath made them so;
        Let bears and lions growl and fight,
        For 'tis their nature too –
        Isaac Watts, *Divine Songs for Children*, xvi 'Against Quarrelling'.

hands at the cold bars, telling over his beads before an empty mercy-seat, laying himself bare in a way that is only not ridiculous because it is done with the grand belief in another's sympathy. So, mind, tell me. I shall know to believe what you say and no more. I shall know if you say 'I still wish this much, and not thus much', but you mean what you say, and are not putting the less for the greater. I want our friendship, my own dearest friend, to be the faithfullest and most candid that ever has been. A shadow of pretence, it seems, would undermine all things; just a little word feigned, and the whole truth is eternally compromised. It cannot be, after all that has been – can it, my dear? After so much that was true and sincere, everything must continue to be splendidly true and sincere. So, you know now what I mean; for I always feel sure that you can read between the lines with me, and see the whole struggle of motives and considerations that has moved me to say anything. And so, you will never be afraid.

Tuesday

I feel somewhat ashamed to send the above; but if I begin destroying, I shall never find myself in a mood that I think worthy of being shown to you; so I am going to send it and shame the devil.

I am working on – slowly, but pretty steadily: I have got over a good deal of ground I think, but dear heart! it seems it will be a long time ere I can see whether there is any parallel at all to be made between Knox and Savonarola; after which (in the affirmative case) I shall have to begin to try to make it.

I am sitting here watching my opportunity to slip up to the Spec. and see if there is anything from you; I find it very difficult to get out of the house alone just now, my father sticks to me pretty closely and yet, wonderful to say, we have not had the shadow of a discussion since I came. My temper is a little better now. Your letter completed my cure – and so I hope we shall keep on good terms for a long time to come. I wish I durst hope, for always.

I wish I had been kinder to Bertie. I have an awful fear of his forgetting me lightly; it would seem somehow like a candle going out before the shrine. Besides which, I like him very much for himself. He did say some such jolly things while we were all in Chepstow Place,[2] that I felt inclined to eat him. Good little Tom Thumb! how valiantly he tilts against the Giant! Do you remember the Sunday's dinner; there was something about those two last days, of peace and perfect reliance that was wanting in anything before. And yet you did look so ill, all the time. I do hope you were not the worse of your journey; at least you will be removed from all

---

[2] The Sitwells lived at 15 Chepstow Place.

those continual aggravations that you have to endure elsewhere.[3] My poor darling, it makes me hot all over to think of your life.

I wonder if I weary you with all this drivel. Ha! There is my father gone out. I am off to the Spec.

11 A.M.

No letter today. Hope for tomorrow or the next day. These good booksellers of mine have at last got me a *Werther* without illustrations. I want you to like Charlotte; she is, in some ways, not unlike one you know. Werther himself has every feebleness and vice that could tend to make his suicide a most virtuous and commendable action; and yet I like Werther too – I don't know why except that he has written the most delightful letters in the world. Note by the way, the passage under date June 21st not far from the beginning; it finds a voice for a great deal of dumb, uneasy, pleasurable longing that we have all had, times without number. I looked that up the other day for 'Roads',[4] so I know the reference; but you will find it a garden of flowers from beginning to end. All through the passion keeps steadily rising, from the thunderstorm at the country-house – there was thunder in that story too – up to the last wild delirious interview; either Lotte was no good at all, or else Werther should have remained alive after that; either he knew his woman too well, or else he was precipitate. But an idiot like that is hopeless; and yet, he wasn't an idiot – I make reparation, and will offer eighteen pounds of best wax at his tomb. Poor devil, he was only the weakest – or, at least, a very weak-strong man; and he is delightful when he tells Lotte to have her speech printed and sent round to the

1.30

I have been cleaning out old drawers and coming across all sorts of traces of the little boy that you did not know, the sickly patient little boy who was often awake all night in this room. I found a forlorn little yellow book into which he used to copy verses of the Bible, on Sundays; the selection begins with 'Thou God seëst me', and ends with 'All men have sinned –'; all laboriously and unevenly printed out, with a six-years-old unsteadiness.[5] I found of course great *débris* of unfinished romances and poems and plays; and among other things, a theological tract of mine, while I was still in the gall of bitterness, in which are some very startling ethical propositions. I found too, in the pocket of an old purse, in company with crests and greasy

---

[3] Mrs Sitwell had gone back to Cockfield Rectory.
[4] RLS quotes this passage from *Werther* on the last page of 'Roads'.
[5] This small book inscribed 'Text Book, R.L.B.S. 1856' containing Bible texts in large printed characters was shown at the Grolier Club Exhibition of Stevenson First Editions in 1914, and pages from it reproduced in the Catalogue (1915) facing p. 16.

little pictures of all sorts, some of young sir's first cards; one of which I send you for the jest's sake. A very pitiful little joke, too, over which I feel more inclined to cry than to laugh.

It is raining now most manfully, and I shall soon have to pick my way out to the post with this; for as long as you are at the Rectory and wish my garrulage, I want you to have the same regularly.

Von[6] Herzen

Good-bye, dear   R.L.S.

138   *To Frances Sitwell*

MS NLS. Partly published in *Letters*, I, 70–72.

Tuesday 9 September 1873   [*17 Heriot Row*]
11.40 P.M.

I was sitting up here, working away at John Knox, when the door opened and Bob came in. At first I thought he was drunk; he came in with his hands over his face and sank down on a chair and began to sob. He was scarcely able to speak at first, but he found voice at last and I then found that he had come to see me, had met my father in the way and had just brought to an end an interview with him. There is now, at least, one person in the world who knows what I have had to face – damn me for facing it, as I sometimes think, in weak moments – and what a tempest of emotions my father can raise when he is really excited. It seems that this poor cousin of mine has hated Bob and me all through his life, that our words have been a sharp poison to him, and our opinions horrible, and our presence an intolerable burthen: he always met us as friends; he was too weak it seemed to show what he disliked and what shocked him, and he led us on, unconsciously I daresay, to play with him cards-down, and keep nothing secret. A little before death, he relieved his feelings to my father; Bob, he said, was a 'blight', a 'mildew'; it was matter of wonder to him 'how God should have made such a man'; I was the one depraved and hideous one who could endure Bob's presence; *und so weiter, in infinitum*. My father's interview with Bob has been long coming; and has now come. I am so tired at heart and tired in body that I can only tell you the result tonight. They shook hands; my father said that he wished him all happiness, but prayed him as the one favour that could be done him, that he should never see him between the eyes again. And so parted my father and my friend. Tomorrow I shall give more details.

[6] This word is blotted out but still legible.

Wednesday

The war began with my father accusing Bob of having ruined his house and his son. Bob answered that he didn't know where I had found out that the Christian religion was not true, but that *he* hadn't told me. And, I think from that point, the conversation went off into emotion and never touched shore again. There was not much said about me – my views according to my father, are a childish imitation of Bob, to cease the moment the *mildew* is removed; all that was said was that I had ceased to care for my father, and that my father confessed he was ceasing, or had greatly ceased, to care for me. Indeed, the object of the interview is not very easy to make out; it had no practical issue except the ludicrous one that Bob has promised never to talk to me about Religion any more. It was awfully rough on him, you know; he had no idea that there was that sort of thing in the world, although I had told him often enough – my father on his knees, and that kind of thing. O dear, dear, I just hold on to your hand very tight, and shut my eyes. I wonder why God made *me*, to be this curse to my father and mother. If it had not been for the thoughts of you, I should have been twice as cut up; somehow it all seems to simplify when I think of you; tell me again that I am not such cold poison to everybody as I am to some. What my poor cousin said of me, what dying testimony he left against me and all my works, I shall now never learn; even if my father attempts to begin, I must stop him. I am going up on another hunt for a letter from you; if I find one, and you are well and happy, the sky will be all blue once more.

3 P.M.

No letter. I hope you are well. To continue the story, I have seen Bob again, and he has had a private letter from my father, apologising for anything he may have said; but adhering to the substance of the interview. There was more in this letter (which Bob, perhaps by rather a breach of confidence, allowed me at my earnest desire to see) of his wailings over a ruined life and hopes overthrown which are intolerable to think about. Moreover I learn that my mother had hysterics privately last night, over it all. If I had not a very light heart and a great faculty of interest in what is under hand, I really think I should go mad under this wretched state of matters. Even the calm of our daily life is all glossing; there is a sort of tremor through it all and a whole world of repressed bitterness. I do not think of it, because it is one of those inevitable Fates that no thinking can mend. As Luther said 'Ich kann nicht anders – hier stehe ich – Gott helfe mir'.[1]

---

[1] 'Here stand I. I can do no other. God help me' – Martin Luther's speech before the Diet of Worms, 18 April 1521.

And yet, my dearest, I did not wish to harm anyone; and don't, and I *would* do what I could, if I could do anything.

Now, don't get bothered about this. It has been as bad before any time this last year, and then I had no one to take the bitterness to. I have just had this cry on your shoulder (so to speak) and I feel better again. Only let need be the excuse for my bothering you with yet another letter. And, at any rate as long as you are away from home I did want to write to you often; for after that I must write very seldom, must I not? Do you think once a fortnight would be too often?

I am afraid this letter is again incoherent a little; but this and yesterday have been rather bad days with me. My dear, how poor all my troubles are after all compared with yours; I am such a scaly alligator and go through things on the whole so toughly and cheerily. I hope you will not misunderstand this letter and think I am *Werthering* all over the place. I am quite happy and never think about these bothers and I am sure if you were to ask my father and mother, they would tell you that I was as unconcerned as any Heathen deity; but 'heartless levity' was always one of my complaints. And a good thing too. 'Werena my heart licht, I wad die.'[2] And now, my darling, I may say just a word about *you* before I end, may I not. I have dreamed about you the last nights often, only I never see you properly. It is worth while to dream of you though, even unhappily, because you come up before me when I waken sometimes very vividly. This is Wednesday the 10th of September; three weeks ago I was not alone in my room here. I take it kind in Nature, having a day of broad sunshine and a great west wind among the garden trees, on this time of all others; the sound of wind and leaves comes in to me through the windows, and if I shut my eyes I might fancy myself some hundred miles away under a certain tree. And that is a consolation, too; these things *have been*.

> 'Tomorrow, let it shine or rain,
> Yet cannot this the past make vain;
> Nor uncreate and render void
> That which was yesterday enjoyed'[3]

I have the proof of it at my heart, my darling; it never felt so light and so happily stirred in the old days. Just now when the whole world looks to me as if it were lit with gas, and life a sort of metropolitan railway, it is a great thing to have clear memory of sunny places and of love. How my mind rings the changes upon sun and sunny! Farewell, my dearest friend

R.L.S.

---

[2] The best-known song by Lady Grisell Baillie (1665–1746).

[3] Sir Richard Fanshawe's translation of Horace, *Odes*, III.xxix.43f. in his *Selected Parts of Horace*, 1652. RLS also copied these four lines into his edition of Horace edited by Joseph Currie (Princeton – see also Anderson, I, 215).

commonly called the 'viper'; friend of the 'mildew' and the 'demon'. O dear I don't feel like a viper to you, do I?

139   To Frances Sitwell

MS NLS. Partly published in *Letters*, I, 72–4.

Friday 12 September 1873   *17 Heriot Row*

I must write you a line or two, my dear friend, although I shall not send it away until I hear from you at least; . . . [1] I was over last night contrary to my own wish, in Leven, Fife; and this morning I had a conversation, of which, I think, some account might interest you. I was up with a cousin who was fishing in a mill-lade; and a shower of rain drove me for shelter into a tumble-down steading attached to the mill. There, I found a labourer cleaning a byre; with whom I fell into talk. The man was to all appearance as heavy, as *hébété*, as any English clod-hopper; but I knew I was in Scotland and launched out forthright into Education and Politics and the aims of one's life. I told him how I had found the peasantry in Suffolk and added that their state had made me feel quite pained and down-hearted. 'It but to do that,' he said, 'to onybody that thinks at a' (all)'. Then again, he said that he could not conceive how anything could daunt or cast down a man who had an aim in life. 'They that have had a guid schoolin' and do nae mair, whatever they do, they have done; but him that has aye something ayont (before) need never be weary.' I have had to mutilate the dialect much, so that it might be comprehensible to you; but I think the sentiment will keep, even through a change of words, something of the heartsome *ring* of encouragement that it had for me. And that from a man cleaning a byre. You see what John Knox and his schools have done.

Tonight my father was talking of how he feared to do what he knew he ought; and I did I think some good to our deplorable condition in this home of ours by what I said. I spoke too to my mother afterwards; telling her how I felt with my father and hoped all good from anything he could do; and only hoped in that, that every man should do what he thought best, as best he could. But I had to stop, as she was growing hysterical. I hope I have done something tonight; although the hitch ever remains; what shall it profit a man if he be as good, and wish as well, and work as strenuously, as he please, and withal lose his own soul?[2]

[1] Two or three words scored out.
[2] An echo of Mark 8:36.

Saturday

This has been a charming day for me from morning to now. (5 P.M.) First I found your letter and went down and read it on a seat in those Public Gardens of which you have heard already. I was very happy and went home and did a good morning's work. After lunch, my father and I went down to the coast and walked a little way along the shore between Granton and Cramond. This has always been with me a very favourite walk. The firth closes gradually together before you, the coast runs in a series of the most beautifully moulded bays, hill after hill, wooded and softly out-lined, trends away in front till the two shores join together. When the tide is out, there are great, gleaming flats of wet sand, over which the gulls go flying and crying; and every cape runs down into them with its little spit of wall and trees. We lay together a long time on the beach; the sea just babbled among the stones; and at one time we heard the hollow, sturdy beat of the paddles of an unseen steamer, somewhere round the cape. I am glad to say that the peace of day and scenery was not marred by unpleasantness between us two; indeed I do think things are going a little better with us; my father I believe has some of the satisfaction consequent upon a good *auto-da-fé* now he has finally quarrelled with Bob and banished him. And although it seems mean to profit by what my own heart feels anxious to resent, I am only too glad of any peace between us although every month of it were to cost me a finger. You will understand the wearying, despairing, sick heart that grows up within one, when things go on as sometimes they do; and how the whole of life seems blighted and hopeless and twilight; although that is no reason why I should make you bear my yoke.

I am glad to hear that you think the V.[3] will be cautious. I should feel little fear if I could think you were to be able to have your own soul in quietness for an occasional holiday. I like to think of you in Hooker's garden,[4] only I wish it had not been so cold.

I am unhappily off my style and can do nothing well; indeed I fear I have marred 'Roads' finally, by patching at it when I was out of the humour. Only, I am beginning to see something great about John Knox and Queen Mary; I like them both so much, that I feel as if I could write the history fairly. Knox is charming in this respect, that his character is always so consistent and strong; like a figure in ink-outline in a pencil sketch. His utterances are pregnant with individuality.

[3] The Vicar, i.e. Albert Sitwell.
[4] Sir Joseph Dalton Hooker (1817–1911), the distinguished botanist who was Director of Kew Gardens 1865–85. RLS visited Kew Gardens with Mrs Sitwell during his visit to London (see Letter 145).

Sunday

It has rained and blown chilly out of the east all day. This was my first visit to church since the last Sunday at Cockfield. I was alone and read the minor prophets and thought of the past all the time; a sentimental Calvinist preached—a very odd animal, as you may fancy – and to him I did not attend very closely. All afternoon I worked until half past four when I went out, under an umbrella, and cruised about the empty, wet, glimmering streets until near dinner time.

I have finished 'Roads' today and send it off to you to see. The Lord knows whether it is worth anything; some of it pleases me a good deal; but I fear it is quite unfit for any possible magazine. However I wish you to see it, as you know the humour in which it was conceived, walking alone and very happily about the Suffolk highways and byeways on several splendid sunny afternoons. If you think it good, I shall be pleased; but I fear I must postpone all hope of honest earnings until I have made something of J.K. and Savonarola.

Tomorrow I hope to find two porridge bickers for Colvin,[5] whose interests I have shamefully neglected. Believe me, Ever your faithful friend
Robert Louis Stevenson

Monday

I have torn this open at the cost of a postage stamp, to add that I have received a very kind letter from Colvin. He tells me not to grind at Savonarola, but to write what I am prepared to write. Advice I am only too glad to receive.

I have looked over 'Roads' again and I am aghast at its feebleness. It is the trial of a very 'prentice hand'[6] indeed. Shall I ever learn to do anything *well*? However it shall go to you, for the reasons given above.

I hope you have already forgiven me for my injudicious world of correspondence last week; but I was really rather wretched. Things are better now.   L.

I am so glad I kept this letter open that I may thank you for yours. It is worth while having been in trouble to be so comforted. I cannot thank you enough, my dearest friend; and I know that you know all I feel at any rate. I shall not post to you again till this day week. I have forgotten, dear,

---

[5] 'Stevenson, while a guest at my Norwood Cottage, had been scandalised at seeing me eat oatmeal porridge for breakfast out of a common soup-plate, and declared that it must absolutely be eaten, *more Scotico*, with a horn spoon out of a wooden bowl or "bicker". And he undertook after his return to Edinburgh to find and send me a couple of such bickers, with their appropriate horn spoons' (Colvin, *ICR*, 92).

[6] Burns, 'Green Grow the Rashes'.

by the way, to fill in the name of Michael Angelo's friend out of Vasari; but you can supply the blank at fancy.[7] You are not often out of my thoughts.

Louis

140 *To Frances Sitwell*

MS NLS. Excerpts published in *Letters*, I, 74–7.

Monday 15 September 1873 *Edinburgh*

You will have seen before you get this that I had so far forestalled your advice in trying to tell my mother that I *did* feel. Yet it is neither easy nor pleasant so to do. There are some sentiments that it is an insult to have to explain. I have a very elastic temper – a good thing to have in this damned world – and it is, I suppose, natural that they should think I care nothing for all they suffer; and yet God knows it is not so. It is so different, dear, dealing with a person who, you know, will be quick to sympathize with what you say and what you have left unsaid, that perhaps you will scarcely understand – indeed I have a difficulty in believing myself – how shy and reserved I have grown with them. I am by nature, and continue to be with others, only a little too open and free; but somehow I cannot speak where I have a fear of being doubted or misunderstood. You see, they think the offence originally wilful; and therefore no protestation of regret can be of the value of so much breath in their eyes. They think me as happy as ever I was – they can see no difference in me. I am still heartlessly light; and so I must let the matter rest. It can never out. I can see no way to an understanding. I see no daylight in front of us, so far as that goes – only continual plodding on, as it were in rain and mire, and the alternative of successful dissimulation and terrible discoveries followed by bitter hopeless despair on the one side and bitter, hopeless sorrow on the other. No, my dear friend, I am terribly calm and critical just at present and I see nothing more than that; a grim alternative, a very unlovely prospect at the best. I feel so much as if I were talking to you just now, in the stiff, didactic vein that I sometimes do fall into, that all these hundred miles of space are as if they were not. What I heard from you, and from Colvin also, this morning has given me a better heart for this unbeautiful struggle – a better heart than, at other times, I should have thought it possible to have. I do lean very much upon your sympathy and you must remember ever that you owe your life to many of us – it is less yours now, than it was even last July – is it not? You have

---

[7] Probably Vittoria Colonna (1492?–1547) to whom Michelangelo wrote some of his finest sonnets. This reference does not appear in the published article.

someone else terribly dependent on you. You have lifted me so much out
of the miry clay and put so beautiful a new song in my mouth,[1] that I fear
I should be a poor waif without some of my deity's continued favour. It is
a thing to thank God for, that there should be someone like you, carrying
so bright a lamp of comfort up and down our dim life, bringing priceless
sympathy to one and to another, giving it, widely and fearlessly, like the
good sun.

I must be very strong to have all this vexation and still to be well. I was
weighed the other day; and the gross weight of my large person was eight
stone six! Does it not seem surprising that I can keep the lamp alight,
through all this gusty weather, in so frail a lantern? And yet it burns cheerily.

Tuesday [16 September]

I made up my mind last night to have a large incremation of letters; but
I failed when it came to the point. Better luck next time! My mother is
leaving for the country this morning and my father and I will be alone for
the best part of the week in this house. Then on Friday, I go south to
Dumfries till Monday. I must write small or I shall have a tremendous
budget by then!

7.20 P.M.

I must tell you a thing I saw today. I was going down to Portobello in
the train, when there came into the next compartment (third class) an
artizan, strongly marked with smallpox and with sunken, heavy eyes – a
face, hard and unkind and without anything lovely. There was a woman on
the platform seeing him off. At first sight, with her one eye blind and the
whole cast of her features strongly plebeian and even vicious, she seemed as
unpleasant as the man; but there was something beautifully soft, a sort of
light of tenderness, as on some Dutch Madonna, that came over her face
when she looked at the man. They talked for a while together through the
window, the man seemed to have been asking money. 'Ye ken the last
time', she said, 'I gave ye two shillin's for your ludgin', and ye said' – it died
off into whisper. Plainly Falstaff and Dame Quickly over again. The man
laughed unpleasantly, even cruelly, and said something; and the woman
turned her back on the carriage and stood a long while so, and, do what I
might, I could catch no glimpse of her expression, although I thought I saw
the heave of a sob in her shoulders. At last, after the train was already in
motion, she turned round and put two shillings into his hand. I saw her
stand and look after us with a perfect heaven of love on her face – this poor
one-eyed Madonna – until the train was out of sight; but the man, sordidly

[1] Psalm 40:2–3.

happy with his gains, did not put himself to the inconvenience of one glance to thank her for her ill-deserved kindness.

O my dear friend, I could not bear to see you used thus. Do you know I wish you had known Leonardo; I think he was the one man full enough, to be worthy of you. But you live now, and poor shadows on a wall are the only men going. By God, I wish I were Leonardo.

I am beastly seedy tonight. Do you know we have found all our drains have been wrong for years; I do hope yours at Chepstow Place are all right. I wish you would ask about them. I have a terrible dread of these secret, subtle poisonings – no Medici could instil death so stealthily and gradually as an indifferent plumber.

Wednesday [17 September]

I went and wrote to Colvin last night when I should have written to you or nobody; and the result is that I have demeaned myself most stagily through two sheets of notepaper. I put in an apology and sent it off at once; for I could not rewrite it. But I feel very much ashamed of myself and doubtful even yet about the wisdom of sending it off. It was really pathetic to hear my father praying pointedly for me today at family worship, and to think that the poor man's supplications were addressed to nothing better able to hear and answer than the chandelier. I could have bit my tongue out, and you know I am good at biting.

I hope Colvin won't contemn me; but I find I cannot vend an expurgated edition of myself and I seem even weaker on paper than I am in speech. Everything will out.

I have been up at the Spec. and there got your note, dear, and looked out a reference I wanted. The whole town is drowned in white, wet vapour off the sea. Everything drips and soaks. The very statues seem wet to the skin. I cannot pretend to be very cheerful; I did not see one contented face in the streets, and the poor did look so helplessly chill and dripping; without a stitch to change or so much as a fire to dry themselves at, or perhaps money to buy a meal or perhaps even a bed. My heart shivers for them. And to look back out of all this on Cockfield! If I were as unscrupulous as Goethe, I believe I could write a book about some events in my life that would rather tickle the long ears. Do you know the more I think of the reading of one of Browning's poems one Sunday afternoon, the more I find it hard to fancy there was not a deal of meaning in it. There are some little turns of demeanour that I don't quite like to recall.

O my dear friend, you know all I have at my lips and so there is no need to say it. *Ich denke immer dein.* I feel as weak as water at present; my heart is melted.

But if I be dear to some else. – Don't blame this little break down; it is a great victory on the negative side; for I want to say worlds more.

10 P.M.   *Queen's Hotel. Bridge of Allan*

My father got alarmed about the open drains and so we are here for the night in a place that I do most dearly affect. Every place round me is saturated with recollections from the time that I was in short clothes up to the miserable days of last winter. I have just taken out my writing materials to say good night to you. I put in my movements, rather by head and shoulders, into my dryasdust note to Bertie, for *your* information. The book I have ordered for him is *Cortes and Pizarro*[2]; I hope it will arrive on the right day. *Schlafen Sie wohl, meine schöne Freundin.*

Thursday   *Helensburgh*

I write under all manner of contrarious circumstances – on my knee, with a very dim light, in a cold room. The wind is wailing without most pitiably; it has been raining violently all day, with only few and insecure intervals of fairness. I have to tell you that before I left home, I made inquisition and burnt all your letters but the first and the last; and these two I carry with me, my beautiful friend, as a sort of pledge of your existence. The time will come when I shall be strong enough to burn one; but there are parts of the other, that point to no one, which I shall cut out and keep forever. I do live very much on these little stray planks of the past, the drift-wood of the old boat. Tomorrow I go south to Dumfries, to stay with a married cousin,[3] and sometime on Monday I shall be back in Edinburgh; so that on Tuesday morning I shall once more have the pleasure of going to the Speculative to seek for a letter from you. Of course now you are back in town among all your friends, I do not expect to hear much from you, or often. But hope is pleasant, if it does not make the heart sick, and that is not possible between you and me. I trust you, my dear friend, to the outside of faith; I don't ask any miracles from my deity; I believe. I cannot deny that I get to long very greatly to see you once again; but only when I am forced to be idle as I am just now; when I am full of work, I am happy and quite content; it is enough, then, to know you where you are and what you are – in the world and yourself.

I sent off 'Roads' to you in a great hurry, because I saw I should have to write it over again if I kept it any longer by me; yet I regret it; I wish I had perfected it before I sent it to you: I am half inclined to think there are

[2] A book for children by William Dalton (1862, reprinted 1872) retelling the stories of the conquest of Mexico and Peru.
[3] Mary Greig.

phrases in it that deserve better company than I am fit to give them – certainly, than I have given them. It would be strange if a man drunken with a beautiful sentiment should not read a thought nearer to Nature's heart, than the obdurate and strong-hearted tourist. I hope you can read my dissolute scribble; it is worse than usual tonight owing to difficulties of position. Good night, dear.

Friday [19 September]   *Terreglestown Dumfries*

What a budget this is growing! You can see anyway what a difference this makes upon my life, that I should have some one to come to every day and speak out, with no fear of misunderstanding or uncertainty as to what is wished; some one to whom I can show myself, in all my humours and not think always that I have committed an indiscretion.

All my thirst for a little warmth, a little sun, a little corner of blue sky, avails nothing. Without, the rain falls with a long drawn *swish*, and the night is as dark as a vault. There is no wind indeed, and that is a blessed change after the unruly, bedlamite gusts that have been charging against one round street corners and utterly abolishing and destroying all that is peaceful in life. Nothing sours my temper like these coarse termagant winds. I hate practical joking; and your vulgarest practical joker is your flaw of wind.

I have tried to write some verses; but I find I have nothing to say that has not been already perfectly said and perfectly sung in *Adelaide*.[4] I have so perfect an idea out of that song! The great Alps, a wonder in the starlight – the river, strong from the hills, and turbulent, and loudly audible at night the country, a scented '*Frühlings-garten*' of orchards and deep wood where the nightingales harbour – a sort of German flavour over all – and this love-drunken man, wandering on by sleeping village and silent town, pours out of his full heart '*Einst, O Wunder, einst*' etc. I wonder if I am wrong about this being the most beautiful and perfect thing in the world – the only marriage of really accordant words and music – both drunk with the same poignant, unutterable sentiment.

I am glad to tell you that I think I am a little better in body and quite recovered in mind. The combination of earthy, sensual and Devilish weather, with a fair spice of uneasiness at home has a good deal put me out.

Today in Glasgow, my father went off on some business and my mother and I wandered about for two hours. We had lunch together and were very merry over what the people at the Restaurant would think of us – mother and son they could not suppose us to be; and I think we were throughout

---

[4] Beethoven's famous song from a poem by Friedrich von Matthison. In 'On Falling in Love' RLS refers to *Adelaide* as 'the absolute expression of this midsummer spirit'. He quotes from it again in *The Ebb-Tide*, ch. 2, calling it 'The masterpiece of love, in which so many have found the expression of their dearest thoughts.'

good friends. In a shop in Buchanan Street, there was exposed a little gold wristlet with 'Phil. I.3' upon it; look up the New Testament and take the text,[5] *meine schöne Freundin*, as a message from me. The violets you sent me some time ago were very sweet; it is a comical enough circumstance that I swallowed one; how it came within reach of such a fate is easier imagined than described, in the good, old, ponderous phrase.

I say, this looks like a week's reading – this Epistle.

I do hope things are going on well with you; you must tell me if anything looks bad. Is the 'spinster' again in town and does she take the snuff-box once more conveniently out of the way? O the happy days! You know what days I mean.

Saturday [*20 September*]

And today it came, warmth, sunlight and a strong, hearty, living wind among the trees. I found myself a new being. My father and I went off a long walk, through a country most beautifully wooded and various, under a range of hills. You should have seen one place where the road suddenly fell away in front of us down a long, steep hill between a double row of trees, with one small fair-haired child framed in shadow in the foreground; and when we got to the foot there was the little kirk and kirkyard of Irongray, among broken fields and woods by the side of the bright, rapid river. In the kirkyard, there was a wonderful congregation of tombstones, upright and recumbent on four legs (after our Scotch fashion), and of flat-armed fir trees. One gravestone was erected by Scott (at a cost, I learn, of £70) to the poor woman who served him as heroine in the *Heart of Mid-Lothian*,[6] and the inscription in its stiff, Jedediah Cleishbotham fashion is not without something touching. We went up the stream a little farther to where two Covenanters lie buried in an oakwood; the tombstone[7] (as the custom is) containing the details of their grim little tragedy in funnily, bad rhyme, one verse of which sticks in my memory: –

> 'We died, their furious rage to stay,
> Near to the kirk of Iron-Gray.'

We then fetched a long compass round about, through Holywood Kirk and Lincluden ruins to Dumfries. But the walk came sadly to grief as a pleasure

---

[5] 'I thank my God upon every remembrance of you.'

[6] In the churchyard at Irongray, seven miles from Dumfries, there is a tombstone bearing an inscription, composed by Scott, in memory of Helen Walker (died 1791) who 'practised in real life the virtues with which fiction has invested the imaginary character of Jeanie Deans.' *The Heart of Mid-Lothian* is one of the 'Tales of my Landlord' allegedly sold to the publisher by Jedediah Cleishbotham.

[7] 'Edward Gordon and Alexander M'Cubine, martyres, hanged without law by Lagg and Cap. Bruce . . . March 3, 1685.'

excursion before our return. My father mentioned that when Burton asked the Royal Society for the use of certain MSS for his life of Hume,[8] my uncle Alan had voted against permission being given, because Hume etc. . . . I expressed melancholy at the idea; and my father in the course of some talk, put the case of something proposed to be published against his memory and asked if I would allow it. I said yes, and further it, because if the MS were extant it must to light sometime and better therefore, while I was there to examine. He was utterly crushed; and tauntingly reproachful. I wished very much to say something as to how I would always try to support his fame; but I *cannot* in such circumstances – it seems too hollow to profess things that should be taken for granted. O it was miserable – utterly miserable. I *did try* to speak, but the thing is impossible – strictly speaking, impossible for me. If you had seen how wretched he was![9]

Sunday [21 September]

Another beautiful day. My father and I walked into Dumfries to church. When the service was done I noted the two halberts laid against the pillar of the church yard gate; and as I had not seen the little weekly pomp of civic dignitaries in our Scotch country towns for some years, I made my father wait. You should have seen the Provost and three baillies going stately away down the sunlit street, and the two town-servants strutting in front of them, in red coats and cocked hats and with the halberts most conspicuously shouldered. We saw Burns's house – a place that made me deeply sad, and spent the afternoon down the banks of the Nith. I had not spent a day by a river since we lunched in the meadows near Sudbury. The air was as pure, and clear, and sparkling as spring water; beautiful, graceful outlines of hill and wood shut us in on every side, and the swift, brown river fled smoothly away from before our eyes, rippled over with oily eddies and dimples. White gulls had come up from the sea to fish and hovered and flew hither and thither among the loops of the stream. By good fortune, too, it was a dead calm between my father and me.

---

[8] John Hill Burton (1809–81), Scottish historian, published his life of David Hume in 1846.
[9] In an incomplete and unpublished poem (MS Yale) written after his father's death, RLS referred to this period:

> Or how in the long roads, half-suited pair
> Day after day we reasoned of the faith . . .
> My heart with sorrow and with joy recalls.
> And most among the wood of Irongray
> One tearing difference, when our two hot heads
> The older and the younger, two warm hearts
> Kindred and yearning both, almost divorced.

Do you know I find these rows harder on me than ever. I get a funny swimming in my head when they come on, that I had not before – and the like, when I think of them.

If I could only think myself fit for anything; but the stimulus of your approval and Colvin's has died a good deal off, and I find myself face to face with the weak, inefficacious personality that I knew before. I am unfit I fear for much; but don't be afraid – I have promised, and I *will* – I shall do something yet, if I have to tear myself in three to do it. And yet I don't know how it is to be managed. As you have seen already, I have greatly failed over 'Roads', which I ought to have been able to do; and indeed, I fear I am unfit as yet to make any money by my pen; and until I make money, you know, I can get no farther forward in my own difficulties. Colvin kindly offered to give me a chance of reviewing anything I wanted for the *Pall Mall*; but I do not think I am fit – that's the short and long of it. I am no good yet; but I shall make myself some good before all's done. I will, dear, for your sake – *and*, you know.

My aunt asked me if I had happened to observe Mrs Sitwell's feet and whether I thought them beautiful. I said, I *had* happened to observe them and thought them very nice. *Et de rire.*

I must tell you in case you are nervous that these two warm days have made me twice as well in health; and my low spirits are only the old business and are only when I come to sit down quietly and think. At ordinary times I am in rather good humour. I do hope you are keeping cheery. I thought today you would be at Hampstead – were you? You know all I mean about that. Outside, it is a splendid night of stars; but (as I once wrote before, in feigning) the full moon is risen over my life. Good night, *meine schöne Freundin.*

Monday [22 September][10]   *Edinburgh*

Great glory on my return to hear from you and Colvin. At least, then, I am not so much out of it as I was thinking. Dear, I am so grieved that you should be vexed at home. Don't bother about me; it is just the old story, only sudden revelations of a whole Hell between people, and such miserable misunderstandings as I have given an instance of, in this very letter. I am very buoyant now; bear up, and we'll come through all of us full sail. I must catch the post with this however. Bertie's book is out of print, I learn; I must look about for another. I shake you by the hand *fiercely*, dear – Good-bye.

[10] RLS and his father returned home from Dumfries on 22 September; MIS stayed on for another week.

141   To Sidney Colvin

MS Yale. Excerpts published by Colvin in 'Stevenson at the Start', *ICR*, 90–93.

Tuesday 16 September 1873   [*Edinburgh*]

My dear Colvin, I have just been having a long talk with my father; and you may cry to the deaf sea or the devil or anything, and hope as soon for something respondent. Always the gulf over which no man can go, always a great hell between people.

I beg pardon. There is no good in burthening people by one's incoherence in these matters, because it leads to no good to oneself, only the above few words have been a bit of an outlet.

Let me say at once that I am awfully obliged to you for your kind letter and all you say in it. My relief at hearing that I need not prosecute Savonarola, you may imagine. I had already foreseen that it would take me from two to four years, supposing me to lay aside every other pursuit and the sin that doth so easily beset me.[1] I shall incontinently betake me to what I had originally meant. I do not know if it will do for anything; it is a portion of what I hope to do afterwards and so I have a better interest in trying my hand at it. Suppose I can work it into anything supportable should I send it to Macmillan,[2] as he told me; and if so, how should I address to him? What is the name that his godfathers and godmothers gave him in the day of his baptism? and where is the place that now knows him and shall shortly know him no more?[3] The latter is (I think) Bedford Street, Covent Garden; but of the former, I know nothing. He is called 'Macmillan & Co,' but '& Co' is hardly a Christian name and might send my modest manuscript through the hands of all manner of unsympathetic subordinates. I don't know (by the way) if I told *you* that he had told *me* to send my MS to him and that he would recommend it to Groves.[4] (Be kind to my spelling – I don't know, if there be two Ms in recomend, or only one; and have therefore betaken me to something like two Ms and a half – though that is scarcely a compromise.) I do not know what to say quite about anything I may do. I am afraid to send anything I can turn out to Macmillan. I know so well that it will be feeble and especially uninteresting; and yet I do not know if it would be quite fair to ask you to look over it first, and tell me whether, by sending it in, I should merely compromise the future. Please understand this one fact about me (for a *fact* it is) that I can stand honesty.

---

[1] Cf. Hebrews 12:1 – 'let us lay aside every weight, and the sin which doth so easily beset us.'

[2] Alexander Macmillan (1818–96), founder with his brother Daniel of the publishing firm.

[3] A combination of the Catechism and Psalm 103:16. I have corrected RLS's slip of the pen in writing 'godfathers' instead of 'godmothers'.

[4] George Grove (1820–1900), knighted 1883, was editor of *Macmillan's Magazine* 1868–83; his enduring fame rests on his *Dictionary of Music and Musicians* (1878–89).

And indeed, I should be more proud of your honest refusal (as a proof that you know I can take the truth in good part, which I can, by God) than of any half-hearted acceptance. Please do not misunderstand me. I am always inclined to put things so that they seem overstated; but the above is no bravado; it is sober choice. And I do not know which answer would make me feel you more friendly; or make me more proud and pleased with myself.

I have been moving in the matter of bickers; and had been too, before your note – bickers are not easy to get I find; and in the meantime you will perhaps allow me to send you two that are not quite of a size. I shall prosecute my enquiries in the meantime and find something else more worthy of a Professor of Fine Art before 'the conversion of the Jews.'[5] I have added (and I trust you will thank me for the addition – spelling is a great trial)[6] – two horn spoons. These spoons, owing to their being really the result of individual handicraft, possess a sort of patriarchal charm. Moreover they are of so rude a workmanship, that one feels himself, on seeing them, several centuries back in the cool, leisurely Middle Ages – far from all bustle and fever of modern competition. I daresay you have heard the Scottish 'taunting proverb'[7] (my Bible quotations are sadly thrown away on so ignorant an unbeliever as you) against the unthrifty and idle, that they are like 'neither to make a spoon, nor spoil a horn.' It seems to me, now, that the artificers of those that I sent you, have simply *spoiled horns*. I hope you will enjoy the unvarnished effrontery of this merchandise as I have done. Please note the forlorn brackets that stand for adornment; and the melancholy bias of the spine in at least one of the two cripple implements that I have the satisfaction of forwarding. Again, please note the whistle in the end; that is to entertain peevish and refractory urchins. If your order had been for *luggies*[8] instead of for *bickers*, I could have shown you another device for the same laudable end, in the shape of certain small shot introduced between the two layers of a double bottom; so that by a judicious change of level, a rattling noise is produced, and a consequent peace in perturbed nurseries.

Please tell me (for I have promptly forgotten) to what Inn of Court and to what functionary thereof, I am to address my 'Humbly Sheweth.' After much inward conflict I will own myself wrong in the matter of the cartoons, and I hope this admission argues me in a more saving state wth regard to the general question. I pray Heaven you may be able to read my hand – *zwölf Seiten eng und* very illegible. I am growing more and more to leave out several tenths of each word – a practice to be manfully withstood.

[5] Marvell, 'To His Coy Mistress'.
[6] RLS first wrote and deleted 'adition'.
[7] Habakkuk 2:6.
[8] A wooden bowl with a projecting handle or handles.

I hope to send off the bickers by tomorrow, as well as the present scribble. Yours very sincerely   Louis Stevenson

P.S. Next day. This letter shows the progress of my temper. When I began I was at white heat so could neither write nor spell nor conduct myself like a . . .[9] gentleman. I would not send it, if I were not too lazy to face so much transcription. Pay no attention, however, to anything in the first sheet except the question about sending things to Macmillan, and his address; and sympathise deeply with all perturbable spirits. I really ought to beg your pardon. It is a sort of insult to send a letter like this – a naked letter; but I mean this apologetic postscript to be a fig leaf.   R.L.S.

You can also believe the passage about telling me the truth; it may be convenient some time.   L.

142   *To Sidney Colvin*

MS Buffalo.

Thursday 18 September [*1873*]   *Helensburgh*

My dear Colvin, I have to write to inform you that I have been suddenly deracinate from home before the bickers could be sent off; so that you may not wonder at their non-arrival. I take the opportunity to apollogise for my last letter. (Bad spelling again I think.) I was not well and besides I was suffering under a new dose of misfortunes that I had the wisdom not to enter upon in such a frame of mind. A cousin, lately deceased, left a dying testimony against the 'horrible atheists' among the connection, and the consequence has been that my greatest friend has been forbidden the house. Under the continued influence of seediness and this cataclysm in the family, I was in a somewhat morbid frame of mind. I have only to ask you to forget that such a letter was ever written. I should not have written to you at all in such a state, and I have to hope that you will simply consider that letter as unwritten.

For your kindness, I have to thank you again. Believe me the very fact of such a letter as you sent me, is a great help to me to be patient and (I hope) kind through all. Believe me, Yours very sincerely   R.L. Stevenson

P.S. Do not regard this palinode as embracing any business question as to the Temple, please.   L.

[9] Two words blotted out, possibly by RLS.

143   To Frances Sitwell

MS NLS. Partly published in *Letters*, I, 77–9.

Monday 22 September [1873]   *Edinburgh*

My dear friend, how could you have fancied any slight; or rather, for I know you did not do so, how could you fail to see the true rationale of what took place. Another of my melancholy little periods of wretchedness having come upon me, I began to write to S.C. (as I had to do) with a heart so full of bitterness that it flowed slaveringly over upon my beard; for which I have since suffered intense shame. I have just had another disagreeable tonight. It is difficult indeed to steer steady among the breakers; I am always touching ground; generally it is my own blame, for I cannot help getting friendly with my father (whom I *do* like) and so speaking foolishly with my mouth. I have yet to learn in ordinary conversation that reserve, and silence that I must try to unlearn in the matter of the feelings. We have both (as you say) a main unpleasant road to travel and we must hold hands firmly and mutually keep up our hearts.

I am more vexed than I can say at having broken out to S.C.; but he has taken it very kindly. One may fall in the mire in the company of gentlemen without much uproarious laughter, thank God. But that is a side to my self – an imbecile, decrepid side – that I hate to think about; and every new illustration of it costs me much pain.

Colvin has taken the trouble to write me six sides of advice about my little paper. I do not know how I shall find words to thank him. In fact I cannot, even to you, say how much obliged I am. The news that 'Roads' would do reached me in good season; I had begun utterly to despair of doing anything. Certainly I do not think I should be in a hurry to commit myself about the Covenanters; the whole subject turns round about me and so branches out to this side and that that I grow bewildered; and one cannot write discreetly about any one little corner of an historical period, until one has an organic view of the whole. I have however, given life and health, great hope of my Covenanters; indeed there is a lot of precious dust to be beaten out of that stack even by a very infirm hand.

What a fool I was to write to Bertie about the book – it is out of print; and he must just have patience; I shall find ultimately something else as good.

I am just going to buckle to, to remodel 'Roads' according to S.C.'s prescriptions.

Much later

I can scarcely see to write just now; so please excuse. We have had an awful scene. All that my father had to say has been put forth – not that it was anything new; only it is the devil to hear. O dear God, I don't know what to do – the world goes hopelessly round about me – there is no more possibility of doing, living, being anything but a *beast* and there's the end of it.

It is eleven, I think; for a clock struck. O Lord there has been a deal of time through our hands since I went down to supper. All this has come from my own folly; I somehow could not think the gulph so impassable and I read him some notes on the Duke of Argyll[1] – I thought he would agree so far and that we might have rational discussion on the rest. And now – after some hours – he has told me that he is a weak man and that I am driving him too far, and that I know not what I am doing. O dear God, this is bad work.

I have lit a pipe and feel calmer. I say, my dear friend, I am killing my father – he told me tonight (by the way) that I alienated utterly my mother – and this is the result of my attempt to start fresh and fair and to do my best for all of them.

I am a beast to bother you, with all your troubles, over this; but tonight has been really very bad – worse than ordinary. If I could only cease to like him, I could pull through with a good heart; but it is really insupportable to see his emotion – an impotent emotion rather, to make things worse – his sort of half threats of turning me out and O God bless the whole thing.

I have a ringing headache so please excuse this scrawl of nonsense. I should not send it off I know and yet I do wish a little consolation. You don't know what a difference it makes; especially now that Bob is very difficult to get at. I *did* mean to make him nearly happy all this time my mother was away; and see the result! O dear God, I wish I could think *he* was happy. It has been a terrible blow to him. He said tonight, 'He wished he had never married', and I could only echo what he said. 'A poor end,' he said, 'for all my tenderness.' And what was there to answer? 'I have made all my life to suit you – I have worked for you and gone out of my way for you – and the end of it is that I find you in opposition to the Lord Jesus Christ – I find everything gone – I would ten times sooner have seen you lying in your grave than that you should be shaking the faith of other young men and bringing such ruin on other houses, as you have brought already upon this' – that is a sort of abstract of one speech. There is a jolly son for you – there is the staff I have been to his declining years. 'I thought,' he said, 'to have had someone to help me, when I was old.' Much help he has had.

I must wait till tomorrow ere I finish. I am tonight too excited.

[1] His Speculative Society essay (see Letter 116, n. 3), 'Law and Free Will – Notes on the Duke of Argyll' – an attack on *The Reign of Law* (1866) by the eighth Duke of Argyll (1823–1900).

Tuesday [23 September]

I shall not read over the foregoing as I know I shall suppress it and I don't want to suppress it. The sun is shining today which is a great matter and altogether the gale having blown off again, I live in a precarious lull. On the whole I am not displeased with last night; I kept my eyes open through it all, and I think, not only avoided saying anything that could make matters worse in the future, but said something that *may* do good. But a little better or a little worse is a trifle. I lay in bed this morning awake, for I was tired and cold and in no special hurry to rise, and heard my father go out for the papers; and then I lay and wished − O if he would only *whistle* when he comes in again! But of course he did not. I have stopped that pipe.

I am going to push on and finish the patching up of 'Roads' according to S.C.'s receipt. I can not amplify as he proposes I should; but I'll do all the suppressing he wants and have it all written over today sometime and ready to send off. I am very glad I have that to busy myself with and be a little hopeful over.

Now please don't think this has been much worse than usual. It is only a second, third, fourth, fifth performance of a piece that can never be stale. I shall always be a good deal interested when that organ is ground, of course, because my own fingers are in among the works.

Now you see I have written to you this time and sent it off, for both of which God forgive me. Ever your faithful friend   R.L.S.

My father and I together can put about a year through in half an hour. Look here, you mustn't take this too much to heart. I shall be all right in a few hours. It's impossible to depress me. And of course, where you can't do anything, there's no need of being depressed. It's all waste tissue.   L.

144   *To Sidney Colvin*

MS Yale.

23 September 1873   *Edinburgh*

My dear Colvin, I am so glad you think something could be made of 'Roads'; and I have tried to follow your directions as fully as I could. The amplifications, however, I have not been in a fit vein to attempt; and indeed I do not know that I could have kept any longer on the literary tight-rope; it was so difficult to avoid falling over into metaphysics or downright, naked extravagance. I don't mean that more could not be said; but only that I could not say more. I have tried however to get rid of the wonderfuls and otherwise pick the thing together; and if it will not do now, I am afraid I must give it up as a bad job for the present. If such should be your melancholy judgement, or that of the S[aturday] R[eview] please return me the *trista vestigia*[1] and I may make something better hereafter.

I have had a very bad time of it with my father I am sorry to say which has miserably put me out. I think he had half a mind to order me out of the house. It is very disheartening that things should go so ill, when I am earnestly solicitous to make it as well for him as I can.

I do not know how to thank you for your very great kindness. Of course, if this thing will do for the *S.R.* it will be something definite at present and will give me much hope for the future. I find nothing so needful as that I should make money and be so far on another footing at once. I have fortunately a great chance of getting on to review a little in the *Scotsman*[2] which will be practice, and always so much coin. As to what you are kind enough to say about the *Pall Mall*, I am too diffident of myself to try, unless something really very much moved me; please do not mistake me, I will try anything that I have any hope of doing, but it is so hard to write anything that is really fit for cold black and white printing.

Accept my very warm thanks and believe me, Yours sincerely

Robert Louis Stevenson

P.S. Bickers and horns are to be immediately looked for.   L.

145   To Frances Sitwell

MS NLS. Brief excerpts published in *Letters*, I, 79–81.

Tuesday evening, 23 September [*1873*]   [*17 Heriot Row*]

I just write to let you know I am thinking of you, although it is scarcely necessary now; you are the very texture of my thought; I am never an hour without you slipping in somewhere, dear. Was my last letter too much for you? It was cruel in me to send it. I repent me much. But I wanted to get all that off my mind, and you are my confessional. I shall not, I trust, have so to vex you often. Good night, *meine schöne, liebe Freundin*. Be happy, my dear; and I shall be happy, in our ruined, miserable house; as ruined and miserable nearly as yours. O dear, be happy and brave and glad through it all; you have been the good sun to me; and it is always something. If I had not known you, where should I have been?

---

[1] *tristia vestigia* – dismal traces.
[2] No reviews in *The Scotsman* have been traced.

Wednesday [*24 September*]

I have found another 'flowering isle',[1] Claire. All this beautiful, quiet, sunlit day, I have been out in the country; down by the sea on my own favourite coast between Granton and Queensferry. There was a delicate delicious haze over the firth and sands on one side, and on the other the shadow of the woods was all riven with great golden wefts of sunshine. A little, faint talk of waves upon the beach; the wild strange crying of sea gulls over the sea; and the hoarse wood-pigeons and shrill, sweet robins full of their autumn lovemaking among the trees, made up a delectable concerto of peaceful noises. I spent the whole afternoon among these sights and sounds with Magnus Simpson[2] – Walter (of whom you have heard) his younger brother. He was very nice and nowise philistine, thank God. And we came home from Queensferry on the outside of the coach and four, along a beautiful way full of ups and downs among woody, uneven country and laid out (fifty years ago, I suppose) by my grandfather, on the notion of Hogarth's line of beauty. You see my taste for Roads is hereditary.

There has been no more trouble here: I don't know how or why; anymore than I know why and how trouble comes when it *does* come.

I am in great hopes of a letter tomorrow. By the bye can you read [the] insufferable scrawl into which my correspondence usually degenerates? Tell me a word or two of that, if it should be to the bad, and I will try and get myself more together in the penmanship direction.

How strangely well and long, Colvin manages to write. He doesn't seem to give way either, as I am always inclined to do when I get talking on letter-paper. He seems always to remember where he is and which side is uppermost. I wish I could learn to do the like. Bob said the other day that I had been working all my life not at literature, but at conversation; perhaps he is right.

I do hope, dear, you have had no more scenes. We both know well enough from bitter, hopeless experience how little is to be said in such matters; but I have learned, since I have had certain letters coming to me now and then, how much sympathy can lighten and alleviate the impotent misery of such accursed junctures. I want you to know, and I feel you know already, how truly and *justly* I feel with you. I have underlined '*justly*' because that is my particular pretension. I do pretend dear to know better what you feel than anybody else – often, at least. I shall not soon forget my pride, when I noticed one day at Cockfield that you were ill, when no one else had yet noticed it. I *do* think that I know you; and I do think, also, that I feel with you as keenly as my nature will let me – and by God! that's as

---

[1] 'Other flowering isles must be/In the sea of Life and Agony,' – Shelley, 'Lines Written among the Euganean Hills', ll. 335–6.
[2] Alexander Magnus Retzious Simpson (1852–84). (See Letter 1334.)

keenly as anybody else can, although I fear not so well or so usefully. Anyway, my dearest friend, you know what my hope and resolute intention is; and I still try feebly after it, and will try in the future, and grow stronger through trial.

Thursday [*25 September*]

Another beautiful day; but I am rather seedy and out of heart. My father said no more than truth about my mother's feelings to me; I see that now very clearly; although it does seem hard to have put it into words. She is quite cold and unresponsive, after all. I try to cheat myself with flimsies; but that's the hard kernel of fact.

I tell you this is just a mere trial of nervous strength between us. The weakest will die first, that is all. And I don't know whether to wish for the one alternative or the other. Both seem horrible; but not much more horrible than the unsightly, hopeless present.

I must be a little more pleasant. I know, my dearest friend, how sad you feel and do not wish to make things worse for you; only your own hard experience must have taught you one thing that, if things turn even to the worst, if all life falls about you in deplorable ruin, you have still happy moments, keenness to feel pleasure, an undisturbed little well of content-ment in the beautiful past, a great faithful hope, through it all, for some good thing yet in the future. You will not, then, exaggerate my unpleasant state; today, I am certainly at the bottom of despondency; but I know it to be a passing humour only and to have as much, perhaps, to do with my digestion as with my troubles.

There is no fear, I think, of my getting up to town in October; but great fear, if I cannot get health and spirits together, that I shall go up only to be plucked. However that I hope will be remedied in a little while. The effect of Monday night must pass off sooner or later; though, it is strange, these scenes seem to tell more and more on me at each repetition. I don't get acclimatised.

I must put away this paper and pray for a better spirit to write to you in tomorrow. This is the letter for next Tuesday morning; it seems a long while before you will read it, my dear friend. All these humours will have gone by, these feelings will be cold; it will be *tant soit peu*, an anachronism. Living speech is better.

> *Das Herz ist mir bedrückt und sehnlich*
> *Gedenke ich der alten Zeit;*
> *Die Welt war damals noch so wöhnlich*
> *Und ruhig lebten hin die Leut.*
>
> *Doch jetzt ist alles wie verschoben*
> *Das ist ein Drängen eine Noth;*

Gestorben ist der Herr Gott oben
Und unten ist der Teufel todt.

Und Alles schaut so grämlich trübe,
So krausverwirrt und morsch und kalt[3]

Thursday 10.30

I have effected my great purpose and have finished, addressed and stamped a second letter to Maud before she has answered my first. It is a lamentable enough letter, and has taken three desponding days to drum out; but *le voilà enfin* and it's being gloomy will be all the better perhaps from a certain point of view. – Did I tell you that I had a hope of getting some reviewing to do for the *Scotsman*? That will be always money and I have not the same timidity for that that I have for S.C.'s kind, but alarming propositions.

Friday [26 September]

I was wakened this morning by a long flourish of bugles and a roll upon the drums – the *reveillé* at the Castle. I went to the window; it was a gray quiet dawn. A few people passed already up the street between the gardens, already I heard the noise of an early cab somewhere in the distance, most of the lamps had been extinguished but not all, and there were two or three lit windows in the opposite *façade* that showed where sick people and watchers had been awake all night and knew not yet of the new, cool day. This appealed to me of course with a special sadness; how often in the old times, my nurse and I had looked across at these, and sympathised! But I thought most of all of a more recent dawn at which I had assisted; of the lilies in the moat; the far-spread, breathing silentness; the grey satisfying light of the early morning.

---

[3] Heine, *Buch der Lieder*, '*Die Heimkehr*', XXXIX wanting the last two lines. Hal Draper's modern translation is as follows:

> My heart is heavy – sad the present;
> I think back to the olden days
> When all the world was still so pleasant
> And people went their peaceful ways.
>
> Now, helter-skelter, elbows shove us,
> Pressure and stress on every side!
> Dead is the good Lord God above us,
> And down below the devil's died.
>
> Everything goes in churlish fashion,
> A rotten, tangled, cold affair;
> [And but for a little love and passion
> There'd be no surcease anywhere.]
>
> [*The Complete Poems of Heinrich Heine*, Boston, 1982]

Only the day began ill with a fanfare; for I somehow took that as the emblem of a letter (which I had already half expected) and of course stumbled over a little disappointment. I hope to God you are not ill.

Dear friend, do not be ready to shy if you find me anyway unworthy; be long suffering with me. I am still so depressed and sick at heart that I am not fit to do more than tell you again and again that I am now miserably dependent, that you have spoiled a certain pretty rough, vulgar and courageous volunteer in the war of life who went south some two months and a half ago and, since you have put a new heart of flesh within him, you must help to keep it warm with sympathy.

I wish – wish – wish for a letter tomorrow – a line – a trifle – a salutation; and this I say for charm. O dear you must surely feel the thrill and longing that I have through these – four hundred miles indeed! – but four hundred miles of living, sensitive, warm air. I feel as if the letter would come tomorrow, now. I have prayed faithfully. I have swung the censer before no empty shrine. I think somehow you will feel my want, the utter polar loneliness of my spirit, at this time; and will send me a raven with just a little phrase of friendship in its bill.

This is a jeremiad indeed, to send to you – not at all a pretty dish to set before my Queen; but I cannot fool with you, and I cannot forego writing either, until I know it will be unpleasant to you. You will not forget your promise I know. Rash as I am, and fool as I made of myself in that letter to Colvin, I would not let anyone but you see all this gray despair – not for worlds; I do so pride myself on priceless cheerfulness; and I cannot yet make up my mind to admit that there is a great chance that it will ultimately desert me.

> Ma gaieté s'en est allée,
> Sage ou fou, qui la rendra[4]

and so forth. And I know what sight, whose voice, whose touch, would bring back the truant at the turn of a second.

I wish you would read Michelet's *Louis Quatorze et la Révocation de l'Edit de Nantes*.[5] I read it out in the garden, and the autumnal trees and weather, and my own autumnal humour, and the pitiable prolonged tragedies of Madame and of Molière, as they look, darkling and sombre, out of their niches in the great gingerbread *façade* of the *Grand Age*, go wonderfully hand in hand.

I wonder if my revised paper has pleased the *Saturday*. If it has not, I shall be rather sorry – no, very sorry indeed – but not surprised and certainly not

[4] Unidentified.

[5] Jules Michelet, *Histoire de France* (1835–67). Three odd volumes of an 1871 reprint from RLS's library are at Yale.

hurt. It will be a great disappointment; but I am glad to say that, among all my queasy, troublesome feelings, I have not a sensitive vanity. Not that I'm not as conceited as you know me to be; only I go easy over the coals in that matter.

4.50

I have been out reading Hallam[6] in the garden; and have been talking with my old friend the gardener, a man of a singularly hard favour and few teeth. He consulted me this afternoon on the choice of books, premising that his taste ran mainly on war and travel. On travel, I had to own at once my ignorance. I suggested Kinglake;[7] but he had read that, and so, finding myself here unhorsed, I turned about and at last recollected Southey's *Lives of the Admirals* and the vols of Macaulay containing the wars of William. Can you think of any other, for this worthy man? I believe him to hold me in as high an esteem as anyone can do; and I reciprocate his respect for he is quite an intelligent companion.

Maud writes to you all right, does she? I hope she bears no malice to me for anything.

Of course, I have not been going on with Claire:[8] I have been out of heart for that; and besides it is difficult to act before the reality. Footlights will not do with the sun; the stage moon and the real, lucid moon of one's dark life, look strangely on each other.

Saturday [27 September]

My violent wishing of yesterday has failed; for all that I am in somewhat better health and spirits; for all which blessings the Lord make us truly thankful, for Christ's sake, Amen.

I have read Morley's second article on Education[9] today; and I can only say that I would give half my forefinger to have written anything so fine, and just and temperate. Surely, they must feel small, after that; but no.

It has been again a lovely, warm day; Bob and I lunched very leisurely off omelettes and a bottle of Burgundy in a sunny restaurant overlooking

---

[6] Probably Henry Hallam's *Constitutional History of England* (1827) from which RLS quotes in his essay on Knox (*Familiar Studies*).

[7] A.W. Kinglake's classic account of travels in the Middle East, *Eothen* (1844).

[8] This passage and a similar one in Letter 149 show that RLS tried to work extracts from his letters to Mrs Sitwell into a novel, presumably an epistolary one in the same form as 'The Edifying Letters to the Rutherford Family' (posthumously published, with an introduction by Roger Swearingen, 1982). Support for this is given in the following entry in Notebook A265A at Yale: 'Claire. 1st letter, life at home. LJR. Absent friends, taken for mad, the book of poems, letter from Tallboys, walk with the friend and conversation about giving over responsibilities.' See also Furnas 395–7.

[9] John Morley's 'The Struggle for National Education' appeared in the *Fortnightly Review* from August to October.

Princes Street. His great hobby at present, my dear friend, is one that I am very glad to tell you. He is more and more strong every day against any dogma of extinction; more and more anxious to pull down the so-called scientific arguments against immortality. I do not know that I can quite agree with him; but what he says is still weighty. So, there is something good.

11 P.M.

I do not quite understand how things lie. I wrote a letter to you, to which I should have thought you would have been anxious to reply; I had also a sort of notion that you would have made Bertie write when you found the book could not be forthcoming (if as nothing else), as a substitute for a letter from you; in addition to this I had sent the bickers to Colvin and half expected an acknowledgement. This seems to me in my morbid state (for I am a little morbid owing still to last Monday night) like a consensus of proof that something has taken place or may have taken place. And so I feel my dear friend that this may be the last letter I shall ever send to you. If my foreboding be right, I wish before all things else in the world that you should understand my feelings; if I be wrong, you will not blame too much a little haste to fancy the worst in one who is most cruelly put to it to keep up his heart at all. I want you to understand, then, once and for all, that nothing can change my view and that I will ever continue my purpose of living as you would have me live. I shall try always to make myself ever worthier of the friendship that I have had; I am merely made another man; that other man I shall continue to be, do not fear. If anything makes you stop your kind correspondence with me (as I half fear something has), do not think that I shall ever forget or feel less. You will always have done your work fully. I shall always desire to do my best, for *your* sake. You understand now, how thoroughly free you will be to follow out what wisdom or necessity may dictate; and how you will still have made a new man of me, changed altogether my life, given me something, dear, to live and work for, even if it can never be thanked by so much as a look.

I daresay I am a fool, in writing thus; that I am merely following where my own desponding humour leads me; if this is so, I know you will not exaggerate the impact of what I say and remember that I do not want much writing, that this is no complaint, that this is a matter born out of an unhappy conjunction; and even so, as you see, has not damped my courage. *Do* understand me. I have a fear that something must have happened, and so I write frankly and fully, because I fear I may never write to you again; but O my dear, you know – you see – you must feel, in what perfect faith and absolute submission I am writing. You must feel that I shall still feel as I have felt and will work as well *for* you and *towards* you, without any recognition, as I could work with all recognition. Remember always that you are my Faith. And now, my dearest, beautiful friend, good night to you. I shall never feel otherwise to you, than now I do when I write myself Your faithfullest friend   R.L.S.

Sunday [28 September]

I brought the unhappy week to a most dolorous end last night, in the scrap above. I shall leave it however, as, right or wrong, they show you how I can take what may come, or (it may be) has come.

Sunday coming again on the back of this has been rather happy for me; I have been reckoning the beads of my rosary of recollection, very piously. Just a month ago, we were sallying forth at this time to K[ew] Gardens, with the nice schoolmaster in our company. O that is a day that I shall never forget; nor the day before; nor so many other beautiful days at Cockfield. And they cannot be taken from me; they, nor their influence. I am not morbid today; nor even wretched; only a little sad, and shaken by a lurking notion that you may be ill; for that would explain and that now puzzles me. I do not want to encourage this; but I shall not send off this letter, until I hear from you again, in case of accidents. Thank God, my last, I think, was quite unexceptionable.

In church this morning, I am ashamed to say I was so superstitious as to pray; I thought I would have the chance at least. They were praying, then, for sick friends.

If I were never to hear from you again. O dear, I hope you are not ill.

8 P.M.

My dear I am now calm and full of work; I have been doing Latin and have just now been trying my hand once again on a paper about W. Whitman; I have no fear or doubt any more. Tomorrow, I wait for without trouble; if there be no letter, I still keep back these sheets; if a letter comes, I send them and you will see in this postscript, that the storm has gone over and that I am once again myself. Not nervous now, or morbid, but quite peaceful. My mother is returned[10] and has been very nice to me; and I have brought myself by all this fervent writing and thinking, into a spirit once again of cheerful acquiescence – to anything, but your illness; *that* of course I exclude, so don't be ill; but you know now how freely you may shake me off, if you should find it desirable; you know now, that even in that case you need not doubt me: I have faced that also, and I see that in the light of what I feel for you, I can bear it gladly and will not lose the good lessons you have taught me.

---

[10] MIS returned home from Dumfries on 27 September.

Monday [29 September]

I have just sent off a sedate little note to you. I dared not send off all this nonsense until I heard and yet I dared not let you go without a word; in case you might be ill, my dear. I must first go along and see my friend who is confined to bed; and then I shall just shut myself up here and work – work – work and keep myself from thinking. If you are ill, as I fear you are, O my dear, how much harm have I not done perhaps by my mad letter of last Tuesday; half out of pique I sent it because you had seemed to blame me for having held my peace before. *O meine liebe Freundin*, go not away – do not be ill; that is the last hardship for us all. If you are ill, however, think of this that the thought of you is just life and air and sunshine to me, even now, even when I am so much in doubt as to you, and know not whether you are well or whether you may not, by some event, be separated from me forever. Still, it is so; I would not forego the knowledge I have had of you, the dear friendship that there has been between us, the great things you have taught me, for – I can find no phrases – for anything. So think of that, if you should be ill and these lines should ever reach you, think of that and be a little happier, think of that – think of how much you have been to me *alone* without thought of others, without thought of how many dark lanes the white moon has looked healingly down into, rather the warm sun has lit up, made cheerful and healthy – and then you will get more strength at the very inspiration of the thought. O blessed life, *O Madonna mia* – no! *nostra* – look down a little gladly on us all.

11 P.M.

I am so sorry that I sent that note off this morning without further thought. It might seem cold to you and unfriendly. I must try and tell you things that might amuse you, if it so chance that you still wish to hear and are well enough to let this be sent.

On Saturday morning, I read Morley's article aloud to Bob in one of the walks of the public garden. I was full of it and read most excitedly; and we were ever, as we went to and fro, passing a bench where a man sat reading the Bible aloud to a small circle of the devout. This man is well known to me, sits there all day, sometimes reading, sometimes singing, sometimes distributing tracts. Bob laughed much at the opposition preachers – I never noticed it till he called my attention to the other; but it did not seem to me like opposition – does it to you? – each in his way was teaching what he thought best.

Last night, after reading Walt Whitman a long while for my attempt to write about him, I got *tête-montée*, rushed out up to Magnus Simpson, came in, took out *Leaves of Grass*, and without giving the poor unbeliever time to object, proceeded to wade into him with favourite passages. I had at least this triumph that he swore he must read some more of him.

You see I am throughly re-established in spirits by these two samples; and yet the first little spirt of enthusiasm was immediately after another disappointment in the letter line. It is wonderful how one accommodates himself. All today even, I have kept up beautifully and have done a lot of work although every time I thought of you I felt my heart drawn together. I do trust you will not be very ill – if I could only think you are well! but that is impossible, or you would have sent me a line after Tuesday's letter. O my dear friend, be strong and well – O be strong and well! I am afraid to think what I sometimes fear.

Tuesday [30 September]

I have written to Bertie today *morne* attempts to be funny. I cannot write to you however or I know I shall get off work; at which I have been steadily but with almost no result, all day, with the exception of the usual walk up to the Speculative, and the somewhat slower walk home again.

Wednesday 1 October

The beginning of another month. It is a whole month now since I left. Please forget all that is gloomy in this letter should it ever be sent. I am quite jolly, and really getting a fairish amount of work through my hands.

I must tell you that I have a new bookcase in my room. I am very proud of my room so I give a plan.

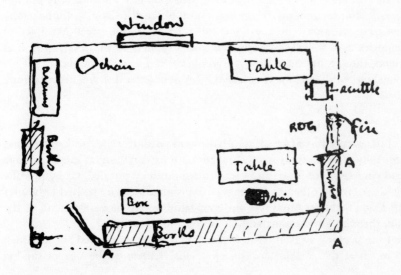

The long Bookcase (A. A. A.) is only about 3 feet 6, so it is nice to sit on the top of, especially in the corner; for I have a thorough child's delight in perches of all sorts. The Box is full of papers. Of course you see where I sit – on the chair that I have cross-hatched, shut in among books and with the light in front during the day and at my right at night. I am going to buy a wicker arm chair so I shall have three chairs soon. I may say that in my sketch it has somehow got bigger than three times its right bigness, which is very odd; for I wish it were just a little smaller. Don't you like the arrangement?

12.50

NO LETTER. Now this is very funny. I should have thought you would have answered my Tuesday's letter; I felt sure you would not have lost an hour in answering Monday's note; and yet, thank God, you are not ill, or Maud would have heard of that. What can this mean, old man? She could not be so brutal as to give you no hint, as to let the whole correspondence cease without a word, and you go day after day up to the College and come back again with the heart-ache. And yet what can it be? O God, God, God, GOD. You are not ill I know, my dear friend; or, at least, I fondly hope; and though I believe that no eye but mine shall ever see these lines and that all that made me so happy is at an end, I must still keep writing to you. I did not wish more than I had; but I find that I had made myself slavishly dependent upon it. And now when it is gone, I do not know quite how I am to face the blank. Yet I shall do it. I am a very good martyr in the quiet, drawingroom signification of one that can live very steadfastly through a pretty troublous life. And if my health will hold out, I shall utterly put this present trouble underneath my feet and look back to you, without bitterness and without regret, as one looks back on the great examples of centuries ago. I shall always live as you would have me; even now dear friend, though my brain swims a good deal, I am going to put myself resolutely to work, and for your sake. O this poor letter that will never be read.

10 P.M.

I have triumphed like a bird. I have worked all day and worked well and hopefully. And I am as strong and resolute for anything as can be. I have read your last letter over, and I remain again utterly puzzled. Can you really be ill? or, is the other notion that I have sometimes entertained right after all? I don't know. Anyway I am your faithful and *submissive* friend to the end, through good report and ill; as you must know.

I am working away at 'Walt Whitman', having determined not to launch so much as the smallest cockboat on what I mean to be one of the big cruises of my life, a reconnaissance in full force with a whole fleet; and although I have not yet had the least visitation of either felicity or facility, I hope to drum something laboriously out which may answer the purpose and be fit for print. No word by the way from Colvin. It is devilish funny. I am afraid to write and ask, although my parents are already beginning to ask whether he has yet acknowledged receipt of the bickers. It is a curious *Zustand*.

Thursday [*2 October*]

The whole affair at once cleared up this morning; I hear from you and you are ill, but worse than that I hear from Colvin of a letter gone astray. I shall take this up with me, when I go, and put in the results of my enquiries before I close it. Good-bye my dear friend. I just send this with a record of my gloomy times as it is written; but it is all blue sky again now.

Spec. Soc.

The letters are both here. I have had all this gloom out of the fatal stupidity of a porter. I do hope you are keeping better; Colvin seems to think it is no more than a cold. Do get strong; I am all right, now the clouds are away; but this succession of anxieties put my brain into an awful state, so please excuse the letter, At least, you will see I was not unworthy of trust; although I was a fool.

My father seems all the better for having cleared himself on Monday last; and I suspect he must have told my mother what he said, because she has been quite changed, has given me a little present, – my father coveted the said gift and I was going to give it up to him, but she would not allow me. Besides this, she wrote me a very kind letter. There may be better times in that. Still it is always a pic-nic on a volcano.

Get better. Ever your faithful friend   Louis Stevenson

146   To James Walter Ferrier

MS Yale.

Thursday 24 September [*1873*][1]   *17 Heriot Row*

My dear Ferrier. Call me all the beasts in the Apocalypse, Gog and Magog, the three frogs, the mill-stone that it would have been better for that man

---

[1] Thursday was 25 September.

to have had about his neck,[2] the scarlet prostitute, or the nondescript animile with crowns and other deformities upon his bloated person; void yourself in injurious language; lay on, and spare not; wade in; behold me, with raised drapery, crouched dutifully over the bench of torment. I have deserved all. I have been a beast. However, old man, what comes late, comes not I hope unwelcomely.

I was in England a bit this summer; but I got involved with people and so failed to get to Malvern. Among others I went to stay with Sidney Colvin, the man who used to do the critical notices for the *Fortnightly*. I have again, through him, some hopes of getting into print. You see as usual I am preluding a literary campaign; there is always about me the sound of trumpets threatening charge, and devil a charge; I am ever, in Milton's phrase 'mewing my mighty youth'[3] and it seems within the limits of the strictest probability that I shall continue to mew (or *mu*) the same until it is an entirely unserviceable article. Still, my hopes are better. Indeed, I wait at present with some trepidation, the judgement of the *Saturday Review* on an article of mine. Many others of course are and have been in the same predicament (and will be too, for the matter of that) without any perceptible effect on their future. However, I sent this in by Colvin's advice and so I may perhaps be of a better hope.

And now for yourself, how are you? how goes the vile tabernacle? is your immortal spirit as pure, supersensual and (to speak without profanity) heavenly as ever? Mine is. I have been converted and am going to devote the latter end, or bum, of my life to the confection of savoury religious tracts – the *tartlet* so to speak of pious literature. I have meditated also a large work, on the Plan of Southey's *Admirals* and Campbell's *Chancellors*, to be called *Lives of the Free Church Moderators*; for which undertaking, let me request your collaboration.

Bob begs to be remembered tenderly to you; he bewails you as the Jews mourned for Barabbas – or somebody else, I think that's a bad shot. He finds Edinburgh but a barren promontory without your company; and to say truth, there are others who do now and then hunger after the racy flesh-pots of your conversation.

Keep up a good pecker, old man, and always keep the head to the wind with a little work. I hope the aspiring blood of Lancaster is going to wade in[4]; only, in the affecting words of the Reverend Keble, you must not

---

[2] The mill-stone reference is in Matthew 18:16 (and related Gospels); the three frogs are unclean spirits in Revelation 16:13; all the other references come from Revelation. I have corrected a slip of the pen of 'God' for 'Gog'.

[3] Milton, *Areopagitica*.

[4] *3 Henry VI*, V.vi.60.

'strive to wind yourself too high
For mortal life beneath the sky;' —[5]

a couplet that suggests being written the morning after the Reverend bard
had exceeded at dinner and overwound his watch for upwards of fifteen
calendar minutes. Calendar minutes is a good phrase, eh?

Stick in 'Sound, sound the clarion! fill the fife! To all the sensual world
proclaim! A small annuity for life, Is worth a handle to your name.'[6] No,
that's not exactly how Scott wrote it, is it? All the same.

Is that dissoloot Writer to the Signet, C. Baxter about there still? Bless
him for me, if he is, and tell him that I pray for him day and night so
vigorously as to [be] a scandal to the neighbourhood. I wish he would
repent. Hoop la! Another religious summersault! Gentlemen, there is no
deception. This sinful brand merely leaps through the small trap-window
labelled 'Grace', and you see him at the other side a spangled and sanctified
harlequin, with the two edged lath of the scriptures in his hand, the mask
of hypocrisy (or self-deception) upon his ugly mug, and shod with the hob-
nailed shoes of the preparation to tramp upon his erring neighbours.

This letter is one wild gambado. The fun in my head becomes fast and
furious. I write faster and faster and have less and less idea what I am writing
about. I wish the dinner bell would ring me down from my wild flight.

Seriously, however, I hope you are keeping in better health. You will
forgive my long, shabby silence and write again soon, won't you? And
meantime, Believe me, your friend   R.L. Stevenson

147   To Frances Sitwell

MS NLS. Excerpts published in *Letters*, I, 81–3.

Thursday 2 October [*1873*]   [*17 Heriot Row*]

I must just begin another letter to you, now the last is sent off. You
cannot fancy the expansion of heart that I feel today; I had a difficulty not
to dance upon the streets. Weather still wet, wet and cold. Yesterday
afternoon about this time, I remember, a man played most pitiably on the
cornet-à-piston in the neighbouring street, and I began to cry; which was
wretched foolishness, but I suppressed it at once and kept on at Wodrow's
Analecta[1] (a Covenanting book) and made my notes as best I could. I am in

---

[5] John Keble, *The Christian Year*, 'Morning'.
[6] The original, though quoted by Scott as the motto to ch. 34 of *Old Mortality*, is actually by Thomas
Mordaunt.
[1] Robert Wodrow, *Analecta: or, Materials for a History of Remarkable Providences; Mostly Relating to
Scotch Ministers and Christians*, 4 vols (Edinburgh, 1842–3). RLS's copy is at Yale.

another world now; and I am afraid cannot be half sorry enough for your being ill. The mere triumph that you must feel at finding another human being so dependent on you for his happiness, will give an *élan* to your health and throw this little cold off, as one would throw a piece of gauze off the shoulders. I am utterly enslaved, and what would become of me without your letters? Well you know what; I told you in my last; I should pull through; I can pull through anything; I had partly pulled through already; and did not know I had been so continuously wretched, until the key of the maze arrived this morning; and I found myself once more really happy. I must get to work now.

11.30

I have been out, tonight, at dinner; and everything, except your seediness, has conspired to put me in a good humour. I had utterly forgotten these last few days what it was to be perfectly happy, to be at peace with one's own heart, to be free from the continual obsession of a carking, uneasy trouble. I would have you understand my dear friend, that I am now *in excelsis*, all black humours fled from me utterly, nothing left but a sunny content and acquiescence in all things. I did not know till last week that I was so dependent; but I was glad to learn at the same time that I was still strong; for strong I was; you saw the weakness and all the dark hours, but you could not see (even in what I honestly wrote) how I turned off these troubles, and was a good man and true, and did my utmost, all the time. I feel as if I had worlds to tell you; and yet nothing comes. You can see the best picture of how much depressed I was, where I tried to be at my ease and to write something that I thought would amuse you. There must be some pitiful bits of such a description in my long last letter. I was so pleased to gather, when I had fairly come to myself, that you were already better. That is a great thing for me, as for others. More than the health of all the residue of mankind could be. Good night. . . .[2] The word I wrote has a nasty secondary meaning and shall out. Be well.

Friday [*3 October*] *10* P.M.

Imagine that this is the first time for ten years that I have not been home until dinner was done. That will give you a better idea of how things go with us than anything else. I was as uneasy as a late schoolboy. Bob got very warm today that I should break and leave my parents. My health is certainly not so good as it might be, and he says I have grown a new wrinkle since I came back this summer. I can only tell you that he was in the humour of even violence, and said if I were to lose my health here my father should

[2] One word blotted out by RLS.

hear some language from him about his religion that he was not capable of thinking possible; and yet, even in this mood, I convinced him that the thing was impossible. I could not, just after they have given me a room for myself and my mother has taken so much interest in it, go off and leave them that same room empty, as a bitter reproach continually in their side, as a harsh proof that, after they had done all, they had not been able to keep their son. If I convinced Bob with these things, I may convince you. And then I shall be away for a day or two in the end of the month – a day or two in the sun.

Saturday [4 October]

I am so glad you have understood my letter. I was sure you would or I would never have sent it. It was of course possible to misunderstand; but I have such confidence in your sympathy with me, that I had no fear.

I have found that it was mere laziness on the part of the porter's servant that sent things wrong; but I have *crossed her loof* and so I hope this will not recur.

It is a little sharp today; but bright and sunny with a sparkle in the air, which is delightful after four days of unintermitting rain. In the streets I saw two men meet, after a long separation it was *plain*. They came forward with a little run and *leaped* at each other's hands. You never saw such bright eyes as they both had. It put one in a good humour to see it.

It was *Auntie*[3] who had heard of the fame of your feet, but how, I know not.

I am sorry to hear you are still on the sofa. That is not good. I do wish I were in London. I am better myself, I think, much better; and of course I have got into a little piece of calm which makes all the odds. *I* can't see any wrinkle or change; but Bob says he sees it, when I am talking about these miserable businesses, so I suppose I do make some sort of ugly mug or another. If you keep well, I will; that's a fair offer.

8 P.M.

I have had a pleasantish day. I made a little more out of my work than I have made for a long while back; though even now, I cannot make things fall into sentences – they only sprawl over the paper in bald, orphan clauses. Then I was about in the afternoon with Baxter (Degray); and we had a good deal of fun first rhyming on the names of all the shops we passed, and afterwards buying needles and quack drugs from open-air vendors and taking much pleasure in their inexhaustible eloquence. Every now and then as we went, Arthur's Seat showed its head at the end of a street. Now today

---

[3] I.e. Jane Whyte Balfour.

the blue sky and the sunshine were both entirely wintry; and there was about the hill, in these glimpses, a sort of thin, unreal, crystalline distinctness that I have not often seen excelled. As the sun began to go down over the valley between the new town and the old, the evening grew resplendent; all the gardens and low-lying buildings sank back and became almost invisible in a mist of wonderful sun, and the Castle stood up against the sky, as thin and sharp in outline as a castle cut out of paper. Baxter made a good remark about Princes Street, that it was the most elastic street for length that he knew; sometimes it looks, as it looked tonight, interminable, a way leading right into the heart of the red sundown; sometimes again, it shrinks together, as if for warmth, on one of the withering, clear, east-windy days, until it seems to lie underneath your feet.

I do hope you are better. The V. has finished his ministrations I suppose, so that one cannot felicitate you much upon tomorrow. I do feel wonderfully ashamed, when I read your letters; they are so full of *me*; mine are so impregnated with myself. However, a person can't help being selfish I suppose, and I won't act so any more than I can help.

Bob was very violent last night, for which I like him none the less, as you may believe.

I want to let you see these verses from an ode to the Cuckoo, written by one of the ministers of Leith in the middle of last century – the palmy days of Edinburgh – who was a friend of Hume and Adam Smith and the whole constellation. The authorship of these beautiful verses has been most truculently fought about; but whoever wrote them (and it seems as if this Logan had) they are lovely.[4]

> What time the pea puts on the bloom
> Thou fliest the vocal vale,
> An annual guest, in other lands
> Another spring to hail.
>
> Sweet bird! thy bower is ever green,
> Thy sky is ever clear;
> Thou hast no sorrow in thy song,
> No winter in thy year.
>
> O could I fly, I'd fly with thee!
> We'd make on joyful wing
> Our annual visit o'er the globe,
> Companions of the spring.

---

[4] The Revd John Logan (1748–88) who edited the poems of his friend Michael Bruce (1746–67) in 1770 claimed the 'Ode to the Cuckoo' as his own, but it has been attributed to Bruce. Burke thought it the most beautiful lyric in the language.

Sunday [*5 October*]

I have been at church with my mother; where we heard 'Arise, Shine' sung excellently well and my mother was so much upset with it that she nearly had to leave church.[5] This was the antidote, however, to fifty minutes of solid sermon, verra heavy. I have been sticking in to 'Walt Whitman'; nor do I think I have ever laboured so hard to attain so small a success. Still the thing is taking shape, I think; I know a little better what I want to say all through; and in process of time, possibly I shall manage to say it. I must say I am a very bad workman, *mais j'ai du courage*; I am indefatigable at re-writing and bettering and surely that humble quality should get me on a little.

I was almost sorry, almost angry with you for having written that last letter to me, when you were tired and so weak. Don't forget that it was not your silence, but your silence at a very curious time coupled with S.C.'s silence also at a curious time, that made the thing so hot for me. Mind and never weary yourself again to write to me.

8 P.M.

I wish you were by to give me advice, dear, for my father wishes me to write something for the papers and I don't quite know whether it would be harmful for the good old cause or no.

I have just been reading your letters over – the last three, I mean, my pocket contingent – and I feel ever so much better, and wish to pour out my thanks before you in grateful libation.

There has not been the stir of a leaf in the house since last Monday, but of course, last Monday is enough of matter for a lifetime. Nothing can efface what has been said already; nothing can put me back again where I once was. If no one else had any interest in it but myself, I would be out of this as fast as possible; only remember this that when I proposed last year the simple and plausible scheme of an English University, I was point-blank refused. I must be kept, don't you see, from persons of my own way of thinking – the same spirit that shut up Huguenot children in convents.

I wish I knew whether to write this for my father or no. I do feel the responsibility of launching some damnèd arrow that may glance aside, as something almost beyond what I can bear.

Bob has been, the few times I have been able to see him, a perfect God for me, all through my troubles; it is a very good thing to have a friend, my dear. And you know what I might go on to say.

---

[5] 'Lou and I at St George's forenoon. The music splendid. "Arise shine for thy light is come" [an aria from Handel's *Messiah*] was almost too much for me' (MIS, *Diary*).

Monday [*6 October*]

Rain again. This letter I have written for my father is the oddest piece of joint stock in the world. My father means it as a defence of Established churches, and I as an assault on all religions; so you may imagine what a trouble it was to write it. I managed very well, and he only made two alterations, both of which, however, compromise *my* meaning a good deal. You can conceive how awkward and bothering this is.[6]

I do hope you are better, and that the weather is more clement with you than it is here. I am I think all right again or very near it; not so well of course as I was when I came north, but that is not to be looked for; and besides black winter is on the road. The gardens are quite russet now, and here and there, even black. The roads begin to collect their permanent winter mire. It is a very early season. I must lay aside everything else and wade into my exam, or I shall infallibly be plucked.

Did you ever see, or dream of anyone who was so gauche at sealing letters. I burn my finger on almost every attempt. I do not know why it is that I am so distrait this morning. I wished to say a lot to you as this is post day but I can get nothing to come out. One reason is that I am as cold as ice. The fire had gone out and has only just been rekindled, and the sloping roof of my garret chills it wonderfully fast.

148   *To Charles Baxter*

MS Yale. Published in *Baxter Letters*, 25–6.

[*? October 1873*]   *17 Heriot Row*

Private

My dear Baxter, I wished to say a little word to you last night, and much of it I managed to say, yet left that unsaid that was made all the more important as I went forward. I wish you to understand that what I said to you is not to be judged exactly as other matters that go betwixt me and my

---

[6] Possibly the long letter signed 'A Hind Let Loose' in the *Edinburgh Courant* of 14 October 1873, headed 'Presbyterian Union on the Basis of Disestablishment'. This contains a favourite RLS quotation from Patrick Walker about 'right hand extremes and left hand defections'. It points out the possible dangers that would follow from the great power and wealth that would be enjoyed by the united Churches unchecked by the State: 'If we imagine this coalition, numbering eighty per cent of the nation, wholly independent of the State, and possessed of immense wealth . . . is it not plain that it would have the undisturbed possession of every hustings, every Town Council, and every School Board over the length and breadth of Scotland? And if such were the case, and the tradition of former Presbyterian ascendancy were followed up, what pleasure in life or freedom of conscience would be left for the other twenty per cent, I leave for the serious consideration of your readers.'

friends; and to ask you, as a very particular act of friendship, two things. (First) that you will not mention anything of what you have heard from me to *anyone* else and (second) that you will not recur to the matter unnecessarily with me.

Please, old man, do not misunderstand this note. You will know how serious I am when I tell you that I had little sleep last night, because I had omitted to add these two requests which I know you will very kindly grant. Indeed it is perhaps better that they should be made to you in writing. You need not answer this note, either by word or in writing. Believe me, Ever your friend (as I hope you to stand mine)   Robert Louis Stevenson

You know there are some things, old man, on which chaff is not quite on the spot. Let this little note of considerable pain on my part, be forever among the number of such things and pardon me for having written it.

R.L.S.

149   *To Frances Sitwell*

MS NLS. A brief excerpt published in *Letters*, I, 83–4, added to Letter 147.

Monday 6 October [*1873*]   [*17 Heriot Row*]

My dear, it is a magnificent glimmering moonlight night, with a wild, great west wind abroad, flapping above one like an immense banner and every now and again swooping furiously against my windows. The wind is too strong perhaps, and the trees are certainly too leafless for much of that wide rustle that we both remember; there is only a sharp angry sibilant hiss, like breath drawn with the strength of the elements, through shut teeth, that one hears between the gusts only. I am in excellent humour with myself for I have worked hard and not altogether fruitlessly; and I wished before I turned in just to tell you that things were so. My dear friend, I feel so happy all over when I think that you remember me kindly. Life is doubled for me. I have been up tonight lecturing to a friend on life and duties and what a man could do; a coal off the altar had been laid on my lips,[1] and I talked quite above my average and I hope I spread, what you would wish to see spread, into one person's heart; and with a new light upon it.

I shall tell you a story. Last Friday, I went down to Portobello, in the heavy rain, with an uneasy wind blowing *par rafales* off the sea (or '*en rafales*' should it be? or what?). As I got down near the beach a poor woman, oldish and seemingly lately, at least, respectable, followed me and made signs. She was drenched to the skin, and looked wretched below wretchedness. You

[1] Cf. Isaiah 6:6–7.

know I did not like to look back at her; it seemed as if she might misunderstand and be terribly hurt and slighted; so I stood at the end of the street – there was no one else within sight in the wet – and lifted up my hand very high with some money in it. I heard her steps draw heavily near behind me and, when she was near enough to see, I let the money fall in the mud and went off at my best walk without ever turning round. There is nothing in the story; and yet you will understand how much there is, if one chose to set it forth. You see, she was so ugly; and you know there is something terribly, miserably pathetic in a certain smile, a certain sodden aspect of invitation on such faces. It is so terrible, that it is in a way sacred; it means the outside of degradation and (what is worst of all in life) false position. I hope you understand me rightly.

Tuesday [7 October]

I wish just to salute you, my dearest friend. I have not done so much today, I am sorry to think; somehow work would not come through my hands. I have received a rather interesting letter from the Miss Crosby[2] I called on when I was staying with you; which I purpose sending along with this as it may interest you.

Tonight it has rained fearfully, and thundered. One peal came loud and sharp, like a single stroke upon some immense drum; it would have been a good piece of 'effect' for some scene in a novel. I do trust you are better, my dear. My heart is as full of you as it can be.

By the way, what a nice person Maud is; her letter to you made me think much per cent more of her even than I had thought before. Good Maud!

Dear if I could but put you up before the world – you don't know what I mean, because no woman could; but I know. I want to make you appear to everyone what you are – do you know? I cannot say it, but I feel it.

9.20

I have finished the first draught of 'Walt Whitman'! *Gloria in excelsis!*

Wednesday [8 October]

My mother took hysterics today at lunch – she had been bothered about some family troubles of which you have heard, and the advertisement of the marriage in today's Scotch papers finally knocked her up[3] – so my father has

---

[2] See Letter 117, n. 1 and Letter 150.
[3] *The Scotsman* of 8 October recorded the marriage at Galle, Ceylon of 'Mackintosh Balfour to Caroline Louisa, daughter of the late Colonel Sissmore, Bengal Army, and widow of the late Lewis Balfour.' Because of this marriage the Stevensons were estranged from Mackintosh and his wife, and were not reconciled until Mackintosh was on his deathbed. Marriage to a deceased brother's wife was forbidden by Church and State. Marriages usually took place abroad.

taken her away with him to Ireland, where he is called on business. I am alone in the house, and so I allowed myself, at dinner, the first light reading I have indulged in since my return in the shape of some Montaigne. And I *have* enjoyed it.

My little triumphant flourish of last night was sadly impertinent. I have looked over the said boasted first draught and it is so bad that I very nearly despaired ultimately. If I could only *write* like Colvin! I have lots to say. However I shall persevere. This 'first draught' let me mention means only the first stringing together of laborious fragments.

I have been all day in the house for I smashed my little toe against the leg of a table while I was *en costume de bain* this morning, and am as lame as Vulcan in consequence.

Do you know, I have been thinking a little of my wretchedness when your letters did not come; and the whole business is knocked most unpleasantly at my conscience. I too left letters unanswered until they ceased to come, from a person to whom the postage even must have been a matter of parsimony; left them unanswered, on purpose that they might cease. O God! a thing comes back to me that hurts the heart very much. For the first letter, she had bought a piece of paper with a sort of coarse flower-arabesque at the top of it. I wish you would write cruelly about this – I wish you would by God! I want something to make me take up arms in my own defence – no I don't. Only I could not help writing this to you because it is in my mind – or my heart; and I hope you won't hate me for it. Only one thing gives me any little pleasure, and it is a very, very faint one. I never showed the letters to anyone, and some months ago they became insupportable to me and I burnt them. Don't I deserve the gallows?

Thursday [*9 October*]

I found one of these letters that I had somehow missed in destroying them, and it has not helped to put me into a better humour with myself. If I were a remorseful person, I should be very useless and mournful, shut up here in the house alone, with a lame foot and the rain and cold. However I am not so; only by God, this is not to happen again. On that I think my mind is made up very resolvedly.

Last night, a friend dropped in about supper time and strangely enough he was in much the same humour as myself and full of regrets for past hard-heartedness, utter, stark inhumanity of the cheerful butterfly order, surely the most abhorrent thing in this shameful world. If there is a 'moral governor of the universe', he must feel heartily ashamed of having ever made me. My friend and I sat up till twelve and mutually confessed each other and strengthened our sense of shame I think much. Montaigne has been a tremendous comfort to me since my people have left; he is the most charming of table-companions. I have not yet heard from you that you are better; but I intend to believe that you are ever improving until I hear the contrary. There is no word of 'Roads'; I suspect the *S.R.* must have looked darkly upon it, in spite of all S.C.'s kind revision and correction. Amen – so be it; we must just try to do something better. 'Walt Whitman' in the meantime is in a pitiable bad way. The style sticks in my throat like badly made toffy.

I hope the V. does not bother you now you are ill. Believe me, my dear friend (and this comes, considering my present mood, from a very unimpeachable witness) you *must* be hard-hearted and firm and, at all prices, take your health out of the shadow of that incubus.

My own health, *à propos*, is I think almost re-established.

I have got your letter, and I do not care now about anything; I am all as full of happiness as I can hold – I feel a perfect ocean of it in my breast, sunlit and living. You know that isn't nonsense, although it looks like it. I have not got my breathing quiet yet, after reading it and so you must excuse what is written. Don't be afraid for me, what I say above is true. I think I am *quite* well again; though of course I am still a little played out.

I shall take your advice about my work, although one feels they can do so little for an exam. In this short time. I have been working about three hours a day for it. I shall try now to work more.

I am sorry to hear S.C. is not so well. I shall write to him soon.

After Dinner

You cannot think how pleasant it is for me to live alone here. I have learned the lost art of solitary life – that of not gulping one's meals and feel myself far on in the apprenticeship for a Hermitage.

A little while ago there was a very distant organ in the streets and, as organs are things rather more rare in Edinburgh than they are with you, the sound of an organ about dinner time when the evening has fallen, carries a great many reminiscences into the market-place of my memory from all sorts of odd corners where they had long lain hid. I sat a long while and brooded on dead and disaffected relatives, and my own childhood; and a whole decameron of little stories came back upon me. It would be impossible to bring before you, what went before me; you would not understand the little symbols that pass current in my memory, any more than I could understand the similar currency in yours. Broadly, however, you can understand that I lived a long while very far back, before people whom I really loved were estranged from me, and a long while before I came suddenly, in my thoughtless journey, upon a corner and, turning it, saw the sun. – There are little local sentiments, little abstruse connexions among things, that no one can ever impart. There is a pervading impression left of life in every place in one's memory, that one can best parallel out of things physical, by calling it a *perfume*. Well, this perfume of Edinburgh, of my early life there, and thoughts, and friends – went tonight suddenly to my head, at the mere roll of an organ three streets away. And it went off newly, to leave in my heart the strange impression of two pages of a letter I had received this afternoon, which had about them a colour, a perfume, a long thrill of sensation – which brought a rush of sunsets, and moonlight, and primroses, and a little fresh sentiment of springtime into my heart, that I shall not readily forget. It is by writing such letters to harassed people that one harmonises the universe in their ears; recalling beautiful things, and a beautiful spirit; lovely things, and love.

What I hear out of the utterances of a certain V. is not to me unfamiliar. The saying has been said to me so often, in all enthusiastic earnestness, that it has lost much of its significance for me. However, it is always respectable here; there, it should be repressed with stern contempt. There will be plenty of trouble there in the future; but the 'sweet, passionate, old idea' will triumph: I believe in the good cause; the good cause fought for by worthy Christ and (in some ways) unworthy Voltaire, and so many others. It shall not die; thrown even on the wayside it shall flourish and fructify.

Friday [*10 October*]

Last night, the fire was let out in my room, so I went down to Portobello, missed the last train and had to walk home, lame foot and all, between twelve and one. A violent west wind blew against me; the whole sky was lit up with the diffused glimmer of the moon, although the moon herself was invisible: the wide wet road returned this light after a fashion ghostly enough. About half-way, I found a man serenading a house by the roadside with a cornet – something almost incredible. He was sent away shortly, I suppose, for he was behind me all the rest of the way up to town and little snatches of music followed me at every lull in the wind. There was something uncanny about the whole walk; I was glad enough when I came near the outskirts and saw the double line of lamps come running out of the town to meet me, as it were servants with flambeaux. In the streets too there was this unpleasant pallid glimmer; it had a sort of resemblance to dawn – a still-born dawn – a dawn with something wrong with it.

I do feel inclined to suppress some sheets of this letter, but I won't. I don't want you to be the friend of any imaginary character, but the friend of R.L.S. So you had better know him for the brute he is.

Sunday [*12 October*]

I have destroyed some of this letter; but I want to preserve out of it, a quotation: –

> *Les yeux par la lune pâlis*
> *Me semblent pleins de violettes.*

To which, I had added: *Bien Sonnent.*

I expect to come to town about the twenty-fifth. The Exam is on the thirtieth, and I require to have made certain preliminary arrangements before the 28th. I shall be plucked, I am sure.

This is the day that is of all days most lovely in Edinburgh. It is raining pitilessly. There is no sound but the fire talking to itself, and the dull patter of the rain; and I have the sense of isolation, of intervals of space, very strongly upon me; this little room is an ark upon the illimitable deluge, or a star in the empty heavens; you know what I mean, don't you? These times make one feel a great hunger and yearning, and I know not what wonderful rehabilitation of the past. Large tracts of one's memory seem lit up with a sudden burst of sunshine. I have been living in Cockfield garden all morning; coming and going in the shrubberies; and leaning a long while over the gate. Every place is sacred; reminiscences gather about my feet like bramble-sprays: I feel if I were there, really, I should not know where to go first.

And this person of fine sentiments is the hero of what has been referred to already; I can't write any more when I think of that; everything sounds like a mockery. And yet, it *is* I: and that wasn't: be not afraid. I had not opened my eyes; but I have opened them now, and I see with blinding clearness. I hope you won't feel hatred for me; and yet I think you ought. I don't know if I can reconcile you again with yourself, if you do not hate me; I think I was a madman for telling you.

Do you see the strange way in which I regard anything I have written, as having reached you already? What I have written, I have written. I have an odd sort of reverence for it; and it requires very strong motives of prudence to make me lay sacrilegious hand (as I have done today already) upon any word.

3 P.M.

I have done my quantum of History; and have just stopped to make my first addition to Claire. I have added some few sentences out of this letter, making the meaning clearer of course and trying to better the loose expression one uses in *really* writing letters to dear friends[4] – those sentences about the organ recalling the 'perfume' of my past life here, and how the thought of your letter came in upon me so strongly.

I have determined to wait till I come to town and let Bert choose for himself.

[4] See Letter 145, n. 8.

What a curious impersonal thing writing a letter is. I don't know that it is so egotistical, after all, to be egotistical as I am, when I write to you. It really seems now to be quite the reverse: I say things about myself, out of a desire that you should hear them. As Montaigne says, talking of something quite different: *'Pour se laisser tomber à plomb, et de si haut, il faut que ce soit entre les bras d'une affection solide, vigoureuse et fortunée.'*[5] It argues a whole faith in the sympathy at the other end of the wire; and an awful want to say these things.

Monday [*13 October*]

I must tell you the bad news I heard last night. Our doctor thinks my father very far from well. You may imagine what this news is to me; and I cannot say it. I am very much better; quite well in health, only below *par* a little. Plainly, 'Roads' is refused, which is a sell: however I am going ultimately, when I am done with my Exam, to make something good out of 'Walt Whitman': I am not depressed about that.

Keep well, my dearest friend. That is the great thing after all. Let me think of you, as you said yourself, still ready to grasp at every corner of happiness, still your own beautiful self. And do not be sad about me: it is enough to know that you still live and have not forgotten me. Ever your faithful friend   R.L.S.

150   *To Elizabeth Crosby*

MS Yale.

7 October [*Postmark 1873*]   *17 Heriot Row*

My dear Miss Crosby, I find I have only this one small sheet of notepaper and so I must write small. It was very good of you to write again, and your letter did me good as any sound of activity must do, when one is surrounded with callous stagnation. The engineering drawing seems a good thing and would be another good opening for women I daresay. I shall ask about it.

I do not know whether you received my card, but I duly called for you at Portland Place and found the bird flown. Your letter telling me when you were to return was forwarded to London and reached me on the night before I had to start for the North; so you see we were at cross purposes. I shall be up in London sometime at the end of this month and I shall make a point of finding my way to see you.

---

[5] Montaigne, 'De la Physionomie': 'To let oneself fall plump down, and from so great a height, it ought to be in the arms of a solid, vigorous, and fortunate friendship' – Cotton's translation, revised by W.C. Hazlitt.

I am anxious that you should not misunderstand my morbid humours. I have just as much of my old capacity for enjoyment, and I am tenfold more industrious than I ever was before. But, you must know, my life is a very distressing one at home, so distressing that I have a great difficulty in keeping up a good heart at all or even in keeping my health together. For nearly a year back, I have lived in the most miserable contention with my parents on the subject of religion. I can do nothing myself, but hold my peace and try to steer away from dangerous subjects; but even with all this, the fires break out every now and again and I am driven to the most wretched state. To be continually told that you have utterly wrecked the lives of your father and mother, and to see that much of this is true – the wretched truth – is not, you must grant, a very favourable circumstance for cheerful thought. However I must, in Scotch phrase, dree my weird as best I can; and in the meanwhile I keep on working to the best of my power.

I made some kind friends, this year, in England: one of whom has some influence in literary circles – much influence, I should say; and he has shown himself very eager and generous in using it for me. However I do not yet know, whether I am strong enough for appearing before the public; so I just work on with one thing and another, and especially with my Covenanters (of whom you may possibly have heard some word in old days) and I hope to do some good work yet, before Heine's handful of earth is thrown into my mouth[1] and the 'studious lamp'[2] is finally put out.

It is very kind of you to have been so industrious in writing to one so unworthy; but I was always a most unregenerate correspondent; so you must not think the neglect – the silence, as of the grave – anything peculiar. I am afraid this note even, seems a little gloomy; but you must attribute that to the fact that I am very sleepy and cold, and that my shoulders ache badly after several hours of writing. Believe me, yours very truly

Louis Stevenson

11.20 P.M.

I mention the hour as a slight excuse for the shortcomings of mine epistle; for I have this qualification for being ultimately healthy, wealthy and wise, that I *go to bed* betimes.[3]

---

[1]
> *Also fragen wir beständig*
> *Bis man uns mit einer Handvoll*
> *Erde endlich stopft die Mäuler –*
> *Aber ist das eine Antwort?*

(So we constantly ask questions, until someone finally stops up our mouths with a handful of earth – but is that an answer?) – Heine, *Gedichte 1853 und 1854*, VIII '*Zum Lazarus*', 1.

[2] Milton, *Areopagitica*.

[3] *Twelfth Night*, II. iii.9, plus the proverbial saying incorporated in a nursery rhyme.

151   To Frances Sitwell

MS NLS. Excerpts published in *Letters*, I, 84–6.

Tuesday 14 October [1873]   *[17 Heriot Row]*

My father has returned in better health and I am more delighted than I can well tell you. The one trouble that I can see no way through is that his health, or my mother's, should give way. Blessedly, this seems at least delayed; although the eternal hopelessness of the position is ever more and more present with me day by day.

Tonight, as I was walking along Princes Street, I heard the bugles sound the recall. I do not think I had ever remarked it before: there is something of unspeakable appeal in the cadence. I felt as if something yearningly cried to me, out of the darkness overhead, to come thither and find rest; one felt as if there must be warm hearts and bright fires waiting for one up there, where the buglers stood on the damp pavement and sounded their friendly invitation forth into the night. And I was feeling at the time so lonely and sad – culpably enough dear friend, with a letter warm in my pocket and the hope of going south so soon to where my summer dwells. However, it is hard to keep up one's heart with all this trouble weighing on one at every moment. Consolation is so vain, although it is none the less pleasant; and the best of it, after all, is the mere strong statement of sympathy, the sense that some one else knows and thrills with one in their sorrows, as I know yours and many a time thrill painfully to think that they should so be. I feel often as if I could take the pillars of our sick world and, with one great heave, pull the whole ponderous building over my head – willingly, a martyr. But this is no age for these blind, easy-hearted heroisms. One must nowadays be wary and considerate over all; there are fathers and mothers under this hideous roof and our heart-strings have been built into the walls and buttresses of the infamous temple. The business is carefully to extricate these involved sentiments – tenderly to lead forth into sunshine and the open air these misled imprisoned loved ones. And I – who cannot – must just settle down into the dyspeptic, mooning, useless brute that is growing gradually here in the north into the usurped personality of Louis Stevenson; against which growth, I must honourably struggle, with your good help.

Wednesday [15 October]

I have to apologise for the gloomy spirit in which I write; I hope however that it will go off. I feel so ashamed of myself whenever I get a letter; but it returns always and always. I may as well tell you exactly about my health. I am not at all ill, have quite recovered; only I am what *M.M. les médecins* call below par; which in plain English is that I am weak. With tonics, decent weather and a little cheerfulness that will go away in its turn and I shall be all right again.

I was down at Portobello tonight on my weekly visit, which puts me always into better heart. However, I could not help grudging when I saw Bob sitting quietly in the drawing room with his mother and sisters, reading Mill's *Logic*. I find it necessary to turn out at night after I have been working all day; for I am then a little fractious and peevish and if I stayed in, there would only be grief. I am so glad to think you like to read my 'thick letter'. It gives me such pleasure to write it. Also, my dear friend, I am glad to hear what you say about the Exam; until quite lately I have treated that pretty cavalierly; for I say honestly that I do not mind being plucked; I shall just have to go up again; I have now, you see, no fear of interference. We travelled with the Lord Advocate[1] the other day and he strongly advised me in my father's hearing to go to the English Bar; and the Lord Advocate's advice goes a long way in Scotland. It is a sort of special legal revelation. Don't misunderstand me. I don't of course want to be plucked; but so far as my style of knowledge suits them I cannot make much betterment on it in a month. If they wish scholarship more exact, I must take a new lease altogether.

Have I – yes, I have told you that my father is well again. I can tell you now another matter, which I can only explain when I see you, that the fire in my room will be most probably suppressed. This is no one's blame; only it is a devil of a nuisance – indeed I can hardly overrate the hindrance it will be to me, putting me back precisely where I was before and nullifying the whole advantage of my room.

When I am to come down I do not know. I wish four or at the very least three days in London before the 30th, and yet Saturday being the 25th, I don't quite know how it is to be managed. If I were quite strong I should come down on Sunday night; but I am afraid I should only be fit for bed for a week after if I did so. Perhaps the simplest way would be to come down on Saturday and go to a hotel until you thought it the right time to receive me; for I do not quite see my way to saddling your household with this Scottish incubus for so long a time. The twenty-second letter of the alphabet (is that right?) must be considered. Let me know please in a letter to 17 Heriot Row, what your views are as to these matters.

My dear, you should not have a cough at all. I hope to hear no sound of that, when I come there. You know you must be well; or you leave me without the best of my strength for anything.

I am so glad that you have taken my last in such good part. I have learned my lesson; so you need not fear to diminish my sentiment in the matter. It

[1] George Young (1819–1907), Scottish judge, Lord Advocate 1869–74; Judge of the Court of Session with title of Lord Young 1874–1905.

is a horrid thing to look back upon; but it is, I think, one of those things on which one should *not* look back.

Thursday [16 October]

My head and eyes both gave in this morning and I had to take a day of complete idleness. I was in the open air all day, and did no thought that I could avoid, and I think I have got my head between my shoulders again: however, I am not going to do much. Nothing but work and botheration is not good for this mortal brain. You must excuse this short note; but I wish to write to Colvin and I have a short note from another that I must answer as it contains an invitation and much good will; and I am afraid to write much tonight, lest I should not be quite fit for work tomorrow.

Later

I don't want you to run away with any fancy about my being ill. Given a person weak and in some trouble, and working longer hours than he is used to, and you have the matter in a nutshell. You should have seen the sunshine on the hill today; it has lost now that crystalline clearness, as if the medium were spring water (you see I am stupid!)[2]; but it retains that wonderful thinness of outline that makes the delicate shape and hue savour better in one's mouth, like fine wine out of a finely-blown glass. The birds are all silent now but the crows. I sat a long time on the stairs that lead down to Duddingston Loch – a place as busy as a great town during frost, but now solitary and silent; and when I shut my eyes I heard nothing but the wind in the trees; and you know all that went through me, I daresay, without my saying it.

11

I want just to say good night to you. I don't know why. My easy constitution has settled the matter for me, by turning it into mild tic; all the muscles over my head are painful, but my eyes and brain are quite relieved;[3] so that I see daylight before me only a very little way. Good night, dear.

Friday [17 October]

I was right in what I prognosticated. I had a night of tic – not very bad; and I am now all right in the head; only tired and *sublimely stupid*. I am going out to lounge and sit on seats and go on tramway cars, for another day's

---

[2] RLS wrote 'like spring water', then deleted 'like' and wrote 'as if the medium were' above it.
[3] MIS records that RLS had severe attacks of neuralgia during this week and was kept awake at night.

idleness, and hope to get to work again tomorrow, a little more carefully than before however.

11

I am now all right, my dear friend; I do not expect any tic tonight and shall be at work again tomorrow. I have had a day of open air; only a little modified by *Le Capitaine Fracasse*[4] before the dining room fire. It is a jolly book; quite untrue and a libel upon God's earth and the ways of the men thereupon; but amply redeeming all its untruthfulness by a degree of the picturesque, by a succession of splendid miniatures, that are as pleasant as true art, although they are miles away from it. This is not sculpture; it can be compared to the gargoyles and wall-carvings of a gothic church. It has the same talent as *Émaux et Camées* and no other. It is not a novel but a series of vigorous and grotesque coloured etchings. I must write no more for I am sleepy after two nights – to quote my book – '*sinon blanches, du moins grises*'; and so I must go to bed and faithfully, hoggishly slumber.

Saturday [*18 October*]

The Saturday R. has resumed its place in my esteem. It has declined 'Roads' – abhorrent and abominable *Saturday*.

I have slept well however and am in better form this morning physically; and so even this fearful instance of the depravity of my native land has not had much influence for worse upon me. I feel able to write a few more words consecutively and indeed I have something to tell you. What still remained to be fulfilled out of Claire, looks very like fulfilment. Bob is coming down with me next Saturday, on his way to Antwerp. So that when I return in November, I shall be in the position of the original fellow. I can't write; but that's all right. I am glad we are going so far together; it would have been horrid just to have seen him off from the station here and gone back alone; so that is one matter to be glad of. Outside, the sun is shining and I am going I think to take a third day of idleness; which is another matter to be glad of. Moreover, I *may* find a letter from you in the Spec., as such things have occurred on the Saturday; and this chance is a third thing to be glad of. For all these thy mercies, O Lord, make us truly thankful.

Going to Bed

I am simply incapable of cohabiting any house with my father. He *would* ring in the Jews on me this evening, and I could not help fighting a little bit in what I thought the cause of truth in all schemes. The person who is

---

[4] Theophile Gautier's novel (1863); *Émaux et Camées* (1853) is a volume of poetry by the same author.

staying with us[5] after having launched at me a certain orthodox reproof (not that I dared to be in any way unorthodox, except implicitly as against the theory of the narrowly miraculous) retired to bed; and I had to sit up, with my father. I tried every wile that I have to thaw him, but he responded only in gruff monosyllables. At last he got up to go to bed. I could not let him go in such a mood, so I asked his pardon and said that I was afraid I had spoken hotly. He said I should know these were subjects on which he felt deeply and that I did nothing to save his feelings; whereupon, with the sublime theatricality of the Stevenson family (O we mean it, when we do it − don't mistake) I kissed his hand and became ruefully tearful. This is a case of a very quiet dissonance; but of course it is not nice; and I am afraid I was rather inconsiderate. Only it is difficult to hold your tongue when people speak at you for ten minutes on end. I daresay my father wishes the Chinese had never existed!

This little unpleasantness has put me somewhat off what I had meant beforehand to tell; about the admirable movements of a boat that I saw 'taking' Leith pier today in a capful of wind and a little seaway; and about how I had gone today to Portobello for the last time on any Saturday and had walked with Bob through a lot of our old ways, for the last time also perhaps. However it is perhaps as well that my humour of writing should run dry just here. I am growing so shamefaced about myself. I had thought myself so brave, and yet, my dear, I find myself so feeble. I was feeble about those letters; I am not feeble, but prostrate, about the future here at home; and I feel a little feeble about Bob's going away. However, you must put a better heart in me when I come south and send me up here again for the long lonely winter full of courage; and that, the sight of you will do amply. I have always known that it was matters with 'fellow creatures' that put me out; for example, I don't mind a bit about 'Roads', except that I wanted the money and had a certain carnal eagerness to see myself in print. A whole universe of 'Roads' could not compromise my serenity; but it is the *devil* when there are other people in the bargain. I must go to bed; good night, my dearest friend, and forget all about your troubles for a little time and, if I thought it worth the breath, I would pray that you might have such beautiful dreams that you would be disappointed to awaken, and that the sun looking into your room and a great stir of hopes and recollections at your heart, might repay you ten-fold for the dreamland you have left.

Sunday [*19 October*]

It is hard to believe that it is not two months yet since I left London; it seems two long ugly years. Cockfield was in a former state of existence. The

---

[5] James and Mary Greig and their baby were staying at Heriot Row.

proud waters have gone over my soul[6] most infernally in the meantime. But I see the shore very near me now – the shore of a small island only and the 'unplumbed, salt, estranging sea'[7] on the other side of it; but I am anxious now to reach it and rest a moment. I wish to get to the end of a stage; and now like the traveller who sees the lit windows along the road, I begin to run and cry Victory. O it makes me feel glad! Surely we shall have much to say to each other.

5

I have had a somewhat curious adventure this afternoon, trying to protect a poor crazy preacher in the Queen's Park from a posse of rude boys and brutal old men. I must wait to tell you about the old man's curious fancies and style, until I can speak with you. Much that he said was real Christianity; as once, 'If any of you has something that anybody else is in want of, and does not share it with him, he is a vile robber'; a proposition that was greeted, in this Christian country, with shouts of derision. After getting a good deal of insult myself, I lost heart and went away, leaving him still thundering on in the midst of his jeering audience.

I shall have a case of conscience to put to you, my dear, when I come south, about my conduct at home.

Monday [20 October]

To recapitulate. I shall arrive on Saturday night. Please write soon if you would like me to stay with you; and if so, name the day for that. Good morning to you. Be happy, Claire. Ever your faithful friend

Louis Stevenson

The above is the whole letter; the rest is maundering principally.

152   *To Sidney Colvin*

MS Yale.

[16 October 1873]   *17 Heriot Row*

My dear Colvin, I am sorry to say that I have a little overworked myself; and in the midst of a continual botheration about my father and mother, my brain is a little easier set off its balance than otherwise it would be. So you must just excuse a very dry note; coming, as is usual from me with a begging

---

[6] Cf. Psalm 124:5.
[7] Matthew Arnold, 'To Marguerite', l. 24.

petition on its brazen forehead. You must please grow used to me in the character of the long remembered beggar, which is so suitable to my circumstances and perhaps my humour.

I find I need the concurrence of two barristers to my petition before I am even allowed to be plucked; there seems a coquetry almost loathsome in thus chaffering with a poor devil on the brink of the oubliette. But so it is. This petition, or whatever it is called, must be lodged upon the 28th at latest. So that you can be of the utmost service to me, if you can find two barristers (with straw in their shoes, in the old fashion) who will be ready on Monday the 27th to certify that I am a gentleman of respect: ability and a proper person etc. Do you think you can manage this? I am ashamed to be every day so beholden to you; but your facility breeds a certain confidence that should be suppressed at once and with every circumstance of brutality whenever it trespasses beyond what becomes.

I shall have something to say to you about McLennan when I see you in London; but both head and eyes are already rebellious at so long a stretch. Sincerely yours   Louis Stevenson

153   To Sidney Colvin

Text: *Letters*, I, 86.

Wednesday [*22 October 1873*][1]   [Portobello]

My dear Colvin, Of course I knew as well as you that I was merely running before an illness; but I thought I should be in time to escape. However I was knocked over on Monday night with a bad sore throat, fever, rheumatism and a threatening of pleurisy, which last is, I think, gone.[2] I still hope to be able to get away early next week, though I am not very clear as to how I shall manage the journey. If I don't get away on Wednesday at latest, I lose my excuse for going at all, and I do wish to escape a little while.

I shall see about the form when I get home, which I hope will be tomorrow (I was taken ill in a friend's house and have not yet been moved).

How could a broken-down engineer expect to make anything of 'Roads'? *Requiescant*. When we get well (and if we get well), we shall do something better. Yours sincerely   R.L. Stevenson

Ye couche of pain.

[1] Misdated 15 October by Colvin.
[2] MIS records that on Monday 20 October RLS went to a musical party at Portobello and stayed the night at Bob's home. He was taken ill and had to remain there until he was well enough to be brought home on the Thursday afternoon.

154   To Sidney Colvin

MS Yale. Partly published in *Letters*, I, 87.

Thursday [23 October 1873][1]   *17 Heriot Row*

My dear Colvin, I am at my wits'-end about this abominable form of admission. I don't know what the devil it is; I haven't got one, even if I did, and so can't sign.

Monday night is the very earliest on which (even if I go on mending at the very great pace I have *made* already) I can hope to be in London myself. But possibly it is only *intimation* that requires to be made on Tuesday morning: and one may possess oneself of a *form of admission* up to the eleventh hour. I send herewith, a letter which I must ask you to cherish as I count it a sort of talisman. Perhaps you may understand it. I don't.

If you don't understand it, please do not trouble and we must just hope that Tuesday morning will be early enough to do all, as I really think it may. Of course, I fear the exam will spin me; indeed after this bodily and spiritual crisis, I should not dream of coming up at all; only that I require it as a pretext for a moment's escape, which I want much. It is now almost worse for me than before, although I can banish it. I have almost no more rows; but at the cost of keeping up a continual, cold distance, that is very unlovely and unpleasant.

I am so glad (to shut the door on the skeleton) that 'Roads' has got in.[2] I had almost as soon have it in the *Portfolio*, as the *Saturday*; the *P.* is so nicely printed and I am *gourmet* in type. I don't know how to thank you for your continual kindness to me; and I am afraid I do not even *feel* grateful enough – you have let your kindnesses come on me so easily.

If you should understand more of Milton's letter than I have done, you will know whether anything can be done or no, but please do not trouble. I hope this note is legible; for I am a little tired. Yours sincerely

Louis Stevenson

May the question of signature stand over till I see *you*?   L.S.

155   To Frances Sitwell

Text: excerpt in AAA Catalogue, 15 January 1926 (720).

Thursday [? 23 October 1873]   *[Edinburgh]*

I am home again; but a little tired and so averse from much writing. Only I wanted to tell you that I was now quite recovered. My throat almost well:

---

[1] Colvin misdates this letter 16 October.
[2] 'Roads' was published under the pseudonym 'L.S. Stoneven' in the November number of the *Portfolio*.

my strength returned to a very large extent, – and that I look little worse, and feel rather better, than I did before I broke down . . . I hope my letter of yesterday did not frighten you; but I did not anticipate so speedy a recovery and there is nothing more unkind than 'Peace Peace where there is no Peace'[1] . . .

[1] Jeremiah 6:14.

V. ORDERED SOUTH: MENTONE
October 1873–April 1874

As we have seen, Stevenson had been considering the possibility of being called to the English Bar and had planned to travel down to London at the end of October 1873 to take the preliminary examination in order to enter one of the Inns of Court.

His mother's diary shows that he left for London without telling his parents. On Friday 24 October she recorded: 'Lou thinks he wants a change and sets off for Carlisle.' On the 28th she wrote: 'Hear that Lou went all the way to London Saturday which I know was too long a journey.'

After that events moved swiftly. Colvin and Mrs Sitwell were worried by Stevenson's ill-health and in particular by the nervous exhaustion largely brought about by the bitter disagreements with his father. At their prompting on 28 October he saw Dr Andrew Clark[1] who forbade him to return home. The next day, in a written opinion, Clark recommended that he should go to Mentone. As soon as they heard the news the Stevensons came to London to consult Clark themselves. They saw him on 4 November, after waiting for three hours, in the course of which Mrs Stevenson nearly fainted. He was quite firm that RLS should go to the South of France, and equally firm that his mother should not accompany him. In her *Diary Notes* written twenty years later (in amplification of her diary) Mrs Stevenson recorded:

> He [Clark] tells us that Lou's nervous system has quite broken down, that his lungs are delicate and just in the state when disease might very easily set in. When I ask if I ought to go with him he said: 'No, he wants a complete change of everything, scene, diet and companionship; strangers will be much more likely to bring him out of himself than if you were with him.'

The next day RLS was on his way to Dover, *en route* for Mentone. His essay 'Ordered South' (published in *Macmillan's Magazine*, May 1874) describes his feelings at this time. It is (as Colvin points out) 'the only one of his writings in which he took the invalid point of view or allowed his health troubles in any degree to colour his work.'

Mentone had become part of France as recently as 1860. Like many of

---

[1] Andrew Clark (1826–93) was a fashionable London physician who specialised in the treatment of lung diseases; President of the Royal College of Physicians 1888; created a baronet 1883.

his contemporaries, RLS usually spelled it in the Italian manner as Mentone but sometimes he used the more correct spelling of Menton. I have followed Colvin in standardizing the spelling as Mentone.

156   To his Mother

MS Yale.

[*28 October 1873*][1]   *15 Chepstow Place [London]*

My dear Mother, Have been to see Dr Andrew Clark, who has peremptorily forbidden me to go up for the Exam and put me on a diet. Colvin and Mrs Sitwell both wanted me to go and consult the great man and I still felt so seedy and weak that I was nothing loath. He forbids me in the meantime to go north again. I shall be able to send you his written opinion tomorrow or next day. He has looked me thoroughly all over and says there is nothing organically wrong; only that I am (what of course I knew I was as well as he) very much landed.

The weather here is fairly warm and I have been driving about in a hansom 'disregardless of expents';[2] I have also gotten me mine own birthday present – a Landor – price £1. So that you stand absolved.

I suppose the Greigs are gone, and with them the obese and silent offspring.[3] I think it was just as well that I got away on Friday; it is my opinion that I should have been ill again, had I not made that rapid diversion on Carlisle.

It's a bore about the exam, but *Dieu dispose.*

How is M'sieur? Ever your affectionate son   R.L. Stevenson

157   To Charles Baxter

MS Yale. Published in *Baxter Letters*, 26–7.

[*? 28 October 1873*]   *15 Chepstow Place, Bayswater, London*

My dear Charles, Your kindness put me in rather an odd little difficulty on Saturday morning. Please send the letters to this address – the first word is 'Chepstow', in case you can't read it – in a large envelope. My paper will appear in the *Portfolio* for December; where you may look for it.

[1] MIS noted receipt on 29 October.
[2] A phrase from Artemus Ward, 'Cruise of the Polly Ann'.
[3] This sentence was deleted by MIS but is still decipherable.

I am really very far from well; and so you must pardon me for writing very briefly. My head swims so devilishly I can hardly see to write. I have been to see a swell London doctor, who thinks I shall pull round, on a diet etc.

The Lord help you in that damned town, whose name even makes me shudder!

Years hence I think I shall be able to tell you something that will make you respect me, although that sentiment sounds somewhat burlesque in connexion with, Ever your friend   R. Louis Stevenson

This is the skeleton of what I would write to you if my head were stronger.

158   To his Parents

MS Yale.

Wednesday 29 October 1873   *15 Chepstow Place*

My dear Father and Mother, I am afraid this letter will surprise you a little but I have to let you know what Dr Clark's opinion is. In the first place, let me repeat that he says I have no disease, nothing organically wrong whatever. In the second place, keep steadily in view that he expects me to recover fast and thoroughly. But in order to [hasten] this recovery, he wishes me to go at once to the Riviera for a little while. He says I shall fall ill if I stay in the North; but his diet, in a more decent climate, he thinks will make me well again quite speedily.

Mrs Sitwell knows a clergyman's family at Mentone already whom she thinks I should like to know. Colvin also, so soon as he shall have finished his lectures at Cambridge, will be going to the continent for his own health and has promised to join me if I am there. So you see I should not want for companions.

I am sorry to think of putting you to this expense, and indeed I do not know whether you can afford it or no. The doctor seemed very decided that I ought to go and said his orders were 'perèmptory'.

Mrs Sitwell is very tyrannical with me and keeps me to the prescribed diet. In the meantime, she will not let me go away; so that you can continue to write here.

Please write soon and tell me. Ever your affectionate son

R.L. Stevenson[1]

---

[1] As soon as they received this letter, on 30 October, his parents arranged (as MIS noted in her diary) to 'go to London to make enquiries.' RLS's letter was evidently accompanied by a letter from Mrs

159   To his Mother

MS Yale.

Thursday [30 October 1873]   *Chepstow Place*

My dear Mother, The telegram *ne s'explique pas beaucoup*. If you mean that I am to do what Clark tells me, I want the following articles of virtu.

1. A velveteen waistcoat.
2. My thin summer coat.
3. Knox's works V vols.
4. McCrie's Life of Same II vols.[1]
5. The papers and books in the two upper shelves of division C of my library do you understand,[2] which I should like moved *without examination.* *
6. Sandars' *Justinian.*[3]

If I am not to go, I suppose I don't want anything. I thought I was quite recovered, but I got a little bad again this forenoon; so I suppose I am a little weak still.

I shall find rooms in some hotel tomorrow. Both Mrs Sitwell and the Vicar profess themselves sorry at the prospect of my leaving; although I have been a somewhat burthensome inmate, owing to diet and bosh.

If all these things come I fear they will be too much for my portmanteau. Oh!

7. Dress boots.
8. More day shirts.

I feel wonderfully cheery in spite of the doctor; so rejoice muchly at that. Ever your affectionate son   R.L. Stevenson

My father must learn Chepstow *Place*. Every letter goes wandering about and comes back with all sorts of lamentations on the outside. 'No such terrace. No Stevenson. Try Chepstow Place.'   L. S.

* *On craignez* what Monsieur would call '*le Poli.*'

Sitwell. MIS wrote to her on 30 October telling her of the planned visit and thanking her for her 'kind note and all your goodness to my boy. I can assure you it has been a great comfort to me to know that he was among kind friends and well cared for, particularly just now when I know he is not strong.' On arrival in London on Saturday 1 November the Stevensons were met at the Paddington Hotel by Colvin who took them to Chepstow Place for a brief meeting with RLS.

[1] Thomas McCrie (1772–1835) – 'the learned and unreadable McCrie' RLS calls him in his preface to *Familiar Studies* – published his *Life of John Knox* in 1812.

[2] A rough sketch of the position of the bookshelves.

[3] *The Institutes of Justinian* edited and translated by Thomas Collett Sandars, 4th edition 1869. RLS's copy is at Yale.

160   *To Charles Baxter*

MS Yale. Published in *Baxter Letters*, 30.

[*? 4 November 1873*][1]   [*? London*]

My dear Charles, *Le grand moment est arrivé. Ce soir, avant que je me couche, je saurai ce que j'ai encore d'espoir. Je me sens au bord du gouffre. Un indicible vertige m'engourdisse toutes les facultés. Une heure – et je serai je ne sais où.* It is my final cast, old man, for happiness in this unhappy world.

And yet I have strength enough to say that I have received your notice and to bid you, O perfidious man, tremble upon your tottering throne.

5.45 – Spec. Rooms. And I dine at six! O what a low and detestable proceeding.

Good-bye. Yours, on the red hot tenterhooks,   R.L.S.

161   *To Frances Sitwell*

MS NLS. Partly published in *Letters*, I, 88.

[*4 November 1873*]   [*London*]
3.30

My dearest friend, Clark is a trump. He said I must go abroad and that I was better alone – 'Mothers' he said, 'just put fancies into people's heads and make them fancy themselves worse than they are.' My mother (with some justice) denied this soft impeachment. However they are evidently bent on my return in six weeks at longest; I hope they may find resignation for methinks I shall manage to disappoint them. All seems to go well; they are rather, I think, pleased than the reverse with what they have heard (I have only seen my mother) and the admirable placidity of their mind does not seem to be at all perturbed. I had a slight spar with my mother this afternoon about my movements tomorrow. She said 'You shall not have everything your own way, I can tell you.' I said 'I don't expect it, but surely I may please myself as to where I am to sleep.' She caved incontinently in and asked it as a favour; wherefore I facilely gave way and promised.

8.30

Your note is come. Thanks. I go tomorrow to Dover. Thursday night I shall be in Paris. Friday Sens. Saturday Macon. Sunday Avignon. I should

---

[1] Both the place and date are conjectural. The letter may have been written on 4 November while RLS was waiting to learn the outcome of his parents' interview with Dr Clark about the journey to the South of France. It was also the date for the first meeting of the new session of the Speculative Society.

like a little note at Avignon, my dear friend. How difficult it is to write on paper that has been folded already! By the way, the whole scheme came out during dinner. I was to have been despatched to Torquay with my mother; Clark disposed of all that at one breath; they think no end of Clark.

Do keep well and be strong and jolly; and let me hear that you are blooming in spite of the World, the Flesh, and the Vicar. I am as jolly as two and have had no return of my homesickness (for what home, you know!) I do look forward to the sun and I go with a great store of contentment – bah! what a mean word! – of living happiness that I can scarce keep bottled down, in my weather-beaten body. Do be happy. Ever your faithful friend

R.L.S.

I like the enclosed. Hugo is a gentleman, isn't he.   L.

162   To Charles Baxter

MS Yale. Published in *Baxter Letters*, 29–30.

[Postmark 4 November 1873]   *[London]*

My dear Baxter, Please redeem my *Democratic Vistas* by W. Whitman from Wilson, Tobacconist, in Leith Street. Miss Mason has charge of it – not old W. himself; so please explain to her my movements and how my health it is all ruinèd and I'm a-goin' south.

In a little while I think you will receive my *Leaves of Grass* also, when you will be decent and cheery enough to do them both up discreetly into a parcel and forward them to the address that I shall have sent you before then.

Let Simpson etc. know of my movements. I think my last blow was that Sunday night. I never got properly well again. My parents utterly puzzle me; I have sometimes a notion that the atheist son is almost in the way. My head is about done for so good-bye old man. Poste Restante, Mentone, is my next address.

R.L.S.

163   To Frances Sitwell

MS NLS. Published (with a few omissions) in *Letters*, I, 89–91.

5 November [1873]   *Dover*

My dear friend, I came down today in company with a man who regaled me with the chronicle of accidents that had befallen him – he had broken in his time seven ribs, a collar bone, a leg and an arm, and seemed not one penny the worse. The country was very lovely; one grand spread of russet and green; and to the Medway, which accompanied us for a little way, I quite lost my heart. Tonight it blows most lamentably, and the noise of both wind and sea dins in my ears. I fear I shall not have a pleasant crossing.

My father was much delighted with you, as I knew of course he would be; but you and S.C. have so lamentably overdone your solemnity that you have given rise to an entirely new theory of my illness. I have been in 'the very worst possible hands'; my illness is almost entirely owing to your society; and so forth. Are they not perplexing persons to deal with?

This is the first day I have not seen you for ten days – 'a faggot's blaze' – but I am still warm and shall keep warm too, although I am now (to use Pan's[1] pathetic phrase) 'out in the night.'

I have an article in my head which I think might do for the *Portfolio*. You see you always inspire me.

6 November   *Paris*

We had a very bad passage; there was weeping and wailing and gnashing of teeth all round me, the table in the centre of the cabin was overset and an avalanche of bags, camp-stools, coats etc., was sent down to leeward, one heavy lurch, to the great discomfiture of many. I was not sick; wherefore I rejoiced greatly. I am very tired or I should have a great deal to say to you, dear. As it is I must just say what I *would* have said. I would have said a lot about the *smell* of foreign towns; which you will be able to supply; and a lot also, about effects of poplars which seem to me sometimes quite perfect. Especially rivers winding hither and thither in a discreet, diplomatic way and always between poplar colonnades. There were two English ladies in the carriage with me going to Italy under the guidance of a man; all three, stolid, obtuse and unemotional. It did make me angry to think that a third of the money that will be spent in hawking these dull creatures through all that is sunny and beautiful would suffice to take you, with all your eager sensibilities and quick nerves. Do you know, I feel as if it were so selfish in me to go and leave you at home there in foggy London; and of course, it's a very foolish feeling with no practical bearing upon anything in the world and so had better be dismissed.

It is not nine yet and I am overcome with sleep. Tonight I arrived tired in a great city after nightfall; and I did the same on the Saturday before last; only how different were the two arrivals! Tonight I was going a stranger among strangers; and on Saturday I was coming home.

I went out and dined at a café and then smoked a pipe up and down the streets, it was cold a little but I could not resist the lights and the pleasant

---

[1] A guess at an illegible word. 'Pan' was a familiar name for Bertie Sitwell (cf. Letters 336 and 341). The word could be 'Jim', but this makes no better sense.

sound of the new language in my ears. MacMahon's address[2] is pasted up everywhere and political pictures fill the windows.

7th [November]

I sleep ten and lie in bed twelve hours consistently. I have had breakfast and have just crawled upstairs to get a rest. My room is on the sixth floor; although they make it out to be the fourth only by dint of calling one the entresol and not calling another anything at all.

Three things I am very anxious to learn: first, the Vicar's little game; second, the particulars of your interview with my father; third ('and it never can be mine') *Clark's* version of my parents and their views on everything.

I just stop to remark upon French dogs, which seem to me more French considerably than the French people. They are charmingly national. I saw two today reading MacMahon's message, or pretending to read it, with patriotic concern.

I am half in doubt whether I shall go on today or not; but I shall if I am able. Paris is cold, and wearies me a little besides. And then I do wish to get settled and have my books and papers all about me once more and be able to write to you in comfort instead of shivering up here among the sparrows. I am very like a sparrow on the housetop by the bye; by a peculiar disposition of the neighbouring roofs, the idea that one is in the open air is almost irresistibly forced upon one in this numero dix-ter, and there is nothing in the temperature to belie it.

I am growing gradually more rested while I gossip with you. I wish to go to the Poste Restante, just in *case*, and thence to some good booksellers to inquire about a lot of books on the French Calvinists which are necessary to my little Covenanting game. It amuses me hugely to go on writing thus. I have sent exactly three lines to my parents dear; so your letter is not so short by comparison, is it? That is a whisper in your ear. I wish it were physically. If I only were not tired I would write such lots; but my spine is beginning to crawl, so good-bye.   R.L. Stevenson

164   *To his Mother*

Text: AAA Catalogue, 8 May 1928 (556).

[*6 November 1873*]   [*Paris*]

In Paris all right. Bad passage. I was not sick, but I am very tired and am going to bed incontinently. 8.30.   R.L.S.

---

[2] Marshal MacMahon (1803–93) second President of the Third Republic (1873–79). A message from him was read at the opening of the Assembly on 5 November seeking a prolongation of the President's power in the interests of peace and stable government.

165   To Frances Sitwell

Text: Colvin's Galleys, Silverado.

6 [7] November 1873[1]   *Hotel de Paris, Sens*

I am delighted. I have been wickedly wandering about this charming town by moonlight. The cathedral dominates everything; and I saw, I think, one of the most curious moonlight effects that I have ever seen – a whole carved front lit by a sidelong glimpse so that only one side of the reliefs was whitened and the gargoyles were left little jets of projecting blackness. The houses ranged up close to it on both sides, but one could see over the roofs a range of misty buttresses on one hand and on the other the mass of the tower piling itself up in serene faintness into the starry sky. Then there are alleys and open lawns all round the town, and the Seine, divided by an island and glorified with moonlight.

7th [8 November]

I was overtaken with sleep last night and could say no more. Sens by daylight has quite come up to the expectations raised by Sens overnight. It is really a charming old town, and I have a good many vignettes to carry away with me in my memory.

By the by, the autumn here is more beautiful than I have ever seen autumn before. The country is so steeped in rich colours that even under a cloudy sky it looks as if it were lit up with evening sunshine; even the poplars cling to their dead leaves as though they were breeches.

I shall probably go no further tonight than Dijon.

8th [9 November]   *Orange*

Here I am in Provence and in very early autumn, or rather late summer. I pushed on last night to Lyons, and was too sleepy to write. I have just arrived, and despatch to catch post. Ever your true friend,   R.L.S.

166   To his Mother

MS Yale.

Sunday [9 November 1873]   *Orange*

All right and happy. Met a sister of Piazzi Smyth's[1] between Dijon and Lyons. I wonder who she is. I can*not* write so you must take what you get

---

[1] Since RLS was in Paris on 6 and 7 November, I assume he was one day out in his dating throughout this letter.

[1] Charles Piazzi Smyth (1819–1900), Professor of Astronomy at Edinburgh University 1846–89; Astronomer Royal for Scotland.

and be thankful. I had a pleasant stage at Sens. Lyons (by the way – where *were* our eyes in old days?)[2] is one of the most lovely towns in the world. I go tomorrow to Avignon; next day to Tarascon, or perhaps Marseilles or perhaps farther. That depends on the body and the spirit.   R.L.S.

167   To Frances Sitwell

MS NLS. Partly published in *Letters*, I, 91–3.

[*10 November 1873*]   *Avignon*

I have just read your letter up on the top of the hill beside the church and castle. The whole air was filled with sunset and the sound of bells; and I wish I could give you the least notion of the *southernness* and *Provençality* of all that I saw. I thought (as I had often thought before though I do not know that I ever put it into words) that I should like to read nothing but letters from you. So you *had* it out with my father; I thought you must have played some strong card; he seemed to think so much more of you than he had done before he left and in the cab (he drove with me to the station) he was continually bringing round the conversation upon you.

I cannot write while I am travelling; *c'est un défaut*; but so it is; I must have a certain feeling of being at home and my head must have time to settle. The new images oppress me, and I have a fever of restlessness on me. You must not be disappointed at such shabby letters; and besides, remember my poor head and the fanciful crawling in the spine.

Your letter has done me so much good. It was just like getting a long breath again. – So it is all true.

I am so glad the lectures are going on all right.[1]

I don't know the day of the month; nor (what is my climax of happiness) the day of the week. I knew the day of the month yesterday or this morning; the other has been gone a good while.

It is wonderful how seldom I consciously think of you; only whenever I try to express anything to myself, it is a letter to you; and whenever I make to myself any scheme for the future, it is always subject to you; and in fact, though it rarely boils over, my mind is in a constant quiet simmer of you and all your belongings.

I am back again in the stage of thinking there is nothing the matter with me, which is a good sign; but I am wretchedly nervous. Anything like rudeness, I am simply babyishly afraid of; and noises, and especially the sounds of certain voices, are the devil to me. A blind poet who I found selling his immortal works in the streets of Sens, captivated me with the

[2] The Stevensons stayed two nights at Lyons in January 1863 on their way to Mentone.
[1] Colvin was giving the Slade lectures at Cambridge during November and December.

remarkable, equable strength and sweetness of his voice; and I listened a long while and bought some of the poems; and now this voice, after I had thus got it thoroughly into my head, proved false metal and a really bad and horrible voice at bottom. It haunted me some time; but I think I am done with it now.

I hope you don't dislike reading bad style like this, as much as I do writing it; it hurts me when neither words nor clauses fall into their places, much as it would hurt you to sing when you had a bad cold and your voice deceived you and missed every other note. I do feel so inclined to break the pen and write no more; and here *à propos* begins my back.

After dinner

It blows tonight from the north down the valley of the Rhone and everything is so cold that I have been obliged to indulge in a fire. There is a fine crackle and roar of burning wood in the chimney which is very homely and companionable, though it does seem to postulate a town all white with snow outside.

I have bought Sainte-Beuve's *Chateaubriand* and am immensely delighted with the critic.[2] What a miraculous ideal of literary demerit Chateaubriand is. Of course, he is clever to the last degree; but he is such a — liar, that I cannot away with him. He is more antipathetic to me than anyone else in the world.

I begin to wish myself arrived tonight. Travelling, when one is not quite well, has a good deal of unpleasantness. One is easily upset by cross incidents, and wants that *belle-humeur* and spirit of adventure that make a pleasure out of what is unpleasant.

What a character you have given me. I should have liked to have heard the interview [with] my poor father; he was in the hands of one that was too strong for him!

Tuesday 11 November

There! There's a date for you. I shall be in Mentone for my birthday with plenty of nice letters to read. I went away across the Rhone and up the hill on the other side that I might see the town from a distance. Avignon followed me with its bells and drums and bugles; for the old city has no equal for multitude of such noises. Crossing the bridge and seeing the brown turbid water foam and eddy about the piers, one could scarce believe one's eyes when one looked down the stream and saw the smooth blue mirroring tree and hill. Over on the other side, the sun beat down so furiously on the white road that I was glad to keep in the shadow and, when

[2] *Chateaubriand et son Groupe Littéraire Sous l'Empire* (1861).

the occasion offered, to turn aside among the olive yards. It was nine years and six months since I had been in an olive yard; I found myself much changed, not so gay, but wiser and more happy. I read your letter a fourth time and sat a while looking down over the tawny plain and at the fantastic outline of the city. The hills seemed just fainting into the sky; even the great peak above Carpentras (Lord knows how many mètres above the sea) seemed unsubstantial and thin in the breadth and potency of the sunshine.

I should like to stay longer here; but I can't. I am driven forward by restlessness, and leave this afternoon – about two. I am just going out now to visit again the church, castle and hill, for the sake of the magnificent panorama, and besides because it is the friendliest spot in all Avignon to me.

Marseilles

You cannot picture to yourself anything more steeped in hard bright sunshine than the view from the hill. The immovable inky shadow of the old bridge on the fleeting surface of the yellow river seemed more solid than the bridge itself. Just in the place where I sat yesterday evening, a shaven man in a velvet cap was studying music – evidently one of the singers for *La Muette de Portici*[3] at the Theatre tonight. I turned back as I went away; the white Christ stood out in strong relief on his brown cross against the blue sky, and the four kneeling angels and four lanterns grouped themselves about the foot with a symmetry that was almost laughable; the musician read on at his music and counted time with his hand on the stone step.

12 November   *Mentone*

One letter only! S.C. is the only person worth anything; and even he is not worth much, seeing he writes as if he might not come. If there is not one from you tomorrow, I shall swear horribly which, considering the holy occasion, would be very wrong.

My first enthusiasm was on rising at Orange and throwing open the shutters. Such a great living flood of sunshine poured in upon me, that I confess to having danced and expressed my satisfaction aloud; in the middle of which the boots came to the door with hot water, to my great confusion.

Today has been one long delight, coming to a magnificent climax on my arrival here. I gave up my baggage to an hotel porter and set off to walk at once; I was somewhat confused as yet as to my directions, for the station of course was new to me and the hills had not sufficiently opened out to let me recognise the peaks. Suddenly, as I was going forward slowly in this confusion of mind, I was met by a great volley of odours out of the lemon

[3] Daniel Auber's opera (1829).

and orange gardens, and the past linked on to the present and, in a moment, in the twinkling of an eye, the whole scene fell before me into order and I was at home. I nearly danced again.

I suppose I must send off this tonight to notify my arrival in safety and good humour and I think good health, before relapsing into the old weekly vein. I hope this time to send you a weekly dose of sunshine from the south, instead of the jet of *snell* Edinburgh east wind that used to was.

By 'holy occasion' I mean my birthday – the festival of St R.L. Stevenson – and not the Lord's day, which – the Lord be praised – I got over without knowing.

I am very curious to hear about you and the Vicar. By the way, I have been exercised in mind about Bert. Keep him out of the way of little French boys. One little French boy – and not a bad little French boy – may do him a lot of harm; he is much safer with little English boys. Good-bye. Ever your faithful friend   R.L.S.

168   To his Mother

MS Bancroft. Partly published in *Letters*, I, 94–5.

[13 November 1873]   *[Mentone]*

Madame, There are *two* roads up the Cabrool, one on each side. The station is perched between the Cabrool and the Turin Road, just where the road used to join the two valleys at that beautiful angle. There is a *place* with arcades and a clamorous cab stand in front (I think) of where P. Amarante's used to be but of this I am not sure. This is my birthday. Many happy returns. I am going out to make more discoveries.

Later

The *Place* is not where I thought; it is about where the old Post Office was. The Hôtel de Londres is no more an hotel. I have found a charming room in the Hôtel du Pavillon, just across the road from the Prince's Villa; it has one window to the south and one to the east, with a superb view of Mentone and the hills, to which I move this afternoon. Can we possibly have called 'Grillières' Grillier?[1] If such an error is conceivable, I have run down my old friend and preceptor, who trained me up in the way that I should go so sedulously in former days, installed as agent of the *Courier de Menton* in a curious box, half bed-chamber, half office, and looking unspeakably suitable to the man, on the Quai Napoléon. He seems still on troublesome terms with the Amarantes who have now increased and mul-

[1] He gave RLS French lessons in 1864 (see Letter 24, n. 5).

tiplied beyond belief; and I shall copy out for you some day (if I am right in supposing this to be M. Charles) an amusing document – a note of dreadful preparation – in the war, which is placarded all over the outside of his little citadel on the Quai Napoléon. In the old great *Place*, there is a *kiosque* for the sale of newspapers; a string of omnibuses (perhaps thirty) go up and down under the plane-trees of the Turin Road on the occasion of each train; the Promenade has crossed both streams and bids fair to reach the Cap St Martin. The old chapel near Freeman's house at the entrance to the Gorbio valley is now entirely submerged under a shining new villa, with pavilion annexed; over which, in all the pride of oak and chestnut and divers coloured marbles, I was shown this morning by the obliging proprietor. The Prince's Palace itself is rehabilitated and shines afar with white window curtains from the midst of a garden, all trim borders and greenhouses and carefully kept walks. On the other side, the villas are more thronged together and they have arranged themselves, shelf after shelf, behind each other. I see the glimmer of new buildings too as far eastward as Grimaldi; and a viaduct carries (I suppose) the railway past the mouth of the bone caves. F. Bacon (Lord Chancellor) made the remark that 'Time was the greatest innovator';[2] it is perhaps as meaningless a remark as was ever made; but as Bacon made it, I suppose it is better than any that I could make. Does it not seem as if things were fluid? They are displaced and altered in ten years so that one has difficulty, even with a memory so very vivid and retentive for that sort of thing as mine, in identifying places where one lived a long while in the past and which one has kept piously in mind during all the interval. Nevertheless, the hills, I am glad to say, are unaltered; though I dare say the torrents have given them many a shrewd scar, and the rains and thaws dislodged many a boulder from their heights, if one were only keen enough to perceive it. The sea makes the same noise in the shingle; and the lemon and orange gardens still discharge in the still air their fresh perfume; and the people have still brown comely faces; and the Pharmacie Gras still dispenses English medicines; and the invalids (*Eheu!*) still sit on the promenade and trifle with thin fingers in the fringes of shawls and wrappers; and the shop of Pascal Amarante still, in its present bright consummate flower of aggrandisement and new paint, offers everything that it has entered into people's hearts to wish for in the idleness of a sanatorium; and the *Château des Morts* is still at the top of the town; and the fort and the jetty are still at the foot, only there are now two jetties; and – I am out of breath. (To be continued in our next.)

For myself, I have come famously through the journey; and as I have written this letter (for the first time for ever so long) with ease and even pleasure, I think my head must be better. I am still no good at coming down

[2] 'Of Innovations'.

hills or stairs; and my feet are more consistently cold than is quite comfortable. But, these apart, I feel well; and in good spirits all round.

I have written to Nice for letters, and hope to get them tonight. Continue to address P. Restante. Take care of yourselves.

This is my birthday, by the way – O, I said that before. Adieu. Ever affectionate son   R.L. Stevenson

169   To Frances Sitwell

Text: Colvin's Galleys, Silverado. Partly published in *Letters*, I, 95–6.

13 November 1873   *Hôtel du Pavillon, Mentone*

I must pour out my disgust at the absence of a letter; my birthday nearly gone, and devil a letter – I beg pardon. After all, now I think of it, it is only a week since I left, and so you are not to blame, as I thought you were; of course the week has seemed more like three to one constantly moving and meeting with things that imperiously demanded his attention.

I have here the nicest room in Mentone. Let me explain. Ah! there's the bell for the *table d'hôte*. Now to see if there is any one conversable within these walls.

In the interval my letters have come; none from you, but one from Bob, which both pained and pleased me. He cannot get on without me at all, he writes; he finds that I have been the whole world for him; that he only talked to other people in order that he might tell me afterwards about the conversation.[1] Should I – I really don't know quite what to feel; I am so much astonished, and almost more astonished that he should have expressed it than that he should feel it; he never would have *said* it, I know. I feel a strange sense of weight and responsibility.

Thursday [Friday 14 November][2]

I am beginning to feel my journey and am rather to smash today; so I can only write a little. My room commands the finest view of Mentone in the place – there. There is rather a nice man here – a man, I mean, who is not a Philistine, who likes Shelley and Keats and Morris. I think he will be nice to talk to. Good-bye just now. I must take a rest.

---

[1] Soon after his arrival in Antwerp, Bob wrote to RLS: 'I have been so accustomed to live entirely with you and see and do everything with, or with reference to you, that the being unable to tell you everything day by day, to hear what you say, and to have you for public audience world and everything that I am now quite stumped. Talking, I find was talking with you. Talking with other people I must have always thought, this I will tell Louis, this I won't, so that it was merely collecting material for my real talk with you. . . . Success means you, life means you, friendship means you, everything means you.'

[2] Since 13 November was a Thursday, I assume RLS got the day of the week wrong.

My dearest friend, I have received your letter, and I write to tell you two things and shall send off the letter tomorrow in spite of what I said in my last.

Now then, think a little of me out here in the sun, among olives, oranges, lemons, canes (or reeds, or whatever they call them), and the Mediterranean lifting up its hoarse voice on the shingle under my windows, and the quiet Alps of the Seaboard standing round about me in the darkness, and all my troubles drowned in oblivion for a bit and a great hope just dawning on me, bit by bit, like another sun (for a great hope is dawning on me – a hope that with a little strength, a little quiet, a little such strong fellowship as you have given me, I shall still be able to do something for this poor, numb Atlas of Humanity and help him some small atom to bear his intolerable burthen).

Friday [*Saturday 15 November*]

I was awake this morning at dawn. A strangely shaped veil of mist hung over the Italian coast; the town was fast asleep in the quiet pure morning light: only the hills sat round it bolt upright – they had been wide awake all night. I can see all this out of my bed. Good-bye, and do take care of yourself. I have to catch the post, having disgracefully slept in this morning. Ever your faithful friend,   L.S.

170   *To Sidney Colvin*

MS NLS.

[*14 or 15 November 1873*]   *Hôtel du Pavillon, Mentone*

My dear Colvin, Many thanks for your letter and the card which I shall probably put in requisition as the Villa d'Adhémar is not a gun shot distant from my hotel.

I am just beginning to recognise how thoroughly all to smash I must have been; the spring has not righted itself at once, as I had hoped. However I eat well and generally sleep well, not quite always; and I can walk fairly, though with much perspiration and subsequent collapse, on even ground. Coming down hills is not my forte.

I am full of all manner of literary schemes; but quite unaffectedly incapable of carrying out the least of them. However, I hope that that will go off; though in the meantime it is enough to make one bite one's fingers to see all this quiet idle time slipping uselessly away, and to know that the big hand is spread and waiting for us, probably only a small way on.

I *do* count on you; and shall ever regard it as a most dastardly breach of contract if you come not. You know your own health requires it; and so does mine; and if the devil were in it, I would find a way.

I have a charming room, a thought near Heaven for one of my materialistic spirit, but commanding out of one window the open sea, and out of another the long trend of the coast and Mentone and the great hills.

If it will not bother you, a note here will not be thrown away, for I grow sometimes dull when I can walk no more and am too stupid to read anything worth reading – although that sounds like a somewhat left handed compliment to your letters!

The motto is charming. With all good wishes for the lectures and an obstinate hope to see you shortly, Believe me, Ever yours sincerely

R.L. Stevenson

171   To his Mother

MS Yale.

*[15 November 1873]   [Mentone]

I just jot down a word or two as the beginning of a note I shall try to finish for you tomorrow.

I have received from Colvin a card to certain Andrews's[1] who live in the Villa d'Adhémar and so are quite close. The Dewars[2] also are quite close; and I met Mrs Dewar and the boy today and was asked very kindly to call. There's a very nice man here called Dowson, with a pretty wife and son;[3] he talks literature heavily with me. I am afraid although not much inclined that I shall have to look out for society a little; for I cannot read much and so sometimes lack for occupation. Little Barber[4] is here; Dowson told him I was here and he recollected me and said he would look me up. I have not yet found courage enough to go into Nice; but must do so shortly I suppose

[1] James Bruyn Andrews (1842–1909), American lawyer who gave up his practice in New York in 1871 because of ill-health and spent the rest of his life in Europe, mainly in Mentone. A student of ethnology, archaeology and folk-lore, he published many articles on these subjects and compiled a grammar and dictionary of the Mentonese dialect. He married (1869), Fanny, daughter of the American financier Cyrus W. Field; she died 1905.

[2] At their London hotel the Stevensons had met Lt.-Col. Alexander Cumming Dewar (1803–80) of Vogrie, Midlothian and his wife. They were taking their son James Cumming Dewar (1857–1908) out to Mentone because of his ill-health. RLS was to meet the son again in the Marquesas in 1888. (See *From Saranac*, 141.)

[3] Alfred C. Dowson (died 1894), London businessman, his wife Annie and their son Ernest (1867–1900) who became the poet of the Nineties. Alfred Dowson spent much time in the south of France and translated *Bordighera and the Western Riviera* (1883), by Frederick Fitzroy Hamilton.

[4] The Revd William Barber (died 1878), vicar of Teynham, Sittingbourne 1872–8 and Chaplain of the English Church, West Bay, Mentone.

and unbosom myself to Bennett.[5] Many thanks for your letters; and the
pamphlets. Tell my father I was very thick with some commercial travellers
at Orange; and that one of them, comparing France with England said I
should never get so much cheated in France. I demurred. 'Well,' he said,
'just look at this – you never get cheated by a cabman in France, or
overcharged at a Railway Station, as you do in England.' Perhaps after this
remarkable inversion of his favourite statement, he will begin to prepare to
commence to believe that no man can judge a foreign nation.

Next day [16 November]

Today it is cloudy a little and cold so I have had to light my fire and
resign myself to the house for the afternoon. I forgot to thank you for Hill
Burton yesterday;[6] *bien obligé.*

There are hereby, on the gate pillars of a villa, two inimitable plaster lions
which are evidently the work of a humorist of the first water. One of them
lies with his jowl on his spread paws, his eyes sleepily half-opened, a greasy
smile on his wide mouth and bathed (so to speak) all over in an atmosphere
of brutal repletion; the other, stretching his neck upward uneasily and
showing his big teeth in the act of dolorous snarling, has plainly carried his
dinner just a degree farther and is now undergoing the pains and penalties
of speedy indigestion. I am sure my father would be delighted with this pair
(*hac in re scilicet una gemelli*)[7] of jolly gormandisers.

Dowson has lent me Clough, which I like a good deal, and I am reading
Miss Edgeworth's *Popular Tales for the Young*[8] with thorough gusto. They are
often clumsy and transparent; but it is fine milk diet for the mind.

A Catholic (Mrs Devinish Walsh) lady, who goes in for being a swell and
whose talk runs much on Princesses and Barons, Lords and Ladies and
people of high degree, has told me of a book which will interest you (*Mrs
Gerald's Niece* by Lady G. Fullerton).[9] It is about Roman Catholic contro-
versies; but the scene is laid in Mentone and I hear that the descriptions are
really charming; you had better see for yourself. Mrs Walsh is a good
natured person. She sits at the head of the table; then, Mr and Mrs Dowson
(and at lunch, their little son); then (at dinner only) a certain Mr and Miss
Moon, who do not much interest me. He, poor fellow, is evidently very ill
however; quite the feeble one of the party; all the rest of us indeed look

---

[5] John Hughes Bennett (1812–75), an Edinburgh physician and physiologist who spent his winters
at Nice; Professor of Institutes of Medicine, Edinburgh University 1848–74.

[6] RLS's copy of John Hill Burton's *History of Scotland, from the Revolution to the Extinction of the Last
Jacobite Insurrection* (2 vols, 1853) is at Yale.

[7] In this one point alike. Cf. '. . . *hac in re scilicet una multam dissimiles*' (quite different), Horace,
Epistles, I.x.2.

[8] Maria Edgeworth's *Moral Tales for Young People* (1801) or her *Popular Tales* (1804).

[9] Lady Georgiana Charlotte Fullerton (1812–85) novelist, philanthropist and Roman Catholic
convert. *Mrs Gerald's Niece* appeared in 1869.

most happily robust. Dowson and I expressed mutual incredulity in each other's bad health; and Mrs Walsh is a jolly, fat, healthy, active, hustling woman of forty-five maybe, who looks as if she had never been ill in her life. (Happy Thought Mrs Devilish Walsh) – a person with a cold in his head, you see![10]

Next day [17 November]

I was down at the Dowsons' room last night, smoking a pipe. Dowson is really a very pleasant man. This morning there is a nasty cold air about; so I went up the Gorbio a good way, thinking a good deal of poor Jessie[11] as you may imagine; and when I came down again presented my card at the Villa d'Adhémar. Andrews seems very pleasant and we had a fierce forenoon of it over meteorology. He has Bookan[12] (as he calls him) and a vol. of the Magazine with him; and he remembered my name from some of my father's papers in the latter.[13] I think tomorrow I must go to Nice; but I shall not go until the wind is warmer. I got a little cold but it is gone again; I do not wish another. I send home one of the letters you forwarded to me (of course I knew that there were stages in depravity – the moral horror that you allude to is, I quite feel, a lower stage than any guilt in which you have hitherto imbrued your hands) as I think somebody might pay for me and intimate that I retire with the greatest relief and thankfulness from the said Edinburgh University Boat Club. Will you kindly ask the person who told you that about Simpson to close their mouths in which case they will probably catch no flies. I wish you would take any opportunity you find to contradict a lie that, I know, will be offensive to him and that cannot fail to be unpleasant for the other person.[14] Ever your affectionate son

R.L. Stevenson

172   To Charles Baxter

MS Yale. Published in *Baxter Letters*, 30–2.

Private

[*15 November 1873*]   *Hôtel du Pavillon, Mentone*

My dear Charles, I feel that I ought to write to you; though after all you never write to me; and yet I [am] not in good enough spirits to be tonight

---

[10] *Happy Thoughts* (1866), and its sequels were a highly popular series of humorous books by Francis Cowley Burnand, originally published in *Punch*.

[11] His cousin Jessie Warden, who had been with the Stevensons at Mentone in the winter of 1863–4 and who died in 1867.

[12] Alexander Buchan (see Letter 107, n. 2).

[13] TS was a frequent contributor to *Nature*.

[14] Apparently a reference to Simpson's irregular marriage. Cf. Letter 468, n. 3.

a very pleasant correspondent. I am only gradually finding out how nearly done for I have been; I am awfully weary and nervous; I cannot read or write almost at all and I am not able to walk much; all which put together leaves me a good deal of time in which I have no great pleasure or satisfaction. However you must not suppose me discontented. I am away in my own beautiful Riviera and I am free now from the horrible worry and misery that was playing the devil with me at home. A friend in London I must tell you, had a conversation with my father (this is in the strictest confidence – I am not supposed to know of it myself) and explained to him a little that I was not the extremely cheerful destroyer of home-quiet that he had pictured to himself, and that I really was bothered about this wretched business and I hope some good out of that if I can only pull my health round. I hope you will write to me and write something amusing. I shall write shortly to J.W.F. and Simpson, and you will oblige if you will announce this my intention (should you have an opportunity) in order that I may enjoy some gratitude *avant le coup* if either of them has any gratitude in him.

If you have any cheerfulness in you, write cheerfully; for all my correspondents I am sorry to say, are in a somewhat chilblained humour. Bob writes sadly from Antwerp where he feels lonely as yet and there are other troubles besides my own that make the pack a little heavy just at present; I wish I could get it off my aching shoulders for half an hour. If I were pious I should pray for a night's sleep; for I slept badly yesterday and that plays one out when one is seedy.

I do not know how I am to apologise to you for this Jeremiad, which is not like the usual run of my correspondence with you at all; but the truth is, I am out of heart at this knock-down blow just when I was beginning to get a possibility of good work and a livelihood. It is beastly to have a bad head like this; and to have to pay for half an hour's thinking with a bad night or an hour or two of miserable nervousness. However, we keep our weather eye open, and still hope greatly. I cannot be a heretic to my own favourite gospel of cheerfulness altogether; and I have my jolly hours too, I can promise you, when the sun shines and the lemon gardens perfume everything about them more sweetly than the most delicate 'air oil.

Next night [*16 November*]

I am placidly ignorant of the day of the week, but I think it is the sixteenth of the month. I had a good night, without specially committing myself to the Powers that be, and woke in time to see a magnificent dawn. I am in somewhat cheerier humour than before. Bob gave me the messages about the *Portfolio*. You will like it, I think; Simpson had better go without his number as he will contemn and loathe the article. It is to be signed L.S.

Stoneven; which makes not a bad name. O! what about the Spec.! Do for the Lord's sake, clear me of responsibility, and write and tell me how you get on this Session. I do think that the Spec. is about the only good thing in Edinburgh.[1] I should like to be present at a meeting tonight – O awfully. I would open a debate about the game-laws, or defend the Christian religion, or make the coffee outside with Clues,[2] or support the secretary in his tyranny, or do anything mean, sordid, and disreputable for that inestimable favour. Shouldn't I have a nice pipe in the lobby – no, up at the far end of the library sitting on the steps. Tell me how many of you are drunk at Barclay's dinner.[3]

I have just put another billet on the fire and it is most cheerful and companionable and gossips and chirps away to me like an old friend. The sea is quieter tonight; but it always wails among the shingle uneasily. It is a quiet, dark night outside with stars. I wonder strangely what everyone is about tonight – friends in London, Antwerp, Edinburgh; and me alone here up at the top of the house, with my two little windows shining, two little lighted beacons over the peaceful Mediterranean.

Talking of which, old man, take care of yourself, like a good chap, won't you? And believe me, Ever your affectionate friend   R.L. Stevenson

When you get *Leaves of Grass*, you'll send the two books off, won't you?

173   To Frances Sitwell

MS Yale. Privately printed by C.R. Ashbee in *Three Letters from Robert Louis Stevenson* (1902), 5–7.

[c. *15 November 1873*][1]   [*Mentone*]

Here is what I have often said in good prose, put into bad verse.

> I read, dear friend, in your dear face
> Your life's tale told with perfect grace;
> The river of your life I trace
> Up the sun-chequered devious bed
> To its far distant fountainhead.

---

[1] Softened in Balfour, I, 78 into 'about the best thing in Edinburgh'.

[2] ' "Clues" our worthy old soldier servitor' (Guthrie, *Robert Louis Stevenson*, 1920, 33).

[3] Thomas Barclay (1851–1940) President of the Spec. 1873–5, advocate 1874, barrister Inner Temple 1876. Baxter explains (*The Outlook*, 19 February 1898) that it was the habit to dine together in small parties before the meeting and that Barclay dispensed 'some splendid hospitality'.

[1] A MS of this poem at Yale (reproduced in Beinecke V, facing p. 2013) is dated Mentone 15 November 1873 and bears a deleted dedication 'To Claire'. The first three stanzas were published as *Underwoods* XX 'To F.J.S.'; the last four first appeared in *Three Short Poems* (1898). G.S. Hellman described the MS in BBS II but ignored the reference to Claire, which would have ruined his theory (see Letter 135, n. 3).

Not one quick beat of your warm heart,
Nor thought that came to you apart,
Pleasure nor pity, love nor pain
Nor sorrow, has gone by in vain;

But, as some lone wood-wandering child
Brings home with him at evening mild
The thorns and flowers of all the wild,
From your whole life, O fair and true,
Your flowers and thorns you bring with you.

And thorns. But did the sculptor spare
Sharp steel upon the marble, ere,
After long vigils and much care
And cruel discipline of blows,
From the dead stone the statue rose?

Think you I grudge the seed, who see
Broad armed the consummated tree?
Or would go back if it might be
To some old geologic time
With Saurians wallowing in fat slime,

Before the rivers and the rains
Had fashioned, and made fair with plains
And shadowy places fresh with flowers,
This green and quiet world of ours,

Where, as the grass in springtime heals
The furrow of the winter's wheels,
Serene maturity conceals
All memory on the perfect earth
Of the byegone tempestuous birth.

I send you this rubbish just to show you, my dear Amalia (which is the name of your *face*, I have found no name yet for your spirit) that I thought of you. Don't criticise it, for the love of Charity, but remember that it was written by a – an imbecile I was going to say and I'm not much better.

R.L.S.

174   To Frances Sitwell

MS NLS. Excerpts published in *Letters*, I, 96–8.

Sunday [*16 November 1873*]   [*Mentone*]

I sat a long while up among the olive yards today, at a favourite corner where one has fair view down the valley and onto the blue floor of the sea;

I had a Horace with me and read a little; but Horace, when you try to read him fairly under the open Heaven, sounds urban and you find something of the escaped townsman in his descriptions of the country, just as somebody said that Morris's[1] sea-pieces were all taken from the coast. I tried for long to hit upon some language that might catch ever so faintly the indefinable shifting colour of olive leaves; and above all, the changes and little silverings that pass over them, like blushes over a face, when the wind tosses great branches to and fro; but the Muse was not favourable. A few birds, scattered here and there at wide intervals on either side of the valley, sang the little broken songs of late autumn; and there was a great stir of insect life in the grass at my feet. The path up to this 'coign of vantage'[2] where I think I shall make it a habit to ensconce myself awhile of a morning, is for a little while common to the peasant and a little clear brooklet. It is pleasant, in the tempered gray daylight of the olive shadows, to see the people picking their way among the stones and the water and the brambles; the women especially, with the weights poised on their heads and walking all from the hips with a certain graceful deliberation.[3]

This thin paper utterly baffles and disconcerts me; it is like trying to write upon vapour. O that I had a pen of iron![4] The good prophet was probably in some similar strait.

Monday [17 November]

Today there was a coldish wind and I took refuge up a valley. Great bunches of reeds and a good many cypresses give somewhat of an oriental look to this valley. In the path, winding up by something between steps and a paved incline, between old walls tufted with green and discoloured with rain, I met a curious little group coming down. On the back of one of the great Mentonese asses (more like mules) were slung two kegs and between the kegs, sitting royally, upright and well back and with her feet thrust straight before her almost on to the ass's head, a girl. As the whole pile swayed with every step of the ass there was something very strange about the look of it all.

Tuesday [18 November]

I must write a little to you; and yet I do not know what to write. In this suspense as to how things stand with you everything seems equally imper-

---

[1] Philip Richard Morris (1836–1902) made an early reputation with his sea pictures but later painted religious subjects.

[2] *Macbeth*, I. vi.7.

[3] Cf. 'Ordered South': 'To some . . . their recollection may be most vivid of the stately gait of women carrying burthens on their heads.'

[4] Job 19:24.

tinent. I have written *des riens* – and very little of them – for two days; but today I must say something more. I have been to Nice today to see Dr Bennett; he agrees with Clark that there is no disease; but I finished up my day with a lamentable exhibition of weakness. I could not remember French, or at least I was afraid to go into any place lest I should not be able to remember it, and so could not tell when the train went. I walked about the streets; in such a rage with every person who came near me, that I felt inclined to break out upon them with all sorts of injurious language; and only didn't, I think, because I knew if I gave way at all, that I should give way altogether, and cry, or have a fit, or something. At last, I crawled up to the Station and sat down on the steps and just steeped myself there in the sunshine, until the evening began to fall and the air to grow chilly. This long rest put me all right; and I came home here triumphantly and ate dinner well. There is the full, true and particular account of the worst day I have had since I left Chepstow Place. I shall not go to Nice again for some time to come.

I have felt lonely sometimes, dear, but generally very happy; and I have been doing all I can not to think about you for some days back or to think of you only in the past. I am so much afraid for your health; I have some experience now of the results of such misery as you must be suffering. You have many friends at least, dear, who will be true to you whatever turns up; and some who think your friendship the greatest boast of their life, and the greatest pleasure. Whatever happens, you will not want for eager sympathy; very eager and warm sympathy, as you know well. The other morning at breakfast, my weak tea had a familiar taste in my mouth; and in a moment, Mentone had passed away and I was breakfasting in C.P. and you were there in the mob cap and the maroon dressing gown. I was very happy.

Ça! There is a little of my say out; and I feel happier.

Wednesday [19 November]

I have been very tired all day; lying outside my bed and crying in that feeble way that you recollect at C.P. Nevertheless your letter was a great comfort to me as it seems to show that some of the gale has gone over. O I do trust all will go well. I am so glad to hear that S.C. will come; so glad and yet so sorry; for you will be very lonely and miserable.

Thursday [20 November]

I am today quite recovered and got into Mentone today for a book which is quite a creditable walk. As an intellectual being I have not yet begun to re-exist; my immortal soul is still very nearly extinct; but we must hope the best. It was good of you to write to me at all, when you were in such distress; please remember in future not to write me a long wearying letter (I mean wearying to the writer, you know) but just drop a courtesy to me and say good morning. How you could have supposed that I was angry, God only knows; I must be even more feeble in the brain that I had thought myself, if I communicated that impression to you in my letter. You must excuse me if my letters are not interesting – I am so stupid. Now do take warning by me. I am set up by a beneficent providence at the corner of the road, to warn you to flee from the *hébétude* that is to follow. Being sent to the South is not much good unless you take your soul with you, you see; and my soul is rarely with me here. I don't see much beauty. I have lost the key; I can only be placid and inert, and see the bright days go past uselessly one after another. Therefore don't talk foolishly with your mouth any more about getting liberty by being ill and going south via the sick-bed. It is not the old free-born bird that gets thus to freedom; but I know not what manacled and hide-bound spirit, incapable of pleasure, the clay of a man. Go south! Why I saw more beauty with my eyes healthfully alert to see in two wet windy February afternoons in Scotland, than I can see in my beautiful olive gardens and grey hills in a whole week in my low and lost estate, as the Shorter Catechism puts it somewhere. It is a pitiable blindness, this blindness of the soul; I hope it may not be long with me. – So remember to keep well; and remember rather any thing than not to keep well; and again I say, *anything* rather than not to keep well.

Not that I am unhappy, mind you; I have found the words already; placid and inert; that is what I am; I sit in the sun and enjoy the tingle all over me, and I am cheerfully ready to concur with anyone who says that this is a beautiful place, and I have a sneaking partiality for the newspapers, which would be all very well, if one had not fallen from Heaven and were not troubled with some reminiscence of the '*ineffable aurore*'.[5] I cannot be quite a beast; and I am fit for nothing else. I have such longings after the clear air and the lights of Eden; but the world is all before me where to choose,[6] I suppose, but I will not be content with any lower sphere.

To sit by the sea and to be conscious of nothing but the sound of the waves and the sunshine over all your body, is not unpleasant; but I was an Archangel once.

Friday [*21 November*]

If you knew how old I felt. I am sure this is what age brings with it, this carelessness, this disenchantment, this continual bodily weariness; I am a man of seventy; O Medea, kill me, or make me young again![7]

---

[5] Cf. '*O l'ineffable aurore où volaient les colombes!*' Victor Hugo, *L'Année Terrible* (1872), '*Janvier 1871*', VI line 46. Colvin quoted this passage in his review of the poem in *Macmillan's Magazine*, August 1872 (partly reprinted in *Memories and Notes*, 266).

[6] *Paradise Lost*, XII. 646–7, describing Adam and Eve leaving Eden.

[7] Cf. in 'Ordered South' the paragraph describing the state of mind of the invalid doubtful of recovery: 'He will pray for Medea; when she comes, let her either rejuvenate or slay'.

Today has been cloudy and mild; and I have lain a great while on a bench outside the garden wall (my usual place now) and looked at the dove-coloured sea and the broken roof of cloud, but there was no seeing in my eye; so once again I have no little flower gathered out of Italian sunshine to put between the leaves for you! Let us hope tomorrow will be more profitable.

Saturday [22 November]

There is my dearest friend a fatality upon me; I did so wish to write to you a letter that would give you some pleasure and I cannot. I have an ignoble cold in my head today, which confines me to the house and shuts the last door upon my hope of amusing you. I can only return to my hopes about you and trust faithfully that the way has become once more plain and sunny before you.

I think a good deal of my future as you may fancy; and one thing I shall change (and one only I think) if I am restored to health and work and pleasure. I shall give my books away as far as I can without loss. That is the one thoroughly selfish taste that I find I have strong within me; a taste irreconcilable with all I hope for the world; and so go it shall. It has always made me recoil with a little shiver of selfishness from what I should otherwise have embraced; and so we must do with it what Christ recommended for right hands and eyes.[8] *Dieu Merci*, there are libraries, and friends are ready to lend. That is the only news I have to give you; what little life I have left, seems to have entered into its closet and shut door and windows, and to live now among colourless moral things.

I do wish a little scrap you know, now and then, to tell me how things go; but do not give yourself any unnecessary fatigue; be very frugal of your strength, cherish the flame with both hands – O God, if it were to go out and leave us in the dark.

I hope my letter will neither weary nor frighten you and that you will remember, now I have written to you in all the deformity of my hypochondriasis and with all the sickly vanities – bed-side flowers after all that amuse and divert the mind – of a person who does not think himself well – remember that I come of a gloomy family, always ready to be frightened about their precious health; and so treat my narrative of today with abatement.

Good-bye, dear friend, do take care of yourself and don't make ship-wreck of your health and cheerfulness and vitality as I have done. Your (I may say without exaggeration) in the hope of a blessed resurrection; and always your faithful friend   R.L.S.

---

[8] Cf. Matthew 5:29–30.

175   To his Mother

MS Princeton.

Thursday [20 November 1873]   [*Mentone*]

Madame you must take what you can get and be thankful this week. I went through to Nice to see Bennett and (seeing doctors is fatal) I have been tired ever since and not up to writing, walking or anything. He gave me a gargle and talks threateningly of my tonsils; he appears to think meanly of my throat generally; but the tonsils he hates; he thinks he wishes them out; as he confessed to me that he had detonsillated his whole family, I minded me of the old fable and laid my finger privily against my nose.

I have called on everybody. Dowson is very nice indeed; I go down to his room for a pipe previous to turning in often. Thanks for the newspapers and especially for having marked them. Baildon has rather got it;[1] I cannot but feel sympathy with the reviewer. You must take this scrap and be as thankful for it as you can.

I have nothing to say and am not in the humour to say that with any good grace.

The weather has been cloudy here but not at all cold. I have not been into town for a long while and so have had no opportunity for finding out if Grillières is Grillier.

I am afraid I shall want some more money shortly. It is astonishing but I am afraid it will not cost me much under £5 a week; this seems very enormous and perhaps it may come less next week. Mentone is very much dearer than most of the places I stayed at. I was abominably swindled at the Hotel Westminster for my one night – above a pound! but that is the only overcharge I have met with. I kept my fires last week under four francs; which was not bad.

I got into town this afternoon as far as a booksellers to whom I *abonné*'d myself for one book at a time being obliged to confess myself in need of some lighter reading than I had.

This hotel is comfortable. All the servants and people are singularly obliging which is a great thing.

Friday

I was much surprised at [what] Charteris said of John Stuart Mill. 'Seemed to have been kind and benevolent' is used where, for any one else,

---

[1] *First Fruits and Shed Leaves*, a book of poetry issued anonymously by H.B. Baildon (see Letter 29, n. 1) was savagely reviewed in *The Scotsman* on 7 November 1873 and the *Edinburgh Courant* on 14 November.

he would have said '"*was*" kind and benevolent'; such locutions show a
certain bias. But the strange part was his attempt to stultify Mill's position,
and almost to pull mouths at him, because he had been singularly faithful in
love. All this sounds so unlike what I should have expected from Charteris
that I suspect bad reporting.[2] You were present, I understand and I should
like to hear what your opinion was. – Also (a wide leap) what about *Monte
Cristo*?

I am now quite rested again from my visit to Nice; and feel all right; only
I can do no work whatever, and can walk only a very little.

Good-bye. Ever your affectionate son   Louis Stevenson

176   *To Frances Sitwell*

MS NLS. One paragraph published in *Letters*, I, 101, added on to Letter 179.

Saturday 22 November [*1873*]   [*Mentone*]

1st. Tell me about your health.

My father – see how my head is mixed – my dearest friend, I have today
answered my father's letter. I attempted when I began to make it calm and
rational and intended to send you a copy, but I got carried away and wrote
those sort of things that one does not copy. It was a fearfully exciting letter
to write, and I am quite *brisé*; I refused to promise because I said such
promises were wrong; I said that nothing would make me return to the life
we had been leading for half a year back and that I had determined, in the
interest of all three of us, to take my life into my own guidance and
implored him to have some confidence in me. It may be difficult to follow,
but I do not think it can be taken amiss. I had my say out anyway, in a
manner I could never have done *viva voce*; and I am glad it is written and
gone, although if I had it in my hand here, I should put in into the fire. He
cannot misunderstand this letter anyhow; and I think it was no less than a
triumph over my pride, my writing it.[1]

---

[2] Archibald Hamilton Charteris (1835–1908), Professor of Biblical Criticism, Edinburgh University
1868–98. In a lecture to the Ladies' Educational Institution in Edinburgh on 11 November, he
commented at great length on the absence of Christian belief in J.S. Mill's upbringing and
philosophy as revealed in his posthumously published *Autobiography*. RLS is referring to the
following passage, as reported in the *Edinburgh Courant*: 'When one turns to look at . . . [Mill] who
seems to have been benevolent and kind, and in the one grand passion of his life a devotee as
unhesitating as the maddest of them all, and sees him trying to reform the world by argument, and
poring over social problems without allowing God to be in all his thoughts . . . it is in sadness and
not in scorn we use our Master's words – "one thing he lacked" but that thing the centre and key
of all.'
[1] This letter must have been destroyed. His mother records laconically in her diary on 24
November: 'Hear from Lou. He seems in low spirits.' See Letter 268.

I have a cold in my head and *en bon garçon* I am going early to bed, immediately in fact (7.30). I have just been reading over all the letters that I have with me (from you). Good night.

Sunday [*23 November*]

A most beautiful day; but I have been in bed almost all day with my cold; and have just risen and am waiting the bell for dinner. This fellow Dowson in the hotel is as good as gold to me; goes every day to the library to change my books for me, does all my messages in fact and came this afternoon and sat by me for about a couple of hours. How very nice everybody is in the world, except *Der* (letter) and a few others.

Monday [*24 November*]

Another day among ten thousand. I have been steeping myself in sun; and think I am well through colds and fatigues and all the rest of it. Even my head has come round a little and I have been working with some little success. I received a letter from S.C. this morning which gave me two pieces of good news: first, that he was veritably coming hither and, second, and yet better, that the troubles were again quieted; and, if only for a time, what does it matter? Let us enjoy the sunshine. O my dear friend, I am so glad to think you are at peace again, and I only trust that your health has not suffered in the least degree from suspense and misery. Do take care of it. I have gone in for a course of George Sand with immense delight and good results to health, spirits and poor bemuddled brains; and am altogether vastly cheerfuller than I was before. However, I still cannot hit upon the way of making a letter interesting.

What a great distance there is between us. It seems a week since I sent away my last; and yet it cannot have reached you yet. It does seem so strange. I cannot *feel* so great a distance as that; I still *feel* within a few hours of you. I wish I were quite certain you were well and happy.

I am as full of morality as ever, and am trying to put together a little decalogue of my own, in some distinct, legible handwriting. I should fancy there must be other people ready to feel the same as I do and be moral in something like my way.

I have never got over to the Miss Wards;[2] they live in the other bay, a great way from here. I went once, but I had been misdirected and could not find the house; and since then I have been too tired to risk so long an excursion.

---

[2] Agnes and Maria Ward, sisters of Humphry Ward (see Letter 632, n. 1). Agnes (died 1953) became Principal of the Maria Grey College for Teachers in London.

Tuesday [25 November]

I knew yesterday when the man came in to the *table d'hôte* with letters in his hand, that there was one from you, for me; I know the look of the envelopes. *Dieu Merci*, things sound better for you. Well, I too may say that things are better for me. My letter to my father has been no mistake. He has answered it by a telegram – 'Quite satisfied with your letter – keep mind easy. Will write.' So that I think I have done good; indeed, that letter could not have failed to bring about an ultimate rupture, if it had not been going to do some good. It is very kind of him to have telegraphed, is it not? It is strange how perfectly I have got over all my feelings of anger to them; no, I never did feel angry – but *the désagrément that I had in thinking of them* – now I am away. I keep perhaps a little corner of anger against my mother for having been rude to you; I should like to let her know how she offended me and how little I thought of her, when she was so; and I am sorely irritated because I must just hold my tongue and silently swallow this resentment. But I have a better hope for the future with regard to them, as I have with regard to everything else. This little time of weakness and idleness has been very useful to me; I have counted my whole moral and intellectual fortune, and I think I can meet my engagements, my dear friend. I do not see myself in any embarrassment, except this plaguey matter of health. I am all very well, I find, if I do nothing; but any exertion plays me out most thoroughly. Even a 21 game of billiards does for me for the rest of the day.

I received a curious visit this afternoon from a little dwarf Englishman whom I used to know and take walks withal when I was here before. I was then thirteen and he some twenty-five, and we were about the same height. It was astonishing how much I had grown. In opening the door to let him out, I passed my arm thoughtlessly right over his head. Poor fellow, the meeting must have been painful for him. When he last knew me, I was something pleasant for him to be with; when he was gone with me alone, he might forget that there was anyone else in the world of a different size; and now to find me so changed, to find a sneer where he had been used to see a sort of silent consolation – he must have felt his heart rather wrung.

Wednesday [26 November]

I have made myself indispensable to the Dowsons' little boy (*aet.* 6) a popularity that brings with it its own fatigues as you may fancy; and I have been fooling about with him all afternoon, playing dominoes, and learning geography with him, and carrying him on my back a little. *Very* little, because though he is not half the weight of Bertie, I am not a quarter as strong.

I have been wondering to myself as to the change that has come over me since I knew you. Great as it is, it is not a change – rather a sudden development; nor even that – it is more as if you had come to me with a sudden great light and, for the first time, I had seen what I am and about what I always had been really. If I never saw you again, and lived all my days in Arabia, I should be reminded of you continually; you have gone all over the house of my mind and left everywhere sweet traces of your passage. It is not possible that our two minds should quite cease; I believe with Théophile Gautier – not a grain of dust that has ever been through my brain in these latter days, but will leap and thrill and waken to recollections if the wind should blow or the rain wash it anywhere near you. It is very *living*, this matter; we let ourselves still be blinded by the old stories that it is something dull and cold and clayey only half-awakened for a while by the strong impulsion of the soul. Dreams and delusions! it is this matter that throbs and thrills and is shaken all through with delicate sympathies, that is obedient to music and colour and love. O I am proud – I am *glorious*! that I have been made of this honourable stuff.

Friday [*28 November*]

Today came a letter from my father which I forward to you. I could not look for more; and yet – to you let me confess it – I was somehow disappointed. I think it was natural. After an hour's work, at white-heat of emotion, writing *my* letter; I have two placid minutes and a half in reading his. This is the one unhappy circumstance that makes people who are easily embittered and not over wise, begin to think themselves misunderstood.

As for what he says about the money he does not understand, as how should he? how miserable this is becoming to me. I cannot endure to be dependent much longer. It stops my mouth.

Something I must find shortly. – Eh! I mean when I am able for anything. However I am much better already; and have been writing not altogether my worst although not very well. 'Walt Whitman' is stopped. I have bemired it so atrociously by trying to work at it when I was out of humour, that I must let the colour dry; and alas! what I have been doing in its place does not seem to promise any money. However it is all practice and it interests myself extremely. I have now received £80 – some 55 of which still remain; all this is more debt to civilisation and my fellow men. When shall I be able to pay it back? O you do not know how much this money question begins to take more and more importance in my eyes every day. It is an old phrase of mine that money is the *atmosphere* of civilised life; and I do hate to take the breath out of other people's nostrils. I live here at the rate of more than three pounds a week and I do nothing for it. If I did not hope to get well and do good work yet and more than repay my debts to the world, I should consider it right to invest an extra franc or two in laudanum. But I *will* repay it.[3]

I hope you do not think me in low spirits. I am not. Only I am grown strangely more sensitive to some points of right and wrong and very eager to do the right myself.

Saturday [*29 November*]

This is the day when my letter has to be sent away; and I always feel a sort of sorrow as of parting again, upon these days; and when the sheets are all sent and the interview so to speak is at an end I feel vastly more alone and am in a hurry to begin to speak to you again. Do you know, my friend, it is as if I could hear your voice when I write to you thus. I feel inclined sometimes to set a chair for you by mine in front of the fire; but that would be to make laughable, what is indeed a very serious pleasure – I am almost afraid lest it should be laughable to speak of it. It does make me so happy to think of you.

Without, the day is lovely, and I am just going out somewhere into the sunshine among the olive gardens when I have said good-bye to you; for I am really better in body and in mind and take every day a pretty fair walk in the afternoon besides playing a game of billiards in the morning. – By the by, does S.C. know of the cholera in Naples. It is very bad we hear, and seems rather to interfere with some of his schemes. I grow impatient for his arrival. I do so want to know him better, as you may fancy. I cannot tell you how much I want to know him thoroughly, and I look forward most eagerly to our time together.

Only, dear, it will be a dull time for you.

And now I think I must make up my mind to shake hands with you and end the talk; but you know I am not always very good at that.

I have nothing more to say and yet I cannot shut up the letter.

I wish I could send it full of the splendid sunshine; sea and sky are as blue as they know how to be and the outline of hill and tree seems just on edge with joy to be so near the Heaven – you should see how the hills reach up

---

[3] In ch. 2 of the posthumously published 'Lay Morals', RLS described his perplexities as a young man over the privileges and advantages he enjoyed because of his father's wealth compared with the hardships endured by more deserving students. His perplexities increased when, because of ill-health, he was sent 'at great expense to a more favourable climate'; he contrasted his favoured position with that of other young men of equal promise who had to remain at home to die: 'Like many invalids, he supposed that he would die. Now should he die, he saw no means of repaying this huge loan which by the hands of his father, mankind had advanced him for his sickness. In that case it would be lost money. So he determined that the advance should be as small as possible; and, so long as he continued to doubt his recovery, lived in an upper room, and grudged himself all but necessaries. But so soon as he began to perceive a change for the better, he felt justified in spending more freely, to speed and brighten his return to health, and trusted in the future to lend a help to mankind, as mankind, out of its treasury, had lent a help to him.'

their bald heads and make themselves as tall as they can, all for the love of the blue!

Read, please read, *François le Champi* by George Sand; it is like a dream of goodness and virtue and still gentle heroism. Ever your faithful friend

Robert Louis Stevenson

177   To Sidney Colvin

MS Yale.

[*? 24 November 1873*]   *Hôtel du Pavillon, Mentone*

My dear Colvin, All right, I shall come. I cannot tell my father yet, as I am in the middle of a correspondence with him of which I shall tell you further – I cannot write tonight, being tired.

Please get a *Portfolio* sent (if the cumbrous publication will send) to R.A.M. Stevenson, Hotel du Cheval de Bronze, Marché aux Oeufs, Antwerp, and hold me indebted to you for the amount.

Many thanks for the introduction. I don't know if I shall find myself in the humour to move to Monaco. I am so little up to any good, that I am afraid I shall be a pitiful fellow traveller. You must just make up your mind from the first to go whithersoever you list without any attention to the sheer hulk[1] who will dully cruise along side of you. I have given up attempting to walk and just sit on a seat in the sun and read George Sand.

Believe me, with aching back, cold feet and addled head, Ever yours sincerely   R.L. Stevenson

178   To his Mother

MS Yale.

Wednesday [*26 November 1873*]   [*Mentone*]

My dear Mother, Your choice of papers is admirable; and your choice of news is also worthy of commendation.

I lead the life of a vegetable; I eat, I sleep, I sit in the sun, I read alas! nothing but novels and newspapers; and I write nothing but the necessities of correspondence. I have found myself much better since I gave up trying to walk and to work, and resigned myself to sitting in the sun and George Sand. How amply rewarded I am for my moderation! I have the whole of

---

[1] 'Here a sheer hulk lies poor Tom Bowling', the opening words of the song by Charles Dibdin (1745–1814), that RLS quotes throughout his letters.

her novels before me. Even *La Petite Fadette*, for as long as it was in the house, I had not read.

Mrs Dewar is very kind indeed; and Dowson is awfully so. I have never got along to the Miss Wards; they live so far away.

Friday [*28 November*]

I have been thoroughly out of the mood for writing; but better, and quite cheerful.

Thank Monsieur ever so much for his letter.

The money has arrived.

Colvin writes to me that he is coming out in the second week of December. I shall probably join him. Sicily, he thinks of; and the sea-voyage thither smiles upon me. I have a notion, I rather want that sort of thing.

Excuse this scrawl.

Disraeli's,[1] Tulloch's[2] and Greyfriars'[3] addresses were all three excellent; Disraeli's brilliant. Did you notice the kinship of style in the two others.

I have one word to say about the controversy that looms obscurely through what you write. This is no case for compromise. It is a question of right and wrong. If my father leaves out any word that he believes to be true, out of respect of persons, it is grossly culpable. There is my strong voice of protest.[4]   (Signed with his own hand)

Robert-Louis Stevenson

179   To Frances Sitwell

MS NLS. Excerpts published in *Letters*, I, 99–101.

Saturday [*29 November 1873*]   [*Mentone*]

My dear friend, Your letter did not come till after mine had been despatched this afternoon and yet I think I had answered it all. Do not be afraid; if I can, *one* life shall not fail you. I will, as I have always said I would, I will do my best and live well in the world and try to make it a better world for others; and you know to whom my work is dedicated – if it goes well and turns out work of any use or beauty, I shall couple it with you in another

---

[1] Disraeli was installed as Lord Rector of Glasgow University on 19 November and gave an inaugural address. The next day he was presented with the Freedom of the City and made another widely reported speech. On 22 November he addressed the Glasgow Conservative Association.

[2] John Tulloch (1823–86), Principal and Professor of Theology at St Mary's College, University of St Andrews, delivered the introductory lecture there at the beginning of the new session on 13 November. The subject was the present tendency to extremes in religion.

[3] Edinburgh magistrates and Council made their 'Annual Visitation' to the Old and New Greyfriars' Churches on Sunday 23 November and there were special sermons.

[4] Apparently a reference to a business quarrel with David Stevenson. Cf. Letter 189.

way, and you know what I mean there too. O your letter made me feel strong and happy.

Today for the first time I saw Mrs Andrews who charmed me and would I think please you to the topmost; she is not so far (as far as I can judge) as some others; but she is interested in all the right things and has the sympathies that we can share; more so than her husband who seems to me less alive and sensitive, although very kind.

Sunday [30 November]

Today is as hot as it has been in the sun; and as I was a little tired and seedy, I went down and just drank in sunshine. A strong wind has risen out of the west; the great big dead leaves from the roadside planes scuttled about and chased one another over the gravel round me with a noise like little waves under the keel of a boat, and jumped up sometimes on to my lap and into my face. I lay down on my back, at last, and looked up into the sky. The white corner of the hotel, with a wide projection at the top, stood out in dazzling relief; and there was nothing else, save a few of the plane leaves that had got up wonderfully high and turned and eddied and flew here and there like little pieces of gold leaf, to break the extraordinary sea of blue. It was bluer than anything in the world here; wonderfully blue, and looking deeply peaceful, although in truth there was a high wind blowing.

I am concerned about the plane leaves. Hitherto, it has always been a great feature to see these trees standing up head and shoulders and chest – head and body, in fact – above the wonderful blue-gray-greens of the olives, in one glory of red gold. Much more of this wind, and the gold, I fear, will be all spent.

I repeat, as the grand result of my morning, 'the sky *was* blue.'

9.20

I must write you another little word. I have found here a new friend, to whom I grow daily more devoted – George Sand. I go on from one novel to another and think the last I have read the most sympathetic and friendly in tone, until I have read another. It is a life in dreamland. Have you read *Mademoiselle Merquem?* I have just finished it and I am full of happiness. Good night. Today you will have been somewhat happier; it is Sunday. I wonder if there was blue sky and sunshine up at Hampstead. If I thought you were alone I should wish somehow to make myself sensible to you over all these miles, and cry good night into your ear. I do think myself getting better, which is more than I have done always; and I hope greatly in the future. I know very well that I have not talent for a success in that way; but one can be good and make a finer life of it and a more splendid and durable success. With your help, I shall do this – I think I shall do this. Good night.

Monday [1 December]

I did not quite know last night what to say to you about *Mademoiselle Merquem*; nor do I quite know today. If you want to be unpleasantly moved, read it; it is in some ways so strangely like your story.[1]

I am gloomy and out of spirits tonight in consequence of a ridiculous scene at the *table d'hôte*, where a parson whom I rather liked, took offence at something I said and we had almost a quarrel. It was mopped up and stifled, like spilt wine with a napkin; but it leaves an unpleasant impression.

I have again ceased all work, because I felt that it strained my head a little, and so I have resumed the tedious task of waiting with folded hands, for better days. But thanks to George Sand and the sunshine, I am very jolly.

That last word was so much out of key, that I could sit no longer and went away to seek out my clergyman and apologise to him. He was gone to bed. I don't know what makes me take this so much to heart. I suppose it's nerves or pride or something; but I am unhappy about it. I am going to drown my sorrows in *Consuelo* and burn some incense in my pipe to the God of Contentment and Forgetfulness.

Tuesday [2 December]

O Consuelo de mia alma,[2] I wish you were here. I am so tired and played out this morning. My head is like lead, and my heart; but I have found the name for you at last – Consuelo. Consolation of my spirit. Consolation. It pleases me to write it and I am as weak as a child this morning; so please excuse this little peal of bells over my triumph. I had waited so long to find a name for you, and I had almost ceased to hope; and it seemed almost like meeting you again or suddenly knowing you better, Consuelo, to have a name that I could think of you by without jar or sense of incongruity. But I am so tired and heavy, I cannot write more.

Later

I cannot read or do anything but write to you. And yet I feel I ought not just at present. And I won't.

---

[1] The heroine of George Sand's *Mademoiselle Merquem* (1868) is under an obligation to marry a man she does not love because he has been kind to her grandfather. Eventually she is able to marry the young man she does love.

[2] In ch. 32 and elsewhere in George Sand's *Consuelo* (1842–3), the young heroine of that name sings what is described as a Spanish canticle taught her by her mother in childhood beginning with the words '*Consuelo de mi alma*' (solace of my soul).

1 P.M.

I have taken a long rest and had *déjeuner* and I can write a little now without playing the fool. I want to tell you something, Consuelo, that made me feel as if some one had struck me in the face; so deadly and so shameless an insult to man and to woman and to that Christ whom they pretend to worship, it is. They have – the Pope has, I mean – taken steps for the entire suppression of a serious abuse. Certain inferior creatures, called women, have lately been permitted to outrage decency by singing God's praises in the houses kept sacred for that purpose; this affront to Heaven shall be suppressed. Is it not maddening! I am thankful my parents are honest Calvinists. Had they been Catholics this crime against humanity would have finished by utterly alienating me from them. I *hate* all Romanists.

Do you ever go by the tree, Consuelo? I wish I could go there today. I feel so lonely and in want of consolation.

Wednesday [*3 December*]

These relapses dishearten me; I am as weary this morning, after a day of perfect rest yesterday, as if I had walked many miles. Fortunately the day is better and I think I shall be able to find a seat in the sun and out of the wind, as these long days in the house when one cannot do any work whatever grow intolerable before night. I shall leave this I think on Monday, and go on leisurely to Marseilles where I shall meet Colvin on Thursday; I am looking forward to his coming very eagerly; I am in want of some one to speak seriously with; for I have arranged my life in my own mind and it needs some talking over.

Thursday [*4 December*]

I see two things in today's paper. One is a review of a novel by that youth Madox Brown;[3] he seems quite a swell. The other is that your Bishopsbourne friend is to go to Gibraltar.[4] I am sincerely sorry for that. I hope you will not feel the want of him. Still I do not know but I hope, if I can only get better, I shall be a help to you soon in every way and no more a trouble and burthen. All my difficulties about life have so cleared away; the scales have fallen from my eyes and the broad road of my duty lies out straight before me without cross or hindrance. I have given up all hope, all fancy rather, of making literature my hold; I see that I have not capacity enough. My life shall be, if I can make it, my only business; I am desirous

---

[3] Oliver Madox Brown (1855–74), novelist and painter, son of the painter Ford Madox Brown. His first novel, *Gabriel Denver*, had just been published.
[4] The Revd Charles Waldegrave Sandford (1828–1903), Rector of Bishopsbourne, Kent 1870–73, was appointed Bishop of Gibraltar in January 1874.

to practise now, rather than to preach, for I know that I should ever preach badly and men can more easily forgive faulty practice than dull sermons. If Colvin does not think that I shall be able to support myself soon by literature, I shall give it up and go (horrible as the thought is to me) into an office of some sort; the first and main question is, that I must live by my own hands; after that, come the others. I think after the letter, that my father will give me an allowance whatever I do, or wherever I live; well that allowance, I must have quite free. I must not depend upon it at all. I must have that for 'my father's business',[5] which I am truly impatient to be about. And now you see, dear friend, how I hope to begin: 'all men must live upon what they make *alone*'; that is the first member of my creed and I am going to begin with carrying out that. There are other commandments to follow; but they cannot be reached until the first is settled.

You will not regard me as a madman, I am sure, or I shall have wrongly called you Consuelo. It is a very rational aberration at least to try to put your beliefs into practice. Strangely enough it has taken me a long time to see this distinctly with regard to my whole creed; but I have seen it at last, praised be my sickness and my leisure! I have seen it at last; the sun of my duty has risen; I have enlisted for the first time and after long coquetting with the shilling, under the banner of the Holy Ghost.[6]

I am glad I have at last found a time in which I could tell you a little of how life looked to me now. It is such a little change from what I thought before – merely the opening of my eyes a thought wider; and yet it makes much difference on all things. And you know, or perhaps you do now know, how much you have had to do in this change. – I am much better today, by the way, although even now, not quite *all* that I could desire.

8.15

Thank you, my dear friend, for your letter; it was too jolly. No, of course I am not angry; I have perfect confidence in you; you will do nothing wrong or unwise. I quite agree with you about the money just now; the first matter is to get well and for that, they must pay. I have made up my mind too that if I do not pick up before Colvin leaves me, I shall try a long voyage and for that also, they must pay. I am quite reasonable; only I regret; *verstehst du, liebe Freundin?*

If you had seen the moon last night. It was like transfigured sunshine; as clear and mellow, only showing everything in a new wonderful significance. The shadows of the leaves on the road were so strangely black that

---

[5] Luke 2:49.

[6] Cf. Heine, *Buch der Lieder*, '*Aus die Harzreise*', '*Bergidylle ii*', where the poet calls himself a Knight of the Holy Ghost (*Ritter von dem heilingen Geist*), the Holy Ghost in this context being the *Weltgeist* or *Zeitgeist*, i.e. the Spirit of the Age.

Dowson and I had difficulty in believing they were not solid, or at least pools of dark mire. And the hills and the trees, and the white Italian houses with lit windows. – O nothing could bring home to you the keenness and the reality and the wonderful *unheimlichkeit* of all these – when the moon rises every night over the Italian Coast, it makes a long path over the sea as yellow as gold.

How I happened to be out in the moonlight yesterday, was that Dowson and I spent the evening with an odd man called Bates, who played Italian music to us with great feeling; all which was quite a dissipation in my still existence. *Je l'ai brulée.*

No, I shall never be a poet; just as I shall never be a swell prose writer (although I may be good enough as averages go, at that); but I may be a good man.

See what a long letter I have written unto you, today!

O! Dowson is a shipbuilder;[7] a member of the Arts Club; fond of Morris, Keats etc. His wife is very pretty, and I should think she was a nice little woman, but she is not very come-at-able. The little boy is also very pretty.

I do hope you will get to Paris, *Consuelo.*

Friday [*5 December*]

You are wrong about my father; he had never bothered me again. The letter I wrote was the answer to the one he wrote to me at C. P.

I have had such a busy day. Breakfast with the Andrews' at twelve; talk, stories, laughter; then about three, away with Andrews to call on some other people, where I met two people, mother and daughter, whom I used to know well enough eight or nine years ago in Edinburgh; but whom I have scarce seen since. I have not thought or read the whole day long; and I see plainly that this is the life for me just now.

Tomorrow will be dissipated likewise; as I find a kind note from the mysterious Bates asking me to go and drive with him to Bordighera and breakfast there. Who Bates is I should like to know. S. Argyll-Bates, his name is,[8] and he or his uncle or somebody has an estate in Berkshire.

Do you know I have a funny fancy that I shall never be any good in Society again; I have not made one joke since I left London, I think. It would be strange enough if I ceased to have any conversation now. So that the last of my social ascendancy was used up in growing acquainted with you. I suppose this is mere nonsense and that I shall talk and laugh again, when once I am recovered; but I don't mind even if it were to be true; I

---

[7] He owned Bridge Dock, Limehouse.
[8] Samuel Argyll-Bates (born 1827), son of a Leicestershire landowner, matriculated at Magdalen College, Oxford in 1851.

don't care much now, if I be a knight of the woeful countenance; because I have got all that I want now, have I not?

Saturday [6 December]

In case I am not back in time, I have to send this off in the morning hurriedly. Good-bye dear friend. Always your faithful friend

Robert Louis Stevenson

180   *To Bob Stevenson*

MS Huntington.

[Sunday 30 November 1873]   *[Mentone]*

I got your capital long letter this morning at breakfast and laughed over it most heartily; I knew that by this time your troubles were ended and you had received a 20 fr. note from me, which would give you 19 fr. at least if you took it to a changer's.[1]

Of course I have nothing of this description to tell you; I don't do anything, but sit in the sun and read George Sand's novels, and write a little in the evening – a very little, and very ill; for my brain is not yet returned to me and I am as stupid as three.

When I begin to move on, I may have something to tell you; but here, it is impossible. There is nothing here but sunshine, and olive gardens, and the sea, and the seaboard Alps. And all one has to look at is the way the shadows change and follow the sun; wonderful shadows they are, away up among the rocky hills, when one throws its fantastic profile in black upon the face of the one behind it. Sunday is a nuisance, because no-one will play a game of billiards with me on Sunday; being all either orthodox, or Grundyites. I am tired today; so must stop.

Tuesday [2 December]

I have been very seedy all day; but I begin again to try to tell you something more of how I live. To begin with, I read George Sand from morning to night in great measure to keep myself from working, and I am more and more delighted with her. If you ever get within reach of *Consuelo*, don't fail to read it; you will find it extremely interesting as a novel, full of the most interesting things about music and with some of the best passages in the way of literary workmanship in the world.

---

[1] In a letter dated 'Wednesday morning 26(?) November' Bob told how he was excluded from the class because he arrived late and the straits to which he was reduced through lack of money – 'I made a bloody error in coming to Antwerp.'

I know some Americans called Andrews; the wife is very charming and the husband too is jolly enough. I had a row with a clergyman at dinner yesterday, owing to having jested about mothers'-meetings (droll cause of war); but I made up with him tonight and we sat an hour together after *table d'hôte* today and liquored up together, and I snuffed out of his snuff box and he told me innocent tales of his college days; very innocent and not very interesting. That has been the one event of today. I went down in the morning and tried to play billiards, but I was so done for that I had to come in again and have been in the house doing nothing all day. Even now I am almost blinded with blood to the head, so that I am not very well able to write.

You have never acknowledged receipt of my 20 fr.; but I hope you got them; I lost no time in sending them off. Why the devil don't you regulate your expenses better, and, I say, for God's love stick to the bloody drawing. The more I look about me and think, and I have nothing else to do just now, the more I see how necessary for you a little course of stiff school-work is. I cannot write any more, owing to blood to the head and eyes.

Wednesday [3 December]

You have got the money. That is good. So are you for writing to me so regularly. I shall leave this about the 7th or 8th and my address then will be Poste Restante Palermo, I believe. I am awfully glad to hear of your life, and it did make me envious. To get a great deal of work done and to be able for healthy exercise – these are my two desires. About my health, it seems to me about an even toss up; my nervous system may be merely fatigued, or it may be exhausted; if the former, I shall begin to perk up again in a month or two; if the latter, I shall never be worth a cuss again – brains or body. That is really good news about your drawing. *Vive der Professor!* Only what the devil is *pouderée*? Powdered?[2]

I suppose I shall just have to send off this letter very much as it is; for I have nothing interesting to say; I am awfully stupid and dull myself and so cannot amuse people about nothing. I don't think I have ever known the full pleasure of being in bed before this bout; so that is always one thing learnt; I am so heavy and inert when I am up, and when I lie down, the mattress supports me all over and I do rest most notably. Also, sitting on one's bum; that is a very fine thing and would be finer if one had not a back. I shall put this away just now and hope for something to put into it ere tomorrow.

---

[2] In a fragment of another letter Bob says that he has gained 'the tardy praise of the professor' for his drawing from life: 'That is very well done. You must have studied from the antique some time. You have done it so fast. . . . The pose is "*très bien ponderée*"'.

Thursday [4 December]

I had rather an amusing evening yesterday. A man called S. Argyll-Bates (Urgle Betts, they call him) a person with an estate I believe, asked Dowson and me to go along and smoke with him. We went last night; and he played Verdi, Bellini and Donizetti and S. Argyll-Bates to us for ever so long. He is death upon Verdi; he knows nothing about German music; '*hates*' sacred music, and does not even admit Rossini without a grudge. It is good to meet with a man who has an opinion of his own. He really plays splendidly; and he gave us Marsala and tobacco *ad lib*. At last we said we must go. He then produced a red manuscript book, tapped it, shook his head and said with a sort of sorrowful leer 'Arabic Romance'. He then sat down and sang a song out of this book; when it was done and we had applauded, he said in the sort of tone of reverential quiet sorrow that one might use for a recently deceased grandparent; 'I have been offered a hundred pound for that songgg (he pronounced it thus: I ave bin offured – a hundred-pound for that songg) – music and words; but I wouldn't separate it from the rest. Incidental song – Arab Romance'; and he tapped the red book again and shook his head. He is somewhat like an educated goat in appearance, with Willy-Murray[3] hair; sort of man that you know will be something odd, from the first glance. *Au reste*, quite a gentleman and awfully kind and friendly, and very fond of damned small jokes, which he tells with admirable light and shade so that you laugh in spite of your teeth. His story of '*Mr Williams of London*' is a thing that depends altogether on the telling; if I were to write it, it would be perfectly idiotic. He is a bloody eccentric card. [*MS incomplete*]

181   To his Mother

MS Buffalo.

Monday 1 December [1873]   [*Mentone*]

My dear Mother, Have I been gone so long then, that there has arisen another generation unknown to me. Who are those persons of whom you write with a familiarity so bewildering – Minnie and Charlotte?[1] Do let me know; I am piqued; you speak as if they were in the house with you and I am blessed if I know who they can be.

I am going to breakfast with the Andrews's on Friday.

---

[3] William Bazett Murray. See Letter 101, n. 7.
[1] MIS records that Minnie and Charlotte Benton stayed at Heriot Row 25–28 November. They seem to have been friends of Jane Balfour, or perhaps children she was looking after.

I am not taking too little stimulant; I find my allowance quite sufficient for me; but I do not make a fetish out of Clark's quantities and I exceed whenever I want to do so – not, I think, to my benefit ever.

If I have never told you whether it was sunny or no, it is because one does not speak weather in a place where there is none–certainly, the sun has been shining and the sky has been blue. I surely implied that when I told you how I employed myself; which is in two words, reading George Sand in the sun. I often rise tired and with a headache in the morning; but when I have once got myself spread out in the sun, like rose leaves on a newspaper, I begin gradually to come round, the headache leaves me, and I drink in strength and a delicious drunkenness; drunkenness almost literally, for when one goes back into the shadow, it takes a minute or two to get steady on one's feet. Colds and fatigue are drawn out of you, as it were in a hot bath. And the best of humours descends at the same time into your heart; so that after an hour or two of such a sun–bath, I am as strong as – no, not *quite* as strong as Hercules, but as good natured and amiable as – I have it in me to do.

Have I been up valleys? I have been once up to the Gorbio a bit; never within sight of the village; and the other valleys are all too far away. You must understand once for all, that I am not athletic nowadays; indeed, there is no one more inert in mind alas! as well as body, I should hope, upon the whole Riviera. At the same time, I am beautifully placid, and since I have been picking up and have got over the nervous irritability that bothered me, I have been as happy as a sand-boy – whatever that favoured individual may be. I am able, you know, to walk much more than the week before last, and have been twice into town; but still my way of life is generally something after this fashion.

9.50 to 10.10. Tea and bread and butter.

Thereafter a game of billiards with Moon or Dowson, and a long sun bath on the beach at the back of the Hotel.

12.30. *Déjeuner.*

An hour's rest – letters, or reading.

1.30 or 2 away up to a seat among some olives whence I have a charming view and where I get the last of the sunshine. It is on the side of the hill at the entrance to the Gorbio, close to the Villa d'Adhémar. Home about 3.30 or 4. Light my fire if I have not lit during my hour's rest after lunch, and read or write letters till

6.30 Dinner.

After dinner, one pipe then read or write letters till about nine when I generally smoke another pipe with Dowson. To bed, about ten.

I scarcely ever vary. My correspondence figures largely I see in the above list; but, as you have seen, I have not been in the humour for much writing.

Tell Cummy that I shall write to her shortly. I must wash my hands now for dinner.

After dinner

You see that my life is not very eventful, and you can understand that even if I were in the best possible vein for writing, I should be rather in want of incidents for my correspondence. Slight differences in the temperature, slight differences in the quality of the meals, the end of one novel or the beginning of another and the arrival of more or fewer letters – these are the only events that distinguish one day from that which follows it or that which went before. Therefore, be charitable and do not lay the whole of the blame of my dull letters on the deterioration of my brains. My father appeared to wish pleasantry; he must go otherwhere; this booth is closed for the present and my five wits are all gone on a holiday, whence I hope they may come back to me perfectly re-established.

Possibly too when I begin to move again, my letters will begin to come easier through my hands; and that is not long to wait for nowadays. I shall probably leave this day week in order to join Colvin at Marseilles and take it easy on the way, stopping at Monaco some time and, it is possible, also at Hyères. Adieu. Ever your affectionate son   Robert Louis Stevenson

182   *To Sidney Colvin*

MS Yale.

1 November [actually December 1873]   *Hôtel du Pavillon, Mentone*

My dear Colvin, I hope you have thought of the possibility of a quarantine. The cholera at Naples has been frightening all the Mediterranean seaboard, and at some ports they have had a quarantine of seventeen days. Three weeks in an Italian lazaretto is not my notion of a very complete holiday; and is, besides, expensive.

I suppose I shall meet you at Marseilles. Have you an attachment for any hotel there? Please send me complete sailing directions. I should not like to miss you in any way; for I am beginning to grow impatient for your arrival. I am glad to be able to give a better account of my health, it is I really think much better. Body and soul are both somewhat more valid than they were; and life is beginning again to be agreeable to me. Never has the *spirit of delight*[1] been so long absent from me. I might as well have been buried, for

[1] Shelley, 'Song': 'Rarely, rarely, comest thou,/Spirit of Delight!'

nearly a week, as far as any living, any pleasurable sensation or even any strong sensation is concerned.

So I trust I shall not be altogether the dead-alive, burthensome companion with whom I threatened you in my last, but that I shall mount from strength to strength and renew my youth like the eagle's.[2] In the blessed hope of seeing you at no very distant date, believe me, yours very sincerely

Robert Louis Stevenon

P.S. Another fact about Sicily is somewhat discouraging. No country walks are possible, owing to brigands. But all agree notwithstanding in commendation of scenery and climate – of Palermo that is, Catania is represented as the very devil.   R.L.S.

183   To his Mother

Text: extract in Anderson III (143).

[*4 December 1873*]   [*Mentone*]

Madame, . . . I am not in the mood for writing. . . . Sicily is, I think given up, and it is like enough that I may never get beyond the Riviera. . . . Your telegram put my back up and I answered only by two words.[1] I thought I had written quite often enough and once for all I shall let you know if I am ill. . . . Wine seems to have no effect in strengthening or exhilarating me. Its principal effect is to give me flushed cheeks and injected eyes. . . .

184   To Charles Baxter

MS Yale. Partly published in *Letters*, I, 103–04; fully in *Baxter Letters*, 35–9.

4 December [*1873*]   [*Mentone*]

My dear Baxter, At last, I must write. I began a letter to you before, but it broke miserably down and when I looked it over it seemed so contemptible a fragment that I have put it in the fire. I must say straight out that I am not recovering as I could wish. I am no stronger than I was when I came here and I pay for every walk beyond say a quarter of a mile in length by one, or two, or even three days of more or less prostration. Therefore let nobody

[2] Psalm 103:5.
[1] MIS, *Diary*, 1 December: 'We have no letter from Lou yet so send a telegram. A letter comes in the evening which relieves us.' 2 December: 'Answer to telegram at 7 P.M. "All right!"'

be down upon me for not writing. I was very thankful to you for answering my letter; and for the princely action of Simpson, in writing to me – I mean before I had written to him, I was ditto to an almost higher degree; I hope one or other of you will write again soon and, remember, I still live in hope of a reading of Graham Murray's address.[1] I do so much want somebody to be rude to me! The *Leaves of Grass* has not, I suppose, turned up. Damn. Not that it matters really as I could do no work to it, even if it were here. Of course, you must keep my cheerful auguries about my health to yourself or any of trustworthy ear who may be interested therein; but I do somewhat portend that I may not recover at all, or at best that I shall be long about it. My system does seem extraordinarily played out.

Yes, I am as moral as ever; more moral.[2] A man with a smashed-up constitution and 'on a diet' can be moral at the lowest possible figure; and then I always was a bit of a Joseph, as you know. My whole game is morality now; and I am very serious about it. Indeed I am very serious about everything, and go to the boghouse with as much solemnity as another man would go to church with. I can't laugh at a mosquito, and I have not made a joke, upon my living soul, since I left London. O! except one, a very small one, that I had made before, and that I timidly repeated in a half-exhilarated state towards the close of dinner, like one of those dead-alive flies that we see pretending to be quite light and full of the frivolity of youth in the first sunshiny days. It was about Mothers' Meetings, and it was damned small, and it was my ewe lamb – the Lord knows I couldn't have made another to save my life –; and a clergyman quarrelled with me and there was as nearly an explosion as could be. This has not fostered my leaning towards pleasantry. I felt that it was a very cold, hard world that night.

My dear Charles, is the sky blue at Mentone? Was that your question? Well, it depends upon what you call blue, it's a question of taste I suppose – it's only about as blue as Hell, that's all, or bluer. Is the sky blue? You poor critter, you never saw blue sky worth being called blue in the same day with it. And I should rather fancy that the sun did shine, I should. And the moon doesn't shine neither. O no! (This last is sarcastic.)

Mentone is one of the most beautiful places in the world and has always had a very warm corner in my heart, since first I knew it eleven years ago. I went back certainly not

---

[1] Andrew Graham Murray (1849–1942), later Viscount Dunedin, had a very distinguished legal career, eventually becoming Lord Justice-General and Lord President of the Court of Session 1905–13. In a letter of 16 November Baxter wrote: 'Graham Murray's opening address was very successful, being not much of a discourse such as we have usually had, but rather a smart satirical attack upon the leading members of the Society, among whom were specially distinguished yourself and your humble friend.'

[2] In the same letter Baxter wrote: 'Are you still suffering from the paroxysm of virtue which characterised your last days here? Write me thereof, and of Mentone: is the sky blue? and does the sun shine?'

11 December

Let us, dearly beloved brethren, start fresh. I got a most charming letter from Simpson today at dinner which has braced up my nerves considerable; and I shall try now to finish mine epistle.

I know here the comicalest of cusses; one in appearance somewhat like an educated goat, with a negro's wig on, called Argyll-Bates, or (in the orthography of the *Courrier de Menton*) Arpel-Batts. Argyll-Bates and I became acquainted while he stayed at this hotel; and both Dowson and I knew he would turn out eccentric. He asked me to go a drive with him to Bordighera; and I expected all sorts of strange manoeuvres; I thought he would bring out a long flute, or fife, in joints, out of different places of concealment about his person (having previously turned up his cuffs so as to convince me that there was no deception, spring or false bottom) and that having put them together, he would pass his fingers through his hair, knock his hat in, hastily black his face and hands with a burnt cork and, standing up in the open carriage, begin to play wild music; or, I thought he would play the banjo; or, that he would bring out globes of water with gold fish in 'em. But he didn't. He only brought out a black bottle and drank Marsala from the neck. He herded much with gipsies when he was young; and he sang me gipsy songs. The other evening, I went along to his rooms and he read aloud to me a burlesque of his own composition. (O Lord! how our sins do find us out, how of our pleasant vices are fashioned the scourges wherewithal our buttocks tingle![3] But I never read anybody *a burlesque*.) He plays very well on the piano and that is about the best of him.

So you read an essay to the Spec.? And they didn't know very much more about J.P. after it than they had known before?[4] And that was damned little, you bet? Well, well, there have been other great works coldly looked upon; and verily, I say unto you, you –, you have your reward. I think I see J.P. rubbing his shadowy palms together in Hell and thanking God that he has been understood at last. When I say I think I see him, I don't mean anything very definite, for I shouldn't know him from Job if I were to see him. He didn't wear a collar, if I remember rightly? That was his best holt, wasn't it? It was very good – ha, ha! He didn't wear a collar! O Lord, that's rich! What a humorist! And the exquisite sense of fitness, too, that kept him from overdoing the pleasantry and not wearing trousers either!

– I wish he hadn't worn trousers, though. I could then have capped the jest so well by kicking his bottom.

– I hope I don't hurt your feelings. That *chef-d'oeuvre* about not wearing a collar is all I know about J.P.; but, as I said before, I think that capital.

---

[3] Cf. *King Lear*, V.iii. 170–71.
[4] Baxter read an essay on Jean Paul Richter to the Spec. on 2 December.

This is the 26th consecutive day without rain or cloud. (That's not English, but that don't matter much.) You see the Mentonese is rather on the spot about weather, isn't he? His wife, about whom you asked with a spasm of ill-concealed Satyriasis,[5] is pretty for a short time, and then goes in for *tempus edax* what'shisname[6] without further scruple. I don't know whether she is faithful to him or not, but I should fancy she had few temptations after a certain age.

I live in the same hotel with Lord Salisbury.[7] Ahem. He has black whiskers and looks not unlike Crum Brown;[8] only rather more of Crum B. than there is in the Edinburgh edition. He has been successful (or his wife has) in making some kids; rather a melancholy success; they are weedy looking kids, in highland clo'. They have a tutor with them who respires Piety and that kind of humble your-lordship's-most-obedient sort of gentlemanliness that noblemen's tutors have generally. They all get livings, these men, and silvery hair, and a gold watch from their attached pupil; and they sit in the porch and make the watch repeat for their little grandchildren, and tell them long stories beginning 'when I was a private tutor in the family of etc.'; and the grandchildren cock snooks at them behind their backs, and go away whenever they can, to get the groom to teach them bad words. – My friends, let us all kneel down and thank God that he has never made us tutors in a nobleman's family: there are some fates too pitiable for tears. I would sooner be a Macer. (Talking of whom, is there anything new about Johnny Adam?[9] Dear man! how my heart would melt within me and the tears of patriotism spring to my eyes, if I could but see him reel towards me, in his dress clo' like a moon at midday and smiling his vulgar, Scotch grin from ear to ear!) Can I do anything for you with Lord Salisbury? Ahem.

Foot-note in small print – Is he a dook, marquis, earl, or paper Lord?[10]

I see with pain that you are still as dissipated as the devil. Upon my word, Charles, I do not think you ought to leave the parent nest. I speak very seriously. I doubt if you would not be much the worse for it. Remember what is the invariable result of their absence, and perpend my man, perpend. Seriously, if it can be managed, stay where you are. It seems a rude thing to say; but I do think the terrors of the law are not unnecessary for you.

---

[5] Baxter: 'Is it better to be a Mentonian (I'm blessed if I know where the place is) than a Scotchman? are his wives prettier? his daughters more virtuous? his life purer, and his end happier?'

[6] '*Tempus edax rerum*' (Time the devourer of all things) – Ovid, *Metamorphoses*, 15.234.

[7] Robert Arthur Talbot Gascoyne-Cecil (1830–1903), third Marquess of Salisbury; later three times Conservative Prime Minister. There were six children, ranging in age at this time from four to fifteen.

[8] Alexander Crum Brown (1838–1922), Professor of Chemistry, Edinburgh University, 1869–1908, half-brother of the author of *Rab and His Friends*.

[9] The drunken Clerk of Court celebrated in RLS's posthumously published 'To Charles Baxter, On the death of their common friend, Mr John Adam, Clerk of Court' (*Collected Poems*, 106–08).

[10] A judge whose title was not hereditary.

I question if anybody ever had such cold hands as I have just now; however, wonderful to state, I have no blood to the head, and so can go on writing.

I am reading Michelet's *French Revolution*; having somewhat surfeited myself on George Sand. Even the most wholesome food palleth after many days banqueting; and History's little dish-full of herbs seemed at last preferable to the stalled ox of pampered fiction.[11]

Sidney Colvin will arrive here on Saturday or Sunday; so I shall have someone to jaw with. And seriously this is a great want. I have not been all these weeks in idleness, as you may fancy, without much thinking as to my future; and I have a great deal in view that may or may not be possible (that I do not yet know) but that is at least an object and a hope before me. I cannot help recurring to seriousness a moment, before I stop, for I must say that living here a good deal alone and having had ample time to look back upon my past, I have become very serious all over: not in religion, as you may fancy, but morally. If I can only get back my health, by God! I shall not be as useless as I have been. By God, or by Satan, or by the Unknowable, or by the Universum, or by Myself (because there is none greater alas!) or however we shall have to swear nowadays, when we have laid aside your religion, my gentle communicant, Ever yours, *mon vieux*,

Robert Louis Stevenson

(Soon to Simpson.) Health really on *the improve*.

185   *To Elizabeth Crosby*

MS Yale.

5 December 1873   *Hôtel du Pavillon, Mentone*

My dear Miss Crosby, do not think me quite so rude as I have certainly seemed. After a very long struggle with illness, I arrived in London so weak that I was incontinently ordered abroad. I had kept up for two months, and gone on working hard into the bargain, to say nothing of an extreme of distressing feelings through which I had to pass; and – in fine – my health has broken down. I am quite unable to work; indeed, I am often unable to write a page of a letter; and I have not walked for more than about a mile since I came here, without paying for it by two or three days of prostration. I am in hopes of course that I shall pick up again; but, in the meantime, I have not made much improvement.

After that, I hope you will see that I was not quite so cavalier as I seemed;

[11] Cf. Proverbs 15:17.

I am still open to blame for not having written to you I know; but you must believe that I have sent many good intentions to finish the *trottoir* of where you know and that writing a letter is to me really a matter of fatigue and some distress. As for writing a good letter, such as could give pleasure to the meanest of souls, it is out of my power; I can but take off my hat, and sign my name.

There – am I pardoned?

And now I must try to say something else, in despite of a head which feels as if it were full of fluid whenever I try to collect my thoughts. O! if you can get hold of this month's *Portfolio* (December) you will find a little paper of mine signed L.S. Stoneven (a pseudonym which I must ask you to respect) which may be more worth reading than this letter. If you do chance to come across it, will you announce to me the oblivion of my many defalcations, by kindly telling me what you think of it? I don't mean politeness, you know, but criticism; and I hope you understand me well enough to say what you do veritably think upon the subject.

At present, I do nothing but read George Sand and sit in the sun by the sea shore. The weather has been better than heavenly, if it can enter into the heart of the unorthodox to conceive what heavenly weather is; and this is (as I daresay you have heard me say) a pet place of mine. Indeed nothing could be more delightful if I had only a little of my old gusto; but I am sometimes so dull and little alive to what I see that I almost feel as if 'nothing *could* bring back the hour of splendour in the grass, of glory in the flower.'[1]

However, we hope the best faithfully, and keep a good heart up in spite of all.

I am afraid, as usual now, that my letter is very dull and a thought gloomy. Please forgive me, and accept my best thanks for your long suffering to my offences. I shall hope to hear from you what you think of my first publication. Meantime believe me, Yours very sincerely

                                                        Robert Louis Stevenson

186   *To his Mother*

MS Buffalo.

Sunday [*7 December 1873*]   [*Mentone*]

My dear Mother, I had a capital lunch with the Andrews's on Friday and a pleasant talk afterwards, when Mr Andrews (somewhat to my disgust, for I should have much preferred to stay and talk with Mrs A., who is very nice)

---

[1] Wordsworth, 'Ode. Intimations of Immortality', x.

removed me to the Moggridges.[1] There were several people in the Moggridge's drawing room, whom as it was growing dusk I did not distinguish at all particularly; but I had scarcely been introduced by my name, when lady sprang up and began shaking my hand and I heard a girl say – 'Is it Louis Stevenson, Mamma?' Who should this be but Mrs Romanes and one of her daughters?[2] They are all over here in a villa on the East bay. Bob, she told me, is getting on well, with his regiment; it was quite true about Bankhead,[3] but he has since been discharged for desertion etc. We were taking afternoon tea, when Sir William and Lady Jardine[4] were announced; so that I found myself surrounded by the Scotch.

Next day (yesterday), I had been invited by Sam Argyll-Bates (of whom I think I have written) to join him on a drive to Bordighera. And as I was going along to his hotel, I met old Romanes himself, who shook me warmly by the hand and invited me to come to see them almost as if he meant it. I shall go.

Bates gave me a swell lunch at Bordighera and we had a very pleasant day; but I am somewhat paying the penalty of two days of gluttony and riotous living; having entirely busted my stomach up.

There is a very stirring chronicle is it not; you see I shall not seemingly want for excitement; indeed if there is a prospect of any long continuance of these sweet-denners, I shall retire. Colvin I think will come here sometime next week and I don't know where we shall go, or whether we shall go anywhere.

Andrews says, one cannot expect to get well soon; that his worst time was six months after he had given up work and begun to take care of himself; that the system continues to go down, a good while, before you can check the momentum, and begin to send it up again. And this must of course be specially true of a case like mine where I kept up to the last and fought for so long with the depression.

I think I should get a letter tonight. One thing that offended me about the telegram was that it arrived just after I had written you the longest letter I had written yet. Ever your affectionate son   Robert Louis Stevenson

Tell me about everybody's health.

You are determined to get bad letters – don't blame me.

---

[1] The family of John Traherne Moggridge (1842–74), who published books on the flora and fauna of Mentone.

[2] Described by Colvin as 'a wealthy and rigidly pious Edinburgh couple'. Their son, Robert John Romanes (1852–1909), an Academy schoolfriend, fought a 'duel' with RLS at Peebles (see *ICR*, 14). He became an officer in the 25th Regiment (King's Own Scottish Borderers). Colvin says that there were long current many anecdotes about his escapades.

[3] William John Coldham Bankhead (born 1852) was in the same class as RLS at the Academy.

[4] Sir William Jardine (1800–74), Scottish naturalist who edited the *Naturalists' Library* 1833–45. He married as his second wife (1871) Hyacinth Symonds (died 1921); she subsequently married Sir Joseph Hooker.

187   *To Frances Sitwell*

MS NLS. Excerpts published in *Letters*, I, 104–06.

Sunday [*7 December 1873*]   [*Mentone*]

The first violet. There is more secret trouble for the heart in the breath of this small flower, than in all the wines of all the vineyards of Europe. I cannot contain myself. I do not think so small a thing has ever given me such a princely festival of pleasure. I am quite drunken at heart; and you do not know how the scent of this flower strikes in me the same thought, as I think almost all things will do now; everything beautiful to me brings back the thought of what is most beautiful to me. My little violet, if you could speak I know what you would say! I feel as if my heart were a little bunch of violets in my bosom; and my brain is pleasantly intoxicated with the wonderful odour. I suppose I am writing nonsense but it does not seem nonsense to me. Is it not a wonderful odour; is it not something incredibly subtle and perishable? The first breath, veiled and timid as it seems, maddens and transfigures and transports you out of yourself; and yet if you seek to breathe it again, it is gone. – It is like a wind blowing to one out of fairy land. – No one need tell me that the phrase is exaggerated, if I say that this violet *sings*; it sings with the same voice as the March blackbird; and the same adorable tremor goes through one's soul at the hearing of it. I am writing much about my little violet; and yet you know how much I am keeping back. It is [one] of these delicate penetrating sensations that passes, like a two edged sword, through your heart; it presents itself in the holy of holies; it is there a sweet incense before the little image that one cherishes most secretly. This violet has known all my past and in a moment in the twinkling of an eye, showed me all that was beautiful and lovable in my bygone life.

I beg pardon for this rhapsody. The violet has turned my whole mind out of doors; and my brain is swept and garnished, an empty house full of nothing but perfume and love.

Since I wrote the above, I have had a little note from you. I cannot explain to you how it is that these little notes of business jar upon me; I suppose, the sight of your hand makes me expect too much and I am tantalised. It is, I suppose, as if I were to visit you and you were to be courteous and dignified and distant. Do you know, I should be almost too much cast down, if ever this should happen. – O I feel sorry just now for a man whom I dislike and distrust more than any one in the world. If I write thus, you need be under no fear that I am foolish; only I feel more and more every day, how necessary your *friendship* is to me and how very vain a show I should be in the world without it. Your sympathy is the wind in my sails. You must live to help me, and I must live to do honour to your help. And yet, my poor Consuelo, when I speak thus, I am selfishly forgetful of your own sad condition. O I wish I could do anything to help, and yet I can do nothing but say so. If some of us are spared, there will be at least eternal honour to your name. Apotheosis is no great consolation for the moment; but it is always something and I do think I could write something durable about the influence you have had upon me. I shall not count the wager lost, till I have written about you and failed: I do not think one could fail, when one felt so strongly and so gratefully. And then there is the other. No, your name will never be quite forgotten but wherever there are humane men and noble women, the one will wish they had lived when they could have known you and been comforted and strengthened by you, and the others will set you before them as a model.

There. If you don't believe that, it is because you doubt those whom you have inspired; and that would be rude –

Monday [*8 December*]

All yesterday, I was under the influence of opium; I had been rather seedy during the night and took a dose in the morning and, for the first time in my life it took effect upon me. I had a day of extraordinary happiness; and when I went to bed, there was something almost terrifying in the pleasures that besieged me in the darkness. Wonderful tremors filled me; my head swam in the most delirious but enjoyable manner; and the bed softly oscillated with me, like a boat in a very gentle ripple. It does not make me write a good style apparently, which is just as well lest I should be tempted to renew the experiment; and some verses,[1] which I wrote turn out, on inspection, to be not quite equal to 'Kubla Khan'. However I was happy; and the recollection is not troubled by any reaction this morning.

I managed, at last, to present my letter and myself to Miss Ward. She is really jolly; and we had a long talk on all manner of subjects. I wish I had made an effort before, and found her earlier; for I have been rather out at elbows for sympathy. Dowson and I nearly came to disagreement last night about women; it is really his only crying sin. However I forgave him, and read him that bit of Walt Whitman about the widowed bird,[2] which I thank God affected him quite tolerably. I think if I read that to a person; and 'the person' remained quite callous that I should tomahawk 'the person', always supposing there were a tomahawk handy. I have been looking back over my opium-rapsodies (eh? how do you spell that? There is something wrong; I think it wants an H.). They are quite true; only a little opiumed about the future; opium seems to be another word for vainglory in my case;

---

[1] The poem beginning 'Swallows travel to and fro' (*Collected Poems*, 75), written to Mrs Sitwell and headed 'Claire', is dated 'Mentone Dec 7th' (MS Yale). This was the poem (first printed in BBS I) from which Hellman created the Claire Myth. See Letter 135, n. 3.
[2] The aria in 'Out of the Cradle Endlessly Rocking'.

still I'm as glad I wrote it; and what I cannot do, you know another may do: you have two strings to your bow; and I hope, a third is in the fashioning.

Wednesday [10 December]

I was so happy on the first of last month and the last of the month before. I cannot expatiate any more or upon anything else, because I am just sitting here trying to recollect all that passed on that Friday and Saturday. I only remember a blot; but it was a blot of happiness.

Do you know I think I am much better; I really enjoy things, and I really feel dull occasionally; neither of which was possible with me before. And tho' I am still tired and weak, I almost think I feel a stirring among the dry bones. O I should like to recover, and be once more well and happy and fit for work! And then to be able to begin really to my life; to have done for the rest of time, with preluding and doubting; and to take hold of the pillars strongly with Samson – to burn my ships with (whoever did it) – O I begin to feel my spirits come back to me again at the thought.

Thursday [11 December]

I sat along the beach this morning under some reeds (or canes – I know not which they are); everything was so tropical; nothing visible but the glaring white shingle, the blue sea, the blue sky, and the green plumes of the canes thrown out against the latter some ten or fifteen feet above my head. The noise of the surf alone broke the quiet. I had somehow got '*Uber allen Gipfeln ist Ruh*'[3] into my head; and I was happy for I do not know how long sitting there and repeating to myself these lines. It is wonderful how things somehow fall into a full satisfying harmony; and out of the fewest elements there is established a sort of small perfection. It was so this morning. I did not want anything further.

Thursday

The night before last, I dreamed that my mother had written to me that they could join me here about Christmas (I think) and I must own that the dream was not agreeable to me and that I awoke from it with relief. Today, Andrews tells me that she has been writing something of the sort to the Bennetts at Nice. Why not to me? It sounds strange and seems to me an awful nuisance. However, I am afraid there are lest there are some real troubles afoot with you; and so I need not grumble over what may never come to anything; besides it is horrible not to wish to see your parents is it not? I ought to be ashamed to confess it to myself; and yet God knows, it

[3] Goethe, *Lieder*, '*Wanderers Nachtlied*' (Over all the mountain tops is peace).

is not that I have lost my regard for them; I shall always try to make things as jolly for them as I can. Now, I fear lest something in S.C.'s letter meant that there was more trouble on the horizon than ever; he said he had reasons for not wishing to go far off which he would tell me. It is wearisome to repeat the formula, and yet you know it is more than a formula, that I feel with you very keenly. But good Heaven! what people there are in the world. I do not want immortality, if it is to be an immortality with the spirits of certain whom I could name. I would rather be put out of pain at once – would not you? Curious – there is a mistake, almost rather of orthography than grammar, that I never observed before. I must make a guilty remark, and that is, that I am afraid we – on second thoughts, as the remark is not guilty, I shall not make it here but make it some other time, without preface.

I want to tell you how thoroughly everything in my life has fallen into order, and how *everything* seems for the best. The prospect looks so quiet and happy, in spite of all, that I have sometimes a little shudder lest it should be a mirage. My own heart is reconciled to itself, that is perhaps the great thing and that no one can take away from me. How much this has been your doing, Consuelo, I can never tell you, for I can never explain it to myself; only, as I said before, you came to me as it were the point of day and I began to see clearly. Now, they cannot rob me of that, my peace of mind is not, I think, such as the world can take away; and they cannot take away from me your precious friendship; and, if they did even, I should not believe it and it would make little difference to me. I should still say firmly that it was a cloud, and that the sun shone ever behind it. And so it will shine, will it not, dear friend? behind all clouds and eclipse. You cannot take away what you have given, nor undo now what you have done. For better or for worse, I have been changed, and if I know myself, O how much for the better. I am very eager for S.C.'s arrival. He must and shall be a dear friend for me: that is written and shall come to pass.

About Miss Ward: I was greatly pleased with her manner. She came in so *directly* and shook my hand as if I were a man, and sate herself down in a chair and crossed her legs with quite amusing nonchalance. It is a blessing to see a girl who looks like a woman, after so many young ladies.

Andrews I am beginning to like very much. There is a wonderful deal of simplicity about him, that offends a little at first because you do not know that it is simplicity.

I have not been quite so well today; but as a whole this week has been much my best and I am beginning to be more hopeful. I was half afraid lest my system might have been quite exhausted and I could not bear to die before I had done any good and after I had done so much harm.

Dowson was so pleased with the 'widowed bird' that he asked me to read it to his wife; I think it must be my *chef-d'oeuvre* – I always shake so, after having read it. Exception always made of 'The Stream's Secret',[4] that being a case of inspiration.

Friday [12 December]

I have had another letter today from my people; no word of coming here. I trust it may be a false alarm. It will be worse for all parties if they come here now. I am a little doubtful as to whether I should attribute your silence this week to more rows or to S.C.'s departure; but I shall cling to the last hypothesis. By the by, if you write to S.C. and I hear from him that my letters have not gone astray and that you are well, you need not bother writing to me; I should almost prefer that you didn't. Writing to two people at the same place is always heartless work. Do you understand? A bit of a message answers my purpose and you must take it easy.

Saturday [13 December]

I received marching orders from Colvin last night for Monaco, which is a bother; but I am of course going. I have not been able to pack up yet; for my head is very bad today. I do not know what it was that excited me but I could not sleep last night; and today I have had tic. It was not very bad in the morning; but now I have to carry my head as if it were a pitcher of water, which is not favourable to letter writing. I went over to the other bay to see the doctor, to call on the Romanes's (people from Edinburgh) and p.p.c.[5] to Miss Ward in case I should not be back for some time. The doctor part was delayed till tomorrow. At the Romanes's I was entertained for some time - with a lecture on the vanity of life, eternity, soul, don't mind not being able to do work, Hell, eternity, Jesus, Soul, eternity, future state, with my tooral ooral i do. You see that I am in a bad humour. Miss W. talked about you very nicely. She said she liked to be able to give reasons for her likes and dislikes, but she could not tell how it was she liked you – There was so much that was responsive to anyone about you – She felt for you very strangely, she imagined men must be strangely fascinated by you (and she looked at me very hard – I was admiring the landscape with continence). You had been so kind to her before she came out here. So. People like to hear their praises. I think I must say good-bye to you, as I have to write a scrap to my parents; and my head is a great obstacle to activity. I have the same difficulty always in finishing. Such a strong reluctance to say good-bye to you for a whole week. I wish I knew how you were and how things went with you; but I shall hear tomorrow. Good-bye. If you knew how I cudgel my brains for a message for Bertie; but I have not the talent

---

[4] Dante Gabriel Rossetti's poem, 'The Stream's Secret'.

[5] *Pour prendre congé*, i.e. to take leave. It was the custom to leave a visiting-card bearing these letters.

for these little attentions. I wish you would invent one for me! Send it out and I'll copy it and send it back. Good-bye again. It *is* so hard to finish a letter. Ever your faithful friend   Robert Louis Stevenson

188   *To his Mother*

MS Yale.

Tuesday [9 December 1873]   [*Mentone*]

Let us have a shy at pleasantry. The parson here – no, in the other bay, is called Marant Brock, which got spelt in his advertisements *Mourant* Brock;[1] whence he was always called 'the dying badger'.

I smoke, you may understand Monsieur, the common French tobacco, and I like it quite as well as any other.

I found my way yesterday to Miss Ward; whom I found very jolly indeed. I think I am really better now; I have far more enjoyment of life and am not quite so easily fatigued.

You will have been glad to learn that I no longer contemplate Palermo. I think it is likely I shall stay here a good while longer.

If I had not burned your letter, I could prove to you that the context entirely prevented my supposing that 'Minnie' was just Beech House Minnie.[2] Our numbers are now somewhat increased.

```
          5
   4 ┌──────┐ 6
   3 │      │ 7
   2 │      │ 8
   1 │      │ 9
  11 └      ┘ 10
```

1.2. Mr and Mrs Dowson. 3.–4. Miss and Mr Moon 5. Mrs Walsh. 6. R.L.S. Now for the new arrivals. 7. Miss Brocklesomething or other. 8. Miss Tidman (Sea Salt) 9.–10. Two Mrs Napiers (Scotch). 11. Mrs Hayes (a friend of the Dowsons). The last is the only nice addition I think and her brother, a card who has overworked himself at Cambridge, is coming shortly. The Napiers are low-bred women from Glasgow, who associate with the Devenish Walsh, and are dazzled with her horrible strings of titled friends and details as to her wonderful luxury and splendour. How a place like this lends itself to scandal. I am ashamed when I reflect how much of my talk consists of animadversion on this insufferable woman. I will not

[1] This was in fact his real name. Mourant Brock (1802–83), Vicar of Christ Church, Bristol 1856–71 and Chaplain of the English Church, East Bay, Mentone 1872–80.
[2] Beech House, Morningside, Edinburgh, where Aunt Jane lived and various members of the Balfour family stayed when home from India.

bate a jot from that expression. If to be vulgar, vainglorious, a Roman Catholic, rude, utterly without sympathy or any sensitiveness, is to be insufferable, Mrs D. Walsh comes up to that. She really is a drawback to the hotel.

The Dowsons are of course my chief people; Mrs Dowson is a pretty little woman, but somewhat inaccessible; Dowson is really very pleasant and kind; and then we are the only two smokers in the house.

There was this morning much excitement, as some people, said to [be] the Earl of Salisbury's family, were looking at rooms. I do not yet know whether they have taken them or no.

Now today has been a model day. I came down about ten. Played two games of billiards – there's a great advance in strength for you by the way – and sat in the sun till breakfast; then I went about at the foot of the Gorbio with Moon, and followed the sunshine from one *bield* to another. In about half past three; sit in front office, read, doze and now (5.10) write this letter.

Yes, the Andrews's was a regular French *déjeuner*. Oysters, two meats, a vegetable, ice and *gâteaux*.

I told you on Sunday I had been paying the penalty of my sweet meals. Thereby, hangs a tale. I took an opium pill on Sunday morning, and for the first time, it took full effect upon me. I lived all Sunday in the most inexpressible bliss; and when I went to bed at night, there was something almost terrifying in the pleasures that crowded upon me in the darkness. I was afraid I should have nightmare; but my sleep was untroubled and I awoke quite well on the Monday morning. I shall send you some violets and maidenhair in this letter. They are the first violets I have found; I got them (or rather little Dowson got them for me) on Sunday afternoon when I was walking in some olive yards with him and his father; and the effect of the perfume on my opium stimulated nerves was something wonderful to look back upon. The real fact I fancy, was that I did not require it: I shall be more careful how I take such a drug again; I am not quite the figure for much opium I think.

Wednesday [*10 December*]

Yes, the Salisbury people have taken two flats; and we are all as glad as if we had a share in the hotel – so much do we like everybody about it.

I am happy to say that I think myself at last really on the mend; and I have been complimented on the improvement I have made in the last week by Dowson and Moon; wherefore rejoice. I am reading Michelet's *French Revolution* with much interest. O! Give my paper to Auntie and Cummy and Greig and Dick and Kingero[3] and the policeman at the corner of the

[3] See Letter 476.

street. The three first are serious; and you may add to them such others as you think right. Ever your affectionate son   Robert Louis Stevenson

Love to Cummy, along with the paper.

189   To his Mother

Text: *Letters*, I, 102.

Saturday [13 December 1873][1]   [*Mentone*]

My dear Mother, I am so sorry you were so long without hearing that time and I have a difficulty in understanding that it could have been so long; I suspect some letter must have miscarried. You never tell me how you keep either of you; and you never tell me how that row with U.D. goes on or has ended.[2]

I am really very much better, quite beginning to come round again. Today, however, you must excuse me from writing more than a line or two, because I took tea yesterday at the Andrews's, was awake in consequence almost all night and have a good deal of tic today. You see the consequence of breaking rules; and yet day and night you do not cease to incite me to break them more! *C'est pas joli.* I lunched yesterday with the Dewars (heavy) and spent the afternoon with the Andrews's – it was their receiving day. I like the Andrews's very much now.

Today I called on the Romanes's and found only Mrs R.; she talked religion to me for some time and then I went away again. She was not very inviting and I do not think I shall build myself a lodge in their garden.[3] Their house is appropriately called the Villa Sahara.

O – if you can learn Wilson's[3] address in Aberdeen, send him one of the papers and send me the address. Send Bisset[5] a *Thermal I[nfluence]*: also.

I expect Colvin shortly. Ever affectionate son,

Robert Louis Stevenson

Tell Cummy I recognized her hand on a *Glasgow News* and that I'll write to her shortly.   R.L.S.

---

[1] Dated 14 December in *Letters*, but this was a Sunday. MIS probably noted the postmark.

[2] Printed as 'V.D.' in *Vailima Edition* where the letter was first published. I assume it is a misreading for 'U.D.' i.e. Uncle David. Cf. Letter 178, n. 4.

[3] Cf. Isaiah 1:8.

[4] George Wilson: see Letter 201 and n. 1.

[5] The Revd Archibald Bissett (1843–1916), minister at Foulden in 1874 and at Ratho 1876–1916. He knew RLS well in his University days and read Classics and Philosophy with him when he was preparing for his Law examination. His reminiscences are in *ICR*.

190   To his Mother

MS Yale. Published in *Letters*, I, 106–07.

Monday [15 December 1873]   *Monaco*

My dear Madame, I am here now with Colvin. Weather as before. Body as before. I shall dine tomorrow I believe with the notorious Sir Charles Dilke,[1] who is here and whom Colvin had to see on business. I am happy to inform you that Mentone-Bennet[2] said nothing could be worse for me than wine, except music and things of that sort. He said –

Tuesday [16 December]

I don't remember what I was going to say. We have just come back from dining with the Dilkes'; where we had a very good dinner and very good wine. Lady Dilke is a first rate mimic and has a waiting maid who is Scotch and not unlike some of our friends in character over whom she made great running.

Wednesday [17 December]

I can't say that Colvin's arrival seems to make me much more of a correspondent. Just there, we got talking and wrote no more till it was time to go to bed. We have very nice rooms here near Monte Carlo; so that we have the gardens at hand and can go and bake ourselves under the palms at a moment's notice. You don't seem to have written to me for some days now; not that I complain, understand; I am only wondering at the two phenomena – Last week's letter every day and the comparative silence of this week. Colvin and I are to go to the Andrews's on Christmas day, breakfast and then a 'tree' in the afternoon.

I must finish this off and get the post or you will be growing impatient. I am really well pleased with my progress just now. I am less tired and dispirited than I was by a great way; and of course, Colvin's being with me is a great amusement. I think you would like Monaco, they are very strict and make you sign a paper – '*Nom de famille – Prénoms – Age – Qualité ou*

---

[1] Sir Charles Wentworth Dilke, second baronet (1843–1911), Radical politician; MP for Chelsea 1868–86; President of the Local Government Board 1882–5. His notoriety at this time was due to his strong expression of republican views. Greater notoriety and the wrecking of his political career came with the Crawford divorce case in 1886. In 1872 he married Katherine Sheil, who died in childbirth in 1874.

[2] James Henry Bennet (1816–91), London physician and specialist in gynaecology, whose recovery from consumption through residence at Mentone made him an advocate of the Riviera for sufferers from lung disease. He is regarded as the discoverer of Mentone as a health resort and it became his permanent winter home.

Profession – Lieu de naissance – Dernière demeure – Domicile habituel.' That is rather hot is it not. Hullo. Time flies. Your affectionate son

R.L. Stevenson

P.S. Be careful what you write to Mrs Bennett;[3] she is not discreet.

191   To Frances Sitwell

MS NLS. Excerpt published in *Letters*, I, 107–08.

Monday [*15 December 1873*]   *Monaco*

S.C. came last night all right, and he is engaged at present in writing (to you most likely) in this very room. He is at the table with one candle; I am on a sofa by the fire with another. He will tell you all about my tabernacle and so I may save myself the trouble. I went to the music today but had to come out, it excited me so much. I am awfully glad he has come, and do not think so badly of the news he brings, as I had feared. Your jolly long letter has just come and has made me very happy; only this cold will be bad for you. You say nothing about the half caste?

Tuesday [*16 December 1873*]

We have been out all day in a boat; lovely weather and almost dead calm, only the most infinitesimal and indeterminate of oscillations moved us hither and thither; the sails were duly set and flapped about idly overhead. Our boatman was a man of a delightful humour; who told us many tales of the sea, notably one of a doctor, who was an Englishman and who seemed almost an epitome of vices, drunken, dishonest and utterly without faith; and yet he was a '*charmant garçon.*' He told us many amusing circumstances of the doctor's incompetence and dishonesty and imitated his accent with singular success. I couldn't quite see that he was a charming *garçon* – 'O oui – comme caractère, un charmant garcon.*' We landed on that Cap St Martin, the place of firs and rocks and myrtle and rosemary of which I spoke to you. As we pulled along in the fresh shadow, the wonderful clean scents blew out upon us, as if from islands of spice; only how much better than cloves and cinnamon! We landed and I sat for a bit on a stone, while S.C. knocked about over the rocks and undergrowth; I daresay he will tell you about the richness and variety of greens, and yet all sober and subdued; and how one had only to pass one's hand over the bush, to take it back embalmed with some healthful, strong, virginal perfume; and how there was a French peek-

---

[3] RLS spelled the names of both doctors with one 't' but the reference in Letter 203 shows that he was referring to the wife of Dr Bennett of Nice (Letter 171, n. 5).

neek on the Cape which much distressed him, and the various other delights of this little excursion. He cannot enjoy anything here without regretting that you are not here also; and I have not quite countenance enough to make any answer. Some things seem to one too obvious to say; how much more to acquiesce in. I do think we are getting on jolly; there seems to be no *gène*, and of course he is very kind.

Wednesday [*17 December*]

I have no notion of your being alone at home. There's no place like H—, you know – which you may understand as you will –

I was interrupted here and take up my wondrous tale,[1] on a seat behind the Casino – palms, aloes, sunshine; and, shortly from within, the band will make itself audible and all this time, your being in the cold and alone or worse; it is not very pleasant to think of.

S.C. is away walking; three people are walking up and down between me and the Casino and laughing as they go, in a quiet middle-aged manner. I have not an idea in my head, except the desire to speak to you. I should have lots to say if you were here; if I should see some one come along the walk; and some one stopped and sat down beside me on the seat – there is plenty of room; not, of course, that I should let some one get so near before I had leaped up and run to meet her. O wouldn't it be Heaven; and then think of S.C. coming back from his walk, thinking nothing of what was awaiting him! It is perhaps cruel to tantalise both of us by writing such things; but I have nothing else in my head. S.C. has lost the white hat, which is detestable of him. By God, you did look jolly in it. I never felt more prattly, with less prattle on hand, than I do this afternoon. I think you would find me nice to talk to though, Consuelo.

It is awfully jolly having S.C. here, I shall be miserably dull I fear when he goes again; however he will go back to you, which will be a comfort, yes, a great comfort.

Last night, we dined with Sir Charles and Lady Dilke, who amused me very much. I like the republican; not his wife, O no. S.C. is evidently enjoying his walk, as he has been gone nearly two hours – time has become a mere jest to me you see.[2] I was glad he went, as I was afraid he was hanging about rather more than was good for him. I am a depressing person to be with for most people. The man sick of a palsy[3] is about the only character in history who could have lived with me without getting bored. My existence is so strictly occupied in sitting down, which is just a good as anything else when once you're used to it but doesn't appeal to the

---

[1] Addison, 'The spacious firmament on high' cf. Letter 80, n. 1.
[2] RLS first wrote and deleted 'three'.
[3] Cf. Matthew 9:2.

imagination at first sight. You can't tell how much I want to see you today – how *badly* I want to see you. Never mind. I am in luck; and soon you will escape for a little and be your old free born bird for a week or two; never mind what fictitious end of imprisoning thread that you carry with you. Ours are the natures that can shut our eyes to such tokens of slavery, that once out of the prison can find all the old pleasure in the open Heaven and fields, although the broken fetters still clank upon our wrists. And you *will* have some happy time at Paris anyway; and go back stronger and happier, as pleasure can only strengthen and renew. It is good to me to think of all this. I hope very keenly in your hope, and shall be happy in your pleasure. The sun is getting low, the gardens are solitary, the air fresh and somewhat chill: from the Casino, the orchestra wails and sobs, and almost brings tears into my eyes – Now, with a thunder of drums and brass, it has wakened up to furious elation. I am afraid I must say good-bye to my seat and our little talk. You *have* been sitting by me here for a long time Consuelo – but now I must go and leave you. The orchestra is again low and plaintive and seems asking me to stay. I have looked over my shoulder, and see a tall ship standing out seaward, in a silver haze, the sails just tipped with sun – cymbals, from within, and a reluctant 'dying fall'[4] of wind instruments. Good-bye!

10.30

I was right in my predictions. S.C. has shown me something that he is doing (I suppose this a breach of confidence so you must not let on) and I am delighted. What I said was true, and I knew some one would do it, and it has been done. *Viva*! Good S.C.! I am as happy as a king about it; I would rather this had happened than a legacy of £3000 a year. I *am* happy. I could not go to bed till I had told you of it.

Friday [18 December]

S.C. and I are sitting on a seat on the battlemented gardens of Old Monaco. The day is gray and clouded, with a little red light on the horizon, and the sea, hundreds of feet below us, is a sort of purple dove-colour. Shrub-geraniums firs and aloes cover all available shelves and terraces, and where these become impossible, the prickly pear precipitates headlong downwards its branches of oval plates; so that the whole face of the cliff is covered with an arrested fall (please excuse clumsy language) a sort of fall of the evil angels petrified midway on its career. White gulls sail past below us every now and then, sometimes singly, sometimes by twos and threes and

---

[4] *Twelfth Night*, I.i.4.

sometimes in a great flight. The sharp perfume of the shrub geraniums fills the air.

I cannot write, in any sense of the word; but I am as happy as can be and wish to notify the fact before it passes. We have not heard from you since our arrival. Your letter must have gone astray. – The sea is blue, gray, purple and green; very subdued and peaceful; earlier in the day it was marbled by small keen specks of sun and larger spaces of faint irradiation; but the clouds have closed together now, and these appearances are no more – Voices of children and occasional crying of gulls; the mechanical noise of a gardener somewhere behind us in the scented thicket; and the faint report and rustle of the waves on the precipice far below, only break in upon the quietness to render it more complete and perfect.

Evening

How little I have written to you this week. Well that is a good sign; and means that I have been occupied and happy. I only hope you have been the like; I feel somewhat a sinner against you in my happiness just now for I fear it has left you rather out of it; others have taken your cloak, and now I have got your coat also.[5] Well, well, – well well. I don't know what to say and that is why I reiterate senseless syllables; for I am sleepy if the truth were known and it is quite on the cards that I am writing nonsense. We are very anxious to hear from you, dear, as you may fancy; but I do not think the other has let himself get uneasy; he has manfully resisted all corrupt imaginations and adhered to the belief that the letter has gone astray and I have never had any doubt: I have got past my stage of fright and miserable anxiety and can go now most stoutly and contentedly without a letter for as long as you may ever find it necessary or convenient to leave me; which does not mean, as you know, that I am changed at all towards my deity; for I cannot change now. If I were dead, I could not change.

Saturday [19 December]

The only authentic address after you receive this is 'Poste Restante, Monaco.' We are going to change our hostelry and go up into the old town, but P.R.'s are always the safest and most manageable; you can change as you will.

Don't let on that I wrote what I did write on Wednesday evening. It was a breach of confidence I suppose.

Last night, I was much awake, early in the night because of bells ringing, and again early in the morning because of work-folk going past in the dark with a great tramp of feet and much whistling and singing; and then finally,

---

[5] Cf. Matthew 5:40.

by one of our fellow lodgers beginning his morning's practising upon the
'cello. Every time I woke, I thought of you; and I wish to say again how
right it all is for me and how (if I were to die tomorrow) you should only
be glad that it was in your power to make one person's life so much more
beautiful – one other person's life. It is now five months ago since I saw you
first; only five months. It seems like my whole life, Consuelo. Ever your
faithful friend   Robert Louis Stevenson

192   *To Bob Stevenson*

MS Yale.

[*17 December 1873*]   [*Monaco*]

My dear Bob, I am at Monaco with Colvin, sitting outside in the sun on a
seat behind the Casino. The band (one of the best in Europe) is just tuning
up, putting me in mind of the tuning before Orosy's concert. Appropriately
enough there is a piece of Chopin's in the programme – a *Marche Funèbre*
from which I expect great things if I can only manage to listen to it, which
is doubtful; the last time I went to the band, I had to come out straight –
the brass made me quite mad and all my nerves got tense and stiff like
whipcord. There is the hour, I am going in to try – a sell. This is not the
classical afternoon, nothing but Adam, Auber, Hervé, Strauss and that lot.
M. Eusèbe Lucas, the director, pleases me awfully, he has jolly shoulders and
a good moustache. Directing a good band is very proud work and gives
opportunity for much grace, if you can be graceful. I feel as if I could be
damned graceful at it, but perhaps the more solid requirements of the metier
might go to blazes. Do you remember an old proposition of the *Messiah*,
with me to conduct and you for tenor, M. Hart soprano etc? The recollection fills me with laughter. Has the sun of Jink[1] then set? God forbid, as St
Paul would say, but rather it is risen again and this mortal has put on
immortality. Shine sweet sun forever upon the dusty ways of life. Thee
often shall the wayfarer, or at the peep of morning or at noon, in devious
error sunken, pause to hail etc. *À propos* of the music I have been hearing,
a purely lyrical idea very sweet and pretty in itself has just been crushed out
of existence by the whole weight of the orchestra. I am beginning to
wonder a little that no letter comes for me from you; have you been
expelled the Academy and sent forth an egregious exile?[2] I suppose not, or
I should have heard of it: I hope you are getting on really well. Do you find

---

[1] The special word used by Bob and RLS for their elaborate jokes. 'As a rule of conduct, Jink
   consisted in doing the most absurd acts for the sake of their absurdity and the consequent laughter.'
   (RLS, *Autobiography*, quoted in Balfour, I, 91.)

[2] '*egregius properaret exsul*' (he hastened away, an honourable exile) – Horace, *Odes*, III. v. 48.

any real difference in the way of teaching and does it seem to you better. Tell me about this like a good soul.

Colvin being here makes things very jolly for me. Yesterday I dined with Sir Charles Dilke and his wife; Sir C. is a joke, awfully *bon garçon* and in such funny clothes – republican clo' I suppose. You know, he is the man who proposed to suppress the monarchy and got so much chaffed a few years ago. He is about thirty; and just Hell on laughing at jokes – his joke, your joke, my joke, anybody's joke.

Sunday 4 January [1874]

I have been a long while – nearly a fortnight since I wrote this last scrap. In the interval, I got your letter which amused me much.

Colvin and I are back again at *Mentone. Hotel Mirabeau.* A man shot himself at the gaming tables, when Colvin was in the room: He was a Pole, and had played everything; this gave us a distaste to the place, so we left.

I did hear Chopin's *Marche Funèbre* and Mendelssohn's *Hebrides Overture*; I enjoyed them awfully, but I was ill for three days after. So you see what it is to have played out your nerves.

Colvin and I get on awfully well; it is very jolly his being here, but he goes shortly and I shall feel very lonely.

There is a French artist here called Robinet,[3] a very decent fellow, a realist rather, perhaps a bit of a praeraphaelite; but as yet we only know him by his talk. He told me some good stories of Courbet, who is (as perhaps you know) *the* realist *par excellence.* He said he had done something that Ingres had never done. What is that? asked Robinet. '*Eh bien,*' he said, '*j'ai peint deux cent cinquante fois mon vase de nuit.*' Several more of his stories would amuse you, but they are long. Colvin tells me that Courbet's grand climax of realism was a picture called *La Baigneuse* of a great, fat, obese *bourgeoise* clambering out of a bath with her big bum turned to you. It was the ugliest thing on record. The Empress had been looking at a picture of Rosa Bonheur's of a lot of percheron horses – those great, white draught horses with immense quarters; and when she saw Courbet's *Baigneuse*, she said: '*Est'ce aussi une percheronne?*'[4]

It is strange how long it takes one to recover, if you have once broken down. I am much better but horridly weak and not able for any work – I have not written above a few pages all these two months and these are not fit for fodder – *à propos*, I am afraid you did not get the *Portfolio*; at least mine

---

[3] Paul Robinet (1845–1932): 'A bush-bearded French landscape painter, sometimes known as "*le Raphael des Cailloux*" from the more than pre-Raphaelite minuteness of his treatment of the foregound detail of pebbled shores; a devout Catholic and reactionary, and withal the best of genial good fellows' (Colvin).

[4] Courbet's painting, *Les Baigneuses* (now at the Musée Fabre, Montpellier) caused a scandal at the 1853 Salon. The anecdote about the Empress seems to be well-authenticated.

was not sent and Colvin ordered the two at the same time: I am afraid it is too bulky for the post.

I have nothing to say, so you must be content with a mere scrap I am afraid. You must have had great sport these days. You do not say how you get on with your work.

How strange it is that you should go back to Mathilde Brand after so long. I certainly would see her if I had a chance; it will either cure you unpleasantly; or will ensure you a great pleasure for the time; and one may be too curious in looking forward and insisting on permanence in what gives our nerves a pleasant shock. No one would refuse to look at a sunset because a sunset cannot last. And besides, old man, the devil is not yet dead; there is life and hope in both of us; and the 'who knows?' may be answered some day with an affirmative.

Colvin thinks rather well of my Covenanting stories[5] and thinks if I string two or three of them out, it looks like coin; so that is a consolation.

Please address Poste Restante, Mentone; it is always better. Ever your affectionate friend   Robert Louis Stevenson

193   To his Mother

MS Yale. Published in *Letters*, I, 108–09.

Thursday [18 December 1873]   *Monte Carlo*

My dear Mother, Colvin has gone walking to Mentone to cash draughts, as we had become penniless. I am sitting on a seat on the low terrace at Monte Carlo; the sea shining in front; on the right old Monaco; on the left Roccabruna, Cap St Martin and the Italian coast; behind me a flower border full of bees, a wall covered with green creepers and a great clump of palms and aloes. One – no, two aloes are in wonderful flower twenty feet high if they are an inch and standing over the palms by a foot or two. Last night it has rained and the air this morning is exceptionally soft and pure, and the sun is a little veiled. Drums and trumpets come to me very faintly from the old town; the Carabiniers of Charles the Third[1] are turning out, or changing guard or something. You remember these Carabiniers of yore, do you not? I think there are more of them now; they are very likely paid

---

[5] RLS projected a series of Covenanting stories. A list of ten stories in an early geometry notebook (Haverford College) is annotated *A Covenanting Story-Book*. It includes 'The Curate of Anstruther's Bottle', 'Strange Adventures of the Reverend Mr Solway', 'The Devil of Cramond' and 'The Story of Thrawn Janet'. A notebook of 1873/74 (Notebook A265A, Yale, uncatalogued) lists six stories under the heading *Covenanting Story Book*. See also Letter 329, n. 3.
[1] Charles III (1818–89), Prince of Monaco from 1856.

by Blanc,[2] and not by Charles Trois. *À propos* (information crowds upon me) Charles Trois is blind and Blanc employs a thousand persons at Monte Carlo. Blanc you know is the ex-King of Homburg. Each of his daughters will have half a million (English). Both the Kings of Monaco (Blanc and Charles Trois) have *châteaux* in Normandy. I owe all this gossip to two sources, somewhat different – a charming French boatman and Lady Dilke.

Colvin being here is certainly a great improvement, and I have been more jocular than I have been for long. The standing[3]

Friday [*19 December*]

It is difficult to take up one's thread again; don't let us try. Today, we have spent the day in old Monaco, breakfasting at a hotel on the *Place*. The day was quite clouded over; but wonderfully soft and warm. One of those days of quiet irradiated light that are lavished upon us in England and for which we are so little thankful. I recollected having been there nearly eleven years ago, and my father throwing stones over the cliff and making me calculate the height. I think I spotted the old Casino. It is to let. The gardens on the edge of the cliff are superlatively delightful and we half think of moving up there away from the bands and gas jets and equivocal company of Monte Carlo. Nothing will reconcile Colvin to the Casino on the Riviera; I speak the words of wisdom continually and say that it is a very nice Casino, as a Casino, and that the gardens are nice; but the pigeon-shooting is certainly horrid to behold and the importunate noise of the guns pervades the garden all afternoon.[4] Tell my father that if he gives up that chapter, he will do a cowardly action; if he didn't know it very well himself, I wouldn't say so.[5] I am glad you liked 'Roads'. I am sleepy and must to bed.
Ever affectionate son   Robert Louis Stevenson

194   To Charles Baxter

MS Yale. Published in *Baxter Letters*, 39–40.

20 December 1873   *Monaco*

My dear Baxter, There is a large wooden chest (plain deal) in my sitting room; in that box many papers, and among these papers two stories, one (which you read a long while ago) called 'The Curate of Anstruther's

[2] François Blanc purchased the gambling concession at Monte Carlo in 1861 and made the Casino a great commercial success.
[3] The sentence breaks off at the bottom of the page. RLS starts again overleaf the next day.
[4] In the shooting-gallery on the lawn just below the terrace of the Casino, overlooking the sea, captive pigeons were released from traps to be shot by rifle-fire.
[5] This sentence was crossed through, presumably by MIS.

Bottle'; the other called 'The Devil on Cramond Sands'.[1] Both are written on single leaves of white ruled foolscap and I should think they would be close together. They cover each about thirty leaves written on one side only – O! the last leaves of the second story are on another sort of paper, not-ruled I think, which you might be apt to forget. If they are not in the chest (but I am almost sure they are), they are in one of the long drawers of the kist of drawers in the same room.

Now, if you will dedicate ten minutes of your time to this brief search, and send the papers to me by Book Post, you will be a very good and acceptable person, and I will forgive you your unaccountable inaction about W.W.[2] and a certain breach of confidence of which I say nothing now.

Do work this off for me, without delay, as it is of a little importance to yours truly, or may be. Please shew the accompanying certificate to my people, as it may amuse them. Ever your friend   R.L. Stevenson

'Admit ————————————————————
—— Charles Baxter, Esq.[s] Writer to Her
Majesty's Signet, ————————————————
————————————————————————
—— to view the Shrine
R. L. Stevenson
On Secret Service

To one Steward (an Stewardess)
of [14] Heriot Row.

195 To his Parents

MS Yale.

Monday 22 December [1873]   *Monte Carlo*

Glad to hear at last how you are. I am still very well; indeed today had been an extraordinary day for me; I have not been so well yet, I think.

Colvin has gone to Nice to get some books and he means to call on the

[1] See Letter 192 n. 5. 'The Curate of Anstruther's Bottle' is presumably the seventeenth-century anecdote recorded by RLS in 'The Coast of Fife' of how the devil came for Mr Thomson, the drunken Curate of Anstruther.

[2] RLS had asked Baxter to send him two of Whitman's books. See Letter 162.

Bennetts. I like the climate of Monaco, I think almost better than that of Mentone; or perhaps it is just that we have been having weather which is more to my taste: the air seems fresher and more bracing and tells its story better, as an air coming off the sea, and there does not seem to be the same difference between the temperature of day and night.

It is a strange place to live at in some ways. *Everybody* gambles; we produce the effect of something unnatural upon the people because we spend our evenings at home. Last night, our landlady (a German body who has been in Edinburgh and who has just learned enough of other languages to corrupt her own) told us how she was cheated right and left; how people disappeared and their baggage found its way, piece by piece, to the *Mont de Piété*; how the waiters spend the whole of their wages at the table; and (this with really great graphic power) how one man had shot himself in the house here six months ago.

We will move I expect in two days, either across the bay to old Monaco, or altogether away somewhere else.

You would not think that I was starving myself, if you could see the bill for my last night's dinner. I agree to tell you this story on the condition that it is never repeated in my hearing and that I am never even to see a smile on your faces when the fatal word is named. You must understand, first, that Colvin and I hang together in the loosest possible way, that our diets and digestions are so diametrically opposite that we are practically never to-gether at meal time, or, when we are, are eating quite different meals. Well, I went down alone to the restaurant last night, skimmed over the *carte* and was doubtful what vegetable to order; in a moment of half stupidity pointed to a word and said '*asperges*'. I had my dinner and when the *addition* was brought, I broke out into a cold perspiration – no, it was a hot one, by the by; it is as well to be physiologically correct – : they cost 10 fr. Ten silver francs.

C. and I are very dangerous for each other dietically; his principal meal is between twelve and one, and if I overeat myself then I am ill for a week; my main meal is at six, and if C. overeats himself then, he is nowhere for a fortnight.

I am nearly done with M'Crie's *Knox*. 'Acushla', as Colvin calls him, is really an awful ass; I have laughed over him sometimes till I was sore. Only, he certainly had read a lot.

Later

Colvin has brought home *Woodstock*[1] from Nice and we have started reading it aloud, which is a huge institution. He has seen Bennett and

[1] Scott's novel (1826).

reported my case and taken sweet counsel[2] with him, but it does not seem to have made any great difference on his views.

I do not think Mrs B. the wisest of persons in all ways; I hear much of her somewhat inconsiderate tattle through the Andrewses who are very thick with the Bennetts. This for your instruction, as it has been for mine.[3] I am glad you both seem pleased with 'Roads'. I do not agree with Monsieur as to its position in relation to the 'Old Scotch Gardener'.[4] 'Roads' is quite the best written thing I have ever done, to my taste. There are things expressed in it far harder to express, than in anything else I ever tried; and that after all is the great point. As for style, *ça viendra peut-être*. You may show it to Hanky[5] if you like: it is yours; you have bought the journal; it ceased to be mine when I parted with it to P.G. Hamerton the editor of the publication.[6]

It is M'Crie, and not Knox, whom Colvin calls 'Acushla' – Acushla Machree, Irish term of endearment. The Irish language, so far as I am acquainted with it (from one representation of *The Colleen Bawn*)[7] consists mainly of the word M'Crie.

I do hope M'sieur will stick to his flag, and not sacrifice again to that unlovely altar.

It was as well you sent me a paper or I should never have known who 'Hanky' was; he is not happily named; these syllables have been already made familiar to the B'r'ish Public in a manner quite the reverse of serious. Nicholson has made great strides surely. How did they get the harmonium in and out?

If I am as well again tomorrow as I have been today, I shall be much elated. Ever your affectionate son   Robert Louis Stevenson

196   To his Parents

MS Yale (filed with Letter 195).

Wednesday [*24 December 1873*]   [*Monaco*]

I suppose I am one of the best invalids in the world; beside occasional unregenerate motions after coffee, I have settled down without difficulty

---

[2] Cf. Psalm 54:14.

[3] These two sentences were scored out by MIS.

[4] Published in the *Edinburgh University Magazine* for March 1871 and reprinted in *Memories and Portraits*.

[5] Probably a joke or a newspaper misprint for Sankey. The revival meetings conducted in Edinburgh November 1873 to January 1874 by the American evangelists Dwight L. Moody and Ira D. Sankey aroused immense enthusiasm. A number of the services were held in St Stephen's Church which at that time had no organ. MIS went to several of the services.

[6] Philip Gilbert Hamerton (1834–94), artist and essayist who founded and edited *The Portfolio* 1869–94.

[7] Dion Boucicault's popular play (1860).

into the discipline of my position. I do not care to walk; I am quite happy to bask; I read and knock about and am as inert and peaceable as a man can be.

It is a long time since you have written; but I saw you had received my letters by the changed address of the newspaper that came this morning. I have been better the last three or four days than I have hitherto been; and count myself altogether a better specimen than I was. However I am not yet tempted to indiscretion by any very notable excess of vitality; such happy difficulties will return in time, I hope. Indeed I am really in far better hope about myself than I have been at some periods; this good fit has not only been better but it has been more permanent.

I have one of Colvin's pens; and it seems to me as if it made me write ridiculously like him; but there has always been noticed a similarity between the hands.

Woodstock is a delight; we read it all afternoon in an olive yard, and all evening over the fire. I would counsel you to get it, if you have not read it already, it is as jolly as can be.

I regret to say that the weather has changed; and that we have, once again bright glaring sun and a chill air, and the customary gymnastic of the thermometer at sunset. There is nothing so charming as the cloudy weather here; the nights are so warm that you can sit out without a greatcoat if you will, and the delightful veiled temperate sunshine of the afternoon is a thing to enjoy before one dies. I had quite forgotten this sort of weather. And you?

Tomorrow being Xmas, we drive over to Mentone to lunch and spend the day with the Andrewses. I own I should just as soon stay where I was; and so I think would Colvin, but the A.'s were very kind to me and the excursion must be made: I don't know how it is that we seem incapable of motion; I call it infirmity of purpose. Colvin repudiates the expression with contempt and sets it down to an aversion for packing.

Certainly the seas of books that we have messed about the two rooms look disheartening. Living here is however somewhat more expensive than I could wish; one lives like a fighting cock, but pays accordingly. I should like, by the way, to hear some more about my father's lecture; was it much on the same rails as the *Good Words* article?[1]

No – I am not doing much intellectually. I am very stupid; so is Colvin. For two people, each with some pretensions to intellect, I am bound to say that we are both very stupid. However we have plenty of fun; and now that we have reached the bogey part of *Woodstock*, we have little thought for much else. The people about, too, have a sort of interest of their own – from the other side of the street. I shall not close this tonight in case I have

---

[1] MIS records that on 4 December TS gave a lecture on British storms to the St Stephen's Young Men's Literary Association. His article 'British Storms' appeared in *Good Words* for June 1868.

a letter from you tomorrow as I expect I shall, and time enough before we start, to put in an answer if any be needed.

Xmas Day

Many happy returns to you all. There is no time to wait. I must just get this posted without waiting to see whether you wish an answer or no. Although it is not much use unless you send to the post on Sunday morning; in case you do so, however, I wish you good-bye. Ever your affectionate son   Robert Louis Stevenson

197   To his Mother

MS Yale.

Sunday 28th [December 1873]   [*Monaco*]

The braces are in London at the Dead Letter Office 'in consequence of not being a *bona fide* Sample or Pattern.' Happily my obedient humble servant G.R. Smith is the Controller at present; and I feel sure he will do everything in his power to oblige me.

The list of persons to whom you sent my paper seems inspired; but you have not sent me Wilson's address.

You may best understand my improved condition by a fact. Yesterday afternoon, profiting by Colvin's absence on a walk, I went down to the band and heard Chopin's *Marche Funèbre* and a long overture of Mendelssohn's, and was able to walk home again at the end of it all; and am none the worse this morning. Whereas, when we first came here, I went in only for a minute and had to flee in a pitiable state of smash at the first noise of brass.

This week sometime, I expect we shall go to Hyères; continue however to address Poste Restante Mentone; only one headquarters is the motto.

By the by, looking over what you said about 'Roads', I was much pleased with it. Excuse a lecture. When one deals with such far-away feelings, *the danger* is to put on approximate colours with a trowel and to get coarse, noisy and high falutin'; it could be said to 'elude' (though I confess it is a paradox) it is likely to be more nearly correct. So I took your criticism as a great encouragement, madame. I wish you would tell me what part of it you liked the best.

I am writing to catch a post today; so you must take what you can get. With all good wishes to both of you, Your affectionate son

Robert Louis Stevenson

198   To his Parents

MS Yale.

[30 December 1873]   *[Monaco]*

We go to Mentone on Thursday. We have had about enough of this.

I wish you to get from some library and send hither to me shortly, *Clément Marot and other Essays* by Prof. Henry Morley.

Also I wish my father would keep his eyes open after two books that I want badly – Ruddiman's *Buchanan* and Chalmers's *Lindsay*.[1]

Adieu-Ever affectionate son   Robert Louis Stevenson

I send a figure★ to my father;[2] it is thought very fine; a Professor of Art has given in his adhesion to it; by bending back a portion of the legs he can be made to remain upright in a kneeling position.   R.L.S.

★ I hereby certify that this is a work of art of the first class, and that I consider it my duty to encourage this kind of exercise in preference to most others. (Signed)

Sidney Colvin, Professor of Fine Arts, M.A. Etc.

199   To his Mother

MS Yale. Published in *Letters*, I, 110–11.

2 January 1874   *Hôtel Mirabeau, Mentone*

Here I am over in the east bay of Mentone, where I am not altogether sorry to find myself. I move so little that I soon exhaust the immediate neighbourhood of my dwelling places. Our reason for coming here was however very simple. Hobson's choice. Mentone during my absence has filled marvellously.

Continue to address P.R. Mentone; and try to conceive it as possible that I am not a drivelling idiot. When I wish an address changed, it is quite on the cards that I shall be able to find language explicit enough to express the desire. My whole desire is to avoid complication of addresses. It is quite fatal. If two P.R.s have contradictory orders they will continue to play

---

[1] George Buchanan, *Opera Omnia*, ed. Thomas Ruddiman, 2 vols (1715); Sir David Lindsay, *Poetical Works*, ed. G. Chalmers, 3 vols (1806).

[2] A figure of a kneeling man drawn and cut out by RLS and mounted on the letter. The 'certificate' is in Colvin's hand.

battledore and shuttlecock with an unhappy epistle, which will never get further afield but perish there miserably.

You act too much on the principle that whatever I do is done unwisely; and that whatever I do not, has been culpably forgotten. This is wounding to my nat'ral vanity.

I have not written for three days I think; but what days! They were very cold; and I must say I was able thoroughly to appreciate the blessings of Mentone. Old Smoko, this winter would evidently have been very summary with me. I could not stand the cold at all. I exhausted all my own and all Colvin's clothing; I then retired to the house, and then to bed; in a condition of sorrow for myself unequalled. The sun is forth again (*laus Deo*) and the wind is milder, and I am greatly re-established. A certain asperity of temper still lingers, however, which Colvin supports with much mildness.

In this hotel, I have a room on the first floor! Luxury, however, is not altogether regardless of expense. We only pay 13 frs. per day – 3½ more than at the Pavillon on the third floor – And beggars must not be choosers. We were very nearly houseless, the night we came. And it is rarely that such winds of adversity blow men into Kings' Palaces.

Looking over what has gone before, it seems to me that it is not strictly polite. I beg to withdraw all that is offensive.

At *table d'hôte*, we have some people who amuse us much; two Americans, who would try to pass for French people and their daughter the most charming of little girls.[1] Both Colvin and I have planned an abduction already. The whole hotel is devoted to her; and the waiters continually do smuggle out comfits and fruit and pudding to her. All well. Ever affectionate son   Robert Louis Stevenson

200   *To his Mother*

MS Yale. Partly published in *Letters*, I, 111–12.

Sunday 4 January 1874   *Mentone*

I got your letter today; but I am not sure that I do remember the Bishop of Toledo.[1] It was something about a sermon; and I take it the allusion was rude, so am not displeased that my memory fails me. You seem to be a long while in receiving my letters; at least, this last seems scarcely quite posted up to the date I should have expected.

Mrs Romanes overtook me yesterday and told me you had written to her. It was very kind of you, although I fear the intercourse will never be

[1] Mr and Mrs Johnstone (or Johnson) and their daughter Marie.
[1] A family joke. Apparently originally a nickname for TS, but later applied to RLS himself.

very familiar. Not but that one of the daughters smiles upon me, as if the graces of my person and the charm of my address pleased her more than they seem to please madame. Poor Mrs R.! With the traces of having once been pretty, there is something very sad about the aspect of her age, if the word be not too strong. The lines in her face are lines of suffering or at least of uneasiness, and not of suffering that has been pleasantly or constantly endured; and when she speaks with you, there is a very painful distraction in her manner, as if she were conscious of some one overhearing her or as if she were keeping an ear for something else. I wonder if her married life has been happy.

We have here fallen on the very pink of hotels. I do not say that it is more pleasantly conducted than the Pavillon, for that were impossible; but the rooms are so cheery and bright and new, and then the food! I never I think, so fully appreciated the phrase 'the fat of the land' as I have done since I have been here installed. There was a dish of eggs at *déjeuner* the other day, over the memory of which I lick my lips in the silent watches.

Now that the cold has gone again, I continue to keep well in body and already I begin to walk a little more. My head is still a very feeble implement and easily set a spinning; and I can do nothing in the way of work beyond reading books that may, I hope, be of some use to me afterwards.

I was very glad to see that McLaren[2] was sat upon, and principally for the reason why. Deploring as I do much of the action of the Trades Unions, these conspiracy clauses and the whole partiality of the Master and Servant Act are a disgrace to our equal laws. Equal laws become a byword when what is legal for one class becomes a criminal offence for another. It did my heart good to hear that man tell McLaren how, as he had talked much of getting the franchise for working men, he must now be content to see them use it now they had got it. This is a smooth stone well-planted in the foreheads of certain dilettante radicals, after McLaren's fashion, who are willing to give the working men words and wind and votes and the like, and yet think to keep all the advantages, just or unjust, of the wealthier classes without abatement. I do hope wise men will not attempt to fight the working men on the head of this notorious injustice. Any such step will only precipitate the action of the newly enfranchised classes, and irritate them into acting hastily; when what we ought to desire should be that they should act warily and little for many years to come, until education and habit may make them the more fit.

[2] Duncan McLaren (1800–86), Independent Liberal MP for Edinburgh 1865–81. He had offended Edinburgh Trade Unionists by refusing to support their agitation for repeal of the Criminal Law Amendment Act, especially those clauses designed to protect non-union workmen who wished to work during a strike. Meetings and demonstrations were held to 'denounce' him and a vote of no confidence was passed at a meeting of electors. In spite of this, he held the seat with an increased majority at the next election.

All this (intended for my father) is much after the fashion of his own correspondence. I confess it has left my own head exhausted; I hope it may not produce the same effect on yours. But I want him to look really into this question (both sides of it and not the representations of rabid middle-class newspapers, sworn to support all the little tyrannies of wealth) and I know he will be convinced that this is a case of unjust law; and that, however desirable the end may seem to him, he will not be Jesuit enough to think that any end will justify an unjust law.

Here ends the political sermon of Your affectionate (and somewhat dogmatical) son   Robert Louis Stevenson

201 To George Wilson[1]

MS NLS.

5 January 1874   *Hôtel Mirabeau, Mentone*

My dear Wilson, By a wonderful *à propos*, your address reaches me now, on the very morning of your dinner. I wish I could be there in person; but you may be sure that I am there in sympathy. I shall never forget all that I owe to you and the many pleasant times we have had together, and you may count upon it that there are not many present this evening at your dinner who were more sincerely happy at your success; or who better knew how well you had deserved it. I know that you won't look upon this as humbug, or I wouldn't write it. Besides as I have been very nearly in kingdom come, and am not, even now, quite out of earshot of the heavenly psalmody, I have a certain right to say what I feel, not given to oily, ruddy, healthful people at home.

Seriously about my health, it was as near a smash as could be. You knew when you were in Edinburgh that I had a good deal to bother me; that went on increasing to a very painful degree; my father was ill – even caused his doctor some alarm – and I blamed myself about that: at the same time, I kept on working about seven hours a day and walking a good deal, thinking that would do me good. The last weeks were weeks of terrible wretchedness, just holding myself together with both hands. At last, when I did get to London, I got there only to have no head in the world, to be hysterical, to have a crawling up my spine if I wrote two sides of a letter and – in fine

[1] A Mr Wilson is mentioned by MIS as being employed as a private tutor from 1868 onwards; he was present at RLS's 21st birthday party. It seems likely that he was the Revd George Wilson (1838–1921), who was ordained and became minister of the Tolbooth Church, Edinburgh in 1873. He was transferred to Cramond in 1878 and in 1887 to St Michael's Mission Church, Edinburgh. The reference to Archibald Bisset, another clergyman, (see Letter 189, n. 5) lends support to this identification.

– to be sent away here and just saved immediate damnation by the thickness of a sheet of note paper. My people do not know how ill I was; nor in fact does almost anyone, so you need not expatiate about that. I am wonderfully better; though I am only able to walk about a mile in the day and the least work, or even writing such a note as this, makes my head swim and fills my eyes with blood. However, I think I am going to give auld clootie the slip for a season; which I did not always expect.

Sidney Colvin is here with me and has been for about three weeks. This is very jolly for me; I shall be damned lonely when he goes. Bob is at Antwerp at the School of Art, where he seems to be getting on fairly well.

I was very much pleased to hear that Bisset had got settled somewhere at last – or rather I fancy I should say so soon. Please tell him of my congratulations.

You will know that when I am here alone, I have sometimes periods of a certain (shall we say?) dullness. Often I cannot read for the two hours between sunset and dinner as then my eyes are at their worst; so that they are not vastly agreeable – these two hours. All this means, that if ever you should find time for a note – just how do you do and good-bye even – it would be very acceptable to sincerely yours. Poste Restante is my address; it is safer than hotels, in case one changes. The same remark applies to the Curate of Foulden.[2]

Have you heard that I have made my first little cookey by literature – I can scarcely say bread – ? A sketch of mine appeared in the *Portfolio*, for which I shall get three guineas or so. I don't think you would much care for it; so I am afraid to suggest that you should look at it. But in case you *did* want to see my first attempt it was in the December part and called 'Roads'. For God's sake, don't tell Bisset about it; it is of that description which is least calculated to please him; and I fear he would despise me thenceforward.

And now I must shut up. I shall drink your health and prosperity today at dinner, and listen for the cheering from Edinburgh. Ever yours sincerely

Robert Louis Stevenson

202   *To his Mother*

MS Yale. Partly published in *Letters*, I, 113–14.

7 January 1874   *Mentone*

Yes. I have been compared already to the Bishop of Toledo. I shall cease further correspondence on the next allusion to this ecclesiastic.

[2] Where Bisset was the minister.

I received yesterday two most charming letters – the nicest I have had
since I left – December 26th and January 1st: this morning I got January 3rd.
Of course it was written by Colvin; this is ridiculous, we don't write so like
as all that comes to. Yes, you are right about *Woodstock*. Let me rehearse the
titles somewhat at greater length. *The Works of George Buchanan*: edit.
Ruddiman. *The Works of Sir David Lindsay of the Mount*: edit. Chalmers.
Now are you pleased. Let them be looked for wherever they are likely to
be found; I am not so very anxious to have them looked for, you know; my
principal anxiety is to get them found. Hamerton has not yet dubbed up.[1]

There is the catechism answered, so far as I remember.

The stories for which I have to thank you are: the Xmas dinner at Uncle
George's;[2] my father's solicitude about your writing too much (a little gem
of anecdote); and your own party with MacGregor as host.[3] You see I am
down upon kids.

Into the bargain with Marie, the American girl, who is grace itself, and
comes leaping and dancing simply like a wave – like nothing else; and who
yesterday was Queen out of the Epiphany cake and chose Robinet (the
French painter) as her *favori* with the most pretty confusion possible. Into
the bargain with Marie, we have two little Russian girls, with the youngest
of whom, a little polyglot button of a three-year-old, I had the most
laughable little scene at lunch today. I was watching her being fed with great
amusement, her face being as broad as it is long and her mouth capable of
unlimited extension; when suddenly, her eye catching mine, the fashion of
her countenance was changed, and regarding me with a really admirable
appearance of offended dignity, she said something in Italian which made
everybody laugh much. It was explained to me that she had said I was very
polisson to stare at her. After this she was somewhat taken up with me and
after some examination, she announced emphatically to the whole table, in
German, that I was a *Mädchen*; which word she repeated with shrill emphasis, as though fearing that her proposition would be called in question –
'*Mädchen, Mädchen, Mädchen, Mädchen.*' This hasty conclusion as to my sex,
she was led afterwards to revise, I am informed; but her new opinion (which
seems to have been something nearer the truth) was announced in a third
language quite unknown to me and probably Russian. To complete the
scroll of her accomplishments, she was brought round the table after the
meal was over and said good-bye to me in very commendable English.

[1] I.e. Hamerton had not paid for the essay 'Roads'.
[2] 'Christmas day – dine at George's. Little Tom has been crying up the chimney to "Sandy Claus"
to bring him a dirk – he gets two! and is out of the body with delight' (MIS, *Diary*).
[3] 'I have a blind man's buff party at home . . . MacGregor is host and proposes Lou's health as "The
Man in the Moon". Very good' (MIS, *Diary*, 3 January 1874). James MacGregor (1832–1910),
minister of St Cuthbert's 1873–1910, enjoyed the reputation of being one of the most eloquent
preachers in the Church of Scotland.

There is a Roland for your Oliver.

O! I remember another question. Why do I cut the sheet in half?[4] Why? Well, because I prefer it so, I suppose.

The weather I shall say nothing about; as I am incapable of explaining my sentiments upon that subject before a lady. But my health is really greatly improved: I begin to recognise myself occasionally, now and again; not without satisfaction.

Will you remember me specially to MacGregor: I look back upon him with especial favour. And O, by the by, I must tell you a curious thing. When I heard that Buchan liked my paper, I was more pleased by far than when I heard it was accepted. I seem to have a curious liking and respect for Buchan.

Please remember me very kindly to Professor Swan; I wish I had a story to send him but story, Lord bless you, I have none to tell, sir;[5] unless it is the foregoing adventure with the little polyglot. The best of that depends on the significance of *polisson* which is beautifully out of place. Ever your affectionate son   Robert Louis Stevenson

203   *To his Mother*

MS Yale. Excerpt published in *Letters*, I, 114–15, linked to Letter 202.

Saturday 10 January 1874   *Mentone*

Yes I think I did get an umbrella; but I think it cost ten bob, not sixteen. Enquire into this. – No, it is not Mrs B. that keeps me from going to Nice; I do not think anything against her, she is good natured, but also she is a facile and *incorrect* tattler. What keeps me from going is simply the fatigue of the journey there and back; it makes a very horrid day. I shall go shortly to Henry B. Indeed I went today and after sitting an hour in his waiting room, came away again without farther success.

The little Russian kid is only two and a half; she speaks six languages. She and her sister (*aet.* 8) and May Johnson (*aet.* 8) are the delight of my life. Last night I saw them all dancing – O it was jolly; kids are what is the matter with me. After the dancing, we all – that is the two Russian ladies, Robinet, the French painter, Mr and Mrs Johnstone, two governesses, and fitful kids joining us at intervals, played a game of the stool of repentance in the Gallic idiom.

[4] At this time RLS was writing on small half-sheets of writing paper.
[5] 'Story! God bless you! I have none to tell, Sir.' – George Canning, 'The Friend of Humanity and the Knife-Grinder'.

O – I have not told you that Colvin is gone;[1] however, he is coming
back again; he has left clothes in pawn to me.

I hear poor accounts of Mrs Sitwell, whom misfortunes and anxieties
seem to pursue. I hope however to hear that she is better shortly.

I lunched with the Andrews's on Friday; today I have called on Miss
Ward, who, I find, has been very seedy but is better; and the Romaneses,
who were out.

So I have a good deal of news for this note. I have not yet heard since
No. 2.[2]

I was so glad to hear about the chapter; it was well done. I throw up my
cap. Bravo! Ever your affectionate son   Robert Louis Stevenson

204   To Sidney Colvin

MS Bristol.

Saturday [10 January 1874]   *Mentone*

When next I lend a clothes brush, it shall be to one of stricter honesty.
Please send me the ticket for Visconti's library, it must be nearly time to
renew it. The Andrews's were offensively sorry for your departure. Confound 'em, they might have been very glad for what they had.

I had such a charming evening with the kids – O beautiful kids – and the
Russians and Johnstonses and Robinet, and then nearly fell asleep over the
Fortnightly. Morley is very jolly; so is Marat.[1] I have written another note to
Mrs. Sitwell, but somehow I had a horrid notion something would go
wrong with it; whence this other to you. I am all right, I think. I have found
out for myself that that game is not kidneys, but some muscle in my back
that seems weak and rather out of it. I am going to see Bennet today; my
finger is d—d sore, so I think it should be ready for dissection – I ceased to
be able to work promptly, isn't that odd. Yesterday, I duly worked my
hour. The net result was three and a half sentences; which, after I had reread
them with preparation and prayer, I did unhesitatingly delete. I shall not
repeat this farce – O! Boyd called yesterday morning, while yet the
threshhold was hot from the passage of your feet; I described your movements in magnificent perspective; I think he supposes you in Cappraria.[2] He
was extremely cheery, he came into the room (figuratively) leaping and

---

[1] Colvin had gone to Paris for a few weeks, probably to see Mrs Sitwell.
[2] The Stevensons were beginning to number their letters in order to check on possible losses.
  Unfortunately their letters from this period have not survived.
[1] The January issue of the *Fortnightly* contained an essay by John Morley on 'Mr Mill's Autobiography' and one on Jean-Paul Marat by F. Bowen-Graves.
[2] Caprera, a small island off the coast of Sardinia where Garibaldi was living in retirement.

singing and praising God[3] that he was not as other men; he seems so unaffectedly happy to be *Boyd*; there is something very pretty about it. He also told me an i–d–c–t anecdote. Ever yours   Robert Louis Stevenson

Mind I hear on Monday.

205   *To his Mother*

MS half at Yale and half at Bancroft. Partly published in *Letters*, I, 115–16.

Sunday 11 January 1874   *Mentone*

In many ways, this hotel is more amusing than the Pavillon. There are the children to begin with; and then there are games every evening, the stool of repentance, question and answer, etc. And then, we speak French, although that is not exactly an advantage in so far as personal brilliancy is concerned.

Today, I got No. 3. I was in a bad humour, was I? Ah, I thought so. If you could ask Colvin, he could tell you something more on that head. Cold weather makes me the most unpleasant of living things; and I snap and snarl and empty vials right and left upon men and beasts and inanimate objects with a heartiness that is refreshing to witness.

I am in lovely health again today: I am very easily put down again. The little excitement of Colvin's departure put me out of gear for a couple of days; but I have got all right again, and feel quite boastful. I walked as far as the Pont St Louis very nearly today, besides walking and knocking about among the olives in the afternoon. I do not make much progress with my French; but I do make a little I think. I was pleased with my success this evening; though I do not know if others shared the satisfaction.

The two Russian ladies (Madame Garschin and Mme — sneeze, and you'll approximate)[1] are from Georgia all the way. They do not at all answer to the description of Georgian slaves however; being graceful and refined and only good looking after you know them a bit. Mme —[2] puts me a little in mind of poor Jessie Warden[3] curiously enough; she has some of the same

---

[3] Cf. Acts 3:8.

[1] Mme Sophie Garschine and her elder sister Madame Nadia Zassetsky. RLS made two false starts at spelling 'Zassetsky' then abandoned the attempt. Colvin says that they were fifteen or more years older than RLS and both he and Furnas make the point that Russian character and temperament were not then as familiar in the West as they have since become through translated plays and novels. In *Memories and Notes*, Colvin writes: 'Both were brilliantly accomplished and cultivated women, one [Madame Z.] having all the unblushing outspokenness of her race; its unchecked vehemence and mutability in mirth and anger, in scorn, attachment, or aversion; the other much of an invalid, consistently gentle and sympathetic, and withal an exquisite musician.'

[2] Another attempt to spell 'Zassetsky', crossed through.

[3] See Letter 171, n. 11.

manner and grimaces; when I see her playing games that I have often played with Jessie, I catch myself often comparing the two.

[4]To do you justice, you do not complain about my correspondence nowadays. I do not yet understand the famous week of the telegram; but I was still very seedy and stupid and used to calculate making the pauses as long as was practicable; for I was very averse from letter-writing.

I find I am much amused by the roll-call of dinner parties. Please remember me very kindly to the Jenkins and thank them for having asked about me. Tell Mrs J. that I am engaged perfecting myself in the 'Gallic idiom', in order to be a worthier Vatel[5] for the future. M. Folleté, our host, is a Vatel by the way. He cooks himself, and is not insensible to flattery on the score of his table. I began of course to complain of the wine (part of the routine of life at Mentone); I told him that where one found a kitchen so exquisite one astonished oneself that the wine was not up to the same form. '*Eh voilà précisement mon côté faible, monsieur,*' he replied with an indescribable amplitude of gesture. '*Que voulez vous? Moi, je suis cuisinier!*' It was as though Shakespeare, called to account for some such peccadillo as the Bohemian seaport, should answer magnificently that he was a poet. So Folleté lives, in a golden zone of a certain sort – a golden, or rather torrid zone, whence he issues twice daily purple as to his face – and all these clouds and vapours and ephemeral winds pass far below him and disturb him not.

He has another hobby however; his garden, round which it is his highest pleasure to lead the unwilling guest. Whenever he is not in the kitchen, he is hanging round loose, seeking whom he may show his garden to. Much of my time is passed in studiously avoiding him, and I have brought the art to a very extreme pitch of perfection. The fox, often hunted, becomes wary. Ever your affectionate son   Robert Louis Stevenson

206   *To Elizabeth Crosby*

MS Yale.

Sunday 11 January 1874   *Hôtel Mirabeau, Mentone*

My dear Miss Crosby, Coming across an old letter of yours, I begin to fear that my last was insufficiently addressed and hasten to write again. In case it has never reached you, I must recapitulate briefly my defence. I have been very ill, and am not yet very well. The trouble that I was going through at

---

[4] The Bancroft MS begins at this point.

[5] In the Jenkin theatricals of May 1873, RLS had played 'Vatel, a cook' in *My Son-in-Law*, translated from Emile Augier's comedy *Le Gendre de Monsieur Poirier*. The historical François Vatel, Steward to the Prince de Condé, committed suicide in 1671 because he thought the fish would not arrive in time for a banquet for Louis XIV.

home, too much work and other causes, produced a complete breakdown, utter nervous prostration, an incapacity for intellectual work quite un-equalled in my experience (should there be two l's in unequaled? O yes, there should surely. The last looks very forlorn. Where was I? O yes) and nearly everything bad except low spirits. I certainly was not far off the dark river, in religious idiom; but I have pulled round wonderfully and do not think I am going to die yet a bit, after all.

Now, I hope this will lead you to pardon me for my long silence. I was not very fit for writing letters to say the truth. As for not calling, I only arrived in London to be sent off here, in a pitiable state really.

I am now, I say, really better. I can walk about a little, and the sense of enjoyment which for more than a month lay quite dormant in me in this beautiful home of my recollections, has at last reawakened; the bandage has been taken from my eyes, and I can see again that these are the same splendid hills and gardens. While it lasted, however, there was nothing more depressing and even irritating; and this effect was increased for me by the fact that I had been there before and knew the whole place by heart. I would trail my poor carcase, with great difficulty, up to some favourite point of view, and wait and wait and no ecstasy would come; it is not much of a figure of speech to say that I was blind.

But now, I am alert again and very quick to enjoy. And by good fortune, there are three children in the hotel here with me that give me an immensity of delight. Two little girls of eight − one of them a model of natural grace and lightness and vitality − and one wonderful little creature of two and a half, who is busily engaged just now in making herself beautiful for the future. The dull body resists; but there are impulses of grace, inspirations of just and appropriate movement, in the little brain that are ever struggling to express themselves outwardly; and that every now and then succeed, and do manage to incarnate themselves in a visible gesture, after a thousand ridiculous fiascos, a thousand laughable, lumpy, fat, babyish failures.

Out of my children and the scenery and the little corner of work that I permit myself, now and again, on red-letter days, I manage to get enough excitement for a tolerably happy life. Still it is often an intolerable thought, to be thus *planté-là* at the very outset of life that one had hoped to make full and beautiful and useful. And the feeling that money is being spent on one, day by day, which one scarcely sees how one is ever to be able to repay to Society, would become a nightmare if it were indulged.

My friend Sidney Colvin, whose name I daresay you may have seen on the cover of the *Fortnightly* or elsewhere, has been staying with me for nearly a month, and his company has been a great pleasure; but he is gone again now, although soon (I hope) to return.

Bob is still at Antwerp, studying. I had a letter from him this morning, written in good spirits but talking of a speedy move to some other school.

I hope you will let me know if this reaches you. I shall put two addresses on in case of accident. Believe me, Yours sincerely

Robert Louis Stevenson

O! my first publication – a paper on 'Roads' appeared, I believe (I have not yet seen it myself) in the *Portfolio* for December.

207   *To Bob Stevenson*

Text: TS copy, BL.

[c. *12 January 1874*]   [*Mentone*]
[*Beginning of letter missing*]

... kid about two and a half years old, and speaks six languages; the words come up all the same, as they come handy, English, French, German, Italian, Russian, etc. She calls me Monsieur Berechino,[1] which is the Italian for *Polisson*. She is a hell of a jolly kid. Also we play games of an evening; and we all talk French which is good practice although suppressive to the *esprit*. I am more *bête* than any array of terms can express, in that language.

Has W.W. paralysis, poor devil?[2] That's what I shall have some of these days. I have no more artisticisms at present. If you see S.C., he will likely be able to tell you some. I shall write to him and tell him that you may perhaps call before he leaves. I should like you to *ménager* him, as he is one of the best of human beings, as kind as boots, and a bloody clever fellow into the bargain and one who hates God and Heaven and the soul and sich.[3]

Edinburgh, they write me, is in high revival. One can go to these prayer meetings every day, if one pleases; and all the world is repenting of sin and bathing in the blood of the lamb without money and without price, world without end, amen, glory glory hallelujah.

I think I may count myself as better, but I am still so easily overset and thrown back that I cannot boast. A few minutes hard walking, a piece of bad news in a letter, a cold day – anything sends me back again and I have to make quite another convalescence before I am myself again. I shall send off this scrap, because I want it to reach you soon. Ever your affectionate friend

Robert Louis Stevenson

---

[1] RLS's misspelling of *birichino* – little rascal. Cf. Letter 202.
[2] Bob had heard from an American of Walt Whitman's partial paralysis.
[3] '[Atheism] was indeed the fashion of the hour; even to the fastidious Colvin, the humblest pleasantry was welcome if it were winged against God Almighty or the Christian Church' (RLS, 'Memoirs of Himself ').

208   To Sidney Colvin

MS Yale. Partly published in *Letters*, I, 130.

[*12 January 1874*]   [*Mentone*]

My dear Colvin, I write to let you know that my cousin may possibly come
to Paris before you leave; he will likely look you up to hear about me, etc.
I want to tell you about him before you see him; as I am tired of people
misjudging him. You know *me* now. Well, Bob is just such another mutton,
only somewhat farther wandered and with perhaps a little more mire on his
wool. He has all the same elements of character that I have: no two people
were ever more alike only that the world has gone more unfortunately for
him, although more evenly. Besides which, he is really a gentleman and an
admirable true friend, which is not a common article.

I write this as a letter of introduction in case he should catch you ere you
leave.

No letters today (Monday). *Sacré chien*, *Dieu de Dieu*, and I have written
with exemplary industry. But I am hoping that no news is good news and
shall continue so to hope, until all is blue.

Imagine my delight to find a footnote in Capefigs[1] thus conceived: –

> ### * Apud M'Cries, 1545.

It was dear old darling Acushla. Doesn't he look handsome with the
terminal s? Immediately after, Capefigues talks of *la grande flotte de Dracke*.

Today is Russian New Year. Robinné (which seems to be how his name
is spelt, confound him) gave bouquets to all the ladies, and tea and music in
the salon; but as I had a little overwalked myself and was bad in the head,
I funked the entertainment. Ever yours   Robert Louis Stevenson

209   To Sidney Colvin

MS Yale.

Tuesday 13th [*January 1874*]   [*Mentone*]

My dear Colvin, I told you I did not hear on Monday. Well, this morning
Venus came to me while I was dressing and offered me two confounded

---

[1] Jean Baptiste Honoré Raymond Capefigue (1802–72), prolific French historian. RLS was reading
his *Histoire de la Réforme, de la Ligue, et du Règne de Henri IV* (8 vols, 1834–5). The references are
in Vol. 4, 19–20.

Scotch newspapers. I asked if there were no letters – was she certain – quite certain? And then I gave her a faint notion of the noise of a certain division of English generally known as language. She immediately bolted; and I stood in the middle of the room, the newly arrived journals in one hand and my toothbrush in the other, and uninterruptedly blasphemed the Lord my God for the space of about a minute and a half. I may sometimes have sworn 'with a better grace', but never, I am sure, 'more natural';[1] it was just one perfect jet of language. I was come to an end of this and was engaged (I assure you) in reorganising my whole nature on the strictest principles of philosophy, when there came a knock at the door, and Venus reappeared, still laughing at the vigour of my last remarks, with one letter in the well known up and down, and another in a suspicious dissipated, drunken, scrawly, uncertain sort of fist unknown to me, which turned out on investigation to be that of Master Bert. I smiled simply from ear to ear; knowing the width of my smile, on even ordinary occasions of delight, I imagine it must have [been] something worth seeing just then.

I am rather afraid that 'Mr Solway'[2] is miscarrying; it is getting very long and the profoundly matter of fact manner peculiar to yours truly, I am afraid, is too heavy for such a class of story. The incidents are not vivid enough to carry off the stolidity of the style.

I am quite thick with the Russians now. The room next door is occupied. The lady coughs, and I tremble lest they should make a row about my smoking. I lost a Philippine[3] to Marie which I duly paid. 'Le Grand Hotel Godam'[4] is in the press. Today, at last, I saw Bennet. He has changed my tonic and given me a villainous acid that deforms my human face divine past recognition. The growth was a wart after all, and it has been cauterised; I did not know a wart could be so sore; the last two or three days, it has really troubled me.

---

[1] 'He does it with a better grace, but I do it more natural.' *Twelfth Night*, II.iii.90.

[2] One of the stories in both lists of the *Covenanting Story Book* described in n. 5 of Letter 192. In Notebook A 265A it is called 'Strange Adventure of Mr Nehemiah Solway'. It is also listed as 'Hylsop and the Coals of Fire being . . . a relation of the strange chances that befell the Reverend Mr. Nehemiah Solway in the year 1687' in 'Notes Practical, Historical and Amusing' (some pages from a notebook of *c.* 1868 at Yale).

[3] A game in which a person finding a nut with two kernels eats one and gives the other to a person of the opposite sex. When the two next meet, the one who first says 'Good morning, Philippine', is entitled to a present from the other.

[4] A small card containing a burlesque hotel advertisement in French and broken English, concocted by RLS at Mentone (apparently with Colvin's help) and printed at a local press. There is a copy at Harvard. This very rare piece of Stevensoniana is reprinted in Lucas, 84–5.

Wednesday [*14 January*]

I have ordered D'Aubigné's *Memoirs*[5] and bought a book by Philarète Chasles on the XVIth century in France[6] and Augustin Thierry's *Histoire du Tiers État* to see what he makes of the Ligue.[7]

Don't bother to answer all my notes, please; it is just a need of babilation to one who knows how I exist. I am pretty well today, only busted up with tea last night which Robinet made me take. Ever yours

Robert Louis Stevenson

210   *To Frances Sitwell*

MS NLS. Excerpts published in *Letters*, I, 116–18.

Tuesday 13th [*January 1874*]   [*Mentone*]

I lost a Philippine to little May Johnson last night; so today I sent her a rubbishing doll's toilet and a little note with it, with some verses telling how happy children made every one near them happy also, and advising her to keep the lines and some day when she was 'grown a stately demoiselle' it would make her 'glad to know, She gave pleasure long ago'; all in a very lame fashion; with just a note of prose at the end telling her to mind her doll and the dog and not trouble her little head just now to understand the bad verses; for, some time when she was ill, as I am now, they would be plain to her and make her happy. She has just been here to thank me, and has left me very happy. Children are certainly too good to be true.

I got Bert's nice letter and yours this morning.

Yesterday, I walked too far and spent all the afternoon on the outside of my bed; went finally to rest at nine and slept nearly twelve hours on the stretch. Bennet (the doctor) when told of it this morning augured well for my recovery; he said youth must be putting in strong; of course I ought not to have slept at all. As it was, I dreamed *horridly*; but not my usual dreams of social miseries and misunderstandings and all sorts of crucifixions of the spirit; but of good, cheery, physical things – of long successions of vaulted, dimly lit cellars full of black water, in which I went swimming among toads

---

[5] Agrippa d'Aubigné (1552–1630), Huguenot soldier who served under Henry of Navarre, poet and historian. RLS's annotated copy of Volume 1 of his *Oeuvres Complètes* (1873) containing 'Sa vie à ses enfants' is at Yale.

[6] Philarète Chasles (1798–1873). RLS's annotated copy of his *Études sur le Seizième Siècle en France* (1848) is at Yale.

[7] Augustin Thierry (1795–1856). RLS's annotated copy of his *Essai sur l'Histoire de la Formation et des Progrès du Tiers État* (1871) is at Yale. The Ligue was an association of French noblemen formed in 1576 to defend the Roman Catholic religion against the Protestants.

and unutterable, cold, blind fishes; now and then these cellars opened up into sort of domed music-hall places, where one could land for a little on the slope of the orchestra, but a sort of horror prevented one from staying long and made one plunge back again into the dead waters. Then my dream changed and I was a sort of Siamese pirate, on a very high deck with several others. The ship was almost captured and we were fighting desperately. The hideous engines we used and the perfectly incredible carnage that we effected by means of them, kept me cheery as you may imagine; especially as I felt all the time my sympathy with the boarders and knew that I was only a prisoner with these horrid Malays. Then I saw a signal being given and knew they were going to blow up the ship. I leaped right off and heard my captors splash in the water after me as thick as pebbles when a bit of river bank has given way beneath the foot. I never heard the ship blow up; but I spent the rest of the night swimming about among some piles with the whole sea full of Malays searching for me with knives in their mouths. They could swim any distance under water, and every now and again, just as I was beginning to reckon myself safe, a cold hand would be laid on my ankle – ugh!

However, my long sleep troubled as it was put me all right again and I was able to work acceptably this morning and be very jolly all day; though as usual after an overfatigue, rather creepy in the back, my hand toward the end of the last paragraph showing pretty definite traces thereof. This evening I have had a great deal of talk with both the Russian ladies; they talk very nicely and are bright likeable women both. They come from Georgia.

Wednesday [14 January]

What a sell this morning's fat letter was; not however unwelcome. I was very glad to think that was so.

I have been out nearly all day, latterly in the front of the hotel with my adorable little child, her nurse and her mother, who is (I think I can spell it now) the Princess Zasetsky. Rather a hard name to call a fellow creature? isn't it? I am very well today; and that little look into a month ago has let me see how much progress I have made and put me in good heart. A somewhat amusing thing reached me this afternoon. The nurse (who is English) lugged in, after so head-and-shoulders a fashion that I suspected she had been told to do so, an assurance to the effect that Mme la Princesse had not been offended by my leaving the room on the occasion of her *fête* but had been quite pleased by the freedom. I confess to having had a difficulty to keep from grinning; at the time, I did not know she was a Princess or anything else and of course never thought twice of going away whenever the music was introduced and never made any apology except to Robinet because he had paid for the hautboys.

Miss Ward leaves on Saturday for San Remo for a fortnight at least. I am afraid she does not improve; tho' she is very plucky about it.

An organ came into the garden this afternoon and played for some time, Nelitchka dancing up and down in front of the hotel, with solemn delight.

10.30

We have all been to tea tonight at the Russians' villa; tea was made out of a samovar, which is something like a small steam engine, and whose principal advantage is that it burns the fingers of all who lay their profane touch upon it. The tea was, I believe all that black tea can be; it costs ten francs to fourteen a pound; the same brand green (if so I translate rightly *fleur de thé*) costs seventy francs a pound. We had also caviar, which is not very good on the whole. After tea Madame Zasetsky played Russian airs, very plaintive and pretty; so the evening was Muscovite from beginning to end. Madame Garschin's daughter danced a tarantella, which was very pretty. Please tell S.C. that the Prince (according to the excellent testimony of his wife) resembles Bonfils[1] to a hair. There, I think that's all very instructive.

I am keeping as cheery as can be, you see; either this hotel is immensely nicer than the Pavillon, or I am much better; I think there is something of both in it.

I blame myself sometimes, when I find that I can always write to you, whereas when I set myself down to write to my people I always plead ill health; but I can't help it: it is so. I want to write to you, and I don't want to write to them; I suppose that's the plain English of it all.

Thursday [15 January]

A jolly letter today from S.C. Tell him he is a bird of paradise, and that his letter made me very cheery in every way. It gave good news of you, and good news to me in many ways.

I have some journals sent me about the Edinburgh *revival* and I have made myself nearly sick over them. It is disheartening beyond expression. I wish I had been there that I might have seen the movement near at hand; but I am afraid I should have taken up a testimony and made everybody at home very much out of it.

Nelitchka brings me a flower generally in the morning which I wear. I do wear flowers when they are given me by certain persons, as you know or ought to know.

---

[1] Stanislas Bonfils (1822–1909), archaeologist; founder and curator of the museum at Mentone. Cf. Letter 246.

I am awfully stupid today; as indeed I have been for some time back; but it is a cheery stupidity. I don't suppose you will mind a gibbering letter, so long as the gibber is in good spirits.

I may remark that I don't understand the Russians at all; not at all; not in the very least. I was simply regaled this afternoon with a family secret; and a very curious story it is. Certainly Madame Zasetsky was a great deal moved immediately before; but at the time she told the story she was as cool as a cucumber. I shall immediately prove how worthy of confidence I am by telling it to you. Bella is not Mme Garschin's daughter; but Madame Zasetsky's. Madame Garschin had no family and was cut up; Madame Z. agreed with her husband that the next should be given to Mme G. It was done, and the child is the curse of the poor adoptive mother's existence. She loves her devotedly and has spoiled her without limit, and Bella repays her with disobedience and drives her into hysterics every day or two. Today, this took place and the scene, that I saw between the mother and daughter – supposed aunt and niece – was very strange. Madame Zasetsky became perfectly resplendent with anger – I did not think she had so much energy in her, tho' I knew she had plenty – and broke forth over the child in the plainest, bitterest language; told her she was killing her mother; imitated her praying for her mother's recovery – '*Vous avez beau prier. C'est trop tard, Mademoiselle, je vous dis que c'est trop tard.*' She almost screamed as she said this, and the girl ran away to complain to her mother (as she supposed) that is her aunt; and Madame turned round to Mr Johnson and me with the sublimest nonchalance – '*Vous ne savez pas – Bella est ma fille, à moi.*' I have intolerably muddled the story; but if you can follow it, it does not want for interest. Mme Garschin lives upon the imposture; cannot bear any one to know. Mme Zasetsky is inconsolable that she should have had anything to do with such a miserable bargain. I do think the child is (what her mother called her) a devil.[2]

7.30

The more I think of it that scene on the beach seems the more striking to me. It is one of the most dramatic situations one can conceive – the mother giving up a child, dedicating it before it was conceived, to complete the happiness of her sister. This child hating her mother, whom she takes for a cross grained aunt, scarcely refraining from putting out her tongue at her today, when she broke out into this righteous indignation. The sister having

---

[2] Strangely enough, Colvin who cut this passage from his published text wrote: 'We never could well make out which child belonged to which sister, or whether one of the two was not the mother of them both' (*Memories and Notes*, 114). It may be as Furnas surmises (428) that they both became so wary of what the Russians said that they 'discounted the whole story as merely another Slavic extravagance.'

set the whole worth of her life upon this child, whom she destroys, on the condition of this fiction, which cannot be long supported. God knows what a tragedy lies before the family.

It is difficult to believe that this nasty girl is the sister of the quite adorable Nelitchka; of whom an anecdote by the way. Whenever she cries, and she never cries except from pain, all that one has to do is to start '*Malbrook s'en va-t-en guerre*', she cannot resist the attraction, she is drawn through her sobs into the air; and in a moment there is Nellie singing, with the glad look that comes into her face always when she sings, and all the tears and pain forgotten.

I have written a great deal to you these past three days, and on the whole (considering the writer) with very little egotism. I am afraid the hand is horrid. I shall write to my people for some photographs, and send one to Bert when they come. I have received a *carte* from Mary Johnson, *voire aussi celle de la poupée*.

The weather has been superb.

I cannot get that story out of my head. I keep trying to figure to myself the evolution of the imbroglio; and, turn it how I may, the future does not look promising for either Mme Garschin or Bella.

10

I cannot keep from writing to you although I have nothing to say. I can just hear the sea on the beach, and I daresay you can hear from where you are 'The same voice of woods and seas' (or however it goes) in the living tides of Paris. We have been playing again at *la Salette* (or *Sallette*)[3]: I am pronounced not at all *drôle*, which is cheery: I must have changed oddly: I thought I was rather given that way. Johnson (Bourbon Whiskey) tells a story better, I think, than almost any man I have ever heard. His anecdotes are full of close observation; the pantomime thoroughly just and significant in conception and admirably brought before one in language. His story of a dog that was lost, has left a series of pictures in my mind, as vivid and characteristic as any I ever got from a book. Why does not a man with so good a faculty, try writing? he would be very successful surely.

S.C.'s note was awfully nice. Good-bye, my dear friend. Ever your faithful friend   Robert Louis Stevenson

It is wonderful, before I shut this up, how that child remains ever interesting to me. Nothing can stale her infinite variety; and yet it is not very various. You see her thinking what she is to do or to say next, with a funny grave air of reserve; and then the face breaks up into a smile, and it

---

[3] I.e. *la sellette*, the culprit's stool, the stool of repentance.

is probably 'Berechino!', said with that sudden little jump of the voice that one knows in children, as the escape of a jack in the box; and – somehow – I am quite happy after that!   R.L.S.

211   *To his Mother*

MS Yale. Published in *Letters*, I, 122–3.

Wednesday 14 January 1874   *Mentone*

The name of the Russian who puts me in mind of Jessie – or rather, I should say, the Russian, not her name, – is the Princess Zasetsky. I do not know what Madame Garschin's title is; so cannot give you any more Burke. They are both very nice, I think: indeed the population of the hotel is all jolly: I like it infinitely better than the Pavillon lot of horrid English. This is such a jolly mixture from the mildest milk and water English clergyman's washed-out daughters to the somewhat roystering yankeedom of Johnson or the jolly fine graceful manners of the Mesdames Russes.

I overwalked myself a hair's breadth on Monday from which I am just recovering. I pay for such excesses in utter uselessness during the day, an enormous proportion of sleep and that sleep troubled with horrible dreams; so I have a considerable interest in not overwalking myself.

Miss Ward goes on Saturday to San Remo for a fortnight – O yes madame, you deserve all credit for your wisdom in the Romanes affair. I suppose it was Mrs Logan who did it: Mrs R. herself had evidently got muddled as to the story; I understood her to say you had written. I have seen and heard no more of them since my visit, and hope it may long be so.

Exercise a certain measure of discretion yourselves about sending books; of course don't let us go to the bankruptcy court. I shall proclaim my desires as they seem to me, but you may temper them with the worldly prudence peculiar to the Scottish climate.

Mrs Sitwell, I am glad to hear, is better again.

I have received Nos. 4 and 5 duly. This is going to be a dull letter in spite of all I can do. O! I lost a Philippine to little May Johnson and gave her a doll's toilet.

I am going to lunch with Dowson on Friday.

I have never seen 'Roads' myself yet. And only part of it even in type at all; for I added a lot in proof. I am glad the Bishop of Toledo is dropped. I felt uneasy in his presence. Partly from not knowing quite what he meant.

Ever your affectionate son   Robert Louis Stevenson

O! a joke. I was informed by the nurse incid-enttally (rum division[1] and wrong spelling) that I gave great satisfaction to Mme la Princesse by treating her without *façons* upon some occasion. No wonder. I only knew she was a Russian with an unpronounceable name. I didn't know she was a Princess then.   R.L.S.

212   *To Charles Baxter*

MS Yale. Published in *Baxter Letters*, 40–42.

[*c. 15 January 1874*]   [*Mentone*]

My dear Charles, I am here in a funny little Society – an American called Johnson, one of the best story-tellers in the world, a man who can make a whole *table d'hôte* listen to him for ten minutes while he tells how he lost his dog and found him again; Mme Johnson, his wife, a good woman, pious, stupid, who removes herself from the contamination of our games on the Sunday night (we play games in the Salon); his daughter May, a little girl of eight, very pretty and wild; M. Robinet, a French painter, a very good fellow; Mme Zasetsky, a Russian Princess, and Mme Garschin, her sister, two very nice women; Mme Garschin's little daughter and Mme Zasetsky's, my adorable little Nelitchka, two and a half years old, talking the wonderfullest jargon of German, English, Italian, Russian and Polish. I shall be better able to tell you of all this when I see you as there are certain things that I do not care to write about. Don't open your eyes – the length they would occupy stands for the better part of my discretion. I hope you will be able to read this scrawly hand. Everybody is very jolly and we live just like a family; d—d like a family in fact – family secrets are produced right and left and I could tales unfold etc. You have no idea of how things are managed in such a Society. The Stool of Repentance, for example, at which we play often, is really a serious censorship: nobody dreams of giving any opinion that they do not mean; and one is told the cheerfullest home truths to one's face, seated on a chair in face of laughing audience. You have no idea what fun it is, especially on the sort of tentative terms on which we all are, to hear what people are thinking about you in the clearest terms – I was going to say English, but it's French. I have scarcely spoken a word of English today; so you may conceive what debauched French I serve myself with.

You are a good fellow to send me all these things; a beastly good fellow. The Lord bless you. Have you been revivalled yet? They sent me magazines about it; the obscenest rubbish I was ever acquainted with. Simpson tells me

---

[1] A false division of syllables at the end of the line.

MacGil[1] has stopped liquoring; he will take to buggery likely. I bless God
I am an infidel when I read of such nervous fiddle-de-dee; and these people
are down upon the spiritualists! Why I saw that bald-headed bummer J.
Balfour[2] had been describing a meeting he was at. He said, 'They then
enjoyed very precious and manifest tokens of the Lord's Presence.' If I had
been there and had sworn upon all the obscene and blasphemous phrases in
my large repertory, that God had *not* been there, they would have told me
it was because my heart was hard; and yet when the poor humble spiritualist
tries to cock up his little tail on the same pretext, they say it's a manifest
imposture and bend their brows on him as if he were a thief. O *sapristi*! if
I had hold of James B. by the testicles I would knock his bald cranium
against the wall until I was sick.

*Eh bien, et comment ça va t-il, mon Ecrivain au Signet? Est-ce que vous vous
portez bien, ou avez vous une —?*

Imagine my position; when we were playing at a game in which one has
to finish a word, I had both *bou* and *fou* given to me; the first time I saved
myself with bou*quet*, but the second I could think of nothing but what thou
wottest of, and so was silent and paid my forfeit. I shall now shut up. *Baisez
mon cul.* Ever yours   Robert Louis Stevenson

213   *To Sidney Colvin*

MS Yale. Partly published in *Letters*, I, 131–2.

Friday [*16 January 1874*]   [*Mentone*]

My dear Colvin, Thank you very much for your note. This morning I am
stupid again; can do nothing at all; am no good '*comme plumitif*'. I think it
must be cold outside. At least that would explain, my addled head and
intense laziness.

O why did you tell me about that cloak.[1] Why didn't you buy it? Isn't
it in *Julius Caesar* that Pompey blames – no not Pompey but a friend of

---

[1] In a letter of 5 November 1881 Simpson records that his friend and fellow-advocate Arthur
  Makgill (1842–99) was one of the few who voted for RLS when he stood for the History Chair
  at Edinburgh University in 1881.
[2] James Balfour, W.S. (1815–98), fourth son of James Balfour, W.S., of Pilrig was MIS's cousin; he
  assumed the surname of Melville in 1893 on succeeding to the estate of Mount Melville, Fife. He
  was one of the signatories (along with leading Edinburgh clergymen and others) of a letter sent to
  all Scottish churches in December 1873 calling for a week of prayer to coincide with that being
  held in Edinburgh during Moody and Sankey's meetings.
[1] 'It had been a very cold Christmas at Monaco and Monte Carlo, and Stevenson had no adequate
  overcoat, so it was agreed that when I went to Paris I should try and find him a warm cloak or
  wrap. I amused myself looking for one suited to his taste for the picturesque and piratical in
  apparel, and found one in the style of 1830–40, dark blue and flowing and fastening with a snake
  buckle' (Colvin).

Pompey's – well, Pompey's friend, I mean, the friend of Pompey – blames somebody else who was his friend – that is, who was the friend of Pompey's friend – because he (the friend of Pompey's friend) had not done something right off, but had come and asked him (Pompey's friend) whether he (the friend of Pompey's friend) ought to do it or no?[2] There, I fold my hands with some complacency: that's a piece of very good narration. I am getting into good form. These classical instances are always distracting. I was talking of the cloak. It's awfully dear. Are there no cheap and nasty imitations? Think of that. If, however, it were the opinion (ahem) of competent persons that the great cost of the mantle in question was no more than proportionate to its durability; if it were to be a joy for ever; if it would cover my declining years and survive me in anything like integrity for the comfort of my executors; if – I have the word – if the price indicates (as it seems) the quality of *perdurability* in the fabric; if, in fact, it would not be extravagant, but only the leariest economy to lay out £5.15. in a single mantle without seam and without price; and if – and if – it really fastens with an agrafe – I would BUY it. But not unless. If not, a cheap imitation would be the move.

I hope the letters come to you all right. I have sent them off with a keen sense of humorous malice, since I was told to stop putting on stamps. If you have to pay *very* much for them I'll pay it back.

Since I began this, I have received another letter from Mrs Sitwell with news of another headache. This has rather checked my gaiety. I say, she must not go back until she is really fit. It is most disheartening.

I am very well. I have got over my morning's stupidity I think. It has been raining, and the day is cloudy and mild.

Saturday [*17 January*]

Heavy rain. I say, you know, Madame *can't* go back until she is really better; but of course you will be quite awake to that.

I am all right, but stupid. Ever yours   Robert Louis Stevenson

214   *To Frances Sitwell*

MS NLS. Published (with a few deletions) in *Letters*, I, 118–22. One paragraph repeated in I, 129–30.

Friday [*16 January 1874*]   [*Mentone*]

I have been altogether upset this evening and my quiet work knocked on the head. I told you I did not understand the Russians; but I didn't tell you altogether why; indeed I don't know if I quite *can* tell you yet. But the

---

[2] 'Ah, this thou shouldst have done, / And not have spoke on't!' *Antony and Cleopatra*, II.vii.79–80.

reason is this: I don't know what Mme G.'s little game is with regard to me. Certainly she has either made up her mind to make a fool of me in a somewhat coarse manner, or else she is in train to make a fool of herself. I don't care which it is (tho' I sincerely hope it is the former) if it would only take a definite shape; but in the mean time, I am damnably embarrassed and yet funnily interested. It is very funny. They must want to make a fool of me; and yet they must suppose me to be *such* a fool. It is too coarse for a joke. I wish you were here to tell me which it is. I have not thought it necessary to say anything about my own opinions in the matter; and I won't.

It is very odd what a fool they must think me. I can*not* get over it. Now tonight Mme Z. asked to examine my hand. It was evidently a put up thing, because I had asked her before and she did not do it. Well, she had hardly looked at it before she gave a little start and a cry (she is a finished actress); then followed some hasty rather excited talk between her and her sister in Russian, and then Mme Z. said: '*Il y a quelque chose ici que ma soeur me défend de vous dire.*' And then after a pause '*Et cependant je crois bien que vous comprenez.*' A chair next Mme G. became vacant, she motioned to me to take it and talked to me for a long time quite seriously and nicely about anything you like. I took the first occasion of leaving the chair and going away; when up gets Mme with a sort of fling and changes her seat also saying something to her sister quite angrily in Russian.

You must understand that since my illness I have grown unspeakably timid, bashful and blushful – I don't know why – and I suppose that that is where the humour of the thing lies.

There is a first report. We shall see how this goes on. I feel easier now I have told you how the thing stood; I did not care to tell you of the very vague and possibly foolish notions that I have had before, but tonight has cleared the matter up so far; and it now must be one of two things – a deliberate plant or an affair, which may bother me. It makes it all the more difficult for me to know how to act, that I really do like Mme G. and am sorry for [her]; feelings that will not be lessened at all by this plant, if only she would be done with it. You know my impersonal way of liking people and how I would no more change my admiration for a person because I suffered from her, than I would for the grace of an aloe because I pricked my finger with it or for the ocean because it drowned for me my dearest friend. Mme G. is a very fine organization whom it gives me pleasure to study, a pleasure which will be neither increased nor diminished by this business, however it turns out.

And now, dear, about yourself. I was awfully vexed this morning to hear that you were ill again; and don't quite know what to say or to think. One thing, however, I do see; and that is, that this life is killing you and that you must not return to Calvary until you are really better. Mind that you *must* not, it would not be right. You must not die for everybody's sake; and if you go back again, you will. If only that man would break his neck! You know very well that my life would not be worth living to me if you were not here; and you know what it would be to another. If you do not get really stronger soon, something definite must be done. I will be a party no longer to any half measures that are to cost me all that is good in life. It must be apparent that this is the voice of wisdom.

> *À quoi bon, hélas!*
> *Rester là si tu me quittes*
> *Et vivre si tu t'en vas?*[1]

Saturday [17 January]

A rainy day has kept the Russians at home, so I know no more than last night. Although I think more and more that Madame's intention was to get up a sorry little flirtation, with as much seriousness as these things admit of, I am still pleased by thinking that the crass, almost brutal, stupidity that I exhibited last night may have put an end to it.

I wish I could hear how you were. I can't make out what has come to my hand; I can't write with it in the old position; and in the new, I can't write legibly. I am very well, but utterly stupid, more utterly stupid than ever. Stupidity can't go farther now, *Dieu Merci*! My head is sewed up altogether. No unpleasant feelings, no fluidity, no creeping; only just like what S.C. used to feel, perfect stupidity; only that he could write when he made himself; whereas I have been trying all day and have not got a single sentence out.

I can't quite get over this disappointment about your health; and yet there is no more to be said. You must not go back; and if Paris does not do, you must go somewhere else. You must take to yourself some of the excellent advice you gave to me. Cost what it may, you have to keep in health. *Cost what it may.* You are evidently not what you ought to be; and if everything else goes to pigs and whistles in the meantime, you must recover.

9 o'clock

Yes, I have succeeded I think, in getting this straightened up. Mme G. has been, as ever, very nice and *interested* with me this evening, and there has

---

[1] Victor Hugo, *Les Contemplations* (1856) XXV.

been no more bosh. This gives me great pleasure. Mme Z., in giving characters all round (for a forfeit), said of me: '*Monsieur est un jeune homme que je ne comprends pas. Il n'est pas méchant, je sais cela, mais après, ténèbres, ténèbres, ténèbres — rien que des ténèbres.*' That I understand for the best also; I believe it means that they are quite puzzled with me and give me up. I am sincerely glad things have turned out thus; for I am very happy here among these people and I was afraid there was going to be a difficulty. I don't think there will be now.

I am very well, feel very much as I did before the breakdown, that is to say quite alive again but useless, shaky and nervous; I think S.C. would find a change in me; but I thought I should have recovered into good health, and not into my old shaky health, as I seem to be doing.

Sunday [18 January]

Yes, I adhere to both my good statements of yesterday; I am better; and the Russian difficulty — the Eastern question, so to speak — is solved. Both of the ladies are very kind and jolly to me today; and this is the second without any foolishness up to now. They are both of them the frankest of mortals; and have explained to me, in one way or other, that I am to them as some undiscovered animal. They do not seem to cultivate R.L.S.'s in Muscovy. It has been rather a curious episode. I say, S.C. must know nothing of this; it would be the deuce if he did. Mind, I'll take it as a real breach of confidence if you tell him.

I must tell you of my evening before I go to bed. There has been one bad sign; hitherto the Princess sat next me at table; today they have changed places and Mme G. sat next me. But with these people one must not think too much of that; they do what they want with perfect frankness; they make Robinet sit between them, for example.

Robinet and I went this evening to tea with them; Mme Johnson was ill; so neither she nor her husband could go. Well, my news is pleasant; the conversation was interesting as usual — Mme Zaseska is certainly a very clever woman. But tonight, it turned out that they know Mill and Spencer; that Mill's death was regarded as a calamity in Russia; that they are people of like views with us. At present, their word is to support the Empire — the people being unfit for power and the Empire lending itself to all advances; but their opinions are most hopeful. It does one's heart good and gives one great hope for Russia. I wish you could know these two women; you would like them. As for me, I think I am at my ease now; they have changed their manner to me greatly and I do think there is an end of the nonsense. I know that Mme Z. has now an exaggerated notion of my talents and character, and that will help. I have ceased to play the stupid and take things as they come, and it seems to pay.

Monday [19 January]

Yes, I am much better; very much better I think I may say. Although it is funny how I have ceased to be able to write with the improvement of my health. I shouldn't wonder if I returned into a schoolboy phase. Do you notice how for some time back you have had no descriptions of anything; the reason is that I can't describe anything. No words come to me when I see a thing just now. I want awfully to tell you, today, about a little '*piece*' of green sea, and gulls, and clouded sky with the usual golden mountain-breaks to the southward. It was wonderful, the sea near at hand was living emerald; the white breasts and wings of the gulls as they circled above – high above even – were dyed bright green by the reflexion. And if you could only have seen, or if any right word would only come to my pen to tell you, how wonderfully these illuminated birds floated hither and thither under the grey-purples of the sky!

I am vexed that S.C. cannot be shewn this letter; but he must not really – you will see that of course yourself. I have written all this to you, because you are you; but I could not write such stuff to anybody else, without being something very nasty and unclean. And yet I should like him to know what I think about your not being so well; also I should like him to know that the reason you do not show him the letter is a reason coming from the outside; I daresay you can manage to let him understand that without being too communicative.

I have been waiting a letter from either of you; and I think one *should* come this morning. I do want badly to know how you are again. My dear, if you do not get better really, you must let the whole thing slide; you must feel that that is your duty. It is very disinterested advice on my part too; except that my interest in keeping you in the world is, I may say, con-siderable. My dear, I write this lightly; but you know very well I do not feel it lightly. O if you were gone what a cold dark place this world would be. *N'en parlons pas.* You must – O if I could write, I could let you know what I feel – If I could speak to you, I could – but I am quite dumb on paper.

Mademoiselle Bella made another attempt at killing her mother (her aunt) but her aunt (her mother) was there and she does seem to have a sort of sway over the child which the other has not; and yet how the child hates her!

I am the worst writer in the world. You can't tell how I hate that; it is a continual series of shameful surprises for me, now, to write, even a letter to you; I don't manage to say what I mean.

I think I may send off this letter today. I have certainly come to a stage; I think to the last stage. However I am quite tranquil and cheery and well. I shall expect with interest a nice wise letter from you. If you are seedy, write two lines on a bit of paper and give them to S.C. to enclose. Ever your faithful friend   Robert Louis Stevenson

215   *To his Mother*

MS Yale.

Saturday [*17 January 1874*]   *Mentone*

6 come in.[1] Do not attempt to understand the posts; it all depends on the
degree of activity of the Postmaster for the moment; here, in the south, the
idea of hurry about a letter is not much *répandue*. In Italy, they are still more
languid. When the Postmaster feels in the humour, he sorts a few letters and
gives them to the *facteur*, and this latter delivers as many as he feels up to,
very much as you might pay visits of an afternoon. It is nice to think that
there are people in the world to whom life is so little serious.

I am sincerely sorry for the perfect and well educated lady.

To judge from your letters, there seems to be little else read in Edinburgh
but the December *prtfl*.[2]

I was at tea with the Russians the other evening. Russian tea is bully.
This stuff cost from 10 to 14 francs a lb; the same brand green would cost
seventy francs, if I am right in translating '*fleur de thé*' as green. I speak little
else but French now; so you may fancy there is not as much grammar comes
from between my teeth in the twenty-four hours as would cover a sixpenny
piece. I am more fluent however. Nelitchka is still the darling of my heart.
Yesterday at dinner, I was attracted by tremendous cries of '*Monsieur*' from
down the table in Nellie's voice. I looked at her and immediately the finger
was up and, with immense gusto, '*Berechino*' was said.

It rains most steadily, but is very warm. It's a blessing there are people in
the house; but the rain kept the Russians from lunch and will keep them,
I fear, from dinner. In some ways the Russians are the rummest people in
the world. Mme Zasetsky is a very fine character, a person for a tragedy, as
I had opportunity of observing; but I prefer Mme Garschin; and Nelitchka
to both of them.

The rain prevents me from being able to write. I don't know why but
you may find out for yourself. *Je vous salue*.

Sunday [*18 January*][3]

In bed – that means before I have got up – don't be alarmed – I do not
rise till eleven; this is Colvin's tip and I think it pays.

When Nelitchka (this is the Russian Nellie) hurts herself and begins to
cry, all that requires to be done is some one to start '*Malbrook s'en va-t-en*

---

[1] Acknowledging receipt of letter No. 6 from his parents.
[2] I.e. the December 1873 *Portfolio*, in which 'Roads' appeared.
[3] The Sunday portion (one sheet numbered 2) is filed at Yale as the fragment of another letter but
it is evidently a continuation of the Saturday letter. It is dated 18 January 1874 by MIS.

guerre'; in a minute she has joined in the air, with the tears still running down her face; and in another, she has forgotten her troubles.

O! about the books. I should like if they were *moveable* to have them. If not to find them at home.

The dish of eggs has not been repeated. I wait eagerly for it; and shall ask when it comes. One disadvantage of living in a house where they can cook, is that the dishes rarely recur.

O I say I want more money some of these days; it's horrible; but so it is £80! in three months! It is not a cheap place; you can't make it cheap here; for I have a good chance of trying as I never spend anything.

I am very much better, but not quite pleased with myself. I had expected to get *well* again; I have only got ill again; that is to say got back to much the same state as I was in before the breakdown. It's a stage, I suppose.

R.L.S.

end[4]

216   To his Mother

MS Yale. Extract published in *Letters*, I, 132–3.

Monday 19 January 1874   *Mentone*

O so Monsieur has managed to write a good letter at last; it was positively pleasant, in spite of the Bishop. I shall answer your questions straight through.

1st. Keep the books for me.

2nd. No, I have not quarrelled with Colvin; he had to leave for business; he will return soon, if all is well, for another month; I thought he was to write to you; he said he would. You must take the news you get and try and be very thankful for it, or you will get less, perhaps.

3. Mrs Sitwell's other trouble has blown over for the time, but still hangs over her. The only sister whom she has in Europe, with whom she is now staying in Paris, has married a Frenchman.[1] This poor man is just alive – frightfully ill, and the business on which he is engaged has a crisis about every week; so that they may be beggars almost any moment. Of course, this is not to be cried at the cross; though I daresay it might be, at Edinburgh Cross, for all the harm it would do.

4. Nelitchka or Nelitska, as you know already by this time, is my adorable kid's name. Her laugh does more good to one's health than a

---

[4] These last three words are squeezed along the top of the first page of the letter.

[1] Susan Fetherstonhaugh (?1835–1917) married a French engineer, M. Ponsarde (Lucas, 58). In 1886–7, when a widow, she was governess to George Meredith's daughter for a short time.

month at the seaside: as she said today herself, when asked whether she was a boy or a girl, after having denied both with gravity, she is an angel.

5. O no, her brain is not in a chaos; it is only the brains of those who hear her. It is all plain sailing for her. She wishes to refuse or deny anything, and there is the English 'No fank you' ready to her hand; she wishes to admire anything and there is the German '*schön*'; she wishes to sew (which she does with admirable seriousness and clumsiness) and there is the French '*coudre*'; she wishes to say she is ill and there is the Russian '*bulla*'; she wishes to be down on anyone and there is the Italian '*Berechino*'; she wishes [to] play at a railway train and there is her own original word 'Collie' (Say the o with a sort of Gaelic twirl). And all these words are equally good.

6. O yes she'll come out of it. Bella (sound that B. almost like P.) the cousin knows one language from another now admirably.

7. I am called M. Stevenson by everybody except Nelitchka who calls me M. Berechino.

8. The weather today is no end as bright and warm as ever. I have been out on the beach all afternoon with the Russians. Mme Garschin has been reading Russian to me; and I cannot tell prose from verse in that delectable tongue which is a pity. Johnson came out to tell us that Corsica was visible, and there it was over a white, sweltering sea, just a little darker than the pallid blue of the sky and, when one looked at it closely, breaking up into sun-brightened peaks.

I may mention that Robinet has never heard an Englishman with so little accent as I have − ahem − ahem − eh? − what do you say to that? I don't suppose I have said five sentences in English today; all French; all bad French, alas!

I am thought to be looking better. Mme Zaseska said I was all green when I came here first, but that I am all right in colour now and, she thinks, fatter.

I am very partial to the Russians. I believe they are rather partial to me. I am supposed to be an '*esprit observateur*'! *À mon age, c'est étonnant comme je suis observateur*!

The second volume of *Clément Marot* has come. Where and O where is the first. Ever your affectionate son   Robert Louis Stevenson

What about the envelope? Stylish?

The latter part of this letter is a small collection of compliments, there are more on hand. The Bishop is looking up, eh?

[2]I have spoiled one of my charming envelopes to add a word.

I want you to order some of my photographs from Moffat;[3] the one you like; and send me two or three.

---

[2] The MS of the rest of this letter (dated 19 January by MIS) has become muddled with the MS of Letter 221.
[3] John Moffat, an Edinburgh photographer.

I have just heard a most horrid account of the Polish Insurrection and the way in which it was suppressed from Mmes Zasetsky and Garschin. Imagine, the rebels were boys of fourteen and fifteen! They said they could not keep from crying as they saw them going off to Siberia in irons. *Cependant, ces garçons n'était pas précisement bons. Quelques uns d'entre eux ont pendu une dame parce qu'elle n'approuvait pas cette révolution insensée. Révolution insensée, c'est là le mot; c'était une révolution dans le genre des révoltes Irlandaises, on ne savait pas ce qu'on voulait.*

For the rest their account of Russia is very hopeful. Did you know[4] that the Emperor Nicholas had poisoned himself?   R.L.S.

I have worn the same necktie for four months; and I am the companion of Princesses. Worthy son of the friend of the aristocracy.

Tuesday [20 January]

Another envelope sacrificed. I have forgotten both times that I want some more money. This hotel costs me about six lbs. a week; that is horrid, and yet I do not care to go away; I am so jolly here; there is no other place in Mentone where one could be so jolly.

I find that 'Pella' and not 'Bella' is the child's name.[5]

This is another beautiful day; and I am going along to the town to cash my last draught and then give the most of it away to Père Folleté.

Sich is Life. Your affectionate son   R.L.S.

Decoration[6]   No extry charge

★ O, Mme Garschin told me the other day that for the greater part of the year at home, she never goes out without coming in wet above the knees. I asked if it was snow. '*O toute bonnement − de boue.*' Imagine such a life.

★ Let my father see if he can find a fault in grammar in the English there. I have found one in his letter like it.

217   *To Sidney Colvin*

MS Yale. First two paragraphs reproduced in facsimile in Stevenson Extra Number of *Bookman* (1913), 106.

[c. *19 January 1874*]   [*Mentone*]

My dear Colvin, Write by all means to my parents. My casual way of giving information raised in them an idea that we had quarrelled; and as I do not

---

[4] MS: 'not'.
[5] Her full name was Pelagie (recorded in official visitors' list at Franzenbad, 15 July 1874).
[6] A scrawl round the initials.

think that is precisely the state of matters, I should like you to write and put them right. I think I said something about the man who shot himself; say what you think about him that will please them.

I am really *very well*; but unfit for work to the last degree; I have even ceased my 'daily stage' of Mr Solway under the reasoned conviction that I was gradually spoiling a good story. It is curious that I am almost unable to write at present; the reason is that I am gradually changing the attitude [of] my hand in writing; and at present both the old and the new position is intolerable to me for any length of time. Calligraphy is horrid to me.

I am glad to hear 'George III'[1] is going to be long, and wait the proof with eagerness. Thank you for what you say about opening the letter; I think I know the feelings of a forger now, or a detected thief.

I have finished *Nanon*[2] and just dally with the end of Capefigs.

Surely anything would be better for Madame than a return to England while she is yet weak; surely *anything*. It will not do for her to go back to the old daily irritations before she has got strength and health and cheerfulness again, to meet them with.

I can write no more, my hand is so villainously uneasy. O Bennet told me nothing; I told him how I was and he pretended to be interested; and then I gave him five and twenty francs, and he was pleased. You credulous in doctors! Ever yours   Robert Louis Stevenson

218   *To Frances Sitwell*

MS NLS. Partly published in *Letters*, I, 125–8.

Tuesday [20 January 1874]   [*Mentone*]

Yesterday, I could not write somehow. Your letter has just arrived – hurray! that sounds better – and the bird of paradise. I have more to tell you, of course, about the Russians. I am just a little afraid I am behaving badly. They amuse and interest me immensely; they are the only nice people really in Mentone; and so I have now given way altogether and spend all my time with them. I do think it is all right, however. I am quite as much with the one as with the other. I will tell you about yesterday; and you can judge for yourself. At lunch Mme Garschin sat next me: in the afternoon they were sitting on the beach, and as Mme Zaseska was writing, I camped on Mme G.'s shawl and talked for I daresay an hour. At dinner Mme Zaseska came and sat next me. And, after dinner, as Nellie had been sick and was at home, she had to go back and asked me to come with her. Until Nellie went to

---

[1] Colvin's 'Some Phases of English Art under George III', the theme of his Slade lectures, was published in the *Fortnightly Review* in March and May 1874.
[2] George Sand's novel (1872).

bed, we amused her and then we sat and smoked cigarettes together and talked marriage and society and all sorts of things, until Mme G. came in from the hotel about nine. I offered to go, as in duty bound, but was made to stay and stopped with the pair of them until half past ten. They really are two of the splendidest people in the world. I will tell you something about both of them that will interest you. First, The Princess. What breaks her heart is Germany. 'I wish,' she says, 'to found Society upon love; and here I find the happiest possible families consisting of a learned professor and a kitchen maid; even Goethe was happiest with his kitchen maid. If I could, I *wouldn't believe* in Germany.' Second, Mme Garschin. All I know about her is from Mme Z.; she is reserved about herself. However, she is so bigoted in the views that we hold, so convinced that all paltering with error only does harm, that she has never been to church since she has married. Consequently, the peasants believe she is a devil. They know, however, that she takes better care of them than anyone else; and this is not an uncommon scene: A woman, in childbirth, sends for her, and beseeches her to make the sign of the cross ('because we know that you have Satan in you') before she touches her. Madame is inflexible. 'I have nothing to do with either God or Satan,' she says always. 'You know *me*; and you know whether I come to you with a good intention or no. If you think I don't, you should not let me come, and I will go away again.' Isn't that a strange person? and a fine person? I *do* wish you could know these two women; you would like them and they would interest you, just as I like them and am interested in them.

(4 o'clock)

Mme Zazeska has had ten kids; this, she says, explains her ignorance; her ignorance does not need much explanation as there is not much of it. I am quite sure that it is all right now about them. Mme Zazeska did not come to lunch; Mme Garschin was there and we had a talk which enlightened me a good deal as to her character. We somehow got onto Christ: *'J'en suis amoureuse,'* she said. 'I have never loved any man I have seen. I want to have been one of those women who did love him and followed him.' This Christ business explains the bigotry.

I have bought a new hat, a brigand sort of arrangement. I don't think it partakes much of the perpetual loveliness of old marbles. There is a delicate bloom upon it that the first shower, I know, will remove. It is probably glue; and if so, God knows what may be the result on the coherency of the whole structure.

For health, on this beautiful day I am perfect. I have been sitting alone by the sea, with a sunshade between me and the sun, and feeling just as happy as I could be and telling myself all manner of nice things. Corsica was just visible on the horizon; and, what was far more lovely, ranges of delicate cloud mountains, white and faint and far away, in the intense pale blue; for the blue has a way of being at once intense and pale; even of ceasing to be blue altogether, and changing into a nameless whiteness, like that at the heart of a violet (I think, or a pansy?), that, somehow, is to me like a perfume. The gulls, as usual, sailed by continually, tilted, and on the watch for fish.

I am so glad to think you are happy again, and beginning to be conscious of where you are and to live in your surroundings. You might have looked at Raphael's portrait of himself when he was young, when you were at the Louvre, and told me whether there was any sense in the old Dutchwoman's astounding compliment.[1] I don't care whether *La Gioconda* is nasty; it should be; the person who had only all the past that there was at the date of Leonardo must have been nasty: the *La Gioconda* that I mean and know, is not. You would have been what they call nasty, had you lived then, do you know that?

10.30

O yes, it's all right. These people like me now, and it's all right, I feel sure. I have spent this evening also with them – Robinet and I. And these has been nothing to disquiet me; I think the thing has passed; and they *are* nice. I am awfully lucky to have found them. Mme Z. says she will let Nelitchka go on the stage if she has the vocation, as seems likely. N. is a darling and no mistake.

Wednesday [*21 January*]
4 o'clock

Nothing today to tell you, except that the weather is lovely and I am well and stupid. I have quite got over my fears about what you know and take the goods that the Gods supply me withal, contentedly and unenquiringly. Nelitchka is still seedy and I have not seen her once today, which is a privation.

Thursday [*22 January*]

Another letter from you, and one that I did not expect. I must say plainly that I do not like the sound of this secretaryship;[2] it sounds like too much

---

[1] Others saw a likeness between RLS and Raphael's self-portrait. A.J. Daplyn in an article in the *Sydney Daily Telegraph* of 5 May 1894 refers to 'the features which in repose remind me of Raphael's portrait of himself in the Louvre'. Fanny Osbourne also described RLS as 'a gaunt Scotchman with a face like Raphael' (see vol II, p. 186).

[2] In 1874 Mrs Sitwell became Secretary of the College for Working Women, 29 Queen's Square, Bloomsbury (founded 1864). In October 1874 when this became the New College for Men and Women, RLS wrote a note about it for *The Academy*. See also Letter 528, n. 1.

to do to begin with; and then it sounds like coarse work – work not good enough for you – work that a person with less sensibility might actually do better than you and that would fill up the measure of such an one's being while it would not fill up yours. However, it is worth keeping in mind that such work is, of all things, the most lethean, the most tranquilising and anodyne: it would likely agree with your health. I mean this seriously. For nervous people, I believe there is nothing so good as routine business. And of course it would be always work in a good direction.

My dear, I am very unwilling to think you should go back again to London. I wish you could stay where you are and forget about your moral nature and your troubles for a good, quiet month or two. These times of easy happiness are like a good night's rest in one's lifetime; and one gets up from them renewed and with the world all changed about one for the better. But of course I quite feel what you feel about money and work. And if you are strong enough. I shall rejoice when you have fairly your own earned bread in your hands.

I hope my last letter did not bother you; I was bothered myself a little when I wrote it. I am not bothered now. Mme Garschine is very nice to me, sweet and serious. Mme Zassetsky[3] has a great idea that I am very clever, I think; indeed they both have. You know it is with me, as with you; people will take me for being cleverer than I feel. Only I understand it in my case. I do say and think nice and true things; people observe that; and they cannot tell the want of *suite* and fibre, the defect of strong continuousness, that there is behind it all.

I wonder if I was wrong to write you, as I did last? I don't think so. I do want always to write what is up in my mind; besides it was a matter about which I wished counsel. And God knows, I don't understand it yet. The extreme niceness that is shown now; far more than before; is still inexplicable to me. I am disoriented – all abroad. However, not unpleasantly now: I am quite easy as to the result, I think.

4

I have been all afternoon in the garden playing with Nellie and talking to Mme Zassetsky. She has written three comedies (almost farces as far as I could judge from her description) which have been very successful. Mme G. did not appear at all upon the scene. It was she who asked me in and she left the moment I accepted the invitation. I wonder if I've been rather a brute. Nellie made my life a burthen to me, playing hide and seek and making me eat bread whether I would or not: we are now excellent friends: Mme Z. demanded '*À quand, les noces?*' But I have a serious rival in M.

<hr />

[3] RLS had finally learned how to spell their names (see Letter 220).

Robinet, whom she calls 'benet', and whom, as he walks with her arm in arm with his legs doubled, she regards as a little boy.

Friday [23 January]

I am in great expectation of another letter today in answer to my last. I talked much with Mme G. last night, and I am almost certain that it's all straight again.

My dear friend, I cannot write this morning, and I wanted to write. You must just take my adieux without any embellishment. I am ever happy in the thought of you. Ever your faithful friend   Robert Louis Stevenson

I hope you are not going back too soon. For God's sake take care of your health. I am very well still; very well.

219   *To Sidney Colvin*

MS Yale. Brief quotation in Masson, 112.

[c. 20 January 1874]   *[Mentone]*

My dear Colvin, The bird of paradise has arrived duly. I shall have it framed. The Ruskies were much amused; I explained the circumstance to them in my best French. I am thought to have vastly improved in my French, by the way. I have spent the last three evenings with them; they are awfully kind and jolly. I have bought a hat. Please send me a cake and some money to buy a cricket bat.

I have worked today at 'Ordered South'. I think 'Ordered South' will have to be ordered to Jericho. I don't mean that, only I am a fool, a cheery, gibberous fool. I am really a little more hopeful about it; I have now got all the stuff together; and perhaps another transcription will get it sort of right.

How was you tomorrow? I feel very humorous and inclined to stand up and wink at myself in the mirror. There is no extry charge. It is odd although I feel so funny, the jokes don't seem to come. If I attempt it with an English quill will you take, O reader, for the deed, the will?[1] Laugh, will you. Why the devil, don't you laugh?

I have felt serious once and twice but at the present moment, I can scarcely say that I do. I don't care a bit about suffering humanity. I am a bird

---

[1] Longfellow prefaced 'The Blind Girl of Castèl-Cuillè' a translation 'from the Gascon of Jasmin' with the following:

> Only the Lowland tongue of Scotland might
> Rehearse this little tragedy aright;
> Let me attempt it with an English quill;
> And take, O Reader, for the deed the will.

of paradise. It's awful humbug having to go to bed. As jolly old Sir Thomas Browne said, 'The huntsmen are already up in Persia';[2] and here at my ear, a cock is crowing for the morning with no apparent sense of incongruity. I have the desire to sit up all night and it contraries me sorely to have to thwart it. But we must be good. May God bless you and keep you and lift up the light of his rubicund countenance upon you, and send his angels to look arter you lest by any chance you should stumble and go a mucker.[3] Amen. Amen. Amen. Amen. Ever yours   Robert Louis Stevenson

Postscriptum. I am not mad, most noble Festus,[4] only gibberous – a malady incident to R.L.S.

220   To his Mother

MS Yale.

Wednesday 21 January [1874]   *Mentone*

Yesterday, I bought a new hat. It created the strongest delight in Mme Zazeska; she has been grinding under the '*laideur impossible*' of my straw, which she says looked as if it had had smallpox. The new one was duly exhibited, fitted and approved. Nelitchka is still a little seedy. The hat, by the way, is what I may call, the 'urbane brigand' type.

No. 8 just arrived. I don't know much about the clergyman; indeed he may not be a clergyman – I only thought the family looked like a clergyman's family: I have only once seen him: he is old and bronchitic. *My* people are the Ruskies chiefly, and then the Johnsons and Robinet; but the Ruskies chiefly. Pella is not nice; but Nelitchka and Mmes Z. and G. are all three very nice.

Do you know that Louise's criticism[1] has nearly put me out of the body with vanity and pleasure. If there's a nice kind of quietness about it, it's all right, I should think. She (Bishop of Toledo) must be a *very* clever child.

4 o'clock

A doll's toilette is a game, with soap boxes and brushes and things; it was bought at Armarante's.

---

[2] 'The Huntsmen are up in America, and they are already past their first sleep in Persia.' From the last paragraph of Browne's *The Garden of Cyrus* (1658).
[3] Echoing Numbers 6: 24–6 and Psalm 91: 11–12.
[4] Acts 26:25.
[1] On 16 January MIS read 'Roads' to a number of relatives. She records Louise's remark: 'I like the way the words go, and there's a nice kind of quietness about it.' This was probably the daughter of George W. Balfour, Louisa Whyte Balfour (born 1859), later Mrs Adam Black.

The Boggi's are at San Remo. I *think* I have heard that old B. is dead. I have never laid my hand on Mr Charles.

I am very desponding as to my Russian orthography. The only name I thought I was right about, I wasn't: it should be Garschine. I suspect Mme La P.'s is Zasetschky, or something like that with more K's and Z's about it, than I somehow see an opening for. I know two words of Russian; I am afraid either to write or say either of them, owing to difficulties of spelling and pronunciation. By the way, do you remember my old General?[2] Mentone seems to bring me always among Muscovites.

I am glad to hear my letters can amuse anybody; I thought they were too twaddley.

The weather is simply heavenly now. Warm as summer. I am still very well; very well. I met old Romanes the other day, and talked to him; he is not unpleasant to speak with.

Thursday [22 January]

Zassetsky is the way to spell it. I have been getting all manner of lessons in Russian. You would have laughed if you had seen Robinet, Johnson and me sitting in a half circle round Mme Garschine and trying to repeat impossible sounds after her with the utmost seriousness. She nearly had a fit with laughing. There is really a horrid letter, a sort of u that you say by putting your tongue as far over your throat as you can. Ever your affectionate son   Robert Louis Stevenson

221   To his Mother

MS Yale.

Saturday [24 January 1874]   [Mentone]

My dear Madam, Let not anyone henceforward speak against my dress. I have been complimented, since the suppression of the straw, or rather *à propos* of the suppression of the straw, on the harmony of my costume by Mme Zassetsky. You see I simply had not been moving in good enough Society: I always knew my ideas on dress were far more beautiful than those of a Baxter, how much more of a Torrie or a J.A. Watson;[1] and, at length, you see I am taken for what I am worth. O this triumph after long

---

[2] Cf. Letter 26. At Davos, 1880–81, RLS planned, but never wrote, an essay, 'My Russians. 1. The old deaf General. 2.The Villa Marina' (MS list of five projected essays, Yale).

[1] Robert Jameson Torrie (1850–1912), a University friend who became a stockbroker. Jane Elderton Warden (1829–1904), daughter of TS's sister Jane, married John Kippen Watson (1816–91), treasurer and manager of Edinburgh Gas Light Company. They had two sons, George and John Adam Watson.

tribulation is unspeakably sweet. What a weapon do I now possess against those, who in the future, accuse my taste – *Bourgeois*; highly respectable perhaps, but *bourgeois*.

The weather here is more superb than one can describe. Yesterday morning I met the girl Romanes and lectured her with considerable fluency for some time; the extreme ease of my native language, when I return to it, is I confess too much for what little discretion I have ever had, and I lecture worse than ever. She appeared gratified however; how good it is of people to appear gratified on these occasions; I wonder how they do it. I met her afterwards, when I was taking a walk with Mme Garschine and was bowed to most graciously.

These two Russians, or rather these three Russians, for I suppose Nelitchka must be counted one, are a very sincere pleasure to me. (In truth, none of them are Russians; the two ladies being Georgians, as I think I have told you.) They are very intelligent, agreeable and frank; easy to a degree unknown in England; and, especially Mme Garschine, really of a very *fine* character. I thought at first that Mme Zassetsky was the finer: she has most *esprit*, but Mme G. is most sympathetic and. . . .[2]

It's no joke about my clothes. Mme Garschine was inveighing against the English want of taste in costume, and, when I told her that I was known, even in England, for one that dressed disgustingly, she told me that, on the contrary, I dressed (for an *Englishman*) very well and employed again the word that Mme Zassetsky had already used – *harmonieusement*. After this, will Edinburgh be silent? Will the Torries and the Watsons and the Mrs T. Stevensons, hold their peace and cover their faces and acknowledge their better with contrition and humility.   R.L.S.

222   *To Sidney Colvin*

MS Yale. Facsimile in J. Christian Bay, *Echoes of Robert Louis Stevenson* (privately printed, 1920), Appendix III, 28–30.

[25 January 1874]   *[Mentone]*

Latine scribere mihi nunc jucundum est; si bene, laudes deo soli reddendae; verum, ut timeo, si male, male sine ulla decenti scribam pudori. Muscovitas semper amabiles inveni, semper ingeniosas amoenasque foeminas. Stopcoxus simplicissimus est et, ut ita dicam, brebisissimus. Currit per arduos, per gramina, et tenuem voculam ad voces montium marisque semper jungit. Heri, in certis tenebrarum penetraliis, remoto in cubiculo suo, multum fertur flevisse, quia Principessa flores eum iterum donaturum more Junonis vetuit.

---

[2] One sheet of this letter is missing. It resumes at sheet 4. MIS dates this last sheet 26 January, presumably from the postmark.

Fere degambolatus sum – O Lord that's good, that's a triumph, it's better
than the English; there *is* no language like Latin after all – *fere degambolatus
sum; spero tandem; et mehercle jam iterum triumpho. Pictor amabilis; puer quoque
bonus; tener, facilis, ab omni parte (nescio quomodo) mihi ridiculus, Stopcoxus, te
absente*,[1] has been asking my advice about his pictures and has taken it and
thinks it good; which pleases me, as I thought I wanted the organ of pictures
altogether.

I have very nearly finished a complete draught of 'Ordered South', but
shall wait your arrival before I transcribe it, lest perhaps it should be unfit for
human food.

Please suit yourself about coming; so long as you do come. I am not to
be pitied at all. I spend my evenings with Robinet and the Ruskies and
knock about, you know how, during the days. My health still wonderful.
Ever yours   Robert Louis Stevenson

O! I tried to get a monogram for myself, and look at the pitiable result.

That is ℞ after many hundred attempts; amongst the unsuccessful, this

was thought to be a success. You may imagine, therefore what the others

were like. If my initials were ' ℭ ' it would be simple enough.

223   *To his Mother*

MS Dartmouth.

Sunday January (?)th [25] *1874*[1]   *Mentone*

What have I never mentioned Paul Robinet, the French painter, to you?
That is unaccountable. He is very nice. All yesterday afternoon, I was up in

---

[1] RLS's Latin is not always easy to make out. The following is an attempt to translate it:

> It now pleases me to write in Latin; if well, praise must be given to God alone; but if badly, as
> I fear, I shall write without any decent sense of shame. I have found the Muscovites to be always
> agreeable, always intelligent and charming ladies. Stopcock [Robinet] is the most artless fellow
> as he is, so to speak, the most sheep-like. He runs over the heights and over the plains, and
> continuously joins his piping little voice to the voice of the mountains and the sea. Yesterday
> in certain innermost nooks of darkness, in his own distant chamber, he is reported to have wept
> copiously because the Princess forbade him, Juno fashion, ever again to present her with
> flowers. [Cf. Letter 208].
>   I am nearly *degambolatus*; but yet I hope; and by Hercules, now I triumph again. The amiable
> painter; a good lad too; Stopcock, gentle, good-natured, and to me (I don't know why) in every
> respect amusing, has, in your absence, been asking my advice . . .

Stopcoxus is the Latinization of Stopcock, RLS's joke English translation of Robinet; in French,
robinet is a tap or stopcock (cf. Letter 223). *Brebisissimus* must have been adapted from the French
brebis (sheep). *Degambolatus* is a baffling word. Perhaps RLS was thinking of gambol in the sense
of frisking or leaping about in a playful manner and meant that his antics in trying to write Latin
were almost over. Another conceivable meaning is that he has 'walked off his feet' (cf. Letter 223);
gamba is late Latin for hoof.

[1] Someone has inserted '26th' but Sunday was 25 January.

his *atelier*, counselling him about his pictures: I was astonished to find that I gave very good advice; when the experiment was tried, the picture was often greatly improved. He was full of gratitude, and I of vanity, before the *séance* was over. Yes, the Russians live in a Villa close by and only come in for meals. Yes, there is a public *salon*. Yes, Nelitchka is the polyglot. Mme Zassetsky is laid up with a gum boil; she is very seedy. Nelitchka is better.

Sincerely yours has again learned that he is mortal. I was so very well last week, that I was again coming round to the opinion that it was all sham, and that I should begin to work again, and walk, and take up the thread of my life where I let it fall. Alas! I walked into Mentone on Friday and then up and down in front of the hotel just a little too long. That night, I could not sleep and, yesterday, I was *accablé* with fatigue. I am better today, but feel considerably humbler for all that. Probably, there is not on record a better invalid than I. The mere fact that I have avoided any cold since immediately after I arrived is an evidence of circumspection that few can produce in this delectable but dangerous climate. I hope the boast may not bring bad luck.

There now is a funny remnant of superstition. I never brag about my health, without appending some such little apology; and after I have appended it, I feel quite easy again.

There are several men; one very nice old Englishman among the number; but Robinet, I know best – Stopcock, as those who are learned in foreign tongues[2] and at the same time dislike the appearance of an alien word in the middle of English, may prefer to call him; or, if you will, Paul; which latter tickles me most chiefly. He has a very large head: and is my rival in Nelitchka's affections, and I must own a serious rival. But today, I have had a triumph. Nellie came to me today after lunch, toddling along in her comic fashion, and kissed my hand. I have been out of the body ever since with satisfaction.

My Russian has caved in. There is a '*и*' in Russian; and there is also an '*ℓ*' in Russian. O yes. It is nothing to Georgian however, as they tell me: I shall not try Georgian, I can promise you.

Kissing a hand, I must explain is Nelitchka's most intimate caress.

Good-bye. Ever your affectionate son   Robert Louis Stevenson

In a fit of imbecility I employed myself trying to find a monogram; the result is horrid.[3]

O you can find out for yourself how much I shall get for 'Roads'. £1 a page, carried out to the most scrupulous extent is the figure; so you can see how much it covers: it should take £3 odds I think: perhaps nearly four.

[2] MS: 'times'.
[3] The same monogram as in Letter 222.

224   To Frances Sitwell[1]

MS NLS. Partly published in *Letters*, I, 135.

Monday [26 January 1874]   [*Mentone*]

I see on reflexion that this can't reach you till Thursday morning.

Last night, I had a quarrel with the American on politics. It is odd how it irritates you to hear certain political statements made. He was excited and he began suddenly to abuse our conduct to America; I, of course, admitted right and left that we had behaved disgracefully (as we had); until somehow I got tired of turning alternate cheeks and getting duly buffeted; and when he said that the *Alabama* money had not wiped out the injury, I suggested, in language (I remember) of admirable directness and force, that it was a pity they had taken the money in that case.[2] He lost his temper at once and cried out that his dearest wish was a war with England; whereupon, I also lost my temper and, thundering at the pitch of my voice, I left him and went away by myself to another part of the garden. A very tender reconciliation took place; and I think there will come no more harm out of it. We are both of us nervous people, and he had had a very long walk and a good deal of beer at dinner: that explains the scene a little. But I regret having employed so much of the voice with which I have been endowed, as I fear every person in the hotel was taken into confidence as to my sentiments, just at the very juncture when neither the sentiments nor (perhaps) the language had been sufficiently considered.

O I have remembered a thing for my Golden Calendar – the Hide and Seek – only on what day it was, I know not. It was a somewhat different amusement from the 'Cou-cou' that I play with Nelitchka; the transparentest of farces, as she hides always in the same place and that is visible to every person in the garden except those who turn their backs to it, but which gives her immense delight. I am rewarded for my exertions by hearing her laugh, which is one of the nicest noises in God's earth.

O my dear, don't misunderstand me; let me hear soon to tell me that you don't doubt me: I wanted to let you know really how the thing stood and perhaps I am wrong, perhaps doing that is impossible in such cases. At least,

---

[1] This sheet (2 pages) is linked in NLS with the MS of Letter 210, but it must be later. It is numbered 4, but the earlier pages have not apparently survived.

[2] The Confederate privateer *Alabama*, built in a British port in breach of strict neutrality, inflicted immense damage on the shipping of the North during the American Civil War. The prolonged negotiations over the US Government's claim for compensation from Britain strained relations between the two countries. In December 1871 an Arbitration Tribunal awarded the USA $15 million compensation for damage by the *Alabama* and two other vessels. In *The Amateur Emigrant* ('New York') RLS wrote: 'The first American I ever encountered after I had begun to adore America, quarrelled with me, or else I quarrelled with him, about the *Alabama* claims.'

dear, believe me you have been as much in my heart these three days as ever you have been, and the thought of you troubles my breathing with the sweetest trouble. I am only happy in the thought of you, my dear – this other woman is interesting to me as a hill might be, or a book, or a picture – but you have all my heart. . . .[3]   R.L.S.

225   To his Father

MS Yale. Partly published in *Letters*, I, 136–7.

Monday [*26 January 1874*]   [*Mentone*]

My dear Father,   *Stevenson & Co*
    Received divers Sola Bills of Exchange (whatever that means) to the amount of £50 (fifty pounds, no shillings and no pence).
    Yours to hand   R.L. Stevenson

Thomas Stevenson Esq.

    Heh! Heh! business letter finished. Receipt acknowledged without much ado, and I think with a certain commercial decision and brevity. The signature is good; but not original.
    I should think I had lost my heart to the wee princess. Her mother demanded the other day '*À quand, les noces?*'; which Mrs Stevenson will translate for you, in case you don't see it yourself.
    I had a political quarrel last night with the American, it was a real quarrel for about two minutes; we relieved our feelings and separated, but a mutual feeling of shame led us to a most moving reconciliation, in which the American vowed he would shed his best blood for England. In looking back upon the interview, I feel that I have learned something: I scarcely appreciated how badly England had behaved and how well she deserves the hatred the Americans bear her. It would have made you laugh, if you could have been present and seen your unpatriotic son thundering anathemas in the moonlight against all those that were not the friends of England. Johnson being nearly as nervous as I, we were both very ill after it, which added a further pathos to the reconciliation.
    There is no good in sending this off today, as I have sent another letter this morning already.
    O a remark of the Princess's amused me the other day. Somebody wanted her to give Nelitchka garlic, as a medicine. '*Quoi? Une petite amour comme ça, qu'on ne pouvait pas baiser? Il n'y a pas de sens en celà!*'

---

[3] Two or three words – possibly 'my darling' – inked over at a later date.

I had to pay 18 sous the other day for a letter from Charlie Baxter; do abuse him.

Tuesday ★[27 January]

I suppose even Lindsay is too big to come out here; so be it; but you might have an eye always open for a second-hand Wodrow.[1]

I am reading a lot of French Histories now; and the spelling keeps one in good humour all day long – I mean the spelling of English names. Very well. Ever affectionate son   Robert Louis Stevenson

226   *To Sidney Colvin*

MS Yale.

[c. 27 January 1874]   [*Mentone*]

My dear Colvin, Many thanks for your adorable children.[1] Blake – is Blake, you know. Stothard, I think, I understand and enjoy with perfect intelligence, and all the more as I remember a little book of hymns which I had when I was a child – no, not hymns, children's songs; one about a cow, for instance – full of charming little nudities among big flowers and grass. As for Flaxman, I have been sick with love, ever since I saw these adorable things; Flaxman is the man for my money.

Will you bring me when you come Sainte-Beuve's *XVIth Century*;[2] any decent book, if you can find one without trouble, about the *women* of the XVIth Century in France, Germany or where you will – if possible France; and, if possible, Brantôme's *Dames*.[3] I smell a possible article which would be all good work for the future. Don't spare coin, for anything good. O *and a good and modern* book about Geneva, Calvin etc. Please forgive me troubling you. I shall bless you forever if you can do this for me. Ever yours
                                                        Robert Louis Stevenson

---

[1] For Lindsay see Letters 198, n. 1 and 202; for Wodrow see Letters 57, n. 2 and 147, n. 1.

[1] Colvin, *Children in Italian and English Design* (1872). After a brief introduction on the art of antiquity and the Italian Renaissance, Colvin discussed the work of William Blake and his contemporaries, Thomas Stothard (1755–1834), the illustrator and painter and John Flaxman (1755–1826), the sculptor and draughtsman whom he considered the greatest of the three. RLS's copy of the book inscribed by Colvin was sold at Sotheby's, 9 May 1949 (7).

[2] RLS's annotated copy of Sainte-Beuve's *Tableau Historique et Critique de la Poésie Française et du Théâtre Français au XVIe Siècle* (1828) is at Yale.

[3] RLS's copy of an edition dated 1868 of Brantôme's *Vies des Dames Illustres* (originally published 1665–6) is at Yale. He quotes from it in his essay on Knox.

227 *To Sidney Colvin*

MS Yale.

[c. *28 January 1874*]   [*Mentone*]

My dear Colvin, Yesterday's was to catch the post. I have a possible article, as I said, before my mind – John Knox and women, but I should need such a lot of erudition to make it right; and to begin with *Brantôme*. Surely there should be a cheap *Brantôme*; it is indecent you know. I know you will be a dear creature and charge yourself with my desires, as, 'naked, helpless, piping loud,'[1] I make them known to you over France.

The Child Essay has interested me very much. Do you know what I mean when I say that it strikes me as being too well written? One slides over good things unconsciously. It has the look of being a *Ptfl* reprint – is that so?[2]

O! do you know why the Russians avoided us? Bourbon Whiskey had told them that we were both drunkards – came down screwed to dinner – and when you did not come, it was because you were dead drunk or unpresentable, at least. Cheery? Curious how, wherever I go, I come trailing clouds of dipsomania. You were also thought to be a Mentone correspondent of a local paper, and the conversation was turned, experimentally, on the subject of one of your supposed communications.

Let me know well beforehand when you mean to come. Ever yours

Robert Louis Stevenson

Bourbon whiskey is gone. Robinet is really an *awful* good soul. Old Long beats the servants, and young Long gives them gratifications after the execution; old L. also beats his nieces: whether or no Bonfils escapes, I know not. A note from Madame seems to indicate that you will be a week yet in Paris. Instruct me.   R.L.S.

228 *To his Mother*

MS Yale.

Friday [*30 January 1874*]   [*Mentone*]

I don't know what to say to you, my life has become so stereotyped again. Yesterday, I had a drive with Mme Zassetsky and Nelitchka; that is

---

[1] Blake, *Songs of Experience*, 'Infant Sorrow'.
[2] The essay had been published in four issues of *The Portfolio* in 1871. Colvin was a regular contributor to the magazine.

my one piece of news. I was rather glad to hear that the students made a row;[1] I thought their poor hearts had been dead within them, since a certain snowball riot:[2] it is good for boys to be violent and unruly and to hate all constituted authority; for it is of such boys that good citizens are made. I am going along to lunch with the Andrews's today, uninvited. But I had to go into town at any rate to draw money, and do a commission for Mme Z.; so I have taken advantage to kill two dogs with one stone.

I have been promised a photograph of Nellie: I have absolutely nothing to say. I still continue well, so long as I confine myself to walking as far as the Society of Antiquaries and back – any further (for example, to College) would knock me into a cocked hat.[3]

Saturday [31 January]

Which, it's very stupid of you, not to tell me the other side. You do not surely fancy that it would put me out? I don't mean that it would interest me to hear that the Traquairs (for example) or the Murrays of Great King Street[4] could see nothing in it; but anything said in condemnation by any person who has the faculties necessary for the appreciation of such stuff, would interest me immensely.

Was it Mrs Murray of Great King St. who had a shock of paralysis? Please remember how many Mrs M.'s there are.

That Clark was quite right in stopping my wine, I know. Today if I liked I could take a lot of liquor and go and do twice as much work, say; that is precisely what has to be avoided. I am very much pleased with my recovery; but if I do not get really stronger, I think I shall end by going to sea; a long voyage is however detestable to me; but one could coast about very jollily. Indeed the *Pharos* would be all my fancy painted for a month or two.

On the whole I suspect my walk is not more than to the Napiers and back, or rather perhaps to Duke Street and back.

I have received news of Bob which has put me nearly out of the body with satisfaction. He is really doing well at Antwerp, and some of the people seem to think he will make a spoon after all. Ever your affectionate son

Robert Louis Stevenson

---

[1] The students held a torchlight parade, in defiance of a ban by the University authorities, to celebrate the marriage of the Duke of Edinburgh and the Grand Duchess Marie of Russia.

[2] See Letter 79, n. 1.

[3] This is the end of the page. There may be a break in the letter but the next two sheets are numbered 2 and 3. They are catalogued at Yale as fragments of two other letters. MIS dates the last page 3 February; this may be the date of receipt.

[4] These two names were crossed out by MIS. See Letter 231, n. 1.

229   To Frances Sitwell

MS NLS.

Friday [*30 January 1874*]   [*Mentone*]

I am glad to write quietly to you again. I think my last letters will have explained the situation. Moreover I am easier than ever as to the difficulty; two days have passed now, with no attempt to meet me, tho' I have been much with the others. My vanity is not so very bad after all, I find; for I am sincerely glad that this is so.

I am beginning to weary a little for S.C.: it is so nice to have a judgement seat at hand.

Yesterday it was so cold that all the world of the hotel came to meals with countenances withered and shrivelled; but this morning I think we are back again in summer – the room is full of pleasant sunshine. A man works all day long at a pump and whistles or sings without intermission, and there is a great noise of children and mothers (coming from whence I know not) about the garden of the hotel.

What are you thinking of the dissolution and the two pitiable manifestos?[1] Which is more disheartening, I know not: – The nullity of Gladstone's, coupled with the disgraceful income tax abolition, or the gamesome immorality of Disraeli's. I regret to say that I feel a malicious joy in the incarceration of Mr Whalley.[2]

Saturday [*31 January*]

I had yesterday news from Bob that nearly took me out of the body with pleasure. He is really making progress; the fellows at the School of Art at Anvers seem to think he will get on; one of them, a deaf and dumb, wrote

---

[1] Gladstone announced the dissolution of Parliament in a long manifesto to the electors of Greenwich on 24 January. His main point was a promise to abolish income tax (then standing at threepence in the pound). Disraeli's counter-manifesto to the electors of Buckinghamshire was issued on 26 January.

[2] George Hammond Whalley (1813–78), Liberal MP for Peterborough and an ardent supporter of the Tichborne Claimant, was fined £250 for contempt of court on 23 January while the Tichborne trial was in progress. He refused to pay the fine and spent the night in prison; he was released the next day when his sister paid the fine. Arthur Orton (1834–98) figured in two of the longest and most celebrated trials of the century. Claiming to be the missing Roger Tichborne, wealthy heir to a baronetcy who was lost at sea in 1854, Orton, who had been 'identified' as her son by Lady Tichborne, brought a civil action against the Tichborne Trustees in 1871–2. When this failed he was prosecuted for perjury and sentenced on 28 February 1874, after a trial lasting 188 days, to fourteen years' penal servitude. Released in 1884, he died in poverty. The trials excited enormous interest and controversy and many people were convinced that he was genuine. Orton, a butcher's son from Wapping, was a man of enormous bulk, completely unlike Tichborne, and in spite of his near-illiteracy and ignorance he showed great cleverness and acuteness during the lengthy cross-examinations.

on his board 'you will be a femous artiste some day.' O I say, it makes me feel well, that. If he does well, I shall do well too. You can fancy how excited I was: it is the first hope I have had given me. He hopes to be in Paris by today, I think; so he will see S.C., which I wanted him very much to do. I am beginning as I said yesterday, to weary for S.C.; is odd how soon he takes a sort of adviser-position in my mind; I feel as if I should never be able to take another step all my life without his advice.

I lunched with the Andrewses and had some agreeable talk with them – with him mostly, I think. . . . [*MS incomplete*]

230   To Sidney Colvin

Text: TS copy, Yale.

Saturday [31 January 1874]   [*Mentone*]

My dear Colvin, I don't understand your complaint of correspondence. I wrote you a letter that resembled the letter of a person of weak mind, and a letter conceived in great part in a dead language, and two other letters in a vein at once mendicant and shrill, all since I heard from you; so that, on the whole, my position is superb as compared with yours and I should counsel you to make no demonstration.

Please, if it is to be the 8th, please send me off per book post Baudelaire's *Petits Poèmes en Prose*,[1] at least I think it – yes, I know it is. Bob may have called on you before you get this. I had another letter from him which put me in immense spirits. It is the first time I have been led to hope that he may really make a spoon. I was so much elated that I had a regular debauch at Andrews's, of wine, coffee, liqueur and tea, and a lesser debauch in the evening, at the Muscovites, upon tea and tobacco. The result is not what might have been desired by the most careful of hygienists; but I am wonderful. I hear that you have a cold; so you had better come south and look after me; besides I want you to tell me whether 'Ordered South' is worth transcription; it is not well written, but I do think some of the stuff is c'rect. I want you to see Bob, though, badly. I hope he will show you some of what he has been doing; if I was sure that he would get on, you know, Colvin, I would be twice the man I am.

I have a real letch after Brantôme, I must read him, and I think he would be the balmiest fellow to possess. O the cloak sounds awful, shall I dare to indue it? By the way, I can show you how to wear a Highland cape

---

[1] RLS's annotated copy (published 1869) is at Yale. See Letter 323, n. 3.

now – 'A Macfarlan' as P. Robinet calls it; my style is much admired. Ever
yours   Robert Louis Stevenson

231   To his Father

MS Yale. Partly published in *Letters*, I, 138–9.

[*1 February 1874*]   [*Mentone*]

I am so sorry to hear of poor Mr Murray's death.[1] He was really so
amiable and kind that no one could help liking him, and carrying away a
pleasant recollection of his simple, happy ways. I hope you will communicate to all the family how much I feel with them.

Mme Zassetsky is Nelitchka's mamma. They have both husbands
and they are in Russia, and the ladies are both here for their health.
They make it very pleasant for me here. Today, we were all [on] a drive
to the Cap St Martin and the Cap was adorable in the splendid
sunshine.

Yes, I am very like you; in my stupid head and even in sleeping before
dinner, which I do now almost always – sometimes for nearly an hour.
I read J.H.A. Macdonald's speech[2] with interest: his sentiments are
quite good, I think. I would support him against McLaren at once.
What has disgusted me most, as yet, about this election is the detestable
proposal to do away with the income tax. Is there no shame about the
easy classes? Will those who have nine hundred and ninety-nine thousands
of the advantage of our Society, never consent to pay a single tax unless
it is to be paid also by those who have to bear the burthen and heat of
the day, with almost none of the reward? And the selfishness here is
detestable, because it is so deliberate. A man may not feel poverty very
keenly and may live a quite self-pleasing life in pure thoughtlessness; but
it is quite another matter when he knows thoroughly what the issues
are, and yet wails pitiably because he is asked to pay a little more, even if it
does fall hardly sometimes, than those who get almost none of the benefit.
It is like the healthy child crying because they do not give him a goody, as
they have given to his sick brother to take away the taste of the dose. I have
not expressed myself clearly; but for all that, you ought to understand, I
think.

[1] William Murray S.S.C. of 78 Great King Street, father of RLS's friend William Hugh Murray,
died on 26 January.
[2] John Hay Athole Macdonald (1836–1919) a distinguished lawyer was the unsuccessful Conservative candidate for Edinburgh in the General Election. He became Lord Justice-Clerk in 1888. In
his *Life Jottings* (1915) Macdonald recorded that he and RLS appeared in the Jenkin theatricals; on
another occasion he played Shylock to RLS's Antonio in the trial scene of *The Merchant of Venice*.

The Bishop of Toledo is pretty well, and he will be joined by Colvin towards the end of the week. I have not dated this letter. It is Sunday, I think the first of February: Sunday anyway. Ever your affectionate son

Robert Louis Stevenson

232   *To Frances Sitwell*

MS NLS. Published in *Letters*, I, 142.

Monday [2 February 1874]   *[Mentone]*

I just wish to say good night to you. Today has been windy, but not cold. The sea was troubled and had a fine fresh saline smell like our own seas, and the sight of the breaking waves and, above all, the spray that drove now and again in my face, carried me back to storms that I have enjoyed, O how much! in other places. Still (as Madame Zassetsky justly remarked) there is something irritating in a stormy sea whose waves come always to the same spot and never further: it looks like playing at passion: it reminds one of the loathsome sham waves in a stage-ocean.

Tomorrow, you go; and tomorrow night, the straits will be again between us. Absence from you brings home distances to me wonderfully, and I have a sort of bird's eye picture of the space that separates us always under my eye. I am afraid my letters will again cease to amuse you, for I have got used to my surroundings and begin to take the people a little more as a matter of course. Of my own difficulty I don't think much. I do think it is tided over. No, my paper is not good; it has the right stuff in it, but I have not got it said: I am afraid S.C. when he comes, will be disappointed. I did not tell you he had written me such a jolly note, saying he hoped a great deal from me, and looked forward to having me to fight with him under all good banners, and under the private flag that we both follow lovingly. It is very nice of him; but I am not so good a card as he thinks; it is very doubtful to me, if I shall ever have wit enough to do more than good paragraphs. However, a good paragraph is a good paragraph and may give tired people rest and pleasure, quite as well as a good book although not for so long; a flower in a pot is not a garden, but it's a flower for all that, and its perfume does the heart good. So let us take heart of grace and be happy.

Tuesday [3 February]

O I have always forgotten to tell you a curious thing. About four nights ago. . . . [*MS incomplete*]

233   To his Mother

MS Yale.

Wednesday *[*4 February 1874*]   [*Mentone*]

I know a book you can send me. Robertson's *History of Scotland*; if possible with Dugald Stewart's life prefixed.[1] Surely that will be sendable. If it be, will you kindly send it off *quickly* as I intend soon to move on to Alassio, and I should not like a book to be hanging between two P.R.'s. D. Stewart's life is mere luxury, you know.

Colvin will arrive any night, beginning with Friday. This is not definite, but I don't know more definitely.

All goes well except the weather. Yesterday was an impossible day, and I was very sorry for myself from morning to night. Some Edinburgh people have arrived in the hotel. I have no desire for their acquaintance; and they have not as yet heard me employ any language but French.

How does the world use you? Silence as to weather characterises your correspondence. Have I missed no frost? By the bye, how nicely, with what inimitable gravity my father introduced the Bishop in his last note.

My photographs are in request; send me three more, and you might frank the letter sufficiently this time, if it's all the same to you. I had to pay upwards of a franc for the last.

You would have laughed if you had heard us trying to compare weights; Robinet in kilograms, I in stones and the Russians in some unknown Muscovite unit; and no means of comparison within reach! It was like people talking 'with tongues'.

The Bishop of Toledo is enormously better in his head; enormously. When I look back at what I was when I came here, I feel very cheery. At the same time, this inability to walk becomes *embêtant*. Before going on into Italy, I shall go to Nice and see Bennett and have a serious talk with him.

Alassio I go to, I think; because there's a sandy beach and a cheap hotel. This is something dear: nothing but the company would have made me stay on so long; but as long as I was alone, I did not want to leave it. Ever your affectionate son   Robert Louis Stevenson

---

[1] William Robertson (1721–93). His *History of Scotland* (1759) met with enormous success. In 'Some Portraits by Raeburn' RLS writes:'You can see whether you get a stronger and clearer idea of Robertson the historian from Raeburn's palette or Dugald Stewart's woolly and evasive periods.' Stewart (1753–1828) was Professor of Moral Philosophy, Edinburgh 1785– 1809.

234   To Frances Sitwell

MS NLS. Partly published in *Letters*, I, 123–4, plus one paragraph I, 135–6 (added to Letter 224).

Wednesday [4 February 1874]   *[Mentone]*

My dear friend, It has snowed today, and blown and been the very devil in the way of weather. Andrews lunched with me and in the afternoon we both had tea at the Villa Marina. I am so sleepy that I see I can write no sense; so I must shut up.

Thursday [5 February]

It is still so cold, I cannot tell you how miserable the weather is. I fear S.C. will feel the change badly. I have begun my 'Walt Whitman' again seriously; many winds have blown since I last laid it down, when sickness took me in Edinburgh. It seems almost like an ill considered jest to take up these old sentences, written by so different a person under circumstances so different, and try to string them together and organise them into something anyway whole and comely; it is like continuing another man's book. Almost every word is a little out of tune to me now, but I shall pull it through for all that and make something that will interest you yet on this subject that I had proposed to myself and partly planned already before I left for Cockfield last July.

I am very anxious to hear from you how you are. My own health is quite very good; I am a healthy octogenarian; very old, I thank you, and of course not so active as a young man, but hale withal: a lusty December. This is so; such is R.L.S.

I am a little bothered about Bob, a little afraid that he is living too poorly. The fellow he chums with spends only 2 francs a day on food, with a little excess every day or two to keep body and soul together; and though he is not so austere, I am afraid he draws it rather too fine himself.

Friday [6 February]

We have all got our photographs; it is pretty fair, they say, of me, and as they are particular in the matter of photographs, and besides partial judges, I suppose I may take that for proven. Of Nellie there is one quite adorable; I shall be so proud to show it to you. The weather is still cold. My 'Walt Whitman', at last, looks really well: I think it is going to get into shape in spite of the long gestation.

You have not yet heard of my book? O yes you will have heard of it perhaps from S.C. *Four Great Scotchmen* – John Knox, David Hume, Robert Burns, Walter Scott.[1] These, their lives, their work, the social media in

---

[1] This is one of the projects listed in Notebook A 265A (uncatalogued MS Yale).

which they lived and worked, with, if I can so make it, the strong current
of the race making itself felt underneath and throughout – this is my idea.
You must tell me what you think of it. The Knox will really be new matter,
as his life hitherto has been disgracefully written, and the events are romantic and rapid; the character very strong, salient and worthy; much interest as
to the future of Scotland and as to that part of him which was truly modern
under his Hebrew disguise. Hume, of course, the urbane, cheerful, gentle-
manly, letter-writing eighteenth century, full of niceness, and much that I
don't yet know as to his work. Burns, the sentimental side that there is in
most Scotchmen, his poor troubled existence, how far his poems were his
personally, and how far national, the question of the framework of Society
in Scotland and its fatal effect upon the finest natures. Scott again, the ever
delightful man, sane, courageous, admirable; the birth of Romance, in a
dawn that was a sunset; snobbery, conservatism, the wrong thread in
History and notably in that of his own land. *Voilà, madame, le menu.
Comment trouvez vous? Il y a de bon viande, si on parvient à la cuire con-
venablement.*

Sunday [8 February]

Still cold; gray and a high imperious wind off the sea. I see nothing
particularly *couleur de rose* this morning: but I am trying to be faithful to my
creed, and hope. O yes, one can do something to make things happier and
better; and to lighten the old intolerable burthens; and to give a good
example before men and show them how goodness and fortitude and faith
remain undiminished, after they have been stripped bare of all that is formal
and outside. We must do that my friend; you have done it already; and I
shall follow and do something nice. I shall make a worthy life, and you must
live to approve me.

Evening

Your letter has come. Thank you, my dear friend. We see the thing with
the same eyes, thank God; it has made me very happy. You see I have
journalised after all, but you are to think of that now, as a chance. You do
not say much of your health; I want truth about it. Mine I assure you, is as
well as if this had not happened. The cold winds are rough upon me but that
is all.

By the way, much that S.C. will tell you about Mme Garschine is true
indeed, but not quite true. She told me the story of her life, herself, at some
length, yesterday and today, although I rather fled the confidence; but she
said she knew her sister had told me a lot already and she wished me to
respect her on just grounds. What astonishes me is the excellent way in
which everybody tells stories; Madame G.'s autobiography was a master-

piece of clear, vivid, interesting narration; I feel with shame that I could not write so well.

Do not fear, dear friend. I will trust you in everything, and wholly. You are my faith, as you know. Ever your faithful friend

Robert Louis Stevenson

235   To Sidney Colvin

MS Yale.

[c. 5 February 1874]   [Mentone]

My dear S.C., I suppose this will be my last note then. I think you will find everything very jolly here. I am very jolly myself. I worked six hours today. I am occupied in transcribing 'The Bottle',[1] which is pleasant work to me; I find much in it that I still think excellent and much that I am doubtful about; my convention is so terribly difficult that I have to put out much that pleases me, and much that I still preserve, I only preserve with a misgiving.

I wonder if my convention is not a little too hard, and too much in the style of these decadent curiosities, poems without the letter E, poems going with the alphabet and the like, that insufferably cumber the artist without producing commensurate power of giving pleasure in the accomplished work. This doubt as to one's fundamental position is very distracting and takes away the satisfaction that I have in what I do to a great extent. And yet the idea seems to attach itself to the realistic movement of the age and, if rightly understood and treated as a convention always and not as an abstract principle, should not so much hamper one as it seems to do. The idea is not, of course, to put in nothing that would not naturally have been noted and remembered and handed down; but not to put in anything that would make a person stop and say – how could this be known. And then, without doubt, it has the advantage of making one rely on the essential interest of the situation and not cocker up and validify feeble intrigue with incidental fine writing, and scenery, and pyrotechnic exhibitions of inappropriate cleverness and sensibility. I remember Bob once saying to me that the Quadrangle of Edinburgh University was a good thing and our having a talk as to how it could be employed in different arts. I then stated that the different doors and staircases ought to be brought before the reader of a story, not by mere recapitulation, but by the use of them, by the descent of different people, one after another, by each of them. And that the grand feature of shadow and the light of the one lamp in the corner should also be introduced only as they enabled people in the story to see one another or

---

[1] 'The Curate of Anstruther's Bottle' (see Letter 194, n. 1).

prevented them to see one another. And finally, that whatever could not thus be worked into the evolution of the action, had [no] right to be commemorated at all. That is the best example of my theory that I can give, and it shows it, I think, in its true light. After all, it is a story you are telling; not a place you are to describe; everything that does not attach itself to the story, is out of place; and the best test of what does attach itself, is precisely what the persons engaged would have been likely to note and remember.

This is a lecture not a letter; and it seems rather like sending coals to Newcastle, to write a lecture to a subsidied Professor. However, I cannot think of anything else at present.

I hope you have seen Bob by this time.[2] I know he is anxious to meet you and I am in great anxiety to know what you think of his prospects – frankly of course –: as for his person, I don't care a damn what you think of it: I am case-hardened in that matter.

I am glad to hear your cold is better. Madame seems dull and sad, in her prison again; but the gaoler is absent.

À revoir bientôt. I wrote a French note to Madame Zassetsky, the other day, and there were no errors in it. The complete Gaul, as you may see.

Ever yours   Robert Louis Stevenson

Write to me as long as it is any good, do.

236   To his Mother

MS Yale. Partly published in *Letters*, I, 137–8.

Thursday [5 February 1874]   [Mentone]

Marot vol. 1. arrived. Thanks. The post has been at its old games. A letter of the 31st and one of the 2nd arrive at the same moment!

I have had a great pleasure. Mrs Andrews had a book of Scotch airs, which I brought over here and set Madame Zassetsky to work upon. They are so like Russian airs that they cannot contain their astonishment. I was quite out of my mind with delight. 'The Flowers of the Forest' – 'Auld Lang Syne' – 'Scots wha hae' – 'Wandering Willie' – 'Jock o' Hazeldean'

---

[2] Bob had arrived in Paris at the beginning of February. On 6 February he wrote to say he had met Colvin. In a later letter he wrote: 'He is very nice indeed, Colvin, very curious and nervous, I should think tho'! In the café after dinner he said, "I suppose you are quite *au fait* as to all that regards Louis." I said, not thinking what was coming, that I was. He said then that he had been much grieved to observe the effect that certain emotions you had gone thro' lately had had upon you. He said it was a first class thing for you to do and that he knew no other man who was so game for being on the spot as you and that whatever you had lost you had gained in him such a friend for life as it is difficult to gain. I thought he was not supposed to be cognizant of what had gone on at all. I am mystified first by you, more by him.'

– 'My boy Tammie', which my father whistles so often – I had no conception how much I loved them. The air which pleased Madame Z. the most was 'Hey Jonnie Cope are ye waukin' yet?' It is certainly no end. And I was so proud that they were appreciated. No triumph of my own I am sure, could ever give me such vainglorious satisfaction. You remember, perhaps, how conceited I was to find 'Auld Lang Syne' popular in its German dress; but even that was nothing to the pleasure I had yesterday at the success of our dear airs.

Yesterday evening, after Madame Z. had been playing a lot of the airs that Jessie[1] used to play – 'Within a mile', 'Aiken Drum', etc – she began walking up and down the room imitating different people and I stood in the corner and laughed till I was sore; it was so like Jessie; had Mary but been the other witness instead of Madame Garschine, I might almost have begun to doubt where I was, and that Jessie was here no more to make me laugh.

The edition is called *The Songs of Scotland without Words for the Pianoforte* edited by J.T. Surenne,[2] published by Wood in George Street. As these people have been so kind to me, I wish you would get a copy of this and send it out. If that should be too dear, or anything, Mr Mowbray[3] would be able to tell you what is the best substitute, would he not? *This*, I really would like you to do: as Madame proposes to hire a copyist to copy those she likes and so it is evident she wants them. Ever your affectionate son

Robert Louis Stevenson

237   To his Mother

MS Yale.

[*5 February 1874*][1]   [*Mentone*]

I have been reading a paper of my father's in *Nature*.[2] Andrews gave me the number. Yesterday it snowed. Today it looks as if it would rain.

[*6 February*]

Yesterday this note broke down, not without shame to its projector as you see by the fragment here preserved. We expect eagerly today, our photographs. The photographer is fully convinced that I am Prince

[1] Jessie Warden (cf. Letter 171, n. 11).
[2] John Thomas Surenne (1814–78), organist and teacher of music in Edinburgh. The book was published in 1842.
[3] John Thomson Mowbray W.S. (1808–92), TS's lawyer.
[1] Dated 14 March by MIS but this cannot be correct. The MS has become muddled with the beginning of Letter 238.
[2] TS had a letter in *Nature* of 29 January 1874 enclosing a letter from the lightkeeper at Dhu Heartach lighthouse about an earthquake on 6 January; but the reference may be to an earlier paper.

Zassetsky junior. He showed the photographs to Robinet: '*Voici,*' he said, '*Madame la Princesse, et voici la petite fille, et voici le jeune homme.*' Robinet immediately pointed to a photograph of another fellow about my age. '*Et celui-là, est-ce aussi un Russe.*' – '*Non, c'est un anglais, celui-là.*' And Robinet came home in great glee at having thus contributed to the imbroglio.

Here is a thing that is like a Warden-story. Madame Z. is tall, very beautiful, dark, and, if anything, a little apalling-looking (hitch in spelling somewhere); she is called in her own class, *la grande pietresse.* Well, after she had been many times photographed, with great preparation and seriousness and in studied attitudes suitable to the dignity of her appearance, she said she wished to be photographed in a way of her own, and sitting down, without further preface, twisted her face into the most detestable grimace of her whole repertory. There were two photographers present; but they were both so discomfited with laughter that neither of them could do anything and she had to go without the photograph (which she really wanted, you know).

I spent a large part of yesterday afternoon in washing Nellie's dolls with her; we each of us had a doll in a little tin bath and a bit of cloth by way of sponge; and between us a tin pail, into which we dipped, the water being *censé* to be there. To complete the picture, figure to yourself that the crown of my head was charged with odds and ends of coloured cloth, lace, silver paper and what not – added piece by piece (this is an almost everyday process) and every addition followed by a moment of critical contemplation and the approving sentence of '*schön cosi*' or '*cosi pitty*' –; also that my button holes were crammed with paper flowers (stop thief! I don't know where this sentence is going to), and you – you – (stop till I see how the sentence began) – yes – and the picture will be complete. Such amusement is not without weariness; but Nellie is imperious and a day of revolt is followed by many days of averted favour; and there are many aspirants to her favour. Ever your affectionate son   R.L. Stevenson

Reviews of my father's book[3] – more news of Anstruther.

238   *To his Mother*

MS Yale.[1]

Wednesday *[11 February 1874]   [Mentone]*

I have been a long time without writing. Forgive me. Colvin came on Sunday afternoon for three weeks. I am much better in mind and body. My

---

[3] TS's *The Design and Construction of Harbours* (second edition, 1874).

[1] The first half of the MS is wrongly linked with Letter 237; the second half is listed at Yale as a separate letter.

mind really almost itself again, and the body aged, but respectable and not decrepid. Indeed, a green old age is the completest idea I can give of my own condition.

I can't remember for the soul of me what was in your last, and here in bed it is inaccessible. I hope there were no queries of haste. It is now very cold, there were spales of ice on the water buckets this morning and last night it blew a tornado out of the hills. On this occasion, I have been able to resist the cold which shows the progress I have made.

The Romanes's: I reserve to myself the pleasure of making a few remarks on the earliest opportunity to Mr R., and in the meantime I shall not do myself the pleasure of visiting again the Villa Sahara; well named residence! Some of them do me the honour to converse about me in public places in a manner which I cannot allow to pass unnoticed. You would be equally savage – no, more so – if I chose to tell you what they said.

Everybody continues well. Nellie, under the benign influence of a vermifuge, has recovered beauty and spirits. O – Madame Z.'s wine has arrived, and I have been given several bottles.

If you could see my cloak, you would have more respect for me: it is magnificent, and drapes one after a fashion inimitable. Don Giovanni is the nearest thing; but I think there's more dignity about R.L.S.

It is astonishing how drained of news I am. Ever your affectionate son

Robert Louis Stevenson

I say, of course, you'll send me the book when it appears, and all reviews.

R.L.S.

239   To Frances Sitwell

MS NLS. Excerpt published in *Letters*, I, 140–41.

Thursday [12 February 1874]　　　　　　　　　　　　　　　[Mentone]

Last night, we had a masquerade at the Villa Marina. Pella was dressed as a contadina, and looked beautiful; and little Nellie, in red satin cap and wonderful red satin jacket and little breeches, as of a nondescript impossible boy; to which Madame Garschine had slyly added a little black tail, that wagged comically behind her as she danced about the room, and got deliciously tilted up over the middle bar of the back of her chair, as she sat at tea, with an irresistible suggestion of puss in boots – well, Nellie thus masqueraded (to get back to my sentence again) was all that I could have imagined. She held herself so straight and stalwart, and had such an infinitesimal dignity of carriage; and then her big baby face, already quite definitely marked with her sex, came in so funnily atop, that she got clear away from all my power of similes and resembled nothing in the world but Nellie in masquerade. Then there was Robinet in a white night gown, old-woman's cap (*mutch*, in my vernacular), snuff-box and crutch, doubled-up and yet leaping and gyrating and flying about the floor with incredible agility; and lastly, Mademoiselle in a sort of elderly walking dress and with blue spectacles. And all this incongruous, impossible world went tumbling, and dancing, and going, hand in hand, in flying circles to the music; until it was enough to make one forget one was in this wicked world, with Conservative majorities[1] and President MacMahons and all other abominations all about one.

Also last night will be memorable to me for another reason, Madame Zassetsky having given me a light as to my own intellect. They were talking about things in history remaining in their minds, because they had assisted them to generalisations; and I began to explain how things remained in my mind, yet more vividly, for no reason at all. She got interested and made me give her several examples; then she said, with her little falsetto of discovery: '*Mais c'est que vous êtes tout simplement enfant!*'

This *mot* I have reflected on at leisure and there is some truth in it. Long may I be so!

Yesterday too, I finished 'Ordered South', and at last had some pleasure and contentment with it. S.C. has sent it off to Macmillan's this morning and I hope it may be accepted; I don't care whether it is or no, except for the all-important lucre; the end of it is good whether able editor sees it or no.

Friday [13 February]

Yesterday afternoon for the first time for a day or two I had a good long talk with Madame Garschine. I wish I could make up my mind to tell you what she said, for I should like to know if you agree with it: I have been quite confused and upset every time I have thought of it since. If I am like what she says, I must be a very nice person! She was very curious to hear about my 'passion' and hoped the 'passion' was impressionable and nowise *Écossaise*: of both of which I was able to certify her. There is not a cloud in the sky, as you may see by this. Poor woman, she seems to be suffering more than ever. I hear that her husband is ill; and as (I have been told) she never means to go back to him, I daresay this may count for something in her changed looks.

S.C. heard yesterday and I was pleased to hear about G. Elliot.[2] Look

---

[1] The Conservatives had won the Election by a majority of fifty-one seats and Disraeli became Prime Minister for the second time.

[2] George William Elliot (1844–95), who had been at Trinity College Cambridge with Colvin, had just become Conservative MP for Northallerton.

here, do you know that I am getting really better? I shall be better soon, and able to work and be about all that you want me, and be to you what you know I wish to be.

Saturday [*14 February*]

I have lost my penholder; so this must go in pencil. I had a bad day yesterday: one of these days, you know, when life seems one *impasse*, one impossibility. Everything looked wrong to me, and I was sick at heart. The weather was gray and blustering, as it might have been in Edinburgh and I went labouring up and down the beach in the wind, in a passion with myself – at least a sort of sham passion, a little froth on the top of a great dead sea of discouragement. I am out of it again a good deal; but you know, there the thing does remain a little. These things do not pass in a night's time; I shall have a bad time again, likely enough, this afternoon. You don't know that about me; when I am discouraged, I am discouraged. I feared I should not be strong enough to take a position, when I went home, and would let myself be drawn into some false one, and everything else in the same way, looked black, and impossible, and blockaded by impenetrable walls.

I may tell you also, while I am in the Jeremy mood, that I am discontented with myself. All that Mme Garschine told me, the other day (and I believe she meant it) – all that you have told me, *all that you feel for me*, Consuelo – is so much better than I feel myself to be that I begin to loathe myself as an imposture. When you see 'Ordered South', you will understand how I prefer 'the shadowy life that we have in the hearts of others', because it is so much more beautiful and noble, to the vulgar little market place of petty passions that I know bitterly to be myself. Is it all a dream, dear? Lift up your eyes and you will see that I am not worthy, and turn away.

I am so glad now to be sure, and thoroughly to understand that past difficulty. It was all, as I see now distinctly, something got up between jest and earnest – three parts at least in jest – by Madame Z.: the other never had a hand or an interest in it.

Sunday [*15 February*]

I wonder how you are. I think we are both a little uneasy about you, and I don't know whether to send this off or wait until I hear from you. I am a little tired and stupid still, this morning, and have nothing to say except that I do not fail to think of you; nor shall ever. Also I begin to be somewhat homesick and impatient – not for Edinburgh as you may fancy; and on the whole, I am somewhat low at heart. This is all because it is February – don't think much of it. If I could only knock, this forenoon, at the door of No. 15!

I shall just send it off. Good-bye, dear. You do believe me now don't you. Ever your faithful friend   Robert Louis Stevenson

240   To his Mother

MS Yale. Partly published in *Letters*, I, 139, linked with Letter 231.

Friday [*13 February 1874*][1]   [*Mentone*]

The wine has arrived and a dozen of it has been transferred to me; it is much better than Folleté's stuff. We had a masquerade last night at the Villa Marina: Nellie in a little red satin cap, in a red satin suit of boy's clothes, with a funny little black tail that stuck out behind her, and wagged as she danced about the room, and gave her a look of Puss in Boots; Pella as a contadina; M. Robinet as an old woman; Mademoiselle as an old lady, with blue spectacles; and to see all these incongruous, impossible people go flitting about the room, leaping, and turning and dancing hand in hand to the music – above all if you keep in view the disproportion of size between Nellie, diminished to the smallest of cats in her tight costume, on the one hand, and Robinet on the other, exaggerated into a giant by his long white drapery – it was as good as a dream, or better. (If you think I have got creditably out of that sentence, I am sure *I* am quite pleased.)

Yesterday, we had a visit from one of whom I had often heard from Mrs Sellar[2] – Andrew Lang. He is good-looking, delicate, boyish, Oxfordish etc. He did not impress me unfavourably; nor deeply in any way.[3]

My cloak is the most admirable of all garments. For warmth, unequalled; for a sort of pensive, Roman stateliness, sometimes warming into Romantic guitarism, it is simply without concurrent: it starts alone. If you could see me in my cloak, it would impress you. I am hugely better, I think: I stood the cold, these last few days without trouble, instead of taking to bed as I did at Monte Carlo. I hope you are going to send the Scotch music.

I am stupid at letter writing again. I don't know why. I hope it may not be permanent; in the meantime you must take what you get and be hopeful. The Russian ladies are as kind and nice as ever. Ever your affectionate son
                                                        Robert Louis Stevenson

---

[1] In view of the reference in Letter 239, it may have been written a day earlier. MIS misdates it 7 February.

[2] Eleanor Mary Denniston (1829–1918), who was MIS's bridesmaid, married (1852) William Young Sellar (1825–90), Professor of Humanity at Edinburgh 1863–90. He was Andrew Lang's uncle.

[3] Andrew Lang (1844–1912), scholar, folklorist, poet and man of letters, was at this time a Fellow of Merton College, Oxford. He, too, had developed lung trouble and was wintering at Mentone. He described the meeting in *Adventures Among Books* (1905), p. 43: 'He looked . . . more like a lass

241   To his Mother

MS Yale.

[*15 February 1874*][1]   [*Mentone*]

My dear Mother, I did not write by yesterday's post, because I had no pen. I am much obliged for the books. I was made to inscribe the song book, '*en souvenir d'un Écossais*'. On the whole, that book has been a gain economically, as Mme now refuses to take payment for the wine she gave me.

I am so stupid, not seedy, but stupid this morning that I have nothing to say. I hope you are all very well. We are all very well. Please send me a cake. The master says I am a good boy.

I was very glad to get Robertson. The portrait is bad.

You must write and tell me how you are; but I hope this will come quite out of date and find you on your feet again and so much as the memory of your dwam[2] forgotten. I am sorry I cannot write you a good letter today: good-bye. Ever your affectionate son   Robert Louis Stevenson

242   To his Mother

MS Yale.

⋆[*17 February 1874*]   [*Mentone*]

My dear Madame, I must try to write a bit today; though even yet I do not feel much like it.

Imagine Nellie noticing my hair. The night before last she came up to me and pulled it saying that it was '*nein schön*'. It was cut the next afternoon and the moment she saw me, she fell into ecstasies of admiration: '*schön, schön*', she cried, and kissed me with unction, and could not take her eyes off me. Surely that is funny in so young a child.

We have had many masquerades. Lastly, Nellie was *à la Tartare*, and Pella as a Marquise. The Tartare dress is charming. Madame Garschine showed me, also, how the Tartar women dance, slowly balancing themselves from side to side with raised arms, and slowly turning round with infinite pliant little changes of posture: this they do, in the moonlight, on

than a lad, with a rather long, smooth oval face, brown hair worn at greater length than is common, large lucid eyes. . . . I shall not deny that my first impression was not wholly favourable. "Here," I thought, "is one of your aesthetic young men, though a very clever one."' Lang remembered, too, RLS's 'big blue cloak' and Tyrolese hat. Lang and RLS soon became warm friends. Lang's letters to RLS survive, but Lang destroyed most of RLS's.

[1] Dated 16 February by MIS, but this must be the postmark.
[2] Swoon, fainting fit.

the flat roofs of the Crimean towns: to complete the idea, remember that there is something sad and a little uncanny in the character of the accompanying music.

Robinet is the best of men – I mean that without exception: I don't think I ever knew such an Israelite indeed, in whom there was no guile.[1] However, he is a very strict Catholic and is just about going to treat us to the unlovely spectacle of a forty days' fast – this being the last day of the *Carnaval*. He and Pella go to Nice to see the braws and ferlies.[2] And the day is beautiful. After a week of cold weather, and wind and rain, we are back in summer, with a sky beautifully clouded and soft, and the sea blond and luminous. I shall do a good deal of lying on my beam ends today, I promise myself.

I was glad to hear you were on the mend. There must have been some sympathy between us, as I was very second rate these past days. However, I'm right again, and I hope *you* will be too, before this reaches you.

This is an improvement and as such will not be hardly judged I would fain hope. Ever your affectionate son   Robert Louis Stevenson

243   To his Mother

MS Yale. Published in *Letters*, I, 141.

★[*22 February 1874*]   [*Mentone*]

My dear Mother, I am glad to hear you are better again: nobody can expect to be *quite* well in February, that is the only consolation I can offer you.

Madame Garschine is ill, I am sorry to say, and was confined to bed all yesterday, which made a great difference to our little society. *À propos* of which what keeps me here, is just precisely the said society. These people are so nice and kind and intelligent, and then as I shall never see them any more I have a disagreeable feeling about making the move. With ordinary people in England, you have more or less chance of re-encountering one another; at least you may see their death in the papers; but with these people, they die for me and I die for them when we separate.

Andrew Lang, O you of little comprehension, called on Colvin.

You had not told me before about the fatuous person who thought 'Roads' like Ruskin – surely the vaguest of contemporaneous humanity. Again my letter writing is of an enfeebled sort. Ever your affectionate son
                                                         Robert Louis Stevenson

[1] Cf. John 1:47.
[2] Fine clothes and marvels.

244 *To his Mother*

MS Yale.

[27 February 1874]   [*Mentone*]

My dear Mother, February has as usual been depressing me; and even yet I
don't feel at all inclined for correspondence. Last night I had a little tic and
this morning in consequence I am stupid and sleepy. The stupidity is proved
by the pattern in which I am writing:[1] at least it's not quite a proof of
wisdom. There has been a coldness between Nellie and me, you will be
grieved to learn. She considers that I was wanting in consideration for her
on a recent occasion; when, as she would not let me go away from her, I
took advantage of a moment and disappeared among the olives, while she
had her back turned. A child of her age ordinarily would have simply
forgotten it, before we met again. But it is now three days ago, and I have
not yet been taken into favour again. *New Pattern.*[2] We play at a curious
game. Everyone writes characters of one individual, he also writing his own
character; in the evening all the portraits are read aloud, and the author of
the best (chosen by vote) is crowned with laurel by Nellie, who keenly
enjoys her own part of the sport. And indeed the rest also. When she hears
the others laughing, she laughs also with much gusto. Which pattern do you
like best? Each has merit. I could invent nicer patterns but it would be so
difficult to write in them. Ever your affectionate son

                                                   Robert Louis Stevenson

Postscript. I cannot leave the page unfinished: it looks so purposeless and
untidy. And I have nothing to say. O, Weather. The weather – broken
down. The weather is improved.   R.L.S.

245 *To his Mother*

Text: *Letters*, I, 143–4.

1 March 1874   [*Mentone*]

My dear Mother, The weather is again beautiful, soft, warm, cloudy, and
soft again, in provincial sense. Very interesting, I find Robertson; and
Dugald Stewart's life of him a source of unquenchable laughter. Dugald

---

[1] On the first page the lines of handwriting are arranged in a pattern of two lines close together
separated by a space.

[2] Written at the end of the first page to announce a change in pattern overleaf: one line, space, three
lines close together then a space.

Stewart is not much better than McCrie, and puts me much in mind of him. By the way, I want my father to find out whether any more of Knox's Works was ever issued than the five volumes, as I have them.[1] There are some letters that I am very anxious to see, not printed in any of the five, and perhaps still in MS.

I suppose you are now home again in Auld Reekie:[2] that abode of bliss does not much attract me yet a bit.

Colvin leaves at the end of this week, I fancy.

How badly yours sincerely writes. O! Madame Zassetsky has a theory that 'Dumbarton Drums' is an epitome of my character and talents. She plays it, and goes into ecstasies over it, taking everybody to witness that each note, as she plays it, is the moral of Berecchino. Berecchino is my stereotype name in the world now. I am announced as M. Berecchino; a German hand-maiden came to the hotel, the other night, asking for M. Berecchino; said handmaiden supposing in good faith that sich was my name.

Your letter come, O, I am all right now about the parting, because it will not be death, as we are to write. Of course the correspondence will drop off: but that's no odds, it breaks the back of the trouble. Ever your affectionate son   Robert Louis Stevenson

246   To his Mother

MS Buffalo.

*[6 March 1874]   [Mentone]

The other day, about half-past three, when I was in my room by some chance, there came a knock at the door. 'Entrez,' quoth I. Enter Alec Ross. 'Hoo's a' wi' ye, Jamie,' said he: this was too much for me, – so I pretended not to know him, and had the best of the jest after all I fancy. He was not disgusting after that any more: his fooling was knocked out of him for that once. He was very kind, and it was good of him to come and see me: he is living four miles out of Cannes on the road to Grasse. He still seems a little in error as to the degree of our intimacy, and a man who stands for a long time with his hand familiarly placed upon my shoulder, whose eyes fill with 'real tears' (as the play bills say) at the tale of my afflictions, and whom, after all and at the bottom of the matter, I *do not know*, is a somewhat bewildering phenomenon to me. However it's all right I suppose: there is no extra charge: I have probably known him in a previous state of existence: I am

[1] In notebook RLS/H (Yale), RLS records probably in May 1874 the purchase of Vol. 6 for £1.1.0.
[2] The Stevensons had visited London 21–25 February.

not mad most noble Festus, although I think I should become so, if I thought too much on this subject.

There is an interesting man here called Bonfils, who has made it his business to realise the stone-age, who makes all manner of stone-age implements and weapons with the aid of stone age appliances alone. Arrow heads, weights for fishing lines, bows, knives, hammers, all manner of things of that sort are in his little museum; also much pickled horror in glass bottles; we went there in a party, and one of the most beautiful sights on earth was Madame Z. overcoming M. Bonfils' delicacy, and craving leave humbly, from the top of Olympus, 'to subscribe towards his interesting collection'. Useless to state, that M. B. capitulated at once, and accepted divers coins in a condition of rosy confusion that was a compliment to Madame's grand airs.

It is relief to have some news to give you. Ever your affectionate son

Robert Louis Stevenson

247   To his Mother

MS Yale. First paragraph published in *Letters*, I, 144–5.

Monday [9 March 1874][1]   [*Mentone*]

We have all been getting photographed and the proofs are to be seen today. How they will look I know not. Madame Zassetsky arranged me for mine, and then said to the photographer: '*C'est mon fils. Il vient d'avoir dix-neuf ans. Il est tout fier de sa moustache. Tâcher de la faire paraître,*' and then bolted leaving me solemnly alone with the artist. The artist was quite serious, and explained that he would try to '*faire ressortir ce que veut Madame la Princesse*' to the best of his ability; he bowed very much to me, after this, in quality of Prince you see. I bowed in return and handled the flap of my cloak after the most princely fashion I could command.

I am better again with Nellie; she was charming last night. She gave an account of Milan for the benefit of the untravelled. She was sitting alone in the middle of an enormous arm chair, and there was a moment's silence; she rose to her knees, and gave the following with great solemnity and accentuating with her head: 'Garten, Miloono, an' Music – Polka; an' Neliska, an' Peliska, an Mamiska look it. An' biches. An' Teatro.' And then after a pause of perhaps ten minutes, and a lot of conversation passing about her in the meantime, she added, 'An' Biches do cosi', imitating how they eat. O another sentence of hers. She has somehow discovered that her nurse, Lotta, is consumed by a secret passion for M. Robinet, and lets concealment feed upon her damask cheek;[2] she therefore electrified the company, the other

[1] Dated 10 March by MIS, evidently from the postmark.

day, with this undeniable proposition: 'Lotta *contente*, Binet kiss Lotta.'
Where I have put "an"', there is only a little whine. Ever affectionate son

R.L.S.

248   *To his Mother*

MS Yale.

Wednesday ★[*11 March 1874*]   [*Mentone*]

I am very nearly through with my money again; it is the deuce; there are
a good many books in, this time, which has run it away quicker I fancy.
This will be £130 in less than five months – something like 300 a year –
something above £300 a year. *Peccavi, Peccavi.* And yet I cannot do it
cheaper. Except these books, I have spent nothing but my lodging, and
necessary clo', and occasional necessary cabs.

I hope you will send me the prodigal some more shortly, as he is always
uneasy with his last ten pounds.

There is no sign of the weather becoming too hot alas, 'all the hills are
covered wi snaw'[1] an' I am frozen rarely. That's to say, the nights are warm
and jolly, but during the day the winds are often horrid. Ever your
affectionate son   R.L.S.

Well.

Letter came, answering to the name of No. 27. As Nellie would say '*No
Fankyou*' for it!

249   *To Alison Cunningham*

Text: TS copy, Yale.[1]

[*mid-March 1874*]   [*Mentone*]

My dear Cummy, There's a letter for you at last. So be thankful. Whom
have I seen, of those you used to know at Mentone?[2] Not very many. The

---

[2] *Twelfth Night*, II.iv.114.

[1]
> Up in the morning's no for me,
> Up in the morning early!
> When a' the hills are covered wi' snaw
> I'm sure it's winter fairly!

Burns (chorus taken from an old song); RLS reminded Cummy in December 1893 (Letter 2663)
how she used to carry him to the window and quote this to him.

[1] I have corrected a few obvious misreadings in the TS copy.

[2] Cummy accompanied the Stevensons on their tour to the Continent in 1863. They stayed at
Mentone from 4 February to 31 March, occupying a flat in Villa Bosano. *Cummy's Diary* of the
tour was published in 1926.

Boggis have all gone to San Remo; and the Hôtel de Londres is now let in flats, much as the Villa Bosano was. The Villa Bosano itself is now joined to the Hôtel de Turin (now called de Russie) and figures as an annexe; nay the front garden even has been built over with a dining room. Right in front of it, on the other side of the road is the new English Church, Mr Barber minister.

One of the donkey women I found the other day and had a longish talk with her; her sister is dead; she remembered us all, or pretended to remember us all with *adresse*.

I know the people of the Villa d'Adhémar very well; have a standing invitation to lunch there when I please; so that's one old house still open to me.

Dr Bennet bowls about in an open carriage with even more assumption than formerly. The French people call him Jupiter, because he is monarch of all he surveys to such a degree.

I cannot find out whether Grillier is alive or dead.[3] I think I saw Marie's[4] father a good way off once, but I could not be sure. I still go to the Pharmacie Gras, where they now have an English Assistant. The Amarantes don't call themselves the Mentone Bazaar now, but 'late Mentone Bazaar', why I can't imagine. The railway of course brings lots of traffic, and about the hour of any train, you may see a score and more of omnibuses go away up the Turin Valley under the plane trees, to fetch down the newcomers from the Station. There is a weekly journal, which licks all journals for not being interesting. There is a pro-fusion of cabs open, shut, two seats, three seats, four seats, one horse or two horses, knocking about in all directions and clamouring to be hired. A band of music plays three times a week, now in the East bay, now in the West, and now in the new square with the gardens and the arcade in the middle of the town. So you see Mentone has been coming to years of discretion, like some others of us, since last we were there. You would not know yourself in some places. You would sing 'This is no my ain Mentone, I ken by the biggin' o't'.[5]

This leaves me very well, and I hope it will reach you ditto. Please remember me to your brother. How is Charlie?[6]

By the way, the person next me at dinner has been fasting all through Lent.[7] He is a deacon at the fasting: I never saw any one else do it (*except you*

---

[3] See Letter 168, n. 1.

[4] The servant-girl who looked after the Stevensons in 1863, frequently mentioned in Cummy's diary.

[5] Cf. the popular Scottish verses beginning 'This is no' my ain house, I ken by the biggin' [building] o't.' RLS quotes them as a heading to his essay 'The Foreigner at Home'.

[6] MIS recorded that Cummy's mother died on 30 May 1870. I have assumed that the TS 'Mother' is a misreading for 'brother'.

[7] Presumably Robinet (see Letter 242). This reference provides an approximate date for the letter.

sometimes); and I assure you it makes me quite empty myself, to see him batten on potatoes and sardines and bread. Ever yours very sincerely, my dear Cummy,   Robert Louis Stevenson

No extra charge for the size of the signature.

250   *To his Mother*

MS Yale.

[16 March 1874]   [*Mentone*]

My dear Mrs Stevenson, Those who criticise the Bishop of Toledo, do so at their peril. You know very well that Ross is a person antipathetic to me; I can't help it, and he can't help it; his colour, a certain look as if he were a dentist, a chastened assumption in his manners, the wife of his bosom above all – are these not enough reasons for a Dr Fell?[1] Now it so happens that he is still more antipathetic to Colvin and that Colvin had been recounting to me all that was bitter against him in his soul the very day before: funny enough. I do not pretend that his visit made me like him, because it didn't, but it softened my heart to him greatly and I indicated that in my letter; it was there for perspicacious eyes to see.

Ludovicus Toledensis

Thank you for communicating Mrs Jenkin's criticism, it is very good and very agreeable to me; I wonder what grammar she will find to claw: I am death on colloquialisms on principle. Our written and spoken speech in English are already far too far apart, a state of matters that tends toward death in the former; however of course there are colloquialisms and colloquialisms.

My day: in the morning nothing, letters, getting up, and a potter in the sun; twelve. Lunch: generally a turn with Madame Zassetsky or Madame Garschine until about one. Then in to work for two hours, or three at the most. Then a walk, or up to the Villa Marina for tea. Six. Dinner, and in the evening Villa Marina, tea, music, kids dancing, reading aloud. About half-past nine or ten, home again, smoke a pipe; in bed always by eleven.

[1] Dr John Fell (1625–86), Bishop of Oxford, immortalised in Thomas Brown's epigram: 'I do not love you Dr Fell.'

Idle, but a man of eighty can't be too active, and that is about my age. Good-bye. Love to Jessie.[2] Ever your affectionate son

Robert Louis Stevenson

251   To Sidney Colvin

MS Yale.

[*Tuesday 17 March 1874*]   [*Mentone*]

My dear Colvin, I have been so stupid you must pardon my silence. I got your letter the day before yesterday; and today, a note from Beauvais addressed to the Reverend Father Stevenson and concluding '*Veuillez agréer, Révérend Père, etc.*' My answer concludes thus '*Du reste, je ne suis ni père (à ce que je sais), ni révérend. Je me signe tout bonnement (à votre service) Robert-Louis Stevenson.*' Had him there?

It is astonishing how both Mmes G. and Z. are wanting in dignity. I was witness (which I should not have been – there was the first mistake) to a scene, in which they tried to set Robinet down kindly and horribly failed. Léon[1] has come today (Tuesday) but I have not yet seen him, as he was dirty and could not come to dinner and I offered myself to keep Robinet out of harm's way for the evening. Robinet alone is a very good companion; we had much talk over his pictures and then he told me lots of amusing things about peasants, Swiss and franc-comtois.

I am so glad to hear you got on with Bob, and also your report as to his stuff, though that was just what I expected and what I thought myself.

I have been working at loathsome 'Walt Whitman'; but all my work was knocked on the head by a dinner with Pretty-well Lang. P.W.L. gave me some blasted champagne, or else there was some blasted food at table, which knocked me entirely out of time. I slept not at all until four o'clock next morning; and since then I have done little else but sleep and very sorrily somnambulate in the more lucid intervals. You will be glad to learn that pretty well Lang did not sleep himself. Revenge ha! ha! Still I conserve a grain of malice against him. 'Damn him' as Walt Whitman says somewhere

---

[2] Josephine Leila Jessie Balfour (1854–77), eldest daughter of MIS's brother John, stayed with the Stevensons 9–26 March.

[1] Prince Lev Sergeevich Golitsyn (Léon Galitzine) (1845–1915), a member of one of the most famous Russian families. Educated at the Sorbonne and the University of Moscow, he was a man of wide interests and many enthusiasms. At this time his ambition was to become a professor of Roman Law in Moscow and he had been studying the subject at Göttingen University (see Letter 258, n. 2). Later in the 1870s he turned to archaeology and took part in excavations. He is now best remembered as a pioneer of the modern Russian wine industry; on his estate in the Crimea he developed a range of fine wines and was appointed winemaker to the Czar at the famous winery of Massandra in the 1890s (see Sotheby Catalogue, 2 April 1990).

in his pleasant way – 'Damn him! how he did defile me!' I have changed the tense to the preterite, and thus the quotation is singularly apposite. I have never been more defiled in my life.

I met a rum old army doctor, called Lewins,[2] who sent me a paper of his, full of matter that would be not very gratifying to the elect: In which paper, he has the following: 'Healthy sensation . . . is thus our only Heaven: morbid sensation, varying as it does from *ennui* or general *malaise* to mental and corporeal agony and anguish, our only Hell.' Thus, you see, I owe pretty well Lang a fairish instalment of hell. Damn him, how he *did* defile me!

Lewins is sport rather; his paper appears to have been written with a view to inducing apoplexy upon my father and those who are like minded with him. It is the least orthodox thing that I ever encountered in the few and weary years of my pilgrimage.

The portraits will slide round, I fancy; but business is intolerable to me. Have the goodness, therefore, to accept this prattle as it was intended, with an English quill,[3] (that reference is not happy perhaps – never mind) and to *Veuillez agréer, Révérend Père*, the assurance of my perfect consideration.

Robert Louis Stevenson

252   To Frances Sitwell

MS NLS. Published in *Letters*, I, 142–3, added to Letter 232.[1]

Tuesday [17 March 1874]   [*Mentone*]

The weather is all right again, soft and sunny and like summer. For some days, I have been off work owing to cold etc; but tomorrow I hope to get to it again; this unhappy Walt Whitman: I generally find myself no good, when it is in the question. O your last letter was just what I wanted.

Thursday [19 March]

I am better again, having been indifferent out of it, these two last days. The work still lies over, my malison upon it all! I send you a picter of me, which I think looks like a hunchback, but they say it is like me when I am looking at people a little puzzled. Mme Garschine says the under lip requires to be doctored up with a little Indian ink, or something, which she is going to do for her copy.

[2] Robert Lewins (died 1895) served in the Army Medical Department 1842–68, and retired with the rank of Surgeon-Major.
[3] Cf. Letter 219, n. 1.
[1] The MS has also become muddled with that of Letter 232.

The Prince Galitzin has arrived (another one, you know). I do not quite know yet if I like him. I am still plodding away at John Knox and doing a pleasanter spell of work over the Waverley Novels. It is so nice that Bob and Colvin seem to have got on. You must tell me, please, all that Colvin says to you anent the other; it all interests me so much, as you can fancy.

I see what they mean about the picture; if you cover the lower part of the face, you will see a hard, funny, puzzled sort of smile round the eyes.

Sunday [22 March]

Yesterday was such an admirable day. I had a long walk (for me) in the olive yards; the coolth was delicious; imagine that in March. It was curious how every person whom I met in the course of my walk spoke a different language – French, English, Russian, Mentonese – it might have been the plains of Heaven with the great multitude made perfect out of all tongues and nations spread abroad in happiness over them.

I am getting really frightened about you; I shall hold on till Monday night and on Tuesday morning I shall telegraph to S.C., if I hear from neither of you up to then. I am very well, believe me; this splendid summer weather suits me admirably.[2]

Yes, I think I rather like this Russian Prince; certainly not so well, however, as the ladies: I have begun to give Pella lessons in English, by the way. Just time to catch post. Ever your faithful friend

Robert Louis Stevenson

253 *To his Mother*

MS Buffalo. Published (with omission of II) in *Letters*, I, 145–6.

[20 March 1874]   *[Mentone]*

I

My Cloak.

An exception occurs to me to the frugality described a letter (or maybe two) ago; my cloak: it would certainly have been possible to have got something less expensive; still it is a fine thought for absent parents that their son possesses simply THE GREATEST vestment in Mentone. It is great in size, and unspeakably great in design; *quâ* raiment, it has not its equal.

---

[2] The MS breaks off at this point. Colvin, who omits this paragraph, concludes the letter with the paragraph which follows.

II

Miss Jardine of Jardine Hall[1]

I met her at the Moggridges the other afternoon at tea (young Moggridge by the way is a remarkably nice fellow). She heard me called Stevenson, and immediately demanded if I were Tom Stevenson's son: she expressed much astonishment at my dimensions. I told her that the name of Jardine and Jardine Hall had been coupled in my mind (since my earliest infancy) with the idea of a breadboard.[2] It was not until after I was gone that it occurred to me that the remark was perhaps not happily chosen, or at least expressed.

III

About Spain. Well, I don't know about *me* and Spain. I am certainly in no humour and in no state of health for voyages and travels. Towards the end of May, (see end)[3] up to which time I seem to see my plans, I might be up to it, or I might not; I think *not* myself. I have given up all idea of going on to Italy, though it seems a pity when one is so near; and Spain seems to me in the same category. But for all that, it need not interfere with your voyage thither: I would not lose the chance if I wanted.

IV

Money. I am much obliged. That makes £180 now. This money irks me. One feels it more, than when living at home. However, if I have health, I am in a fair way to make a bit of a livelihood for myself. Now please don't take this up wrong; don't suppose I am thinking of the transaction between you and me; I think of the transaction between me and mankind. I think of all this money wasted in keeping up a structure that may never be worth it – all this good money sent after bad. I shall be seriously angry if you take me up wrong.

V

'*Roads*'. The familiar false concord is not certainly a form of colloquialism that I should feel inclined to encourage. It is very odd; I wrote it very carefully and you seem to have read it very carefully, and yet none of us found it out. The Deuce is in it.

VI

Russian Prince. A cousin of these ladies is come to stay with them – Prince Léon Galitzin. He is the image of – whom? – guess now – do you give it up? – Hillhouse.[4]

[1] Helen (died 1902), daughter of Sir William Jardine (see Letter 186, n. 4). She married (1875) Col. Charles Ratcliffe.
[2] Thomas Jardine, 25 Brougham Street, Edinburgh, was a baker.
[3] An inserted reference to the note at the end of the letter.
[4] John Underwood Hillhouse, M.A., the assistant to the Professor of Mathematics at Edinburgh University. MIS recorded that RLS attended his lectures in 1870.

VII

Miscellaneous. I send you a pikter of me in the cloak. I think it is like a hunchback. The moustache is clearly visible to the naked eye – *Ah diable!* what do I hear in my lug? A mosquito – the first of the season. Bad luck to him!

I am very glad to hear that Ellie Balfour is better; I hope she will pull round, for the sake of that brave competent woman, her mother.

There I think I have exhausted what I had to say.

Good nicht and joy be wi' you a'. I am going to bed. Ever your affectionate son   Robert Louis Stevenson

Note to III

I had counted on being back at Embro', by the last week or so of May.

254   *To his Mother*

MS Folger.

[23 March 1874]   [*Mentone*]

My dear Mother, You sometimes suffer it seems to me from Falstaff's malady of not attending,[1] and make it a point of honour to misapprehend me; however as it is usually so only in matters of small importance and as I owe you one for a nice letter, I say no more about that.

I have something interesting to tell you. Yesterday, I was sitting at the tea table with Mme Garschine when I began to say that the profile of an English lady who came the day before for the first time to *table d'hôte*, resembled yours; after I began the sentence, however, I thought it would give so nasty an idea of you, that I changed my venue, and said merely that it had interested me somewhat painfully. '*Oui*' she replied, '*ça doit être, en effet, le profil de votre mère.*' The blood went to my head with astonishment; and she continued to criticise the face; to say that this woman's mouth was weaker and that her eyelids were different from yours, in such a way as showed that she had actually divined you, even into details. Is it not rather uncanny and frightening? However, Mme Garschine is a very second-sighty person indeed; I have heard many instances of that already: seemingly, the Circassians are like the Highlanders herein.

O do you know there is to be another Franco-German war. Prince Galitzin says they make no secret about it in Germany, that they are leaping

---

[1] 'The disease of not listening, the malady of not marking' – *2 Henry IV*, I.ii.138–40.

at every pretext to force a war on the poor Gauls, and the said Gauls are at present baffling them by continual submission.

I have read one after another *Waverley* and *The Fortunes of Nigel*. It is difficult to believe they are by the same hand. *Waverley* is so poor and dull; the other so very strong and mature. King James is one of Scott's best bits, without doubt.

It arrives to me often to dine with Lang at the Anglais, and not infrequently I fail to sleep after such a festival. Yesterday I repeated the experiment; but I did get some sleep last night. I don't understand it.

I send you one of my characters:[2] it is the only one I have by me. Ever your affectionate son   Robert Louis Stevenson

255   To his Mother

MS Yale. Partly published in *Letters*, I, 146–7.

★[*28 March 1874*]   [*Mentone*]

My dear Mother, Beautiful weather, perfect weather; sun, pleasant cooling winds; health very good: only incapacity to write.

The only new cloud on my horizon (I mean this in no menacing sense) is the Prints.[1] I have philosophical and artistic discussions with the prints. He is capable of talking for two hours upon end, developing his theory of everything under Heaven from his first position, which is that there is no straight line. Doesn't that sound like a game of my father's – I beg your pardon, you haven't read it – I don't mean my father, I mean Tristram Shandy's. He is very clever and it is an immense joke to hear him unrolling all the problems of life, philosophy, science, what you will, in this charmingly cut-and-dry, here-we-are-again kind of manner. He is better to listen to, than to argue withal. When you differ from him, he lifts up his voice and thunders; and you know that the thunder of an excited foreigner often miscarries; one stands aghast marvelling how such a colossus of a man, in such a great commotion of spirit, can open his mouth so much and emit such a still small voice at the hinder end of it all. All this while, he walks about the room, smokes cigarettes, occupies divers chairs for divers brief spaces, and casts his huge arms to the four winds like the sails of a mill. He is a most sportive prints.

We are to have a dinner of Russian food some of these days; to which I look forward with some curiosity. Be calm about this letter. I know there might be more of it; but circumstances over which control etc.

[*signature cut away*]

[2] See Letter 244.
[1] An Artemus Ward comic mis-spelling of Prince ('Interview with the Prince Napoleon').

256   To Frances Sitwell

Text: *Letters*, I, 147–8.

Monday [30 March 1874]   *[Mentone]*

My last night at Mentone. I cannot tell how strange and sad I feel. I leave behind me a dear friend whom I have but little hope of seeing again between the eyes.

Today, I hadn't arranged all my plans till five o'clock: I hired a poor old cabman, whose uncomfortable vehicle and sorry horse make everyone despise him, and set off to get money and say farewells. It was a dark misty evening; the mist was down over all the hills; the peach-trees in beautiful pink bloom. Arranged my plans; that merits a word by the way if I can be bothered. I have half arranged to go to Göttingen in summer to a course of lectures. Galitzin is responsible for this. He tells me the professor is to Law what Darwin has been to Natural History, and I should like to understand Roman Law and a knowledge of law is so necessary for all I hope to do.[1]

My poor old cabman; his one horse made me three-quarters of an hour too late for dinner, but I had not the heart to discharge him and take another. Poor soul, he was so pleased with his pourboire, I have made Madame Zassetsky promise to employ him often; so he will be something the better for me, little as he will know it.

I have read 'Ordered South'; it is pretty decent I think, but poor, stiff, limping stuff at best – not half so well straightened up as 'Roads'. However the stuff is good.

God help us all, this is a rough world: address Hotel St Romain, rue St Roch, Paris. I draw the line: a chapter finished: Ever your faithful friend

Robert Louis Stevenson

The line.

_____

That bit of childishness has made me laugh, do you blame me?

257   To his Mother

MS Yale. Published in *Letters*, I, 148.

[6 April 1874]   *Hôtel St Romain, Paris*

My dear Mother, I got a telegram the night of my arrival here, saying you disapproved of the move; well I didn't approve of it particularly myself; I

[1] Rudolf von Jhering (1818–92), who was a professor at the University of Göttingen from 1872, gained an international reputation for his views on Roman Law and his books were translated into many languages. See also Letter 258, n. 2.

only did it to be the sooner able to come home. And now – well now (I beg pardon if I am enigmatical, I can't help it just now, I hate talking about schemes that are in the wind) – well now, I may ask you to join me abroad after all: but this depends on health and various considerations.

The weather here is much colder, but not unpleasant. Bob seems to me to have improved very much in his work; he regrets much that he had not studied at Antwerp from the first.

By the bye, there will be an article of mine in *Macmillan* for (I think) May: it's not very well done – not nearly so well as 'Roads' – but I believe people find it interesting.

I intend going to Fontainebleau, or down the Seine, or somewhere thereabouts, shortly. I was awfully sorry to leave Mentone and the Russians – awfully. Ever your affectionate son   Robert Louis Stevenson

258   To his Mother

MS Yale.

[Early April 1874]   *[Paris]*

My dear Mother,[1] . . . I write now that I have really turned the thing over in my mind about a scheme I had half matured at Mentone. Prince Galitzin, who wanted to talk about everything with me, was always trying to get me on to Law; I had to reply to him that I had no ideas about Law, I didn't know why, I couldn't form any. Well, he had been in precisely the same state himself; he is professor to be, in the University of Moscow; and he told me that he had only understood law when he heard [a] professor at Göttingen. This professor is getting Galitzin to edit his lectures for him and gives his course this year, with quite new detail and care; and Galitzin promises me all help and the use of his notes for so long as I shall not be able to follow the card speaking.[2]

This is a great chance, and I am very anxious to profit by it. It seems to me you could very easily join me there; there are many English there, Professor Blackie every summer (of whose singing at table, Galitzin gave a lively imitation): please write soon and tell me what you can do. Whether

[1] The opening paragraph (about eighty words) thoroughly scored out by MIS.
[2] Léon Galitzine was a law student at Göttingen University from May 1873 until the end of the summer term 1874. He became a friend and devoted disciple of Professor von Jhering (Letter 256). Jhering dedicated vol. I of his major work *Der Zweck im Recht* (1877) to Galitzine and another former student. In August 1892, when Jhering was celebrating the fiftieth anniversary of his law doctorate, Galitzine made a special journey from Russia to Germany and delivered a moving speech at the dinner held in honour of the famous scholar. Galitzine does not appear to have edited Jhering's lectures, but he edited three volumes of lectures on Roman Law given by Professor N. I. Krylov (Moscow, 1868–71) and offered to finance the publication of one of Jhering's works in Russian translation in 1875.

I am able to work or no, remains to be seen of course; but I can be idle, one place as well as another; and the climate is warm, the life cheap and the opportunity one that will never recur. . . .[3] Ever your affectionate son

Robert Louis Stevenson

259   To Frances Sitwell

MS NLS.

[Early April 1874]   Address Hôtel de Russie, 4 Rue Racine [Paris][1]

My dear friend, I got your letter only today and hasten to answer it as well as I can. I cannot say that my letter will be cheerful. My parents have ceased to write to me now for nearly a fortnight: I can say nothing about them; if they do not write in four days, I shall telegraph for a definite answer to the Göttingen question.

This is not agreeable; but my great doubt is my health, which has certainly suffered by the change and needs nice handling just now. This is an awful nuisance just at the time when I ought to be most able to act and think. Work, I cannot: that is flat. I have had a work by me that I wanted to review for a week now; and not a sentence can I write.

I am very much vexed to hear that the waters are coming over you again. You must be brave and take things by the teeth; I promise you, I shall not want for courage, if I have but health; since I began this letter, I have changed my place of abode, having at last found a sunny room

Hôtel du Globe
Rue des Écoles.

Please be strong; and have no fear for me. I shall take care of my affair to the best of my ability.

Do please pull through and be brave, and excuse this note. Ever your faithful friend   Robert Louis Stevenson

260   To Frances Sitwell

MS NLS. Published in J.C. Bay, Echoes (1921), 45–50; Letters, I, 149–51.

[? 11 April 1874]   [Paris]

My dear friend, I am up again in an arm chair by the open window, the air very warm and soft and full of pleasant noise of streets. I have had a very violent cold; the chirruppy French-English doctor who attended me, said I

---

[3] Last sentence (about ten words) deleted by MIS.
[1] Bob's address. It has been blotted out by RLS.

might compliment myself on what I had, as I might just as well have had small pox or typhoid fever or what you will. Now, look here, with all this violent cold my chest remains unaffected: I am bronchial a bit and cough, and I have my mucus membrane raw over the best part of me and my eyes are the laughablest deformed loopholes you ever saw; and withal my lungs are all right. So you see that's good.

I have not had a letter from home since I left Mentone. You know, I was doing what they didn't want; but I put myself out of my own way to make it less unpleasant for them; and surely when one is nearly twenty-four years of age one should be allowed to do a bit of what one wants without their quarrelling with me. I would explain the whole thing to you, but believe me I am too weary. Also, please show Colvin this letter and explain to him that whenever I can, I will write to him; and that in the meantime, if it will not bore him, a note from him will always be most agreeable.

Nothing can be done to assist me: if I get permission, I shall probably go straight away to Germany without delay: by permission, I mean money.

I cannot pretend that I have been very happy this while back; but this morning, I was relieved from a great part of my physical sufferings and at the same time heard you speak more determinedly about your troubles. For God's sake carry these through; if you do, I'll promise to get better and do my work in spite of all.

Monday [? 12 April]

Last night I set to work and Bob wrote to my dictation three or four pages of 'V. Hugo's Romances'[1]: it is d—d nonsense, but to have a *brouillon* is already a great thing. If I had the health of a (simile wanting) I could still rake it together in time.

Yesterday afternoon, I got quite a nice note from my father (after a fortnight's silence), with scarcely a word of anger or vexation or anything: I don't quite know what to make of that. But it does not matter; as I see clearly enough that I must give up the game for the present: this morning I am so ill that I can see nothing else for it than to crawl very cautiously home; the fact is, the doctor *would* give me medicine, and I think that has just put the copestone on my weakness. I just simply perspire without ceasing in big drops that I can hear falling in the bed, and I have a fine generous tic that makes my forehead into that sort of hideous damned-soul mask of bitterness and pain with which the public are already acquainted – I mean such of the public as know *me*. I am going to cut the doctor and sort myself; and the first warm day, I shall fly: a change of air is the only thing that will pull me through. But the north is such an error; cold I am unfit for,

---

[1] 'Victor Hugo's Romances' became RLS's first contribution to the *Cornhill Magazine* in August 1874; it was reprinted in *Familiar Studies*.

I cannot come cold at all. My spirits are not at all bad, I thank you; but my temper is a little embittered, and I have employed more French oaths this morning, in order to try to awaken the placid imperturbable *garçon de chambre* to the fact that I was angry, than I thought that I had in me.

It is curious how in some ways real pain, is better than simple prostration and uneasiness. I seem to have wakened up to meet this tic, it has put me on the alert, I come on smiling. It is so odd; a day ago, I did not care at all for life and would just as soon have died; pain comes, and – I beg pardon, sir, you have made a mistake, I shall pull through in spite of you and be d—d to you – that is my sentiment; I also want to make it a fact.

Tell S.C. that the instant my health is anyway together again, I shall prefer to take to plays than to anything else. I have already a good subject in Gibbon; or rather it was suggested long ago by the *Corpus Juris*;[2] and has been recalled to me by Gibbon: a sort of domestic drama under the low empire; tax gatherers, slaves, cheatery, chicane, poverty; suddenly drums and sunlight and the pageantry of imperial violence: an admirable contrast, and one just suited for the stage. So you see, I shall just be in the humour to consider Diana of the Ephesians.[3] Ever your faithful friend

Robert Louis Stevenson

I shall be in London shortly, if I can; I shall seek rooms at the Paddington Hotel, where my people were, so that on the first opportunity I can come along and see you; if you can, I should like to see you alone, but of course that must be how it can. I shall see you, and S.C., and show Clark my carcase and lift coins from *Portfolio*, and then slowly north by easy stages. And O! if I could get into a sort of clean wide bed in an airy room, and sleep for months, and be wakened in mid July by birds and the shadows of leaves in the room, and rise and dress myself and be quite well and strong and find that dozens of things had been dreams and were gone away for ever!

R.L.S.

261   To Sidney Colvin

Composite text from extracts in AAA Catalogue, 6 February 1929 (476) and a cutting from an unidentified James F. Drake Catalogue (with facsimile of second page).

[*mid-April 1874*]   [*Paris*]

In a very few days I will send you the introduction, *Notre Dame*, *Les Misérables* and *Les Travailleurs de M[er]*; all that is wanting, then, will be

---

[2] *Corpus Juris Civilis*, the Emperor Justinian's great compilation of Roman law.
[3] 'Some of our talk at Mentone had run on the scheme of a spectacle play on the burning of the temple of Diana at Ephesus by Herostratus, the type of insane vanity *in excelsis*' (Colvin).

the *Laughing Man*, *Ninety Three* and a paragraph of postscript and picking together. I suppose you will be able to show this to Stephen.[1] If he doesn't like it he's wrong. It is not very well written, but there is a devil of a lot in it, I can tell you; any intelligent man will be rather stumped by this paper. I wish you would send me as soon as you can *Laughing Man*, or a cheap English translation that would do as well . . . so that I may finish this article while I'm in the vein. I would prefer the translation too, as I'm just a thought weary of V. Hugo just now.

[2]You see I'm giving you enough to do for me: you ought to be happy.
Ever yours   Robert Louis Stevenson

O also for *God's* sake, send a *Portfolio*. I shall end by hating you about this: I *do* want to see 'Roads'. It is the middle of April now; and we are 'strangers yet'.   . R.L.S.

I say, I never thanked you at all for having got me the chance of the *Cornhill* thing.[3] I do thank you though; I am very glad I had this chance I can tell you, and Stephen must be a hass if he doesn't take me.   R.L.S.

262   *To his Mother*

MS (fragment) Yale.

★[*17 April 1874*]   [*Paris*]

[*Part of MS cut away*]

. . . It is a very great pity that I cannot make out Göttingen as that would have done me an immensity of good however, health will not permit so there is no need of speaking about that.

O your letter has come. Thanks. It is funny enough that it should have come just as I was writing . . . [*part of MS cut away*]

Curious, awfully good, French pen, with which however I write rather a bad hand, let those who can explain the incongruity. Ever your affectionate son   Robert Louis Stevenson

---

[1] Leslie Stephen (1832–1904), man of letters, mountaineer and agnostic, father of Virginia Woolf; knighted 1902. He was editor of the *Cornhill Magazine*, 1871–82 and first editor of the *Dictionary of National Biography*, 1882–91.

[2] The rest of the text is taken from the facsimile.

[3] Colvin, who had been asked by Stephen on 20 March 1874 to write an essay on Hugo's novels, secured the commission for RLS.

263   To Sidney Colvin

MS Yale. Partly published in *Letters*, I, 151–2.

[April 1874]   *[Paris]*

My dear Colvin, I am a great deal better, but still have to take care. I
have got quite a lot of 'Victor Hugo' done; and I think not so badly:
pitching into this work has straightened me up a good deal. It is the devil's
own weather; but that's a trifle. I must know when *Cornhill* must see it. I
can send some of it to *Cornhill* in a week easily; even most of it. But I still
have to read the damned *Laughing Man*, and I mean to wait till I get to
London and have the loan of that from you; if I buy anything more this
production will not pay itself. Besides *Cornhill* may refuse, which would be
cruel. The first part is not too well written, though it has good stuff in it.
I wish you would write something and send it to me. I weary to see
something of yours.

My people have made no objection to my going to Göttingen; but my
body has made I think very strong objections. And you know if it is cold
here, it must be colder there. It is a sore pity; that was a great chance for me;
and it is gone. I know very well that between Galitzin and this swell
professor I should have become a good specialist in law, and how that
would have changed and bettered all my work, it is easy to see; however I
must just be content to live, as I have begun, an ignorant, chic-y penny-a-
liner. May the Lord have mercy on my soul.

Response. Amen. And on thy body.

Priest. Bloody Hell!

People, devoutly kneeling. O my God! O pretty well God remove and
exacerbate your immortal spirit!

Priest. O Lord hear our God-damned petitions.

People. And be attentive unto these our pretty well supplications.

During these prayers, the vestrymen shall wade into taking the offertory

I have already spoken about taking the offertory, however. (Jocular
reference to raising coin from the *Portfolio*.)

Going home not very well is an astonishing good hold for me; I shall
simply be a prince.

Have you had any thought about Diana of the Ephesians. I'll straighten
up a play for you. But it may take years. A play is a thing just like a story,
it begins to disengage itself and then unrolls gradually in block. It will
disengage itself some day for me, and then I'll send you the nugget and you
can see if you can make anything out of it. Ever yours

                                                        Robert Louis Stevenson

You seem to have sworn upon your knightly sword that you would not
write to me.   R.L.S.

My letters may have been poor; but they are now *two*.   R.L.S.

You should be ashamed of yourself.   R.L.S.

264 To his Mother

MS Berg. Brief quotation published in Balfour, I, 115.

★[*19 April 1874*]¹   [*Paris*]

My dear Mother, Mont St Michel smiles a good deal upon me; but I want
to see Clark; so there's a difficulty, like everything else.

The paper in *Macmillan* is what I thought felt and saw during the first
two months or six weeks at Mentone; I don't think it particularly well
written, but it interests me, because I mean it a great deal: it is scrupulously
correct. I don't know how you may like it. I just noticed last night a
curious example of how I had changed since I have been a little better;
I burn two candles every night now; for long, I never lit but one, and
when my eyes were too weary to read more I put even that out and
sat in the dark. Any prospect of recovery changed all that; but I
know nobody ever will understand my point of view, so I stow the
remainder.

Weather pretty tolerable. I live just opposite the Sorbonne, in the court
of which I see the trees growing more wealthy of leaves every day; and I feel
awfully anxious to go and hear some of the lectures. One R.P. who reads
on the heresies of the Ligue,² would just be all my fancy painted him. I must
try and find some person answering to Chapman and ask if I can go in for
a bit.

I am awful death on going round in the *Pharos* this summer – I don't
mean with the Commissioners you know; I mean with oil or something –;
it would be very placid and jolly for my health and I could make it pay I fancy,
which is a consideration. Ever your affectionate son

                                                    Robert Louis Stevenson

¹ An envelope so postmarked addressed to his mother by RLS is at Yale.
² Jesuits used to lecture at the Sorbonne and 'R. P.' may therefore mean 'Révérend Père'. For the
Ligue see Letter 209, n. 7. I cannot explain 'Chapman'.

265 *To Frances Sitwell*

MS NLS.

[Sunday ? 19 April 1874] *[Paris]*

My dear friend, I have got 'Roads' sent to me at last; it is worth about two hundred of 'Ordered South' or of this 'Victor Hugo' game that I am playing at present. I cannot write like that now; I am the only judge, I know what there was to say, and I find it said there so well that I am astonished and cannot believe that it was I who did it. And anyway, it was not I: that was conceived and written when my life was in flower. I look back upon it, as an old man looks back to his youth, with admiration and love, but no rivalry. How full it is of Cockfield! I have been thinking of nothing else but Cockfield since I read it.

I hope you are keeping brave and happy and I do hope you will soon find some work. If not you know, you must press matters somehow; by the by, here is a thing that I must say: Remember there is no person in the world who has more claim, more right toward you, than I have now: none, I repeat it; and so remember this that I have the right to help you if ever I can and you should want it. Remember it will be treating me *damned ill*, treating me *shamefully* I think, if you do not let me help you whenever I can, if ever I can. Now, I know you must feel that to be true. You must leave me *something*, dear.

I suppose you have heard of my gradual re-establishment through S.C. I am very much better. All right, I may say, though not powerful, of course. I should like to live alone in a country inn always, not too far away for people to come occasionally to see me; an inn with a garden in which I could sit when there was sun, and fine big trees about it. That is my ideal now, and to settle down there for good, among books and papers. I suppose something more or less like that, I shall manage to carry out, if I live; it will suit me beautifully.

I got a nice long letter this morning from Mme Garschine. Mme Ponsarde was so kind as to send me a doctor's address; but as she put no address in her own letter, I took it into my head I had better take no notice of her kindness; if this is humbug, you will explain I daresay, if you think she would care.

O my dear friend, I want to see you badly and I have no fear now I have told you how it was with me. I feel so weary of things, and I daresay so do you sometimes; only people must not give way: it is a pity there is no way out of the web – we are all so involved and tied up with others. O if life were but simple, and one could faithfully follow impulse! But one can't. Good-bye, dear friend, Ever your faithful friend Robert Louis Stevenson

About that thing, you know I do not wish to feel *altogether* a stranger. (Do you remember how I used to write before about that? I mean centuries ago, in a previous state of being as one might say? do you?) I do wish to feel always as if I were a little more intimate with you than the first-comer. Please excuse this stupid letter: it is Sunday, a strong day in my life.

265A   To his Mother

MS Yale.

★[23 April 1874][1]   *Great Western Royal Hotel,*
                                                            London Terminus

My dear Mother, Here all right. Shall see Clark tomorrow and then shall form definite plans.

The Dilkes,[2] Colvin tells me, are convinced beyond possibility of deconviction, that I wrote *Prince Florestan*.[3] If you have read that production and understand that Dilke is a person much sorted in the same, you will understand how much they ought to love me. I don't know that I feel flattered; I am perfectly certain, looking back on the imperturbable stupidity of my condition whenever they saw me, that the real author would be the reverse of flattered. Ever affectionate son   Robert Louis Stevenson

O, I say, you had better send me two £5 notes, in case of accident.

[1] In her diary for Friday 24 April MIS wrote:'Hear that my dear boy is in London. Telegraph to Tom and him that they may meet.' TS arrived home on the Saturday and that evening the Stevensons had a telegram telling them that RLS would be home the next morning.

[2] Sir Charles and Lady Dilke (see Letter 190, n. 1).

[3] *The Fall of Prince Florestan of Monaco*, an anonymous satire, was in fact written by Dilke himself.

INDEX OF CORRESPONDENTS

GENERAL INDEX

writing compared to, 485; *Modern Painters*, 37–8

Russel, Adam Sedgwick (Wick), 155, 156

Russel, Hamilton, 155 & n, 156

Russel, Mary Poole (*née* Blackburn), 155 & n, 156, 163, 173

Russel, Sara Elizabeth Walrond, 155 & n, 156, 159, 162–3

Rutherford, Gilbert Brydone (Wick), 138 & n, 147, 150, 155, 160–61

Rutherford, Miss, 155–6

Sainte-Beuve, Charles Augustin: *Chateaubriand et son Groupe Littéraire sous l'Empire*, 360; *Tableau Historique et Critique de la Poésie Française et du Théâtre Français au XVIe Siècle*, 466

Saintsbury, George Edward Bateman: praises RLS as a letter-writer, 16; on Henley, 57

Salisbury, Robert Arthur Talbot Gascoyne-Cecil, 3rd Marquess of, 397 & n, 407

Sanchez, Nellie (*née* Vandegrift; Fanny's sister): her biography of Fanny, 62n, 63, 65

Sand, George: RLS reads, 378, 389, 398, 399; *Consuelo*, 385–6; *François le Champi*, 382; *La Petite Fadette*, 383; *Mademoiselle Merquem*, 384–5; *Nanon*, 454

Sandars, Thomas Collett (ed. and tr.): *The Institutes of Justinian*, 353

Sandford, Revd Charles Waldegrave, 386n

Sankey, Ira D., 420n, 444n

Saturday Review: Henley writes for, 57; RLS sends 'Roads' to, 314, 318, 326, 336; declines 'Roads', 344, 348

Saunders, Revd Alexander Reid (Lerwick), 184

Savile Club (*formerly* New Club), London, 45

Savonarola, Girolamo, 292, 299, 308

Scapa Flow, Orkney, 176

Scarborough: RLS's parents visit, 195n, 197

Scots Observer, The see *National Observer, The*

Scotsman, The (newspaper), 314, 317, 334, 376n

Scott, Cyril, *Bone of Contention*: on Bob's wife, 37n

Scott, George, 197

Scott, Sir Walter: on tour of inspection of lighthouses, 186n; erects tombstone for Helen Walker, 305; RLS's proposed study of, 474–5; 'The Eve of Saint John', 165; *The Fortunes of Nigel*, 497; *The Heart of Mid-Lothian*, 305; *The Pirate*, 177n, 186–7; *Woodstock*, 419, 421, 428; *Waverley*, 494, 497

Scottish Meteorological Society, 30, 275–6n

Scrabster, 146, 173–4

Sellar, Eleanor Mary (*née* Denniston), 483 & n

Sellar, William Young, 483n

Sens, France: RLS at, 358–9

Shakespeare, William: *The Winter's Tale*, 152; *Macbeth*, 261

Sharp, James, Archbishop of St Andrews, murder of, 87n, 120n

Shelley, Percy Bysshe, 193n

Shetland islands, 117, 173n, 179–87

Shorter, Clement K., 251n

Shorting, Elizabeth Harriet (*née* Cobbald), 101n, 102

Shorting, Revd Charles, 101 & n

Sicily, 394

Siegfried, Count of Brabant, 240

Simpson, Alexander Magnus Retzious (Sir W.G.'s brother), 315, 322

Simpson, Sir James Young, 229n

Simpson, Sir Walter Grindlay: friendship with RLS, 41, 48, 209, 355, 369; trip to Germany with RLS, 229n, 231, 233–8, 242, 245–7, 250, 253, 258, 264; marriage, 368 & n; writes to RLS in Mentone, 395–6; on Makgill, 443–4

Simpson, William (Sir W.G.'s brother), 250

Sinclair, Amy Camilla (*later* Udny), 200–204

Sinclair, Sir John, 6th Baronet, 155

Sinclair, Sir John George Tollemache, Bart, 200–201

Sitwell, Revd Albert Hurt ('the Vicar'; 'V.'): marriage to Frances, 46; death, 50; breakdown of marriage, 281, 298 & n, 330, 336, 337, 362; chaplaincy, 288n; RLS stays with in London, 353

Sitwell, Frances Jane (*née* Fetherstonhaugh; *later* Colvin): Colvin meets and falls for, 45–8; life and career, 45–8, 50; at Cockfield, 46, 281–6, 293n; first marriage and children, 46, 50; character and personality, 47; RLS's relations with, 47–8, 281–3, 314–25, 404; marries Colvin, 50; death, 54; RLS praises feet, 307, 329; anxiety over RLS's health, 350–52; RLS stays with in London, 351–3; RLS's parents meet, 356, 359; RLS poems to, 370–71, 402n; health, 430, 445, 447; as Secretary of College for Working Women, 456n

Sitwell, Francis Albert (Frances's younger son; Bertie; 'Pan'): born, 46; death, 50; with mother in Cockfield, 281; RLS promises book to, 311, 320; RLS writes to, 323; RLS warns against French boys, 362; writes to RLS, 436–7

Sitwell, Frederick (Frances's elder son): born, 46; death, 46, 281

Sitwell, Isla Ashley, 46

Sitwell, Sidney Mary Beckwith (*née* Wilson;